VBScript™

Petroutsos, Schongar, et al.

201 West 103rd Street
Indianapolis, IN 46290

UNLEASHED

Trademarks

Publisher and President: *Richard K. Swadley*

Publishing Manager: *Greg Wiegand*

Director of Editorial Services: *Cindy Morrow*

Assistant Marketing Managers: *Kristina Perry, Rachel Wolfe*

Acquisitions Editor
Christopher Denny

Development Editor
Anthony Amico

Software Development Specialist
Brad Myers

Production Editor
Mary Inderstrodt

Copy Editors
Heather Butler
Keith Davenport
Karen Letourneau

Indexer
Johnna VanHoose

Technical Reviewer
Greg Guntle

Editorial Coordinator
Katie Wise

Technical Edit Coordinator
Lynette Quinn

Resource Coordinator
Deborah Frisby

Editorial Assistants
Carol Ackerman
Andi Richter
Rhonda Tinch-Mize

Cover Designer
Gary Adair

Book Designer
Gary Adair

Copy Writer
Peter Fuller

Production Team Supervisor
Brad Chinn

Production
Sonja Hart
Michael Henry
Timothy Osborn
Gene Redding

Contents

About the Authors

Bill Schongar and **Paul Lagasse** are the Senior Multimedia Developers at LCD Multimedia Creations, Inc., in Nashua, NH (bills@lcdmultimedia.com and paull@lcdmultimedia.com). Paul is an experienced Visual Basic programmer, with a design background that he's having fun putting to use in a variety of online endeavors. Bill somehow ended up in the computer industry, learning and teaching things about the online world, and contributing to other books such as *CGI Programming Unleashed.* Just don't ask Paul to recommend any movies, or Bill to show you how to juggle axes.

Evangelos Petroutsos has a M.S. degree in Computer Engineering and works as a freelance writer and consultant. He is the author of *Interactive Web Publishing with Microsoft Tools* and co-author of *Visual Basic Power Toolkit.*

Craig Eddy resides in Richmond, VA, with his wife and two children. Craig holds a B.S. in Electrical Engineering from Virginia Tech. He is currently employed as Senior Developer for Pipestream Technologies, Inc., where he is responsible for the continuing development of ContactBuilder and Sales Continuum. He is also the architect and chief programmer for the two-way synchronization between SQL Server and remote versions of Pipestream's sales force automation products. Craig specializes in Visual Basic, SQL Server, and Access development. He has been an author for *Access 95 Unleashed* and *Office 95 Unleashed,* as well as being co-author of *Web Programming with Visual Basic.* Craig's hobbies include private business development and relaxing at the Outer Banks in North Carolina. Craig can be reached at craige@richmond.infi.net.

Keith Brophy is the Software Release Coordinator at X-Rite, Incorporated, and has had many years of experience in the design, development, and testing of software systems. In addition, he has taught advanced programming courses both at Grand Rapids Community College and Northern Virginia Community College. Keith has tech edited *Real-World Programming with Visual Basic* and co-authored *Visual Basic 4.0 Performance Tuning and Optimization* and *Teach Yourself Visual Basic Script in 21 Days,* both from Sams.

Owen Graupman has been working as a system integrator for various firms since he entered the workforce. A programmer by trade, he's written many custom financial applications using Visual Basic. He is currently employed as an independent consultant based in Los Angeles, California.

Brian Johnson is a freelance writer and programmer in Orlando, Florida. He has been involved in Internet development and Visual Basic programming for more than three years. You can usually find him answering questions in the Microsoft ActiveX newsgroups or find out more about him by hitting his Web site at http://home.sprynet.com/sprynet/bjjohnson.

Timothy Koets is a software engineer at X-Rite, Incorporated. He has extensive experience with Visual Basic, VBScript and Web Page development. He is currently teaching Advanced Visual Basic at Grand Rapids Community College. He also has experience with Visual C++, Delphi, Java, PowerBuilder and Lotus Notes. Timothy is the co-author of *Visual Basic 4.0 Performance Tuning and Optimization* and *Teach Yourself Visual Basic Script in 21 Days*, both from Sams.

Tell Us What You Think!

As a reader, you are the most important critic and commentator of our books. We value your opinion and want to know what we're doing right, what we could do better, what areas you'd like to see us publish in, and any other words of wisdom you're willing to pass our way. You can help us make stronger books that meet your needs and give you the computer guidance you require.

Do you have access to CompuServe or the World Wide Web? Then check out our CompuServe forum by typing GO SAMS at any prompt. If you prefer the World Wide Web, check out our site at http://www.mcp.com.

> **NOTE**
>
> If you have a technical question about this book, call the technical support line at (800) 571-5840, ext. 3668.

As the publishing manager of the group that created this book, I welcome your comments. You can fax, e-mail, or write me directly to let me know what you did or didn't like about this book—as well as what we can do to make our books stronger. Here's the information:

FAX: 317/581-4669

E-mail: programming_mgr@sams.mcp.com

Mail: Greg Wiegand
         Sams.net Publishing
         201 W. 103rd Street
         Indianapolis, IN 46290

I
PART

VBScript:
The Language

Introducing HTML Scripting

by Brian Johnson

IN THIS CHAPTER

CHAPTER 1

Introduction

To understand VBScript, you should first have a fairly good understanding of Hypertext Markup Language (HTML). If you are already well versed in HTML, you can probably skim this chapter. We'll start to get into the details of the VBScript language in Chapter 2, "The VBScript Language."

In this chapter, you will

- Learn about active Web pages
- Review concepts that you should be familiar with
- Get a quick tutorial on HTML
- Learn about objects in your HTML pages
- Learn about ActiveX controls on the World Wide Web

Designing Web Pages

There are too many important facets to the language of the World Wide Web to say that any one is the most important. That language is called HTML. In the years since its inception, the HTML specification has been fairly dynamic. So far, each feature added to the standard has made HTML better. Succeeding specifications make pages more attractive, more informative, and richer in content—so much so that Web pages are quickly becoming the interface of choice for retrieving information from computer screens.

This book is about a scripting language called VBScript. VBScript is used to control content and objects in HTML pages designed for the World Wide Web and corporate intranets. VBScript is not about creating applications; it's about creating active HTML. If your pages look and work like applications, that's fine. The most important thing that you're doing when you're using VBScript in your Web pages is bringing the pages to life. Dead, static pages on the Web are about as exciting as slides on television. In the future, pages will be designed on the fly, tailored to the profile of the individual user.

Definitions

If you're new to creating content for the World Wide Web, there are a few concepts that you should be familiar with. The first is the URL, or Uniform Resource Locator. The URL is the address of a particular item on the Internet. This address can be part of either a domain name or an IP (Internet Protocol) address. A URL using a domain name would look something like www.microsoft.com, and the file you're looking for might be in the directory /vbs. You can just as easily use the IP address to get the file you're looking for. For the address www.microsoft.com, the numbers would be 198.105.232.5. A complete URL contains a protocol prefix, such as http:// or ftp://, followed by the address and a port number—for example, http://www.microsoft.com:80.

The second concept that you should understand is client/server. The *server* is a machine that contains the content and the associated server software. The *client* is a machine that is usually not a server but that connects to the server to retrieve content. In this book, you'll read a lot about what's happening on the server side versus what's happening on the client side. In the case of the World Wide Web, the server is the machine that contains your published Web pages, and the client machines are those of people who are viewing your pages.

The final concept that you should be familiar with is bandwidth. *Bandwidth* determines speed at which you can move an amount of data between machines. Three broad types of bandwidth exist: low bandwidth, middleband, and broadband. Low-bandwidth connections are analog connections with modems. Analog connections use sounds that must be translated into digital signals before a machine can understand them. A middleband connection might be an ISDN or other digital connection. Digital connections are faster because they require no translation step, and the signal itself is usually cleaner. A broadband connection might be a T1 connection or a cable modem. Right now, most client machines hook into the Internet in the low-bandwidth connection range. Over the next few years, middleband and broadband connections will become much more common. This should open up great opportunities for you as a content author.

First Things First—HTML

Scripting is about controlling objects. In the same way that a movie script helps to determine what actors do and say, the scripts that you write to control your HTML pages are plans for what the objects in your pages will do. To start, let's quickly review HTML.

HTML isn't really a computer language in the strictest sense of the term. For the most part, HTML is a page-description language that determines how a page will look on the screen.

The page defined in Listing 1.1 and shown in action in Figure 1.1 can be described as static, because it doesn't do too much. It can take you somewhere else, but the point of designing pages isn't so much to send someone somewhere else (although half the Web probably does that). You design a page so that people will come to the page and stick around for a while. You want to distribute information, you want to entertain, and most importantly you want your page to be worthy of a link on someone else's page.

Listing 1.1. A basic HTML page.

```
<HTML><HEAD>
<TITLE>Basic HTML Page</TITLE>
</HEAD>
<BODY>
<H1>This is a level 1 Heading</H1>
<BR>
This is a <A HREF="HTTP://WWW.MICROSOFT.COM/">hyper-link</A> to Microsoft.
</BODY>
</HTML>
```

FIGURE 1.1.

*Listing 1.1, as viewed
from Internet Explorer.*

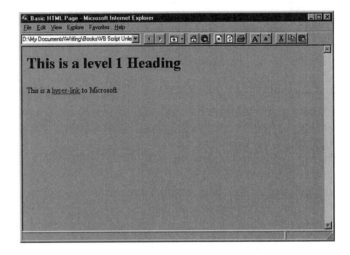

Scripting can help to make this happen. The scripts that you write will control the objects on your page.

Look at Listing 1.1. What tag in that listing do you think is most important? If you do a lot of writing, you might say that the Heading 1 <H1> tag is most important. If you're new to HTML and you're not sure how it works, you might think that the <HTML> tag is most important. If you consider what HTML offers, you'll realize that the most important tag in the listing is the <A HREF="... tag. This tag allows your document to be linked to any other document on the Web. This is important, because before HTML there was no standard way of linking two different document files on the Internet.

HTML is a standard that is maintained by the World Wide Web Consortium (W3C). W3C is a group of individuals and companies that develop and approve standards for the Web. HTML isn't the only standard maintained by W3C. Transport protocols, graphics formats for the Web, objects for the Web, and of course the implementation of scripting languages such as VBScript are also maintained by W3C.

Before you begin writing in Visual Basic Script, you need a little expertise in HTML. Let's review the basics now. For more detailed information, you can check out the reference information and links on the CD.

The <HTML> Tag

The way most HTML is written is with tags. Most of the time you will use two tags, placing your content between them.

The base tag for an HTML document is the <HTML> tag. All tags are enclosed by the less than (<) and greater than (>) characters. Closing tags are usually the same as opening tags except that they're preceded by a slash:

```
<HTML></HTML>
```

This line produces a legal HTML document. Of course, there is nothing to see in the document. The point is that the tags don't show up in the document; only the formatted text does.

The <HEAD> Tag

The <HEAD> tag sets initial document information off from the rest of the document. That information can include <TITLE>, <META NAME>, and other document administration tags.

The <TITLE> Tag

The <TITLE> tag tells the browser what you've named your page. The title of the page usually shows up in the title bar of the browser with which you're viewing the page. The <TITLE> tag is part of the <HEAD> tag in the HTML page.

The <BODY> Tag

The <BODY> </BODY> tags hold the content of your HTML document. Text that is between these tags is formatted to the browser's default style. Listing 1.2 shows a document that contains a line of body text. The style of text in the body of a document is determined by the tags that surround the text.

Listing 1.2. HTML page with a title and body text.

```
<HTML>
<HEAD>
<TITLE>Document Titles</TITLE>
</HEAD>
<BODY>
This is a titled document.
</BODY>
</HTML>
```

Headings

Heading levels in HTML documents range from <H1> to <H6>. In most browsers, the size and weight of heading text is largest at <H1> and smallest at <H6>. (See Figure 1.2.) Listing 1.3 shows you how the heading levels are set in the HTML document.

FIGURE 1.2.

Heading levels in an HTML document.

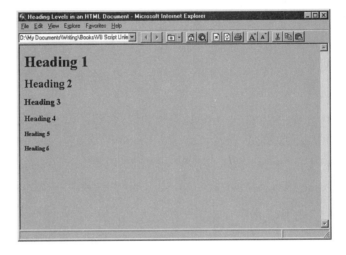

Listing 1.3. Headings in an HTML document.

```
<HTML>
<HEAD>
<TITLE>Heading Levels in an HTML Document</TITLE>
</HEAD>
<BODY>
<H1>Heading 1</H1>
<H2>Heading 2</H2>
<H3>Heading 3</H3>
<H4>Heading 4</H4>
<H5>Heading 5</H5>
<H6>Heading 6</H6>
</BODY>
</HTML>
```

TIP

Don't use heading tags to change the size of text on the page. There are other, more appropriate tags for that task. Use the heading tags as needed, in documents where an outline makes sense.

Heading tags are handy for setting off heading levels in an HTML page. Keep in mind, though, that what someone viewing your document sees can be completely different from what you see when you review your pages in your own browser.

Paragraphs

Paragraphs are the default groupings of text in an HTML page. The paragraph tag, <P>, can be used with or without a closing tag. Like the heading tags, the <P> tag can be used to create a break, but so can the break (<BR>) tag. It's up to you to choose the tags for your own pages, but as with the heading tag, logic should override aesthetics. The paragraph tag should be used to separate groups of text. If you're creating a break just so that the next item is on the following line, you should probably use the break tag.

The <FONT> Tag

The <FONT> tag is used with attributes to set the properties for text inside the tags. Let's go over some of the properties that you can easily change inside the font tags.

Size

The SIZE= attribute is similar to the heading tag. The size of the text inside the tags is set in the same manner. The difference is that the size tag is a formatting tool, as opposed to an organizational tool. It sets the size of text from 0 (smallest) to 7 (largest):

```
This is a <FONT SIZE=6>Large</FONT> example.  This is a <FONT SIZE=1>small</FONT>
one.
```

Face

The FACE= attribute allows you to set the font that is displayed in your reader's browser. For this tag to work, the font that's called must be installed on the client machine. Several different fonts can be specified. If one of the specified fonts is not installed on the client machine, the default font is used:

```
<FONT FACE="Arial, Sans">This text is displayed in Arial or Sans Serif if these
fonts are installed.</FONT>
```

Color

The COLOR= attribute allows you to set the color of text inside the font tags. There are two ways to set the color of a particular font. First, you can use the RGB value of a color, converted to hexidecimal:

```
<FONT COLOR=#FFFFFF>
```

You can also set the color of text by using color names. (See Table 1.1.) By using these names, you can be sure that colors are the same across machines.

Table 1.1. Color names in Explorer 3.0.

Black	White	Green	Maroon
Olive	Navy	Purple	Gray
Red	Yellow	Blue	Teal
Lime	Aqua	Fuchsia	Silver

These color names can also be used with other tags, including the BODY, HR, MARQUEE, and TABLES tags. If you view Listing 1.4 in your browser, you can get a look at these colors. (See Figure 1.3.)

Listing 1.4. Colornames.htm.

```
<HTML>
<HEAD>
<TITLE>Colornames in Explorer 3.0</TITLE>
</HEAD>
<BODY>
<FONT SIZE=6>These are the colornames available to you using the COLOR tag.</FONT>
<P>
<FONT COLOR="BLACK">BLACK</FONT><FONT COLOR="WHITE">WHITE</FONT>
<FONT COLOR="GREEN">GREEN</FONT><FONT COLOR="MAROON">MAROON</FONT>
<P>
<FONT COLOR="OLIVE">OLIVE</FONT><FONT COLOR="NAVY">NAVY</FONT>
<FONT COLOR="PURPLE">PURPLE</FONT><FONT COLOR="GRAY">GRAY</FONT>
<P>
<FONT COLOR="RED">RED</FONT><FONT COLOR="YELLOW">YELLOW</FONT>
<FONT COLOR="BLUE">BLUE</FONT><FONT COLOR="TEAL">TEAL</FONT>
<P>
<FONT COLOR="LIME">LIME</FONT><FONT COLOR="AQUA">AQUA</FONT>
<FONT COLOR="FUCHSIA">FUCHSIA</FONT><FONT COLOR="SILVER">SILVER</FONT>
</BODY>
</HTML>
```

FIGURE 1.3.

Colorname *values in*
Internet Explorer 3.0.

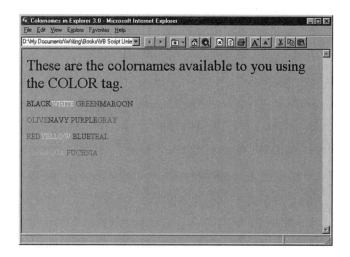

Links in Your Documents

Links are the basis of HTML. They allow you to jump to different documents on the Web or at your local web site. In addition, links enable you to jump to specific parts of documents.

A link works by specifying the URL of the linked file. You use the <A> tag along with the HREF= attribute:

```
This is a link to <A HREF="HTTP://www.microsoft.com/">Microsoft</A>.
```

TIP

Some UNIX Web servers are case-sensitive. For this reason and others, you should get used to calling URLs in a precise manner. For example, a URL that doesn't specify a filename should always end with a forward slash.

To link to a specific location within an HTML file, you need to have tags inside the file to set the places to which you would like to go. These tags are called *anchors.* You set an anchor using the NAME= attribute with the <A> tag:

```
<A NAME="Anchor">This line will be at the top of the page</A>
```

To set a link to that anchor, simply reference the anchor as you would a URL, using the HREF= attribute:

```
<A HREF="#Anchor">Link to Anchor</A>
```

If the anchor is in another file, place the URL to the file in the reference, followed by the anchor:

```
<A HREF="http://www.someaddress.com/anchor.htm#anchor">Link</A>
```

For files that are at the same Web address as the file containing the link, all that is needed to open a particular file is the relative path and filename:

```
<A HREF="page.htm">Page in same directory.</A>
<A HREF="\docs\page.htm">Page in subdirectory.</A>
<A HREF=".\pages\page.htm">Page in another directory.</A>
```

Graphics

Graphics in Web pages are what has made the Internet popular. Before the Web and its graphically rich HTML, the Internet was useful mostly for its newsgroups and Gopher database. Graphics have put a face on the Internet, and the graphics you put into your Web pages should receive careful consideration.

The two most popular graphics types on the Internet are GIF (Graphics Interchange Format) and JPEG (Joint Photographic Experts Group). There are subtypes of each of these formats that progressively render the graphic image. We'll take a quick look at graphics now, but you should get a good HTML reference to study the subtleties of graphics in HTML. One of the best is *Teach Yourself Web Publishing with HTML 3.2 in 21 Days* by Laura Lemay, published by Sams.net.

GIF

GIF was designed by CompuServe. It is able to use only 256 colors, so it is usually reserved for certain items on the page, such as logos and icons. To display a photograph in a page, you'll most likely use the JPEG format.

To place a graphic image into your HTML file, you use the <IMG> tag. The SRC= attribute contains the URL to the file you want to display:

```
<IMG SRC="logo.gif">
```

You can use the ALT= attribute to display a name for the file while it's being loaded by the browser. If the reader is using a nongraphical browser, the text in the ALT= attribute is displayed instead of the image.

Other attributes that you might find useful are ALIGN= and VALIGN=. These attributes determine how text next to an image will be displayed. Possible values for the ALIGN= tag are top, middle, and bottom.

JPEG

Images in JPEG format are displayed in exactly the same way as images in GIF. JPEG images are different from GIF images in a few ways, though:

- JPEG images can contain more than 256 colors.
- JPEG images use lossy compression.
- You can choose the amount of compression you want to use.

As mentioned, in most cases you'll want to use JPEG for photographic images. Keep in mind that increasing the amount of compression in a JPEG file will affect the clarity of the image. Take a look at your JPEG image at a number of compression ratios to determine the best amount of compression for your needs.

Other Graphics Formats

In addition to JPEG and GIF, a new standard file format has been created for the Web: the PNG (Portable Graphics Network) format. PNG was created when questions arose about whether GIF was legally usable in the public domain or whether CompuServe had retained rights to the format. Even though CompuServe has said that GIF is usable on the Internet, the development and adoption of PNG has gone forward. PNG promises to add JPEG-like compression capabilities to GIF-like files.

The BMP or bitmap format should be familiar to most Windows users. Because these images are uncompressed, they're usually not suitable for anything less than middleband use. On a local system, though, the bitmap format could prove useful to companies that don't want to convert large catalogs of existing images.

Linking from Images

Creating a link from an image file is much like creating a hyperlink in text. Simply place the `<IMG SRC= >` tag in the same place that you would usually have text:

```
<A HREF="http://www.microsoft.com/"><IMG SRC="bestwith.gif" ALT="Internet Explorer
3.0" BORDER=0></A>
```

Notice that we've added the BORDER=0 attribute to keep a border from being displayed around the link. In addition, we've added the ALT= attribute so that text will be displayed during the graphics download and in case the user stops loading the page before the download is complete.

Multimedia in HTML

Multimedia is one of the main topics of this book. A large part of creating active content in HTML has to do with utilizing the multimedia features of HTML.

Sound

In HTML, there are two ways to use sound in native formats with Internet Explorer 3.0. One way is to simply link a URL to a sound file in the Web page for playback on the client machine. The other way is with the <BGSOUND= > tag, which allows you to specify a WAV or a MID file to be played as a background sound while the page is being viewed. The file can be played once (by default) or repeated.

Video

Video files can be used within a Web page in the same way as image files. The <IMG> tag, along with the DYNSRC= attribute, is used to place an AVI file into a Web page, as shown in Listing 1.5. Placing an SRC= attribute in the tag allows an image to be placed in the file for browsers that aren't capable of playing AVI files or for low-bandwidth machines where the user has opted to turn off the browser's video capabilities.

Listing 1.5. Inline AVI.

```
<HTML>
<HEAD>
<TITLE>Inline AVI Example</TITLE>
</HEAD>
<BODY>
<H1>AVI file plays inline.</H1>
<HR COLOR="RED">
<IMG DYNSRC="myvideo.avi" SRC="myvideo.gif" CONTROLS>
</BODY>
</HTML>
```

> **NOTE**
>
> One of the characteristics that sound and video files share is large file size. Current bandwidth considerations make multimedia a tough sell on the Internet. Because it takes longer, in most instances, to download a multimedia file than it does to view it, specialized formats have been developed to make using multimedia in Web pages worthwhile. These new formats enable *streaming* of audio and video. Streaming allows video and audio to be played on the client machine before the file is completely downloaded. Streaming formats include Internet Wave, RealAudio, and VDOLive. The clients for these new applications are usually free. These formats require specialized server applications, though, which cost money.

If you want to make a small file play indefinitely, you would use the LOOP=INFINITE attribute. You can set the starting point of an AVI file with the START= attribute. Choices for the START=

attribute include FILEOPEN, which runs the file as soon as it's loaded, or MOUSEOVER, which runs a file when the mouse passes over it.

Tables

It's amazing how creative Web page designers have become with an element as simple as a table. Tables are now used to place content nearly anywhere on a Web page, with a fair amount of control on the designer's part.

The <TABLE> tag is fairly straightforward but not as intuitive as some of the other tags. You create a table by inserting a table tag and then inserting tags for the rows in your table. You can then place content in the cells of your table and set other parameters. Listing 1.6 shows a simple table.

Listing 1.6. A simple table.

```
</HTML>
<HEAD>
<TITLE>Simple Table Page</TITLE>
</HEAD>
<BODY>
<H1>This is a simple table</H1>
<HR COLOR="BLUE">
<TABLE BORDER>
<TR>
      <TD>Cell 1,1</TD>
      <TD>Cell 1,2</TD>
</TR>
<TR>
      <TD>Cell 2,1</TD>
      <TD>Cell 2,1</TD>
</TR>
</TABLE>
</BODY>
</HTML>
```

The BORDER attribute in this table creates a grid into which the table data tag, <TD>, is inserted. Another row would be added with another <TR> tag containing the <TD> tags.

In addition to deciding whether you want a grid to show up in your page, you can set the width of cells. To do this, you use the WIDTH= attribute in the <TD> tag. You can set the width value either in pixels or as a percentage of table size:

```
<TD WIDTH="50%">Wide cell</TD>
```

Other attributes available to you when working with tables include CELLCOLOR=, BORDERCOLOR=, and BACKGROUND=. The BACKGROUND= attribute takes a URL to a graphics file as a value. CELLCOLOR= and BORDERCOLOR= can use either a color name or a HEX value.

HTML 3.0 tags include the THEAD, TBODY, and TFOOT attributes. Listing 1.7 creates a table using these features.

Listing 1.7. Table with header and footer.

```
<HTML>
<HEAD>
<TITLE>HTML Table with Header and Footer</HEAD>
</HEAD>
<BODY BGCOLOR=WHITE>
<H1>Table with Header and Footer Attributes</H1>
<TABLE>
<THEAD>Header for the table.
<TR>
     <TD>Data 1 in Header</TD>
     <TD>Data 2 in Header</TD>
</TR>
</THEAD>
<TBODY RULES=ROWS>
<TR>
     <TD COLSPAN=2>Data in Body 1</TD>
</TR>
</TBODY>
<TFOOT>
<TR>Throughout the book you'll see examples of
     <TD></TD>
     <TD>This is my footer</TD>
</TR>
</TFOOT>
</TABLE>
</BODY>
</HTML>
```

> **TIP**
>
> As you browse the Web, you'll see all sorts of HTML layouts using tables. Whenever you see something that strikes you as interesting, take a look at the source code and save it. Later on, if you need to do something similar, you'll have a library of demo code to browse for ideas.

Finally, what makes HTML tables extremely versatile is that you can place a table within a table for a desired effect. For example, say that you want to use a table that contains a large graphics image and you want to set up some links in a table right next to the graphics image. Listing 1.8 shows how you would accomplish this task, and Figure 1.4 shows the results.

Listing 1.8. Table in a table.

```
<HTML>
<HEAD>
<TITLE>Table in a Table</TITLE>
</HEAD>
<BODY BGCOLOR=WHITE>
<H1>A nested table</H1>
<HR COLOR=RED>
<TABLE BORDER>
<TR>
    <TD><IMG SRC="myimage.gif" ALT="My Image"></TD>
    <TD>
    <TABLE>
        <TR>
            <TD>ITEM 1</TD>
        </TR>
        <TR>
            <TD>ITEM 2</TD>
        </TR>
        <TR>
            <TD>ITEM 3</TD>
        </TR>
        <TR>
            <TD>ITEM 4</TD>
        </TR>
    </TABLE>
    </TD>
</TR>
</TABLE>
</BODY>
</HTML>
```

FIGURE 1.4.

Table within a table.

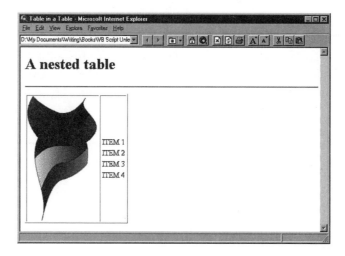

Forms in HTML

In the past, if you were doing anything interactive on the Web, it was usually with HTML forms. For the most part, forms allow for client input that is processed on the server machine. Output from an HTML form is usually sent to the Web server's CGI_BIN directory, where it is processed by a CGI script. A CGI script is a program that runs on the server and usually processes parameters sent from forms on the Web. CGI scripts can be written in any language that can be compiled or run on the server. The most popular languages for creating CGI scripts have been Perl and Bourne shell, a batch-processing language on UNIX machines.

Form Tags

To create a form in an HTML document, you enclose the graphical elements of the form in the <FORM> </FORM> tags. The ACTION= attribute contains the URL of the CGI script to be run. Using METHOD=, you can determine how things are sent to the server. Possible values for this attribute are GET and POST.

Form Components

Forms are created with the basic elements of the graphical user interface common to most GUI operating systems. These elements include buttons, textboxes, radio buttons, checkboxes, and listboxes.

The form elements are named differently in HTML than in a language such as Visual Basic. Most of the elements are created by setting the TYPE= attribute of the <INPUT> tag. Let's go over each element and then run through a few scenarios in which you might use HTML forms.

Buttons

Buttons are created by setting the value of the TYPE= attribute of the <INPUT> tag to SUBMIT. You can set the caption of a button using the VALUE= attribute. The NAME= attribute is passed to the CGI script along with the value. Listing 1.9 shows these tags and attributes at work.

Listing 1.9. Form with a button.

```
<HTML>
<HEAD>
<TITLE>Form with button</FORM>
</HEAD>
<BODY>
<H1>This is a button</H1>
<FORM>
<INPUT TYPE="SUBMIT" NAME=Button1 VALUE="This is Button1">
</FORM>
</BODY>
</HTML>
```

Textboxes

A textbox is created using the TYPE=TEXT attribute. The name of the textbox is set with the NAME= attribute, and the returned value is held in the VALUE= attribute:

```
<INPUT TYPE="TEXT" NAME="Text1" VALUE="(default value)">
```

Additional attributes associated with the TEXT type include SIZE=, which determines the size of the textbox, and MAXLENGTH=, which sets a limit on the amount of text that can be typed into the control.

Textareas

A textarea is like a textbox except that it contains more than a single line of text. Like a textbox, a textarea has a NAME= attribute and a VALUE= attribute. In addition, because the textarea is multilined, you can specify the number of columns and rows in the control using the COLS= and the ROWS= attributes:

```
<INPUT TYPE=TEXTAREA NAME="TextArea1" COLS=25 ROWS=20>
```

Radio Buttons and Checkboxes

Radio buttons are also created using the <INPUT> tag. The TYPE= attribute is set to RADIO, and the NAME= and VALUE= attributes set the name and return value of the control. A caption for the radio button is set by placing text outside the <INPUT> tag, to the left or right:

```
<INPUT TYPE=RADIO NAME=Radio1 VALUE="YES" CHECKED>Question here.
```

Radio buttons are usually set in groups, and only one of the buttons can be set to CHECKED at a time. In forms, groups are determined by control placement. To create a group of radio buttons, you code them together, with no other controls in between.

A checkbox is different from a radio button in that any number of checkboxes may be set to CHECKED at the same time, whether they're grouped or not. To create a checkbox, you set the TYPE= value of the <INPUT> tag to CHECKBOX. The NAME= and VALUE= attributes work the same way for both radio buttons and checkboxes.

Listboxes

Listboxes are set up in HTML forms using the <SELECT> </SELECT> pair. Items between the <SELECT> tags become the items in the list. The NAME= attribute sets the name value of the listbox, and <OPTION> indicates an item within the listbox. The <SELECTED> attribute sets the default return value for the list. SIZE= determines the number of elements to display. If there are more elements than the SIZE= attribute value, the box will scroll automatically. Finally, the VALUE= attribute returns the selected item(s) from the list. Listing 1.10 shows how to set up a listbox, and Figure 1.5 shows the results.

Listing 1.10. Form with a listbox.

```
<HTML>
<HEAD>
<TITLE>Form with a Listbox</TITLE>
</HEAD>
<BODY>
<H1>This is a listbox</H1>
<SELECT NAME=List1 SIZE=5>
     <OPTION SELECTED>Item 1</OPTION>
     <OPTION>Item 2</OPTION>
     <OPTION>Item 3</OPTION>
     <OPTION>Item 4</OPTION>
     <OPTION>Item 5</OPTION>
     <OPTION>Item 6</OPTION>
     <OPTION>Item 7</OPTION>
</SELECT>
</BODY>
</HTML>
```

FIGURE 1.5.

A form containing a listbox.

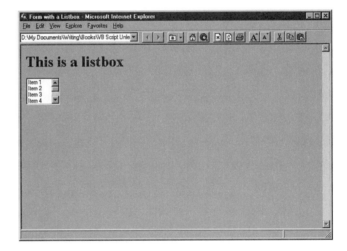

Text Area

The text area in an HTML form is a multiline text-entry field. As with the text input control, the NAME= and VALUE= attributes are passed to the CGI script for processing. To set up the text area on the form, use the ROWS= and COLS= attributes to set the number of rows and columns that show in the form:

```
<TEXTAREA NAME="MyText1" ROWS="20" COLS="75">This is a text area.</TEXTAREA>
```

Using CGI Scripts in HTML

As mentioned, CGI scripts are executed on servers. What CGI programs do depends on what values you send to them via the METHOD= value of a form in an HTML document.

Listing 1.11 is like any common form you might find on the Web. This page uses a script called formmail.pl that takes all the values submitted through the form and returns them to an e-mail address.

Listing 1.11. Form that returns its values via e-mail.

```
<HTML>
<HEAD>
<TITLE>ABC FX Survey</TITLE>
</HEAD>
<BODY>
<H1>ABC FX Survey </H1>
<HR>
<P>
You can help create a better site by answering the following questions.
These are simply questions to determine where most of our readers
are in terms of experience with ABC Graphics Suite for Windows
95 and where they would like more help.
<FORM ACTION="/cgi-bin/formmail.pl" METHOD="POST">
<P>
<INPUT NAME="recipient" VALUE="kattdev@gate.net" type=hidden>
<INPUT NAME="subject" VALUE="ABC FX Reader Survey" type=hidden>
<P>
What is your current experience level with Windows graphics tools?
<P>
<INPUT TYPE="RADIO" NAME="Experience" VALUE="Expert">Expert <INPUT TYPE="RADIO"
 NAME="Experience"
 VALUE="Advanced">Advanced
<INPUT TYPE="RADIO" NAME="Experience" VALUE="Beginner">Beginner
<INPUT TYPE="RADIO" NAME="Experience" VALUE="Help!">Help!
<P>
What application from ABC Graphics Suite do you use the most?
<P>
<INPUT TYPE="RADIO" NAME="Application" VALUE="Picture Publisher 6.0">Picture
Publisher <INPUT TYPE="RADIO" NAME="Application" VALUE="Designer 6.0">Designer
<INPUT TYPE="RADIO" NAME="Application" VALUE="ABC FlowCharter">FlowCharter
<INPUT TYPE="RADIO" NAME="Application" VALUE="ABC Media Manager">Media
Manager
<P>
What types of tips are you most interested in seeing?
<P>
<INPUT TYPE="RADIO" NAME="Tips" VALUE="Picture Publisher">Picture
Publisher <INPUT TYPE="RADIO" NAME="Tips" VALUE="Designer">Designer
<INPUT TYPE="RADIO" NAME="Tips" VALUE="Flowcharter">FlowCharter
<INPUT TYPE="RADIO" NAME="Tips" VALUE="Media Manager">Media Manager
<P>
Are you a graphics professional?
<P>
<INPUT TYPE="RADIO" NAME="Pro" VALUE="No">No <INPUT TYPE="RADIO" NAME=
```

continues

Listing 1.11. continued

```
"Pro" VALUE="Yes">Yes
<P>
If you are using plug-ins, which ones?
<P>
<TEXTAREA NAME="plug-ins" ROWS=10 COLS=75>
</TEXTAREA>
<P>
Do you have any suggestions or tips you'd like to submit?
<P>
<TEXTAREA NAME="suggestions/tips" ROWS=10 COLS=75>
</TEXTAREA>
<P>
<INPUT TYPE=SUBMIT VALUE="Send Info">
</FORM>
</BODY>
</HTML>
```

Other HTML Tags

The tags that we've discussed so far by no means compose an exhaustive list of those that you can use with HTML. Table 1.2 lists a number of text formatting tags that you might find useful.

Table 1.2. Character formatting tags.

Tag	Purpose
`<EM></EM>`	Emphasis
`<CODE></CODE>`	Monospace type
`<KBD></KBD>`	Monospace
`<DFN></DFN>`	Definition
`<CITE></CITE>`	Citation
`<B></B>`	Bold
`<I></I>`	Italic
`<TT></TT>`	Typewriter text
`<ADDRESS></ADDRESS>`	Signature
`<BLOCKQUOTE></BLOCKQUOTE>`	Long citation

Some of these tags may seem redundant, but having precise tags available can be very helpful when converting HTML to and from a typeset format.

One last type of tag that should be mentioned is the tag that creates lists. The `<OL>` `</OL>` combination creates a numbered list automatically. Terms within the list are separated by the `<LI>` tag:

```
<OL>
<LI>First
<LI>Second
<LI>Third
<LI>Fourth
</OL>
```

Other types of lists available to you include menu (`<MENU>`), directory (`<DIR>`), and unordered (`<UL>`) lists.

Frames

The frame tag allows you to open multiple HTML documents and OLE-enabled applications inside the same browser window. Frames can be complicated, but they offer a level of flexibility that's not available in tables to lay out pieces of an HTML document.

To set up a page with frames, you first need to decide how you want the frames to be inserted. The `<FRAMESET>` `</FRAMESET>` tag pair encloses `<FRAME>` tags. The `<FRAMESET>` tags determine how the group of frames will be displayed on the page. Like tables, frames are set up by column and row. The `COLS=` attribute allows you to set up your frameset by percentage, relative size, or pixels. The dimensions for `ROWS=` can be set in the same way.

Using the `<FRAME>` tag itself is fairly straightforward. The `SRC=` attribute names the URL of an HTML document to be placed in the frame. You can use the `MARGINWIDTH=` and `MARGINHEIGHT=` attributes to place the document within the frame. The `FRAMESPACING=` attribute determines spacing between frames. The `FRAMEBORDER=` attribute sets the width of the border between frames, if a border exists. If you want to give the frame scrolling capabilities, use `SCROLLING="YES"`. Finally, the `NAME=` attribute allows you to take control of a frame from within a script. Using the `NAME=` attribute, you can change the URL of the document in the frame or change other attributes. Listing 1.12 shows HTML pages in frames.

Listing 1.12. HTML pages in frames.

```
<HTML>
<HEAD>
<TITLE>HTML Pages in Frames</TITLE>
</HEAD>
<BODY>
<FRAMESET COLS=25%>
    <FRAME SRC="list.htm">
</FRAMESET>
<FRAMESET COLS=75%>
    <FRAME SRC="content.htm">
```

continues

Listing 1.12. continued

```
</FRAMESET>
<NOFRAMES>
Sorry, you need a frames based browser to see this page.
</BODY>
</HTML>
```

Notice in Listing 1.12 that the <NOFRAMES> tag is used to set content for the document if the page is being viewed in a browser that's not capable of using frames. We'll use frames a lot when working with HTML and VBScript.

Scripting

Scripting allows you to take control of content in an HTML document. Like any other tag in HTML, the <SCRIPT> tag uses attributes and allows you to define a scripting language to control the objects in your document. Objects in your document can range from active controls and Java applets to OLE server applications.

The LANGUAGE= attribute sets the scripting language in the <SCRIPT> tag. For VBScript, the language tag is "VBScript". The VBScript code itself is closed with the </SCRIPT> tag. To keep browsers that cannot use the code from displaying the code in a page, comment tags should surround the code:

```
<SCRIPT LANGUAGE="VBScript">
<!--
    SUB Button1_OnClick()
     MsgBox "Welcome to the future.", 0, "Internet Explorer 3.0"
    END SUB
-->
</SCRIPT>
```

When the HTML document is loaded into the browser, the browser sees the <SCRIPT> tag, and the code is sent to the interpreter. VBScript then compiles the code and runs the program.

Although VBScript is the subject of this book, any language can be used to add scripting capabilities to your Web pages, if you have an interpreter installed. If you're using Internet Explorer 3.0 or later, you also have the choice of using the Java Script interpreter.

Objects

Objects are controls or small programs that you can add to your HTML document. They are inserted with the <OBJECT> tag and are defined by their class identification number as stored in the Windows 95 Registry. An object can be an ActiveX control, a Java applet, or an OLE server program. (For Java applets, the <APPLET> tag is used.) In addition to the class id number, other properties can be set for the control that's being inserted. A property is the value for a part of a control. For example, the color property for a circle control might be "RED".

Taking what you've learned so far, here is what it would look like to insert a control into our HTML document:

```
<OBJECT
clsid="clsid{clsid goes here}"
height=20
width=20
id=Btn1
</INSERT>
```

OBJECTS IN INTERNET EXPLORER 3.0

If you've been using Explorer 2.0 for a while, you might wonder how Microsoft was able to add so many features to Explorer 3.0 so quickly. Microsoft converted Internet Explorer 2.0 from a single, do-all program into a shell that hosts components. The components are everything that make up an HTML page. So instead of a GIF routine being coded into the browser, it is a component that does the job just as easily. The same has been done with object controls and the scripting engine. The scripting engine doesn't really know anything about VBScript; all it knows is that it has hit a scripting tag for a language called VBScript. If it finds a script with the VBScript language tag, it hands off to VBScript, which takes over processing of the script.

Any type of object can be placed into an HTML document. As long as the object is on the client machine or can be downloaded from the Internet, it can be run on the client. That's where VBScript comes in. The VBScript language enables you to take an object in your HTML page and control it with a subset of the Visual Basic language. It's a subset of the language because, with HTML documents being loaded dynamically from the Internet, you want to be sure that the page itself isn't capable of any mischief. For example, you wouldn't want the scripting language to be able to format a hard drive, insert a virus, or gather information from your machine without your knowledge.

ActiveX Controls

ActiveX controls are what used to be called OCXs or OLE Custom Controls. The OCX replaced the VBX (Visual Basic Control) in 32-bit programs for Windows 95 and Windows NT. ActiveX controls are special because they are programmed with an interface that allows them to be used in other programs.

ACTIVEX CONTROLS AND THE WEB

The interesting thing about ActiveX controls is that they weren't really developed to be distributed network objects, but they fit into that role rather nicely. As interest in the Web grew, Netscape took a leading role in the browser market, partly by making its browser extensible through the use of plug-ins. Using Netscape's plug-in technology, a software developer can create programs that can run inside the Netscape browser. When Microsoft took a hard look at its own technology, the company decided that it already had a great pluggable technology in the form of OLEs and OCXs, which it renamed ActiveX to better reflect the larger role that the controls would play in HTML authoring.

Chapter 7, "Using ActiveX Controls," takes a closer look at ActiveX controls and how they can be used in your HTML pages.

Review

In this chapter, you read about creating HTML documents. You learned that documents and files on the World Wide Web are found using a URL. You also learned that a client machine usually retrieves data from a server. You took a look at HTML and reviewed the common tags and the layout of an HTML page. We also discussed scripting and how it is used to control objects in active HTML pages. Finally, we discussed ActiveX controls for the Internet.

In the next chapter, you'll learn more about the VBScript language and how it's connected to content in HTML pages.

The VBScript Language

by Brian Johnson

IN THIS CHAPTER

CHAPTER 2

Introduction

VBScript is a member of Microsoft's Visual Basic family of development products. Other members include Visual Basic (Professional and Standard Editions) and Visual Basic for Applications, which is the scripting language for Microsoft Excel. VBScript is a scripting language for HTML pages on the World Wide Web and corporate intranets.

In this chapter, you'll learn about

- The differences between Visual Basic and VBScript
- The syntax of the VBScript language
- Program flow in VBScript
- Interaction between the program and the user in VBScript

Differences Between Visual Basic and VBScript

If you know Visual Basic, you'll probably not have any trouble at all with VBScript. The parts of the language we cover in this chapter are basically the same in Visual Basic, with a few subtle differences. Let's talk briefly about these differences and what you should be aware of as you read this chapter.

One of the things you should be interested in is the safety and security of client machines that access your Web site. Microsoft took this consideration into account when creating VBScript. Potentially dangerous operations that can be done in Visual Basic have been removed from VBScript, including the capability to access dynamic link libraries directly and to access the file system on the client machine.

These security precautions are important because access to the client machine's operating system and internal processes could be disastrous. Of course, people run software that they download from the Internet every day. For some reason, though, people who simply use the Internet, as opposed to those of us who create it, are leery of active content. For that reason, there is a special feature of active controls for the Internet—a digital signature.

A digital signature is a file or piece of code that verifies the authenticity of a program or file. Two distinct things must happen in a secure transaction such as this: The client must be sure of where the active control is coming from and that it hasn't been tampered with along the way.

Programming in VBScript

This section of the chapter doesn't assume that you know anything about programming in Visual Basic. If you're well versed in the language, you can use this section as a review. If you haven't programmed before at all, you'll get the introduction that you need.

To start, we'll create a template that you can use to test various concepts in VBScript. We'll then talk about the things that make up a program and what you need to understand in order to create active HTML pages.

Creating a Test Page

Many new programmers learn how to program by writing small programs that run from the command line. In HTML, there is no command line, so we'll set up a skeleton page that we can use to test some of the concepts and functions covered in this book. We'll call the skeleton program `tester.htm`. Listing 2.1 contains the code that makes up the skeleton program.

Listing 2.1. `tester.htm`.

```
<HTML>
<HEAD>
<TITLE>Tester Page</TITLE>
</HEAD>
<BODY>
<H1>Tester Page for VBS</H1>
<HR COLOR="BLUE">
<INPUT TYPE="SUBMIT" NAME="Btn1" VALUE="Click to test the code">
<SCRIPT LANGUAGE="VBS">
<!--
Sub Btn1_OnClick()
End Sub
-->
</SCRIPT>
</BODY></HTML>
```

In most VBScript programs, you'll need to attach the initialization of a program to some sort of action. In the `tester.htm` page, use the button click event to trigger the action that takes place. To be able to see what happens, we need to change the property of a control on the page, or we can use a message box. Once we have the skeleton program in place, we can test code in the browser.

To start, we'll create a Hello World program. Hello World is a traditional program created in various forms to test input and output techniques. The first Hello World program is fairly simple. To create the script, the following code is added to the `Btn1_OnClick` event in `tester.htm`:

```
Sub Btn1_OnClick
Dim Message
Message="Hello World!"
MsgBox Message, 0,"Tester Result"
End Sub
```

To test the new code, save `tester.htm` and then open it in Explorer 3.0. You'll see the result when you click the button, as shown in Figure 2.1.

FIGURE 2.1.

Tester program with message.

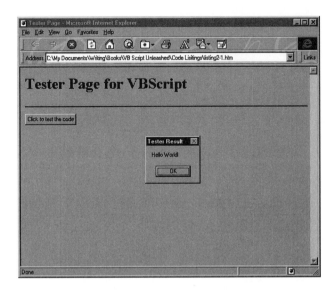

The great thing about having a program like `tester.htm` available is that you can test any small piece of code you want. By saving the file to your desktop, you can easily open the file in Notepad and Internet Explorer 3.0 at the same time, as shown in Figure 2.2. You can then edit and save the file and see the results immediately.

FIGURE 2.2.

Notepad and Internet Explorer working together.

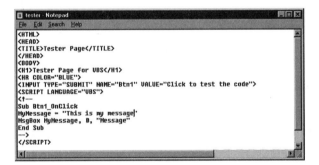

Let's take a look at what's happening in `tester.htm`. The browser reads in the file just as with any HTML document. Notice that the button we've created on the page is no different from the buttons that we create for forms. Microsoft did this so that the same objects created for forms could easily be used for interaction with scripts. This method also helps HTML designers who are used to working with forms.

So, the `<H1>` text shows in the browser, followed by a horizontal rule and finally our button. The browser now hits the `<SCRIPT="VBS">` tag. Here the browser hands off to the scripting engine, which in turn hands off to the VBScript interpreter. The VBS code is then parsed by VBS, compiled on the fly, and run. Our result shows up in the form of the message box.

If some of this isn't quite clear to you now, it should be by the end of the chapter.

What a Program Is

At this point, it might be a good idea to discuss what constitutes a program. Thinking about what's going on with the machine will help you later when you're trying to come up with applications for VBScript in your Web pages.

A computer program is a set of mathematical instructions that perform a task. To make it easier for programmers to get computers to do things, languages have been developed to allow programmers to write instructions for the computer in terms that humans can deal with.

Many computer languages exist. They can be broken into two broad categories: low level and high level. Low-level languages deal directly with what's going on inside the computer, whereas high-level languages keep the programmer thinking at a different level. Low-level languages get closer to the chip. Assembler is an example of a low-level language. When you write a program in Assembler, you do the same sorts of things that you do in a language such as Visual Basic, except that you are much more precise with the chip. Assembler tends to be a little cryptic to people just getting to know it:

```
MOV    BX,0001H
LEA    DX,Msg
MOV    CX,My_Msg
MOV    AH,40H
INT    21H
```

Writing programs in a high-level language such as Visual Basic is much more like writing instructions in plain English. The conceptual buffer between a language that is close to the chip and a higher-level language is called *abstraction*. You know more about what's going on when you read an assembly language program, but you could do it in Basic and not have to worry about moving blocks of memory around yourself.

We can add a layer of abstraction to Visual Basic itself. To teach programming concepts, some instructors use a tool called *pseudo code*. Pseudo code is simply an instruction translated into plain English. I don't use pseudo code much, but I'll cover it briefly here so that you're familiar with the concept.

If you translated the code in Listing 2.1 into pseudo code, it would look like the code shown in Listing 2.2.

Listing 2.2. tester.htm translated into pseudo code.

```
Create a button on the page called Btn1
This is the start of a script in the VBS language
This comment hides the code from browsers that can't understand it.
When the user clicks the button:
Create a space in memory called Message
Set the value of Message to "Hello World"
Create a dialog box containing the value of Message
End the routine
End of the comment
End of our script
```

I won't use this method much in this book because it essentially makes you read the same program twice. I mention it, though, because it shows how you should be thinking when you read through code listings.

When you think about a computer language being mathematical, you don't really need to worry that there are big concepts that you need to understand before you begin to program. To think about what a computer needs to do to process information, think of the game 20 Questions. In 20 Questions, one person has the magic word. Everyone else is allowed to ask 20 questions with a "Yes" or "No" answer. The person who knows the magic word decides whether the question deserves a "Yes" or a "No."

If the magic word is "cow," and the question is, "Is it an animal?", the answer would be "Yes." This is about the level on which the computer works. It remembers things, it compares things, and it can tell you whether two things are the same. Languages such as Visual Basic add features that can work on the things that the machine stores in memory. Programmers are the people asking the questions. The better the question, the more likely it is that you'll get to the ultimate answer.

Concepts You Should Understand: Variables and Procedures

You should understand some simple concepts before you begin to program. Among these concepts are variables and procedures.

A variable is a value stored in memory. If you wanted to get technical, you could say that variable is a name that represents an address containing information stored in memory. For our purposes, thinking of a variable as being equal to a value is fine.

A program is made up of one or more procedures. A procedure is an instruction block in VBScript. Regular procedures, or Subs, simply act on data, but a special procedure called a Function returns a value to the procedure that called it. Be aware that all your scripts will be made up of procedures and Function blocks.

You know that your VBScript programs will begin with a `<SCRIPT>` tag and end with a `</Script>` tag. Your procedures and `Function`s will work the same way. The procedure is created and it is ended. Your program code goes in between.

The Anatomy of VBScript Code

Let's take a look once again at our `tester.htm` file. The script section of the page has a definite structure as shown in Figure 2.3.

FIGURE 2.3.

A VBScript code block is broken down.

```
<SCRIPT LANGUAGE="VBS">
<!--
Sub Btn1 OnClick
      Dim Message, x
      x=100
      Message="Sub Btn1 OnClick"
      MsgBox Message, 0,"Procedure Result"
      Message="Sub MySub"
      MySub(Message)  ■
      x=ReturnCount(x)    ←
      Message="Function returned" + CStr(x)
      MsgBox Message, 0, "Procedure Result"
End Sub
Sub MySub(Msg)   ←
      MsgBoxMsg, 0, "Procedure Result"
End Sub
Function ReturnCount(Num)   ←
        ReturnCount=Num + 1
End Function
-->
</SCRIPT>
```

The first thing you'll notice in the VBScript code block is the `<SCRIPT LANGUAGE="VBS">` line. Keep in mind that you must close out your script code block with a `</SCRIPT>` tag. If you don't add this tag, your script usually won't run and you won't know what's going on because you aren't going to see any error messages. Errors like this are tough to track down because if your code block is large, you might start hacking away at perfectly good code to see if you can figure out what's wrong. An error like this can waste a lot of time because nothing you try works.

> **TIP**
>
> If your script isn't running and you're not getting error messages from your browser, check your HTML.

The next tag that you should get used to adding to a script block is the comment tag. You won't run into a problem with most browsers if you don't add this tag, but it's a good idea to get used to adding it anyway. If nothing else, this tag helps you to see your scripting blocks more easily in your HTML documents. Like the `<script>` tag, the comment tag should have a closing tag, although not having a closing tag will not affect your script in a browser that recognizes the `<SCRIPT>` tag.

Procedures make up most of the rest of a script code block. They have opening and closing lines and are accessible from one another. The first procedure run in a script depends on what events take place within the HTML page. An event is usually an action taken by a user, such as clicking on a button, but other events can also be triggered within an HTML page. Other possible events include timer events, mouse movement, and messages sent from controls.

To review, an HTML script is enclosed by the `<SCRIPT>` `</SCRIPT>` tag pair. The `LANGUAGE="VBS"` attribute sets the scripting language to VBScript. The VBScript script code should be written inside a comment tag, `<!-- -->`. Procedures are blocks of code within the script that make up the program.

Data Types

As mentioned, a variable is a name that represents the contents of some space in memory. Thinking of a variable in terms of memory space will help you to understand an important concept in programming: data types.

All variables in VBScript are of the type variant. A variant is a variable that is simply the name for a piece of data. The variant type doesn't differentiate between types of data until the time comes to process that data. This means that a variable can represent literally any value or type of value. We'll talk more about this ahead.

Subtypes of Variant Types

The variant type has a number of subtypes. Let's go through each of the subtypes and discuss how a variable of any given subtype will take up space in memory.

Boolean

One of the most basic data types in programming is the Boolean data type. This subtype in VBScript can have a value of either `true` or `false`. The Boolean type takes up very little space in memory.

Byte

The byte subtype can be a whole, positive number in the range of 0 to 255. Like the Boolean subtype, the byte subtype takes up very little space in memory.

Integer

The integer subtype takes up 2 bytes in memory and can be an integer value in the range of –32,768 to 32,767. An extra byte of storage makes a big difference in the value that a variable can hold.

Long

The long variable subtype is 4 bytes in size and can be a whole number in the range of –2,147,483,648 to 2,147,483,647.

Single

The single subtype contains a single-precision, floating-point number. Precision refers to the number of bytes of fractional value storage allotted to the variable. A single-precision number allots 2 bytes for fractional value storage. It takes 4 bytes to store a variable of the subtype single. The range of values that a single can hold is –3.402823E38 to –1.401298E-45 for negative values and 1.401298E-45 to 3.402823E38 for positive values.

Double

The double subtype takes up 8 bytes of storage, 4 bytes of which are reserved for a fractional value. The double subtype is extremely precise and is usually reserved for advanced mathematical and scientific operations. It has a range of -1.79769313486232E308 to -4.94065645841247E-324 for negative values and 4.94065645841247E-324 to 1.7976931348632E308 for positive values.

String

The string subtype is a group of up to approximately 2 billion characters. The size of the string variable depends on the length of the string.

Date

The date subtype is a number that represents a date in the range of January 1, 100 to December 31, 9999.

Empty

The empty subtype is returned for variants that aren't initialized. If the variable is a number, the value is 0. If it's a string, the value is " ".

Object

The object subtype contains the name of an OLE Automation object. The object can then be manipulated using the variable.

Error

The error subtype contains an error number. You can use the generated error number to generate an expanded explanation of the error.

Using Variables

Now that you know what variables are all about, let's take a look at how they are used in your VBS scripts.

Declaring Your Variables

Strictly speaking, you don't need to declare your variables in VBScript. You could simply set the variables that you need on the fly:

```
MyString="This is my string"
```

One of problems with setting the value of variables without first declaring them is that the variables become difficult to track. For example, you set the value of a variable somewhere in code, but you can't remember where the variable started. In addition to just being good programming practice, declaring your variables will make it easier for you to read and maintain your code.

To declare a variable in a VBS script, you use the Dim statement. Dim stands for dimension:

```
<SCRIPT LANGUAGE="VBS">
<!--
    Option Explicit
    Dim MyString
    MyString="This is my string"
-->
</SCRIPT>
```

Notice that in addition to declaring our variable with the Dim statement, we added the Option Explicit statement to the beginning of the code. Adding Option Explicit will require you to declare all variables in your script. Using this statement is completely up to you. If you use Option Explicit but don't declare a variable, your script will generate an error when run.

You can declare more than one variable at a time. Just use the Dim statement and put a comma between every new variable name:

```
<SCRIPT LANGUAGE="VBS">
<!--
    Dim Name, Address, City, State, Zip
-->
</SCRIPT>
```

Assignment

To assign a value to a variable, place the variable on the left followed by an equals sign and the value on the right:

```
Name="Brian Johnson"
```

Remember that variables in VBScript are variants. VBScript determines the nature of the variable when you run the script. There are really only two types of data: strings and numbers. String data is always held in quotation marks.

Scope

The scope of a variable refers to where in the script the variable is available for processing. A variable declared inside a procedure is limited in scope to that procedure. If a variable is declared outside of the procedures in the script, it is available to all the procedures in the script. Listing 2.3 illustrates the scope of variables in VBS scripts.

Listing 2.3. Scope of variables in VBS scripts.

```
<HTML>
<HEAD>
<TITLE>VBS Variable Scope</TITLE>
</HEAD>
<BODY>
<H1>Tester Page for VBS</H1>
<HR COLOR="BLUE">
<INPUT TYPE="SUBMIT" NAME="Btn1" VALUE="Local Variable">
<INPUT TYPE="SUBMIT" NAME="Btn2" VALUE="Script Wide Variable">
<INPUT TYPE="SUBMIT" NAME="BTN3" VALUE="Out of Scope">
<SCRIPT LANGUAGE="VBS>
Option Explicit
Dim MyGlobal
MyGlobal="Access Ok"
Sub Btn1_OnClick()
Dim MyLocal
MyLocal="Local access Ok!"
MsgBox MyLocal,0,"Btn1 Clicked"
End Sub
Sub Btn2_OnClick
MsgBox MyGlobal,0,"Btn2 Clicked"
End Sub
Sub Btn3_OnClick
MsgBox MyLocal,0,"Btn3 Clicked"
End Sub
-->
</SCRIPT>
</BODY>
</HTML>
```

If you run the code, you'll see that you can access the local variable by clicking Btn1. If you click Btn2, you'll access the variable that we declared globally. Finally, if you click Btn3, you'll get an error (see Figure 2.4) because the Btn3_OnClick procedure tries to access the variable declared in the Btn1_OnClick procedure.

FIGURE 2.4.

An out-of-scope variable generates an error.

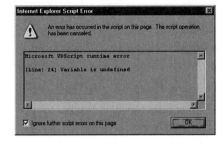

When discussing the scope of a variable, you'll often hear the term *lifetime*. Lifetime refers to the amount of time that the variable exists in memory. At the procedure level, the lifetime of the variable is as long as it takes to run through the procedure. At the script level, the variable is live for as long as the script is live. You can extend the lifetime of a procedure-level variable by declaring the variable as static. A static variable will retain its value between calls to the procedure. To declare a variable as static, simply use the Static keyword:

```
Static MyVariable
```

Scalar

The types of variables we have talked about so far have been *scalar* variables. A scalar variable has only one value assigned to it at a time. Depending on the types of programs you write, you'll probably use scalar variables often in your scripts. When modeling the world, though, you often need to work with sets of values. To work with these values, you need to use a different type of variable known as an *array*.

Array

An array is like a list. When you go to the grocery store, you often carry a list of the items that you need to purchase. If you were to assign the list to a scalar value, it might look something like this:

```
MyList = "peas, carrots, corn"
```

Although it's easy enough to have MyList contain the contents of the list, it's not very easy to figure out which item is which. That's where an array comes in. An array lets you easily specify items in the list and retrieve those items individually. Let's take a look at a simple array.

You declare an array variable in VBScript the same way you do a scalar variable. The difference is that you specify the number of items in the array:

```
Dim MyList(4)
```

Arrays in VBScript start their count at zero, so an array is declared with the highest count number in the array. In this case, `MyList` has a total of five items.

Looking at Listing 2.4, you can see that we've drawn five buttons on the page. An array variable, `MyList`, is declared with five items, and each item is assigned a different value. In the click event for each button, we attach the value of an array item to a local scalar variable called `Item`. We then call a procedure named `ShowMessage`, passing `Item` as a parameter. The `ShowMessage` procedure takes the value of `Item` and plugs it into the `MsgBox` function, which brings up the message box containing the value of the particular array item.

Listing 2.4. Shopping list of items.

```
<HTML>
<HEAD>
<TITLE>Tester Page</TITLE>
</HEAD>
<BODY>
<H1>Tester Page for VBScript</H1>
<HR COLOR="BLUE">
<INPUT TYPE="SUBMIT" NAME="Btn1" VALUE="Item 1"><BR>
<INPUT TYPE="SUBMIT" NAME="Btn2" VALUE="Item 2"><BR>
<INPUT TYPE="SUBMIT" NAME="Btn3" VALUE="Item 3"><BR>
<INPUT TYPE="SUBMIT" NAME="Btn4" VALUE="Item 4"><BR>
<INPUT TYPE="SUBMIT" NAME="Btn5" VALUE="Item 5"><BR>
<SCRIPT LANGUAGE="VBScript">
<!--
Option Explicit
Dim MyList(4)
MyList(0)="Corn"
MyList(1)="Carrots"
MyList(2)="Peas"
MyList(3)="Chicken"
MyList(4)="Cake"
Sub Btn1_OnClick
 Dim Item
 Item=MyList(0)
 ShowMessage(Item)
End Sub
Sub Btn2_OnClick
 Dim Item
 Item=MyList(1)
 ShowMessage(Item)
End Sub
Sub Btn3_OnClick
 Dim Item
 Item=MyList(2)
 ShowMessage(Item)
End Sub
```

continues

Listing 2.4. continued

```
Sub Btn4_OnClick
 Dim Item
 Item=MyList(3)
 ShowMessage(Item)
End Sub
Sub Btn5_OnClick
 Dim Item
 Item=MyList(4)
 ShowMessage(Item)
End Sub
Sub ShowMessage(SelItem)
MsgBox SelItem,0,"Item picked"
End Sub
-->
</SCRIPT>
</BODY>
</HTML>
```

You can also create multidimensional arrays. A 2-D array is declared like this:

```
Dim MyArray(4,9)
```

This declaration creates a table containing five rows and 10 columns. You can pull a particular value from the array using `MyArray(row,column)`. The upper limit for multidimensional arrays is 60 dimensions.

One final note on arrays: You can declare what are called *dynamic arrays* that change sizes as the script is run. To declare a dynamic array, use the `Dim` or `ReDim` statement without adding a size value to the array name:

```
Dim MyDynamicArray()
```

To use this array, you would `ReDim` the array, adding a size value to the name:

```
ReDim MyDynamicArray(14)
```

You can `ReDim` an array as many times as needed.

Naming Conventions

The names that you give variables in VBScript are the same as for any other named item in a script. Variable names must begin with an alphabetical character:

```
'  This is Ok
Dim MyVariable
' This is not Ok
Dim @Variable
```

In addition, variables cannot contain embedded periods and are limited to 255 characters. Finally, you cannot use the same name for two different values in the same scope. It's okay to have the same variable name declared in many different procedures, but the same variable name cannot be declared globally, and it cannot be declared twice in the same procedure.

When you declare variables, you should consider a few naming conventions. Table 2.1 lists these conventions.

Table 2.1. Naming conventions in VBScript.

Variable Subtype	Prefix
Boolean	bln
Byte	byt
Date	dtm
Double	dbl
Error	err
Integer	int
Long	lng
Object	obj
Single	sng
String	str

To use these naming conventions properly, you need to know the probable data subtype of the variables you declare. To name a variable that you know will contain a string, use the prefix along with a descriptive name for the variable:

```
Dim strName
```

The same rules follow for values that you know will be of a specified subtype:

```
Dim dblMiles
Dim blnEmpty
Dim intTotal
```

Using a convention such as this can save you time in the long run. It's much easier to see that you're about to make a mistake when you see an equation like `strValue + dblMiles` than if you simply saw `Value + Miles`.

The scope of a variable also has a naming convention. If you have a script-level variable, you can add an s to the prefix:

```
Dim sdblMyNumericValue
```

We'll talk more about coding conventions throughout the book. As new conventions are introduced, they will be incorporated into the sample code.

Constants

A constant is a named value that doesn't change throughout a script. For example, the value of the speed of light through room-temperature air at sea level is about 760 miles per hour. To use this constant in a script, you simply declare it, assign it, and use it like a variable. To differentiate a value that you want to be a constant in your script, you should use your own naming conventions, so that you don't try to reassign the value of the constant that you've created.

```
'vbSOL Speed of Light
Dim vbSol
vbSol = 760
```

Once you set the value of the constant, you can use it in your script as if it were the actual number. Keep in mind though that constants in VBScript are essentially just variables that you don't change in your program. Unlike other languages that allow you to set the value of a constant to static, there's no way to make a variable in VBScript unchangeable.

Program Flow

Program flow has to do with how your program moves from one line or procedure to another. To illustrate the flow of a program, many programmers use a flowchart.

The specifics of program flow have mostly to do with decision-making in scripts. Next, we'll talk about decision-making steps in VBScript and how different conditional and looping statements affect your script.

Operators

Before we can talk about how flow control works in a program, you need to be familiar with the operators used in the logic operations that control flow. Most of these will be familiar to you if you have a rudimentary background in math. Others might not be quite as obvious.

Table 2.2 contains the operators you can use in VBScript programs.

Table 2.2. VBScript operators.

Operator	Purpose
+	Addition
And	Logical And
&	Concantation operator
/	Division
Eqv	Logical Equivalence
^	Exponential

Operator	Purpose
Imp	Logical Implication
\	Integer Division
Is	Logical Is (Refer to same object)
Mod	Modulus Operator (Remainder)
*	Multiplication
-	Negation and Subtraction
Not	Logical Not
Or	Logical Or
Xor	Logical Xor

You'll be using some of the logic operators in the next sections. The mathematical operators are used for math operations and, in some cases, concatenation. For example:

```
MyString = "Now is the time" & " for all good men…"
```

is functionally equivalent to

```
MyString = "Now is the time" + " for all good men…"
```

Decision-Making in Programs

Decision-making in programs is what programming is all about. Keep in mind that computers aren't really that good at thinking things through. You have to tell the program what to do every step of the way. Humans use a method of thinking that has what are known as *fuzzy logic* characteristics. If you were to ask more than one person to name the color of a particular scarf, you might get the answers red, pink, orange, and scarlet. If you ask a computer to name the color of an element on the screen, you'll get back the exact color name. Taking it one step further, if you ask the same group of people if the scarf is red, they all might answer "Yes." If you ask a computer if the screen element is red, it will return a yes value only if the item is exactly red.

Always keep in mind the limitations of the machine. Write good questions and you'll get good answers.

If...Then...Else

The If...Then...Else statement is one of the basic capabilities of a computer language. This statement tests for the truth of a statement and, depending on the answer, processes information or moves on to another piece of code. Let's look at an example of an If...Then...Else statement in a program (see Listing 2.5) and then talk about what's happening in the code.

Listing 2.5. If...Then...Else in a VBS script.

```
<HTML>
<HEAD>
<TITLE>Tester Page</TITLE>
</HEAD>
<BODY>
<H1>Tester Page for VBScript</H1>
<HR COLOR="BLUE">
<CENTER>
<FONT COLOR=RED SIZE=5>Question:</FONT><BR>
<FONT COLOR=BLUE SIZE=6>Who is buried in Grant's tomb?</FONT><BR>
<INPUT TYPE="SUBMIT" NAME="Btn1" VALUE="Click to test the code">
<INPUT TYPE="TEXT" NAME="Txt1">
</CENTER>
<SCRIPT LANGUAGE="VBSCRIPT">
<!--
Sub Btn1_OnClick()
Dim Message
If Txt1.Value = "Grant" then
Message="You're right!"
Else
Message="Try again"
End If
MsgBox Message, 0,"Tester Result"
End Sub
-->
</SCRIPT>
</BODY></HTML>
```

The example in Listing 2.5 is simple yet powerful. First of all, it's our first useful program. We answer a question, and the computer tells us if we are right or wrong. Immediate feedback and interaction are what it's all about. Let's break down the Btn1_OnClick procedure to see what's happening up close.

When Btn1 is clicked, the If...Then...Else statement asks if the value of the Txt1 text input box is Grant. If the answer to that question is true, the program sets the value of the variable Message to You're right. (See Figure 2.5.) If the answer is false, the value of Message is set to Try again. Notice that there is absolutely no room for error when answering this question. If the user enters grant, GRANT, or US Grant, the program will skip to the Else part of the program, and the message will be "Try again." Later you'll learn how to make If...Then...Else statements a little more tolerant.

If you have a simple If...Then statement, the statement can be just a single line:

```
If x=4 then y=12
```

When the statement takes more than one line, you need to close it off with an End If statement.

FIGURE 2.5.

Outcome of a quiz answer.

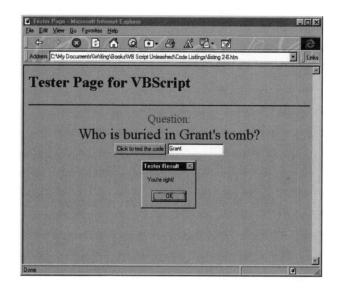

For...Next

The For...Next statement is used to run a block of code statements a certain number of times:

```
Dim x
For x = 1 to 10
Edit1.Value = x
Next
```

In this example, the counter starts at 1 and repeats Edit1.Value = x 10 times. You can also specify the way that the value of x is counted, using the Step keyword. You can use an If...Then statement to exit the loop, if necessary:

```
Dim x
For x = 5 To 50 Step 5
Edit1.Value=x
If x > 20 Then Exit For
Next
```

In this case, the counter starts at 5 and stops at 50 for a total of 10 iterations. The loop is exited after five iterations, because x is greater than 20.

You could also use the Step value to count down, using negative numbers. Starting with a higher number and counting down to a lower one would look something like this:

```
Dim x
For x = 10 to 1 Step -1
Edit1.Value = x
Next
```

Do...Loop

Another common looping statement is Do...Loop. A Do...Loop statement is usually better to use than a For...Next and Exit For combination. The Do...Loop statement allows you to create a loop that runs an infinite number of times. You need to be careful when using this statement—you don't want to accidentally get your script into a loop that it can't get out of:

```
Dim x
x=1
Do Until x = 25
x = x + 1
Loop
```

In this example, the place where you need to be careful is in Do Until x = 25. If the initial value of x was 30, the code would loop continuously without the x = 25 value ever being met.

There are two ways to test for a true value in the Do...Loop statement. You can use the Until keyword to repeat the loop until a condition is true or the While keyword to repeat while the condition is true:

```
Dim x
x = 10
Do While x < 100
x = x + 10
Loop
```

By placing the While or Until keyword after the Loop statement, you can make sure that the code inside the loop is run at least once:

```
Dim x
x = 1
Do
x = x + 1
If x > 30 Then Exit Loop
Loop Until x = 30
```

The code in this Do...Loop block is run at least once before it's ended. We've also added a safety feature in the form of an Exit Loop command that's issued if x is found to be greater than 30. If x is greater than 30, there is no chance that the value will ever be 30.

For Each...Next

The For Each...Next loop is used like the For...Next loop. It is used to test conditions in collections of objects. Objects have properties that are specified by keywords that are appended to the object name after a period. If I had an object with the property of color, you could access that property with MyObject.Color. Groups of objects are called collections, and you can test each of the objects for the truth of a statement using For Each...Next:

```
For Each Car in Lot
     if Car.Color = "Red" then
     MsgBox "Red car!", 0, "Answer"
     End If
Next
```

In this example, the collection of objects is called `Lot`, and the objects are of the type `Car`. We go through the cars in the lot, and when we get to a red one we see a message. You'll learn more about objects in Part II of this book.

While...Wend

According to Microsoft, `While...Wend` is included in VBScript for those programmers who are familiar with its usage, but it's not well documented. Microsoft recommends using `Do...Loop` instead, but let's take a quick look at the `While...Wend` statement to become familiar with its usage:

```
Dim x
x = 1
While x < 10
x = x + 1
Wend
```

The `While...Wend` statement repeats until the value of the `While` portion of the statement is true.

Review

In this chapter, we talked about the differences between Visual Basic and VBScript. You learned that a script is a set of instructions that control the behavior of objects in your Web pages. You learned about data types and that all variables in VBScript are variants. Finally, you learned about program flow and the statements used to loop through a program.

VBScript Functions

by Brian Johnson

IN THIS CHAPTER

CHAPTER 3

Introduction

Procedures are the building blocks of VBScript. So far, we've created a number of scripts in HTML documents. We've used procedures in most of them, but we haven't really discussed the topic in detail. We'll do that in this chapter.

In this chapter, you will

- Learn about procedures and how they are used in VBS scripts
- Learn about the difference between a `Sub` procedure and a `Function` procedure
- Learn about VBScript's intrinsic functions
- Learn how to utilize VBS functions in your own scripts

Procedures in Scripts

Procedures are the logical parts into which a program is divided. The code inside a procedure is run when the procedure is called. A procedure can be called with a `Call` statement in another procedure, or it can be triggered by an event such as a button click.

Events are triggered when messages are sent from the operating system to VBScript. In graphical operating systems, such as Windows, the way that different applications interact with the operating system is by sending and receiving. The operating system is the controlling force in the graphical environment, and the scripts that you write will depend in large part on the resources and messages made available to you from Windows. You'll learn more about events in Chapter 4, "Intrinsic Controls."

`Sub` Procedures and `Function` Procedures

There are two types of procedures in VBScript: `Sub` procedures and `Function` procedures. `Sub` procedures are blocks of code that are wrapped in the `Sub...End Sub` keywords. A `Sub` can take arguments and process them within the `Sub` procedure. A `Sub` can call other procedures, but it can't return a value generated to the calling procedure directly.

A `Function` procedure works just like a `Sub` procedure. It can take arguments and call other procedures. Most importantly, `Function` procedures return a value to the calling procedure. Figure 3.1 shows the relationship between procedures in a typical script. The value returned is then processed by the calling procedure as if the code had been in the same block.

FIGURE 3.1.

Calling one procedure from another.

```
<SCRIPT LANGUAGE="VBS">
<!--
Sub Btn1 OnClick
     Dim Message, x
     x=100
     Message="Sub Btn1 OnClick"
     MsgBox Message, 0,"Procedure Result"
     Message="Sub MySub"
     MySub(Message)  ■
     x=ReturnCount(x)  ◄
     Message="Function returned" + CStr(x)
     MsgBox Message, 0, "Procedure Result"
End Sub
Sub MySub(Msg)  ◄
     MsgBoxMsg, 0, "Procedure Result"
End Sub
Function ReturnCount(Num)  ◄
     ReturnCount=Num + 1
End Function
-->
</SCRIPT>
```

Let's take a look at some sample code. Listing 3.1 contains three procedures. We'll use message boxes to track the program flow.

Listing 3.1. Flow.htm.

```
<HTML>
<HEAD>
<TITLE>Tracking Procedures</TITLE>
</HEAD>
<BODY>
<H1>Tester Page for VBS</H1>
<HR COLOR="BLUE">
<INPUT TYPE="SUBMIT" NAME="Btn1" VALUE="Click to test the code">
<SCRIPT LANGUAGE="VBScript">
<!--
Sub Btn1_OnClick
    Dim Message, x
    x=100
    Message="Sub Btn1_OnClick"
    MsgBox Message, 0,"Procedure Result"
    Message = "Sub MySub"
    MySub(Message)
    x = ReturnCount(x)
    Message = "Function returned " + CStr(x)
    MsgBox Message, 0, "Procedure Result"
End Sub
Sub MySub(Msg)
    MsgBox Msg, 0, "Procedure Result"
End Sub
Function ReturnCount(Num)
    ReturnCount = Num + 1
End Function
-->
</SCRIPT>
</BODY>
</HTML>
```

Let's track Listing 3.1 and see where it's going. Using our tester template, we create two procedures to go with the Sub Btn1_OnClick procedure that was already in place. The MySub procedure takes an argument called Msg and in turn passes that value to a MsgBox function. The other new procedure is the Function ReturnCount, which simply takes an argument, Num, and adds 1 to it.

If you take a look at how the program flows, you'll see that it all begins in Sub Btn1_OnClick. The variable Message is assigned the name Sub Btn1_OnClick, and a MsgBox function is called with Message as one of the arguments. Notice that the flow of the Sub Btn1_OnClick procedure is halted until the message box is dismissed.

After the message box is closed, the value of Message is set to the name of the second procedure in the script, Sub MySub. The MySub procedure is called, with Message as an argument. The argument Message is then called in another MsgBox function call from within MySub. Again, program flow is stopped while the message box is displayed.

Finally, the variable x, having previously been set to a value of 100, is used as an argument in the call to the function ReturnCount. ReturnCount adds 1 to x and returns the value to the calling procedure. We then make x part of the Message variable. Notice that the argument we pass to the MsgBox function must be a string, so we need to convert the value of x to a string before it can be made part of Message. The message box is then displayed with the message "Function returned 101." When the message box is closed, End Sub is hit, and the script ends.

Arguments to Procedures

Arguments can be used to pass data to either Sub or Function procedures. When calling a procedure, you can simply use the procedure name followed by arguments, which are separated by commas:

```
MyProcedure Arg1, Arg2, Arg3
```

Or you can use the Call statement, in which case the argument list must be enclosed by parentheses:

```
Call MyProcedure(Arg1, Arg2)
```

You can also call the procedure without the Call statement and still include parentheses.

Creating and Calling Functions

When you create and use a function, the return value of the function is held by a variable with the name of the function. For example, if you create a function that converts pennies to dollars, you might name the function Dollar:

```
Function Dollar(Cents)
    Dollar = Cents/100
End Function
```

The function returns the value of `Dollar` to the calling procedure.

To call the `Dollar` function from another procedure, you must use a variable of some sort to hold the return value. If you call `Dollar` from the following code, the value `Dollars` will hold the returned value of the function:

```
Dollars = Dollar(2456)
```

Function procedures are great tools for working with data in a VBS script. When you create functions that you know you might want to use again, be sure to save them, so that you can easily reuse them in new scripts.

Intrinsic Functions

In addition to creating your own function procedures for use in your scripts, you can use a number of intrinsic function procedures that are built into VBScript. These functions include string operations, conversions, math functions, time and date functions, and Boolean functions. Understanding these functions will benefit you greatly as you begin to write larger and more complex scripts.

First, let's talk about the basic utility functions available to you.

Basic Functions

The intrinsic functions in VBScript aren't actually broken into categories, but I've divided them up so that you'll remember them more easily. What I've called the basic functions don't easily fit into any of the other categories I've created.

The message box is one of the most useful functions in VBScript. The two types of message boxes available to you are the message box and the input box.

InputBox

The `InputBox` function makes it possible for you to get input from a user without placing a text control on the form. (See Figure 3.2.) It takes seven possible parameters:

```
InputBox(prompt, title, default, xpos, ypos, helpfile, context)
```

All the arguments of the `InputBox` function are optional except `prompt`. Let's take a look at each of these parameters in detail.

3

VBSCRIPT
FUNCTIONS

FIGURE 3.2.

The input box in a
VBScript-enabled page.

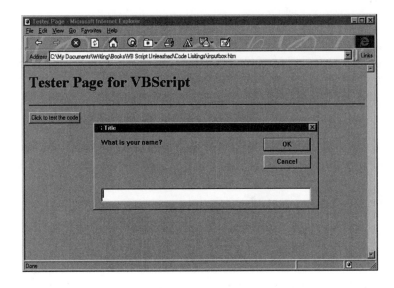

prompt

The prompt argument is a string containing the question that you are asking your user:

```
InputBox("What is your name?")
```

Title

The Title argument determines the title of the dialog. This argument must be a string expression. If the title isn't specified, the title of the dialog defaults to the application name.

default

The default argument specifies a string that appears in the input box on the dialog when the dialog is displayed. Leave this parameter blank if you don't want the dialog to display default text.

xpos and ypos

The xpos and ypos arguments specify where in relation to the screen the dialog is displayed. These arguments are made in twips. The xpos argument specifies the horizontal value, and the ypos argument specifies the vertical value.

helpfile and context

The helpfile argument specifies a Windows Help file to open if the user presses the F1 button. If you specify a Help file, you also need to specify a context id.

The `context` argument specifies a Help context id number for the file called in the `helpfile` argument. The Help context id number opens the corresponding Help topic.

len

The `len` function returns the length of a string or the number of bytes in a variable.

MsgBox

You've been using the `MsgBox` function to test the VBScript language features that we've discussed so far. The message box is useful when you want to notify a user that an event has occurred. You can specify the buttons shown in the dialog, and the function returns a value that indicates which button was clicked:

```
MsgBox(prompt, buttons, title, helpfile, context)
```

The `helpfile` and `context` arguments in the `MsgBox` function are optional.

prompt

The `prompt` argument is a string value of up to 1024 characters. As with the `InputBox` function, you can use the carriage return line-feed combination (`Chr(13)& Chr(10)`), a carriage return (`Chr(13)`), or a line feed (`Chr(10)`) to break the prompt into multiple lines:

```
Dim Message
Message = "This text is broken" + (Chr(13)& Chr(10)) + "into multiple lines."
MsgBox (Message, 0, "Message Title")
```

FIGURE 3.3.

Message box with a multiline caption.

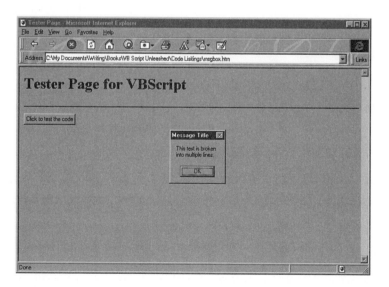

buttons

The buttons argument is a VBScript constant or a numeric value that determines which buttons are displayed on the dialog. Table 3.1 lists the values and constants that you can use when calling this function.

Table 3.1. Settings for the buttons argument.

Value	Buttons shown
0	OK
1	OK, Cancel
2	Abort, Retry, Ignore
3	Yes, No, Cancel
4	Yes, No
5	Yes, No, Cancel
16	(Critical Message Icon)
32	(Warning Query Icon)
48	(Warning Message Icon)
64	(Information Message Icon)
0	(First button default)
256	(Second button default)
512	(Third button default)
0	(User must respond before continuing with application)
4096	(User must respond before continuing with the operating system)

title

The title argument is a string that specifies the text shown in the titlebar of the message box. If no title is specified, the title of the calling application is displayed.

Helpfile and Context

These arguments work the same as for InputBox. Helpfile specifies a Windows Help file, and context specifies the Help context id for the topic.

Return Values

The return values for the MsgBox function are the numeric or constant values of the button pressed. Table 3.2 lists the possible return values for the MsgBox function.

Table 3.2. Possible return values for the MsgBox function.

Button Clicked	Value
OK	1
Cancel	2
Abort	3
Retry	4
Ignore	5
Yes	6
No	7

Let's take a look at a procedure, shown in Listing 3.2, that does something with the return value from a MsgBox function.

Listing 3.2. MsgBox return value.

```
<HTML>
<HEAD>
<TITLE>The MsgBox Returns</TITLE>
</HEAD>
<BODY>
<H1>Tester Page for VBS</H1>
<HR COLOR="BLUE">
<INPUT TYPE="SUBMIT" NAME="Btn1" VALUE="Click to test the code">
<SCRIPT LANGUAGE="VBScript">
<!--
Sub Btn1_OnClick()
Dim strQuestion, intReturn
Do Until intReturn = 7
strQuestion = "Do you want to see another dialog?"
intReturn=MsgBox(strQuestion, 4, "Question" )
Loop
End Sub
-->
</SCRIPT>
</BODY>
</HTML>
```

In this script, the button on the page is clicked, and a yes/no message box is displayed asking whether the user wishes to see the message box repeated. If the answer stored in intReturn holds a value of Yes (6), then the dialog is redisplayed. If the user clicks No (7), the message box is closed and the script is ended until the button is pushed again.

VarType

The VarType function returns the subvalue of a variable. This function is useful for verifying the contents of a variable or for checking the type of variable before trying to operate on it. Table 3.3 shows the possible return values for the VarType function.

Table 3.3. Possible return values for the VarType function.

Subtype	Value
(empty)	0
(null)	1
Integer	2
Long	3
Single	4
Double	5
Currency	6
Date	7
String	8
OLE Object	9
Error	10
Boolean	11
Variant	12
Non-OLE Object	13
Byte	17
Array	8192

You can use either the value or the constant to determine the return type. When the variable on which you're running the function is an array, the function returns the vbArray value added to the variable type in the array.

String Functions

The following string functions act on string data to allow you to manipulate and parse strings. Parsing textual data means dividing it into logical divisions. Let's take a look at the various string-related functions and then look at an example that utilizes some of the functions.

Asc

The Asc function takes a string as a parameter and returns the ASCII character code for the first character in the string:

```
Dim strData, intCharCode
strData = "This is a string"
intCharCode = Asc(strData)
```

In this code example, the function returns the value of T, which is 84. If you run this function on an empty string, it generates a runtime error.

Chr

The Chr function takes a character code as a parameter and returns the corresponding character. Keep in mind that the characters for codes 0 to 31 are nonprintable:

```
StrMyString = "This is my two line" + (Chr(13) + Chr(10)) + "text string example."
```

In this example line, the string has a carriage return and a line feed added to the middle of the text. This will cause a break in the string, displaying it on two lines.

InStr

The InStr function is a powerful text-searching tool that finds the position of text substrings within strings of text. This is a fairly complex function, so you should first be familiar with the function's syntax:

```
position = InStr(startpos, string1, string2, type)
```

The InStr function returns the position of the substring within the string. In this case, the return value is held by the variable position. Let's go through the other arguments individually.

Startpos

The startpos argument is a numeric value that tells the function where to start searching. This is an important argument because if you're thinking about adding search functions to your own string operations, you'll need to adjust the number as you find multiple occurrences of the search string in a large body of text.

String1

The string1 argument is the string in which you are searching for the string2 string.

String2

String2 is the text for which you're searching.

Type

The type argument specifies the string comparison that you're performing. This argument can have a value of 0 (default) or 1. A type 0 comparison is a binary comparison. The function will return a position only in the case of an exact match. An argument of 1 will do a non-case-sensitive, textual search.

We can see the difference between the two types of searches in the following code:

```
Dim strBigString, strSearchString, intReturn0, intReturn1
strBigString = "This is the BIG string"
strSearchString = "big"
intReturn0 = InStr( , strBigString, strSearchString, 0)
intReturn1 = InStr( , strBigString, strSearchString, 1)
```

In this sample, the intReturn0 variable is set to 0 because the function does not find the string "big" in strBigString. The variable inReturn1 is set to 13 because strSearchString is found in the non-case-sensitive search.

Table 3.4. Return values for the InStr function.

String Values	Return Values
mainstring length is 0	0
mainstring is Null	Null
searchstring length is 0	startpos
searchstring is Null	Null
searchstring not found	0
searchstring found	(position of string in mainstring)

If the value of startpos is greater than the length of mainstring, the function returns a 0.

LCase

The LCase function takes a string and converts all the characters to lowercase. It takes a string as an argument and returns the converted string.

Left

The Left function returns a string containing the characters from the left side of the string, up to a specified number. The function takes two arguments, string and length:

```
Dim strMyString, strMain
strMain = "The rain in Spain..."
strMyString = Left(strMain, 15)
```

In this sample, the string variable strMyString would be set to The r, the first five characters of the string. If the number you specify in the length argument is greater than or equal to the length of the string, the function will return the entire string.

LTrim

The LTrim function returns a copy of the string argument with the leading spaces removed from the string:

```
Dim strMyString, strMain
strMain = "    There are four leading spaces here."
strMyString = LTrim(strMain)
```

In this example, the functions returns the string, "There are four leading spaces here."

Mid

The Mid function returns a substring of a specified length from another string. This function takes three parameters: string, start, and length. The length argument is optional.

```
Dim strMyString, strMain
strMain = "Ask not what your country can do for you..."
strMyString = Mid(strMain, 8, 10)
```

In this example, we're looking for a string that starts at character 8 and is 10 characters in length. The string value contained in strMyString is equal to what your .

Right

The Right function works like the Left function, but it returns a specified number of characters starting from the last character in the string. This function takes the number of characters as an argument and returns a string:

```
Dim strMyString, strMain
strMain = "How now brown cow?"
strMyString = Right(strMain, 10)
```

In this example, strMyString is set to the last 10 characters of strMain, or brown cow?.

3

VBSCRIPT
FUNCTIONS

RTrim

The Rtrim function works like the Ltrim function. It removes trailing spaces from a string. It takes a single argument, string, and returns a string.

Str()

The Str() function takes a number as an argument and returns a string value representing the number. The first character in the resulting string is always a space that acts as a placeholder for the sign of the number. If you want to use a numeric value in a string or a function that takes a string as a parameter, you'll need to use this function or the CStr function to make the conversion first.

StrComp

The StrComp function takes two strings as arguments and compares them, based on the third argument, which defines the type of comparison:

```
Dim RetVal, strString1, strString2
strString1 = "This is a string."
strString2 = "This is a STRING."
RetVal = StrComp(strString1, strString2, 1)
```

The StrComp function returns a numeric value that indicates whether the items are the same. The comparison type has two possible values: 0 (default) is a binary comparison, and 1 is non-case-sensitive. Table 3.5 show the return values for the StrComp function.

Table 3.5. Return values for the StrComp function.

Return Value	Description
-1	String1 < String2
0	String1 = String2
1	String1 > String2
NULL	One of the strings is null

String

The String function takes a number and character code argument and returns the character, repeated a number of times:

```
Dim strRetString
strRetString = String(3, 97)
```

This example returns the string `"aaa"`. If the character code argument is greater than 255, the code is automatically converted to a valid character using the `formula charcode = (char Mod 256)`.

Trim

The `Trim` function returns the string argument, with leading and trailing spaced removed.

UCase

The `UCase` function converts all the characters in the string argument to uppercase.

Val

The `Val` function takes a string argument and returns numbers from the string. The function stops retrieving numbers as soon as it hits a non-numeric character:

```
Dim MyNumber, strMyString
MyString = "300 South Street"
MyNumber = Val(strMyString)
```

In this example, the function returns the number 300. The `Val` function recognizes decimal points and radix prefixes. A radix prefix is a prefix that defines an alternative numbering system. The `&O` prefix is used for octal values and `&H` for hexadecimal.

Conversion Functions

Conversion functions enable you to change the subtype of a variable. Although VBScript uses the variant type for all variables, in many cases an argument of a certain type is required. An example would be a function that takes a string argument. If you want to be able to use numeric data, you'll need to convert it to a string before calling the function.

CByte

The `CByte` function converts an expression to the subtype byte.

CDbl

The `CDbl` function converts an expression to the subtype double.

CInt

The `CInt` function converts an expression to the subtype integer.

CLng

The CLng function converts an expression to the subtype long.

CStr

The CStr function returns a string from a valid expression. Table 3.6 lists the return values for various expression types.

Table 3.6. Return values for the CStr function.

Return Value	Expression Type
True or False	Boolean
Short-Date	Date
Runtime Error	Null
" "	Empty
Error(#)	Error
Number	Number

CVErr

The CVErr function returns the subtype error. It takes any valid error number as an argument.

Math Functions

Math functions enable you to perform operations on numbers in your VBS scripts. You'll find these functions fairly straightforward.

Abs

The Abs function takes a number as a parameter and returns its absolute value. The absolute value of a number is the numerical value of a number without considering its sign. An argument of -7 would return the value 7.

Array

The Array function returns a variant value containing an array. The array can be of any subtype. This function takes a list of values separated by commas as a parameter.

Atn

The Atn function returns the arctangent of a number, a trigonometric function that is used to determine angles in triangles. This function is the inverse of tangent (Tan), which calculates the ratio of sides in a right triangle. It takes a number as an argument.

Exp

The Exp function takes a numeric argument and returns e (the base of natural logarithms) raised to a power.

Hex

The Hex function returns a string value containing the value of an argument converted to hexadecimal form. If the argument is a fractional value, it is rounded to the nearest whole number before the function returns the string.

Keep in mind that this function returns a string. If you want to perform mathematical operations on the returned value, you must first convert the string back into a numerical value. Hexadecimal numbers are represented in VBScript using the &H prefix.

Int

The Int function returns the whole number portion of an argument. If the argument is negative, Int returns the first integer value that is less than or equal to the argument.

Fix

The Fix function works like the Int function, returning the whole number portion of an argument. The difference is that if the number argument is negative, Fix returns the first integer value that is greater than or equal to the argument.

Log

The Log function returns the natural logarithm of a numeric argument. The numeric argument that this function processes must be greater than zero.

Oct

The Oct function returns a string representing the octal value of a numeric argument. If the numeric argument is fractional, it is rounded up before the function returns a value. As with the Hex function, the returned string must be converted back to numeric form before you can perform mathematical operations on it. To use an octal value mathematically, you use the &O prefix.

Rnd

The Rnd function takes a numeric argument and returns a value between zero and one. The number generated depends on the numeric argument in relation to the values in Table 3.7.

Table 3.7. Number value determines generation technique.

Number Value	Generates
<0	Same number every time
>0	Next random number
=0	Last generated number
" "	Next random value in sequence

If you want to generate a range of random numbers, use the following formula:

```
Int((upperbound - lowerbound + 1)*Rnd + lowerbound)
```

Let's use the Rnd function to create a program (see Listing 3.3) that generates random numbers. Random numbers are often used in computer games and simulations. We'll use this function to create a page that generates random Lotto numbers. Figure 3.4 shows the page in action.

Listing 3.3. Lotto.htm.

```
<HTML>
<HEAD>
<TITLE>Play 3 Generator</TITLE>
</HEAD>
<BODY><CENTER>
<H1>Play 3 Generator</H1>
<HR COLOR="BLUE">
<INPUT TYPE="SUBMIT" NAME="Btn1" VALUE="Click for the lucky numbers!"><BR><BR>
<INPUT TYPE="SUBMIT" NAME="BtnBall1" VALUE="">
<INPUT TYPE="SUBMIT" NAME="BtnBall2" VALUE="">
<INPUT TYPE="SUBMIT" NAME="BtnBall3" VALUE="">
<SCRIPT LANGUAGE="VBScript">
<!--

Sub Btn1_OnClick()
    BtnBall1.Value = RndBall()
    BtnBall2.Value = RndBall()
    BtnBall3.Value = RndBall()
End Sub

Function RndBall()
    RndBall = (Int((9-0+1)*Rnd+0))
End Function

-->
```

```
</SCRIPT>
</CENTER>
</BODY>
</HTML>
```

FIGURE 3.4.

The Play 3 generator in action.

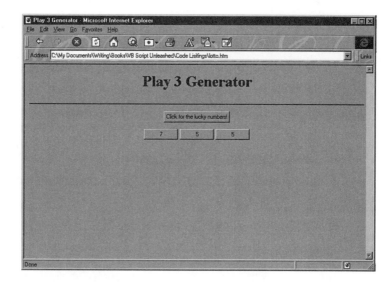

You'll find that random number generation can really spice up your pages. You'll see more random number examples later in this book when we work with other controls that can be manipulated dynamically.

Sgn

The sgn function returns a numeric value representing the sign of a number argument. It returns 1 if the number is greater than zero, 0 if equal to zero, and -1 if less than zero.

Sqr

The sqr function returns the square root of a numeric argument. The argument value must be greater than or equal to zero.

Sin

The sin function returns the sine of an angle.

Tan

The Tan function returns the tangent of an angle.

Time and Date Functions

You'll find time and date functions extremely useful in customizing your Web pages. You can add automatic time and date stamping to pages, and you can write programs that provide useful calendar functions.

Date

The Date function takes no arguments and returns the current system date. In Figure 3.5, the Date function returns the date value in the tester page.

FIGURE 3.5.

The Date *function returns the date value in the tester page.*

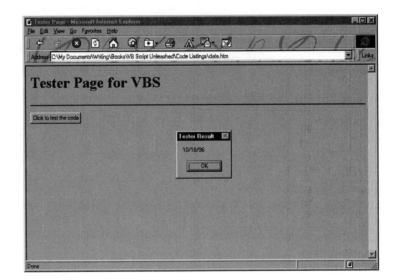

DateSerial

The DateSerial function takes year, month, and day arguments and returns a variant of subtype date. The year argument can be any year between 100 and 9999. The month and day arguments are numeric values.

DateValue

The DateValue function takes a string argument containing a valid date and returns a variant of subtype date. This is an extremely useful function, because it interprets a number of formatted date strings. For example, you could use "January 1, 1999," "1/1/99," or "Jan 1, 1999" as an argument. Once the date is a variant of subtype date, other date functions can be used on it.

Day

The Day function takes a date argument and returns the day as a numeric value between 1 and 31.

Hour

The Hour function takes a time argument and returns an hour value between 0 and 23.

Year

The Year function takes a date value and returns the year.

Weekday

The Weekday function takes a date and optionally a firstdayofweek argument and returns a numeric value representing the day of the week. If firstdayofweek isn't specified, the function defaults to Sunday. The settings for firstdayofweek are shown in Table 3.8.

Table 3.8. Day constants.

Day	*Numeric Value*
System *	0
Sunday	1
Monday	2
Tuesday	3
Wednesday	4
Thursday	5
Friday	6
Saturday	7

*This value is used only in the firstdayofweek argument and is not a return value.

Listing 3.4 takes a string that you enter, converts the string to date format, and then runs the Day function against the date. The return value is then converted to a string that sends the day of the week to the message box. There is no error checking built into the script, so a nonvalid date entry will result in a runtime error. Figure 3.6 shows the results of Listing 3.4.

Listing 3.4. Day.htm.

```
<HTML>
<HEAD>
<TITLE>Day of the week</TITLE>
</HEAD>
<BODY>
<H1>What day did it happen?</H1>
<HR COLOR="BLUE">
Enter any valid date and click the button to find out what day it was!<BR>
<INPUT TYPE="TEXT" NAME="TxtDate"><BR>
<INPUT TYPE="SUBMIT" NAME="Btn1" VALUE="Tell me the day of the week">
<SCRIPT LANGUAGE="VBScript">
<!--
Sub Btn1_OnClick()
    Dim DayVal, Message, MyDate
    MyDate = DateValue(TxtDate.Value)
    DayVal = Weekday(MyDate)
        If DayVal = 1 then Message = "Sunday"
        If DayVal = 2 then Message = "Monday"
        If DayVal = 3 then Message = "Tuesday"
        If DayVal = 4 then Message = "Wednesday"
        If DayVal = 5 then Message = "Thursday"
        If DayVal = 6 then Message = "Friday"
        If DayVal = 7 then Message = "Saturday"
    Message = "It happened on a " + Message + "."
    MsgBox Message, 64,"When did it happen?"
End Sub
-->
</SCRIPT>
</BODY>
</HTML>
```

FIGURE 3.6.

What day did it happen?

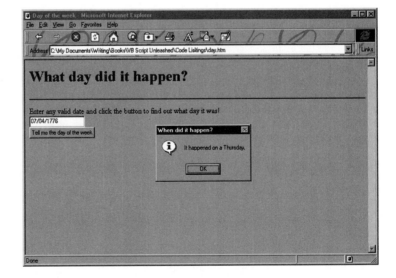

Minute

The Minute function retrieves the minute value of a time value.

Month

The Month function returns a numeric value for the month from a valid date.

Now

The Now function returns the current date and time from the client machine. This function takes no arguments.

Second

The Second function returns the seconds value from a time value.

Time

The Time function returns the current system time as a date subtype variant.

TimeSerial

The TimeSerial function takes hours, minutes, and seconds as arguments and returns a variant of subtype date. The hour argument is an integer between 0 and 23.

TimeValue

The TimeValue function takes a string containing a valid time and returns a variant of subtype date containing the time.

You can use this function to get input from the user and convert it to a date format. Valid values for the time argument include times from 12- and 24-hour clocks.

Boolean Functions

Boolean functions always return a value of true or false. Each of the functions listed in Table 3.9 tests for the truth of a condition.

Table 3.9. Boolean functions.

Function	Tests
IsArray	Is variable an array?
IsDate	Is expression a date?
IsEmpty	Has the variable been initialized?
IsError	Is this an error value?
IsNull	Is this a null value?
IsNumeric	Is this a numeric value?
IsObject	Is this variable an object?

These Boolean functions are important because VBScript has little built-in error checking and no debugger other than Internet Explorer. You can use the Boolean functions to test data before trying to feed the data into functions where it might cause an error.

Listing 3.4 had no built-in error checking. Listing 3.5 shows the same program with a feature to check whether the data from the text input box is a valid date.

Listing 3.5. DayChk.htm.

```
<HTML>
<HEAD>
<TITLE>Day of the week</TITLE>
</HEAD>
<BODY>
<H1>What day did it happen?</H1>
<HR COLOR="BLUE">
Enter any valid date and click the button to find out what day it was!<BR>
<INPUT TYPE="TEXT" NAME="TxtDate"><BR>
<INPUT TYPE="SUBMIT" NAME="Btn1" VALUE="Tell me the day of the week">
<SCRIPT LANGUAGE="VBS">
<!--
Sub Btn1_OnClick()
    Dim DayVal, Message, MyDate, blnCheck
blnCheck = IsDate(TxtDate.Value)
If blnCheck = True then
    MyDate = DateValue(TxtDate.Value)
    DayVal = Weekday(MyDate)
        If DayVal = 1 then Message = "Sunday"
        If DayVal = 2 then Message = "Monday"
        If DayVal = 3 then Message = "Tuesday"
        If DayVal = 4 then Message = "Wednesday"
        If DayVal = 5 then Message = "Thursday"
        If DayVal = 6 then Message = "Friday"
        If DayVal = 7 then Message = "Saturday"
    Message = "It happened on a " + Message + "."
    MsgBox Message, 64,"When did it happen?"
Else
```

```
Message = "You must enter a valid date."
MsgBox Message, 48,"Error"
End If
End Sub
-->
</SCRIPT>
</BODY>
</HTML>
```

If you run DayChk.htm and enter an invalid date, instead of having the script crash with a runtime error, you'll see a message box telling you that the date you entered was not valid. You'll learn more about techniques that you can use to deliver error-free code in Chapter 11, "Optimizing Code."

Review

In this chapter, you learned about procedures in VBScript. You read about functions intrinsic to VBScript and looked at some examples that illustrate the usefulness of functions.

In the next chapter, you'll learn about VBScript's built-in controls and how these basic controls are used to create powerful HTML documents.

Intrinsic Controls

by Brian Johnson

IN THIS CHAPTER

CHAPTER 4

Introduction

VBScript's intrinsic controls are the same ones that you are using if you're working with forms in HTML documents. I'll talk about each of these controls and how they can be used to create interactive Web pages using VBScript.

This chapter covers

- Controls and messages in VBScript
- Using intrinsic controls with VBScript
- Each of the intrinsic controls in detail
- Client-side validation

Events in VBScript

So far, you've created active pages with code that runs when the user clicks a button. Clicking a button generates an event. Events in Windows generate messages. Messages in Windows tell the applications and the operating system what to do and what's going on.

Most of the objects that you place into your HTML documents will have events to which you can attach script code. The Button control you've been using so far has an onClick event. When this event occurs, code in the onClick procedure runs.

Visual Basic is an inherently graphical programming language. The way most information is retrieved and processed from the user is through graphical user interface (GUI) objects that you create for your user. Once the GUI is in place, the user causes the functions and procedures within your program to be initiated through keystrokes or mouse clicks. Table 4.1 defines these terms that I've just used.

Table 4.1. Interaction terms.

Term	Definition
Data	Information that is retrieved, manipulated, and returned to the user
GUI	Graphical User Interface—the buttons, boxes, labels, and other elements of your program that you use to interact with your user
Event	An action by the user, such as a mouse click or a keystroke
Messages	Sent back and forth from the operating system to the program in response to events

Messages in a GUI Environment

Events generate messages in a GUI environment, but not all events are initiated by the actions of the user. There are a number of other ways that events are triggered.

Timers generate messages by default at the end of their timing cycles. These cycles are set by the programmer at design time but can be manipulated by the user at runtime.

Hardware can also generate messages. For example, a message is sent to the operating system when a CD is inserted in the CD-ROM. If the CD is built up for Windows 95, a program on the disk runs automatically. Likewise, if your machine is set up to receive faxes, a message is sent when your phone rings.

Multimedia generates its own types of messages. The multimedia system in the Windows operating system includes high-resolution timers that keep count of frames and time while a sound or video file is playing. During the start and completion of multimedia files, messages are also sent.

Depending on the types of control that you're using in your Web pages, you can write code that reacts to these types of messages. When dealing with the intrinsic controls though, the messages that you will deal with most often include mouse clicks, mouse movements, and keystrokes.

Placing Controls in HTML

You can put these intrinsic controls on your page just as you would regular forms controls. The usual syntax is to place the `<INPUT>` tag into your HTML and use the appropriate TYPE= attribute for the control that you're creating. Placement of the controls on your page is entirely dependent on the HTML code. Listing 4.1 is an HTML page that contains a number of Internet Explorer's intrinsic controls. You can see the result in Figure 4.1.

Listing 4.1. HTML document with controls.

```
<HTML>
<HEAD>
<TITLE>Tester Page</TITLE>
</HEAD>
<BODY>
<H1>Intrinsic Controls in VB Script</H1>
<HR COLOR="BLUE">
<CENTER>
<TABLE>
<TR>
    <TD><FONT SIZE=5 FACE=ARIAL COLOR=BLUE>Controls...</FONT></TD>
    <TD><INPUT TYPE="SUBMIT" NAME="Btn1" VALUE="This is button #1"></TD>
    <TD><INPUT TYPE="TEXT" NAME="Txt1" VALUE="TEXT" ></TD>
```

4

continues

Listing 4.1. continued

```
</TR>
<TR>
    <TD></TD>
    <TD><INPUT TYPE="RADIO" NAME="Rad1">Radio Button</TD>
    <TD><INPUT TYPE="TEXTAREA" NAME="TextArea1"
        ROWS=50 COLS=25 VALUE="TEXTAREA"></TD>
</TR>
<TR>
    <TD><INPUT TYPE="PASSWORD" NAME="Pass1" VALUE="PASS"></TD>
    <TD><INPUT TYPE="RESET" NAME="Reset1" VALUE="Reset #1"></TD>
    <TD><INPUT TYPE="CHECKBOX" NAME="Radio1" VALUE="Checkbox">Checkbox</TD>
</TR>
</TABLE>
</CENTER>
<SCRIPT LANGUAGE="VBS">
<!--
Sub Btn1_OnClick()
Dim Message
Message="Hello World!"
MsgBox Message, 0,"Tester Result"
End Sub
-->
</SCRIPT>
</BODY>
</HTML>
```

FIGURE 4.1.

*VBScript intrinsic
controls in HTML.*

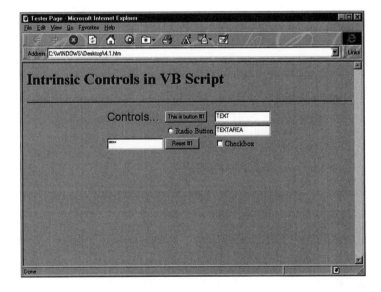

In the preceding example, controls are displayed in an HTML table. Tables offer fairly good control over where your controls are placed on a form, but it takes a little work to get the controls placed where you want them. Microsoft FrontPage allows you to create WYSIWYG (what you see is what you get) tables in Web pages. It's much easier to use a program like FrontPage to lay out a table visually, as shown in Figure 4.2.

FIGURE 4.2.

Laying out an HTML document with controls in Microsoft FrontPage.

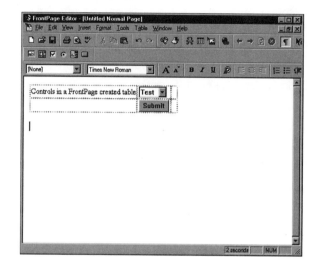

Intrinsic Controls

Button

I've used the button input type, Submit, to test most of the code we've played with so far. It's an easy control to use because users know what to do with it automatically: see a button and click it. What could be easier? Table 4.2 shows the properties for a Button control.

Table 4.2. Button properties.

Property	Description
enabled	Control is enabled (1) or disabled (0)
form	Name of the form to which the control belongs
name	Name used to identify the button in code
value	Caption of the button

Most of the intrinsic controls are created as a parameter of the `<INPUT>` tag. To create an instance of a Button control in HTML, insert an `<INPUT>` tag with the type set to BUTTON or SUBMIT:

```
<INPUT TYPE=SUBMIT NAME=Button1 VALUE="Click Me">
```

The SUBMIT type can be used interchangeably with BUTTON. The RESET type works the same way but is used to clear all the values in a current page.

Properties for the Button control can be set at load time and changed at runtime. Take a look at how properties are set for an intrinsic control at load time in Listing 4.2. Clicking the button causes the runtime event to occur, changing the value of the button.

Listing 4.2. Setting properties for the Submit control.

```
<HTML>
<HEAD>
<TITLE>Tester Page</TITLE>
</HEAD>
<BODY>
<H1>Tester Page for VBScript</H1>
<HR COLOR="BLUE">
<INPUT TYPE="SUBMIT" NAME="Btn1" VALUE="Click to test the code">
<SCRIPT LANGUAGE="VBScript">
<!--
     Sub Btn1_OnClick
     Btn1.Value = "Value is changed!"
     End Sub
-->
</SCRIPT>
</BODY>
</HTML>
```

We've done this before. Here, we set the type, name, and value of the <INPUT> tag when a document is loaded into the browser. Notice how we can change the value property of Btn1 in the Btn1_onClick event. This change takes place at runtime.

The Button control has two events: onClick takes place when the user clicks the button with the mouse, and onFocus occurs when the button receives focus. A button with focus will usually have a small line drawn around the perimeter of the control. A button with focus generates an onClick event when the user presses the Enter key.

Checkbox

The Checkbox control allows you to give the user a choice to check on a page. The user is able to select any or all checkboxes on a page because their checked values are independent of other Checkbox controls. The Checkbox is very useful when you want to allow a user to choose multiple items. Table 4.3 lists the Checkbox properties.

Table 4.3. Checkbox properties.

Property	Description
checked	Checkbox is checked
defaultChecked	Checkbox is checked by default
enabled	Control is enabled (1) or disabled (0)
form	Name of the form to which the control belongs
name	Name of the checkbox
value	Checkbox value

The checkbox control has two events, onClick and onFocus, and two methods, click and focus. Listing 4.3 uses the click method and the onClick event to change the properties among various checkboxes.

Listing 4.3. Checkboxes in HTML.

```
<HTML>
<HEAD>
<TITLE>Tester Page</TITLE>
</HEAD>
<BODY>
<H1>Tester Page for VBScript</H1>
<HR COLOR="BLUE">
<TABLE BORDER>
<TR><INPUT TYPE="CHECKBOX" NAME="TChk1">
    <INPUT TYPE="CHECKBOX" NAME="TChk2">
    <INPUT TYPE="CHECKBOX" NAME="TChk3">
    <INPUT TYPE="CHECKBOX" NAME="TChk4">
    <INPUT TYPE="CHECKBOX" NAME="TChk5">
</TR>
<TR>
<INPUT TYPE="RADIO" NAME="Rad1">Code 1<BR>
<INPUT TYPE="RADIO" NAME="Rad2">Code 2<BR>
<INPUT TYPE="RADIO" NAME="Rad3">Code 3<BR>
<INPUT TYPE="RADIO" NAME="Rad4">Code 4<BR>
<INPUT TYPE="RADIO" NAME="Rad5">Code 5<BR>
</TR>
</TABLE><BR><BR>

<SCRIPT LANGUAGE="VBScript">
<!--
Sub ClrChecks
TChk1.Checked = False
TChk2.Checked = False
TChk3.Checked = False
TChk4.Checked = False
TChk5.Checked = False
End Sub
```

4

INTRINSIC CONTROLS

continues

Listing 4.3. continued

```
Sub Rad1_OnClick
ClrChecks
TChk1.Checked=True
TChk3.Checked=True
TChk4.Checked=True
End Sub
Sub Rad2_OnClick
ClrChecks
TChk2.Checked=True
TChk4.Checked=True
TChk5.Checked=True
End Sub
Sub Rad3_OnClick
ClrChecks
TChk1.Checked=True
TChk2.Checked=True
TChk3.Checked=True
End Sub
Sub Rad4_OnClick
ClrChecks
TChk3.Checked=True
TChk4.Checked=True
TChk5.Checked=True
End Sub
Sub Rad5_OnClick
ClrChecks
TChk1.Checked=True
TChk3.Checked=True
TChk5.Checked=True
End Sub
-->
</SCRIPT>
</BODY>
</HTML>
```

Hidden

The Hidden input type is used to store a value in a form that is invisible to the user. This field isn't really needed with VBScript, because you can store most values with a variable. Before the advent of scriptable controls though, the Hidden type was useful for storing values in CGI-generated pages. This control has name and value properties that can be accessed in VBScript.

Text

The Text type input control is used to retrieve input from the user. Its use is fairly straightforward, and because it is the default type for the Input control, you don't even need to explicitly declare it. The following two lines of code are functionally equivalent:

```
<INPUT TYPE=TEXT NAME=Txt1>
<INPUT NAME=Txt2
```

Setting the value property for the control inserts text into it. You can set the defaultValue property initially to place text into the control. Table 4.4 contains the properties for the Text control.

Table 4.4. Text properties.

Property	Description
defaultValue	Value of control at creation
enabled	Control is enabled (1) or disabled (0)
form	Form to which the control belongs
name	The name of the control
value	Content of the control

The Text input type has three methods that can be called in VBScript, as shown in Table 4.5.

Table 4.5. Text methods.

Method	Description
focus	Give control input focus
blur	Remove focus from control
select	Select text in control

Listing 4.4 uses the Text methods listed in Table 4.5. You can use these methods to help lead your user through a form. For example, instead of placing text on a form that says, "If no, then go to question 4," you can have the focus skip to the appropriate question.

Listing 4.4. Setting focus in a form.

```
<HTML>
<HEAD>
<TITLE>Tester Page</TITLE>
</HEAD>
<BODY>
<H1>Tester Page for VBScript</H1>
<HR COLOR="BLUE">

<INPUT TYPE="SUBMIT" NAME="Btn1" VALUE="Text 1">
<INPUT TYPE="SUBMIT" NAME="Btn2" VALUE="Text 2">
<INPUT TYPE="SUBMIT" NAME="Btn3" VALUE="Text 3">
<BR><BR>
```

4

INTRINSIC
CONTROLS

continues

Listing 4.4. continued

```
<INPUT TYPE="TEXT" NAME="Txt1" VALUE="This is text 1"><BR>
<INPUT TYPE="TEXT" NAME="Txt2" VALUE="This is text 2"><BR>
<INPUT TYPE="TEXT" NAME="Txt3" VALUE="This is text 3"><BR>
<SCRIPT LANGUAGE="VBScript">
<!--
Sub Btn1_OnClick
    Txt1.Focus
End Sub
Sub Btn2_OnClick
    Txt2.Select
End Sub
Sub Btn3_OnClick
    Txt3.Focus
End Sub

-->
</SCRIPT>
</BODY>
</HTML>
```

Table 4.6 lists the events common to the controls that I'm talking about.

Table 4.6. Text events.

Events	Description
onFocus	Control gets focus
onBlur	Control loses focus
onChange	Value property of the control changes
onSelect	Control is selected

Listing 4.5 tracks these events among a number of controls in an HTML page.

Listing 4.5. focus and blur.

```
<HTML>
<HEAD>
<TITLE>Tester Page</TITLE>
</HEAD>
<BODY>
<H1>Tester Page for VBScript</H1>
<HR COLOR="BLUE">
<INPUT TYPE="Text" NAME="Txt1" VALUE="Text 1">

<SCRIPT LANGUAGE="VBScript">
<!--
Sub Txt1_OnFocus
    MsgBox "Text 1 Focus!"
```

```
End Sub
-->
</SCRIPT>
</BODY>
</HTML>
```

You'll notice that when you run this listing you can't do very much with the Txt1 control. This is because a message box pops up every time it receives focus. When the message box shows up, the text box loses its focus, so there is no way to enter data. This code effectively prevents you from using your browser.

Textarea

The Textarea control is similar to the Text type control in that you can use it to enter text on a page. The textarea allows you to enter multiple lines of text, making it more suitable for larger data input. The textarea is not usually an input tag with a type attribute, although that form is allowed. The textarea is a two-sided tag consisting of a <TEXTAREA></TEXTAREA> tag pair. The initial value of the textarea is contained between these tags.

The Textarea attributes are set in the first tag. Table 4.7 contains the Textarea properties.

Table 4.7. Textarea properties.

Method	Description
cols	Number of columns in control
defaultValue	Value of control at creation
enabled	Control is enabled (1) or disabled (0)
form	Form to which control belongs
name	Name of the textarea
rows	Number of rows in control
value	Content of the control

The rows and cols properties allow you to control the size of the textarea:

```
<TEXTAREA NAME=Text1 ROWS=30 COLS=40></TEXTAREA>
```

Figure 4.3 shows how the code above will look in your Web page.

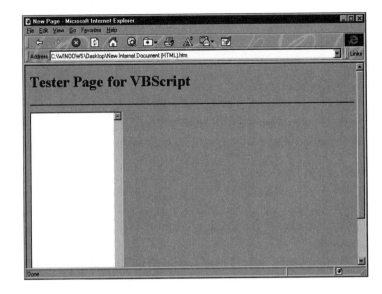

The textarea shares most of the events and methods of the Text type input control. You can use focus and blur to set or remove focus from the control and select to select the text inside it. You can use onFocus, onBlur, onChange, and onSelect to write code for events that have occurred.

Select

The Select control is instantiated in code using the `<SELECT></SELECT>` tag pair. It is similar to a Windows Listbox control. You set the items in the Select control using the `<OPTION>` tag. You can determine the item that your user selects, using either the selectedIndex property or the options property. The control is referenced in code through the name property. You can get the number of items using the length property. Table 4.8 contains the properties for the Select control.

Table 4.8. Select control properties.

Property	Description
name	Name of the control
length	Number of items in the control
options	Array of options for the control
selectedIndex	Index of the currently selected item
size	Number of items displayed (default is 1)

The methods available to the Select control are `focus` and `blur`. Events for the Select control include `onBlur`, `onFocus`, and `onChange`.

The easiest way to use this control in VBScript is to get the `selectedIndex` from the control and then to act on that value using a `Select Case` statement.

Listing 4.6 contains code that displays a message that depends on the item selected in the Select control.

Listing 4.6. Select control with VBScript.

```
<HTML>
<HEAD>
<TITLE>VBScript Select Control</TITLE>
</HEAD>
<BODY>
<SELECT NAME="Sel1">
<OPTION>Option 1
<OPTION>Option 2
<OPTION>Option 3
</SELECT>
<INPUT TYPE=SUBMIT NAME=Btn1 Value="Test">

<SCRIPT LANGUAGE=VBSCRIPT>
<!--
Sub Btn1_onClick
Select Case Sel1.selectedIndex
    Case 0
       Msg = "You selected option 1"
    Case 1
        Msg = "You selected option 2"
    Case 2
        Msg = "You selected option 3"
End Select
MsgBox Msg

End Sub

-->
</SCRIPT>
</BODY>
</HTML>
```

Using Controls in Your Documents

Now, we'll take what has been done so far with controls and try to come up with a less trivial example of what can be done with them.

You might already be using forms and CGI scripts to retrieve and utilize data from users and customers. Data is usually passed to a script as a set of parameters. The script runs on the server, and the result is piped back to the user. In many cases, the script is checking to see that all the necessary entries are completed, or that the entries are valid, before it actually processes the data.

Using VBScript, you can take some of the load off your server by performing the data validation before information is sent across the Net.

Suppose, for example, you are offering free software to customers. If you want to keep track of who is downloading and using the software, you might have the users fill out a registration form before they download the software. In many cases, we know that a lengthy form is going to drive customers away, so we make some fields optional. You want to keep some sort of control over the registration process, so you require a name or handle and an e-mail address. If the user fills out the entire form, great. To get the software, though, the user must provide at least the minimal amount of information.

Listing 4.7 is a standard registration form that you might find on the Internet, and Figure 4.4 shows the results of that code. Notice that the required fields are marked by the asterisks. Normally, if you fill in the form and leave one of the required fields blank, the script on the server processes the information and kicks back a page that tells you to fill in the required fields. If you move this functionality to the HTML document and process the information on the user's machine, you can save yourself some hits on the server. This might not make much difference if your software giveaway doesn't generate too much interest, but it might make a difference if you have a large number of visitors downloading software from your site.

Listing 4.7. Form that validates data before sending it to the server.

```
<HTML>
<HEAD>
<TITLE>ACME Software's Registration Page</TITLE>
</HEAD>
<BODY BGCOLOR=WHITE>
<CENTER><FONT SIZE=7 FACE="Arial" COLOR=BLUE>ACME</FONT><FONT SIZE=5
 COLOR=BLACK>Registration</FONT></CENTER>
<HR COLOR="BLUE">
<FONT FACE="COMIC Sans MS">
Thank you for taking the time to download and test our new product. In order to
serve you well, we ask that you submit the folliong information before downloading
<FONT FACE=ARIAL COLOR=BLUE>ACME</FONT>software.
<HR COLOR=RED WIDTH=75%>
<CENTER>
<TABLE BORDER BORDERCOLOR="BLUE">
<TR><TD ALIGN=RIGHT>*Name:</TD><TD><INPUT TYPE="TEXT" NAME="TxtName"></TD></TR>
<TR><TD ALIGN=RIGHT>*E-Mail:</TD><TD><INPUT TYPE="TEXT" NAME="TxtEMail"></TD></TR>
<TR><TD ALIGN=RIGHT>Address:</TD><TD><INPUT TYPE="TEXT" NAME="TxtAddress"></TD></
TR>
<TR><TD ALIGN=RIGHT>City:</TD><TD><INPUT TYPE="TEXT" NAME="TxtCity"></TD></TR>
```

```
<TR><TD ALIGN=RIGHT>State:</TD><TD><INPUT TYPE="TEXT" NAME="TxtState"></TD></TR>
<TR><TD ALIGN=RIGHT>Zip:</TD><TD><INPUT TYPE="TEXT" NAME="TxtZip"></TD></TR>
<TR><TD ALIGN=RIGHT>Country:</TD><TD><INPUT TYPE="TEXT" NAME="TxtName"></TD></TR>
<TR><TD COLSPAN=2 ALIGN=CENTER><INPUT TYPE="SUBMIT" NAME="Btn1" VALUE="Send It!"><BR>
<FONT SIZE=2>* Required Field</FONT></TD>
</TABLE>
<HR COLOR=RED WIDTH=75%>
<FONT SIZE=2>Thanks!</FONT>

<SCRIPT LANGUAGE="VBScript">
<!--
Sub Btn1_OnClick
If TxtName.Value="" Or TxtEMail.Value="" Then
Dim MyMessage
MyMessage = "Please enter your name and e-mail address."
MsgBox MyMessage, 0, "Incomplete Form Error"
Else
location.href = "/cgi-bin/reg.cgi?Name=" + TxtName.Value + "&EMail=" + TxtEMail.Value +
                "&Address=" + TxtAddress.Value + "&City=" + TxtCity.Value + "&State=" +
                TxtState.Value + "&Zip=" + TxtZip.Value + "&Country=" + TxtCountry.Value
End If
End Sub
-->
</SCRIPT>
</BODY>
</HTML>
```

FIGURE 4.4.

A form with client-side validation.

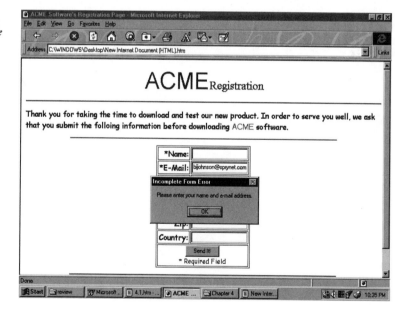

4

INTRINSIC
CONTROLS

Notice here that, rather than using a conventional form in which the information would be piped directly to the server, I call the CGI script in the VBScript code block. This allows the code to be validated on the user's machine before being sent across the Net.

Review

In this chapter I talked about messages and events and how they are related to the code that you write. I talked about Internet Explorer's intrinsic controls and how they can be used in your VBScript programs. I also talked about ways that VBScript code can be used to validate information before that information gets to the server. In the next chapter, you'll learn about the Internet Explorer Object Model for Scripting, which will allow you to take control of the browser using VBScript in Web pages.

VBScript in Web Pages

by Craig Eddy

IN THIS CHAPTER

CHAPTER 5

As you'll see throughout this book, using VBScript within your Web pages enables you to create a very dynamic and interactive experience for the Web surfers who visit your site. This is true whether you have a site that is visible to the entire Internet or an intranet site visible only to users of your company's LAN or WAN.

In the early days of the Web, all that was possible was a page containing text and some links to other documents. From there, the Web evolved to use a graphical interface, enabling Web page designers to embed pictures and graphics in their pages. Along came Netscape and Java, and the Web now has the capability to use various plug-ins and client-side applications. Finally, Microsoft introduced the concept of *active content*, which enables the user, browser software, and Web server to communicate and interact in harmony with one another. Although this chapter doesn't go into the depth necessary to create such a harmonious Web page completely, you will learn how you can combine the capabilities of your Web server with the capabilities of VBScript to create a more dynamic site.

This chapter starts by discussing the use of VBScript to generate HTML content. You will see an example that enables users to build Web pages and display them within Internet Explorer. Next comes a discussion about combining VBScript with CGI and ISAPI applications, which are types of server-side applications. You'll see how you can use these applications to generate HTML with embedded VBScript. Not only are the Web pages generated by such applications dynamic, but the VBScript code embedded in the pages can be different with each invocation of the server-side application as well. Finally, the chapter winds up with a discussion about combining VBScript with database access. This is done using the Microsoft Internet Database Connector to generate pages based on a database query.

Using VBScript and HTML

One of the coolest features of VBScript is its capability to generate HTML on-the-fly. You can use the programming capabilities of VBScript to decide what should appear on the page and how it should appear. Then the script code can output the HTML for display within the browser window.

You can use three methods to generate HTML using VBScript: within the window_onLoad event (which fires when the page loads), embedded anywhere within the HTML file, and as a new page created on demand within the browser window. This section explores all three methods. An example is provided for the third method. More examples of this technique are presented in Chapter 13, "Dynamic Web Page Building."

Using the onLoad Event

When a page is loaded into the Internet Explorer, an event named window_onLoad fires. You can write code in your script to handle this event by adding a code section such as the one shown in Listing 5.1.

Listing 5.1. Code for the `window_onLoad` event.

```
<SCRIPT LANGUAGE="VBScript">
<!--
sub window_onLoad()
...
end sub
-->
</SCRIPT>
```

Any code you place within this procedure is executed when the page is loaded. You also can use the `document.writeln` method to output any HTML text to the page. After you finish writing the HTML, use the `document.close` method to close the document's output stream and actually display the HTML generated by the script.

Embedding VBScript in the HTML

In addition to using the `onLoad` event, you can embed VBScript code anywhere within your page's HTML. This is useful when most of your page is based on static HTML but you want to use VBScript code to display some HTML that changes with varying conditions. A good example of this is displaying the current date on the page. You also can use this technique to embed different graphics and messages, depending on any variable information to which VBScript has access: time of day, type of Web browser the user is running, and even the history list that contains the last few pages the user visited. An example of embedding the current date and time within the page is presented in Chapter 13.

Creating a New Page with VBScript

The final method discussed here involves actually creating a new Web page on-the-fly. When this method is used, the current page is cleared and the new page is displayed in its place. This technique can be used to create slide shows, for example, by embedding VBScript code within HTML generated by VBScript code. Doing so, however, eventually makes you feel like you're aiming a video camera at a monitor that's displaying the camera's output; it creates a neat effect, but you'll get dizzy if you try it for too long!

Instead, in this section you'll create a Web page that enables viewers to create their own customized pages. The example has input controls that users can interact with to decide how their pages should look. When they're ready, they click the Display Page button and the page they specified is generated and displayed. The original page is shown in Figure 5.1. The HTML for the page is given in Listing 5.2. This file also is included on the accompanying CD-ROM as `5-1.htm`.

FIGURE 5.1.
The Create Your Own Web Page entry form.

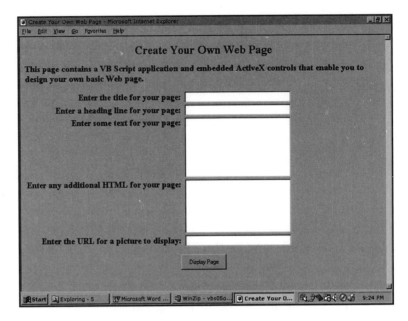

Listing 5.2. The HTML and VBScript for the Create Your Own Web Page page.

```
<HTML><HEAD><TITLE>Create Your Own Web Page</TITLE></HEAD>
<BODY>
<CENTER><H2>Create Your Own Web Page</H2></CENTER>
<p>
<H3>This page contains a VBScript application and embedded ActiveX controls
that enable you to design your own basic Web page.<H3>
<p>
<table><tr><td align=RIGHT><H3>Enter the title for your page: </H3></TD><TD>
<OBJECT ID="txtTitle" WIDTH=225 HEIGHT=23
    CLASSID="CLSID:8BD21D10-EC42-11CE-9E0D-00AA006002F3">
        <PARAM NAME="VariousPropertyBits" VALUE="1749567515">
        <PARAM NAME="Size" VALUE="5962;600">
        <PARAM NAME="FontCharSet" VALUE="0">
        <PARAM NAME="FontPitchAndFamily" VALUE="2">
        <PARAM NAME="FontWeight" VALUE="0">
    </OBJECT>
</TD></TR>
<TR><TD ALIGN=RIGHT><H3>Enter a heading line for your page: </H3></TD>
<TD>
    <OBJECT ID="txtHeader" WIDTH=225 HEIGHT=23
     CLASSID="CLSID:8BD21D10-EC42-11CE-9E0D-00AA006002F3">
        <PARAM NAME="VariousPropertyBits" VALUE="675825691">
        <PARAM NAME="Size" VALUE="5962;600">
        <PARAM NAME="FontCharSet" VALUE="0">
        <PARAM NAME="FontPitchAndFamily" VALUE="2">
        <PARAM NAME="FontWeight" VALUE="0">
    </OBJECT>
</TD></TR>
<TR><TD ALIGN=RIGHT VALIGN=TOP><H3>Enter some text for your page: </H3></TD>
<TD>
```

```
        <OBJECT ID="txtMiscText" WIDTH=225 HEIGHT=125
         CLASSID="CLSID:8BD21D10-EC42-11CE-9E0D-00AA006002F3">
            <PARAM NAME="VariousPropertyBits" VALUE="2831697947">
            <PARAM NAME="ScrollBars" VALUE="2">
            <PARAM NAME="Size" VALUE="5962;3307">
            <PARAM NAME="FontCharSet" VALUE="0">
            <PARAM NAME="FontPitchAndFamily" VALUE="2">
            <PARAM NAME="FontWeight" VALUE="0">
        </OBJECT>
</TD></TR>
<TR><TD ALIGN=RIGHT VALIGN=TOP><H3>Enter any additional HTML for your page: </H3></
TD>
<TD>
        <OBJECT ID="txtHTML" WIDTH=225 HEIGHT=112
         CLASSID="CLSID:8BD21D10-EC42-11CE-9E0D-00AA006002F3">
            <PARAM NAME="VariousPropertyBits" VALUE="2831697947">
            <PARAM NAME="ScrollBars" VALUE="2">
            <PARAM NAME="Size" VALUE="5962;2963">
            <PARAM NAME="FontCharSet" VALUE="0">
            <PARAM NAME="FontPitchAndFamily" VALUE="2">
            <PARAM NAME="FontWeight" VALUE="0">
        </OBJECT>
</TD></TR>
<TR><TD ALIGN=RIGHT><H3>Enter the URL for a picture to display: </H3></TD>
<TD>
        <OBJECT ID="txtPicture" WIDTH=225 HEIGHT=23
         CLASSID="CLSID:8BD21D10-EC42-11CE-9E0D-00AA006002F3">
            <PARAM NAME="VariousPropertyBits" VALUE="675825691">
            <PARAM NAME="Size" VALUE="5962;600">
            <PARAM NAME="FontCharSet" VALUE="0">
            <PARAM NAME="FontPitchAndFamily" VALUE="2">
            <PARAM NAME="FontWeight" VALUE="0">
        </OBJECT>
</TD></TR>
</TABLE>

<SCRIPT LANGUAGE="VBScript"> <!--
Sub cmdSubmit_Click()
Document.Open
document.writeln "<HTML><TITLE>" & txtTitle.Text & "</TITLE>"
document.writeln "<BODY><H1>" & txtHeader.Text & "</H1>"
document.writeln "<P>" & txtMiscText.Text & "<P>"
document.writeln txtHTML.Text
if Len(txtPicture.Text) then
    document.writeln "<P><CENTER><IMG SRC=" & txtPicture.Text
    document.writeln "></CENTER>"
end if
document.writeln "</BODY></HTML>"
document.close
document.close
end sub
--> </SCRIPT>
<CENTER>
    <OBJECT ID="cmdSubmit" WIDTH=96 HEIGHT=32
     CLASSID="CLSID:D7053240-CE69-11CD-A777-00DD01143C57">
        <PARAM NAME="BackColor" VALUE="12615935">
        <PARAM NAME="Caption" VALUE="Display Page">
```

5

VBSCRIPT IN
WEB PAGES

continues

Listing 5.2. continued

```
        <PARAM NAME="Size" VALUE="2540;846">
        <PARAM NAME="FontCharSet" VALUE="0">
        <PARAM NAME="FontPitchAndFamily" VALUE="2">
        <PARAM NAME="ParagraphAlign" VALUE="3">
        <PARAM NAME="FontWeight" VALUE="0">
    </OBJECT>
</CENTER></BODY></HTML>
```

Most of Listing 5.2 is straightforward HTML with some ActiveX text boxes embedded in it. The interesting part as far as this chapter is concerned is in the script code that appears near the bottom of the listing. This code is for the Display Page button's `Click` event, as can be seen from the procedure's definition: `Sub cmdSubmit_Click()`. The code in this procedure takes the data entered in the text boxes and outputs it to a new document.

The new document is started using the `document.open` method. This opens a new output stream into which you can write HTML text. It also clears the document currently displayed in the browser. After this comes various `document.writeln` method invocations. Notice that the code is inserting HTML directly into the output stream. This capability enables you to create any type of Web page you want; you can embed video, pictures, and even ActiveX controls into the new document. Finally, the `document.close` method is invoked to close the output stream and display the new document.

Figure 5.2 shows the data entry page after the text boxes are populated with some sample information. Figure 5.3 shows the page created using the entries shown in Figure 5.2.

FIGURE 5.2.

Sample data entered into the page.

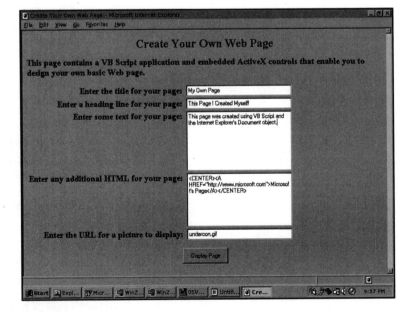

FIGURE 5.3.

The page resulting from the sample data.

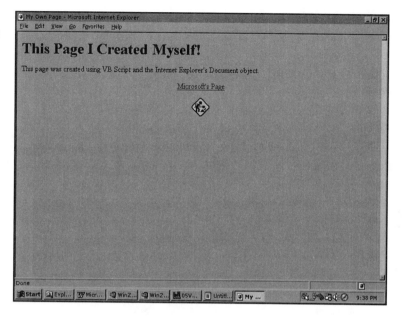

Using VBScript and CGI/ISAPI

Most Web servers provide the capability to launch applications from a Web page and pass the application information that was entered onto the Web page. The application then produces some sort of output page based on the data it received. These applications usually are *common gateway interface* (CGI) or *Internet server API* (ISAPI) applications. They must be written to accept input from the Web server and to return data to the server in the proper format.

VBScript can be tied to CGI/ISAPI applications in both directions. First, the CGI/ISAPI application can generate an HTML document containing VBScript code. This code may depend on the data that was input into the CGI application. A user logon screen for an order entry Web site might request the country in which the user resides, for example. Then, depending on the country's standard address format, both the HTML required to create an address entry form and the VBScript code that will validate the entered address information changes. This data is output by the CGI/ISAPI application differently, depending on the country entered. A user from the United States receives a different order entry page than a user from the United Kingdom, for example, complete with the address validation code appropriate for the country.

In the other direction, it is possible to use VBScript to alter the way the Web page interacts with the CGI/ISAPI application. The script code could change the data before it is submitted to the application, for example. This is useful when the server-side application is expecting a field to be in a specific format but the Web page gives the user more flexibility in entry. The script code then can interpret the entered data and format it properly for submission.

Another use along these lines would be to expand the types of input controls that can be used to enter data. On your HTML form, for example, you might have a drop-down listbox that displays text in a verbose format, but your server-side application is expecting the data in a code format. This is almost always the case for database lookup tables such as titles or ratings. Your listbox might contain the values Chief Executive Officer, Manager, and so on, which has corresponding code values of CEO, MGR, and so on. When the HTML form is submitted, VBScript code can be used to determine which entry is selected in the listbox (using the listbox's ListIndex property) and then to submit the proper code value to the server application (probably using an array that's indexed with the ListIndexes of the corresponding listbox item). This type of page probably is generated originally by another back-end process that has access to the database where the lookup table resides.

Providing Database Access

In addition to interacting with server-side applications using VBScript, you can interact with databases located on the Web server. By using the Microsoft *Internet Information Server* (IIS) with the *Internet Database Connector* (IDC) provided with the server software, you can create a very dynamic database query and reporting tool.

This section doesn't discuss all the details of using the IDC, but you will learn how to set up an IDC script file and an output template file. This output template file embeds some pretty useful VBScript code into the page displayed in response to the IDC script. An *IDC script* is a file used by the IDC to generate a database query. This query can be based on HTML form input variables, or it always can execute the same SQL statement. The example presented here uses the latter method to retrieve a list of all people who have registered in a demo request database.

Defining an ODBC Datasource

Let's start by setting up an IDC connection on your IIS machine. You should have 32-bit ODBC installed on the machine. If not, you need to install it in order to use the IDC features. Run the ODBC administrator and create a system datasource by clicking the System DSN button. The IDC will work only with system datasources. In the dialog that appears, click the Add button, select the driver appropriate for the database you'll be accessing, and click OK. In the dialog that appears next, enter the information required to connect to the database. Be sure to remember the *datasource name* (DSN) you assign, because it is necessary for the IDC script. Click OK to return to the System Data Sources dialog. Click OK to return to the ODBC administrator and exit the application.

Creating the IDC Script File

Next, you'll set up an IDC script to use in querying the database. The script consists of database logon information, the name of the output template file, and a SQL statement to be executed. Listing 5.3 shows the IDC script I used to create this example. This file is provided on the CD-ROM included with this book; the filename is `view.idc`.

Listing 5.3. The IDC script for querying the demo request database.

```
Datasource: Web SQL
Username: sa
Template: view.htx
SQLStatement:
+SELECT FirstName, LastName, Company, Address,
+City, State, Postal, Phone, EMail, ReqID
+FROM DemoRequests
```

The first line specifies the DSN for the ODBC datasource I created. The second line is the logon user name. This datasource points to a Microsoft Access database that has no security specified. If you are using a secured database, you can also use `Password:` to specify the logon password.

The third line in the script specifies the output template file to be used. This is a specially formatted HTML file that contains placeholders for the database fields returned by the query as well as other information available from the IDC itself. (This file is discussed in the next section.)

The next several lines provide the SQL statement to be executed whenever the script is loaded by the IIS Web server. You can specify just about any type of SQL statement as long as it's valid for the database type and structure you're using. Here, you're selecting several fields from a table named `DemoRequests`. You can have the SQL statement span multiple lines by placing a plus sign (+) at the start of the new line.

Creating the Output Template File

This section discusses the meat of this example: the output template file. Listing 5.4 presents the contents of this file; it is included on the CD-ROM as `view.htx`.

Listing 5.4. The output template for the demo request display page.

```
<html><title>Example Database Connection</title>
<BODY BGCOLOR="FFFFFF">
<font size=2>
<h1>These are the folks in the database:</h1>
<h2>Click the Details button for more details:</h2>
<CENTER><TABLE border=1>
<tr>
<%begindetail%>
<TD>
Name: <b><%FirstName%> <%LastName%></b><br>
```

continues

Listing 5.4. continued

```
Company: <b><%Company%></b><br></TD>
<TD>
<OBJECT ID="cmdDetails<%ReqID%>" WIDTH=96 HEIGHT=32
 CLASSID="CLSID:D7053240-CE69-11CD-A777-00DD01143C57">
    <PARAM NAME="Caption" VALUE="Details">
    <PARAM NAME="Size" VALUE="2540;846">
    <PARAM NAME="FontCharSet" VALUE="0">
    <PARAM NAME="FontPitchAndFamily" VALUE="2">
    <PARAM NAME="ParagraphAlign" VALUE="3">
    <PARAM NAME="FontWeight" VALUE="0">
</OBJECT>
<SCRIPT LANGUAGE="VBScript">
<!--
sub cmdDetails<%ReqID%>_click
Dim lTemp
lTemp = "Address: " & "<%Address%>" & Chr(13)
lTemp = lTemp & "City/State/Zip: " & "<%City%>, <%State%> <%Postal%>" & chr(13)
lTemp = lTemp & "Phone: " & "<%Phone%>" & chr(13)
lTemp = lTemp & "EMail: " & "<%EMail%>" & chr(13)

MsgBox lTemp, 0, "<%FirstName%> <%LastName%>"

end sub
--></SCRIPT>
</TD></tr>
<%enddetail%>
</table></CENTER></font>
</body></HTML>
```

The beginning of this file looks like standard HTML. If you look closely, however, you'll see some hybrid HTML tags such as <%begindetail%>, <%FirstName%>, and <%enddetail%>. These are tags interpreted by the IDC when it is returning the output page to the user's Web browser. The <%begindetail%> and <%enddetail%> tags delineate the beginning and end of a section of the file where results from the SQL query will be placed. The HTML that appears between these two tags is repeated for each record returned by the SQL SELECT statement. Tags such as <%FirstName%> and <%LastName%> are the field names returned by the SQL SELECT statement contained in the IDC script. (Refer to Listing 5.3.)

All the details are displayed using an HTML table with two columns. The first column displays the name and company returned from the query. This is done by using these lines:

```
<TD>
Name: <b><%FirstName%> <%LastName%></b><br>
Company: <b><%Company%></b><br></TD>
```

The second column is where you start to see some VBScript creep onto the scene. First, you see the insertion of an ActiveX command button:

```
<OBJECT ID="cmdDetails<%ReqID%>" WIDTH=96 HEIGHT=32
 CLASSID="CLSID:D7053240-CE69-11CD-A777-00DD01143C57">
```

Notice the ID property; it includes one of the fields returned in the IDC script (ReqID). Because VBScript does not allow for control arrays, the template must generate a unique name for each ActiveX control to be placed in the output page. Because the ReqID field is the unique primary key in the table, it's an appropriate field to use. The IDC replaces the text <%ReqID%> with the field's value each time a record is output using the template.

After the object's definition comes some VBScript code for its Click event. Notice again that <%ReqID%> appears in the control's name. The event procedure uses more of the fields from the query to create a string. This string then is displayed using the MsgBox statement.

Finally, you come to the end of the table's row and the <%enddetail%> tag. Then the closing HTML tags appear, and the </HTML> tag ends the template.

Viewing the Results

This template produces a very compact listing of the records returned from the database. If more detail about a particular record is needed, the user can click the Details button to display the message box containing those additional details.

To view the results, enter the URL to the IDC script file into Internet Explorer's address box and press Enter. After the IDC churns a minute or so (depending on the size of the database being accessed), the results page appears. Figure 5.4 shows the results for a sample database on my Web server. Figure 5.5 shows the message displayed for Dilbert Bates after I click his Details button.

FIGURE 5.4.

The page resulting from the IDC script.

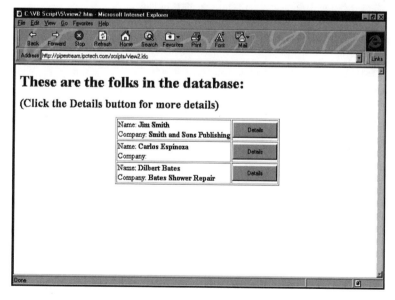

5

VBSCRIPT IN
WEB PAGES

FIGURE 5.5.

The message box created using VBScript.

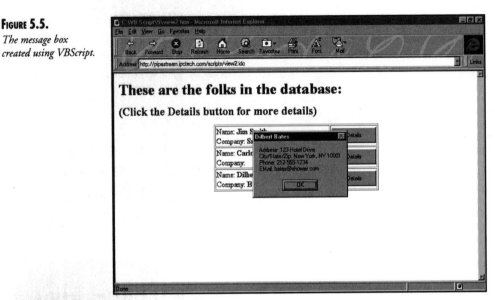

Listing 5.5 shows the HTML generated by the IDC. You can compare this listing with Listing 5.4 to determine that the IDC has indeed properly embedded the SQL query results into the template file and the VBScript code. Listing 5.5 is included on the CD-ROM as `view.htm`.

Listing 5.5. The HTML source for the IDC-generated page.

```
<html>
<title>Example Database Connection</title>
<BODY BGCOLOR="FFFFFF">
<font size=2>
<h1>These are the folks in the database:</h1>
<h2>(Click the Details button for more details)</h2>
<CENTER><TABLE border=1>

<TR><TD>
Name: <b>Jim Smith</b><br>
Company: <b>Smith and Sons Publishing</b><br>
</TD><TD>
    <SCRIPT LANGUAGE="VBScript">
<!--
sub cmdDetails825961365_click
Dim lTemp
lTemp = "Address: " & "123 Book Way" & Chr(13)
lTemp = lTemp & "City/State/Zip: " & "New York, NY 10001" & chr(13)
lTemp = lTemp & "Phone: " & "212-555-1212" & chr(13)
lTemp = lTemp & "EMail: " & "" & chr(13)

MsgBox lTemp, 0, "Jim Smith"
```

```
  end sub
--></SCRIPT>
<OBJECT ID="cmdDetails825961365" WIDTH=96 HEIGHT=32
 CLASSID="CLSID:D7053240-CE69-11CD-A777-00DD01143C57">
    <PARAM NAME="Caption" VALUE="Details">
    <PARAM NAME="Size" VALUE="2540;846">
    <PARAM NAME="FontCharSet" VALUE="0">
    <PARAM NAME="FontPitchAndFamily" VALUE="2">
    <PARAM NAME="ParagraphAlign" VALUE="3">
    <PARAM NAME="FontWeight" VALUE="0">
</OBJECT>
</TD></tr>

<tr><TD>
Name: <b>Carlos Espinoza</b><br>
Company: <b></b><br>
</TD><TD>
    <SCRIPT LANGUAGE="VBScript">
<!--
sub cmdDetails826028414_click
Dim lTemp
lTemp = "Address: " & "Route 102 Box 12" & Chr(13)
lTemp = lTemp & "City/State/Zip: " & "Panama City, Panama" & chr(13)
lTemp = lTemp & "Phone: " & "" & chr(13)
lTemp = lTemp & "EMail: " & "esp@panama.net" & chr(13)

MsgBox lTemp, 0, "Carlos Espinoza"

end sub
--></SCRIPT>
<OBJECT ID="cmdDetails826028414" WIDTH=96 HEIGHT=32
 CLASSID="CLSID:D7053240-CE69-11CD-A777-00DD01143C57">
    <PARAM NAME="Caption" VALUE="Details">
    <PARAM NAME="Size" VALUE="2540;846">
    <PARAM NAME="FontCharSet" VALUE="0">
    <PARAM NAME="FontPitchAndFamily" VALUE="2">
    <PARAM NAME="ParagraphAlign" VALUE="3">
    <PARAM NAME="FontWeight" VALUE="0">
</OBJECT>
</TD></tr>

<TR><TD>
Name: <b>Dilbert Bates</b><br>
Company: <b>Bates Shower Repair</b><br>
</TD><TD>
    <SCRIPT LANGUAGE="VBScript">
<!--
sub cmdDetails825961369_click
Dim lTemp
lTemp = "Address: " & "123 Hotel Drive" & Chr(13)
lTemp = lTemp & "City/State/Zip: " & "New York, NY 10001" & chr(13)
lTemp = lTemp & "Phone: " & "212-555-1234" & chr(13)
lTemp = lTemp & "EMail: " & "bates@shower.com" & chr(13)

MsgBox lTemp, 0, "Dilbert Bates"
```

continues

Listing 5.5. continued

```
end sub
--></SCRIPT>
<OBJECT ID="cmdDetails825961369" WIDTH=96 HEIGHT=32
 CLASSID="CLSID:D7053240-CE69-11CD-A777-00DD01143C57">
    <PARAM NAME="Caption" VALUE="Details">
    <PARAM NAME="Size" VALUE="2540;846">
    <PARAM NAME="FontCharSet" VALUE="0">
    <PARAM NAME="FontPitchAndFamily" VALUE="2">
    <PARAM NAME="ParagraphAlign" VALUE="3">
    <PARAM NAME="FontWeight" VALUE="0">
</OBJECT>
</TD></tr>

</table></CENTER></font>
</body></HTML>
```

Review

This chapter discussed several ways to combine VBScript and HTML. Although the examples weren't earth-shattering, they did demonstrate the basics needed to fully integrate VBScript with your Web pages, your server-side applications, and your existing databases you want to publish on your Web site.

Part II of this book, "Objects in VBScript," examines embedding ActiveX controls and other objects into your Web pages and VBScript code. You'll begin by looking at document objects in Chapter 6, "The Scripting Model."

The Scripting Model

by Evangelos Petroutsos

CHAPTER 6

In the previous chapters, you learned how to write applications with VBScripts and how to program the controls to activate your pages. VBScript can also help control the browser's window, which is the container where your pages get displayed and your code is executed. In this chapter, you explore the objects that let you control the environment in which your VBScript applications will be executed. In terms of traditional programming, you've learned the language. In this section, you learn how to program the environment of the application, too.

ActiveX controls, the objects you use to build the interface of the application, are manipulated through their properties and methods. Internet Explorer provides another set of objects, with their own properties and methods. These objects enable you to manipulate the environment of Internet Explorer itself. Because Internet Explorer is the operating system for your VBScript applications, you can think of these objects as the operating system's controls. The browser's window is such an object. So far, this window has served as nothing more than the container for your application. It was the environment in which VBScript applications were executed. Now, you learn how to control the window object programmatically. You will see that it is possible to load another document in the browser from within your code; it's even possible to create pages on the fly with VBScript code. You will also learn how to control some of the browser's functionality, such as moving back and forward through the history list from within your applications. This process is equivalent to clicking the Back and Forward buttons on your browser, but you'll be able to perform these actions from within your VBScript application.

The material of this chapter assumes a basic knowledge of HTML authoring. You should understand the structure of an HTML document and the HTML tags used in the examples and their attributes. Some topics that are fairly new to Web authoring, such as floating frames, will be explained in the course of the chapter. To make the best of the HTML object model, however, you should at least have a familiarity with HTML authoring.

Windows, Documents, and Frames

The Internet Explorer scripting model is made up of a hierarchy of objects, with the window representing the most important object, the document and the frames objects. The discussion of the Internet Explorer scripting model begins with an overview of these three objects, the properties and methods they provide, and how you can use them to control Internet Explorer. The following sections discuss all the objects of the scripting model and give a number of examples to illustrate them. If you're wondering why Internet Explorer is controlled through objects and why the objects have a hierarchy, you need to read this chapter. Internet Explorer is an OLE control that exposes certain objects, such as its window and the current document. These objects, in turn, expose certain properties, and by manipulating these properties you can actually manipulate Internet Explorer itself.

The various objects through which you can control the behavior of Internet Explorer form a hierarchy. The window object is the top level object in this hierarchy and acts as a container for all other objects. This object is the browser's window you see on-screen; moreover, every parameter of the window you can adjust through VBScript code is a property of the window object. For example, the name of the window is a property of the window object. You can find out the name of the window from within your script with a statement like the following one:

```
wName=window.name
```

Another property of the window object is the status property, the text displayed in the status bar of the browser window. You can find out the current status message with the statement:

```
statusMessage=window.status
```

You can also set the status message with statements like these:

```
window.status="Thanks for visiting our site!"
```

or

```
window.status="Date "& date & " Time " & time
```

The window object's property you will use the most is the document property, which represents the document displayed on the window. This property is actually another object, with its own properties. The document has a background color, whose value can be manipulated with the document's bgColor property. To access the bgColor property of the document object, you can use a statement like the following one:

```
window.document.bgColor=red
```

Because the document object is the default property of the window object, you can omit the window identifier in the previous line:

```
document.bgColor=red
```

The window and the document objects are visible on-screen. Other objects exist that are not visible, but which enable you to control the behavior of Internet Explorer through their properties. The location object is a property of the document object, which enables you to manipulate the URL of the document displayed in the window. One property the location object provides is called href, and is the URL of the document being displayed. This is the URL displayed in Internet Explorer's Address box. To find out the URL of the current document, you must access the href property of the location object of the document object:

```
thisURL=window.document.location.href
```

As usual, you can omit the window identifier. Even so, you have a rather lengthy statement, but don't let it intimidate you. The URL is a location property and the location object applies to the document object. Thus, the location is a property of the document, and not the window. href is a property of the location object, which in turn is a property of the document object, which in turn is a property of the window object. You must write down a sequence of objects, starting with the top level object (the window object) and work your way down to the lower-level object whose property you want to access.

A window can also contain frames, which you can access through the frames object. The frames object is an array of objects, the first frame being frames(0), the second one frames(1), and so on. To control the background color of the document in the first frame, you must access the bgColor property of the document of the first frame. Each frame has its own document property similar to the window object. This time we want to access the document of a frame, which in turn is a property of the window object. Instead of getting the window.document.bgColor property as you saw earlier, you must access the document.bgColor of the frames(0) property of the window object:

```
window.frames(0).document.bgColor
```

Likewise, you can specify the URL of a document to be displayed in a frame. You start with the href property of the location object, which now must be applied to a frame, and not the window's document. To cause another document to be displayed in the first frame of the window, you must use a statement like:

```
window.frames(0).location.href
```

As you can see, the same object can be attached to multiple containers (which are also objects). The window has its own document object, and the document has a location property. If the window contains frames, however, each frame in the window has its own location property. You may find this behavior confusing at first, but you will soon get the hang of it.

In Microsoft's colorful terminology, each entity you see on the browser's window is an object. Objects "expose" some of their properties, which enables you to manipulate them. Some of these properties represent objects themselves, which expose their own properties. The window object exposes the name property, which enables you to examine the name of a window from within your code. To manipulate the background color of the document on the window, you must first access the document property of the window (window.document) and then the bgColor property of the document object (window.document.bgColor).

In the following sections, you explore the objects of the scripting model and their properties, as well as their methods, which enable you to control the Internet Explorer's environment from within your code. The text begins with the window object and one of its most important properties, the document object. As you will realize, the document object offers tremendous flexibility over the appearance and function of your Web pages, and it appears in many examples for this section.

The following list provides the other objects of the window object, which you will explore in this chapter:

history	history is an object you can use to access the history list of the current window. This is a list of the URLs visited already.
navigator	The navigator object contains information about the browser, such as the name of the browser and its version.
location	The location object provides information about the window's current URL.
document	The most important object of all. It's the actual document in the current window.

The window Object's Properties

The following paragraphs explain the various properties of the window object and offer short examples that demonstrate the syntax of the various properties. In the sections that describe the other objects of the scripting model, you will find more elaborate examples of the various properties of the window object's properties.

name

name is a read-only property that returns the name of the window. To create a named window, you must use the TARGET attribute with one of the HTML tags to which it applies. For example, the <A> tag is frequently used with the TARGET attribute, which tells the browser to display the destination HTML document in another window. The HTML line

```
Click <A HREF="http://www.microsoft.com">here</A> to visit the Microsoft Web site.
```

generates a hyperlink, which displays the root document of Microsoft's Web site when activated in the same window that contains the hyperlink. If you specify the TARGET attribute, however, the same document will appear in a separate window:

```
Click <A HREF="http://www.microsoft.com" target="MS">here</A> to visit the
Microsoft Web site.
```

If a window with the name MS exists already, the document will be displayed in it. If such a window doesn't exist, a new window opens and the document appears there. You can later refer to this window by its name. For example, you can set the string to appear in the window's status bar using the status property.

parent

The parent property returns the name of the parent window, which contains the specific window. The parent property of the window object is an object itself, and through its properties, you can adjust the appearance of the parent window.

opener

The opener property returns the window object that opened the current window. The opener property does not return a window name or another window property. It returns an actual object that you can use to access the properties of the window from which the current window was opened. To find the name of the opener window, use the Name property, as in the following line:

```
MsgBox "My parent window is " & opener.name
```

self

self is a window object that represents the current window, but, although mentioned in Microsoft's documentation, it's not yet supported by Internet Explorer 3.0. This property operates similarly to the parent and opener properties, in the sense that it returns a window object, and not the name of the window. To find out the status message of the current window, you could use the status property of the self object:

```
If self.status = "VBScript" Then
    self.status = "ActiveX"
Else
    self.status = "VBScript"
End If
```

If you place this If structure in a Timer event's handler, the message on the browser's status bar would alternate between the strings VBScript and ActiveX.

top

The top property returns an object that represents the topmost window.

location

The location property returns another object, the location object, which is described in detail in a later section. The most important property of the location object is the href property, which returns or sets the URL of the current window. The statement

```
MsgBox window.location.href
```

displays the URL of the current window in a message box. To activate another URL from within your code (in other words, without relying on the user to click on a hyperlink, or the browser's Back button), use a statement such as:

```
window.location.href="www.microsoft.com"
```

defaultStatus

This property sets the default text in the status bar. See the description of the status property to find out how you can display a message in the browser's status bar.

status

The status property returns or sets the text displayed in the status bar. The statement

```
window.status = Now
```

displays in the status bar the date and time the document was opened. To update the status bar, use the previous statement form within a Timer event handler. Figure 6.1 shows two windows with different status messages. The two status messages were displayed with the statements

```
window.status="Welcome to SAMS Publishing"
```

and

```
window.status="Today's date is " & date & " and the time is " & time
```

FIGURE 6.1.

With the status property of the window object, you can control the message displayed in the browser window's status bar.

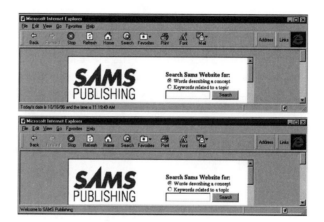

frames

This property returns an array of objects, which are the frames in the current window. Use it to access the various properties of a frame object, such as its name or its URL:

```
MsgBox "The name of the first frame is " & window.frames(0).location.href
MsgBox "The document displayed in the first frame is located at " &
window.frames(0).location.href
```

The location property of the window object controls the contents of the window (through its property href). When you apply the location property to a frame object, it controls the contents of the specific frame.

Methods

Apart from its properties, the window object provides several methods. The methods are predetermined actions that the window object knows how to perform, such as how to display a message and get input from the user, or how to navigate through the history list (the Web sites visited during the current session) of the window. The window object's methods appear next:

alert

The alert method displays an alert message box. The alert message box is very similar to the regular message box of the Windows 95 user interface. It displays a message and remains on the screen, and the execution of the script is suspended until the user clicks the OK button. You can use the alert method for displaying messages to the user; its syntax is

```
alert("Thanks for visiting our site")
```

confirm

confirm displays a message box similar to the alert method, only this box has two buttons, OK and Cancel. The confirm method returns the value True if the OK button is clicked and the value False if the Cancel button is clicked. This method frequently is used to notify the user that an unusual or irrevocable action is about to take place, such as the transmission of Form data to the server. Here's how the confirm method is typically used:

```
x=window.confirm("Do you want to submit the data?")
if x=True Then Form.submit
```

FIGURE 6.2.

The alert, confirm, *and* prompt *methods display boxes that operate similarly to the VBScript* MsgBox() *and* InputBox() *functions.*

prompt

The prompt method prompts the user for data, much like the InputBox() function. The prompt method accepts two arguments, the prompt for the user and an optional default response, and returns the data supplied by the user. The following statement prompts the user for the name of the browser:

```
browserName=window.prompt("What's your favorite browser?", "Internet Explorer")
```

Whatever the user has entered in the box gets stored in the browserName variable, which can later be used in the code. If the user simply clicks OK without entering any information, the default response is returned.

open

The open method opens an existing window, or creates a new one and displays a document in it. This method syntax can become quite lengthy because it accepts a number of arguments:

```
[newwindow = ][window.]open url, target, ["[toolbar=bool] [, location=bool]
[, directories=bool][, status=bool][, menubar=bool][, scrollbars=bool]
[, resizeable=bool][, width=pixels][, height=pixels]"][, top=pixels][, left=pixels]
```

The arguments in square brackets are optional. The simplest form of the open method is

```
window.open url, target
```

where url is the URL of the document to be displayed in the new window and target is the name of the window in which the document will appear. If the window specified with this name exists, this window's contents get replaced by the new document. If not, a new window with this name is opened and the document displays in it. This argument is identical to the TARGET attribute of the <HREF> tag.

The remaining arguments are set to Boolean values (yes/no, or 1/0) and control the appearance of the window. To hide the new window's toolbar, use the argument "toolbar=no", and to prevent the user from resizing the window, use the argument "resizeable=no". The last four arguments, which are specified in pixels, don't need to be enclosed in quotes. The arguments width and height determine the window's dimensions, and the arguments top and left determine the window's position on-screen, measured from the screen's top-left corner.

The return value is a window object, which you can use later to close the window. The statement

```
window.open "http://www.microsoft.com", "MSwindow", "toolbar=no", "menubar=no",
"resizeable=no", width=600, height=400
```

opens the window MSwindow (or creates a new one by that name, if it doesn't exist) and displays the home page of the Microsoft Web site. The MSwindow window has no toolbar and menu. Furthermore, it is 600 pixels wide and 400 pixels tall, and can't be resized. The width, height, top, and left arguments are all mentioned in Microsoft's documentation, but they don't work with version 3.0 of Internet Explorer. If you create a script with the previous line, Internet Explorer 3.0 will produce an error message. Omit the size specification for the new window (the last two arguments), and the open method will work fine. It will display Microsoft's Web site in a window without the usual menu or the toolbar.

You can find the document WindowOpen in this chapter's folder on the CD. The WindowOpen document contains a number of command buttons that act as hyperlinks to various sites. Every time the user clicks one of the buttons, the home page of the corresponding Web site appears in a separate window.

The HTML code of this document is straightforward. It displays a heading and the instructions, and places six command buttons next to its other. The code in each command button's Click event handler invokes the open method to display a URL in a separate window. The contents of the WindowOpen.htm file appear in the following code:

```
<HTML>
<HEAD>
<TITLE>WindowOpen</TITLE>

<SCRIPT LANGUAGE=VBS>

Sub MS_onClick()
    window.open "http://www.microsoft.com", "window1"
End Sub

Sub SAMS_onClick()
    window.open "http://www.mcp.com/sams", "window2"
End Sub

Sub MSN_onClick()
    window.open "http://www.msn.com", "window3"
End Sub

Sub CLGRI_onClick()
    window.open "http://www.caligari.com", "window4"
End Sub

Sub INTEL_onClick()
    window.open "http://www.intel.com", "window5"
End Sub

Sub NSCAPE_onClick()
    window.open "http://www.netscape.com", "window6"
End Sub

</SCRIPT>

<BODY>
<FONT FACE="Verdana">
<CENTER>
<H1>Top Web Sites</H1>
<H4>Click on the following buttons to see some of the best Web sites around.
Each Web site will be displayed in a separate window and, if you wish, you
can open them all at once.</H4>

<P>
<INPUT TYPE=BUTTON NAME="MS" VALUE="Microsoft">
<INPUT TYPE=BUTTON NAME="SAMS" VALUE="SAMS">
<INPUT TYPE=BUTTON NAME="MSN" VALUE="MS Network">
<INPUT TYPE=BUTTON NAME="CLGRI" VALUE="Caligari">
<INPUT TYPE=BUTTON NAME="INTEL" VALUE="Intel">
<INPUT TYPE=BUTTON NAME="NSCAPE" VALUE="Netscape">
</P>
</CENTER>
</BODY>
</FONT>
</HTML>
```

Only the first two command buttons and their code appear here. The other ones function in a similar way.

Open the WindowOpen project and experiment with the various arguments of the open method. Try opening the Internet Explorer window without the toolbar and menubar; you can also make them resizeable or not.

The open method has a behavior similar to that of hyperlinks inserted with the <A> tag; however, it gives you more control over the appearance of the new window. The real benefit of using the open method, though, is that it enables you to specify the target at runtime. On the other hand, the destination of the <A> tag must be furnished at design time and can't change when the document is viewed. With the open method, you can navigate to any URL, even a user-supplied URL.

close

The close method closes an open window. If you have opened a window with the following statement

```
newWindow=window.open "www.msn.com" "w1"
```

you can close it by calling the close method of the newWindow object:

```
newWindow.close
```

setTimeout

The setTimeout method sets up a timer to call a function after a specified number of milliseconds. The syntax of the method is

```
ID = window.setTimeout expression, msec, language
```

where ID identifies the timer object, and can be used with the clearTimeout method, which cancels the timer. expression is the name of a function that will be called when the timer object times out; msec is the number of milliseconds that must pass before the function is called; and language identifies the scripting language of the function (VBScript or Javascript). As usual, the window prefix is optional.

If the user hasn't already switched to another document, you can use the setTimeout method to take some action on a document after so many seconds. For example, you can invoke the method

```
window.setTimeout GoURL, 10000, VBScript
```

and supply the following GoURL() subroutine:

```
Sub GoURL()
    window.document.location.href="http://www.someserver.com"
End Sub
```

If the user hasn't followed a hyperlink to another page within 10 seconds after the window is opened, the browser will display the home page at the site www.someserver.com.

clearTimeout

This method clears the timer with a particular ID. Its syntax is

```
window.clearTimeout ID
```

where ID is the value returned by the setTimeout method.

navigate

The last method of the window object switches to a particular URL, which is supplied as an argument. The statement

```
window.navigate "http://www.msn.com"
```

instructs the browser to connect to the Microsoft Network site and display the site's home page. This method operates identically to setting the window's location.href property to the desired URL.

The document Object

The next object in the scripting model is the document object. You will use this object most often in programming your Web pages, and this section discusses its properties and methods in detail. The document object represents the HTML document displayed on the browser's window or one of its frames. Through its properties and methods you can manipulate the appearance or even the contents of the document. The bgColor property, for example, enables you to read or set the document's background color, and the title property enables you to read the document's title.

The document object has an extremely flexible method, the write method, which you can use to write strings on the current document. This method enables you to create documents on the fly; you'll see quite a few examples of this technique in action in this and following sections.

The document Object's Properties

The following paragraphs explain the various properties of the document object and offer short examples that demonstrate the syntax of the various properties. In the sections that describe the other objects of the scripting model, you find more elaborate examples of the various properties of the document object.

linkColor

linkColor returns or sets the color of the links in the document. This property is equivalent to the LINK attribute of the `<BODY>` tag. To set the color of the links on the current document to a value other than the default value, assign the hexadecimal value of a color, or a color name, to the linkColor property:

```
document.linkColor=yellow
document.linkColor=#00FFFF
```

Both statements set the color of the hyperlinks in the current document to yellow.

aLinkColor

Returns or sets the color of the active link in the document. The active link represents the one under the mouse pointer as the mouse button is pressed and not released. The current implementation of Internet Explorer does not support this property, and the `<BODY>` tag has no equivalent attribute. For the syntax of the property and an example, see the linkColor property.

vLinkColor

Returns or sets the color of the links that have been visited already. vLinkColor is equivalent to the VLINK attribute of the `<BODY>` tag. For the syntax of the property and an example, see the linkColor property.

bgColor

Returns or sets the document's background color. To change the background property of the current document, set the document's bgColor property to a color value. Both statements set the document's background color to green:

```
document.bgColor =#00FF00
document.bgColor="green"
```

fgColor

Returns or sets the document's foreground color. It has the same syntax as the bgColor property.

anchor

anchor is a property of the document object, and like some other properties, it's an object. The length property of the anchor object returns the number of anchors in the document. The individual anchors are stored in the anchors array, whose elements can be accessed with an index. anchors(0) is the name of the first anchor in the document (its value is the NAME attribute of the <A> tag that inserted the anchor in the document), anchors(1) is the second anchor, and so on. The following statements display the number of anchors in the current document in a message box:

```
TotalAnchors = Document.Anchors.Length
MsgBox "The document contains "& TotalAnchors & "anchors"
```

You can also scan all the anchors in a document with a loop like the one that follows:

```
For i=0 to TotalAnchors-1
    ThisAnchor=Document.Anchors(i)
    {do something with this anchor}
Next
```

Scanning the anchors of the current document from within the same document's script section doesn't seem very practical. You can, however, open another document in a frame and access the anchors of the frame with the Frame(1).Document.Anchors array. For another example, see the DocumentLinks example later in this chapter.

link

The link property functions similarly to the anchor property, but instead of the anchors, it represents the hyperlinks in the current document. Like the anchors array, the links array is a property of the document, which represents the only object that may contain links.

form

The form object represents a form in an HTML document. All the form objects on the document can be accessed through the forms array, whose index starts at zero. forms(0) is the first element, forms(1) is the second form, and so on. The form object's properties are as follows.

action

Returns a string containing the current form action, which is the URL of a CGI application.

encoding

Returns or sets the encoding for the form. Its value must represent a valid MIME type, such as text/html.

method

Returns or sets the method for submitting the form data to the server, and its value must be GET or POST.

target

Returns or sets the name of the target window where the result of the form processing will appear.

elements

The `elements` property is an array with the controls on the form. The `length` property of the `elements` object returns the number of controls on the form. The following lines scan all the controls on the first form on the current page:

```
For i=0 to forms(0).elements.length
    ControlName=forms(0).elements(i).name
    {do something with the current element}
Next
```

The `form` object has a method too, the `submit` method. This method causes the form data to be submitted to the browser. Chapter 20, "CGI and VBScript," discusses the `submit` method.

lastModified

Returns the date the current document was last modified. You can use the `lastModified` property of the `document` object to display the date and time it was last modified, without having to hard-code this information in the document itself.

title

The `title` property returns the current document's title. This property is read-only and won't allow you to change the document's title at runtime.

cookie

The `cookie` property enables you to set up client-side cookies. A cookie represents a message you can store on the client computer and read from another page, or the next time the same client loads your page. Cookies enable you to customize your pages for each client by maintaining information between sessions. The `cookie` property makes it possible for your script to actually store a string (or cookie) on the client computer and recall it at a later time. Because this property provides such a flexible and powerful mechanism in Web authoring, this text has devoted an entire chapter to the topic. (See Chapter 14, "Customize Your Web Page with Cookies.")

referrer

Returns the URL of the referring document.

The document Object's Methods

Apart from its properties, the `document` object provides five methods, through which you can manipulate its contents. The methods of the `document` object may not number as many as its properties; however, these methods provide enough to make the document the most flexible object among the HTML scripting objects. This section provides a short description of the `document` object's methods, as well as a few examples that demonstrate how these methods get used. Actually, most of the examples make use of the methods; consequently, this chapter gives you a thorough explanation of the `document` object's methods.

write string

Writes the `string` variable to the current document. The string gets inserted in the current document at the current position, and it doesn't appear until the `close` method is called.

writeLn string

Places the `string` variable into the current document with a new-line character appended to the end. The new-line character is ignored by the browser, so the `writeLn` method operates practically the same as the `write` method.

open

Opens the document for output. The current contents of the document are cleared, and new strings can be placed in the document with the `write` and `writeLn` methods.

close

Updates the screen to display all of the strings written after the last `open` method call.

clear

Clears the contents of the document.

The common sequence of methods used to place data in the current document is

```
Document.open
Document.write "Welcome to VBScript Unleashed"
Document.close
```

Instead of using a string enclosed in quotes, you can write a variable to the document, which could be the result of a calculation or a string that's calculated on the fly at the client's side (an expression that depends on the current day, for instance). The most interesting aspect of the `write` and `writeLn` methods is that their argument may also contain HTML tags. For instance, the statements

```
Document.write "<CENTER>"
Document.write "<H1>Welcome to VBScript Unleashed</H1>"
Document.write "<H3>by SAMS"</H3>"
Document.write "</CENTER>"
```

will cause level 1 and level 3 headings to appear and be centered on the browser's window. The `document` object's methods are quite flexible, and the following sections will present a few more examples.

Using the document Properties and Methods

This section shows a few interesting authoring techniques that make use of the properties of the `Document` object. You start with the color properties, which are the `fgColor`, `bgColor`, `linkColor`, `aLinkColor`, and `vLinkColor`. You can assign a value color to these properties, either by name (red, yellow, orange, and so on) or by hexadecimal representation. Only 16 color names exist, and they represent the names of the basic colors. To assign a color value by name, use one of the color names shown in Table 6.1. The color names are not case-sensitive, but you can't make up other color names. You must use one of the valid names.

Table 6.1. Valid names for the document's color properties.

Color property	*Hex value*
Aqua	#00FFFF
Black	#000000
Blue	#0000FF
Fuchsia	#FF00FF
Gray	#00E000
Green	#008000
Lime	#00FF00
Maroon	#800000
Navy	#000080
Olive	#808000
Purple	#800080
Red	#FF0000
Silver	#C0C0C0
Teal	#008080
White	#FFFFFF
Yellow	#FFFF00

Specifying colors by name is the most flexible method because you are limited to 16 colors. You can also specify colors by their hexadecimal values, and this method enables you to specify any color value you can imagine. The problem with this approach, however, is coming up with the proper hexadecimal value.

To handle color, computers use three basic colors: red, green, and blue. Each color is represented by a triplet, or RGB triplet, with the intensities of these three colors. The intensities are usually expressed as percentages, with 0 corresponding to the absence of a color component and 1 corresponding to full intensity. The triplet (0.25, 0.5, 0.20) represents a color in which the red component has 25% of the full intensity, the green component has 50% of the full intensity, and the blue component has 20% of the full intensity. Because computers internally use one byte for each color component, it's also common to express the three color components with byte values (a number from 0 to 255). The previous RGB triplet could also appear as (64, 128, 51). The triplet (1, 0, 0) shows a pure red tone, because the red component has full intensity and the other two components are missing. The triplet (0.5, 0.5, 0) represents a mid-magenta tone, as it contains equal percentages of the red and green components and no blue. Even the colors black and white can appear as RGB triplets. The triplet (0, 0, 0) is black, because all colors are missing, and the triplet (1, 1, 1) is white, because it contains all three components in full intensity.

If you start with the byte form of the RGB triplet and place the hexadecimal representation of each color component next to each other, you come up with a hexadecimal number that represents the corresponding color. The hexadecimal value of the decimal number 128 is 80, and the hexadecimal number for the RGB triplet (128, 128, 128) is 808080. To use this value as color value in HTML, you must prefix it with the symbol #, as in #808080.

VBScript provides the Hex() function, which accepts a decimal number as an argument and returns its hexadecimal representation as a string. To specify a mid-yellow tone, such as (0, 128, 128), use the Hex() function to convert these values to hexadecimal numbers and then append them to each other, with the following statement:

```
colorValue="#" & Hex & Hex(128) & Hex(128)
```

Then, you can assign this value to any of the color properties of the document object (bgColor, fgColor, aLinkColor, and so on).

Armed with this information, you can now look at a few examples that show how to use the document object's properties and methods.

A Self-Modifying Document

Now look at a couple of examples that use the color properties of the document object. The page shown in Figure 6.3, called WeeklyPage, is in this chapter's folder on the CD. This page has a different background color for each weekday. As you can guess, it combines the WeekDay() VBScript function with the bgColor property of the document object. The WeekDay() function returns a number between 1 and 7, which corresponds to the weekday. The script uses the value returned by the WeekDay() function to select one of seven colors for the document's background color.

FIGURE 6.3.

This document has a different background color, depending on the day of the week it was opened.

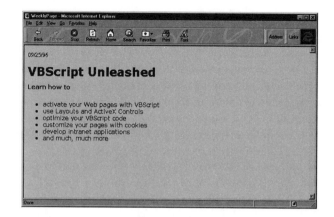

The following HTML code shows the script that produced this page:

```
<HTML>
<HEAD>
<TITLE>WeeklyPage</TITLE>
<SCRIPT LANGUAGE=VBS>
Dim BColor(7)

BColor(1)="Red"
BColor(2)="Blue"
BColor(3)="Teal"
BColor(4)="Yellow"
BColor(5)="Orange"
BColor(6)="Cyan"
BColor(7)="Silver"

Document.bgColor=BColor(WeekDay(Date))

Document.write "<BODY>"
Document.write Date
Document.write "<P>"
Document.write "<FONT FACE='Verdana'>"
Document.write "<H1>VBScript Unleashed</H1>"
Document.write "<B>Learn how to</B><P>"
Document.write "<UL>"
Document.write "<LI>activate your Web pages with VBScript<BR>"
Document.write "<LI>use Layouts and ActiveX Controls<BR>"
Document.write "<LI>optimize your VBScript code<BR>"
Document.write "<LI>customize your pages with cookies<BR>"
Document.write "<LI>develop intranet applications<BR>"
Document.write "<LI>and much, much more"
Document.write "</UL>"
Document.write "</BODY>"
</SCRIPT>
</HTML>
```

Notice that the code sets the color value of the document's bgColor property as soon as it's loaded and then places all the other elements on the page. The entire document is generated on the fly with the write method. This example shows exactly what makes the document such a flexible object. Of course, outputting the HTML commands that will produce the desired output with the write method takes quite a bit of typing, but you can automate this process with a simple program that reads actual HTML code and creates write statements whose arguments are the lines of the HTML code. You must make sure that the HTML code uses single quotes (see the line that changes the font of the document), which will not interfere with the double quotes surrounding the write method's arguments.

Color Cycling

Another interesting trick is to rapidly cycle the background color through a range of colors right before loading a new page. If the page's background color is red, you can start with a black background color, which swiftly changes from black to red and then remains red for the rest of the session. Unfortunately, this effect can be depicted on a page, so you must open the FadeColor page and see how it behaves as it loads the page. It starts with a black background that gradually shifts to red. The entire effect lasts less than a second, but it's quite impressive. To see the effect again, click on the Refresh button.

The code that produces this effect is surpassingly simple. It cycles the background color through a range of color values from black to red, with a For...Next loop:

```
<SCRIPT LANGUAGE=VBS>
For i=0 to 255 step 3
    colorVal= "#" & Hex(i) & Hex(0) & Hex(0)
    Document.bgColor=colorVal
Next
</SCRIPT>
```

You can change the step to make the effect faster or slower, and you can also change the arguments of the Hex() function to cycle the background color from any initial value to any final value. This code is placed in the <SCRIPT> tag and outside any procedure so that it will be executed as soon as the HTML document starts loading and before any other element appears. If you attempt to cycle the background color after placing the strings or any other element on the page, the entire page will flicker. The smoothest color cycling is achieved with gray tones. For example, you can start from white and move slowly to a mid-gray tone with a loop like this one:

```
For i=0 to 128 step 2
    colorVal= "#" & Hex(i) & Hex(i) & Hex(i)
    Document.bgColor=colorVal
Next
```

A characteristic of gray tones is that all three color components are the same.

A Yearly Calendar

The previous example shows how to send straight HTML code to the current window. It's an interesting technique, but you can achieve the same by supplying the equivalent HTML document. The example in this section demonstrates the flexibility of the document object's write method, namely how to create documents that produced different output on different systems, depending on the user's actions. The Calendar project displays a tabular arrangement of Command buttons with the names of the months, as shown in Figure 6.4. The user can click on a month's name and see the corresponding calendar. (See Figure 6.5.) The monthly calendar is generated on the fly with VBScript code. The actual calendar doesn't react to a mouse click, but once you understand how it was generated, you can enhance the application by making certain days hyperlinks to other files on the server (for example, you can display major events, project deadlines, and so on). You can even add code behind the digits of the days.

FIGURE 6.4.

The Calendar *application starts by displaying the months of the year. To see a month's calendar, click the corresponding button.*

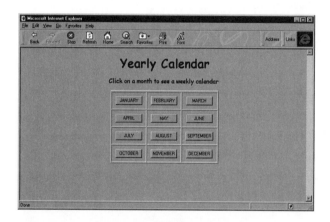

FIGURE 6.5.

A monthly calendar, as displayed by the Calendar *application. To return to the previous screen, click the Refresh button.*

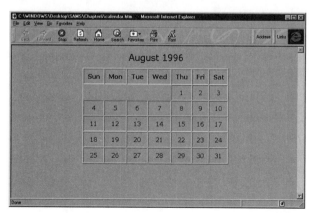

The complete listing of the project is shown here. The HTML lines that display the twelve month names as command buttons are the document's body, and the rest of the code is the script that creates the current month's calendar.

```
<HTML>
<HEAD>
<TITLE>Yearly Calendar</TITLE>
<SCRIPT LANGUAGE=VBS>
Sub JANUARY_onClick()
    DisplayMonth(1)
End Sub

Sub FEBRUARY_onClick()
    DisplayMonth(2)
End Sub

Sub MARCH_onClick()
    DisplayMonth(3)
End Sub

Sub APRIL_onClick()
    DisplayMonth(4)
End Sub

Sub MAY_onClick()
    DisplayMonth(5)
End Sub

Sub JUNE_onClick()
    DisplayMonth(6)
End Sub

Sub JULY_onClick()
    DisplayMonth(7)
End Sub

Sub AUGUST_onClick()
    DisplayMonth(8)
End Sub

Sub SEPTEMBER_onClick()
    DisplayMonth(9)
End Sub

Sub OCTOBER_onClick()
    DisplayMonth(10)
End Sub

Sub NOVEMBER_onClick()
    DisplayMonth(11)
End Sub

Sub DECEMBER_onClick()
    DisplayMonth(12)
End Sub
```

```
Sub DisplayMonth(imonth)
dim MonthName(12)
MonthName(1)="January"
MonthName(2)="February"
MonthName(3)="March"
MonthName(4)="April"
MonthName(5)="May"
MonthName(6)="June"
MonthName(7)="July"
MonthName(8)="August"
MonthName(9)="September"
MonthName(10)="October"
MonthName(11)="November"
MonthName(12)="December"

document.clear
document.write "<CENTER>"
document.write "<FONT FACE='Verdana' SIZE=5>"
document.write MonthName(imonth) & " " & Year(date)
document.write "<P>"
document.write "<TABLE CELLPADDING=10 BORDER><TR>"
document.write
"<TD><B>Sun<TD><B>Mon<TD><B>Tue<TD><B>Wed<TD><B>Thu<TD><B>Fri<TD><B>Sat"
document.write "<TR>"
    firstdate=DateSerial(year(date), imonth, 1)
    thisdate=firstdate
    nextday=1
    For cday=1 to 7
        If WeekDay(thisdate)>cday Then
            document.write "<TD></TD>"
        else
            document.write "<TD ALIGN=CENTER><FONT SIZE=3>" & nextday & "</TD>"
            nextday=nextday+1
            thisdate=DateSerial(year(date), imonth, nextday)
        End If
    Next
    document.write "<TR>"
    weekDays=1
    while month(thisdate)=imonth
        document.write "<TD ALIGN=CENTER><FONT SIZE=3>" & nextday & "</TD>"
        nextday=nextday+1
        weekDays=weekDays+1
        If weekDays>7 then
            WeekDays=1
            document.write "<TR>"
        End If
        thisdate=DateSerial(year(date), imonth, nextday)
    wend
document.write "</TABLE>"
document.write "</CENTER>"
document.close
End Sub
</SCRIPT>
</HEAD>
<BODY>
<FONT FACE="Comic Sans MS">
<CENTER>
<H1>Yearly Calendar</H1>
```

```
Click on a month to see a weekly calendar
<P>
<FONT FACE="Verdana" SIZE=6>
<TABLE CELLPADDING=10 BORDER>
<TR>
<COLGROUP>
<COL ALIGN=CENTER>
<COL ALIGN=CENTER>
<COL ALIGN=CENTER>

<TD><INPUT TYPE=BUTTON NAME="January" VALUE="JANUARY">
<TD><INPUT TYPE=BUTTON NAME="February" VALUE="FEBRUARY">
<TD><INPUT TYPE=BUTTON NAME="March" VALUE="MARCH">
<TR>
<TD><INPUT TYPE=BUTTON NAME="April" VALUE="APRIL">
<TD><INPUT TYPE=BUTTON NAME="May" VALUE="MAY">
<TD><INPUT TYPE=BUTTON NAME="June" VALUE="JUNE">
<TR>
<TD><INPUT TYPE=BUTTON NAME="July" VALUE="JULY">
<TD><INPUT TYPE=BUTTON NAME="August" VALUE="AUGUST">
<TD><INPUT TYPE=BUTTON NAME="September" VALUE="SEPTEMBER">
<TR>
<TD><INPUT TYPE=BUTTON NAME="October" VALUE="OCTOBER">
<TD><INPUT TYPE=BUTTON NAME="November" VALUE="NOVEMBER">
<TD><INPUT TYPE=BUTTON NAME="December" VALUE="DECEMBER">
</TABLE>
</BODY>
</HTML>
```

The 12 command buttons that correspond to the months of the year are placed on the page with straight HTML code. Each button's name corresponds to a month's name, and its onClick event handler displays the actual month calendar. The handler for the onClick event of the JANUARY button is

```
Sub JANUARY_onClick()
    DisplayMonth(1)
End Sub
```

The handlers of the other Click events are similar. They all call the DisplayMonth() subroutine with the proper arguments. The DisplayMonth() subroutine goes through the days of the specified month and prints them under the appropriate day column.

The program first displays the days of the week as headings. The next step is the display of the days of the first week with a For...Next loop. The first week in the month is usually incomplete and the first few cells in the table must remain blank. This loop goes through the seven days in the week until it hits the first day in the month, which happens when the weekday of the first day in the month is the same as the current cell. Until this happens, the program displays empty cells by writing the string <TD></TD> to the document. After the first day in the month is found, the program creates cells where it places the value of the variable nextday, which is increased with every iteration. The string that produces a cell with a number is:

```
"<TD ALIGN=CENTER><FONT SIZE=3>" & nextday & "</TD>"
```

This is HTML code, and any references to variables will be replaced with the actual variable value. If the value of the `nextday` variable is 24, the line that is written to the document is

```
<TD ALIGN=CENTER><FONT SIZE=3>24</TD>
```

which is straight HTML.

After the first week of the calendar has been displayed, the program continues with the following ones. These weeks are complete, except for the last one, of course.

The remaining days of the month are handled with a `While...Wend` loop. With each iteration, the `nextday` variable increases by one day, and the loop keeps going as long as you are in the same month (the condition `while month(thisdate)=imonth`). This loop makes use of an additional variable, the `weekDays` variable, which increases by one with each iteration and is reset back to 1 when it reaches 7. At the same time, the program inserts a `<TR>` tag to the output to start a new row in the table.

The code of the `DisplayMonth()` is fairly straightforward, and you can use it as a starting point for any application that needs to display a calendar. You can easily turn each day of the month into a hyperlink, pointing to a file on the server. If you maintain a separate document for each day of the month on the server, you can modify the application so that each day is a hyperlink to this date's file. Instead of writing the number of the day to the output, you could write a string that will turn it into a hyperlink. If you use the following string as the `write` method's argument:

```
"<A HREF=" & imonth & "-" & nextday & ".htm>" & nextday & "</A>"
```

the actual string that will be written to the output file is

```
<A HREF=1-21.htm>21</A>
```

which is indeed a hyperlink to the file `1-21.htm` on the server. This file must reside on the same folder as the `Calendar` application, or you must prefix the filename with a relative pathname.

The `history` Object

The `history` object is an invisible object that provides methods for navigating through the document's history. It provides the functionality of the browser's navigational buttons, with the added benefit that you can access this functionality through programming. The following text explains the `history` object's methods.

Back *n*

Moves back in the history list by *n* steps, as if the user has clicked on the browser's Back button *n* times. To move to the most recently visited URL, use the statement

```
window.history.back 1
```

Forward *n*

Moves forward in the history list by *n* steps, as if the user has clicked on the browser's Forward button *n* times.

Go *n*

Moves to the *n*th item in the history list. The statement

```
window.history.go 1
```

will take you to the first URL in the list.

The `history` object also provides a property, the `length` property. This property represents the number of URLs in the history list. The current implementation of Internet Explorer always returns the number zero as the history list's length.

The `HistoryObject` Project

The `HistoryObject` document contains a floating frame and three command buttons, which enable you to control the contents of the floating frame. The first button enables the user to type the URL he or she wants to visit in an Input box; it then sets the frame's URL to the string entered by the user. The example uses a frame to display the various URLs, because if the window were updated using the `write` method, the new document would replace the original contents, including the command buttons. A frame makes it possible to provide the controls for manipulating the frame's URL via the `history` object's methods. You could also display the URL in a different window (see the `open` method of the `window` object), but this approach requires that the viewer moves back and forth between two windows.

You can enter a few URLs to visit manually. (Just remember to enter a fully qualified URL, including the protocol identifier, such as `http://www.mcp.com/sams`.) You can also follow the hyperlinks in the first URL, which appear when the project is opened for the first time. Then, you can test the Previous URL and Next URL buttons, which simply call the `Back` and `Forward` methods of the frame's `history` object. The document that produced the page in Figure 6.7 appears in the following code:

```
<HTML>
<HEAD>
<SCRIPT LANGUAGE=VBS>
Sub GoURL_onClick()
    newURL=InputBox("Enter the URL of the location you want to visit")
    Window.frames(0).location.href=newURL
End Sub
```

```
Sub NextURL_onClick()
    window.frames(0).history.forward 0
End Sub

Sub PreviousURL_onClick()
    window.frames(0).history.back 0
End Sub
</SCRIPT>
<CENTER>
<TABLE WIDTH=500>
<TR>
<TD ALIGN=CENTER><INPUT TYPE=BUTTON VALUE="Get me to this URL" NAME="GoURL" >
<TD ALIGN=CENTER><INPUT TYPE=BUTTON VALUE="   Previous URL    " NAME="PreviousURL" >
<TD ALIGN=CENTER><INPUT TYPE=BUTTON VALUE="     Next URL      " NAME="NextURL" >
</TABLE>
<P>
<IFRAME WIDTH=500 HEIGHT=400 NAME="MyFrame" SRC="http://www.microsoft.com">
</CENTER>
</HTML>
```

To display the URL entered in the Input box, the program assigns the string returned by the InputBox() function to the href property of the frame's location object. The other two buttons invoke the back and forward methods of the frame's history object.

When the page is first loaded, it connects to the Microsoft Web site, which appears in the frame. You can follow the hyperlinks of this document to switch to any other page within the same Web site or to visit another site. Some hyperlinks, however, cause the destination page to be displayed on the parent page (with the <A> tag's TARGET attribute), in effect removing your page from the browser's window. If this happens, the page with the command buttons will be replaced on the browser's window, and you must click on the browser's Back button to return to the LocationObject page, or click the Refresh button to reload the original page.

The navigator Object

This object, also invisible, returns information about the browser. You can access this information through the properties exposed by the navigator object, which are all read-only. An explanation of these properties appears in the following section:

appCodeName
Returns the code name of the application. Internet Explorer 3.0 returns Mozilla.

appName
Returns the name of the application. Internet Explorer 3.0 returns Microsoft Internet Explorer.

appVersion

Returns the version of the application. Internet Explorer 3.0 returns `2.0` `(compatible; MSIE`
`3.0A; Windows 95)`.

userAgent

Returns the user agent of the application. Internet Explorer returns `2.0` `(compatible; MSIE`
`3.0A; Windows 95)`.

The most practical use of the `navigator` object involves detecting whether the client is using
Internet Explorer or another browser. Say that you have prepared an HTML page that can be
viewed with any browser, and a more advanced version of the same page that makes use of
floating frames and style sheets. These two features are currently supported by only Internet
Explorer 3.0. You can easily detect which browser the client has running and display the appropriate page.

The `BrowserInfo` project you explore in the next section demonstrates the use of the `navigator`
object's properties. The next example, NavigatorObject, shows you how to detect whether the
browser used on the client is Internet Explorer and adjust the contents of the page accordingly.

The BrowserInfo Project

The BrowserInfo project demonstrates the properties of the `navigator` object. The BrowserInfo
page, which you can find in this chapter's folder on the CD, contains a floating frame. This
frame displays the Sams Web site and four command buttons with the four properties of the
`navigator` object. Click the corresponding command button, and you see the values of the
`navigator` object's properties, as reported by Internet Explorer. You should also open this project
with other browsers to examine its behavior.

The code of the BrowserInfo page appears in the following text:

```
<HTML>
<HEAD>
<SCRIPT LANGUAGE=VBS>
Sub BrowserName_onClick()
    MsgBox window.navigator.AppName
End Sub

Sub BrowserCodeName_onClick()
    MsgBox window.navigator.AppCodeName
End Sub

Sub BrowserVersion_onClick()
    MsgBox window.navigator.AppVersion
End Sub

Sub BrowserAgent_onClick()
    MsgBox window.navigator.UserAgent
End Sub
```

```
</SCRIPT>

<CENTER>
<TABLE WIDTH=500>
<TR>
<TD><INPUT TYPE=BUTTON VALUE="Browser Name" NAME="BrowserName" >
<TD><INPUT TYPE=BUTTON VALUE="Browser Code" NAME="BrowserCodeName" >
<TD><INPUT TYPE=BUTTON VALUE="Browser Version" NAME="BrowserVersion" >
<TD><INPUT TYPE=BUTTON VALUE="Browser Agent" NAME="BrowserAgent" >
</TABLE>
<P>
<IFRAME WIDTH=550 HEIGHT=400 NAME="MyFrame" SRC="http://www.microsoft.com">
</CENTER>
</HTML>
```

The <IFRAME> tag inserts a so-called floating frame. A floating frame looks like a regular frame, but it can be placed anywhere on a page, like an image or any other HTML element. Floating frames are ideal for opening windows in a document, where other URLs can be displayed. In the previous listing, we placed a floating frame centered on the window and below the command buttons, where the Microsoft Web site is displayed. The document to be displayed in the floating frame is specified with the SRC attribute, which is similar to the <IMG> tag's attribute with the same name, only instead of an image, the <IFRAME> tag's SRC attribute specifies a Web site's URL.

The NavigatorObject Project

This example reads the browser's application name and uses it to decide whether to display a generic page or the same page enhanced with Internet Explorer 3.0 features. The NavigatorObject page, seen in Figure 6.6, contains the HTML description of the generic page and a few lines of VBScript code, which uses the navigator object's properties to detect the browser. The SCRIPT section of this page appears next:

```
<SCRIPT LANGUAGE=VBS>

If window.navigator.appname="Microsoft Internet Explorer" Then
    window.document.write "<CENTER>"
    window.document.write "<H1>A Web site in a floating frame</H1>"
    window.document.write "<IFRAME WIDTH=500 HEIGHT=400 NAME='MyFrame' SRC='http://
    www.mcp.com/sams'>"
    window.document.write "<\CENTER>"
End If

</SCRIPT>
```

If the browser can handle VBScript (if not, the browser probably can't handle floating frames and other Internet Explorer 3.0 specific features, either), it will execute the script and will display the page in a floating frame. If the browser doesn't recognize the SCRIPT section, or if it's not Internet Explorer, nothing will happen, and in effect, the entire script will be ignored. The following text shows the entire HTML document, which consists of a SCRIPT section that displays the Sams Web site in a floating frame, and the HTML description of the generic page that prompts the user to download Internet Explorer:

```
<HTML>
<HEAD>
<SCRIPT LANGUAGE=VBS>
If window.navigator.appname="Microsoft Internet Explorer" Then
    window.document.write "<CENTER>"
    window.document.write "<H1>A Web site in a floating frame</H1>"
    window.document.write "<IFRAME WIDTH=500 HEIGHT=400 NAME='MyFrame' SRC='http://
    www.mcp.com/sams'>"
    window.document.write "<\CENTER>"
End If
</SCRIPT>
<CENTER>
<H1>This site is optimized for Internet Explorer 3.0</H1>
<P>
Click <A HREF="www.microsoft.com/ie">here</A> to download the browser.
<A HREF="http://www.microsoft.com/usa/ie/rm/supernet.htm"><IMG BORDER="0"
SRC="ie_animated.gif" WIDTH="88" HEIGHT="31" VSPACE="7" ALT="Microsoft Internet
Explorer" ></A><BR>
</CENTER>
</HTML>
```

FIGURE 6.6.

If you view the NavigatorObject with Internet Explorer 3.0, the page displays a Web site in a floating frame.

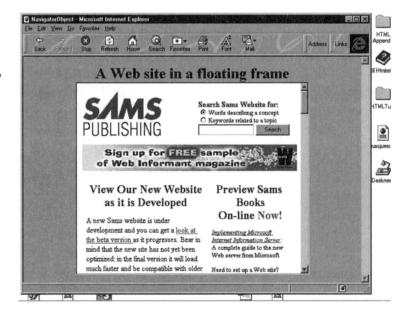

The generic page used in this example, shown in Figure 6.7, is too generic. It doesn't display any actual content; it just prompts the viewer to download Internet Explorer and provides a link to the download site. You can open this project with other browsers to see how it works.

The code for this example has a small bug; namely, it doesn't distinguish between versions 2.0 and 3.0 of Internet Explorer. Internet Explorer 2.0, for example, doesn't support frames. If you anticipate that some of your viewers still use Internet Explorer 2.0, you must also check the version of the browser from within your application to make sure it will not attempt to display floating frames using Internet Explorer 2.0.

FIGURE 6.7.

If the NavigatorObject page is opened with a browser other than Internet Explorer, it displays this generic page.

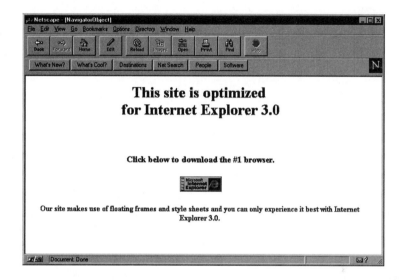

The location Object

The location object provides information about the window's current URL. You have already seen examples of the location object, but all of its properties have not been discussed. This section provides the complete list of the properties of the location object.

href

Returns or sets the compete URL for the location to be loaded into the browser's window. Use this property to connect to another location through your VBScript code.

To find out the current document's URL, use a statement such as this one:

```
MsgBox "You are currently viewing " & document.location.href
```

You can also cause another document to appear on the window, or a frame, with the statement:

```
document.location.href="http://www.microsoft.com"
```

The following properties set the various parts of the URL:

protocol

Returns or sets the protocol of the URL (usually http).

host

Returns or sets the host and port of the URL. The host and port are separated with a colon, as in host:port.

hostname

Reads or sets the host of a URL, which can be either a name or an IP address.

port

Returns or sets the port of the URL (you rarely have to specify the port number in a WWW URL).

pathname

Returns or sets the pathname of the URL. Use this property when you want to specify a document, other than the Web's root document, to be displayed.

search

Returns or sets the search portion of the URL, if it exists. The search portion of the URL is the string that follows the question mark in the URL when the browser submits data to the server. If the URL is

```
http://www.someServer.com/cgi/RegisterUser.exe?UName="Peter Evans"
```

the search portion of this URL is UName="Peter Evans". If the URL doesn't contain a search portion, the search property is an empty string.

hash

Returns or sets the hash portion of the URL.

The LocationObject Project

The LocationObject page on the CD demonstrates the location object's properties. The page LocationObject has a structure similar to that of the previous examples. It contains a floating frame and a few command buttons that demonstrate the properties of the location object. The floating frame of the page shown is a container into which any HTML can be loaded and displayed. To display a new page in the floating frame, the user must click the Get me to this URL button and is prompted to enter the desired URL. The program expects the full name of the URL, including the protocol identifier. The URL of the page is http://www.mcp.com/sams.

The second command button displays the URL of the document in the floating frame in a message box. Finally, the Location Properties button displays several of the location's properties in a message box, as shown in Figure 6.8. Notice that the root document on a Web site doesn't have a pathname property. For the pathname property to have a value, you must follow a hyperlink to another document.

FIGURE 6.8.

The location properties of a page on the Sams Web site as displayed from within the LocationObject page.

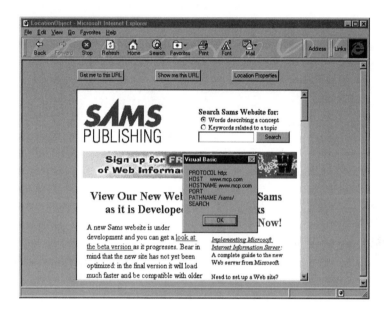

The actual code of the LocationObject page appears next:

```
<HTML>
<HEAD>
<SCRIPT LANGUAGE=VBS>
Sub GoURL_onClick()
    newURL=InputBox("Enter the URL of the location you want visit")
    Window.frames(0).location.href=newURL
End Sub

Sub ShowURL_onClick()
    MsgBox "You are currently viewing the URL " & Window.Frames(0).location.href
End Sub

Sub LocationProps_onClick()
    str="PROTOCOL " & Window.Frames(0).location.protocol
    str=str+chr(10)+"HOST     " & Window.Frames(0).location.host
    str=str+chr(10)+"HOSTNAME " & Window.Frames(0).location.hostname
```

```
         str=str+chr(10)+"PORT      " & Window.Frames(0).location.port
         str=str+chr(10)+"PATHNAME  " & Window.Frames(0).location.pathname
         str=str+chr(10)+"SEARCH    " & Window.Frames(0).location.search
     MsgBox str
End Sub
</SCRIPT>

<CENTER>
<TABLE WIDTH=500>
<TR>
<TD><INPUT TYPE=BUTTON VALUE="Get me to this URL" NAME="GoURL" >
<TD><INPUT TYPE=BUTTON VALUE="Show me this URL" NAME="ShowURL" >
<TD><INPUT TYPE=BUTTON VALUE="Location Properties" NAME="LocationProps" >
</TABLE>
<P>
<IFRAME WIDTH=500 HEIGHT=400 NAME="MyFrame" SRC="http://www.microsoft.com">
</CENTER>
</HTML>
```

The code behind the GoURL button sets the href property of the location object of the window's first frame. The code of the ShowURL button reads this property and displays it in a message box. The code behind the third button's click event becomes lengthier, as it creates step by step the string with all the properties of the location object before displaying them in the message box. chr(10) is the new-line character and is used to cause each new property to appear on a separate line.

The link Object

Another invisible object, the link object, represents a link in an HTML document and exposes various properties through which you can find out the destination of the link. The basic property of the link object is the length property, which returns the number of the links in the document. Each link is a member of the links array. The first link is links(0), the second one is links(1), and so on. Because the hyperlinks in a document are destinations, the link object's properties are identical to the properties of the location object; however, they are read-only this time. A brief explanation of each property follows, but for a more detailed discussion of these properties, see the "The location Object" section.

href

Returns or sets the compete URL for the location to be loaded into the frame.

protocol

Returns or sets the protocol of the URL (usually HTTP).

host

Returns or sets the host and port of the URL.

hostname
Reads or sets the host of a URL, which can be either a name or an IP address.

port
Returns or sets the port of the URL.

pathname
Returns or sets the pathname of the URL.

search
Returns or sets the search portion of the URL, if it exists.

hash
Returns or sets the hash portion of the URL.

target
The last property of the `frames` object is the target that may have been specified in the `<A>` frame. The target of the link is the window, or frame, where the destination document will appear.

The LinksObject Project

The LinksObject document demonstrates the use of the `link` object and the `links` array. The LinksObject page contains a floating frame, where a user-supplied URL appears, and a number of command buttons. The first three command buttons are navigational (you have seen the code behind those buttons in the previous examples of this chapter), and the other three manipulate the `links` and `anchors` arrays. The Count Hyperlinks button displays the number of hyperlinks and anchors in the document displayed in the floating frame. The other two buttons display, on a new page, all the hyperlinks and anchors on the current document, respectively.

The hyperlinks and anchors of the document appear on the same page as the LinksObject document, in effect replacing the original document.

Instead of repeating the code of the entire document, the text shows only the subroutines that count the hyperlinks and display the list of hyperlinks and anchors. The `CountLinks()` subroutine uses the `length` property of the `links` object to get the number of hyperlinks in the document and the `length` property of the `anchor` object to get the number of anchors. Then, it combines them in a string which is displayed with the `MsgBox()` function:

```
Sub CountLinks_onClick()
    str="This document contains" & chr(10)
    str=str & window.frames(0).document.Links.Length & " links and" & chr(10)
```

```
    str=str & window.frames(0).document.Anchors.Length & " anchors"
    MsgBox str
End Sub
```

The `ShowLinks()` and `ShowAnchors()` subroutines open a new document on the same window and write the elements of the `links` and `anchors` arrays, respectively, there. Notice that the links are placed on the document as hyperlinks so that you can also follow them from this page.

```
Sub ShowLinks_onClick()
    Document.clear
    Document.open
    For i=0 to window.frames(0).document.Links.Length-1
        Document.write "<A HREF=" & window.frames(0).document.Links(i).href & ">" &
window.frames(0).document.links(i).href & "</A><BR>"
    Next
    Document.Close
End Sub

Sub ShowAnchors_onClick()
    Document.open
    For i=0 to window.frames(0).Document.Anchors.Length-1
        Document.write window.frames(0).Document.Anchors(i)
    Next
    Document.Close
End Sub
```

To return to the previous window, you must click the browser's Refresh button. The Back button won't work because no previous document is in use. It's the same document! When you use the `write` method to send output to the current window, you're not creating a new page, you just change the contents of the page that contains the script dynamically.

Review

The Internet Explorer scripting object model is a collection of objects through which you can control Internet Explorer and the HTML documents displayed in it programmatically. As demonstrated in several examples in this chapter, it is even possible to create the content to be displayed on the fly, with the methods of certain objects of the scripting model (in particular, the document object, which is the flexible one).

The scripting model is a hierarchy of objects, each one of which exposes certain properties and methods. Some of the properties are objects, and they can apply to more than one object. The document object, for instance, is a property of the window object and represents the document currently displayed in the window. If the current document contains frames, each frame has a document property as well, which represents the document of the individual frame.

The document object provides the write method, which lets you control the actual contents of the document from within your script. When the document object is used as a property of the window object, the write method applies to the document displayed on the window, regardless of whether or not it contains frames. When the document object is used as a property of a frame, the write method applies to the specific frame.

The objects of the scripting model are arranged in a hierarchy that reflects their function and their role in scripting. The topmost object in this hierarchy is the window object, which is the container for HTML documents, forms and scripts. Most of the window's properties are objects, too, such as the frames object (a collection of all the frames in the current document, if any), the history object (an object that exposes the navigational methods, such as Back and Forward), the location object (which lets you connect to any URL via its href property), and so on. The document object is the most flexible object in the hierarchy, in the sense that it allows you, the programmer, to generate HTML pages on the fly, based on conditions such as user preferences, dates, or the browser used to display the page on the client.

PART

II

IN THIS PART

Objects in VBScript

Using ActiveX Controls

by Brian Johnson

IN THIS CHAPTER

Custom controls have revolutionized Windows programming. If you're new to programming, you might not appreciate the impact custom controls have had on software development. In this chapter, you'll examine the ways ActiveX controls can be used to enhance your Web development efforts.

Looking at a Brief History of Custom Controls

ActiveX custom controls, or OCXs, are the 32-bit descendants of the dynamic link library (DLL) and, more recently, the Visual Basic Control (VBX). In order to understand these controls and what they do, it might help to take a brief look at how Windows controls have evolved over the last few years.

Microsoft Windows was developed with the understanding that software developers needed a way to easily take advantage of the features and functions built into the operating system. Developers used DLLs to meet this need. DLLs are programs that provide functions and procedures to other programs. DLLs changed the way programmers thought about adding features to their programs. Instead of saying, "We need some information about memory; let's ask the machine about it," the thinking changed to, "We need some information about memory; let's see what Windows knows." In the first case, programmers were asking for information directly from the processor; in the second case, the program was asking for information from Windows. Not much difference, but it did provide a layer of abstraction to the process of getting the information.

After Visual Basic hit the market, a specification for the VBX control turned a very simple programming system into an extensible, world-class development tool. The VBX control is also a DLL, but with special features that enable people to use the control seamlessly in the Visual Basic development environment.

The Win32 API brought another form of custom control: the OLE custom control (or OCX). We now call these ActiveX controls. An ActiveX control is different from a VBX or DLL because the control is registered with the operating system when it is installed. After an ActiveX control is registered, it can be used as a component by any application developed, using any one of many different development environments (subject to certain licensing restrictions), including VBScript.

Examining the Anatomy of an ActiveX Control

Remember that an ActiveX file is basically the 32-bit cousin of the VBX control and can be used in both Visual Basic and VBScript. An ActiveX control is more advanced and flexible in that it implements OLE in process servers as DLLs. In other words, it supports some very useful OLE features, such as in-place activation, automation, and event notification. Table 7.1 lists the library types used in Windows.

Table 7.1. DLLs and custom controls.

Control	Extension	Function
Dynamic link library	`.DLL`	Enables users to access functions, routines, and resources from other applications.
Visual Basic	`.VBX`	Provides the same custom control capabilities as a DLL. Can be used graphically in a development environment, such as Visual Basic 3.0, MSVC++ 1.52, and Delphi 1.0.
ActiveX control	`.OCX`	Provides the same services as a DLL or VBX. In addition, the OCX can take advantage of extremely powerful OLE features.

Registering Your ActiveX Controls

Like other OLE objects, when you install an OCX file, it is registered with the operating system in a system database called the Registry. When an OCX file is registered, its unique *class ID* (CLSID) number is placed in the system Registry. The CLSID number called from your HTML Web page *instantiates* (or creates an instance of) the object on the page on the client machine.

OLE significantly adds to the flexibility and capabilities of a Web page in a client/server environment like the Internet. The potential might not be obvious to you yet, but consider this for starters: An OLE object or an OCX can do anything that can be done on the client machine. The possibilities are exciting, but there are risks, and we'll talk about some of these later.

All ActiveX controls are referenced by their CLSID numbers stored in the Registry. Table 7.2 contains some of the CLSID numbers you'll use to insert ActiveX controls into your HTML.

Table 7.2. CLSID numbers for common controls.

Control	CLSID
Chart	FC25B780-75BE-11CF-8B01-444553540000
Label	99B42120-6EC7-11CF-A6C7-00AA00A47DD2
Menu Control	52DFAE60-CEBF-11CF-A3A9-00A0C9034920
Preloader	16E349E0-702C-11CF-A3A9-00A0C9034920
Popup Menu	7823A620-9DD9-11CF-A662-00AA00C066D2
StockTicker	0CA4A620-8E3D-11CF-A3A9-00A0C9034920
Timer	59CCB4A0-727D-11CF-AC36-00AA00A47DD2

7

Using ActiveX Controls

Keep in mind that some custom controls require licenses for development use and distribution. You can't necessarily use these objects in your own Web pages without a proper license. In these cases, the control vendor will provide you with a file that must be kept in the same directory as the control or Web page for the control to work on a user's machine.

THIRD-PARTY CONTROLS

A large cottage industry of programmers has developed with the widespread use of VBX files. These developers were able to create and distribute controls and still make money from them by requiring license (.LIC) files to be installed on the machines of developers but not redistributed with the controls. License files enable programmers to use the controls in the development environment. The same sort of licensing capabilities were created for ActiveX controls, but instead of a license file being added to the developer's Windows/ System directory, a license code is added to the Registry. The code stored in the Registry is not redistributable and is subject to the same sorts of restrictions as the LIC file.

Putting an ActiveX Control in Your Web Page

An ActiveX control is inserted into an HTML page by using the <OBJECT> tag, followed by the <CLASSID> tag and the CLSID number:

```
<OBJECT ID="pmenu1" WIDTH=0 HEIGHT=0
CLASSID="CLSID:52DFAE60-CEBF-11CF-A3A9-00A0C9034920">
```

Initial parameters are set before the CLSID number, along with an <ID> tag that sets the size and gives the control a name (ID). Control of the OCX is managed by using the ID. The HEIGHT and WIDTH properties of the ActiveX control set a rectangle in which visual controls are displayed. Placement of the control on the Web page is dependent on HTML formatting.

You can set the property values for the object by using the <param> tag inside the <OBJECT> </OBJECT> pair, as in this example:

```
<param name="angle" value="90">
<param name="BackStyle" value="0">
```

ActiveX controls are programmed just like any other object on your Web page. You set the properties of the control, and then your script reacts to messages sent by the user interacting with the objects in the browser. Because this is happening mostly on the client machine, the speed of the operation is limited only by your client's hardware.

Each ActiveX control has a set of properties and actions that can be set and reacted to. Suppose that you use the Label control to create some text on your page. You might set up the label like this:

```
<OBJECT ID="Label1" WIDTH=104 HEIGHT=27
  CLASSID="CLSID:99B42120-6EC7-11CF-A6C7-00AA00A47DD2">
     <PARAM NAME="_ExtentX" VALUE="2752">
     <PARAM NAME="_ExtentY" VALUE="714">
     <PARAM NAME="Caption" VALUE="Label Control">
</OBJECT>
```

You then can respond to the Click event in your code:

```
Sub Label1_Click()
Dim a
a = Label1.Caption
If a = "Start" Then
  a = "Stop"
Else
  a = "Start"
End If
Label1.Caption = a
End Sub
```

In this example, you can see that an ActiveX object works and behaves just like any VBScript intrinsic control. This is one of the great benefits of using ActiveX controls in Web pages. The broad base of current custom control developers will eventually make it very easy to find just the control you need for your particular purpose. If you're using a particularly popular control, such as one of the Microsoft controls discussed in this chapter, the user might already have the control installed on his or her system. The use of such controls is then seamless to the user.

Installing and Distributing ActiveX Controls

Most ActiveX custom controls will have to be downloaded and installed on the user's machine before they can be viewed in the user's browser. ActiveX controls are automatically downloaded to the user's machine if the CODEBASE parameter of the <OBJECT> tag is specified. The CODEBASE parameter specifies a URL to the ActiveX control. The CODEBASE tag is used like this:

```
<OBJECT
ID=iexr2
TYPE="application/x-oleobject"
CLASSID="clsid:0CA4A620-8E3D-11CF-A3A9-00A0C9034920"
CODEBASE="http://activex.microsoft.com/controls/iexplorer/iestock.ocx#Version=4,
70,0,1161"
WIDTH=300
HEIGHT=50>
```

When the user hits the page containing this tag, Internet Explorer checks to see if the control is already registered on the user's machine. If it is not, the security of the control is verified and, depending on the user's security preferences, the user is given the option of installing the control on his or her machine. If the user answers in the affirmative, the control is installed by Internet Explorer.

After distributed ActiveX objects are downloaded and installed, they usually are stored in an object cache on the client machine.

Examining ActiveX Controls

Microsoft has made available a number of controls that you can use in your own VBScript HTML pages. Keep in mind that in order for these controls to work, it's up to the client (your reader) to install them on his or her machine. These controls are freely distributable and can be made available to people interested in seeing and using your implementation of the object on their machines.

Animated Button Control

The Animated Button control takes a small Video for Windows (.AVI) file and allows you to use various combinations or frames for different button states. For example, if a file has 15 frames, the first five frames may be played in the button's default state. The second five frames can be reserved for the Mouseover state and the last five for the Mousedown state. This is a powerful control that offers more control than an animated GIF file. Table 7.3 lists the properties for the Animated button control.

Table 7.3. Animated button control properties.

Property	Description
DefaultFrStart	Starting frame for default state
DefaultFrEnd	Ending frame for default state
DownFrStart	Starting frame for mousedown state
DownFrEnd	Ending frame for mousedown state
FocusFrStart	Starting frame for focus state
FocusFrEnd	Ending frame for focus state
MouseoverFrStart	Starting frame for mouseover event
MouseoverFrEnd	Ending frame for mouseover event
URL	Address of the AVI file used

The Animated button control has only one method, AboutBox. This method will call up the About box for the control. This control has five events. Table 7.4 lists these events, along with a description of each.

Table 7.4. Animated button control events.

Event	Description
ButtonEvent_Click	The user clicks the button.
ButtonEvent_DblClick	The user double-clicks the button.
ButtonEvent_Enter	The mouse pointer passes over the button.
ButtonEvent_Leave	The mouse pointer leaves the button area.
ButtonEvent_Focus	The button gets focus.

One drawback to the Animated button control is that the AVI file format isn't well compressed. This can make the size of the files that you would like to use a little too large for use on the Internet. As bandwidth increases for home users, this will become less of a problem.

Chart Control

The Chart control works just like any chart you might use in Excel or Visual Basic. You provide a matrix of numeric values, and a chart is created that models those values. Using the Chart control, you can provide your user with up-to-the-minute feedback regarding a set of numbers. Table 7.5 shows the properties of the Chart control.

Table 7.5. Chart control properties.

Property	Description
BackStyle	0 for transparent; 1 for opaque
ChartType	One of the following:
	0=Simple Pie
	1=Pie with wedge out
	2=Point Chart
	3=Stacked Point
	4=Full Point
	5=Simple Line
	6=Stacked Line

continues

Table 7.5. continued

Property	Description
	7=Full Line
	8=Simple Area
	9=Stacked Area
	10=Full Area
	11=Simple Column
	12=Stacked Column
	13=Full Column
	14=Simple Bar
	15=Stacked Bar
	16=Full Bar
	17=HLC Stock
	18=HLC Stock WSJ
	19=OHLC Stock
	20=OHLC Stock WSJ
ColorScheme	One of three predefined values: 1, 2, or 3
ColumnIndex	Index value of the current column
Columns	Number of columns in the matrix
DataItem	Data value for a RowIndex, ColumnIndex pair
DisplayLegend	0 shows legend; 1 hides legend
HorizontalGrid	0=No Grid, 1=Lines
GridPlacement	One of the following: 0=None 1=Lines
RowIndex	Index value of the current row
Rows	Number of rows in the matrix
Scale	Percentage scale; default is 100%
VerticalGrid	0=No Grid, 1=Lines
URL	Data file to be read into control

You can set the values in the chart at load time and change them at runtime. The Chart control supports only one method, AboutBox, and doesn't generate any events.

Listing 7.1 shows how you can use the Chart control in an HTML document. Entering numeric values in the text boxes changes the style of the chart in the page. (See Figure 7.1.)

Listing 7.1. Using the Chart control in a reference document.

```
<HTML>
<HEAD>
<TITLE>Chart Explorer</TITLE>
</HEAD>
<BODY BGCOLOR=WHITE>
<CENTER>
<FONT FACE="Comic Sans MS">
<H1>Chart Explorer</H1>
<HR COLOR="BLUE" WIDTH=85%>
<TABLE BORDER BORDERCOLOR=RED>
<TR><TD COLSPAN=2>

<OBJECT ID="chart1" WIDTH=220 HEIGHT=155
 CLASSID="CLSID:FC25B780-75BE-11CF-8B01-444553540000">
    <PARAM NAME="_ExtentX" VALUE="5821">
    <PARAM NAME="_ExtentY" VALUE="4101">
    <PARAM NAME="Rows" VALUE="4">
    <PARAM NAME="Columns" VALUE="3">
    <PARAM NAME="ChartType" VALUE="0">
    <PARAM NAME="Data[0][0]" VALUE="9">
    <PARAM NAME="Data[0][1]" VALUE="10">
    <PARAM NAME="Data[0][2]" VALUE="11">
    <PARAM NAME="Data[1][0]" VALUE="7">
    <PARAM NAME="Data[1][1]" VALUE="11">
    <PARAM NAME="Data[1][2]" VALUE="12">
    <PARAM NAME="Data[2][0]" VALUE="6">
    <PARAM NAME="Data[2][1]" VALUE="12">
    <PARAM NAME="Data[2][2]" VALUE="13">
    <PARAM NAME="Data[3][0]" VALUE="11">
    <PARAM NAME="Data[3][1]" VALUE="13">
    <PARAM NAME="Data[3][2]" VALUE="14">
    <PARAM NAME="HorizontalAxis" VALUE="0">
    <PARAM NAME="VerticalAxis" VALUE="0">
    <PARAM NAME="hgridStyle" VALUE="0">
    <PARAM NAME="vgridStyle" VALUE="0">
    <PARAM NAME="ColorScheme" VALUE="0">
    <PARAM NAME="BackStyle" VALUE="1">
    <PARAM NAME="Scale" VALUE="100">
    <PARAM NAME="DisplayLegend" VALUE="1">
    <PARAM NAME="BackColor" VALUE="16777215">
    <PARAM NAME="ForeColor" VALUE="32768">
</OBJECT>

</TD>
</TR>

<TR>
    <TD ALIGN=RIGHT>Chart Type:</TD><TD><INPUT TYPE="TEXT" NAME="CT"></TD>
</TR>
<TR>
    <TD ALIGN=RIGHT>Chart Colors:</TD><TD><INPUT TYPE="TEXT" NAME="CC"></TD>
```

continues

Listing 7.1. continued

```
</TR>
<TR>
    <TD COLSPAN=2 ALIGN=CENTER>
    <INPUT TYPE="SUBMIT" NAME="BtnTest" VALUE="Test It!"></TD>
</TR>
</TABLE>
<HR COLOR="BLUE" WIDTH=85%>

<SCRIPT LANGUAGE="VBScript">
Sub BtnTest_OnClick
    If CT.Value = "" then CT.Value = "0"
    If CC.Value = "" then CC.Value = "0"
    chart1.ChartType=CT.Value
    chart1.ColorScheme=CC.Value
End Sub
</SCRIPT>

</BODY>
</HTML>
```

FIGURE 7.1.

The Chart Wizard in Internet Explorer.

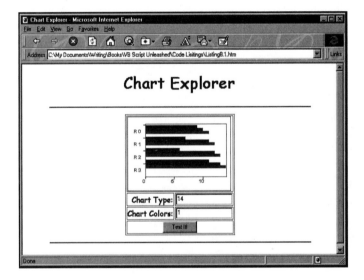

Label

The Label control is a simple, elegant control that gives you quite a bit of flexibility when working with text. You can use the Label control to insert angled text into your HTML documents. (See Figure 7.2.) Using a Timer control or any other event, you can change the properties of the Label control at runtime. Table 7.6 lists the properties for the Label control.

FIGURE 7.2.

The Label control can do things that normal HTML cannot.

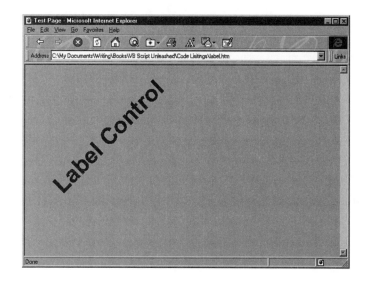

7

Table 7.6. Label control properties.

Property	Description
Alignment	One of the following: 0=Left 1=Right 2=Centered 3=Top 4=Bottom
Angle	Angle at which text is displayed
BackStyle	One of the following: 0=Transparent 1=Opaque
Caption	Label text
FontBold	One of the following: 0=False 1=True
FontName	Name of the font
FontSize	Font size
FontStrikeout	One of the following: 0=False 1=True

continues

Table 7.6. continued

Property	Description
FontUnderline	One of the following: 0=False 1=True
frcolor	Font forecolor (as an RGB hexadecimal triplet)

The Label control has a Click event and has one method: About.

Listing 7.2 uses the Label control to enhance the look of a page.

Listing 7.2. Using the Label control.

```
<HTML>
<HEAD>
<TITLE>Tester Page</TITLE>
</HEAD>
<BODY BGCOLOR=WHITE>
<H1>Tester Page for VBScript</H1>
<HR COLOR="BLUE" WIDTH=85%>

<OBJECT ID="label1" WIDTH=75 HEIGHT=400 vspace=0
    align= ALT="<H1
 CLASSID="CLSID:99B42120-6EC7-11CF-A6C7-00AA00A47DD2">
    <PARAM NAME="_ExtentX" VALUE="1984">
    <PARAM NAME="_ExtentY" VALUE="10583">
    <PARAM NAME="Caption" VALUE="VBScript">
    <PARAM NAME="Angle" VALUE="90">
    <PARAM NAME="Alignment" VALUE="7">
    <PARAM NAME="Mode" VALUE="1">
    <PARAM NAME="FillStyle" VALUE="0">
    <PARAM NAME="FillStyle" VALUE="0">
    <PARAM NAME="ForeColor" VALUE="#000000">
    <PARAM NAME="BackColor" VALUE="#C0C0C0">
    <PARAM NAME="FontName" VALUE="Times New Roman">
    <PARAM NAME="FontSize" VALUE="36">
    <PARAM NAME="FontItalic" VALUE="0">
    <PARAM NAME="FontBold" VALUE="0">
    <PARAM NAME="FontUnderline" VALUE="0">
    <PARAM NAME="FontStrikeout" VALUE="0">
    <PARAM NAME="TopPoints" VALUE="0">
    <PARAM NAME="BotPoints" VALUE="0">
</OBJECT>

<OBJECT ID="label2" WIDTH=51 HEIGHT=400 vspace=0
    align= ALT="<H1
 CLASSID="CLSID:99B42120-6EC7-11CF-A6C7-00AA00A47DD2">
    <PARAM NAME="_ExtentX" VALUE="1349">
    <PARAM NAME="_ExtentY" VALUE="10583">
    <PARAM NAME="Caption" VALUE="UNLEASHED">
```

```
        <PARAM NAME="Angle" VALUE="90">
        <PARAM NAME="Alignment" VALUE="6">
        <PARAM NAME="Mode" VALUE="1">
        <PARAM NAME="FillStyle" VALUE="0">
        <PARAM NAME="FillStyle" VALUE="0">
        <PARAM NAME="ForeColor" VALUE="#000000">
        <PARAM NAME="BackColor" VALUE="#C0C0C0">
        <PARAM NAME="FontName" VALUE="Arial">
        <PARAM NAME="FontSize" VALUE="36">
        <PARAM NAME="FontItalic" VALUE="0">
        <PARAM NAME="FontBold" VALUE="1">
        <PARAM NAME="FontUnderline" VALUE="0">
        <PARAM NAME="FontStrikeout" VALUE="0">
        <PARAM NAME="TopPoints" VALUE="0">
        <PARAM NAME="BotPoints" VALUE="0">
</OBJECT>
</BODY>
</HTML>
```

You might have noticed that Listing 7.2 contains no VBScript code. I did this to show you that you can use some of these objects without writing any code at all. The really nice thing about the Label control is that you can create this vertical-text effect without making it a GIF or a JPG file. Saving bandwidth is always a good thing.

Popup Menu Control

The Popup Menu control is used to create a popup menu when the user clicks a named control or image link with the mouse on a Web page. This control is used mostly for navigational purposes. If you have a lot of links on a Web page that contains other important data, you can place those links in a popup, giving your page a cleaner look.

The Popup Menu control has only one property, `ItemCount`. The `ItemCount` property is set to the number of items in the menu. The `Menuitem[]` parameter tag is used to label the individual items on the page. You can then use a script to call the URL of the page that you want to navigate to.

There are five methods associated with the Popup Menu control:

- `AboutBox`: Brings up the About box for the control
- `Additem`(item, index): Adds item at specified index
- `Clear`: Clears all menu items
- `PopUp`(x, y): Where x and y are position values
- `RemoveItem`(index): Removes item at specified index

The one event for the Popup Menu control is `Click(item)`. The index of the item clicked is passed to the event.

Listing 7.3 contains a script that uses the Popup Menu control. A Label control's `click` event is used to call `Pop1.Popup`. Notice that we use a `Select Case` block to retrieve the number of the item called.

Listing 7.3. Popup Menu control example.

```
<HTML>
<HEAD>
<TITLE>Test Page</TITLE>
</HEAD>
<BODY BGCOLOR=WHITE>
<H1>Popup Menu Control</H1>
<HR COLOR=NAVY>

<Table BORDER BGCOLOR=YELLOW></TR><TD>
<OBJECT ID="Label1" WIDTH=165 HEIGHT=44
 CLASSID="CLSID:99B42120-6EC7-11CF-A6C7-00AA00A47DD2">
    <PARAM NAME="_ExtentX" VALUE="4366">
    <PARAM NAME="_ExtentY" VALUE="1164">
    <PARAM NAME="Caption" VALUE="Popup Menu">
    <PARAM NAME="Angle" VALUE="0">
    <PARAM NAME="Alignment" VALUE="4">
    <PARAM NAME="Mode" VALUE="1">
    <PARAM NAME="FillStyle" VALUE="0">
    <PARAM NAME="FillStyle" VALUE="0">
    <PARAM NAME="ForeColor" VALUE="#000000">
    <PARAM NAME="BackColor" VALUE="#C0C0C0">
    <PARAM NAME="FontName" VALUE="Arial">
    <PARAM NAME="FontSize" VALUE="18">
    <PARAM NAME="FontItalic" VALUE="0">
    <PARAM NAME="FontBold" VALUE="1">
    <PARAM NAME="FontUnderline" VALUE="0">
    <PARAM NAME="FontStrikeout" VALUE="0">
    <PARAM NAME="TopPoints" VALUE="0">
    <PARAM NAME="BotPoints" VALUE="0">
</OBJECT>
</TR></TD></TABLE>
<OBJECT ID="Pop1" WIDTH=5 HEIGHT=5
 CLASSID="CLSID:7823A620-9DD9-11CF-A662-00AA00C066D2">
    <PARAM NAME="MenuItem[0]" VALUE="Microsoft Home Page">
    <PARAM NAME="MenuItem[1]" VALUE="C¦Net Online">
    <PARAM NAME="MenuItem[2]" VALUE="PCWeek">
</OBJECT>

<Script Language=VBScript>

Sub Label1_Click
    call Pop1.PopUp()
End Sub

Sub Pop1_Click(byVal X)

Select Case X
    Case 1
        top.Location="http://www.microsoft.com"
```

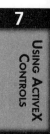

```
    Case 2
        top.Location="http://www.cnet.com"
    Case 3
        top.Location="http://www.pcweek.com"
End Select

End Sub
</Script>
</BODY>
</HTML>
```

Figure 7.3.

Popup Menu control navigates to popular URLs.

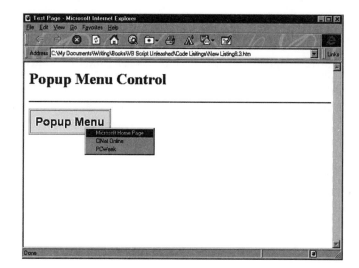

The Menu control is very similar to the PopupMenu control. The Menu control is essentially a button control that pops up a menu for the user. This control has two properties, `ItemCount` and `Caption`. `ItemCount` refers to the number of items in the menu. The `Caption` property sets the caption of the button used to show the menu.

To add items to the menu, you use the `Menuitem[ ]` parameter. You can also set the caption for the control as a parameter.

The Menu control has the same methods and events as the Popup Menu control and can be programmed the same way.

Preloader Control

You can use the Preloader control to anticipate the desires of your users and to download what, presumably, will be the next page they want to see. When they're ready to look at the page, it will pop up instantly and they will be amazed.

You need to be careful with this control. It won't do much good to preload a page unless that page is going to take a significant time to download, or any delay will cause the user to lose a feel for the flow of a number of pages.

The Preloader control has five properties:

- Bytes: Amount of data read in
- CacheFile: Name of the locally cached file
- Enable: Enables the Preloader control (1=enable, 2=disable)
- Percentage: Percentage of data read in
- URL: The URL for the next page to be loaded

The Preloader control has a single method, About, and two events:

- Completed: Indicates that the download has completed
- Error: Indicates that an error occurred during the operation

StockTicker Control

The StockTicker control downloads information and displays it at preset intervals. The data files displayed can be in either text format or XRT format. To create a file to be used by the StockTicker control in text format, place the letters XRT on the first line and then specify the data as name-tab-value-CR/LF lines. For example:

```
XRT
Item1      Value1      Value2      Value3
Item2      Value1      Value2      Value3
Item3      Value1      Value2      Value3
```

The StockTicker control has the properties listed in Table 7.7.

Table 7.7. StockTicker properties.

Property	Description
BackColor	Background color
DataObjectName	URL of the data file
DataObjectActive	1=Active; 0=Inactive
ForeColor	Foreground color
OffsetValues	Vertical offset from name in pixels
ReloadInterval	Reload interval for the data file
ScrollWidth	Amount of scroll for each redraw
ScrollSpeed	Interval at which the display is scrolled

The StockTicker control has only one method, AboutBox, and no events.

Timer Control

You can use the Timer to control time-based events in your code. The timer is especially useful if you need to track a repetitive event. If you don't have a timer to use in your pages, you have to use a loop in code, which bogs down your system.

The Timer control has two properties:

- Enable: Starts or stops the timer (0=disabled, 1=enabled)
- Interval: Specifies the interval in milliseconds at which a Timer event will be triggered

The Timer control supports only one event: Timer. The Timer event is triggered when the value of the Interval property has been passed.

The only method supported by the Timer control is About, which provides information about the control.

Listing 7.4 uses the Timer control to activate the controls on the page. Remember that you can't directly control the HTML content of a page without reloading. You can change the properties of active controls on a page, though, and those changes are reflected immediately. Listing 7.4 provides such an example.

Listing 7.4. Controlling objects with the timer.

```
<HTML>
<HEAD>
<TITLE>Changing Message Example</TITLE>
</HEAD>
<BODY BGCOLOR=WHITE>
<H1>Changing Message</H1>
<HR COLOR="YELLOW">
<TABLE BORDER BORDERCOLOR=GREEN>
<TR>
<TD>
    <OBJECT ID="label1" WIDTH=555 HEIGHT=40 align= vspace=0
 CLASSID="CLSID:99B42120-6EC7-11CF-A6C7-00AA00A47DD2">
    <PARAM NAME="_ExtentX" VALUE="14684">
    <PARAM NAME="_ExtentY" VALUE="1058">
    <PARAM NAME="Caption" VALUE="       Message Box">
    <PARAM NAME="Angle" VALUE="0">
    <PARAM NAME="Alignment" VALUE="4">
    <PARAM NAME="Mode" VALUE="1">
    <PARAM NAME="FillStyle" VALUE="0">
    <PARAM NAME="FillStyle" VALUE="0">
    <PARAM NAME="ForeColor" VALUE="#000000">
    <PARAM NAME="BackColor" VALUE="#C0C0C0">
    <PARAM NAME="FontName" VALUE="Arial">
    <PARAM NAME="FontSize" VALUE="14">
```

continues

7

USING ACTIVEX
CONTROLS

Listing 7.4. continued

```
    <PARAM NAME="FontItalic" VALUE="0">
    <PARAM NAME="FontBold" VALUE="1">
    <PARAM NAME="FontUnderline" VALUE="0">
    <PARAM NAME="FontStrikeout" VALUE="0">
    <PARAM NAME="TopPoints" VALUE="0">
    <PARAM NAME="BotPoints" VALUE="0">
</OBJECT>
</TD>
</TR>
</TABLE>

    <OBJECT ID="Timer1" WIDTH=39 HEIGHT=39
     CLASSID="CLSID:59CCB4A0-727D-11CF-AC36-00AA00A47DD2">
        <PARAM NAME="_ExtentX" VALUE="1032">
        <PARAM NAME="_ExtentY" VALUE="1032">
        <PARAM NAME="Interval" VALUE="3000">
    </OBJECT>
<SCRIPT LANGUAGE="VBScript">
Dim x
x = 0
Sub timer1_timer
Dim Msg(3)
Msg(0)="     This is the first message.  Number 2 is coming up!"
Msg(1)="     The second message is finally here."
Msg(2)="     Message 3, time to go back to the first."
label1.caption = Msg(x)
x = x + 1
If x > 2 then x = 0
End Sub
    </SCRIPT>
</BODY>
</HTML>
```

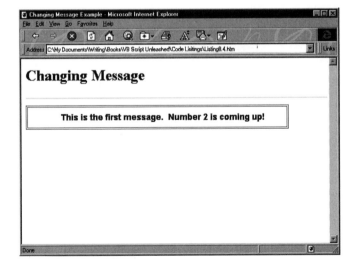

FIGURE 7.4.

The message changes in the Timer example.

Listing 7.4 uses a timer and a Label control to display a series of messages. This is a nice effect, but with a little more code, you can make it more useful.

Suppose that you create a Web game and you want to give users a choice of places to which they can jump. You can use the index value of the message array to set up a URL for each message, as shown below:

```
Sub Label1_Click
timer1.enable = 0
If x=0 then MyUrl = "http://www.thespot.com"
If x=1 then MyUrl = "http://www.yahoo.com"
If x=2 then MyUrl = "http://www.cnet.com"
Self.Location.href=MyUrl
End Sub
```

In this subroutine, you use the `Click` event for the Label control to interrupt the timer. Because x was declared as a global variable, its value is available to all the procedures in the script. In this case, the value of x is used to determine the value of `MyUrl`, which is then loaded in the browser.

Using Third-Party Controls

Using controls that you purchase in your pages isn't much different than using controls that are freely available. You must make the control available to your user as an ActiveX control that loads itself, or you need to make sure that the control is registered on your user's machine. You also must adhere to the licensing requirements for the control. Check with the vendor for the details about using their controls in your Web pages.

Using Signed Controls

Because ActiveX controls are potentially such powerful components, you must consider some security issues. Remember that an ActiveX control can do anything that can be done on a client machine. You want users to take advantage of the ActiveX controls that you've linked into your document, so the question is, "How can my reader be sure that the control is safe?"

If you make sure that the controls you use are signed, you'll stand a much better chance of having casual browsers see what you've added to your page. Code signing lets the user know who produced the code and whether that code has been changed since the control was signed. Users can set the level of security for the controls that are loaded into their browsers. They can accept all controls from a particular company, accept controls after a confirmation dialog, and accept or reject all controls to be loaded on to their machines. If the controls you're using are not signed, Internet Explorer notifies those users who are concerned about network security or simply rejects the control outright.

Creating ActiveX Controls

One of the great things about using OCXs in your Internet documents is that OLE controls themselves are written in a language that's familiar to many programmers: C++.

If you're a C++ programmer, you're probably already familiar with creating OLE custom controls. If you're not a C++ programmer, but you think you might like to become one in order to create OLE controls, this quick look at OCX development might interest you. Here, you'll look at creating the default custom control with Microsoft Visual C++ 4.0.

Programming in C++ is not very much like programming in Visual Basic or VBScript. C++ is a programming language developed by Bjarne Stroustrup in the early 1980s. It's a version of the C language that contains extensive object-oriented features.

Because C++ is a language based on reusable and extensible code, Microsoft has encapsulated the Win32 API, along with many other features, into the *Microsoft Foundation Classes* (MFC). The MFC is the C++ wrapper around the Win32 API and the basis for development in the VC++ IDE (Integrated Development Environment) using a feature called the OLE Control Wizard. (See Figure 7.5.)

FIGURE 7.5.

The OLE Control Wizard automates the process of creating ActiveX controls.

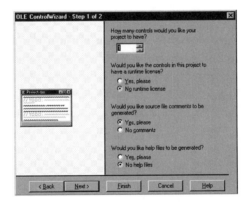

Using the Control Wizard to Create the Skeleton Files

The Control Wizard is the part of Developer Studio that generates the files needed to create an MFC-based ActiveX control. To create the basic files for an OCX control, follow these steps:

1. Choose File | New. In the New dialog, double-click Project Workspace.
2. In the Name text box, type Circle. (The Circle is the default ActiveX control.)
3. Select OLE Control Wizard as the project type and then click Create. The OLE Control Wizard appears.
4. Click Finish to exit the New dialog.

The Control Wizard now spends some time generating the skeleton files you'll need for your new control.

Compiling a Control

To build a control, choose Build from the Build menu. Again, this isn't Visual Basic or VBScript, so you'll have to wait a few seconds while your new control is compiled and linked. When it's all over, you'll have a nice CIRCLE.OCX file that you can register with your system.

Registering Your Control

Registering your control from Developer Studio is easy. Simply choose Tools | Register Control and it's done. Now you can test the new control.

Testing Your Control

You can test your new control with the OLE control test container, which you start from the Tools menu in Developer Studio. After the container opens, choose Edit | Insert OLE Control to add the CIRCLE.OCX file to the container. You can manipulate the file within the test area.

If you're thinking about getting into custom control development with C++ and MFC, you should keep some things in mind:

■ You'll hear C++ described as an "elegant language" by experienced programmers (who like it <G>). Don't let that fool you into thinking that C++ is easy to use.

■ C++ is a powerful, complex language that you'll spend months—even years—learning.

■ If you do decide to take the C++ plunge, you will find that your efforts are rewarded—eventually.

This simple control is the default created by the Control Wizard. To get a control to do even a little more takes a bit of work.

Creating Non-MFC ActiveX Controls

Though the size of the ActiveX controls created with the Control Wizard is modest, for users to access this control in their own browsers, they need to have installed the MFC runtime library, which is quite large. In addition, because ActiveX controls are designed to eventually run on Windows, Macintosh, and UNIX computers, Microsoft wrote a non-MFC specification so that ActiveX controls could be made smaller and more portable. Check the ActiveX Software Development Kit for details.

Signing Your Objects for Internet Use

To have the controls that you create certified for Internet use, you'll have to visit an ActiveX control Certificate Authority and carefully read through the procedures for having your controls certified. Once you've received credentials from such an authority, you'll need to prepare your code for signing. Details and tools for doing this are included with the ActiveX Development Kit. As of this writing, details regarding obtaining credentials could be found at `http://www.microsoft.com/intdev/sdk/docs/com/comintro-f.htm`.

Review

In this chapter, you learned about ActiveX controls and how you can use them to enhance your Web pages. You saw that ActiveX controls are extremely powerful, and that verification should be considered when using them. You then examined the controls that are freely available to Web designers and VBScript programmers. Finally, you took a quick look at part of the Microsoft Developer Studio called the Control Wizard, which helps C++ programmers create their own custom controls.

The ActiveX Control Pad

by Brian Johnson

IN THIS CHAPTER

At a certain point, the potential complexity of the content you can create using ActiveX controls becomes so great that you need specialized tools to easily do what you want. To assist you in the creation of complex ActiveX content, Microsoft has released a tool that enables you to insert and script ActiveX controls in HTML. The name of that tool is the ActiveX Control Pad.

In this chapter, you'll look at the ActiveX Control Pad and how you can use it to create ActiveX-enabled HTML pages. You'll also learn how to use the ActiveX Control Pad to insert and script ActiveX controls. And, finally, you'll learn about HTML layout files and how you can use them to create precise control layouts in Web documents.

Taking a Tour of the ActiveX Control Pad

The ActiveX Control Pad provides an editing environment that makes it easy for you to create or edit HTML files that contain ActiveX objects or ActiveX layouts. The ActiveX Control Pad is a Windows 95 application that runs in Windows 95 or Windows NT. Figure 8.1 shows the ActiveX Control Pad application. This section gives you a quick tour of the application and then discusses how you can use it to create ActiveX-enabled HTML documents and layouts.

FIGURE 8.1.

The ActiveX Control Pad application.

The ActiveX Control Pad consists of four major components:

■ Text editor
■ Object editor
■ Page editor
■ Script wizard

This section discusses these components in general and then describes in detail how to use the ActiveX Control Pad.

Text Editor

The ActiveX Control Pad text editor is basically the same tool you get with Windows Notepad. A significant difference is that the ActiveX Control Pad editor doesn't suffer from the 64KB file size limit that Notepad does. Unfortunately, other than creating a skeleton HTML file by default when opening a new file, there aren't any added HTML helpers such as the ones found in commercial HTML tools. You might find it easiest to create your base HTML files in a program like Microsoft FrontPage and then insert your ActiveX controls into the HTML using the Control Pad.

Object Editor

The object editor makes it easy for you to insert ActiveX controls into your HTML pages. The most difficult thing about using ActiveX controls usually is getting the CLSID numbers right in your HTML code. In addition, you usually need to look up and include the parameters of each control you put into your documents. The object editor automatically places the correct CLSID number into HTML and makes setting parameter values visual and simple.

Page Editor

The World Wide Web Consortium specification for two-dimensional layouts describes methods you can use to place 2-D material into HTML pages. The page editor of the ActiveX Control Pad enables you to create HTML pages that behave and look very much like stand-alone applications created with a programming tool such as Microsoft Visual Basic. In addition to layout capabilities, the page editor contains its own set of ActiveX controls that you can use in special HTML files called *HTML Layouts*. HTML Layout files have an ALX extension and are embedded into standard HTML files.

Script Wizard

The Script Wizard automates the creation of VBScript and JavaScript code in HTML or ALX files. The Script Wizard gives you easy, graphical access to the methods, properties, and events of ActiveX controls and ActiveX layout components. Figure 8.2 shows the Script Wizard in Code view. Users of Visual Basic will notice that the editing window is very similar to the editor in VB. You'll see later how an ActiveX control and VBScript code were added to the HTML page.

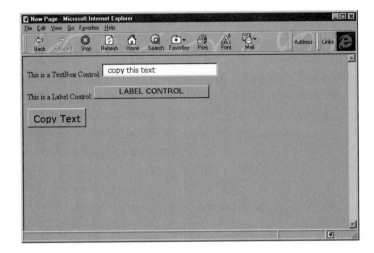

Using ActiveX Controls

Adding ActiveX controls to your HTML documents is fairly straightforward. You first need to
open the HTML document in the ActiveX Control Pad and place the cursor in your HTML
code at the point where you want the control to appear. You then choose Edit | Insert ActiveX
Control and select the control that you want from the dialog that appears. Figure 8.3 shows
the Insert ActiveX Control dialog. You can select any ActiveX control that's registered on your
machine.

FIGURE 8.3.

*Inserting an ActiveX
control in HTML with
the ActiveX Control
Pad.*

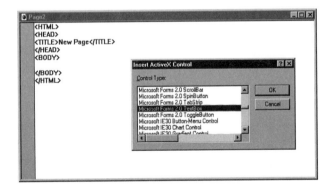

After you select a control, it appears in its own window along with a Properties dialog for the
control. Figure 8.4 shows a Label control in a window. You can size the control inside the window
and change the other properties in the Properties dialog. Closing the window containing the
control places the control code in the HTML file.

After you have your control in place, you can open it again in the object editor by clicking the Object button next to the HTML code in the editor. (See Figure 8.4.)

FIGURE 8.4.

Editing control properties.

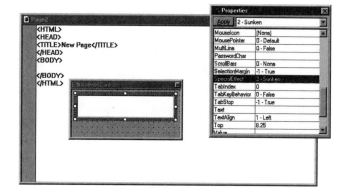

FIGURE 8.5.

Clicking the icon opens the ActiveX control.

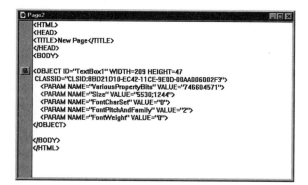

Using these steps to insert ActiveX controls in your HTML documents is much faster and is more efficient than trying to manually insert a control, complete with CLSID number and parameters. The next section takes a look at how the ActiveX Control Pad can help you generate your VBScript code.

Creating VBScript with the Script Wizard

After you have your controls in place, you can use the Script Wizard to create the VBScript code that will control the ActiveX objects. The *Script Wizard* is a tool that enables you to graphically manipulate and use the properties, methods, and events for ActiveX objects in HTML. To create a VBScript code block using the Script wizard, you first place your objects in HTML by choosing Edit | Insert ActiveX Control. You then invoke the Script Wizard by clicking the Script Wizard icon (the one that looks like a scroll at the end of the toolbar) or by choosing Tools | Script Wizard.

The Script Wizard window contains three panes. The first, Select an Event, lists the events available to the programmer based on the controls loaded in the document. Each element is listed in this window with its events shown in outline form.

The second pane, Insert Actions, offers properties and methods that you can access and manipulate. Like the Select an Event pane, Insert Actions is in outline form, and you can expand and collapse the objects listed to access their events.

The final pane in the Script Wizard is where the generated code is displayed and edited. Two radio buttons appear at the bottom of the window that enable you to select List View or Code View. You can see what your program is going to do by running through it in List View, but if you want to create more than very simple scripts, you'll want to use Code View.

Let's create a VBScript page that contains a Label control that changes after it's clicked.

To create a scripted event for the Label control using the Script Wizard, follow these steps:

1. Create a new page and insert a Microsoft IE30 Label Control.
2. In the Properties window, set the Angle property of the label to 90 and change the caption property to "My Cool Label." Set the font size to 35 and resize the control in the preview window so that it fits.
3. Run the Script Wizard. Open the IeLabel1 node in the Select an Event pane and then select click.
4. In the Insert Actions pane, open the IeLabel1 node and double-click caption. An input box appears.
5. In the input box, type I've been clicked!
6. Open the HTML file in Internet Explorer and click the label. You'll see the caption change.

This isn't a very heavy duty example, but it does show you some of the power of the ActiveX Control Pad. Without this tool, you would have to write all the code yourself. Take a look at Listing 8.1 to see how much actual code is generated.

Listing 8.1. Code generated from the Label control example.

```
<HTML>
<HEAD>
<TITLE>New Page</TITLE>
</HEAD>
<BODY>
    <SCRIPT LANGUAGE="VBScript">
<!--
Sub IeLabel1_Click()
IeLabel1.Caption = "I've been clicked!"
```

```
end sub
-->
    </SCRIPT>
    <OBJECT ID="IeLabel1" WIDTH=100 HEIGHT=368
     CLASSID="CLSID:99B42120-6EC7-11CF-A6C7-00AA00A47DD2">
        <PARAM NAME="_ExtentX" VALUE="2646">
        <PARAM NAME="_ExtentY" VALUE="9737">
        <PARAM NAME="Caption" VALUE="My Cool Label">
        <PARAM NAME="Angle" VALUE="90">
        <PARAM NAME="Alignment" VALUE="4">
        <PARAM NAME="Mode" VALUE="1">
        <PARAM NAME="FillStyle" VALUE="0">
        <PARAM NAME="FillStyle" VALUE="0">
        <PARAM NAME="ForeColor" VALUE="#000000">
        <PARAM NAME="BackColor" VALUE="#C0C0C0">
        <PARAM NAME="FontName" VALUE="Arial">
        <PARAM NAME="FontSize" VALUE="35">
        <PARAM NAME="FontItalic" VALUE="0">
        <PARAM NAME="FontBold" VALUE="0">
        <PARAM NAME="FontUnderline" VALUE="0">
        <PARAM NAME="FontStrikeout" VALUE="0">
        <PARAM NAME="TopPoints" VALUE="0">
        <PARAM NAME="BotPoints" VALUE="0">
    </OBJECT>
</BODY>
</HTML>
```

Using HTML Layouts

HTML layouts are an exciting new addition to the World Wide Web. These 2-D layouts give programmers precise control over the placement of objects, such as ActiveX controls, on the page. The ActiveX layout then is inserted into a standard HTML document and is displayed much like a floating frame. The layout itself is contained in a text file with an ALX extension. Using the ActiveX Control Pad to create layout files is very much like creating programs in Visual Basic. This section takes a look at how it's done.

You create a layout by choosing File | New HTML Layout. This opens an empty layout area and a toolbox. To add items to the layout, click the control in the toolbox and drag the item onto the layout with the mouse. You also can drag and drop controls from the toolbox to the layout. Figure 8.6 shows an ActiveX layout with a couple of controls added. You set the properties for the controls that you place on the page by double-clicking the control or by clicking the control and choosing Properties. After you set the controls and properties, you can run the Script Wizard to generate code for the layout.

FIGURE 8.6.
*Creating a layout with
the Control Pad.*

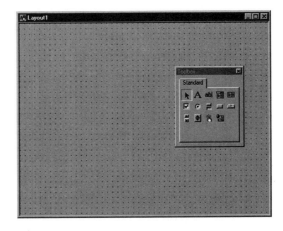

The amount of control that layouts give you is really quite extraordinary. The rest of this chapter looks at HTML layouts and how you can tap some of the potential for your own Web documents.

Looking at the Available Controls

The HTML Layout control has its own set of ActiveX objects that you can use in your layouts. Because these controls are different than any of the controls discussed so far, they are covered here. In cases in which an HTML Layout control has an intrinsic control counterpart, those characteristics unique to the HTML Layout control are discussed.

Tables 8.1 through 8.3 list the properties, methods, and events common to most of the HTML Layout controls. The size of the properties list alone gives you an idea of the richness of these controls.

Table 8.1. Common HTML layout properties.

Property	Description
Accelerator	Accelerator character for object
Alignment	Position of control relative to caption
AutoSize	Object sized to caption automatically
BackColor	Background color to object
Caption	Caption visible to user
ControlTipText	Hint text for object

Property	Description
Enabled	Control is enabled
Font Object	Font object for caption property
ForeColor	Color of caption text
GroupName	Group that contains control
Height	Height of object in points (1/72 inch)
LayoutEffect	Determines movement of object
Left	Left position of object in layout
Locked	Object locked into position
MouseIcon	Icon when mouse is over object
MousePointer	Sets pointer for object
Name	Name of object
OldHeight	Previous height of object in points
OldLeft	Previous left position in points
OldTop	Previous top position in points
OldWidth	Previous width of object in points
Parent	Name of parent object of control
Picture	Bitmap displayed on object
PicturePosition	Location of picture
SpecialEffect	Visual style of object
TabIndex	Index number in tabbing order
TabStop	Object is in the tabbing order (Boolean)
Top	Top position of object in layout
TripleState	Allows a True/False/Null selection
Width	Width of object in points
Value	Value for object

8

THE ACTIVEX
CONTROL PAD

A few properties mentioned here deserve some explanation. First of all, the Font Object property refers to an object that describes the font used to display the Caption property or the Value property for the various controls.

The Font object has the properties `Bold`, `Italic`, `StrikeThrough`, `Underline`, `Weight`, and `Name`. You easily can specify the value of a font used for a control by setting these attributes individually and then accessing the `Font` object property by name, as shown in this code:

```
Dim BigFont
BigFont.Bold = True
BigFont.Size = 36
Label1.Font = BigFont
```

Remember that you can change the font of a control at design time by using the Properties dialog. Clicking the button adjacent to the value entry box for the font displays a Font dialog. You then can choose the font and style for the control.

`ControlTipText` refers to the small pop-up message that appears when the mouse pointer is held over a control at runtime. You should use this control only when necessary. You usually don't need to specify a value for this property in Label controls, for example. Labels, by definition, are self-explanatory. You might want to add a `ControlTipText` value to a button that contains only a picture or a `Picture` control with an associated `Click` event. Just try to imagine where your users might be looking for help.

The `TripleState` property refers to items that can contain a null value in addition to `True` or `False`. An example of this is when two or more radio buttons are grouped and none are selected.

Table 8.2. HTML layout control methods.

Method	Description
Move	Moves the item in the layout
SetFocus	Gives the item the focus
Zorder	Specifies the depth of the object in the layout

You can call the `Move` method with this argument:

```
Object.Move(Left, Top, Width, Height, Layout)
```

`Left` and `Top` refer to the position of the control within the layout. `Width` and `Height` refer to the size of the control. `Layout` refers to the parent's layout event and whether that event is initiated after the move.

The `SetFocus` method gives the calling control the focus in the layout.

The `Zorder` in the layout refers to the 3-D placement of controls within the layout. Setting the `Zorder` value of a control to `0` brings the control to the front. Setting this value to `-1` sends the control to the back. You can set or change this value at design time by right-clicking the control and choosing Bring to Front or Send to Back.

Table 8.3. HTML layout control events.

Event	Description
AfterUpdate	Event occurs after a change
BeforeDragOver	Event occurs before a dragover event
BeforeDrop	Event occurs before a drop event
BeforePaste	Event occurs before a paste event
BeforeUpdate	Event occurs before an update event
Change	Object has changed
Click	Object is clicked
DblClick	Object is double-clicked
Enter	Before object gets focus
Error	Error occurs
Exit	After object loses focus
KeyDown	Key code and Shift state pressed
KeyPress	Key code pressed
KeyUp	Key code and Shift state released
MouseDown	Mouse button is held down
MouseMove	Mouse is moved over object
MouseUp	Mouse button is released

8

THE ACTIVEX CONTROL PAD

The events for objects in HTML layouts are very rich. You can capture keys and Shift states the user presses in addition to standard events such as Click and DblClick.

Key and *Shift state* refer to the keycode of the key clicked by the user and the Shift state or Ctrl key being held down during that event. Suppose that you write code to capture the keys pressed when a particular object in the layout has focus. It might look something like this:

```
Sub object_KeyDown(KeyCode, Shift)
```

This procedure gives you the numeric code for the key pressed and returns information on the Shift state. If Shift is held down, the value of Shift is 1. If the Ctrl key is held down, the value of Shift is 2. Finally, if the Alt key is held down, the value of Shift is 4. To retrieve the ANSI character that was returned, you can use the value returned from the key press event.

Where appropriate, this section points out added methods, properties, and events for the controls that follow. You should use the Help file for the latest version of the ActiveX Control Pad to learn about additions and corrections.

OptionButton

You use the OptionButton control to select a single item from a group of items. This control works just like the intrinsic OptionButton control. A single option usually is selected from a group of these controls. The item selected is determined through the Value property of the control; -1 is True or selected, and 0 is False or not selected.

TabStrip

You use the TabStrip control to place content into layers accessed through tabs or buttons. You can choose between the two by using the Style option in the Properties dialog. You can set the placement of the tabs by choosing the Tab Orientation option. You can choose Top, Bottom, Left, and Right.

You set up your tabs by selecting a tab, right-clicking, and choosing Insert, Delete, Rename, or Move. Insert creates a new tab item. Delete removes the currently selected tab. You can change the caption, accelerator key, and hint text by choosing Rename. Finally, you can change the order of tabs by choosing Move. Getting your tabs straight is half the battle when you're using this control in your layouts. After you have everything set up, you just place the controls you want to display on the page that's in the front.

Figure 8.7 shows the TabStrip control in an HTML Layout. The controls on TabStrip control pages are displayed when the visible property for them is set to true. You can do this in the Change event for the TabStrip control.

FIGURE 8.7.

Using the TabStrip *control in the ActiveX Control Pad.*

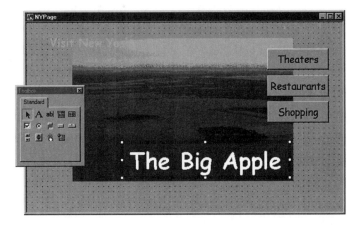

ScrollBar

The ScrollBar control in a GUI environment such as Windows 95 generally is used to view areas larger than the display area. You also can use scrollbars to visually change numeric values. You do this by setting the Min and Max properties or setting the Value property. You can set the degree of change when the scrollbar is used with the LargeChange property. You can display the ScrollBar control horizontally or vertically. The event associated with the ScrollBar control is the OnScroll event.

Spinner

The Spinner control lets your user change a value using only a mouse. It's very handy when used to change values in a particular range. Like the ScrollBar control, the Spinner control has a Min and Max value. The increment of change is set through the SmallChange property.

Label

The Label control is very much like the Microsoft IE30 Label Control discussed earlier in this book. The major difference is that you can't change the display angle of this Label control, making it more like the standard VB Label control. This control is still very useful in ActiveX layouts, though. One property of note is the BackStyle property, which you can set to Opaque or Transparent. This is important when you want to make the label look like it's just letters over a background image, or you want it to have an opaque background for easier reading. Another very handy property is Border, which can be turned on or off. Figure 8.8 shows various labels in an HTML layout with different properties set for each.

FIGURE 8.8.

Various labels in an ActiveX layout.

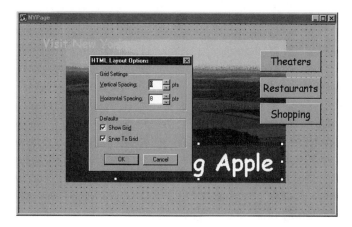

Image

Image controls are very important in layouts because they not only display image information—they can be moved as well. This makes it possible to create Shockwave-like content using only

ActiveX controls and layouts. Shockwave is a plug-in/ActiveX control from Macromedia that enables the use of Macromedia Director movies over the Web. The capability to control the movement of images on-screen is essential for creating truly compelling interactive content.

The movement of images inside a layout depends on three things: drawing, placement of the image, and timing. Take a look at Listing 8.2. It's an ActiveX layout that contains a command button, a timer, and an Image control. It uses the command button to start the timer and the Timer event to position the Image control. Figure 8.9 shows the two visible controls in the layout.

Listing 8.2. Moving an image in an ActiveX layout.

```
<SCRIPT LANGUAGE="VBScript">
<!--
Sub CommandButton1_Click()
IeTimer1.Enabled = -1
end sub
-->
</SCRIPT>
<SCRIPT LANGUAGE="VBScript">
<!--
Sub IeTimer1_Timer()
Image1.Height = Image1.Height + 1
end sub
-->
</SCRIPT>
<SCRIPT LANGUAGE="VBScript">
<!--
Sub Image1_MouseDown(ByVal Button, ByVal Shift, ByVal X, ByVal Y)
IeTimer1.Enabled = False
end sub
-->
</SCRIPT>
<DIV STYLE="LAYOUT:FIXED;WIDTH:515pt;HEIGHT:277pt;">
    <OBJECT ID="Image1"
     CLASSID="CLSID:D4A97620-8E8F-11CF-93CD-00AA00C08FDF"
STYLE="TOP:0pt;LEFT:0pt;WIDTH:66pt;HEIGHT:50pt;ZINDEX:0;">
        <PARAM NAME="PicturePath" VALUE="diamond.bmp">
        <PARAM NAME="AutoSize" VALUE="-1">
        <PARAM NAME="BorderStyle" VALUE="0">
        <PARAM NAME="Size" VALUE="2328;1746">
        <PARAM NAME="VariousPropertyBits" VALUE="19">
    </OBJECT>
    <OBJECT ID="CommandButton1"
     CLASSID="CLSID:D7053240-CE69-11CD-A777-00DD01143C57"
STYLE="TOP:173pt;LEFT:41pt;WIDTH:83pt;HEIGHT:33pt;TABINDEX:0;ZINDEX:1;">
        <PARAM NAME="Caption" VALUE="CommandButton1">
        <PARAM NAME="Size" VALUE="2911;1164">
        <PARAM NAME="FontCharSet" VALUE="0">
        <PARAM NAME="FontPitchAndFamily" VALUE="2">
        <PARAM NAME="ParagraphAlign" VALUE="3">
        <PARAM NAME="FontWeight" VALUE="0">
```

```
    </OBJECT>
    <OBJECT ID="IeTimer1"
      CLASSID="CLSID:59CCB4A0-727D-11CF-AC36-00AA00A47DD2"
STYLE="TOP:124pt;LEFT:8pt;WIDTH:50pt;HEIGHT:33pt;TABINDEX:1;ZINDEX:2;">
        <PARAM NAME="_ExtentX" VALUE="1746">
        <PARAM NAME="_ExtentY" VALUE="1164">
        <PARAM NAME="Interval" VALUE="1">
        <PARAM NAME="Enabled" VALUE="False">
    </OBJECT>
</DIV>
```

FIGURE 8.9.

*An image movement
example in Internet
Explorer.*

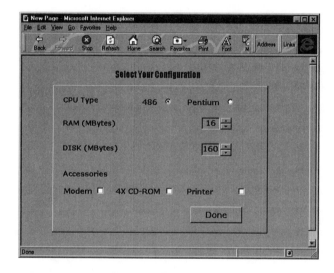

This example doesn't do that much. The VBScript code added is only three lines. It's fairly amazing, though, when you consider standard HTML. You simply can't move pictures around like this without special tools or plug-ins. ActiveX layout makes it fairly simple.

HotSpot

The HotSpot control is invisible to the end user, but it's an extremely useful tool when you're working with the type of content typical of layouts. Like image maps, hot spots enable you to write code in response to user interaction that wouldn't normally have its own events.

To use the HotSpot control, you just draw a rectangle with the control anywhere in your layout in the Control Pad. You then can access the methods, properties, and events of the control through the Script Wizard and the Properties dialog. Most often, you'll use this control with an Image control and the Click event. You'll find the MouseOver event to be quite useful also.

TextBox

The TextBox layout control works just like its intrinsic counterpart. You can use this control to retrieve data from your user. You can retrieve data from a text box through the Text property or the Value property.

For example:

```
MyString = Text1.Text
```

is the same as

```
MyString = Text1.Value
```

The other properties, methods, and events are similar to the intrinsic Edit control, but the HTML layout TextBox control provides a much larger set from which to work. These are all accessible from the Properties dialog and the Script Wizard.

You define the type of the TextBox control with the Multiline and Wordwrap properties. If Multiline and Wordwrap are set to True, you have a control that functions like a multiline entry field. Setting the Autosize property to True changes the size of the control depending on the size of its contents.

The HTML layout TextBox control is more like the VB TextBox control than the intrinsic TextBox control. It offers a few methods that are extremely handy if you're using the control for any sort of editing. The SelText method enables you to insert text into the TextBox control. If text inside the box is selected, it is replaced by the SelText value; otherwise, text is inserted at the cursor.

Finally, you'll notice a SpecialEffect property for the TextBox control. This property enables you to define the display characteristics for the control. Figure 8.10 shows TextBox controls with the various settings for the SpecialEffect set.

FIGURE 8.10.

An HTML layout containing various styles of TextBox *controls.*

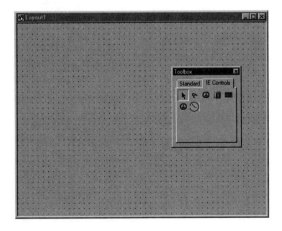

ListBox

The HTML layout `ListBox` control is like the `TextBox` control because it has many value-added features you won't find in the intrinsic `ListBox` control. The `SpecialEffect` property is part of most of the HTML layout controls, and by using this property with all your controls, you can create a layout with a distinctive, consistent style. Besides the visual enhancements, there are features that make the `ListBox` control more useful and customizable.

One of the features of the HTML layout `ListBox` that really adds value to the control is the capability to divide the contents of the `ListBox` into columns. This is done by setting the value of the `Column` property. The contents of the `ListBox` are added and retrieved using a column, row value. You can add many items to a `ListBox` all at once by using a 2-D array.

Listing 8.3 contains the code for adding columns of data to a listbox. You need to set the ColumnCount property as in Figure 8.11 to make this work.

Listing 8.3. Adding an array to a listbox.

```
<SCRIPT LANGUAGE="VBScript">
<!--
Sub CommandButton1_Click()
Dim ListArray(2, 5)

ListArray(0, 0) = "1"
ListArray(0, 1) = "2"
ListArray(0, 2) = "3"
ListArray(0, 3) = "4"
ListArray(0, 4) = "5"

ListArray(1, 0) = "Apples"
ListArray(1, 1) = "Bananas"
ListArray(1, 2) = "Grapes"
ListArray(1, 3) = "Oranges"
ListArray(1, 4) = "Pears"

Listbox1.List() = ListArray
ListBox1.Column() = ListArray
end sub
-->
</SCRIPT>
```

FIGURE 8.11.

A listbox with columns in HTML layout.

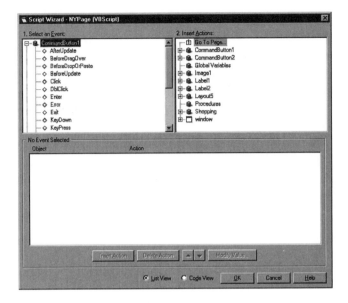

ComboBox

The ComboBox control is used like the ListBox control, but it has the added advantage of being more compact. It's called a ComboBox because a value can be retrieved from the TextBox portion of the control.

CheckBox

The CheckBox control is similar to the RadioButton control. The major difference is that the checkbox usually answers a simple yes/no question instead of being a choice among items. A checked checkbox returns a value of -1; an unchecked box returns 0.

CommandButton

The CommandButton's default event is the Click event. The button is fairly customizable, and you can use the features of the CommandButton control to create some interesting effects. If you set the Wordwrap property to True, you can display multiple lines of text on the button. One very useful property is TakeFocusOnClick, which enables you to write code that uses button clicks and keeps focus on the control where the user is entering information.

ToggleButton

The ToggleButton control works as a visual switch, like a RadioButton or CheckBox control. The ToggleButton control is *sticky*; when the button is clicked by the user, it stays down to indicate that it is in a state of selection. You'll recognize this control if you use a program such as a word processor, where the Bold button would be down to indicate that the characters typed will be bold until the button is clicked again.

The Value property determines whether the control has been activated or selected. If this property is True or -1, the ToggleButton is in its down state. If it is False or 0, the ToggleButton is not selected. To use ToggleButton, you'll usually check for the state of the button and write different code for each state, as in this example:

```
If ToggleButton1.Value = True then
Do Something
Else
Do Something Else
End If
```

WebBrowser

The WebBrowser control enables you to insert HTML files into your HTML layout files. You do this through the CodeBase property for the WebBrowser control. This control works like an embedded frame, and can be controlled through scripting in a similar manner.

Adding Controls to the Toolbox

You can add any ActiveX control you want to the HTML layout toolbox. To add a control, right-click the toolbox and select additional controls. From there, you can select the ActiveX controls you want to use. Figure 8.12 shows a control being added through the Additional Controls dialog.

FIGURE 8.12.

Selecting a control to add to the toolbox.

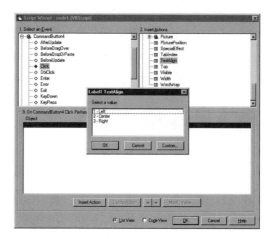

In addition to adding controls to the toolbox, you can add pages to the toolbox so that you can organize your controls. To add pages to the toolbox, right-click outside the tab area and choose New Page.

The new page is inserted into the toolbox with the default name New Page, as shown in Figure 8.13. To change the name, right-click the tab for the page and choose Change Name.

FIGURE 8.13.

The Control Pad toolbox with a new page added.

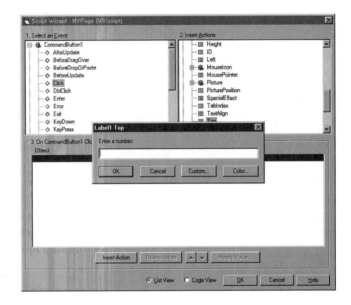

Now that you've seen how to customize the toolbox, keep in mind that one of the best ways to use custom toolbox pages is for storing controls that you've customized. After you place a control on a page, you can set the properties for the control and save those properties by dropping the control back on the page in the toolbox.

By customizing controls and saving pages of controls, you can keep HTML layout designs consistent across Web pages. Suppose that you make a Label control that uses a particular font and color style to display the name of your company. Instead of resetting the properties for the control each time you use it, you just drop in your saved control.

Creating Interactive Content

At first glance, it might look like there isn't much that you can do with an HTML layout that you can't do in plain HTML and VBScript. As far as things like simple forms go, that's probably true. The strength of HTML layouts comes in the flexibility and maneuverability of the controls and objects in the layouts. You can't change an image in HTML without reloading the entire page, for example. It's very simple, though, to change an image in an HTML layout.

The one thing that's very easy to do when working with HTML layouts is to forget that what you create will be running and loading across the Internet. This means that you need to consider the size and availability of the controls that you're using in your layouts. You also need to keep in mind the size of the graphics used in the layout. People probably won't mind spending a couple of extra minutes downloading a game or a useful utility layout, but they might not care for a large layout that's simply embedded in your Web pages for decoration.

Using VBScript with ActiveX Layouts

You probably should think of your HTML layouts as you would HTML documents in floating frames. If you think about your layouts this way, you'll have a better understanding of how things are working in the HTML page when it comes to scripting the layouts and controls on your pages.

When a layout is inserted into an HTML document, it has a Name property. Using the ID property, you can control the content of the layout from outside the layout, in the hosting HTML document. You do this by calling the object you want to access through its parent:

```
Parent.LayoutID.ContolID.Property = NewValue
```

Listing 8.4 uses this technique to change the value of a control inside an HTML layout from outside the layout. The HTML layout used is called remote.alx. The remote.alx file contains only one TextBox control with the ID TextBox1. The On_Click event for the Submit button, MyButton, in the HTML file contains the code that changes the Value property of remote.TextBox1.

Listing 8.4. Changing the value of a layout control from outside the layout.

```
<HTML>
<HEAD>
<TITLE>Remote property change</TITLE>
</HEAD>
<BODY>
<H1>Remote control</H1>
<HR Color=Blue>
This example demonstrates changing the property of an item in an HTML layout
from outside the layout file. In this case, text is inserted into a TextBox control
in an HTML layout from an intrinsic button control.

<OBJECT CLASSID="CLSID:812AE312-8B8E-11CF-93C8-00AA00C08FDF"
ID="remote" STYLE="LEFT:0;TOP:0">
<PARAM NAME="ALXPATH" REF VALUE="file: remote.alx">
</OBJECT>

<INPUT TYPE=SUBMIT NAME=MyButton VALUE="Send Text">
<SCRIPT LANGUAGE=VBScript>
Sub MyButton_OnClick
remote.TextBox1.Value = "This worked!"
End Sub
</SCRIPT>
</BODY>
</HTML>
```

Review

In this chapter, you learned about the parts of the ActiveX Control Pad. You saw how to use the ActiveX Control Pad to insert ActiveX objects. You examined the Script Wizard and how you can use it to generate VBScript code. Finally, you looked at HTML layouts and how they can be created, scripted, and manipulated in your own HTML files.

More ActiveX Controls

by Evangelos Petroutsos

IN THIS CHAPTER

The ActiveX controls explored in the previous chapter come with Internet Explorer. Since the release of Internet Explorer and the ActiveX Control Pad, Microsoft introduced a number of additional ActiveX controls, and there will be many more in the future, both from Microsoft and from third-party companies. In this chapter, we are going to explore a few additional ActiveX controls, which we believe you'll find very useful in VBScript programming. These are the Popup Menu and Menu controls, which let you incorporate menu structures in your documents; the Marquee control, which lets you scroll a page within another page; the Popup Window control, which can display a URL in a window without switching the browser to another URL; and the Chart control, which presents numeric data to the viewer as graphs.

AUTOMATIC COMPONENT INSTALLATION

As mentioned, the additional ActiveX controls we are going to explore in this chapter, as well as a large number of ActiveX controls that will become available in the future from Microsoft and third-party companies, are not automatically installed with Internet Explorer 3.0. So, what will happen if the users of your application don't have the controls already installed on their systems? A common property of all ActiveX controls is called `CodeBase`, and is the URL of the control's code. If the control hasn't been installed on a given client, Internet Explorer will connect to the URL specified by the `CodeBase` property and download and install the control.

The first time you open any of this chapter's projects, you might experience a delay while the message "Downloading components" appears in the browser's status bar. Internet Explorer is downloading the missing components from the appropriate URLs. Once a component (an ActiveX control) has been installed on your system, Internet Explorer won't download it again. When an ActiveX control is installed, it's registered in the Windows Registry and other applications can find it there. The URL for the Chart control, for instance, is

```
"http://activex.microsoft.com/controls/iexplorer/
iechart.ocx#Version=4,70,0,1161"
```

Of course, the missing components won't be installed unless you are already connected to the Internet. If you are testing the examples locally, you must first establish a dialup connection to your Internet service provider, so that Internet Explorer can connect to the URL specified by the `CodeBase` property.

When the Downloading components message is displayed on your browser's window, you needn't worry about your system's security. No components will be installed directly from this book's CD; the ActiveX controls will be installed directly from Microsoft's Web site.

The values of the `CodeBase` property for the ActiveX controls covered in this chapter are listed next. In general, every time you include an ActiveX control in your projects, you should find out the value of the `CodeBase` property from the control's manufacturer and include it in the control's definition with a line similar to the following ones:

```
Menu control:

CODEBASE="http://activex.microsoft.com/controls/iexplorer/
btnmenu.ocx#Version=4,70,0,1161"

Chart control:

CODEBASE="http://activex.microsoft.com/controls/iexplorer/
iechart.ocx#Version=4,70,0,1161"

Popup menu:

CODEBASE="http://activex.microsoft.com/controls/iexplorer/
iemenu.ocx#Version=4,70,0,1161"

Popup window:

CODEBASE="http://activex.microsoft.com/controls/iexplorer/
iepopwnd.ocx#Version=4,70,0,1161"
```

The Popup Menu and Menu Controls

ActiveX controls provide all the functionality of a typical Windows application from within Internet Explorer's environment. But there is one function, which is so common among Windows applications, that isn't available to your VBScript applications—the menu bar. HTML layouts don't have a menu bar, and there's no ActiveX control you can place on a layout that would provide the functionality of a menu bar. There are, however, two ActiveX controls that provide a similar functionality. They are not as convenient or flexible as the elaborate Windows menu structures, but they provide the basic functionality of a menu structure. They are the Popup Menu control, which causes a popup menu to be displayed anywhere on the browser's window, and the Menu control, which is a like a custom command button that displays a dropdown menu every time it's clicked.

The Popup Menu

Let's start our discussion with the Popup Menu control, which is the simpler one. Figure 9.1 shows a popup menu that acts as a shortcut menu. (It's displayed when the user right-clicks a specific area of the layout.) The layout of Figure 9.1 contains three Image controls, each with a picture of a different city. Each time the user right-clicks one of the images, a popup menu is displayed with choices about the specific city. The shortcut menus are also context-sensitive, because each one can be invoked only when the pointer is on top of an Image control.

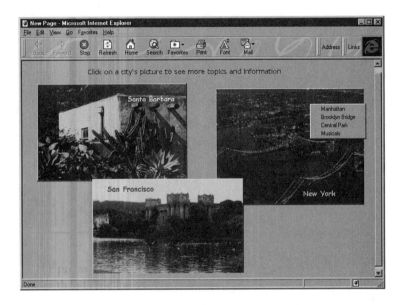

The Popup Menu control provides four methods that let you manipulate its contents and display it:

`Clear`	This method clears the menu (removes any existing options) in preparation for a new menu structure. If you must change the items of a Popup Menu control at runtime, you must first clear its current contents.
`AddItem menuItem`	Appends another option (command) to the popup menu. *menuItem* is the string you want to appear in the menu. To insert an option at a specific location in the menu, supply the item's index in the menu. (The first option has index 1.) The statement

`IEPop1.AddItem "This is the third choice", 1`

will insert the specified string at the first menu item. `IEPop1` is the default name for the first Popup Menu control placed on a layout or form.

`RemoveItem index`	Removes the item at the specified index. The statement

`IEPop1.RemoveItem 1`

removes the first item in the menu. The popup menu has two properties, one of them being the `ItemCount` property, which reports the number of items in the menu. To remove the last item, use the statement

`IEPop1.RemoveItem IEPop1.ItemCount`

`PopUp (x, y)`	This method causes the Popup Menu control to pop up on the screen. x and y are the coordinates of the upper-left corner of the

control, and you can use them to control the popup menu's location. Both arguments are optional, and if you omit them the menu will pop up at the pointer's location. The values of the x and y coordinates are relative to the window, with the origin being the window's upper-left corner.

To display a popup menu from within a command button's `Click` event, insert a statement like the following in the button's `Click` event handler:

```
Sub CommandButton1_Click()
    IEPop1.Popup
End Sub
```

To find out whether the user has clicked a menu item, use the `Click` event of the control, which reports the index of the item that was clicked:

```
Sub IEPop1_Click(index)
    MsgBox "Item # " & index & " was selected"
End Sub
```

The Popup Menu Project

After this introduction to the Popup Menu control, you can look at the implementation of the Popup Menu project, which you will find in this chapter folder on the CD. Create a layout with the three Image controls and then place a Popup Menu control somewhere on the layout. The popup menu is not in the toolbox, so you'll have to customize your toolbox by adding an extra control. Right-click an empty area of the current page (or create a new page, if you plan to add many new controls) and from the shortcut menu select Additional controls. In the Insert ActiveX dialog box that will appear, locate Popup Menu Object and click OK. The icon of the new control will be added to the toolbox's current page. Select the tool and draw a small rectangle on the layout.

The size of the Popup Menu control on the layout has nothing to do with its actual size when it pops up. The actual size of the control depends on the number of choices it contains—and it will be large enough to accommodate them all. One thing you should keep in mind is that the current implementation of the control isn't invisible. Instead, a white stripe with the size of the control at design time will remain visible on the layout. Once the Popup Menu control has been placed on the layout, reduce it to a single line to avoid this white stripe on the layout at runtime. The Popup Menu control doesn't have many properties you can set at design time through the Properties window anyway.

If you save the layout now and look at its code, you'll see that the following definition was inserted by the Control Pad:

```
<OBJECT ID="IEPOP1"
    CLASSID="CLSID:7823A620-9DD9-11CF-A662-00AA00C066D2">
STYLE="TOP:239pt;LEFT:355pt;WIDTH:17pt;HEIGHT:0pt;TABINDEX:0;ZINDEX:3;">
        <PARAM NAME="_ExtentX" VALUE="582">
        <PARAM NAME="_ExtentY" VALUE="0">
    </OBJECT>
```

The menu inserted with the previous OBJECT definition doesn't contain any item yet. Instead, you must add its items with the AddItem method from within your script. To assign some initial items to the popup menu, insert additional PARAM tags with the MenuItem property, as follows:

```
<PARAM NAME="MenuItem[0]" value="First menu item">
<PARAM NAME="MenuItem[1]" value="Second menu item">
<PARAM NAME="MenuItem[2]" value="Third menu item">
<PARAM NAME="MenuItem[3]" value="Fourth menu item">
<PARAM NAME="MenuItem[4]" value="Fifth menu item">
```

The MenuItem property is an array with as many elements as there are options in the menu. Notice that where the indexing of the menu item starts at 1, the MenuItem array's indexing starts at zero.

Before you display the popup menu you just placed on the layout, you must populate it with the AddItem method. Use the Script Wizard or your favorite text editor to edit the Click event handler for each Image control. We could have used three Popup Menu controls in our design, one for each image. But because we want to demonstrate how to manipulate popup menus dynamically with VBScript, we used a single one, which will be invoked when the user right-clicks an image. As soon as the code detects a right-click operation on one of the images, it must clear the menu and append the items for the specific image with the AddItem method. Here's the MouseDown event handler for Image1:

```
Sub Image1_MouseDown(Button, Shift, X, Y)
    If Button<>2 Then Exit Sub
    IEPop1.Clear
    IEPop1.AddItem "Manhattan"
    IEPop1.AddItem "Brooklyn Bridge"
    IEPop1.AddItem "Central Park"
    IEPop1.AddItem "Musicals"
    IEPop1.PopUp
End Sub
```

(The Click event can't be used because it's not invoked with the right mouse button.) The code tests which button was pressed, and if it wasn't the right button it exits the subroutine. (You would probably execute a different command for the Click event.) Then the IEPop1 menu is cleared and populated with the menu items that apply to the image of New York City. The last statement causes the popup menu to be displayed on the window. The MouseDown event handlers for the other two Image controls are quite similar. They simply add different options to the popup menu.

After the user has made a selection, the popup menu's Click event is triggered, which reports the index of the selected item:

```
Sub IEPOP1_Click(item)
    MsgBox "You 've selected option " & item
End Sub
```

The Popup Menu control doesn't provide a property that would return the actual string of the selected item, just its index. If you need access to the actual string from within your code, you must store the options in a global array and use the index returned by the Click event to access the values. Listing 9.1 is the complete listing of the PopMenu layout.

Listing 9.1. The PopMenu project's source code.

```
 1: <SCRIPT LANGUAGE="VBScript">
 2: <!--
 3:
 4: Sub Image1_MouseDown(Button, Shift, X, Y)
 5:     If Button<>2 Then Exit Sub
 6:     IEPop1.Clear
 7:     IEPop1.AddItem "The beaches"
 8:     IEPop1.AddItem "Santa Barbara Peer"
 9:     IEPop1.AddItem "Riviera"
10:     IEPop1.PopUp
11: End Sub
12:
13: Sub Image3_MouseDown(Button, Shift, X, Y)
14:     If Button<>2 Then Exit Sub
15:     IEPop1.Clear
16:     IEPop1.AddItem "Golden Gate Bridge"
17:     IEPop1.AddItem "Fisherman's Wharf"
18:     IEPop1.AddItem "Alcatraz"
19:     IEPop1.AddItem "Sausalito"
20:     IEPop1.PopUp
21: End Sub
22:
23: Sub Image2_MouseDown(Button, Shift, X, Y)
24:     If Button<>2 Then Exit Sub
25:     IEPop1.Clear
26:     IEPop1.AddItem "Manhattan"
27:     IEPop1.AddItem "Brooklyn Bridge"
28:     IEPop1.AddItem "Central Park"
29:     IEPop1.AddItem "Musicals"
30:     IEPop1.PopUp
31: End Sub
32:
33: Sub IEPOP1_Click(item)
34:     MsgBox "You 've selected option " & item
35: End Sub
36: -->
37: </SCRIPT>
38: <DIV ID="Layout1" STYLE="LAYOUT:FIXED;WIDTH:545pt;HEIGHT:330pt;">
39:     <OBJECT ID="Image1"
40:       CLASSID="CLSID:D4A97620-8E8F-11CF-93CD-00AA00C08FDF"
          STYLE="TOP:33pt;LEFT:17pt;WIDTH:243pt;HEIGHT:153pt;ZINDEX:0;">
41:         <PARAM NAME="PicturePath" VALUE="mission.bmp">
42:         <PARAM NAME="BorderStyle" VALUE="0">
43:         <PARAM NAME="SizeMode" VALUE="3">
44:         <PARAM NAME="SpecialEffect" VALUE="1">
45:         <PARAM NAME="Size" VALUE="8571;5396">
46:         <PARAM NAME="PictureAlignment" VALUE="0">
47:         <PARAM NAME="VariousPropertyBits" VALUE="19">
```

9

**MORE ACTIVEX
CONTROLS**

continues

Listing 9.1. continued

```
48:     </OBJECT>
49:     <OBJECT ID="Image2"
50:      CLASSID="CLSID:D4A97620-8E8F-11CF-93CD-00AA00C08FDF"
        STYLE="TOP:41pt;LEFT:305pt;WIDTH:243pt;HEIGHT:183pt;ZINDEX:1;">
51:         <PARAM NAME="PicturePath" VALUE="bridges.bmp">
52:         <PARAM NAME="BorderStyle" VALUE="0">
53:         <PARAM NAME="SizeMode" VALUE="3">
54:         <PARAM NAME="SpecialEffect" VALUE="1">
55:         <PARAM NAME="Size" VALUE="8571;6454">
56:         <PARAM NAME="PictureAlignment" VALUE="0">
57:         <PARAM NAME="VariousPropertyBits" VALUE="19">
58:     </OBJECT>
59:     <OBJECT ID="Image3"
60:      CLASSID="CLSID:D4A97620-8E8F-11CF-93CD-00AA00C08FDF"
        STYLE="TOP:182pt;LEFT:107pt;WIDTH:243pt;HEIGHT:153pt;ZINDEX:2;">
61:         <PARAM NAME="PicturePath" VALUE="lake.bmp">
62:         <PARAM NAME="BorderStyle" VALUE="0">
63:         <PARAM NAME="SizeMode" VALUE="3">
64:         <PARAM NAME="SpecialEffect" VALUE="1">
65:         <PARAM NAME="Size" VALUE="8571;5396">
66:         <PARAM NAME="PictureAlignment" VALUE="0">
67:         <PARAM NAME="VariousPropertyBits" VALUE="19">
68:     </OBJECT>
69:     <OBJECT ID="IEPOP1"
70:      CLASSID="CLSID:7823A620-9DD9-11CF-A662-00AA00C066D2"
        STYLE="TOP:239pt;LEFT:355pt;WIDTH:17pt;HEIGHT:0pt;TABINDEX:0;ZINDEX:3;">
71:         <PARAM NAME="_ExtentX" VALUE="582">
72:         <PARAM NAME="_ExtentY" VALUE="0">
73:     </OBJECT>
74:     <OBJECT ID="Label1"
75:      CLASSID="CLSID:978C9E23-D4B0-11CE-BF2D-00AA003F40D0"
        STYLE="TOP:8pt;LEFT:58pt;WIDTH:396pt;HEIGHT:17pt;ZINDEX:4;">
76:         <PARAM NAME="Caption" VALUE="Click on a city's picture to see more
            topics and information">
77:         <PARAM NAME="Size" VALUE="13970;582">
78:         <PARAM NAME="FontName" VALUE="Verdana">
79:         <PARAM NAME="FontHeight" VALUE="220">
80:         <PARAM NAME="FontCharSet" VALUE="0">
81:         <PARAM NAME="FontPitchAndFamily" VALUE="2">
82:         <PARAM NAME="ParagraphAlign" VALUE="3">
83:         <PARAM NAME="FontWeight" VALUE="0">
84:     </OBJECT>
85:     <OBJECT ID="Label2"
86:      CLASSID="CLSID:978C9E23-D4B0-11CE-BF2D-00AA003F40D0"
        STYLE="TOP:50pt;LEFT:165pt;WIDTH:91pt;HEIGHT:17pt;ZINDEX:5;">
87:         <PARAM NAME="ForeColor" VALUE="65535">
88:         <PARAM NAME="VariousPropertyBits" VALUE="8388627">
89:         <PARAM NAME="Caption" VALUE="Santa Barbara">
90:         <PARAM NAME="Size" VALUE="3202;582">
91:         <PARAM NAME="FontName" VALUE="Comic Sans MS">
92:         <PARAM NAME="FontEffects" VALUE="1073741825">
93:         <PARAM NAME="FontHeight" VALUE="220">
94:         <PARAM NAME="FontCharSet" VALUE="0">
95:         <PARAM NAME="FontPitchAndFamily" VALUE="2">
96:         <PARAM NAME="FontWeight" VALUE="700">
```

```
97:      </OBJECT>
98:      <OBJECT ID="Label3"
99:       CLASSID="CLSID:978C9E23-D4B0-11CE-BF2D-00AA003F40D0"
         STYLE="TOP:190pt;LEFT:132pt;WIDTH:91pt;HEIGHT:17pt;ZINDEX:6;">
100:          <PARAM NAME="ForeColor" VALUE="255">
101:          <PARAM NAME="VariousPropertyBits" VALUE="8388627">
102:          <PARAM NAME="Caption" VALUE="San Francisco">
103:          <PARAM NAME="Size" VALUE="3202;582">
104:          <PARAM NAME="FontName" VALUE="Comic Sans MS">
105:          <PARAM NAME="FontEffects" VALUE="1073741825">
106:          <PARAM NAME="FontHeight" VALUE="220">
107:          <PARAM NAME="FontCharSet" VALUE="0">
108:          <PARAM NAME="FontPitchAndFamily" VALUE="2">
109:          <PARAM NAME="FontWeight" VALUE="700">
110:      </OBJECT>
111:      <OBJECT ID="Label4"
112:       CLASSID="CLSID:978C9E23-D4B0-11CE-BF2D-00AA003F40D0"
         STYLE="TOP:198pt;LEFT:446pt;WIDTH:91pt;HEIGHT:17pt;ZINDEX:7;">
113:          <PARAM NAME="ForeColor" VALUE="16776960">
114:          <PARAM NAME="VariousPropertyBits" VALUE="8388627">
115:          <PARAM NAME="Caption" VALUE="New York">
116:          <PARAM NAME="Size" VALUE="3202;582">
117:          <PARAM NAME="FontName" VALUE="Comic Sans MS">
118:          <PARAM NAME="FontEffects" VALUE="1073741825">
119:          <PARAM NAME="FontHeight" VALUE="220">
120:          <PARAM NAME="FontCharSet" VALUE="0">
121:          <PARAM NAME="FontPitchAndFamily" VALUE="2">
122:          <PARAM NAME="FontWeight" VALUE="700">
123:      </OBJECT>
124: </DIV>
```

In a practical situation, the popup menu's Click event handler will do something more meaningful than simply displaying the index of the selected item. The project RTF Editor makes use of the popup menu to display the usual shortcut menu of a text editor, which implements the Cut, Copy, and Paste operations.

The Menu Control

The Menu control is quite similar to the Popup Menu control, only closer to the actual structure of a menu bar. Each Menu control remains visible on the screen at all times and looks like a command button, as shown in Figure 9.2. When the mouse pointer is moved over the Menu control, the control's caption takes a three-dimensional look. In addition, an arrow pointing down suggests that the menu leads to a submenu. It is possible to have menus without submenus, which behave similarly to command buttons, but they have the same look as the other Menu controls.

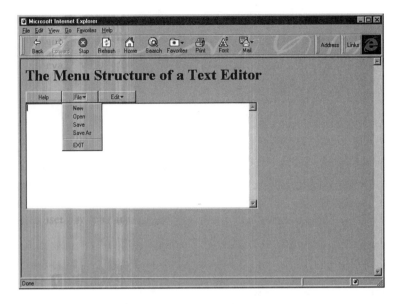

To implement the project Menu, shown in Figure 9.2, we aren't going to use the Control Pad as usual, because Control Pad doesn't insert a meaningful definition in the HTML file. Start a new HTML document and manually insert the following definition:

```
<OBJECT
     id=menu1
     classid="clsid:52DFAE60-CEBF-11CF-A3A9-00A0C9034920"
     width=80
     height=25
     align=middle
>
<param NAME="Caption" value="Menu">
</OBJECT>
```

This definition doesn't attach any items to the menu; you'll have to insert them manually with PARAM tags. The second Menu control (the File menu) in the Menu document was defined with the following OBJECT definition:

```
<OBJECT
     id=menu1
     classid="clsid:52DFAE60-CEBF-11CF-A3A9-00A0C9034920"
     width=80
     height=25
     align=middle
>
<param NAME="Menuitem[0]" value="New">
<param NAME="Menuitem[1]" value="Open">
<param NAME="Menuitem[2]" value="Save">
<param NAME="Menuitem[3]" value="Save As">
<param NAME="Menuitem[4]" value="">
<param NAME="Menuitem[5]" value="EXIT">
<param NAME="Caption" value="File">
</OBJECT>
```

Notice the similarities between the Menu and Popup Menu controls. Moreover, the Menu control provides the same methods for manipulating the contents of the menu at runtime. The `Clear`, `AddItem`, `RemoveItem`, and `PopUp` methods work with the Menu control as well. It's doubtful that you'll ever need to call the `PopUp` method to expand a Menu control, but it's an option.

The Menu control has an `ItemCount` property that returns the number of items in the control, as well as a `Caption` property that sets the menu's title (the caption of the button). The index of the selected item is reported back to the program from within the control's `Click` event handler. This event is triggered when a menu option is selected. Because some menus might not lead to submenus, the Menu control recognizes the `Select` event, which is triggered only when the user clicks a Menu control without a submenu. (The arrow-down symbol will be missing from such a menu.) The Menu document contains three Menu controls and a multiline textbox (inserted with the `TEXTAREA` tag). The first Menu control is a single command that doesn't lead to a submenu. The other two have their own submenus that are the typical File and Edit submenus of a text-editing application. (VBScript can't save data on the local disk, so what's the point in a File menu? It is possible to store data on the local disk with VBScript; it just isn't a recommended, or common, practice yet. The options of the menus of this project were not implemented, of course. This example is meant to demonstrate how to manipulate the Menu control at runtime.)

The complete listing of the Menu document is shown in Listing 9.2.

Listing 9.2. The Menu document.

```
<HTML>
<HEAD>
<TITLE>Menu demo</TITLE>

<SCRIPT LANGUAGE=VBS>
Sub Menu1_Select(i)
    MsgBox "You selected item # " & i & " from the File menu"
End Sub

Sub Menu2_Select(i)
    MsgBox "You selected item # " & i & " from the Edit menu"
End Sub

Sub Menu0_Click()
    MsgBox "You clicked on the Help menu!"
End Sub

</SCRIPT>
</HEAD>

<H1>The Menu Structure of a Text Editor</H1>
<P>
 <OBJECT
    id=menu0
    CODEBASE="http://activex.microsoft.com/controls/iexplorer/
btnmenu.ocx#Version=4,70,0,1161"
```

9

MORE ACTIVEX CONTROLS

continues

Listing 9.2. continued

```
    classid="clsid:52DFAE60-CEBF-11CF-A3A9-00A0C9034920"
    width=80
    height=25
    align=middle
>
    <param NAME="Caption" value="Help">
</OBJECT>

 <OBJECT
    id=menu1
    classid="clsid:52DFAE60-CEBF-11CF-A3A9-00A0C9034920"
    CODEBASE="http://activex.microsoft.com/controls/iexplorer/
btnmenu.ocx#Version=4,70,0,1161"
    width=80
    height=25
    align=middle
>
    <param NAME="Menuitem[0]" value="New">
    <param NAME="Menuitem[1]" value="Open">
    <param NAME="Menuitem[2]" value="Save">
    <param NAME="Menuitem[3]" value="Save As">
    <param NAME="Menuitem[4]" value="">
    <param NAME="Menuitem[5]" value="EXIT">
    <param NAME="Caption" value="File">
    </OBJECT>

 <OBJECT
    id=menu2
    classid="clsid:52DFAE60-CEBF-11CF-A3A9-00A0C9034920"
    CODEBASE="http://activex.microsoft.com/controls/iexplorer/
btnmenu.ocx#Version=4,70,0,1161"
    width=80
    height=25
    align=middle
>
    <param NAME="Menuitem[0]" value="Copy">
    <param NAME="Menuitem[1]" value="Cut">
    <param NAME="Menuitem[2]" value="Paste">
    <param NAME="Menuitem[3]" value="Select All">
    <param NAME="Menuitem[4]" value="">
    <param NAME="Caption" value="Edit">
    </OBJECT>
<BR>
<TEXTAREA rows=15 cols=100></TEXTAREA>
</HTML>
</HTML>
```

The Click event handlers of the File and Edit menus are quite similar. They simply report the index of the item selected. The Help menu's Click event handler reports in a message box that the menu was clicked.

The Popup Window Control

The Popup Window control is a small browser in a window that lets you display any valid URL without leaving the current page. Figures 9.3 and 9.4 show how the Popup Window control works. The page of Figure 9.3 contains two command buttons. When they are clicked, they display the MSN and Netscape pages in a separate window, like the one shown in Figure 9.4. The large window is a Popup Window control that contains the home page of the MSN site. The user can't do anything with it—can't click on hyperlinks, for example, or execute any scripts that happen to be on the page. In fact, as soon as a key is pressed the popup window disappears. Its sole purpose is to provide the user with a preview of an Internet site or document, from within another page.

FIGURE 9.3.

The PopupWin document lets the viewer preview two popular sites without actually switching to another site.

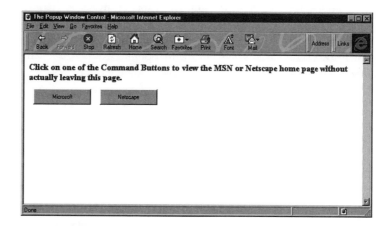

FIGURE 9.4.

This is the MSN home page viewed in a popup window.

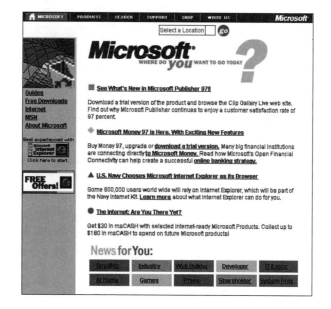

The OBJECT definition for the Popup Window control is

```
<OBJECT ID="PreVu1" WIDTH=1 HEIGHT=1
    CLASSID="CLSID:A23D7C20-CABA-11CF-A5D4-00AA00A47DD2"
    CODEBASE="http://activex.microsoft.com/controls/iexplorer/
iepopwnd.ocx#Version=4,70,0,1161>"
    <PARAM NAME="_ExtentX" VALUE="5054">
    <PARAM NAME="_ExtentY" VALUE="3519">
</OBJECT>
```

The control's dimensions in the OBJECT definition don't matter, because it will be resized to fit the page that's displayed on it. To display the window, use the control's Popup method, which accepts two arguments: the URL of the document to be displayed in the popup window and an optional argument that determines whether the destination document will be resized to fit the popup window or not. The complete syntax of the Popup method is

```
PreVu1.Popup URL, True¦False
```

where *PreVu1* is the default name of the first popup window, *URL* is the URL of the document to be displayed on the window, and the last argument can be True or False value, which determines how the document will fit into the window: whether the document will be resized to fit the window, or the window will be resized to display the document in actual size. The popup window in Figure 9.4 was invoked with the statement:

```
PreVu1.Popup "http://www.microsoft.com", False
```

Figure 9.5 shows the same popup window, only this time it was invoked with the line

```
PreVu1.Popup "http://www.microsoft.com", True
```

FIGURE 9.5.
*You can specify that the
destination document
will be resized to fit in
the available space.*

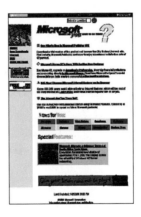

There is also a Dismiss method, which does the opposite. It closes the popup window programmatically. Any user action will close the popup window so the Dismiss method is used rarely, most likely from within a Timer event to close a popup window that remained on the screen for a long period.

The PopupWin example was created with Control Pad, as an HTML document. Start Control Pad, create a new HTML file, and using the Insert ActiveX control command, put two command buttons and a popup window on the document. The text was entered directly on the HTML document (it's not on a label or other control). Once the HTML file is generated for you (the PopupWin document you will find on the CD was edited a little to arrange the buttons), enter the following event handlers in the document's SCRIPT section:

```
Sub CommandButton1_Click
    PreVu1.Popup "http://www.microsoft.com", True
End Sub

Sub CommandButton2_Click
    PreVu1.Popup "http://www.netscape.com", False
End Sub
```

The two popup windows are invoked with a different URL and a different value for scaling. You can change the values True and False to see how they affect the appearance of each site. The code listing of the PopupWin document is in Listing 9.3.

Listing 9.3. The PopupWin document.

```
 1: <HTML>
 2: <HEAD>
 3: <TITLE>The Popup Window control</TITLE>
 4: <SCRIPT Language="VBSCRIPT">
 5: Sub CommandButton1_Click
 6:     PreVu1.Popup "http://www.microsoft.com", True
 7: End Sub
 8:
 9: Sub CommandButton2_Click
10:     PreVu1.Popup "http://www.netscape.com", False
11: End Sub
12:
13: </SCRIPT>
14: </HEAD>
15: <BODY BGCOLOR=WHITE>
16: <H3>Click on one of the command buttons to view the MSN or Netscape
17: home page without actually leaving this page.
18: <P>
19: <OBJECT ID="PreVu1" WIDTH=10 HEIGHT=10
20:  CLASSID="CLSID:A23D7C20-CABA-11CF-A5D4-00AA00A47DD2">
21:   <PARAM NAME="_ExtentX" VALUE="5054">
22:   <PARAM NAME="_ExtentY" VALUE="3519">
23: </OBJECT>
24:
25: <OBJECT ID="CommandButton1" WIDTH=123 HEIGHT=32
26:  CLASSID="CLSID:D7053240-CE69-11CD-A777-00DD01143C57">
27:   <PARAM NAME="Caption" VALUE="Microsoft">
28:   <PARAM NAME="Size" VALUE="3254;846">
29:   <PARAM NAME="FontCharSet" VALUE="0">
30:   <PARAM NAME="FontPitchAndFamily" VALUE="2">
31:   <PARAM NAME="ParagraphAlign" VALUE="3">
32:   <PARAM NAME="FontWeight" VALUE="0">
```

9

MORE ACTIVEX CONTROLS

continues

Listing 9.3. continued

```
33: </OBJECT>
34:
35:    
36:
37: <OBJECT ID="CommandButton2" WIDTH=123 HEIGHT=32
38:  CLASSID="CLSID:D7053240-CE69-11CD-A777-00DD01143C57">
39:    <PARAM NAME="Caption" VALUE="Netscape">
40:    <PARAM NAME="Size" VALUE="3254;846">
41:    <PARAM NAME="FontCharSet" VALUE="0">
42:    <PARAM NAME="FontPitchAndFamily" VALUE="2">
43:    <PARAM NAME="ParagraphAlign" VALUE="3">
44:    <PARAM NAME="FontWeight" VALUE="0">
45: </OBJECT>
46: </BODY>
47: </HTML>
```

The popup window is similar to the keywords of a Windows 95 help file. Although most keywords act as hyperlinks to other pages (or topics, in the case of help files), some keywords cause a small frame with a short explanation to be displayed. This should give you an idea of the kind of functionality you can place on your pages with the Popup Window control. Instead of displaying an entire new page (which, admittedly, isn't very practical), you can display a short HTML document that further explains a term on the current page. In this capacity, the Popup Window control is very useful, if you consider how many times you clicked on a hyperlink only to be taken to a small page with a few lines of text.

The Marquee Control

The Marquee control is Microsoft's first attempt to provide the means for simple animation on Web pages. This control has a function similar to that of the MARQUEE tag, only instead of scrolling a piece of text, it can scroll an entire HTML page in a rectangular area on the document. Moreover, the Marquee control can scroll its contents in all directions, even diagonally. The document displayed and scrolled in a Marquee control is a regular HTML document that can contain images, any HTML tags (including the MARQUEE tag), and even its own animation. The only limitation is that it can't handle hyperlinks and can't contain embedded HTML layouts.

To place an ActiveX Marquee control on your page, use the Insert ActiveX control command on the HTML Editor's Edit menu or insert a definition like the following one in the document:

```
<OBJECT ID="Marquee1" WIDTH=408 HEIGHT=160 BORDER=2
 CLASSID="CLSID:1A4DA620-6217-11CF-BE62-0080C72EDD2D">
    <PARAM NAME="ScrollStyleX" VALUE="Circular">
    <PARAM NAME="ScrollStyleY" VALUE="Circular">
    <PARAM NAME="ScrollPixelsX" VALUE="0">
    <PARAM NAME="ScrollPixelsY" VALUE="-2">
```

```
    <PARAM NAME="ScrollDelay" VALUE="100">
    <PARAM NAME="LoopsX" VALUE="-1">
    <PARAM NAME="LoopsY" VALUE="-1">
</OBJECT>
```

The Marquee control comes with Internet Explorer 3.0 and you needn't specify its `CodeBase` property in the control's definition.

Do not add the Marquee control to the Control Pad's toolbox, because any attempt to place a Marquee control on a layout will crash the program. Just type in the definition or open the Marquee project in this chapter's folder on the CD, copy the definition of the object, and paste it in your HTML document. The various properties of the Marquee control are explained shortly.

ScrollStyleX, ScrollStyleY

These properties set the scrolling style of the marquee, and their values can be

Circular	The document is wrapped around the control. When it reaches the end of the control, the document enters the control from the other end.
Bounce	The document bounces in the control. When it reaches the end of the control, it starts scrolling in the opposite direction.

ScrollPixelsX, ScrollPixelsY

The direction of the scrolling is controlled with the `ScrollPixelsX` and `ScrollPixelsY` properties. Assign the number of pixels by which the contents of the control should scroll in each direction. Positive values cause the contents of the control to scroll right and down. Negative values cause the contents of the controls to scroll in the opposite directions. The contents of the Marquee can scroll in both directions simultaneously, which is equivalent to a diagonal movement.

ScrollDelay

The `ScrollDelay` property is the delay between successive movements of the control's contents, and its value is expressed in milliseconds. This property, along with `ScrollPixelsX` and `ScrollPixelsY`, determines how fast the contents of the Marquee will scroll. Consider two Marquee controls with the following properties:

Marquee 1	*Marquee 2*
ScrollPixelsX=0	ScrollPixelsX=0
ScrollPixelsY=10	ScrollPixelsY=20
ScrollDelay=100	ScrollDelay=200

9

MORE ACTIVEX CONTROLS

Both controls scroll their contents at the same speed. The first control scrolls its contents by 10 pixels vertically every 100 milliseconds (10 times per second), while the second one scrolls them by 20 pixels at a time, but twice as frequently. Both controls scroll the document by 100 pixels per second, but the movement is smoother in the first control.

LoopsX, LoopsY

The LoopsX and LoopsY parameters specify how many times the contents will scroll in each direction. The value -1 causes the document to loop forever.

szURL

This is the name of the HTML document to be scrolled. The value of this property can be a local file or a URL of any page on the Web.

WhiteSpace

This property defines how much white (blank) space will appear between successive scrolls. If you want some extra space to appear before the next appearance of the document displayed in the Marquee control, set this property to the number of pixels of white space. The WhiteSpace value is expressed in pixels.

Zoom

The document displayed in the Marquee control can be larger or smaller than normal size. The Zoom property reduces or enlarges the document by a percentage value. Its default value is 100 and corresponds to actual size. The value 200 will cause the document to appear twice as large as normal.

WidthOfPage

The WidthOfPage property is identical to the WhiteSpace property but applies to the horizontal direction. It determines the width of an empty area that will be drawn between horizontal scrolls.

The Marquee ActiveX control provides two methods for controlling the scrolling, the Pause and Resume methods, which pause and resume scrolling respectively.

The Marquee control recognizes a number of events, too, which give you control over the control's operation. Some of the Marquee events aren't working with the current implementation of the control, but they are documented and you should expect to find a revised version of the control on Microsoft's Web site. Here are the descriptions of the Marquee control events:

OnStartOfImage, OnEndOfImage

The OnStartOfImage event is triggered immediately before the document starts scrolling and the OnEndOfImage event is triggered immediately after the URL has completely scrolled. Both event handlers accept an argument, the HorizontalOrVertical argument, which is H for horizontal scrolling and V for vertical scrolling.

OnBounce

The OnBounce event is triggered when the document bounces off one end of the control, if the scroll style is set to Bounce (properties ScrollStyleX, ScrollStyleY). This event handler accepts an argument (SideBouncedOff) that tells you on which of four possible sides the document bounced (L for left, R for right, T for top, and B for bottom).

OnLMouseClick

You can capture mouse clicks on the control, too, with the OnLMouseClick event. This event is the same as the Click event of other ActiveX controls, but it's named differently.

The Marquee Example

Figure 9.6 shows the Marquee page (which you'll find in this chapter's folder on the CD). The Marquee page contains two Marquee controls, which both display the Sams Web site. One of them scrolls its contents vertically and the other one horizontally. The two command buttons next to the Marquees demonstrate the Zoom property and the Pause/Resume methods. When the user clicks the ZOOM button, the contents of the top Marquee control are enlarged to 120% and the button's caption becomes NORMAL. If clicked again, it restores the contents of the first control to normal size.

FIGURE 9.6.

The Marquee example demonstrates the Zoom *property and the* Pause/Resume *events.*

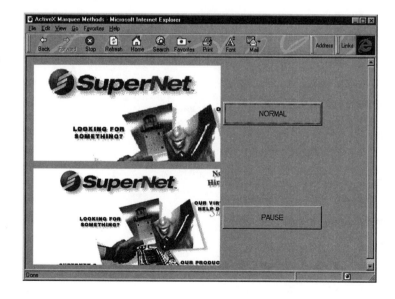

9

MORE ACTIVEX
CONTROLS

The second button temporarily stops the scrolling of the document in the Marquee control, and its caption becomes RESUME. If clicked again, the scrolling resumes and the button's caption becomes PAUSE again. The code of the Marquee document is shown in Listing 9.4.

Listing 9.4. The Marquee document.

```
 1: <HTML>
 2: <HEAD>
 3: <TITLE>ActiveX Marquee Methods</TITLE>
 4: <SCRIPT LANGUAGE="VBScript">
 5: <!--
 6: Sub CommandButton1_Click()
 7: If CommandButton1.Caption="ZOOM" then
 8:     Marquee1.Zoom = 125
 9:     CommandButton1.Caption="NORMAL"
10: Else
11:     Marquee1.Zoom = 100
12:     CommandButton1.Caption="ZOOM"
13: End If
14: End Sub
15:
16: Sub CommandButton2_Click()
17: If CommandButton2.Caption="PAUSE" Then
18:     Marquee2.Pause
19:     CommandButton2.Caption="RESUME"
20: Else
21:     Marquee2.Resume
22:     CommandButton2.Caption="PAUSE"
23: End If
24:
25: End Sub
26: -->
27: </SCRIPT>
28:
29: </HEAD>
30: <BODY>
31: <OBJECT ID="Marquee1" WIDTH=400 HEIGHT=200 align=CENTER BORDER=1 HSPACE=5
32:     CLASSID="CLSID:1A4DA620-6217-11CF-BE62-0080C72EDD2D">
33:     <PARAM NAME="WhiteSpace" VALUE="42">
34:     <PARAM NAME="szURL" VALUE="http://www.sams.com">
35:     <PARAM NAME="_ExtentX" VALUE="124">
36:     <PARAM NAME="_ExtentY" VALUE="125">
37:     <PARAM NAME="Zoom" VALUE="100">
38:     <PARAM NAME="ScrollPixelsX" VALUE="0">
39:     <PARAM NAME="ScrollPixelsY" VALUE="4">
40:     <PARAM NAME="WidthOfPage" VALUE="300">
41:    </OBJECT>
42: <OBJECT ID="CommandButton1" WIDTH=215 HEIGHT=48
43:     CLASSID="CLSID:D7053240-CE69-11CD-A777-00DD01143C57">
44:     <PARAM NAME="Caption" VALUE="ZOOM">
45:     <PARAM NAME="Size" VALUE="5689;1270">
46:     <PARAM NAME="FontName" VALUE="Arial">
47:     <PARAM NAME="FontHeight" VALUE="220">
48:     <PARAM NAME="FontCharSet" VALUE="0">
49:     <PARAM NAME="FontPitchAndFamily" VALUE="2">
50:     <PARAM NAME="ParagraphAlign" VALUE="3">
51:     <PARAM NAME="FontWeight" VALUE="0">
```

```
52:    </OBJECT>
53:    <P>
54:    <OBJECT ID="Marquee2" WIDTH=400 HEIGHT=200 align=CENTER BORDER=1 HSPACE=5
55:       CLASSID="CLSID:1A4DA620-6217-11CF-BE62-0080C72EDD2D">
56:          <PARAM NAME="szURL" VALUE="http://www.sams.com">
57:          <PARAM NAME="_ExtentX" VALUE="124">
58:          <PARAM NAME="_ExtentY" VALUE="125">
59:          <PARAM NAME="Zoom" VALUE="100">
60:          <PARAM NAME="ScrollPixelsX" VALUE="4">
61:          <PARAM NAME="ScrollPixelsY" VALUE="0">
62:    </OBJECT>
63:
64:    <OBJECT ID="CommandButton2" WIDTH=215 HEIGHT=48
65:       CLASSID="CLSID:D7053240-CE69-11CD-A777-00DD01143C57">
66:          <PARAM NAME="Caption" VALUE="PAUSE">
67:          <PARAM NAME="Size" VALUE="5689;1270">
68:          <PARAM NAME="FontName" VALUE="Arial">
69:          <PARAM NAME="FontHeight" VALUE="220">
70:          <PARAM NAME="FontCharSet" VALUE="0">
71:          <PARAM NAME="FontPitchAndFamily" VALUE="2">
72:          <PARAM NAME="ParagraphAlign" VALUE="3">
73:          <PARAM NAME="FontWeight" VALUE="0">
74:    </OBJECT>
75:    </BODY>
76:    </HTML>
```

The Chart Control

The Chart control presents numeric data as graphs, and supports a variety of different types and styles of graphs, such as pie charts and bar graphs. You supply the data and the parameters of the graph, and the Chart control generates the graph on-the-fly. Figure 9.7 is a collection of various chart types generated with the Chart control.

Figure 9.7.

Various types of graphs produced by the Chart control.

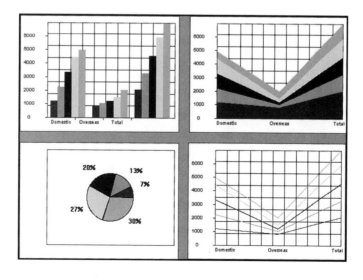

There are seven chart types you can produce with the Chart control: Pie, Point, Line, Area, Bar, Column, and Stocks. In addition, there are more than one flavor of each of these styles. Most of these types have the following variations: Simple, Stacked, and Full. Use the Chart document, which we will present shortly, to experiment with the various graph types and styles.

The Graph control is in essence a mechanism for plotting data. Because of the numerous parameters a data plot can have, the Chart control has a long list of properties. Yet, there are no methods (short of the About method, which displays information about the control) and no events. Let's start with the simpler properties that control the appearance of the chart.

Rows, Columns

These two values determine the total number of data points to be plotted. Obviously, you must supply Rows × Columns data points to the control. (In the section "Manipulating the Chart Control's Data," you'll see how to specify the data to be plotted.)

HGridStyle, VGridStyle

These two properties determine the type of horizontal and vertical grid that will be placed on the graph, and they can have one of the following values:

0 No grid
1 Solid grid
2 Bold grid
3 Dotted grid
4 Bold dotted grid

ChartType

The ChartType property determines the graph's type and may have one of the following values:

0 Simple pie chart
1 Special pie chart
2 Simple point chart
3 Stacked point chart
4 Full point chart
5 Simple line chart
6 Stacked line chart
7 Full line chart
8 Simple area chart
9 Stacked area chart
10 Full area chart
11 Simple column chart
12 Stacked column chart

13 Full column chart
14 Simple bar chart
15 Stacked bar chart
16 Full bar chart
17 HLC (high low close) simple stock chart
18 HCL WSJ stock chart
19 OHLC (open high low close) simple stock chart
20 OHCL WSJ stock chart

ColorScheme

There are five predefined color schemes (0, 1, 2, 3, and 4), and you can set one of them for your chart by setting the `ColorScheme` property.

BackStyle

This property determines whether the graph's background will be transparent (`BackStyle=0`) or not (`BackStyle=1`).

Scale

This is a scaling factor for the graph data and it can go up to 100%, but no more.

RowName

This property specifies a row name. (The row names are the legends that appears along the Y axis.)

ColumnName

This property specifies a column name. (The column names are the legends that appear along the X axis.)

DisplayLegend

Use this property to view (`Legend=-1`) or hide (`Legend=0`) the chart's legend.

GridPlacement

This property controls how the grid is drawn. The grid lines can be drawn either over the chart (foreground) or below the chart (background), and it can have one of the two values

0 Grid lines drawn behind the graph
1 Grid lines drawn on top of the graph

Manipulating the Chart Control's Data

To manipulate the chart's data, the Chart control provides the `RowIndex` and `ColumnIndex` properties. Imagine that the data to be plotted is stored in a tabular arrangement, with `Rows` rows and `Columns` columns. Each row of data in the table corresponds to one line in a line graph, one color in an area graph, or one set of bars with a common color in a bar graph. Successive data for each row is stored in successive columns. To address a specific data point, you must first set the `RowIndex` and `ColumnIndex` properties of the control. To address the second data point of the fourth data set, use the following statements:

```
Chart1.RowIndex=3      ' 4th row
Chart1.ColumnIndex=1   ' 2nd column
```

To set the value of this point, use the `DataItem` property:

```
Chart1.DataItem=1002
```

In other words, you must first select the data point you want to access and then set its value. To assign values to an entire row (which is a data set), use a loop like the following one:

```
Chart1.RowIndex=3     ' 3rd data set
For i=0 to Chart1.Rows-1
    Chart1.ColumnIndex=i
    Chart1.DataItem=DataPoints
Next
```

You can also set the legends of the chart in a similar way. The `ColumnName` and `RowName` properties are the legends of each dataset and each point along the dataset, respectively. The row names appear along the X axis, and the column names appear in a small box on the graph, as shown in Figure 9.8.

FIGURE 9.8.

The legends on the chart are specified with the `RowName` *and* `ColumnName` *properties.*

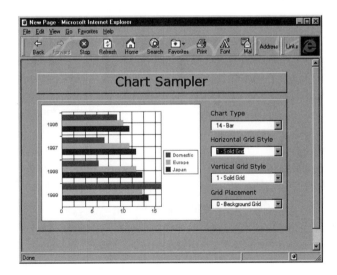

Supplying Data Over the Internet

The URL property of the Chart control lets you specify the data to be plotted with the remaining parameters of the graph in a file, which you can specify by means of its URL. In other words, if you want to post data that changes daily on your Web, you don't have to reprogram your pages. You can just create a file with the new data and have a Chart control on one of your pages request them from the server. This is done with the URL property, which is assigned the URL of the file with the control's data on the server.

The format of this data file is as follows:

The first line describes the ChartType property and contains a number between 0 and 20, as described earlier.

The second line contains an integer, which is the number of rows.

The third line contains another integer, which is the number of columns, followed by the optional column names (separated by tab characters).

The fourth line, and any additional lines beyond the fourth, contains the data for each row. The first element in each of these lines can be the name of the row (optional). Successive data points are separated by tab characters.

The following data file specifies a chart type 9 (stacked area) with 3 rows and 5 columns. The column names are 1996, 1997, 1998, 1999, and 2000. The first row's name (first dataset) is Domestic, the second row's name is Overseas, and the third row's name is Total.

```
9
3
5       1996    1997    1998    1999    2000
Domestic    1234    2242    3342    4434    4954
Overseas    845     1045    1212    1504    2045
Total       2079    3287    4554    5938    6999
```

If you save these lines to a file on the server and assign its name to the Chart control's URL property, the graph described by these values will be plotted automatically. You can also combine this technique with the control's Reload method, which forces the Chart control to read the data again and replot them; you can provide your viewers with graphs based on real-time data. The titles for the graph's columns and rows are optional, and you can omit them. They are used for displaying a legend; a graph can have no legends, legends for one axis only, or legends for both axes.

The Chart Example

Figure 9.9 shows the Chart project, which demonstrates several of the properties of the Chart control. The Chart1 example is simple, but it lets you experiment with the various properties of the control we discussed so far.

FIGURE 9.9.

The Chart document lets you adjust many of the parameters of a graph.

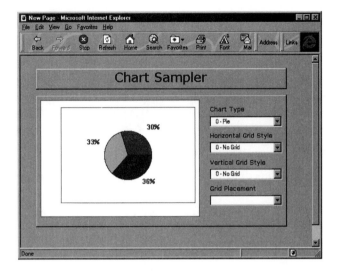

The layout of Figure 9.9 contains a Chart control and four drop-down List controls. Each list contains all the settings for a specific property. The first list controls the type of the graph, the second and third lists control the style of the grid, and the last list controls whether the grid will be drawn in front of or behind the graph. Drop down each list, select a setting, and see how it affects the graph.

Start the ActiveX Control Pad application and create a new layout. To place the Chart control on it, you must add its icon to the toolbox. The Chart control is called Chart Object in the Insert ActiveX control dialog box. Once the Chart control has been placed on the layout, the following definition is inserted in the ALX file. (You can copy this definition and paste it in your own projects.)

```
<OBJECT ID="iechart1"
        CLASSID="CLSID:FC25B780-75BE-11CF-8B01-444553540000"
STYLE="TOP:58pt;LEFT:25pt;WIDTH:256pt;HEIGHT:182pt;ZINDEX:0;"
CODEBASE="http://activex.microsoft.com/controls/iexplorer/
iechart.ocx#Version=4,70,0,1161">
        <PARAM NAME="_ExtentX" VALUE="9022">
        <PARAM NAME="_ExtentY" VALUE="6429">
        <PARAM NAME="Rows" VALUE="4">
        <PARAM NAME="Columns" VALUE="3">
        <PARAM NAME="ChartType" VALUE="8">
        <PARAM NAME="Data[0][0]" VALUE="9">
        <PARAM NAME="Data[0][1]" VALUE="10">
        <PARAM NAME="Data[0][2]" VALUE="11">
        <PARAM NAME="Data[1][0]" VALUE="7">
        <PARAM NAME="Data[1][1]" VALUE="11">
        <PARAM NAME="Data[1][2]" VALUE="12">
        <PARAM NAME="Data[2][0]" VALUE="6">
        <PARAM NAME="Data[2][1]" VALUE="12">
        <PARAM NAME="Data[2][2]" VALUE="13">
```

```
        <PARAM NAME="Data[3][0]" VALUE="11">
        <PARAM NAME="Data[3][1]" VALUE="13">
        <PARAM NAME="Data[3][2]" VALUE="14">
        <PARAM NAME="HorizontalAxis" VALUE="0">
        <PARAM NAME="VerticalAxis" VALUE="0">
        <PARAM NAME="hgridStyle" VALUE="0">
        <PARAM NAME="vgridStyle" VALUE="0">
        <PARAM NAME="ColorScheme" VALUE="0">
        <PARAM NAME="BackStyle" VALUE="1">
        <PARAM NAME="Scale" VALUE="100">
        <PARAM NAME="DisplayLegend" VALUE="1">
        <PARAM NAME="BackColor" VALUE="16777215">
        <PARAM NAME="ForeColor" VALUE="32768">
    </OBJECT>
```

Notice that except for a few standard properties, this definition includes sample data points. The Data array is where all data points are stored. You can edit this definition to change the data or add more data points (and datasets, if you have to). The first index corresponds to the Rows property and the second index to the Columns property.

When the layout is loaded, it populates the drop-down lists and assigns legends to the chart's rows and columns via the RowName and ColumnName property. The actual code of the application, which changes the graph's properties, is quite simple. It picks the property number from the list and assigns it to the appropriate property. The Change event of the first ComboBox control signals that the user has changed the graph's type. Here is the event handler for the event:

```
Sub ComboBox1_Change()
    IEChart1.ChartType=CInt(left(ComboBox1.Text,2))
End Sub
```

Because the Text property of the ComboBox control begins with the setting for the ChartType property, the program isolates this value, converts it to an integer value, and assigns it to the ChartType property of the Chart control.

The complete listing of the Chart project is shown in Listing 9.5.

Listing 9.5. The Chart project.

```
 1: <HTML>
 2: <HEAD>
 3:     <SCRIPT LANGUAGE="VBScript">
 4: <!--
 5: Sub ComboBox1_Change()
 6: IEChart1.ChartType=CInt(left(ComboBox1.Text,2))
 7: end sub
 8:
 9: Sub ComboBox2_Change()
10: IEChart1.HGridStyle=CInt(left(ComboBox2.Text,2))
11: End Sub
12:
```

9

MORE ACTIVEX
CONTROLS

continues

Listing 9.5. continued

```
13: Sub ComboBox3_Change()
14: IEChart1.VGridStyle=CInt(left(ComboBox3.Text,1))
15: End Sub
16:
17: Sub ComboBox4_Change()
18: IEChart1.GridPlacement=CInt(left(ComboBox4.Text,1))
19: end sub
20:
21: Sub Layout1_OnLoad()
22: ComboBox1.AddItem "0 - Pie"
23: ComboBox1.AddItem "2 - Point"
24: ComboBox1.AddItem "5 - Line"
25: ComboBox1.AddItem "8 - Area"
26: ComboBox1.AddItem "11 - Column"
27: ComboBox1.AddItem "14 - Bar"
28: ComboBox1.Text= "8 - Area"
29: ComboBox2.AddItem "0 - No Grid"
30: ComboBox2.AddItem "1 - Solid Grid"
31: ComboBox2.AddItem "2 - Bold Grid"
32: ComboBox2.AddItem "3 - Dotted Grid"
33: ComboBox2.AddItem "4 - Bold Dotted Grid"
34: ComboBox2.Text= "0 - No Grid"
35: ComboBox3.AddItem "0 - No Grid"
36: ComboBox3.AddItem "1 - Solid Grid"
37: ComboBox3.AddItem "2 - Bold Grid"
38: ComboBox3.AddItem "3 - Dotted Grid"
39: ComboBox3.AddItem "4 - Bold Dotted Grid"
40: ComboBox3.Text= "0 - No Grid"
41: ComboBox4.AddItem "0 - Background Grid"
42: ComboBox4.AddItem "1 - Foreground Grid"
43:
44: IEchart1.RowIndex = 0
45: IEchart1.RowName = "1996"
46: IEchart1.RowIndex = 1
47: IEchart1.RowName = "1997"
48: IEchart1.RowIndex = 2
49: IEchart1.RowName = "1998"
50: IEchart1.RowIndex = 3
51: IEchart1.RowName = "1999"
52:
53: IEchart1.ColumnIndex = 0
54: IEchart1.ColumnName = "Domestic"
55: IEchart1.ColumnIndex = 1
56: IEchart1.ColumnName = "Europe"
57: IEchart1.ColumnIndex = 2
58: IEchart1.ColumnName = "Japan"
59:
60: end sub
61: -->
62:     </SCRIPT>
63: </HEAD>
64: <BODY>
65: <CENTER>
66:     <DIV ID="Layout1" STYLE="LAYOUT:FIXED;WIDTH:428pt;HEIGHT:300pt;">
67:         <OBJECT ID="iechart1"
68:          CLASSID="CLSID:FC25B780-75BE-11CF-8B01-444553540000"
             STYLE="TOP:58pt;LEFT:25pt;WIDTH:256pt;HEIGHT:182pt;ZINDEX:0;">
```

```
69:                    <PARAM NAME="_ExtentX" VALUE="9022">
70:                    <PARAM NAME="_ExtentY" VALUE="6429">
71:                    <PARAM NAME="Rows" VALUE="4">
72:                    <PARAM NAME="Columns" VALUE="3">
73:                    <PARAM NAME="ChartType" VALUE="8">
74:                    <PARAM NAME="Data[0][0]" VALUE="9">
75:                    <PARAM NAME="Data[0][1]" VALUE="10">
76:                    <PARAM NAME="Data[0][2]" VALUE="11">
77:                    <PARAM NAME="Data[1][0]" VALUE="7">
78:                    <PARAM NAME="Data[1][1]" VALUE="11">
79:                    <PARAM NAME="Data[1][2]" VALUE="12">
80:                    <PARAM NAME="Data[2][0]" VALUE="6">
81:                    <PARAM NAME="Data[2][1]" VALUE="12">
82:                    <PARAM NAME="Data[2][2]" VALUE="13">
83:                    <PARAM NAME="Data[3][0]" VALUE="16">
84:                    <PARAM NAME="Data[3][1]" VALUE="13">
85:                    <PARAM NAME="Data[3][2]" VALUE="14">
86:                    <PARAM NAME="HorizontalAxis" VALUE="0">
87:                    <PARAM NAME="VerticalAxis" VALUE="0">
88:                    <PARAM NAME="hgridStyle" VALUE="0">
89:                    <PARAM NAME="vgridStyle" VALUE="0">
90:                    <PARAM NAME="ColorScheme" VALUE="0">
91:                    <PARAM NAME="BackStyle" VALUE="1">
92:                    <PARAM NAME="Scale" VALUE="100">
93:                    <PARAM NAME="DisplayLegend" VALUE="0">
94:                    <PARAM NAME="BackColor" VALUE="16777215">
95:                    <PARAM NAME="ForeColor" VALUE="32768">
96:               </OBJECT>
97:               <OBJECT ID="ComboBox1"
98:                CLASSID="CLSID:8BD21D30-EC42-11CE-9E0D-00AA006002F3"
                   STYLE="TOP:83pt;LEFT:297pt;WIDTH:116pt;HEIGHT:17pt;TABINDEX:0;
                   ZINDEX:1;">
99:                    <PARAM NAME="VariousPropertyBits" VALUE="746604571">
100:                   <PARAM NAME="DisplayStyle" VALUE="7">
101:                   <PARAM NAME="Size" VALUE="4092;600">
102:                   <PARAM NAME="MatchEntry" VALUE="1">
103:                   <PARAM NAME="ShowDropButtonWhen" VALUE="2">
104:                   <PARAM NAME="FontCharSet" VALUE="0">
105:                   <PARAM NAME="FontPitchAndFamily" VALUE="2">
106:                   <PARAM NAME="FontWeight" VALUE="0">
107:              </OBJECT>
108:              <OBJECT ID="ComboBox2"
109:               CLASSID="CLSID:8BD21D30-EC42-11CE-9E0D-00AA006002F3"
                  STYLE="TOP:124pt;LEFT:297pt;WIDTH:116pt;HEIGHT:17pt;TABINDEX:1;
                  ZINDEX:2;">
110:                  <PARAM NAME="VariousPropertyBits" VALUE="746604571">
111:                  <PARAM NAME="DisplayStyle" VALUE="7">
112:                  <PARAM NAME="Size" VALUE="4092;600">
113:                  <PARAM NAME="MatchEntry" VALUE="1">
114:                  <PARAM NAME="ShowDropButtonWhen" VALUE="2">
115:                  <PARAM NAME="FontCharSet" VALUE="0">
116:                  <PARAM NAME="FontPitchAndFamily" VALUE="2">
117:                  <PARAM NAME="FontWeight" VALUE="0">
118:              </OBJECT>
119:              <OBJECT ID="ComboBox3"
120:               CLASSID="CLSID:8BD21D30-EC42-11CE-9E0D-00AA006002F3"
                  STYLE="TOP:165pt;LEFT:297pt;WIDTH:116pt;HEIGHT:17pt;TABINDEX:3;
                  ZINDEX:3;">
```

9

**MORE ACTIVEX
CONTROLS**

continues

Listing 9.5. continued

```
121:                    <PARAM NAME="VariousPropertyBits" VALUE="746604571">
122:                    <PARAM NAME="DisplayStyle" VALUE="7">
123:                    <PARAM NAME="Size" VALUE="4092;600">
124:                    <PARAM NAME="MatchEntry" VALUE="1">
125:                    <PARAM NAME="ShowDropButtonWhen" VALUE="2">
126:                    <PARAM NAME="FontCharSet" VALUE="0">
127:                    <PARAM NAME="FontPitchAndFamily" VALUE="2">
128:                    <PARAM NAME="FontWeight" VALUE="0">
129:            </OBJECT>
130:            <OBJECT ID="ComboBox4"
131:             CLASSID="CLSID:8BD21D30-EC42-11CE-9E0D-00AA006002F3"
                 STYLE="TOP:206pt;LEFT:297pt;WIDTH:116pt;HEIGHT:17pt;TABINDEX:2;
                 ZINDEX:4;">
132:                    <PARAM NAME="VariousPropertyBits" VALUE="746604571">
133:                    <PARAM NAME="DisplayStyle" VALUE="7">
134:                    <PARAM NAME="Size" VALUE="4092;600">
135:                    <PARAM NAME="MatchEntry" VALUE="1">
136:                    <PARAM NAME="ShowDropButtonWhen" VALUE="2">
137:                    <PARAM NAME="FontCharSet" VALUE="0">
138:                    <PARAM NAME="FontPitchAndFamily" VALUE="2">
139:                    <PARAM NAME="FontWeight" VALUE="0">
140:            </OBJECT>
141:            <OBJECT ID="Label1"
142:             CLASSID="CLSID:978C9E23-D4B0-11CE-BF2D-00AA003F40D0"
                 STYLE="TOP:66pt;LEFT:297pt;WIDTH:99pt;HEIGHT:17pt;ZINDEX:5;">
143:                    <PARAM NAME="Caption" VALUE="Chart Type">
144:                    <PARAM NAME="Size" VALUE="3493;600">
145:                    <PARAM NAME="FontName" VALUE="Verdana">
146:                    <PARAM NAME="FontHeight" VALUE="200">
147:                    <PARAM NAME="FontCharSet" VALUE="0">
148:                    <PARAM NAME="FontPitchAndFamily" VALUE="2">
149:                    <PARAM NAME="FontWeight" VALUE="0">
150:            </OBJECT>
151:            <OBJECT ID="Label2"
152:             CLASSID="CLSID:978C9E23-D4B0-11CE-BF2D-00AA003F40D0"
                 STYLE="TOP:107pt;LEFT:297pt;WIDTH:116pt;HEIGHT:17pt;ZINDEX:6;">
153:                    <PARAM NAME="Caption" VALUE="Horizontal Grid Style">
154:                    <PARAM NAME="Size" VALUE="4092;600">
155:                    <PARAM NAME="FontName" VALUE="Verdana">
156:                    <PARAM NAME="FontHeight" VALUE="200">
157:                    <PARAM NAME="FontCharSet" VALUE="0">
158:                    <PARAM NAME="FontPitchAndFamily" VALUE="2">
159:                    <PARAM NAME="FontWeight" VALUE="0">
160:            </OBJECT>
161:            <OBJECT ID="Label3"
162:             CLASSID="CLSID:978C9E23-D4B0-11CE-BF2D-00AA003F40D0"
                 STYLE="TOP:149pt;LEFT:297pt;WIDTH:99pt;HEIGHT:17pt;ZINDEX:7;">
163:                    <PARAM NAME="Caption" VALUE="Vertical Grid Style">
164:                    <PARAM NAME="Size" VALUE="3493;600">
165:                    <PARAM NAME="FontName" VALUE="Verdana">
166:                    <PARAM NAME="FontHeight" VALUE="200">
167:                    <PARAM NAME="FontCharSet" VALUE="0">
168:                    <PARAM NAME="FontPitchAndFamily" VALUE="2">
169:                    <PARAM NAME="FontWeight" VALUE="0">
170:            </OBJECT>
171:            <OBJECT ID="Label4"
172:             CLASSID="CLSID:978C9E23-D4B0-11CE-BF2D-00AA003F40D0"
                 STYLE="TOP:190pt;LEFT:297pt;WIDTH:99pt;HEIGHT:17pt;ZINDEX:8;">
```

```
173:                    <PARAM NAME="Caption" VALUE="Grid Placement">
174:                    <PARAM NAME="Size" VALUE="3493;600">
175:                    <PARAM NAME="FontName" VALUE="Verdana">
176:                    <PARAM NAME="FontHeight" VALUE="200">
177:                    <PARAM NAME="FontCharSet" VALUE="0">
178:                    <PARAM NAME="FontPitchAndFamily" VALUE="2">
179:                    <PARAM NAME="FontWeight" VALUE="0">
180:                </OBJECT>
181:                <OBJECT ID="Label5"
182:                 CLASSID="CLSID:978C9E23-D4B0-11CE-BF2D-00AA003F40D0"
                     STYLE="TOP:8pt;LEFT:17pt;WIDTH:404pt;HEIGHT:33pt;ZINDEX:9;">
183:                    <PARAM NAME="Caption" VALUE="Chart Sampler">
184:                    <PARAM NAME="Size" VALUE="14252;1164">
185:                    <PARAM NAME="SpecialEffect" VALUE="1">
186:                    <PARAM NAME="FontName" VALUE="Verdana">
187:                    <PARAM NAME="FontHeight" VALUE="400">
188:                    <PARAM NAME="FontCharSet" VALUE="0">
189:                    <PARAM NAME="FontPitchAndFamily" VALUE="2">
190:                    <PARAM NAME="ParagraphAlign" VALUE="3">
191:                    <PARAM NAME="FontWeight" VALUE="0">
192:                </OBJECT>
193:                <OBJECT ID="Image1"
194:                 CLASSID="CLSID:D4A97620-8E8F-11CF-93CD-00AA00C08FDF"
                     STYLE="TOP:50pt;LEFT:17pt;WIDTH:404pt;HEIGHT:206pt;ZINDEX:10;">
195:                    <PARAM NAME="BorderStyle" VALUE="0">
196:                    <PARAM NAME="SizeMode" VALUE="3">
197:                    <PARAM NAME="SpecialEffect" VALUE="1">
198:                    <PARAM NAME="Size" VALUE="14252;7267">
199:                    <PARAM NAME="PictureAlignment" VALUE="0">
200:                    <PARAM NAME="VariousPropertyBits" VALUE="19">
201:                </OBJECT>
202:        </DIV>
203: </BODY>
204: </HTML>
```

Figure 9.10 shows the ChartURL document, which is a variation on the Chart document. This time we've added a command button that causes the Chart control to read its data and settings from a local file. The file with the data and settings is called CHARTDATA.TXT, and it contains the sample data of the section titled "Supplying Data Over the Internet." When the user clicks this command button, the Chart control reads the data from the CHARTDATA file and updates the graph accordingly. The code behind the Load from File button simply assigns a value to the Chart control's URL property:

```
Sub ComboBox1_Change()
IEChart1.ChartType=CInt(left(ComboBox1.Text,2))
End Sub
```

On the CD you will find the CHARTDATA.TXT file, and you can experiment with it. If you can automate the generation of similar files, you can post graphs with live data on the Web. For example, you can write an application that retrieves numeric data from a database and prepares a file with the information needed by the Chart control to graph the data, including the headings. And as you probably know, it takes much less space to store a few dozen numbers than it takes to store the image of the graph that corresponds to these data.

FIGURE 9.10.

*The ChartURL
document can read its
data and settings from
a local file or a URL.*

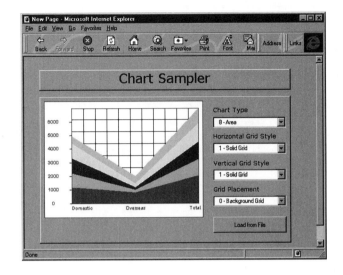

Review

The Chart control is the last of the new ActiveX controls we are going to cover in this book. If you are using some visual programming tools in the Windows environment, you have realized that the ActiveX controls are nothing more than the regular OLE controls that make up the Windows user interface. You are probably wondering whether you should attempt to use the OLE controls already installed on your system. Most of the OLE controls can be used, and we'll look at a few of them in the last part of the book. However, they are not ActiveX controls and the viewers will get a warning every time they open a page that contains old OLE controls (implemented in OCX files). You can use the existing OLE controls on your pages in an intranet environment, and you are going to find interesting examples in the last section of this book.

The ActiveX controls released by Microsoft after the release of Internet Explorer 3.0 and the ActiveX Control Pad are posted at Microsoft's ActiveX Component Gallery at www. microsoft.com/activex/controls. The ActiveX Gallery is the site to visit when you need an ActiveX control for your projects. You will find there a list of all available ActiveX controls from Microsoft and other companies, descriptions of the controls, and the actual controls. Microsoft's ActiveX controls are free, but most of the other ActiveX controls aren't—and you should read the documentation and distribution notes before you download and use them.

IN THIS PART

PART

Advanced VBScript

Error Handling

by Craig Eddy

IN THIS CHAPTER

It seems no matter how hard you try to avoid them, errors are inevitable in any program. Even if your application is coded perfectly, those pesky users always will discover some idiosyncrasy in the application that you never even dreamed possible. Fortunately, because your VBScript applications typically are hosted by the Internet Explorer, the system damage that errors (user- or code-induced) can cause is minimal.

On the other hand, an error that occurs within a VBScript page more than likely will cause the entire page to malfunction. This is akin to an untrapped runtime error in a Visual Basic application. In this case, the user sees a message box describing (to some extent) the error that occurred, and then the user is summarily thrown out of the application. In a VBScript Web page, if an untrapped error occurs, a similar message box is presented to the user.

Although it's impossible to eliminate every error, this chapter describes some methods for coding your VBScript applications that should help avoid most coding errors. It also covers that extremely important part of coding: error handling. In the "Looking at Examples of Error Handling" section later in this chapter, you'll learn how to trap runtime errors in your scripts. The chapter concludes with some scripts that provide examples of error handling.

Because error handling and debugging go hand in hand, you will see some overlap with Chapter 12, "Debugging." Although both chapters look at error handling, they explore different approaches. This chapter emphasizes error handling exclusively, while Chapter 12 looks at error handling as a component of the larger debugging problem.

Handling Errors in Your VBScript Pages

When your VBScript code runs within the Internet Explorer, you can be pretty certain that errors won't have a grievous effect on the user's system. Internet Explorer and the current limits within VBScript code confine the damage your code can do to the user's computer.

The same might not be true, however, of ActiveX components you might use within your Web pages. Because users have to retrieve any ActiveX controls used on your pages, you must ensure that you're using these controls properly. Also, you should feel good about the controls themselves—that they don't contain viruses and that they can't harm your users' systems in any way. As a Web page designer, you have a responsibility to those who will be viewing your pages to make sure that no damage can be done to their systems or to the files on their systems.

This section looks at some of the possible errors that might crop up within your VBScript code. It discusses syntax errors, errors with ActiveX controls, and general runtime errors. The next section, "Coding to Avoid Errors," presents ways to avoid these common errors.

Syntax Errors

Unlike the Visual Basic development environment, there is no syntax checker for VBScript code. If you enter your VBScript code using Notepad or the Microsoft ActiveX Control Pad, you'll have to make sure that there are no syntax errors within your script code. You also can use the Visual Basic development environment to enter your script code and then cut and paste it into your HTML pages. This might be preferable if you have a lot of code, but usually is more trouble than it's worth.

If syntax errors are present within your scripts, Internet Explorer displays a syntax error dialog, such as the one shown in Figure 10.1.

FIGURE 10.1.

A syntax error displayed in Internet Explorer.

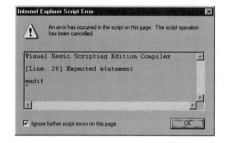

You can specify whether other errors in the script should be ignored by enabling the Ignore further script errors on this page checkbox at the bottom of the dialog. By disabling the checkbox, you're informing the script compiler that it should continue parsing the script code and inform you of additional errors. In the version of Internet Explorer I had at the time of this writing (IE 3.0 beta 2), however, this feature did not seem to work.

Typical syntax errors include misspellings and combining two words into one, such as "endif" instead of "end if." I run into this one all the time, because I'm used to Visual Basic replacing my typing of "endif" with the correct "end if." The easy way around this error is to run a search-and-replace operation before saving your code.

You also can cause syntax errors by misplacing or mismatching operators within an expression. For example, the code

```
MsgBox "Hello " & txtName.Text &
```

causes a syntax error, because the VBScript compiler is expecting something to follow the last ampersand.

> **WARNING**
>
> Because the VBScript compiler ignores white space (such as space characters and carriage returns), a syntax error generated by "hanging" operators is flagged on the line following the offending line.

Another common source of syntax errors is leaving the Then off of an If...Then expression. This typically is done by those of us who also code SQL Server Transact-SQL procedures, which don't use Then. This particular syntax error also is flagged on the line following the If, but the dialog at least tells you that the Then is missing.

Errors with ActiveX Controls

VBScript lets you embed ActiveX (formerly OLE) controls within your Web pages. These ActiveX controls operate just like custom controls in Visual Basic applications: They have properties that can be set, methods that can be invoked, and events that can fire based on user interaction within your page. Because you have programmatic access to all these features within your VBScript code, you also have the potential to cause a lot of errors if you use the controls improperly. This section discusses a few possible errors to watch out for.

The most common error results from incorrectly coding the <OBJECT> HTML tag used to insert an ActiveX control into the Web page. Because this tag contains many of its own elements, such as CODEBASE and ID, along with elements for the properties of the ActiveX control, it is very easy to mistype a setting or leave an important setting off all together.

The <OBJECT> tag also requires that you specify the globally unique class identifier for the control in the CLASSID element. The *globally unique identifier* (GUID) is a unique alphanumeric string assigned to OLE controls when they are created. It not only identifies the control but also makes sure that the correct version of the control is being used. A typical GUID looks like this:

```
0BA686AA-F7D3-101A-993E-0000C0EF6F5E
```

This string must be entered for each ActiveX control you place on your Web page. Of course, if you mistype any character within the class ID, you're not going to get the ActiveX control you intended. Fortunately, the ActiveX Control Pad, discussed in the next section, inserts the GUID and control properties into your HTML code for you.

It also is possible to create runtime errors when using ActiveX controls. This happens when you assign an invalid value to a control property, for example. When using an ActiveX control within your VBScript code, make sure that you understand the properties and methods you're using. This helps you avoid many common runtime errors. Fortunately, most controls you'll use are published by commercial software vendors who almost always provide adequate documentation.

Runtime Errors

Unlike syntax errors, runtime errors do not occur until your VBScript code executes. These errors, unless they are trapped by your code, cause the script to halt after the error dialog appears.

Runtime errors can result not only from mistakes within your code but also from user interaction. The most common cause of this occurs when using data the user has entered into a control on the Web page. If you have a standard text box for entry of a numeric value, for example, the user may enter any alphanumeric character. If you then attempt to use this value as-is with a function or procedure that expects a numeric parameter, a runtime error results.

The section "Coding to Handle Errors," later in this chapter, discusses how to write your VBScript code to properly handle runtime errors.

Coding to Avoid Errors

Although it is nearly impossible to avoid all runtime errors, there are some steps you can take when writing VBScript code to minimize the number that slip through the cracks. This section highlights a few of the pointers I've uncovered while creating scripts.

The famous Save Often commandment is missing, however, because you currently *always* have to save the HTML pages containing VBScript before you can open them in Internet Explorer. Hopefully, Microsoft will soon release a version of Internet Explorer that enables you to edit and debug VBScript code. VBScript code editing is planned for the Internet Studio, but I'm not aware of that product including any debugging tools.

Using the ActiveX Control Pad

For the moment, the best tool available for coding VBScript applications is Microsoft's ActiveX Control Pad. You can download this tool from Microsoft's SiteBuilder Web site. At the time of this writing, the URL for the download page is

```
http://www.microsoft.com/workshop/author/cpad/download.htm
```

If you haven't already downloaded this tool, I highly recommend doing so.

This section discusses a few of the features of the Control Pad and illustrates how these features help you avoid many of the common VBScript coding errors. The Control Pad is covered in depth in Chapter 8, "The ActiveX Control Pad." Here I cover it only enough for a demonstration of error handling. Read Chapter 8 for complete coverage of the Control Pad.

10

ERROR HANDLING

Examining the ActiveX Control Pad

The ActiveX Control Pad has been jokingly referred to as *Visual N++* or *Visual Notepad*, because it strongly resembles the Notepad application, but with a toolbar and a few extra visual elements. Figure 10.2 shows the initial screen of the Control Pad. Although it might resemble Notepad on the surface, it has a lot of power under the hood.

FIGURE 10.2.

The ActiveX Control Pad's opening screen.

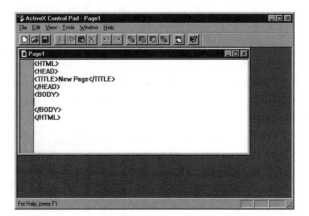

As you can see in Figure 10.2, when the Control Pad starts a new HTML file, it already has entered the standard HTML wrapper codes. This enables you to quickly start creating the HTML and VBScript code specific to the page you are creating.

The Control Pad functions just like Notepad. You can type in the open window, use the text-editing features (Cut, Copy, and Paste), print the file, and save and open other files. Unlike Notepad, the Control Pad sports a toolbar and a multiple document interface that enables you to open multiple HTML files at the same time.

Using ActiveX Controls

The most useful feature of the Control Pad is its capability to insert all the necessary HTML code for an ActiveX control. You even can edit the properties of a specific control that has been inserted into your page, by using an interface similar to the Visual Basic Properties dialog.

To insert an ActiveX control onto your page, follow these steps:

1. Position the cursor at the point where you want to insert the control.
2. Choose Edit | Insert ActiveX Control. The Insert ActiveX Control dialog appears.
3. Select the desired control in the Control Type list and click the OK button. Two windows appear: the Edit ActiveX Control window and the Properties window. (See Figure 10.3.)

FIGURE 10.3.
Editing ActiveX controls in the Control Pad.

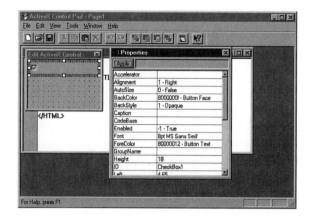

4. Use the Edit ActiveX Control window to size the control. Use the Properties window to edit any other properties as necessary. The Properties window provides popup dialogs for font and color properties, as well as drop-down listboxes for enumerated properties such as Alignment.

5. After you finish editing the control, close the two windows by clicking their Close buttons (the box with the X at the right of the title bar). The HTML code matching the control and its properties is inserted into the page, as shown in Figure 10.4.

After you insert the control into your page, you might need to edit some of its properties. You can do this by directly modifying the text associated with the PARAM elements of the control's <OBJECT> tag. This requires that you know the proper settings for the properties you're modifying, however. Fortunately, you also can return to the Properties window by clicking the button next to the <OBJECT> tag. This button is in the left margin of the ActiveX edit window and has a picture of a cube.

FIGURE 10.4.
HTML code for an ActiveX control.

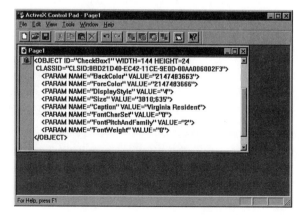

A quick way to insert a copy of the same control is to select everything from the <OBJECT> tag to the </OBJECT> ending tag. Then choose Edit | Copy, place the cursor at the location for the new copy of the control, and choose Edit | Paste. Then be sure to change the ID element of the <OBJECT> tag to a unique name, because VBScript does not support control arrays.

Editing VBScript Code

The ActiveX Control Pad's script-editing features are even more powerful than its control property-editing features. The Control Pad has a Script Wizard that enables you to enter and edit code in a manner similar to code entry with Visual Basic, but with a slightly different interface, as shown in Figure 10.5.

FIGURE 10.5.

The ActiveX Control Pad's Script Wizard.

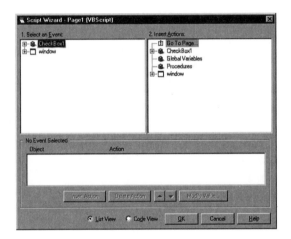

To open the Script Wizard, choose Tools | Script Wizard or click the Script Wizard toolbar button (the one with the picture of an unfurled scroll). The Script Wizard operates in an application modal window. This means that you cannot do anything else in the Control Pad while the Script Wizard is active.

To select which event you want to write script code for, use the tree control at the top left of the Script Wizard. Clicking the box with the plus sign (+) displays a list of the available events for the selected object. Then simply select the event of interest by clicking it.

At the top right of the window is a tree list labeled Insert Actions. This list is similar to Visual Basic's object browser, because it lists all the available controls and their properties, as well as everything available in the Internet Explorer's window object. It also lists any global variables and procedures that have been created in the page's script. To insert an item, select it in the list and double-click it.

Code is actually entered into the script at the bottom of the window. As you can see in Figure 10.6, there are two possible views for this area: List View and Code View. *List View* enables you to view the script in a high-level, more English-like manner. *Code View* is similar to Visual Basic's Code View. You'll probably use Code View more often than List View because it gives you much more flexibility in entering VBScript code.

The easiest way to learn how to use the Script Wizard is to "just do it." Enter some controls onto your page and open the Script Wizard. Select an event from the Event list, and then select Code View and enter some code for that event. Use the Insert Actions list to quickly insert references to properties and other objects.

After you insert a <SCRIPT> tag, either manually or by using the Script Wizard, a Script Wizard button appears next to it. This button appears in the left margin of the Control Pad's editor window. Clicking it takes you to the Script Wizard.

Using Option Explicit

Probably the worst type of error to track down is the improper naming of a variable. If your fingers, like mine, tend to be dyslexic, you probably find yourself constantly swapping letters as you type. Often, I don't even notice that I've done this. When my code runs with such a mistake in it, it never seems to work quite right. It's not until I discover the misspelled variable name that the code works properly.

To avoid such problems, use the Option Explicit directive. This forces you to declare every variable used within your script code. This way, when you misspell a variable, it is flagged as an undefined variable when your script executes. Figure 10.6 shows an example of the dialog displayed.

FIGURE 10.6.

The Undefined Variable Error dialog.

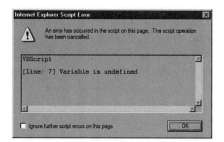

WARNING

The Script Wizard often breaks up your scripts into several parts within the HTML page. You must have an Option Explicit directive within each <SCRIPT> ... </SCRIPT> pair. If you omit the Option Explicit directive, you may not catch a misspelled variable name in that section.

Using Coding Conventions

Another technique that can help you avoid errors is to use a coding convention. Coding conventions help you write code that is easily readable and understandable. As you'll see, they also keep you on your toes when naming and using variables.

The most important coding convention involves naming conventions for variables. The convention I tend to use is a single-character prefix that represents the data type of each variable. Microsoft, on its VBScript Web site, recommends a three-character prefix. The extra characters are necessary to uniquely identify each of the possible data types available in VBScript. I typically only use a few of these data types in my coding, so the one-character prefix is fine for me. Table 10.1 lists the Microsoft-recommended prefixes.

Table 10.1. Microsoft's recommended variable name prefixes.

Data type	*Prefix*	*Example*
Boolean	bln	blnStateResident
Byte	byt	bytCharacter
Date/Time	dtm	dtmStartDate
Double	dbl	dblProductCost
Error	err	errFileError
Integer	int	intQuantity
Long	lng	lngCount
Object	obj	objWordDoc
Single	sng	sngAverage
String	str	strFileName

Microsoft also recommends a naming convention for naming ActiveX objects you insert into your Web pages. Table 10.2 lists these prefixes.

Table 10.2. Microsoft's recommended ActiveX object-naming prefixes.

Object type	*Prefix*	*Example*
3-D panel	pnl	pnlStatus
Animated button	ani	aniStateButton
Checkbox	chk	chkResident
Combobox	cbo	cboContactType

Object type	Prefix	Example
Command button	cmd	cmdSubmit
Common dialog	dlg	dlgFiles
Frame	fra	fraGrouping
Horizontal scrollbar	hsb	hsbBrightness
Image	img	imgContactPicture
Label	lbl	lblFormLabel
Listbox	lst	lstNames
Slider	sld	sldScale
Spin	spn	spnValue
Text box	txt	txtLastName
Vertical scrollbar	vsb	vsbHeight

Coding to Handle Errors

Despite the best efforts of any programmer, errors still can occur, even in flawless code. These errors can result from any number of causes. The preceding section described how to structure your VBScript code in order to avoid as many errors as possible. In this section, you learn how to handle runtime errors.

Runtime errors occur, obviously, when your script is being executed by the host application. In the case of Internet Explorer, runtime errors that aren't trapped within your script cause the Internet Explorer Script Error dialog to be displayed. Figure 10.7 provides an example of such an Error dialog.

This section describes the two VBScript features provided for handling errors in your scripts. The first section describes how you can specify the actions taken when a runtime error occurs. The second section describes the Err object, which provides information about the error that occurred. The properties and methods of the Err object are described here, including the masochistic method Raise, which enables you to create a runtime error within your script. Examples of error handling are provided in this section.

Specifying Error Trapping

In order to trap runtime errors within your script, you must inform the script host (such as Internet Explorer) that you want to do so. You do this by using the On Error statement.

The current syntax for this statement is actually a subset of the Visual Basic On Error statement. In VBScript, there is no support for any construction other than On Error Resume Next or On Error Goto 0. This means that there is no support for a centralized error-handling mechanism that typically is found in most applications. I suppose that this is because of the lack of labels within script code; you cannot specify On Error Goto ErrorLabel, for example.

To trap errors, you first specify On Error Resume Next. Then, after each line of script code for which errors are possible, you must check the value of the Err object to see whether it's greater than zero. The following snippet of script code shows an example:

```
On Error Resume Next
MsgBox Left("The Quick Brown Fox", intCount)
If Err > 0 Then MsgBox "Error: " + Err.Description
```

If the value of intCount is less than 0 when the second line is executed, an error condition occurs. If errors aren't being trapped, a message box is displayed and the script's execution ends at that point. Because the script is handling errors, however, a message box is displayed and the code continues execution.

Any error trapping becomes inactive when another procedure is called, so you should place an On Error Resume Next statement in each procedure if you want to include error trapping within that procedure.

To turn off error trapping and allow the script's host application to decide how to handle any runtime errors, use the statement On Error Goto 0. This opens your script up to the possibility that a runtime error will halt its execution, however.

Using the Err Object

When an error occurs (from a runtime error, an OLE object, or the Raise method executing), the Err object is used to interpret the cause and context of the error condition. The Err object always is available to your scripts and is global in scope.

The generator of the runtime error is responsible for setting the Err object's properties before raising the error condition. The only property required is the Number property. The other properties are optional.

This section describes the properties and methods available with the Err object.

The Err Object's Properties

The Err object has several properties that help describe the error that occurred, as well as the source of the error. This section describes those properties.

Number Property

The `Number` property is the default property for the `Err` object. This means that the following two lines of code are identical:

```
If Err.Number > 0 Then
If Err > 0 Then
```

The `Number` property specifies the error number assigned to the error that occurred. When you are using the `Raise` method to generate a runtime error, add the constant `vbObjectError` to your error number in the `Raise` method's `Number` parameter.

In your script, you should check the `Number` property (explicitly or by simply using `Err`) against any known error numbers relevant to the code that caused the error. If you're using the Microsoft Common Dialog control within your Web page, for example, and the user clicks the Cancel button, the `Err` value is 32755 (assuming that you have set the common dialog's `CancelError` property to 1). The following code illustrates trapping this error:

```
Sub Button1_onClick()
On error resume next
CommonDialog1.CancelError = 1
CommonDialog1.Action = 1
If Err = 32755 Then Msgbox "Cancelled!"
end sub
```

Description Property

The `Description` property provides a human-readable description of the error that occurred. This short description can and should be displayed to the user, especially if the error was a result of user interaction. In this case, the user probably can correct the mistake that generated the error.

Source Property

This property is a string that provides the name of the object or application that caused the error condition to be raised. This string can be displayed to the user, but it's not as useful as the `Description` property.

If an OLE object generated the error, the `Source` property typically is in the form *project.class*.

HelpFile and HelpContext Properties

When the `HelpFile` property is specified by the generator of the runtime error, it should be set to the fully qualified filename of a valid Windows Help file. If the user presses the F1 key when the error dialog is open, the Help file specified is opened. The `HelpContext` property defines a valid context ID for a topic within the Help file. This topic should be specific to the error that was generated.

The Err Object's Methods

Like all useful objects, the Err object also has a few methods that enable you to control the behavior of the object. Methods are invoked in a manner similar to calling a procedure, but without the Call keyword. To invoke one of an object's method, you simply code *object.method* [*parameter_list*], where the optional *parameter_list* specifies the parameters that may be required by the method.

The Err object provides two methods: Clear and Raise. These are discussed in the following sections.

The Clear Method

The Clear method is used to clear all the properties of the Err object. The method takes no parameters and is invoked using Err.Clear.

You need to invoke the Clear method whenever you have trapped a runtime error and your script will continue execution. If you don't execute a Clear, the next time you check for an error condition, the Err object's properties still will contain the values from the previous error condition.

For example, the following code can cause problems:

```
On Error Resume Next
MyObject.InvokeMethod
If Err > 0 then MsgBox Err.Number & ": " &  Err.Description
MyObject.InvokeAnotherMethod
If Err > 0 then MsgBox Err.Number & ": " &  Err.Description
```

If MyObject.InvokeMethod caused a runtime error, the values of the Err object are set accordingly, and the first If Err > 0 Then statement is executed, displaying a message box. However, the second If Err > 0 Then also appears, regardless of whether MyObject.InvokeMethod caused a runtime error. Of course, because the Err object is global, it is possible that MyObject.InvokeMethod might execute the Err.Clear method, but it's better to be certain. The following code is more graceful:

```
On Error Resume Next
MyObject.InvokeMethod
If Err > 0 then
   MsgBox Err.Number & ": " &  Err.Description
   Err.Clear
End If
MyObject.InvokeAnotherMethod
If Err > 0 then
   MsgBox Err.Number & ": " &  Err.Description
   Err.Clear
End If
```

> **TIP**
>
> Notice that I used the ampersand (&) to concatenate the strings in the `MsgBox` calls. This behaves differently than the plus sign (+) because it causes the VBScript compiler to convert the expressions on both sides of the ampersand to strings. The plus sign does not perform this datatype conversion, so you have to use the `CStr` function to convert the expressions to strings.

The Raise Method

The `Raise` method enables you to create runtime errors within your scripts. This method really is designed to allow ActiveX component developers to create a runtime error condition within their component's code. These then are trapped by the script, as described in the section "Specifying Error Trapping," earlier in this chapter. Because the `Err` object is a generic object, however, the `Raise` method also can be used in VBScript code. One of the examples presented later in the chapter (in the section titled "Using the `Raise` Method") demonstrates using the `Raise` method in a subroutine to immediately cause an error condition.

The `Raise` method is invoked with this code:

```
Err.Raise number[,source[, description[, helpfile[, helpcontext]]]]
```

The values specified as parameters will be assigned to the respective properties of the `Err` object. The *number* parameter is the error number to be raised. The *source* parameter is a string that specifies the process that generated the error. In Internet Explorer, if this parameter is left empty, the `Err.Source` property value is `VBScript`. The *description* is a string describing the error condition. The *helpfile* and *helpcontext* parameters generally aren't used within VBScript code, but they specify the name of a *local* Help file and a context ID within that Help file. The specified Help file is displayed if the user presses F1 from within the default VBScript Error dialog.

The only required argument is *number*. If you don't specify the other values, however, the `Err` object's properties retain the values that were present in the object when you invoked the `Raise` method. You can use the `Clear` method described earlier to clear these properties before invoking the `Raise` method.

Looking at Examples of Error Handling

This section provides two sample VBScript pages. The first demonstrates the handling of runtime errors within a script. It uses the `On Error Resume Next` statement described earlier to trap runtime errors. The second example illustrates the use of the Err object's Raise method to programmatically create runtime errors. Although this might seem like a sadistic action for a programmer to take, the example presented shows how doing so in subroutines actually can be useful.

Trapping Runtime Errors

This example demonstrates how to use the On Error Resume Next statement to trap runtime errors. Listing 10.1 shows the HTML code for the sample page. This section discusses what's going on in the VBScript code as it relates to error trapping.

Listing 10.1. HTML for the runtime error-trapping example.

```
<HTML>
<HEAD>
<SCRIPT LANGUAGE="VBScript">
<!--
Option Explicit

Sub window_onLoad()
Dim intTemp
On error resume next

intTemp = -1
MsgBox Left("Quick Brown Fox", cint(intTemp))
if Err then
    MsgBox "Error: " & Err.description
    Err.clear
end if

intTemp = 5
MsgBox Left("Quick Brown Fox", cint(intTemp))
if Err then
    MsgBox "Error: " & Err.description
    Err.clear
else
    MsgBox "No error occurred!"
end if
end sub
-->
</SCRIPT>
<TITLE>Test Page</TITLE>
</HEAD>
<BODY>
</BODY>
</HTML>
```

Starting with the first <SCRIPT> tag, the first line of VBScript code (following the start of the HTML comment), is the Option Explicit directive, discussed earlier in this chapter. This prevents you from using a variable without declaring it first. You then come to the definition of the onLoad event for the main window. This is where all the code for this example is executed.

The first line of code within this event defines a variable named `intTemp`. This is followed by the `On Error Resume Next` statement. Then the value –1 is assigned to the `intTemp` variable, and the code attempts to use this variable as a parameter for the `Left()` function. Because the expression `Left(string, -1)` is invalid, a runtime error is produced. The next line of code following the `MsgBox` statement is where you check for the occurrence of a runtime error. The statement `If Err then` is equivalent to `If Err.value > 0 then`, so any value other than 0 in the `Err` object's `value` property causes this statement to evaluate to `True`.

A message box then is displayed, showing a description of the error. The `Err` object then is cleared using the `Clear` method. This ensures that any other references to the `Err` object's properties don't inadvertently use old property values.

After `end if`, the value of `intTemp` is set to 5. The same `MsgBox` statement is attempted again. This time, however, a valid value is passed to the `Left()` function, and no runtime error occurs. The `Else` portion of the code is executed and a box with the `No error occurred!` message is displayed.

Enter the HTML into the Control Pad or Notepad, save it to a file, and then open the file with the Internet Explorer. You should see a total of three message boxes: one for the runtime error, one with the message `Quick`, and the final one with the message `No error occurred!`

Using the Raise Method

The final example of this chapter illustrates how you can use the `Raise` method within your VBScript code. Although this method might not always be the best way to control the flow of your code, it can prove useful at times. Listing 10.2 contains the HTML code for this example.

Listing 10.2. HTML for the Raise method example.

```
<HTML>
<HEAD>
<SCRIPT LANGUAGE="VBScript">
<!--
Option Explicit

Sub TestRaise(blnRaiseError)
if blnRaiseError then
   Err.Raise 9000, "TestRaise", "Error from TestRaise"
end if
MsgBox "Error not called for"

end sub

Sub window_onLoad()
on error resume next

call TestRaise(1)
if Err then
   MsgBox "Error occurred: " & Err.description
```

continues

10

ERROR HANDLING

Listing 10.2. continued

```
    Err.clear
end if

call TestRaise(0)
if Err then
    MsgBox "Error occurred: " & Err.description
    Err.clear
end if
end sub
-->
</SCRIPT>
<TITLE>Testing Raise Method</TITLE>
</HEAD>
<BODY>
</BODY>
</HTML>
```

This code is very simple. The procedure TestRaise takes a single parameter, blnRaiseError. If this variable's value is greater than 0, the Raise method is invoked with some hard-coded values. This causes the procedure to immediately exit back to the calling routine. If the value is 0, a message box is displayed.

The code for the onLoad event of the main window is where you call the TestError procedure. The On Error Resume Next statement is used to trap the errors. Then TestError is called with a parameter of 1. This causes the Raise method to be invoked and the If Err then block to be entered, displaying the appropriate message box.

The code then calls TestError again, but this time with a parameter of 0. The Raise method is not invoked and the message box within the TestError procedure is displayed. No error condition exists, so when execution returns to the onLoad event, no error message box is displayed.

After this page is loaded into Internet Explorer, you see two message boxes. The first is the error message dialog stating that Error occurred: Error from TestRaise. The second is the message box within TestRaise that states Error not called for.

Review

This chapter covered the basics of error handling within VBScript code. The best way to experience how errors are handled within a particular host application (such as Internet Explorer) is to experiment with error-handling code, such as that provided in Listings 10.1 and 10.2.

From this chapter, you move on to learn how to optimize your VBScript code and then debug your code and create dynamic Web pages. By the time you finish reading this part of the book, you'll have more than enough background to proceed through the final two parts of the book.

Optimizing Code

by Bill Schongar and Paul Lagasse

IN THIS CHAPTER

CHAPTER 11

Let your VBScript code be the best it can be. No, you don't send it into the armed forces; instead, you send it to VBScript boot camp. Teach your code some discipline, make it work as part of a team, and turn out code that you can depend on to do the job you set it to, and do it right the first time. You're already starting out with good material; you just have to make it as suitable as possible for your needs.

Optimizing VBScript isn't a daunting task; it's just a combination of a dash of common sense, along with a hefty dose of what's best in your situation. Unlike its bigger cousins, Visual Basic and Visual Basic for Applications, VBScript doesn't have a lot of room for gray areas about what will make it faster, slower, or better. The subset of functionality limits the extent that you can "tweak" code, but it does present a couple of new things to consider.

This chapter takes a look at what kinds of things you can do to make your VBScript application run a little better and speed up your development cycle. This includes

- Organizing your code
- Use of functions and syntax
- Development tools

If you're already a Visual Basic guru, much of the stuff you'll see here will be pretty familiar, and you might even have your own special tricks you want to add in your own development. If you've never touched Visual Basic before, don't worry. Everything in this chapter is first and foremost aimed right at you, to give you the edge you need to make great, clean code.

Organizing Your Code

There's a lot to be said for being able to read your own writing, and the same holds true for code. HTML pages in and of themselves can often be a mess, and when you add source code for a program, it gets to be a little bit chaotic. That can either work for or against you, depending on what you have in mind.

Chaos Theory 101

One of the wonders of embedded scripting is that what you write is out there for everyone to see. All your functions, all your tricks, and all your work and source code are just one download away from just about everyone's view. Like a business interview, what you present in that first impression may give people an impression (accurate or not) of the quality of your code. If it sprawls all over the HTML source, they'll just be glad it works. If, on the other hand, the code is cleanly spaced out and thoroughly commented, it shows a sense of organization.

Keeping code orderly is an easy task as long as you start at the beginning. Record why you used particular functions, so that if you have to fix a problem or change the code later you'll be ready to make the changes without trying to decipher possibly cryptic entries. Don't go overboard, though! Remember that anything you type has to get downloaded by the end user, and they don't appreciate several hundred lines of comments taking up download time on every page.

Code Behind the Scenes

If you'd like to make folks work a little harder to see your source code or are just more organized by nature, there are options available to you. The most complex would be to roll all your VBScript code into an ActiveX control, and make people download it if they want to use your code. Since that kind of defeats the purpose of using VBScript in the first place and brings a whole new level of programming complexity into the mix, you'll probably want to avoid that route.

A much more efficient and convenient method is to take advantage of Microsoft's HTML Layout files (.ALX files). These are files that combine all the ActiveX control tags and assorted details so that they don't show up on the main page. This gives you two benefits: First and foremost, it gives you a separate file in which to organize the VBScript portion of your HTML file. If you're using repetitive code (on forms validation as an example), you may not want the same information cut and pasted into every HTML file. If you update the ALX file once, any HTML page that references it will automatically get the update.

To show what kind of difference this makes in readability, Listing 11.1 shows a small HTML page with VBScript embedded in it, while Listings 11.2 and 11.3 show the same HTML page with a Layout control object and its associated ALX files. The more complex the script, the better off you are removing it from the HTML page. Once you start using ActiveX controls, it's almost impossible to do much without going this route.

Listing 11.1. HTML and VBScript in one page.

```
<HTML>
<HEAD>
<TITLE>New Page</TITLE>
</HEAD>
<BODY>

    <SCRIPT LANGUAGE="VBScript">
<!--

Dim Index
Dim Caption(5)

Caption(1) = "See the Caption has changed"
Caption(2) = "Of Course you could do a lot more"
Caption(3) = "With this type of control structure"
Caption(4) = "Like Moving the text across the screen"
Caption(5) = "And allow the user to set the speed"

Sub IeTimer1_Timer()
```

continues

Listing 11.1. continued

```
Index = Index + 1
If Index = 6 then Index = 1

IeLabel1.Caption = Caption(Index)
end sub
-->
    </SCRIPT>

    <OBJECT ID="IeTimer1" WIDTH=39 HEIGHT=39
     CLASSID="CLSID:59CCB4A0-727D-11CF-AC36-00AA00A47DD2">
        <PARAM NAME="_ExtentX" VALUE="1005">
        <PARAM NAME="_ExtentY" VALUE="1005">
        <PARAM NAME="Interval" VALUE="2000">
    </OBJECT>
    <OBJECT ID="IeLabel1" WIDTH=368 HEIGHT=27
     CLASSID="CLSID:99B42120-6EC7-11CF-A6C7-00AA00A47DD2">
        <PARAM NAME="_ExtentX" VALUE="9737">
        <PARAM NAME="_ExtentY" VALUE="714">
        <PARAM NAME="Caption" VALUE="This text will change at regular intervals">
        <PARAM NAME="Angle" VALUE="0">
        <PARAM NAME="Alignment" VALUE="4">
        <PARAM NAME="Mode" VALUE="1">
        <PARAM NAME="FillStyle" VALUE="0">
        <PARAM NAME="FillStyle" VALUE="1">
        <PARAM NAME="ForeColor" VALUE="#E8FD00">
        <PARAM NAME="BackColor" VALUE="#000000">
        <PARAM NAME="FontName" VALUE="Arial">
        <PARAM NAME="FontSize" VALUE="12">
        <PARAM NAME="FontItalic" VALUE="0">
        <PARAM NAME="FontBold" VALUE="0">
        <PARAM NAME="FontUnderline" VALUE="0">
        <PARAM NAME="FontStrikeout" VALUE="0">
        <PARAM NAME="TopPoints" VALUE="0">
        <PARAM NAME="BotPoints" VALUE="0">
    </OBJECT>

</BODY>
</HTML>
```

Listing 11.2. HTML page with the Layout control.

```
<HTML>
<HEAD>
<TITLE>New Page</TITLE>
</HEAD>
<BODY>

<OBJECT CLASSID="CLSID:812AE312-8B8E-11CF-93C8-00AA00C08FDF"
ID="sample2_ALX" STYLE="LEFT:0;TOP:0">
<PARAM NAME="ALXPATH" REF VALUE="file:J:\temp\sample2.ALX">
 </OBJECT>

</BODY>
</HTML>
```

Listing 11.3. ALX file containing VBScript.

```
<SCRIPT LANGUAGE="VBScript">
<!--
dim Index

dim Caption(5)

Sub IeTimer1_Timer()

Index = Index + 1

If Index = 6 Then Index = 1

IeLabel1.Caption = Caption(Index)

end sub
-->
</SCRIPT>
<SCRIPT LANGUAGE="VBScript">
<!--
Sub Layout1_OnLoad()

Caption(1) = "See the Caption has changed"
Caption(2) = "Of Course you could do a lot more"
Caption(3) = "With this type of control structure"
Caption(4) = "Like Moving the text across the screen"
Caption(5) = "And allow the user to set the speed"
end sub
-->
</SCRIPT>
<DIV ID="Layout1" STYLE="LAYOUT:FIXED;WIDTH:389pt;HEIGHT:26pt;">
    <OBJECT ID="IeLabel1"
     CLASSID="CLSID:99B42120-6EC7-11CF-A6C7-00AA00A47DD2"
    ➥STYLE="TOP:0pt;LEFT:41pt;WIDTH:281pt;HEIGHT:17pt;ZINDEX:0;">
        <PARAM NAME="_ExtentX" VALUE="9922">
        <PARAM NAME="_ExtentY" VALUE="609">
        <PARAM NAME="Caption" VALUE="This text will change at regular intervals">
        <PARAM NAME="Angle" VALUE="0">
        <PARAM NAME="Alignment" VALUE="4">
        <PARAM NAME="Mode" VALUE="0">
        <PARAM NAME="FillStyle" VALUE="0">
        <PARAM NAME="FillStyle" VALUE="0">
        <PARAM NAME="ForeColor" VALUE="#E8FD00">
        <PARAM NAME="BackColor" VALUE="#000000">
        <PARAM NAME="FontName" VALUE="Arial">
        <PARAM NAME="FontSize" VALUE="12">
        <PARAM NAME="FontItalic" VALUE="0">
        <PARAM NAME="FontBold" VALUE="0">
        <PARAM NAME="FontUnderline" VALUE="0">
        <PARAM NAME="FontStrikeout" VALUE="0">
        <PARAM NAME="TopPoints" VALUE="0">
        <PARAM NAME="BotPoints" VALUE="0">
    </OBJECT>
    <OBJECT ID="IeTimer1"
     CLASSID="CLSID:59CCB4A0-727D-11CF-AC36-00AA00A47DD2"
    ➥STYLE="TOP:0pt;LEFT:8pt;WIDTH:25pt;HEIGHT:25pt;ZINDEX:1;">
```

continues

Listing 11.3. continued

```
        <PARAM NAME="_ExtentX" VALUE="873">
        <PARAM NAME="_ExtentY" VALUE="873">
        <PARAM NAME="Interval" VALUE="2000">
    </OBJECT>
</DIV>
```

Something to keep in mind, though, is that anytime you add a control to the page, you increase download time if the user doesn't have it on his system. When you add an ALX file, you also add the delay while that file is retrieved. If absolute performance is your goal, and you don't use any HTML Layout controls to add functionality to your script, you would be better off avoiding the use of ALX files to store your code. However, since the chances of the HTML Layout control being on a user's system are very high if they've ever visited another site, it's your call.

Error Checking and Debugging

One of the most effective pieces of optimization is to take a piece of code that doesn't run, and then fix it. Sound obvious? You'd be surprised how many people and how many pages put together functions or code, and then don't check the whole thing, or don't check it after that one last "quick change." After all, it worked when it was tested the first time; what's going to stop it from working with that insignificant modification? Yep, you guessed it... practically anything.

The simplest test case for any VBScript application is to load it into whatever is supposed to run it, and see if any errors pop up. The great thing about Microsoft's VBScript runtime is that for safety's sake it's going to perform some checks on script validity before it does anything with the information it contains. So, in about the time it takes you to double-click the HTML file, you can find out if something's wrong. Most of the time this kind of spot-check is only going to spot very basic syntax errors, like missing a comment tag, or spelling a variable differently in a few places, but it's also the kind of stuff that a pair of tired eyes passes over far too easily.

There are a wide variety of error-checking and debugging steps you can take, which you can find explained in detail in Chapters 12, "Debugging," and 14, "Customize Your Web Page with Cookies." Once your code is error-free, then you'll be ready to tweak it to meet your needs.

Use of Functions and Syntax

If VBScript is a subset of Visual Basic for Applications (VBA), and VBA is a subset of the full Visual Basic package, it stands to reason that there just isn't as much that can possibly go wrong or need improvement when you're creating your code, right? Yes and no.

Being a subset of any language definitely means that lots of the problem-causing elements are missing, but it also leaves adventurous developers in search of a way to implement a function that just isn't there. The classic "just sit down and code around it" method may or may not work, depending on just what it is you're trying to sneak past the interpreter, but it may certainly make some tasks a lot harder than they might otherwise have been. What do come into play are many of the same tips and techniques that programmers have been availing themselves of in Visual Basic for a number of years now.

Variables Versus References

With so many ways to address informational components, such as the text in an HTML form element, you might not be too concerned about what methodology you use. You could directly reference the element through a unique name in a statement such as newtext = MyText1. Text, or you can use any combination of Form.Element.Property or Document.Form. Element.Property to recurse your way through different levels of naming. If you're going to be using that property several times, though, you're better off storing the data to a variable in memory, and then referencing that data in the form of a variable later. As an example, Listings 11.4 and 11.5 show two different ways of attacking the same use of data from a form's text input element (named Department) inside a form named UserForm1. While both snippets of code would work inside a real VBScript function, Listing 11.5 uses variables, and would end up being faster. Note that the code examples aren't complete working VBScript programs, just small parts of a larger application.

Listing 11.4. Using Document references instead of variables.

```
 1: Sub Btn1_onClick
 2:      if (Document.UserForm1.Department.Text = Human Resources) then
 3:      {
 4:          call HRValidate(Document.UserForm1.Department.Text)
 5:      }
 6:      if (Document.UserForm1.Department.Text = Engineering) then
 7:      {
 8:          call EngValidate(Document.UserForm1.Department.Text)
 9:      }
10:      if ....
11: end sub
```

Listing 11.5. Using variables instead of Document references.

```
 1: Sub Btn1_onClick
 2:      Dim dept = Document.UserForm1.Department.Text
 3:      if (dept = Human Resources) then
 4:      {
 5:          call HRValidate(dept)
 6:      }
 7:      if (dept = Engineering) then
 8:      {
```

continues

Listing 11.5. continued

```
 9:        call EngValidate(dept)
10:    }
11:    if ....
12: end sub
```

Besides making the code more readable, the use of the variable `dept` substituting for `Document.UserForm1.Department.Text` reduces the underlying number of recursive and repetitive object calls, significantly improving overall performance. This type of optimization is very important when dealing with looping structures like `While...Wend` and `For...Next` loops. Storing the value of a property in a variable and then incrementing that value using a variable is much faster than retrieving data from the property each pass around the loop. One of the great things about objects is that they internally store all the functions that can be used to modify them. This code makes data corruption impossible because the object knows exactly what it wants. However, depending on the quality of the code, getting the text property of an object consecutively can take much longer than getting the property once and then maintaining it in a variable. The extra layer of code that makes objects safe and secure can also make them much more cumbersome for fast operations.

Data Types

One of the most convenient reductions present in VBScript is that of the single data type—the `variant`. Instead of `Dim`ing strings and integers all over the place, VBScript considers all data to be more or less generic. When you begin to use outside functions, such as those in ActiveX controls, you can certainly continue to use the variant data type to pass information to controls, and then have them convert it, but it's often more efficient to use the built-in data conversion routines that VBScript provides, saving one more step. It is a good idea to use functions like `Cint`, `CLng`, and `Csng` and `VarType` to check the values that your variants contain. An even better way of keeping track of the types of variables you are using is to standardize your variable name declarations. Use a prefix that describes the data type in the name of the variable as you define, so that in the future you are able to easily identify the type of data you are referencing.

For example, if you want to store the state of a particular control property as a Boolean, you can define your storage variable as `blnButtonState`. The prefix that you use in the variable name will help you determine just what type of data you will expect to find inside. If you are trying to store currency information for a banking application in a variable, make sure that all of the variables dealing with funds are prefixed with `cur`. That is, `CurTotal` will hold the current total for a user's account with the currency data type. There is no hard and fast standard for this, so work out what works best for you.

ActiveX Controls

Optimizing ActiveX controls is roughly equivalent to trying to compress a brick. They're self-contained and precompiled, and you have only a certain amount of control about the way they handle things. What you do have control over is how you use them, both in quantity and functionality.

Quality, Not Quantity

Before you run out and place every ActiveX control ever made into the HTML on your page, consider the lowest common denominator for connection speeds and download times. If your Internet connection comes in the form of a T-1 line, a 200KB control is an insignificant amount of download time. If you're on ISDN or a dedicated 56.6KB line, controls around 100KB aren't excessive. If you're on a 28.8 modem, or stuck on a 14.4, file sizes start to become extremely important. Having recently downgraded from a T-1 line, we can tell you from experience that people on slow connections won't be too thrilled about waiting a minute or more just for text animation or a PowerPoint slide show.

The task you're faced with is minimizing the supporting files you need in order to get the functionality you want. This often involves a good deal of research, and a bit of design brainstorming. Do you take the chance that someone has a specific control, or is this page's primary duty speed of display and response? Do you embed an Excel spreadsheet, or do you convert the file into an HTML table? You have to make the decisions as to where a change is necessary for speed, and where such a change would detract from functionality and appearance. But sometimes you can make things easier on yourself.

If you look at some of the ActiveX controls out there, you'll notice that there are a variety of different ways of getting a particular task done. While a number of individual controls could be downloaded, the HTML Layout control contains a bunch of useful controls all bundled together. Although you might not need them all, you might need two or three of them, and it's more efficient to download the one CAB file and have it installed than it is to initiate multiple downloads and installations, as long as the single CAB file isn't more than about 30KB bigger than the individual controls.

The trick is to see where one control can serve multiple purposes, and where a control could be replaced with clever (but efficient) coding. Do you need an Image control, or can you get by with an animated GIF? Don't skimp on functionality, though. If you need control over an animated image, you need ActiveX controls to do it. If you have large sequences of images to display, you could end up being better off to start up an `ActiveMovie` control and stream the images as AVI, controlling their playback rate. It's all a matter of give and take.

Divide and Conquer

Remember that speed on the Internet is relative to the amount of data that must be sent over your network connection. The fastest code in the Internet is the code that makes it from your Internet service provider to your local machine in the shortest time. Deadly wait times while a program is downloading can make an early end of an ambitious project. It may actually be a good idea to divide your application into smaller segments and have the user navigate between HTML pages. This keeps the download time at a minimum between parts of your application and will give the best response time to your users who only have 14.4 modem connections. Because VBScript programming and HTML code is realistically just pages and pages of text, the less text you have to transfer, the faster your application will be downloaded to the local machine and processed. Try to keep your applications as tight as possible without giving up your standards. Keep in mind that making your users navigate a little more to get where they are going can often be seen as a higher level of interactivity.

Development Tools

Creating interactive applications can be easy or hard, depending on the tools you have available to you. Developing with VBScript and ActiveX was, like anything else, not a walk in the park when it first came out. But even just a few months after you catch on, a number of options exist for you to get the job done.

Still Using a Text Editor?

Okay, there are a lot of us out there who just refuse to "modernize" certain aspects of our development process. I'll admit to being one of them when it comes to things like HTML page creation, and wanting to do HTML coding all "by hand," instead of relying on someone else's stab at what everyone wants in an HTML editor. If you know the syntax, and type pretty fast, your run-of-the-mill text editor (like Notepad, the old standby) can crank out some useful stuff pretty quickly, and on any system you choose. No quirky development environments, costs, or cryptic interfaces… just you and a heck of a lot of text.

ActiveX Control Pad

While the romance and mystique of the text-editor-using code-creating guru may be something you want to continue to inspire in public, don't be too resistant to certain changes. Advanced interactions, such as those between VBScript and ActiveX controls, require the entry of dozens of parameters and incredibly weird sequences of numbers, which you really don't want to try to memorize, do you? Microsoft likes to call them Globally Unique Identifiers (GUIDs), but you can just call them a pain to type in.

Each ActiveX control has a GUID in the form of a `ClassID`, which tells the client system a lot of things about the control and allows the system to check and see if it has it on hand. If you're up to the task of memorizing 32-bit numbers for every control you plan on integrating, and you would rather type those sequences by hand every time you use each control, you can consider yourself a pretty die-hard ASCII editor fan. You'd also be very wealthy if you got paid by the hour for that.

The next rung up the evolutionary ladder of coding is the ActiveX Control Pad. While not really an Integrated Development Environment (IDE), it does take the first step toward making development easier, and the Control Pad is free. Both of those weigh heavily in its favor, no matter what kind of quirks or drawbacks people may associate with its use.

The Control Pad provides a toolbox for putting together the most commonly used pieces of your HTML page. Objects, properties, positioning… they're all there for your benefit, if you're willing to give it a try. If you don't know the `ClassID`s of the objects you were planning to use, it cuts the time even more significantly. By the time you hunt through and look up the `ClassID` for use with a text editor, you could have placed three distinct classes of objects on your page with Control Pad.

Visual Basic to VBScript Converters

Going even further in optimizing your development time, you can take an existing Visual Basic application and convert it, or the majority of it, to VBScript. The first publicized tool of this sort, VBNet, came out at the time of this writing. It takes existing Visual Basic applications and converts them into VBScript-based applications instead—at least mostly. There are two conflicting schools of thought when it comes to applications like this, because of one simple fact; since VBScript is a subset of a subset of Visual Basic running in a special environment, not all applications (and certainly not all functionality) can transfer from the original application. On one hand this leaves developers saying, "Well, if it can't handle my specific function, then what good is it?" But on the other hand, it makes a large number of other developers smile because it does at least some of the work for them.

The most important thing to do when considering conversion is to take a long, hard look at the original application, and see what kind of functions it needs. File I/O and a pile of other common functions will either end up requiring links to a server-side CGI program or the use of ActiveX controls. Remembering the earlier discussion on download times and the number of controls being used, this could be a problem.

For the moment, treat Visual Basic to VBScript converters as a good step to getting rid of the basic time-consuming steps, but definitely short of a fully optimized and fully functional porting tool. There's no doubt that the tools that currently exist will improve, and that future tools will continue to fuel the competition for the most effective converter on the market. But don't bet the farm on the perfect tool... be prepared to do some of the conversion tune-up yourself.

Future Integrated Development Environments?

Is there a real Integrated Development Environment in VBScript's future? Considering the market that Microsoft is trying to push VBScript into, the sheer number of possible users would seem to be too lucrative for some developers to pass up. As other applications and corporations decide whether to begin hosting VBScript in their applications, each may end up with its own special integration and specialty interfaces.

With Visual Basic 5.0, Visual Basic for Applications, and VBScript to consider, Microsoft may well end up turning Visual Basic into an all-purpose IDE that could use a project wizard to make anything from a full-blown Visual Basic application all the way down to the simplest of VBScript functions. Embedding a Visual Basic/VBA to VBScript converter wouldn't be a bad thing either, considering that they would have an instant inventory of what ActiveX controls were available to provide necessary functionality. While VBScript may be free to the public, rest assured that Microsoft will certainly aim to make a profit from related components, as will countless other developers.

Review

The right amount of optimization is the amount that feels comfortable to you. You don't want to spend all your time tweaking something when there won't be any discernible improvement, but you shouldn't leave code up that could be significantly improved. Since your VBScript source code is there for the world to see, it's their first indication of your work, and they get to see it all, from the organization to the finished results. You only get one chance to make a first impression.

As you begin to integrate more advanced functionality, make sure that you standardize as much as possible. If you have ever worked in a workgroup environment, you know what it is like to look at someone else's code and have absolutely no idea how they got where they are going. A good set of rules set at the beginning of a project and followed through to completion will get your work out the door faster and make your code reusable. There may not be much that you can do to increase VBScript performance-wise, but the performance of your application can be greatly dependent on how it is maintained and reused. A lot of unnecessary hacking into a program to fix undocumented problems will definitely cut back the efficiency of your work.

Debugging

by Keith Brophy and Timothy Koets

IN THIS CHAPTER

If you have been a programmer for very long, you probably realize that writing programs is sometimes the easy part of software development. It's getting the bugs out that can be the real challenge! Judgment is needed to effectively sift through many hundreds or thousands of possible causes of a problem and hone in on a specific bug. At the same time, a great deal of logical, objective analysis must be applied to a debugging problem to scientifically pinpoint a bug and *prove* its existence. As a result, the process of bug-hunting often requires a special focus and concentration seldom encountered in other aspects of life. And, as anyone with experience debugging an application will quickly realize, the frustration involved can be enormous! The good news is that problem-solving techniques and top-notch tools can make this process much easier. The not-so-good news, however, is that such top-notch tools do not come with VBScript. Nevertheless, the tips and techniques suggested in this chapter will go a long way toward minimizing your debugging pitfalls.

Handling VBScript Errors

In order to effectively debug applications, you first must learn a bit about what errors are, what forms they take, and how to handle them when they occur. Once you know how to effectively handle them, you will be more effective in recognizing and preventing them. This first section gives you the background you need to learn about debugging techniques. The techniques themselves are presented in the next section of this chapter.

Unfortunately, VBScript offers little in the way of sophisticated debugging tools and error handling when your program is running. Most commercial language products, including Visual Basic 4.0, offer a development environment that is tremendously helpful when you're debugging programs. Later in this chapter, you'll learn more about those capabilities and what debugging tools VBScript lacks. But first, you should examine what VBScript *does* provide when errors occur. To do this, you should take a look at the various types of errors that can occur in a VBScript program.

Syntax Errors: Say What You Mean!

Errors come in a variety of shapes and sizes. The easiest ones to picture and correct are simple typing or language-usage errors in your VBScript code. For example, consider what would happen if you mistakenly type

```
Dimwit C
```

instead of

```
Dim C
```

in order to declare a variable named C. Because the word Dimwit is not part of the VBScript language or syntax, the first statement can't be processed. This kind of error commonly is called a *syntax error.*

Obviously, if you have a syntax error, your program is not going to work as intended. Fortunately, a program with a syntax error normally won't even run, and the problem can be spotted right away! Such stubborn behavior is fortunate, because the sooner you find a problem, the better. You'd probably rather have your program go "on strike" immediately than have the problem pop up when a user is interacting with your script or, worse yet, when your program gives your user an incorrect result that he's not even aware of!

So how does VBScript respond to a syntax error? Suppose that you have the statement

```
Dim c, c, c
```

This statement, too, contains a syntax error. This time, the error consists of an illegal duplicate definition instead of an incorrectly typed keyword. This statement is not legal according to the rules of VBScript, because a variable name can be used only once; here, it is defined three times in a row. When you attempt to load the page containing this program into the browser, you are greeted with the message shown in Figure 12.1.

FIGURE 12.1.

A syntax-checking script error message.

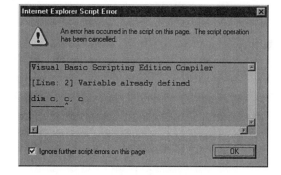

This particular error is identified as soon as the page is loaded in the browser, but other syntax errors might not be caught until after the Web page is loaded. Suppose that a certain code statement is carried out only after a specific button is clicked. In the script event-handler routine associated with that button, suppose that a series of other calculations precedes the statement

```
a = b / c
```

Now, assume that the variable c already has been computed before this statement and that the value stored in c varies from one calculation to another. This statement might work perfectly well for the first several times the button is clicked. If, however, the value of c ever turns out to be 0, this statement fails. Because the computer is unable to divide by 0, VBScript generates a message box similar to the one in Figure 12.1. This brings your program to a screeching halt.

NOTE

When you are presented with the runtime error message from the Internet Explorer browser, you have the option of enabling a checkbox to suppress notification of future runtime errors. If you enable the Ignore further script errors on this page checkbox, notification of future errors in other scripts on the page is suppressed. Loading of the specific script that caused the problem still is halted when errors occur.

These are just two examples of many possible errors that can be detected when VBScript tries to run your program. The errors shown in these examples are referred to as *runtime* errors. Hopefully, your user never sees any runtime errors. Ideally, you would write perfect, error-free code! However, given the complexity of programming, the odds of producing a perfect program are slim. Therefore, you must be able to thoroughly test your programs to remove all their problems before you turn them over to your users. You also can take steps when writing your code to make it more robust if a runtime error occurs during development.

NOTE

When a browser runs your VBScript code embedded in HTML, it does so by passing the VBScript statements to a separate component of software called the *VBScript Interpreter*. This interpreter checks and runs the VBScript code.

Unfortunately, no standard VBScript interactive development environment exists from Microsoft to make the debugging task easier. This makes the task of error-proofing your programs a considerable challenge. VBScript does provide some help in recovering from errors and pinning them down, however. You can write code that helps a program robustly continue after an error occurs. The On Error Resume Next statement serves this purpose. After an error occurs, a convenient source of information called the Err object is available for use in your code as well. With the Err object, you can write program logic that prints error information or takes a code path based on an analysis in code of what error occurred. These techniques for dealing with runtime errors are covered in "Using Simple Debugging Techniques" later in this chapter. But first, take a look at another type of error.

Semantic Errors: Mean What You Say!

By now, you might be feeling a little more at ease, comforted by the idea that there is some support in the VBScript language to help you handle errors. Don't get too comforted, though! First of all, VBScript support for runtime errors might help you handle them, but it won't help you prevent or eliminate them. Second, semantic errors can pose an even bigger problem than syntax errors. A *semantic error* is an error in meaning (that is, you fail to write the program to achieve the purpose you intended). Suppose that you want to add a 4 percent sales tax to the cost of an item. You provide the following code statement:

```
total = orig_price + orig_price * 4
```

4 is used here in place of .04. The result is that this incorrect statement doesn't add 4 percent to your total sale, but it does add four times the cost of your item to your total sale! This is clearly an error. As far as the VBScript Interpreter can tell, however, this statement is fine. VBScript doesn't know what a sales tax rate is. It obediently carries out the calculation you give it.

With a semantic error, the problem rests squarely on your shoulders. VBScript, or any other language for that matter, is not able to automatically highlight this kind of an error for you. Instead, after noticing an incorrect result, you must work backward until you hone in on the problem. Semantic problems do not directly cause runtime errors; they just lead to bad results. And although bad results might suggest that you have a problem, they don't tell you where it is. Often, you must trace through your program line by line, ensuring that each line is correct and produces valid results before proceeding to the next line.

Some languages offer support for this kind of tracing. In the case of VBScript, however, you must put together your own traces. Trace tactics that can be used to address errors are discussed in the following section, and there you'll get a closer look at runtime error-handling techniques you can use to tackle syntax errors. For now, recognize that it is not too important that you know the textbook description of *semantic* versus *syntax* errors. It *is* important, however, that you are aware of the techniques available for dealing with them. You also should realize that the most important tools for debugging—patience and persistence—can be provided only by *you.*

Using Simple Debugging Techniques

Now that you have a feel for the type of error support in VBScript, it's time to observe it in action. The program used to illustrate debugging principles throughout this chapter is the Pace-Pal program. *Pace-Pal* is a standard HTML Web page with embedded VBScript code. The program is shown in Figure 12.2.

Pace-Pal enables you to specify a distance in miles or kilometers and a time in minutes/seconds format. (Hours also can be provided optionally if you're willing to run that long!) With this information, a pace per mile can be calculated. If you run a 26.2 mile race (10k) in three hours and supply that information to Pace-Pal, for example, Pace-Pal calculates that you averaged 6:52-minute miles. This scenario is shown in Figure 12.2.

12

DEBUGGING

FIGURE 12.2.

The Pace-Pal program.

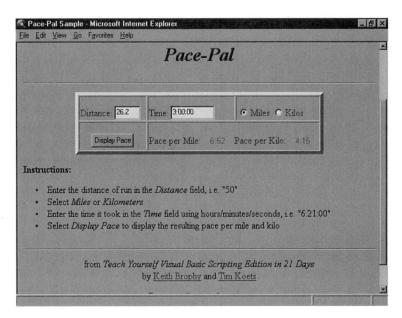

Pace-Pal does its job very nicely when it has perfect, well-mannered, never-make-a-mistake users. It runs into problems, however, when faced with the more typical user who occasionally makes mistakes. Specifically, Pace-Pal does a poor job of handling nonstandard input.

Pace-Pal can derive a 10k pace from a time of 37:12 faster than you can blink an eye. But if you accidentally type 37:12AA rather than 37:12 for the time, disaster strikes. Pace-Pal's code is not constructed to deal with a time in such a format. The code doesn't check the data integrity. Instead, it tries to process the data, causing the VBScript Interpreter to attempt the impossible with the current statement. An attempt is made to carry out a calculation based on character data. The poor VBScript Interpreter is left holding the bag, asked to carry out a statement that makes no sense and will lead to an incorrect result! Needless to say, the interpreter balks, tossing up the famed runtime error window. Figure 12.3 shows the runtime error window generated after Pace-Pal attempts to process a time of 37:12AA.

VBScript is nice enough to clue you into the problem. The error message displayed tells you that the problem is related to an attempted type conversion that is illegal under the rules of VBScript. Unfortunately, VBScript doesn't tell you where this error occurred. And, even worse from the user's point of view, VBScript halts execution of the script because it detected problems there. If you go back and specify good input and click the Display Pace button, nothing happens. Until the page is reloaded, VBScript considers this a bad script and doesn't process any of it.

FIGURE 12.3.

Bad input data causes a runtime error in the Pace-Pal program.

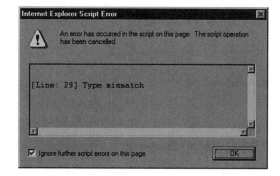

In certain cases, VBScript does provide you with the location of statements that contain errors. In many cases, fundamental flaws in language definition can be detected and pointed out with line-number information when a page is loaded. This is the case with the error shown in Figure 12.3. More subtle errors, or errors that only show up when there are certain data conditions, cannot be predetected. The 37:12AA bad-data-induced error falls into this category. Debugging then becomes considerably more complicated, because half the battle is simply determining which statements caused VBScript to balk.

Take a look at the code in Listing 12.1, for example. This is just one section of the rather lengthy Pace-Pal program. Even after you've gotten a hint that the culprit statement lurks somewhere in this subset of the code, does it easily jump out at you?

> **NOTE**
>
> The source file for the Pace-Pal program is located on the accompanying CD-ROM in the pace-pal.htm file.

Listing 12.1. Source code that contains an error.

```
Function ConvertStringToTotalSeconds (ByVal sDuration)

' -----------------------------------------------------------------------
' Purpose: Takes HH:MM:SS format string and converts to total seconds
' -----------------------------------------------------------------------

Dim iPosition      ' Position of ":" seperator
    Dim vHours         ' Number of hours required
    Dim vMinutes       ' Number of minutes required
    Dim vSeconds       ' Number of seconds required

    ' Start working from right of string, parsing seconds
    sMode = "Seconds"
```

continues

Listing 12.1. continued

```
' Get leftmost time component
iPosition = InStr(sDuration, ":")
If iPosition = 0 Then

    ' No more time info, assume time info just in ss format
    vSeconds = sDuration

Else ' More time info is in string

    ' Store first portion in hours for now, assume hh:mm:ss format
    vHours = Left(sDuration, iPosition - 1)

    ' Parse string for further processing
    sDuration = Right(sDuration, Len(sDuration) - iPosition)

    ' Get middle time component
    iPosition = InStr(sDuration, ":")
    If iPosition = 0 Then
        ' No more time info, must just be mm:ss format
        vMinutes = vHours
        vSeconds = sDuration
        vHours = 0
    Else ' Time info must be in hh:mm:ss format
        vMinutes = Left(sDuration, iPosition - 1)
        vSeconds = Right(sDuration, len(sDuration) - iPosition)
    End If

End If

' Represent all components in terms of seconds
vHours = vHours * 3600
vMinutes = vMinutes * 60

' Return total seconds value
ConvertStringtoTotalSeconds = CInt(vHours) + _
    CInt(vMinutes) + CInt(vSeconds)

End Function 'ConvertStringtoTotalSeconds
```

As you can see even from this relatively straightforward example, isolating a bug by visually inspecting the code is an inexact process as well as a slow, tedious way to solve problems. Fortunately, there are better, easier, more precise ways to hunt down the error.

Using the MsgBox Statement

The debugging difficulty presented by Pace-Pal is that you can't tell where things start to go wrong. As a matter of fact, "start" to go wrong is rather misleading. Things really go wrong all at once, with no gradual transition, because VBScript treats any runtime error as fatal! So the first step is to hone in on your error. Many languages come with development environments that help you easily monitor the flow of your program and pinpoint such errors. Unfortunately, VBScript does not.

If you've debugged in other environments, however, one obvious tool to pinpoint the rogue statement might come to mind: the `MsgBox` statement.

> **NOTE**
>
> The `MsgBox` statement displays a message box on top of the Web page that the user must respond to before the program continues. In debugging, `MsgBox` is useful because it interrupts the normal flow of the program, and that interruption easily can be seen by the user. What's more, the program can provide useful debugging information to the programmer, as you will see later in this section.

When this function is encountered, the designated message is displayed to the user and the flow of your program halts until the user clicks the message box button to acknowledge the message and proceed.

That means that the `MsgBox` statement gives you a way to tell where your program's execution is. Therefore, it gives you a way to get insight into the exact location of a runtime error. Suppose that you're chasing an error in your program. You insert the following statement in the middle of your program and rerun it:

```
MsgBox "I made it this far without my program choking!"
```

If your program displays this message when you rerun it, you have some additional insight into the error you're chasing. You know the runtime error was *not* caused by any statement preceding the `MsgBox` call. The error lurks in some statement after that point in your code. For the next step, you can shift the `MsgBox` statement down a line and rerun the test. If that works, do it again. And again. And again—until you hit the line that causes the runtime error.

Alternatively, you can take the tried-and-true "narrow it down one step at a time" approach. You put your `MsgBox` statement halfway through your code and see whether it is reached. If so, you know the problem must be in the last half of your code statements. Put it halfway through the remaining statements. If that test is successful, put it halfway through the new, smaller remaining section of statements. And again. And again—until you hit the runtime error. If the flow of code is not sequential, the process of isolating the problem is even tougher. Suppose that a line of code calls another routine that branches to one path of a `Select Case` statement, which in turn calls another routine as the result of an `If` condition. In such a case, determining where to put the message box traces in advance becomes very difficult, not to mention complex!

If both these approaches sound similarly tedious and time-consuming, that's because they are! You can save yourself a few test runs by starting right out with a MsgBox statement after each and every statement, each with a different message. Suppose that your program consists of these statements:

```
Sub Test_OnClick

    Dim a, b, c

    a = text1.text * 3
    c = text2.text * 4
    d = a + c

End Sub
```

You then can modify it to get a MsgBox-based program flow trail:

```
Sub Test_OnClick

    Dim a, b, c

    MsgBox "Point 1"            ' We've made it to point 1
    a = text1.text * 3
    MsgBox "Point 2"            ' We've made it to point 2
    c = text2.text * 4
    MsgBox "Point 3"            ' We've made it to point 3
    d = a + c
    MsgBox "Point 4"            ' We've made it to point 4

End sub
```

If your program runs and then dies with a runtime error, the MsgBox statement that last appeared on-screen tells you right where the problem is. This method of tracking down the rogue statement does work, but it takes time to insert all the statements and then remove them after you finish debugging. There is nothing wrong with this approach if your program is small. If your program is large, however, there are better, sleeker, quicker ways to chase down the bug. You just have to reach deep into the VBScript bag of tricks and pull out another language construct: the On Error Resume Next statement.

Using the On Error Resume Next Statement

It would be nice if a program could simply continue after it caused a runtime error. That way, at some later point in the script, you could use code statements to learn whether the end of a procedure was reached successfully to print the values of variables for you to inspect, or to show you the result of calculations. If a program had the perseverance to forge on after it hit rough waters so that you could retrieve this information, the debugging task would be easier.

There's another reason, too, that you might wish your program could survive a runtime error. Although VBScript is trying to save you from bad data or results when it produces a runtime error, there are cases in which you might prefer to continue execution after the error occurs, even if it means living with bad results. Your program might calculate extra information such as the number of calories a runner burns or how much perspiration the runner generates, for example. If so, it could be quite annoying to your user to halt the whole program just because he entered one piece of extraneous information incorrectly.

If you want to perform additional debugging after the rogue statement, or if you don't want the program to crash if an error occurs, you need a way to override the abort. Fortunately, VBScript gives you this override power. It comes in the form of the On Error Resume Next statement. This statement tells the VBScript Interpreter that, when an error is encountered, it should simply ignore it and continue with the next statement. Listing 12.2 shows an example of this statement applied to the Pace-Pal problem.

Listing 12.2. Code made more robust with an On Error statement.

```
Function ConvertStringToTotalSeconds (ByVal sDuration)

    '----------------------------------------------------------------------
    ' Purpose: Takes HH:MM:SS format string and converts to total seconds
    '----------------------------------------------------------------------

    ' When error occurs, continue with next statement
    ' rather than halting program
    On Error Resume Next

    Dim iPosition      'Position of ":" seperator
    Dim vHours         ' Number of hours required
    Dim vMinutes       ' Number of minutes required
    Dim vSeconds       ' Number of seconds required
```

> **NOTE**
>
> The modified Pace-Pal program with the change shown here is located on the accompanying CD-ROM in the file Ppalerr1.htm.

When the On Error Resume Next statement is used, you don't get any frightening messages of gloom and doom, and your program doesn't come to a screeching halt. Instead, the VBScript Interpreter continues with the next statement, leaving your user none the wiser. Figure 12.4 shows the results of running Pace-Pal with this modification. Note that the program manages to provide a final pace result, albeit an incorrect one, in the pace box. But it will work correctly on any valid input that is subsequently entered, even without reloading the page.

FIGURE 12.4.

The Pace-Pal program faced the bug and lived to tell about it!

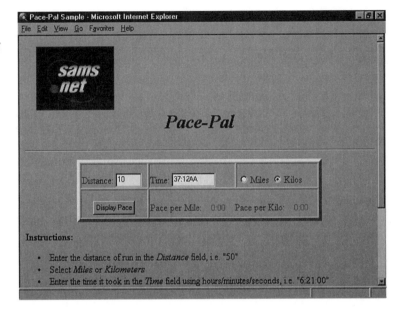

Alas, all is not perfect; there is a problem with the On Error Resume Next approach. The On Error Resume Next statement gives you a way to ignore errors when they occur, as the Pace-Pal example demonstrates. Unfortunately, when you use this statement, you run the risk that you won't find out about a problem in your program that you really *do* care about. For that matter, unless you know specifically what caused an error, it rarely is safe just to ignore it.

If you've used other languages with error handling, particularly VBA or Visual Basic 4.0, you might realize that most error-handling systems provide additional flow-control capabilities when errors occur. In Visual Basic 4.0 or VBA, for example, you can use the On Error Goto statement to direct your program flow to a specific area of error-handling code. For example, On Error Goto Shared_Error_Handling directs the program flow to one specific block of error-handling code labeled Shared_Error_Handling whenever an error occurs. This capability is *not* available in VBScript. The only thing you can do with the On Error statement is to tell it to Resume next—that is, to continue on to the next statement. If an error occurs in a procedure while this statement is in effect, your program simply moves on to the next statement in the procedure. Once again, though, the VBScript language comes to your rescue. There is a way to use On Error Resume Next wisely. You must couple it with the power of the Err object.

Using the Err Object

If you combine On Error Resume Next with a special VBScript object called the Err object, your program not only can survive runtime errors, but it can even incorporate program logic that analyzes these errors after the fact. The Err object is useful for two reasons: It can be a great help in debugging and, in some cases, it can be a feature you want to incorporate into your final program to make it more robust. When an error occurs in VBScript, the Err object analyzes the error to see what kind of a problem, if any, occurred within a body of code. You can display the error code and description after an error occurs and still let your program continue on for further debugging after you display this information. You even might choose to directly build recovery techniques into your programs. If the Err object tells you that data of the wrong type was used in a calculation, for example, you can prompt the user to reenter the data.

> **NOTE**
>
> For an in-depth treatment of the Err object, refer to Chapter 10, "Error Handling." In this chapter, the Err object is considered specifically with respect to debugging your VBScript applications.

The Err object is an intrinsic VBScript object. That means that you don't have to do any work to use it. No special declarations are required. You can simply reference it anywhere in your code and inspect the current error-related property values of this object. These properties provide several important pieces of information:

- **Number:** The numerical error code. This value is set by the VBScript Interpreter when an error occurs. 0 represents no error, and any other number means that an error has occurred. Each type of error has its own specific error code. Type-conversion errors, for example, always generate an error code of 12. Error codes can range from 1 to 65535 for VBScript.

- **Description:** A description of the error that corresponds to the error number. When Err.Number contains 12, Err.Description contains the corresponding Type conversion text description. Note that a description doesn't necessarily exist for every number.

- **Source:** Tells what caused the error. This can be the VBScript page if the error was caused within VBScript, for example, or the name of an OLE automation object if it was caused by an OLE automation component.

- **HelpFile:** The path and filename of a Help file, if relevant, containing more details on the error.

- **HelpContext:** A Help file context ID (topic index) that corresponds to the Help file error information. The Help file and context information can be used to make your program open a relevant Help file containing further information on the error.

There are two methods for using the Err object, which are explained more fully in the next section:

- **Raise:** Generates an error.
- **Clear:** Resets the contents of the error object.

12

DEBUGGING

Using the information from the Err object, you can check whether an error occurred and then examine relevant information to aid you in debugging a detected error. It's easy to check whether an error has occurred. If Err.Number equals 0, no problems were detected. Any other value represents an error code. If you do find an error code, the Err.Description field provides the standard text description of the error. This message is the same one that pops up on the runtime message error box when the program screeches to a halt if you aren't using On Error Resume Next to ignore the errors. You can even look at the originator of the error in the Source property. Most often, the source is the name of your VBScript file itself if it was your VBScript code that caused the problem. In some cases, however, you might find that the error source is a component you have integrated, such as an ActiveX control. You can even get information on associated Help files for errors, although this information is less likely to be of use to you in structuring your error-recovery code. The code sequence in Listing 12.3 shows one example of how you might check to see whether an error has occurred.

Listing 12.3. Checking the Err object to see whether an error has occurred.

```
Sub Test_OnClick

    On Error Resume Next

    Dim a

    a = text1.text / text2.text

    If Err.Number <> 0 Then
        Msgbox "Error : " & Err.Description & " from " & Err.Source
    End If
End Sub
```

Code analysis of the Err object like that shown in Listing 12.3 also can be applied to debugging problems like the Pace-Pal situation. If On Error Resume Next is used to turn off runtime error reporting and aborting, you can look at the end of the suspect procedure to see whether any errors occurred within it. If errors did occur, you can use the Err object to print full details. One important consideration with this approach, however, is that if more than one error occurred within the procedure, you see information only on the most recent error. Still, this is helpful when you simply want to know whether a block of code is error free. If an error occurred, you can add additional error checks and debug further to determine whether there were multiple errors. Listing 12.4 shows an example of the Pace-Pal code with a check inserted at the end of a procedure.

Listing 12.4. Code with additional error diagnostics from the Err object.

```
            vMinutes = Left(sDuration, iPosition - 1)
            vSeconds = Right(sDuration, Len(sDuration) - iPosition)
        End If
    End If
```

```
' Represent all components in terms of seconds
vHours = vHours * 3600
vMinutes = vMinutes * 60

' Return total seconds value
ConvertStringtoTotalSeconds = CInt(vHours) + CInt(vMinutes) + CInt(vSeconds)

If Err.Number <> 0 Then
    Msgbox "Error #:" & Err.Number & " Description:" & Err.Description _
        & " Source:" & Err.Source, 0, "Error in ConvertStringtoTotalSeconds!"
End If

End Function ' ConvertStringtoTotalSeconds
```

NOTE

The source file for Pace-Pal with the change shown here is located on the accompanying CD-ROM in the file `Ppalerr2.htm`.

Notice that this code prints information *only* if the error occurred. If the error did not occur, the user is not disturbed by error information. Figure 12.5 shows the results of this error check. As the figure shows, the error check added to the Pace-Pal code does detect an error within the procedure. The cause is identified clearly as a type-conversion error, and the source is pegged to be the script itself.

FIGURE 12.5.

Information about the error.

Bolstered by the assistance of the Err object, the Pace-Pal code is more robust and provides you with more insight. It is more robust because, despite the error, the program still continues through its code path and produces results without aborting. In this case, a pace of `00:00` is presented as the result because there is no valid data to work with. You have more insight because you can be certain that an error occurred in the ConvertStringtoTotalSeconds function. Additionally, you know precisely which error occurred within that function and that error's source. Armed with this information, you can isolate the cause of the error using the following tracing techniques. But before tackling the isolation steps, it helps to fully understand the intricacies of these error-handling mechanisms. Next, you'll learn a few more advanced details of the Err object and the On Error Resume Next statement, and then look at more tracing techniques. You'll then return to the quest for your Pace-Pal bug.

Taking the Err Object Further

The On Error Resume Next statement, also called an *error handler*, is a procedure-level statement. It remains in effect only within the procedure that contains the On Error declaration. Imagine that a higher-level procedure that uses On Error Resume Next calls a lower-level procedure that does not use it. If an error occurs in the lower level procedure, the flow of statements in that procedure halts immediately. VBScript prepares to alert the user of the error, but before doing so, it checks whether any higher level procedures with an On Error Resume Next function were in the process of calling this lower level procedure. If they were not, the error is treated as a normal runtime error, halting the program and displaying the runtime error to the user. However, if a higher-level procedure with an On Error Resume Next function was calling a lower-level procedure with no error handling, when the lower-level procedure causes the error, it is addressed by the higher-level procedure.

This commonly is termed *raising the error*. The VBScript Interpreter, like many languages, raises an error to higher calling levels until it finds a procedure with error handling. If none is found, the script halts and the user is presented with the error results by the interpreter.

After the error is passed to that higher-level procedure, that procedure's error-handling Resume Next rule goes into effect. That procedure provides instructions to continue to the next statement when an error occurs, so execution picks up right after the call to the lower-level procedure that went awry.

You can't expect to analyze Err object information within a procedure unless that procedure contains the On Error Resume Next statement. As long as this statement exists within the procedure, errors do not cause the procedure to be halted. If the VBScript Interpreter finds that no higher-level procedure with an error handler that was calling the procedure caused the problem, the entire program halts. The bottom line is that if you want to use the Err object to carry out any error analysis in a procedure, make sure that an On Error Resume Next first appears within that procedure.

The Err object itself has a couple more interesting capabilities: the Clear and Raise methods. The Raise method generates an error. More precisely, it simulates an error. In other words, you can tell Raise what kind of error you want to simulate. To simulate a certain type of conversion error, for example, you can use the statement

```
Err.Raise 13
```

to have VBScript respond in its normal fashion, just as if it had encountered an actual code statement that caused an error of error code type 13. Raising an error causes the program to behave exactly as if it had encountered a real error. If any procedure in the active lineup of the current and calling procedures has an On Error Resume Next statement, the program flows to the next applicable statement. In such a case, the Err object then contains the appropriate information for the error raised. For example, Err.Number equals 13. On the other hand, if there is no On Error Resume Next in the active lineup of calling and current procedures, the program treats the raised error as a regular runtime error, displaying a message to the user and terminating the program.

You might be thinking that it would take a pretty twisted programmer to purposely inject a simulated error into his code. Such a tactic is warranted, however, in some situations. (Naturally, the VBScript development team at Microsoft wouldn't have included this method if it could be used only for evil purposes!) One way you might use this method for good is to evaluate the Err object within a procedure to determine the severity of potential problems. You might write code that inspects Err.Number to determine whether the problem is a minor one that won't affect results or a major one that presents critical problems to the program. In the event of a minor problem, you might decide to write code that continues with the normal flow of statements in the current procedure.

For a major problem, however, it might be imprudent to continue with the program after the detection of an error. In that case, you might want the calling procedures at higher levels to address the error without going any further in the current routine. There is an easy way to redirect the program flow back to the error-handling code in the higher-level procedures. If those calling procedures have On Error Resume Next defined, you can simply raise the error with Err.Raise, and control flows to the first higher level calling procedure that has an active error handler.

To have full mastery of VBScript error handling, one more technique remains: the Clear method. A little insight into the Err object and the way it gets cleared is necessary to understand what Clear does. The Err object, as you have learned, keeps a record of information on the last error that occurred. When an error occurs, the appropriate information is loaded into the Err object by the VBScript Interpreter. If this information lingers forever, though, it can cause some headaches. If an error were set in Err.Number indefinitely, you would end up addressing the same error over and over.

For this reason, VBScript clears the Err object whenever your flow of statements reaches the end of a subroutine or function that contains an On Error Resume Next, or whenever an On Error Resume Next statement itself is encountered. All fields are set to their initial state. Any Err.Number containing an error code resets to 0 (indicating no error). Using On Error Resume Next at the start of each procedure guarantees that old errors from previous procedures no longer will be stored in the Err object. You get a clean slate.

This works fine if you just check the value of the Err object once within each procedure. But what if you have multiple places within the same procedure where you check Err.Number? What if your code checks the value after each and every statement? Then, if the first statement causes an error, Err.Number is set accordingly. If you check Err.Number immediately after that statement, you will correctly detect the error, such as a type-conversion error. But all the subsequent statements within the same procedure that check Err.Number still will find the old type-conversion error indicator for the error that already was analyzed, even if the most recent statement caused no error.

If you use Err.Number many times within a procedure, you should ensure that you're not reacting to leftover error data. Fortunately, VBScript provides a means to do this: the Err.Clear method. This method resets all fields of the Err object and assigns Err.Number back to 0 to indicate no error. So when you want to make sure that you are starting with a clean error slate, simply insert an Err.Clear into your code. Typically, this is carried out right after an error is detected and addressed. Some caution must be exercised with this method, however. There is nothing to prevent you from clearing errors that have not yet been addressed. Make sure that you use Err.clear only after checking the Err.number and carrying out any handling needed.

There are many error-handling strategies that can be built on the On Error Resume Next statement and the Err object. If you don't use On Error Resume Next at all, your runtime errors will show through to you (or your user) loud and clear! If you do use the On Error Resume Next statement, you risk inadvertently ignoring errors, unless you diligently check the status of the Err object in every routine that uses On Error Resume Next. When you check error codes, you must remember that error codes still may be set from previous statements unless some action has occurred to clear them.

When writing your error-handling code for higher level procedures that use On Error Resume Next, you must remember that errors can trickle up. This is true whether those errors are natural errors or "simulated" errors caused by Err.Raise. Errors that occur in lower-level procedures can trickle up into your higher-level procedure if lower levels do not use On Error Resume Next. That means that you might need to insert statements that give you more details about an error to pinpoint the cause of it. Fortunately, additional, hand-crafted techniques are available to trace and understand your code. So next you'll learn about what tracing code is really all about.

Using Advanced Debugging Techniques

Thus far, you have learned how to use the message box statement, the Err object, and On Error Resume Next statements to handle errors. To better isolate errors in your code, you need more sophisticated ways to trace your code.

Tracing your code is the act of following the flow of statements as your program progresses. Usually, code is traced to isolate bugs and solve problems. You also might trace code simply to better understand the inner workings of a block of code. You already saw a rudimentary form of tracing earlier in the lesson—simply insert MsgBox function calls into the code, run your program, stand back, and watch where message boxes pop up. Because you know where you inserted the MsgBox calls, you easily can follow the progression of the code.

This approach works reliably and is easy to implement, but it does have some drawbacks. It takes some effort to insert the statements. Then, when you run the program, you must interact with every message box you insert, even if no error occurs. If you've inserted 150 message boxes to trace the flow of your program, it can be rather tedious to respond to each and every one!

There are more powerful, elegant ways to trace code, however. Inserting and responding to a series of message boxes can be a cumbersome task. In addition, an important part of code tracing can consist of watching the values of variables while tracking the flow of statements. Data values and knowledge of the last statement processed often must be viewed in tandem to understand the state of your program and its behavior. There are ways to achieve this type of tracing in VBScript, which is the subject covered in this section.

Tracing Your Code Using the Message Box

There is an easy way to avoid responding to each and every message box in the course of tracing a program. This alternative method consists of combining two aspects of the VBScript language. You've already looked at both halves of the equation; now you just need to join them. If you use `On Error Resume Next` in your program, you have seen that not only will your program survive any errors, but you also will have ready access to error information through the `Err` object. This object tells you whether an error occurred. The message box gives you an easy way to display that status.

If you can be assured that you will see a message after an error occurs, there is no need to view the status of the program if no problems have been detected. You can make the message box trace more elegant by displaying only trace information if an error actually occurred. You achieve this by placing a pair of message box statements around the line of code you suspect contains errors. When the trace feedback is displayed, full details on the type of error can be provided. This technique is shown in the modified Pace-Pal code in Listing 12.5.

Listing 12.5. Tracing the flow with a message box statement.

```
' . . . SAME CODE UP TO THIS POINT AS SHOWN IN PREVIOUS LISTINGS

        vMinutes = vHours
        vSeconds = sDuration
        vHours = 0
    Else ' Time info must be in hh:mm:ss format

        vMinutes = Left(sDuration, iPosition - 1)
        vSeconds = Right(sDuration, Len(sDuration) - iPosition)

    End If
End If

' Represent all components in terms of seconds
vHours = vHours * 3600
vMinutes = vMinutes * 60

If Err.Number <> 0 Then Msgbox "An error is present prior"

' Return total seconds value
ConvertStringtoTotalSeconds = CInt(vHours) + _
    CInt(vMinutes) + CInt(vSeconds)
If Err.Number <> 0 Then Msgbox "An error is present here"
```

An informative tracing message is generated when this script is run, as shown in Figure 12.6.

FIGURE 12.6.

*Output from the
message box trace.*

Now to trace your program, you no longer have to click on trace message boxes when everything is going okay. If you see a message box come up, you know it's coming from an area of your code that detected an error.

> **NOTE**
>
> The modified Pace-Pal program with the change shown here is located on the accompanying CD-ROM in the file `Ppalerr3.htm`.

Saturating Your Code with the Message Box

Using a single pair of message box trace statements might be sufficient if you have a pretty good idea where your problem is. But if you have a really tough problem and want to make sure to cover all the bases, it might be just as easy to insert a trace after each and every statement. That way, you virtually guarantee that you will pinpoint the exact statement that causes the problem.

When you take this approach, remember to clearly and uniquely identify each trace statement through the message box text. It does little good to add 200 trace statements to a program if they all just say `Error has been detected!`. If you run the program and only `Error has been detected!` pops up on your screen, you have no idea which statement the message originated from!

The more descriptive the trace messages, the better. If you have messages spread across more than one procedure, it is helpful to identify the procedure name in the message. The idea is that when you see the message, it quickly leads you to the corresponding location in the program. Listing 12.6 shows the Pace-Pal program with extensive trace messages added. Each is uniquely identified within the message text.

> **NOTE**
>
> The modified Pace-Pal program with the change shown here is located on the accompanying CD-ROM in the file `Ppalerr4.htm`.

Listing 12.6. Tracing the flow with many message box statements.

```
' . . . SAME CODE UP TO THIS POINT AS SHOWN IN PREVIOUS LISTINGS

        vMinutes = vHours
        If Err.Number <> 0 Then Msgbox "Error occurred prior to Point A!"
        vSeconds = sDuration
        If Err.Number <> 0 Then Msgbox_"Error occurred prior to Point B!"
        vHours = 0
        If Err.Number <> 0 Then Msgbox "Error occurred prior to Point C!"

    Else ' Time info must be in hh:mm:ss format

        vMinutes = Left(sDuration, iPosition - 1)
        If Err.Number <> 0 Then Msgbox "Error occurred prior to Point D!"
        vSeconds = Right(sDuration, Len(sDuration) - iPosition)
        If Err.Number <> 0 Then Msgbox "Error occurred prior to Point E!"

    End If

  End If

  ' Represent all components in terms of seconds
  vHours = vHours * 3600
  If Err.Number <> 0 Then Msgbox "Error occurred prior to Point F!"
  vMinutes = vMinutes * 60
  If Err.Number <> 0 Then Msgbox "Error occurred prior to Point G!"

  ' Return total seconds value
  ConvertStringtoTotalSeconds = CInt(vHours) + CInt(vMinutes) + CInt(vSeconds)
  If Err.Number <> 0 Then Msgbox "Error occurred prior to Point H!"

  If Err.Number <> 0 Then
      Msgbox "Error #:" & Err.Number & " Description:" & Err.Description _
         & " Source:" & Err.Source, 0, "Error in ConvertStringtoTotalSeconds!"
  End If

End Function ' ConvertStringtoTotalSeconds
```

The message resulting from this modified code runs with the same program input presented earlier is shown in Figure 12.7.

FIGURE 12.7.

*Output from tracing
with sequential message
boxes.*

From reading this trace message and looking at Listing 12.6, it should be clear exactly which statement caused the problem: the `ConvertStringtoTotalSeconds =` statement. If you had inserted just one trace statement at a time, it might have taken many debug iterations to come to this conclusion. Although you spend more time editing the code when you insert multiple trace statements, you can hone in on the specific problem statement after many fewer iterations.

Watching Your Code Using Variables and the Message Box

So you've located the statement that is causing the problem, but you don't know why the error is occurring or how to fix it. That often takes further debugging; it typically requires a look at the contents of the variables if those variables are involved in the rogue statement. One way to get this information is to print the contents of the variables and the variable subtypes right before the problem statement. This technique is applied to the Pace-Pal program in Listing 12.7.

Listing 12.7. Tracing variable contents with a message box statement.

```
    ' Return total seconds value

    MsgBox "vHours = " & vHours & " with type = " _
& vartype(vHours) & _
         "     vMinutes = " & vMinutes & " with type = " _
       & vartype(vMinutes) & _
         "     vSeconds = " & vSeconds & " with type = " _
       & vartype(vSeconds),0, "Var Dump"

    ConvertStringtoTotalSeconds = CInt(vHours) + _
      CInt(vMinutes) + CInt(vSeconds)

    If Err <> 0 Then
        Msgbox "Error #:" & Err.Number & " Description:" & Err.Description _
          & " Source:" & Err.Source, 0, "Error in ConvertStringtoTotalSeconds!"
    End If

End Function   ' ConvertStringtoTotalSeconds
```

Figure 12.8 shows the results of this variable trace.

FIGURE 12.8.

Output from the message box variable trace.

A full description of the variables is now available. One variable is empty, another has an integer value, and another contains string data. Even after viewing this information, you might be confused over exactly what causes the error. You can take yet one more step to shed light on the problem.

Breaking Apart Complex Statements to Find Bugs

The problem now has been isolated to one statement, and the values and subtypes of the variables prior to that statement are known. In the problem statement, the CInt (convert to an integer) function is applied to both a variable that is empty and to a variable that contains a string. How can you see which of these is the problem conversion, or whether both are to blame? The problem statement consists of multiple pieces or expressions, any of which might be the cause of the problem. Your next goal should be to isolate the problem to just one of these pieces. Therefore, the next step is to break it down into smaller pieces, and then apply the same trace techniques to those subpieces. Listing 12.8 shows the modified Pace-Pal script with the problem statement broken down into smaller pieces that can be traced individually.

Listing 12.8. The complex statement broken down into multiple simpler statements.

```
Loop

    ' Temporary code to isolate problem to one statement

    If Err.Number <> 0 Then Msgbox "Error prior to debugA: " _
         & Err.Description
    debugA = CInt(vHours)
    If Err.Number <> 0 Then Msgbox "Error after debugA: " _
         & Err.Description
    debugB = CInt(vMinutes)
    If Err.Number <> 0 Then Msgbox "Error after debugB: " _
         & Err.Description
    debugC = CInt(vSeconds)
    If Err.Number <> 0 Then Msgbox "Error after debugC: " & _
         Err.Description
    ConvertStringtoTotalSeconds = debugA + debugB + debugC

    ' Return total seconds value
    '   ***Decomposed above for Debug ConvertStringtoTotalSeconds = _
    ' CInt(vHours) + CInt(vMinutes) + CInt(vSeconds)

    If Err.Number <> 0 Then
        Msgbox "Error #:" & Err.Number & " Description:" & Err.Description & _
            "Source:" & Err.Source, 0, "Error in ConvertStringtoTotalSeconds!"
    End If

End Function  ' ConvertStringtoTotalSeconds
```

When the script is run after this change, the message box specifically highlights which piece causes the error. Figure 12.9 shows the error message generated when the CInt function, when applied to a string that contains non-numeric characters, causes VBScript to generate an error.

FIGURE 12.9.

Output from the first message box trace after the error, with a trace on decomposed statements.

This is the cause of the original runtime calamity first encountered at the start of the chapter.

Using Other Tools to Help You with the Debugging Task

The example in Listing 12.8 shows the use of many trace statements in just one area of code. In some cases, you might find that inserting one or more trace statements and moving them around is an effective strategy. If you have a 100-line script but suspect that the problem is somewhere in the first five lines, for example, you might put the error check after line 5. If the trace indicates an error at this location, it simply means that the error occurred somewhere on or prior to that line. To prove exactly where within the first five lines the error occurs, your next step might be to move the trace statement so that it comes right after line 4, and so on.

This type of trace statement movement actually is quite typical of debugging efforts. A statement is moved in the HTML page editor, the browser is activated, and the page is reloaded to test the effect of the change. The same cycle is repeated as often as necessary. As a result, you might find that much of your debugging time is spent in transition between your page editor and browser. It is worth noting that the mechanics of making such changes and testing them can consume a significant part of your debugging time. Take careful stock of the tools you have available, and find a process that works well for you.

One approach that works well in the Windows environment is to simply have the Notepad text editor loaded with your source file. You can specify View–Source from the Internet Explorer 3.0 menu to launch Notepad. Then you can use Notepad to modify your script and save it. After you save the script, however, *don't* close Notepad. It doesn't hurt to leave it up and running. Simply activate the browser, and then reload your page to pick up the new modifications. You can do this in Internet Explorer by pressing the F5 function key. After your modified page is loaded, you can test your script. When you find that more changes are needed, just shift back to the still-open Notepad and repeat the cycle. You avoid the time hit of reopening the editor by using this method. You can take a similar approach with the ActiveX Control Pad editor from Microsoft.

This Notepad scenario is outlined here not to emphasize how to best work with Notepad, but to stress that, whatever your tool, you need to put some thought into how you are applying it.

The idiosyncrasies of interacting with it will be multiplied many times over, because debugging, and particularly tracing, often is a tedious, repetitive process. As more tools become available, choosing the right tool is likely to become more and more critical.

Because technology and tool sets are evolving almost on a daily basis, simply finding out about the right tools for debugging can be a challenge. The best way to get an up-to-date view of available tools for VBScript is to search the Web for current information. Resources such as `www.doubleblaze.com` present you with a summary of many of the important and useful tools. Microsoft's Web site, `www.microsoft.com`, provides additional sources of information.

Using VBScript Versus Traditional Debugging Environments

When you get a browser that supports VBScript, you do not get a VBScript development environment along with it. You are left to your own devices to decide how to construct the segments of VBScript code you insert in your Web pages. You might build VBScript programs in an HTML-generation tool, Microsoft's ActiveX Control Pad editor, or you could generate them directly in a text editor. No matter how you're doing it, odds are it's not in a dedicated VBScript development environment with the full-fledged debugging features of Visual Basic 4.0. Although such tools may materialize over time, they do not exist currently. By contrast, almost all high-end computer languages do have their own sophisticated development environment. Typically, a special editor is used for producing programs; the editor sometimes can help check syntax as you type the programs. Also, these environments often include powerful debugging environments that assist with the task of tracing a program and isolating problems. The Visual Basic 4.0 environment and VBA 5.0 offer a rich set of debugging facilities. Although you can't use these debugging facilities directly with VBScript, you can apply some of the same concepts with the "build-it-yourself" trace techniques you'll learn about later in this chapter.

Using Visual Basic to Debug VBScript Applications

Visual Basic 4.0 has a wealth of debugging tools and capabilities that VBScript does not have. If you are a Visual Basic programmer, however, you can take advantage of Visual Basic to debug your VBScript programs. How is this done? This section gives you the answers.

Using Visual Basic 4.0 Trace Capabilities

The Visual Basic 4.0 programmer has no excuse for not having keen insight into all areas of his source code. Visual Basic 4.0, the high-end member of the Visual Basic family, has powerful, easily controlled debugging facilities. Visual Basic 4.0, for example, enables you to stop the program at any location simply by selecting a line of source code in the program editor and pressing a function key to designate the line as a temporary breakpoint. Upon hitting this breakpoint, the running program screeches to a halt, enabling you to spring into debugging action. You can inspect the value of variables in a special debugging window provided by the Visual Basic 4.0 design environment. You can even type more complex expressions in the window. This enables you to evaluate any other statements that might help you understand the problem. You can use this window to inspect the current state of variables even as your program remains suspended. Figure 12.10 shows a view of the Visual Basic 4.0 development environment with a suspended program that has reached a breakpoint.

FIGURE 12.10.

The Visual Basic 4.0 debugging environment.

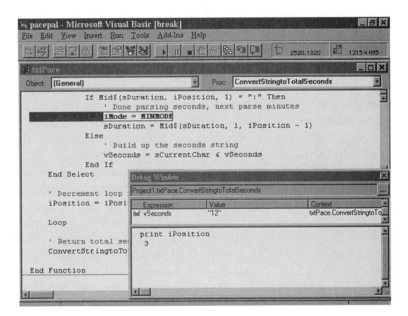

After you check out the state of your suspended program, you can send it on its merry way, right where it left off. You can have it proceed one statement at a time, providing you with the opportunity to query its state line by line. You also can just let it continue until program completion or some other predefined breakpoint. You can even tell it to pick up at an entirely different program location than the one where it stopped. And if you're even nosier about what is going on, you can make arrangements to automatically monitor the contents of your favorite variables as the program chugs along. As variable values change, the new values are displayed automatically in the debug window without stopping your program. You can even provide instructions for your program to stop and show you the last statement it carried out if a variable reaches a certain value.

By now, your head probably is spinning from this dizzying array of debugging weapons, and you're wondering how many of them apply to VBScript. Unfortunately, the answer is that virtually none of these whiz-bang Visual Basic 4.0 debugging features is available to you as you develop VBScript programs. No inherent means exists through the browser or standard text editor to place breakpoints on VBScript programs, to pop up a debug window, to make your program leap to a new location from a suspended state, or to automatically monitor the contents of variables.

On the other hand, several rays of encouragement offset this lack of tools. One comforting thought for the long term is that, as the language matures, tools will likely come. True, that doesn't help you for the short term, but even today's VBScript provides the foundation you need to build similar trace and monitoring capabilities right into your programs. It takes a little extra effort, but as you'll see in the sections that follow, the techniques are really quite easy to apply.

12

DEBUGGING

> **NOTE**
>
> You can find further information on some VBScript development tools as they become available at www.DoubleBlaze.com. Many utilities also are available for various aspects of Web page authoring at the Microsoft site at www.microsoft.com/intdev.

Debugging VBScript Code Within Visual Basic

If you happen to be one of the million plus Visual Basic 4.0 or Visual Basic for Applications programmers, you have a secret weapon you can use in developing VBScript code. Try writing the code in Visual Basic first, and then move it to VBScript! You can take full advantage of the rich debugging capabilities of Visual Basic as you get the bugs out of your program. Then, when it is stable, you can move it to VBScript.

A note of caution, however: There's no such thing as a free lunch. Likewise, there's also no such thing as a free debugger (or at least so it seems). Language differences exist between Visual Basic and VBScript. A program that works fine in Visual Basic 4.0 can be obstinate in VBScript. VBScript is a *subset* of VBA, so much of what works in your Visual Basic application will not work in your script. Depending on your knowledge of the two languages, it can take some work to weed out the syntax differences as you move the code over from Visual Basic 4.0 to VBScript. Some of the language differences are subtle and might not be immediately obvious, even if you know both languages fairly well. The bottom line is that if you debug your code in Visual Basic first and get it running in Visual Basic, don't assume that you're home free. Porting work still might lie ahead in moving the code to VBScript. Nevertheless, Visual Basic's debugging tools make the "debug, then port" process more effective for larger or more complex scripts.

Handling HTML Errors

So far, you have been looking at techniques to debug VBScript applications. You should be aware of the fact, however, that your programs typically are contained within HTML documents. In this case, VBScript works hand-in-hand with HTML, and you must write both VBScript and HTML code to present a Web page to the user. One thing HTML *does* have going for it is a rich set of tools that can aid in quickly developing well-structured Web pages. If you don't have one of those tools, however, or if you have a low-end tool, debugging HTML itself can be the cause of serious hair pulling and grimacing.

It is just as easy to create errors in VBScript as it is in HTML. So how does HTML resolve errors? Consider the HTML shown in Listing 12.9, and note the <A that marks the beginning of an anchor reference.

Listing 12.9. Normal HTML.

```
<H1><A HREF="http://www.mcp.com"><IMG ALIGN=BOTTOM
SRC="../shared/jpg/samsnet.jpg" BORDER=2></A>
<EM>Pace-Pal Sample 3</EM></H1>
```

Suppose that this markup language had been mistakenly entered with just one character different. Assume that the < was inadvertently omitted from in front of the A, as shown in Listing 12.10.

Listing 12.10. HTML missing a tag.

```
<H1>A HREF="http://www.mcp.com"><IMG ALIGN=BOTTOM
SRC="../shared/jpg/samsnet.jpg" BORDER=2></A>
<EM>Pace-Pal Sample 3</EM></H1>
```

The effects of such an omission are ugly indeed, as you can see in Figure 12.11.

Instead of creating the anchor, the internal details of creating the anchor are displayed on-screen. To make matters worse, not only are the results ugly, but they also result in a Web page that doesn't work as intended. The page now has a nonfunctioning link. HTML has no runtime sequence of logic to step through to help pinpoint the error. Instead, it is just a markup or page-generation instruction set. In the absence of sophisticated authoring tools for HTML, the only way you can debug the code is the old method of inspecting it visually. You must look at the page, visually scan it, and review each tag, one by one, for proper syntax. As a general rule, you first should ensure that your HTML code is clean by making a visual inspection before proceeding to debug the VBScript code itself.

FIGURE 12.11.

*Pace-Pal with a
missing tag.*

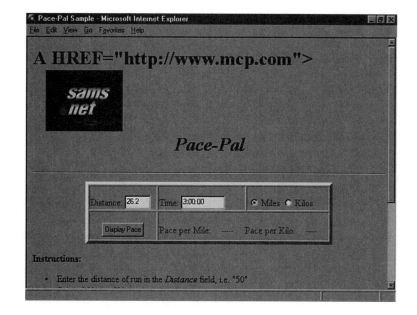

Making Sure the Bugs Are Dead

Once you know the cause of the bug, fixing it is often easy. First, decide what type of fix you
want to put in place. In most programs, like Pace-Pal, many solutions are available. Pace-Pal
can immediately check that data entered by the user is in the correct format and demand that
the user reenter the data if it is invalid, for example. Alternatively, Pace-Pal can check the data
and drop illegal extra characters without telling the user. Then again, Pace-Pal simply can convert any invalid data to 0 and let the user know. The possibilities are many.

For the sake of simplicity, the last solution mentioned is used in this example. Although this
solution isn't necessarily the best way to handle the fix when viewed in the context of the whole
program, it does eliminate the error. A check for invalid data is made right before the problem
statement. If invalid data is found, the user is informed and all times are forced to be 0. Because this is a legal numeric representation, the type-conversion problem is avoided and no
error occurs. Listing 12.11 shows this solution.

Listing 12.11. The fix that our trace pointed us to!

```
' If there is invalid string data, warn the user and
' reset data to prevent more errors
If (Not IsNumeric(vHours)) Or (Not IsNumeric(vMinutes)) _
    Or (Not IsNumeric(vSeconds)) Then
      Msgbox "Time contains character when digits expected. " & _
          " Please respecify!", 0,"Invalid time"
```

continues

Listing 12.11. continued

```
            vHours = 0
            vMinutes = 0
            vSeconds = 0
    End If

    ' Return total seconds value
    ConvertStringtoTotalSeconds = CInt(vHours) + CInt(vMinutes) + CInt(vSeconds)

    If Err.Number <> 0 Then
        Msgbox "Error #:" & Err.Number & " Description:" & _
            Err.Description & " Source:" & Err.Source,
            0, "Error in ConvertStringtoTotalSeconds!"
    End If

End Function   ' ConvertStringtoTotalSeconds
```

With this fix, the program will be robust enough to continue even if a user enters invalid input. Figure 12.12 shows the resulting message box. The program informs the user of the error, substitutes a time of 0 in place of the input, and calculates a pace of 0 seconds per mile.

FIGURE 12.12.

User feedback from the bug-proofed Pace-Pal.

The next step after inserting the fix is to verify that it worked. In this case, that verification is relatively easy. This fix addresses a type-conversion error that prevented Pace-Pal from calculating a final pace. Because the code that checks the error status is still in place at the end of the procedure, simply rerun the procedure. If you don't get an error message, you know the type-conversion error has been eliminated. Likewise, the fact that a pace of 00:00 shows up in the pace text box indicates a complete calculation. So, in this case, verifying that the fix really solves the problem is relatively easy. For some bugs, you might have to add more trace statements or variable analyses after the fix is in place to verify that it had the intended results.

It is important to note that this fix keeps the program from crashing when the user enters an invalid time such as 37:12AA. A similar problem still exists in the code with distance rather than time, however. If the user enters 6.2AA rather than 6.2 miles, a type-conversion-induced runtime error results from a different procedure in Pace-Pal that calculates the final pace. Because the type of problem present in dealing with time also is present in dealing with distance, more than one fix is needed in Pace-Pal to address all the areas where this type of problem occurs. This, it turns out, is very common in debugging, especially in data-handling code. If you find a bug in one place, check for it in other areas of the program too. If wrong assumptions or coding techniques led to problems once, they very likely will lead to problems again.

If you think you have a problem area that you need to check throughout your application, you should be able to pinpoint it quite easily if it results in an error condition. You can use the techniques presented earlier in this lesson. Insert On Error Resume Next in every procedure. At the end of every procedure, check the Err object and display a message if an error occurred within that procedure. This level of tracing gives you a clear indication of any procedures in which the error occurs.

Creating Your Own Debug Window for Tracing

By now, the value of good tracing should be clear. Good debugging usually comes down to good program tracing. Several approaches to tracing are available. The technique of tracing the flow of every statement by displaying message boxes was presented in the sections "Using Simple Debugging Techniques" and "Using Advanced Debugging Techniques." This method can be a bit cumbersome because it requires interaction with a series of message boxes each time you do a trace. The technique of simply displaying a message box only if an error occurs also was illustrated earlier in this chapter. This approach is quite effective, but you might want to monitor the flow of your program at times even if an error has not occurred.

Tracing all statements, even under non-error conditions, can provide a helpful overall picture of what the code is really doing. Understanding the flow of the code and gaining insight into the state of the variables as the code execution progresses helps you better understand the behavior of a program. The more you understand the overall behavior of a program, the better code you can write for it. Likewise, you'll be able to make better intuitive decisions when chasing problems. So what's the best approach when you want to trace normal program flow? As established earlier, the "always display message box" approach can be rather cumbersome. And the "display message box only after error" approach doesn't give the full level of feedback you might be looking for in every case.

You really need a separate debug window that lets you peek into the program as it progresses, much like Visual Basic 4.0's debug window. It turns out that you can build at least some of those capabilities right into your page with VBScript. You just add a rather large form text area input control at the bottom of your page. A debug text box typically is used as a temporary debug tool, and is removed before you release your final version of the code. But in the meantime, during the script-development phase, it can be a considerable help during debugging. Listing 12.12 shows the Pace-Pal HTML source code with an <INPUT> tag added to define this type of debug text box. The sample program Ppalerr5.htm on the accompanying CD-ROM uses this same approach, but it additionally formats the input controls in a table for better visual presentation on-screen.

Listing 12.12. Adding a form text area input control to capture debug trace statements.

```
<FORM NAME="frmPace">
<PRE>
<FONT COLOR=BLUE FACE="Comic Sans MS" SIZE=6>
Distance:     <INPUT NAME="txtDistance" VALUE="" MAXLENGTH="5" SIZE=5>
<INPUT TYPE="RADIO" NAME="Dist" CHECKED VALUE="Miles"
onClick=SetDistance("Miles") > Miles
<INPUT TYPE="RADIO" NAME="Dist" VALUE="Kilos"
onClick=SetDistance("Kilos")>Kilos
Time:         <INPUT NAME="txtTime" VALUE="" MAXLENGTH="11" SIZE=11>
in minute:second format
<INPUT TYPE=BUTTON VALUE="Display Pace" SIZE=30 NAME="Calc">
Pace per Mile: <INPUT NAME="txtPaceMiles" VALUE=""
MAXLENGTH="5" SIZE=5>     Pace per Kilo:
<INPUT NAME="txtPaceKilos" VALUE="" MAXLENGTH="5" SIZE=5>

Debug Window: <TEXTAREA NAME="txtDebug" ROWS="10" COLS="60" >
</TEXTAREA>

</FONT>
</PRE>
</FORM>
```

The `textarea` control, which is named `txtDebug` in this example, provides a convenient place
to log trace information. You can add code to your script to display debug information in this
control wherever you want logging to take place in your program. As a matter of fact, if you
want, you can print debug information after each and every script statement. This logging takes
place in an unobtrusive manner and doesn't require the interaction of the message box. You
can even provide variable and code-location information when you display information in the
`txtDebug` control. Listing 12.13 shows an example of Pace-Pal modified to use this style of tracing.

Listing 12.13. Tracing program flow and variables with form text area input control.

```
document.frmPace.txtDebug.Value = document.frmPace.txtDebug.Value & _
    "Prior to assignment, vSeconds =" & vSeconds & vbCrLF

' Return total seconds value
ConvertStringtoTotalSeconds = CInt(vHours) + CInt(vMinutes) _
        + CInt(vSeconds)

document.frmPace.txtDebug.Value = document.frmPace.txtDebug.Value & __
    "After assignment, vSeconds =" & vSeconds & vbCrLf
```

When Pace-Pal is run with these modifications, a clear trace appears in the `txtDebug` `textarea`
control as the program progresses. Figure 12.13 shows a sample of the trace.

FIGURE 12.13.

Output from the textarea *trace.*

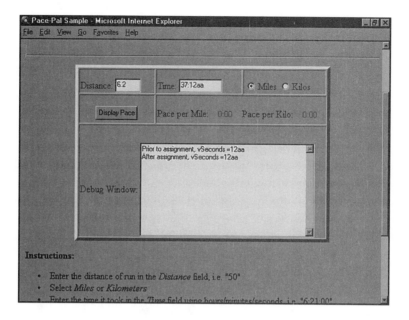

This trace can provide great insight into code behavior. Another advantage of storing trace output in the `txtDebug` control is that you can use this information to review your program history even after your script execution completes. Suppose that your script generates 200 lines of trace information in response to a button click. After the block of code associated with the button click completes, all this information still is available in the `txtDebug` control. You can scroll through the data and reconstruct what happened to the script by looking at this trace. Notice that the variable `vbCrLf` is used here. This is declared to contain the standard line-separator characters—specifically, `Chr$(10) & Chr$(13)`.

Building Your Own Tracing Routines

The technique of placing trace statements in a `textbox` control is handy, but you can make it even more convenient. The statements that log information are not difficult to understand, but they are a bit lengthy. Also, you want to ensure that you take the same approach with every log statement. If you generate one type of trace information in one area of code, and then generate trace information in another format somewhere else in your script, it will be more confusing to analyze the trace results. So it is more convenient to simply call an easy-to-use subroutine every time you want to log trace messages. That way, the subroutine can contain the code to handle all aspects of logging the trace information. Listing 12.14 shows a sample trace debug subroutine.

12

DEBUGGING

Listing 12.14. The definition for a simple trace routine.

```
Sub DebugMsg(Info)
'-------------------------------------------------------
' Print debug message to textarea used for debug display
    Document.frmPace.txtDebug.Value = _
        Document.frmPace.txtDebug.Value & info & vbCrLf
End Sub
```

This procedure takes a string, which is provided as a parameter at the time the procedure is called, and adds that string to the current contents of the `textbox` control. This procedure may be called many times from different locations in the program. The string, which is provided as data to this procedure, should describe the program from which the call is made in order to provide a meaningful trace history. For clear output, new information provided by the trace procedure should be displayed as a new line in the text box. That is the purpose of the `vbCrLf` constant variable in Listing 12.14. `vbCrLf` is a variable for the intrinsic VBScript constant containing the carriage-return/line-feed characters that cause a new line to be generated. The assignment statement appends the new information after the existing contents of the `textbox` control. Then, a carriage return/line feed is appended to the end of that. Any information that follows appears on a new line.

Using this type of subroutine doesn't just save you from repeatedly typing the same trace code. It also ensures that all trace output is generated in a standard, consistent manner. After all, every trace message comes from the same place with this approach. Then the rest of the code simply uses this common subroutine wherever traces are needed. Listing 12.15 shows an example of Pace-Pal, modified to use calls to the trace procedure to carry out a trace.

Listing 12.15. The call to a simple trace routine.

```
DebugMsg "Prior to assignment, vSeconds =" & vSeconds
    ' Return total seconds value
    ConvertStringtoTotalSeconds = CInt(vHours) + CInt(vMinutes) _
        + CInt(vSeconds)
DebugMsg "After assignment"
```

Because any expression can be passed for subsequent display to `DebugMsg`, you have the flexibility to send information about any variable and have that recorded with your program trace. Notice that in the first call to `DebugMsg`, the descriptive string passed to the procedure contains the contents of a variable as well as indicates the location where the call was made. The benefits of this type of flexible trace are tremendous. You can monitor the changes in variables as your program executes, and monitor the current location and progression of the code. You can gain very keen insights from the program-monitoring this trace procedure provides.

12

NOTE

You might have noticed that the calls to the debug trace procedure are not indented, unlike the rest of the program. This is a convention that can be used to make temporary calls stand out. All the debug trace calls here are temporary calls only. Normally, you add them just to aid your debugging efforts during design time and remove them prior to releasing your final product. The practice of left-aligning the debug statements makes it easy to spot the statements and remove them later.

Looking at a Sample Variable Analysis Routine

The information provided by the DebugMsg procedure is good, but even that might not tell you everything you want to know. If you're chasing a problem in a script, it might not be enough just to see the program flow. You might even use DebugMsg to display the contents of a variable and find that it still doesn't quite fill you in on the whole story of the state of your program. One other piece of the picture that can be very important is determining what subtype of data a variable represents, as well as the current value of that data.

A variable that prints as 23 in the trace log, for example, may be stored in a variant variable with subtype string, or a variant variable with subtype integer. For some types of problems, it can be very important to understand which subtype data representation a variable currently has. If you write elegant code to look at the variant subtype and interpret it for logging, the code can be rather lengthy. It's certainly not something you want scattered all over your program. Fortunately, you can apply the same trace procedure solution to this problem. An expanded trace procedure can be defined to provide a "power trace." This procedure not only accepts a descriptive parameter indicating the program location, but it also accepts a parameter that contains a variable to analyze. The procedure then logs an informational string to the textbox control based on these parameters. Part of the information logged in the textbox control displays the program location. The other portion reflects the value and subtype of the variable. An analysis of the variable is carried out to determine the subtype of the variant. This type of debugging procedure provides a very detailed and powerful trace history. Listing 12.16 shows an example.

Listing 12.16. The definition for a variant variable analysis routine.

```
Sub VarAnalyzeMsg(InfoMsg, VarToAnalyze)
'-------------------------------------------------------
' Print debug info message to textarea used for debug display;
' print out type and value of VarToAnalyze

    Dim VarMsg ' Used to build up info about VarToAnalyze
```

continues

Listing 12.16. continued

```
        ' Determine type of variable
        '   Note: If this code was in Visual Basic 4.0, the VB
        '         intrinsic constants such as vbEmpty could be
        '         used instead of the hardcoded values shown
        '         (not defined in beta VBScript)
        Select Case VarType(VarToAnalyze)
            Case 0    ' vbEmpty
                VarMsg = "Empty"
            Case 1    ' vbNull
                VarMsg = "Null"
            Case 2    ' vbInteger
                VarMsg = "Integer, Value=" & VarToAnalyze
            Case 3    ' vbLong
                VarMsg = "Long, Value=" & VarToAnalyze
            Case 4    ' vbSingle
                VarMsg = "Single, Value=" & VarToAnalyze
            Case 5    ' vbDouble
                VarMsg = "Double, Value=" & VarToAnalyze
            Case 6    ' vbCurrency
                VarMsg = "Currency, Value=" & VarToAnalyze
            Case 7    ' vbDate
                VarMsg = "Date, Value=" & VarToAnalyze
            Case 8    ' vbString
                VarMsg = "String, Len=" & Len(VarToAnalyze) _
                    & " Value=" & VarToAnalyze
            Case 9    ' vbObject
                VarMsg = "OLE Automation Object"
            Case 10   ' vbError
                VarMsg = "Error"
            Case 11   ' vbBoolean
                VarMsg = "Boolean, Value=" & VarToAnalyze
            Case 12   ' vbVariant
                VarMsg = "Non-OLE Automation Object"
            Case 13   ' vbDataObject
                VarMsg = "Byte, Value=" & VarToAnalyze
            Case 17   ' vbByte
                VarMsg = "Byte, Value=" & VarToAnalyze
            Case 8194 ' vbArray + vbInteger
                VarMsg = "Integer Array, Ubound=" & Ubound(VarToAnalyze)
            Case 8195  ' vbArray + vbLong
                VarMsg = "Long Array, Ubound=" & Ubound(VarToAnalyze)
            Case 8196 ' vbArray + vbSingle
                VarMsg = "Single Array, Ubound=" & Ubound(VarToAnalyze)
            Case 8197 ' vbArray + vbDouble
                VarMsg = "Double Array, Ubound=" & Ubound(VarToAnalyze)
            Case 8198 ' vbArray + vbCurrency
                VarMsg = "Currency Array, Ubound=" & Ubound(VarToAnalyze)
            Case 8199 ' vbArray + vbDate
                VarMsg = "Date Array, Ubound=" & Ubound(VarToAnalyze)
            Case 8200 ' vbArray + vbString
                VarMsg = "String Array, Ubound=" & Ubound(VarToAnalyze)
            Case 8201 ' vbArray + vbObject
                VarMsg = "Object Array, Ubound=" & Ubound(VarToAnalyze)
            Case 8202 ' vbArray + vbError
                VarMsg = "Error Array, Ubound=" & Ubound(VarToAnalyze)
```

```
        Case 8203 ' vbArray + vbBoolean
            VarMsg = "Boolean Array, Ubound=" & Ubound(VarToAnalyze)
        Case 8204 ' vbArray + vbVariant
            VarMsg = "Variant Array, Ubound=" & Ubound(VarToAnalyze)
        Case 8205 ' vbArray + vbDataObject
            VarMsg = "vbDataObject Array, Ubound=" & Ubound(VarToAnalyze)
        Case 8209 ' vbArray + vbByte
            VarMsg = "Byte Array, Ubound=" & Ubound(VarToAnalyze)
        Case Else
            VarMsg = "Unknown"
    End Select

    VarMsg = "...Var type is " & VarMsg
    ' Print to textarea used for debug trace, must use vbCrLf
    ' to advance lines
    Document.frmPace.txtDebug.Value = _
        Document.frmPace.txtDebug.Value & InfoMsg & vbCrLf
    Document.frmPace.txtDebug.Value = _
        Document.frmPace.txtDebug.Value & VarMsg & vbCrLf
End Sub   ' VarAnalyzeMsg
```

12

DEBUGGING

STYLE CONSIDERATIONS

If you're really alert, you might have noticed that a check is made to see whether the variable is represented in several storage types that VBScript does not support. These include currency and arrays of nonvariants that are supported by Visual Basic. Because it doesn't hurt to check for these extra types, and it could even provide added insight if there was an internal VBScript error that resulted in a bad type, these checks are left in here. This also makes for *upward-compatible* code that can be ported to VBA or Visual Basic 4.0 programs without change.

Listing 12.17 shows a modified sample of the familiar Pace-Pal example. Pace-Pal has been modified to make calls to the VarAnalyzeMsg routine. These calls have been added both before and after the statement that earlier samples indicated was the problem statement. Because three variables are involved in the problem statement (vHours, vMinutes, and vSeconds), all three should be inspected prior to the problem statement to help determine the cause of the problem. Therefore, three different calls to VarAnalyzeMsg are used—one to analyze each specific variable. Likewise, the same three calls to VarAnalyzeMsg are made after the problem statement. This is to ensure that none of the variables has unexpectedly changed value or subtype.

NOTE

You can pretty well determine by looking at the code involved in the incorrect section of Pace-Pal that no variables will be changed after the problem statement. The post-statement calls to VarAnalyzeMsg, however, ensure that you are not making any mistaken assumptions about values not changing. This is a good standard debugging practice to follow, and the calls are included here to illustrate that point. You should scientifically verify the contents of variables during debugging rather than making potentially faulty assumptions. If you've decided that a full trace is in order, you can never assume that a value will not change. It is always best to check debugging information before and after a given statement. Even if you think that nothing will have changed, there is always a chance that you're wrong, and the extra debugging procedure costs you only the time it takes to enter it.

Listing 12.17. The call to the variant variable analysis routine.

```
Call VarAnalyzeMsg("Analyzing vHours prior to ConvertString",vHours)
Call VarAnalyzeMsg("Analyzing vMinutes prior to ConvertString",vMinutes)
Call VarAnalyzeMsg("Analyzing vSeconds prior to ConvertString",vSeconds)

    ' Return total seconds value
    ConvertStringtoTotalSeconds = CInt(vHours) + CInt(vMinutes) + _
        CInt(vSeconds)

Call VarAnalyzeMsg("Analyzing vHours after call to ConvertString",vHours)
Call VarAnalyzeMsg("Analyzing vMinutes after call to ConvertString",vMinutes)
Call VarAnalyzeMsg("Analyzing vSeconds after call to ConvertString",vSeconds)
```

NOTE

The source file for the Pace-Pal program modified to contain the change shown here is available on the accompanying CD-ROM in the file `Ppalerr5.htm`.

The modified Pace-Pal program with the `VarAnalyzeMsg` trace statement generates the output shown in Figure 12.14.

The `txtDebug` text box trace area is filled with meaningful trace information that can help you understand the behavior of the program. Although this trace facility might not be as powerful as the trace capabilities built into other languages, such as Visual Basic 4.0, it does give you ample power to get to the root of just about any VBScript-generated error.

Figure 12.14.

Output from the variant variable analysis routine.

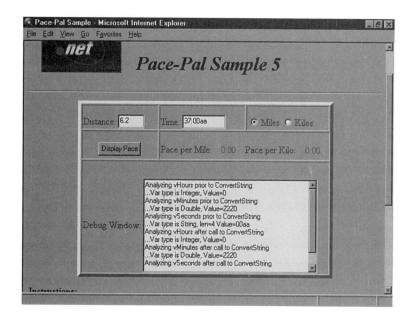

Looking at More Reasons Why VBScript Can Be Tough to Debug

As if all these debugging challenges weren't enough, there are still a few more that haven't been discussed yet. It's important to be aware of these additional challenges—not so that you will spend sleepless nights worrying about them, but so that you will have a broad view of what to expect as you start to chase VBScript-related problems.

VBScript is what sometimes is called a *glue* language. It is great at gluing many components together to provide a powerful programmatic interface. You easily can weave a masterpiece of ActiveX controls, Java applets, intrinsic form controls, and OLE automation components into one tapestry when building your script. Opening the door to such easy integration of components, however, also opens the door to potential problems with them. A third-party control might have a bug in it. The Java applet provided by your coworker might be riddled with hideous errors in logic. The possibilities for problems are endless. And if your VBScript program incorporates those pieces, the problems will be visible to the user through your program. When such a problem occurs, the user considers it your script's problem. Then it falls to you, the debugger, to isolate areas of code to prove that a problem is caused by one specific component.

And now the good news that will save you from those sleepless nights: The very same skills discussed in this lesson that will help you hone in on VBScript errors also will help you hone in on component-related errors. You still need to trace through the program, isolating the problem to one specific area of the code. You still might need to display the value of variables, or even component property values, to monitor the state of the program before and after the statements related to the components that might be causing the errors. You still might need to break down one large VBScript statement involving components into a series of smaller statements to isolate the problem. In every case, the same tools and techniques already discussed still apply.

The Moral of the Story

The best advice to give for debugging and error handling is, "Don't make mistakes!" The outcome is no more probable than if you told the sun to rise in the north and set in the south, though. Mistakes are an inherent and unavoidable part of today's programming model. If you're a programmer, you will make plenty of them. A big part of the task of producing VBScript programs is getting out the bugs and making your programs shield the user from the bugs. The real moral of the story, then, is to apply these debugging, tracing, and error-handling techniques vigorously. Make use of debug tracing and variable analysis routines like those provided in this chapter. They will add efficiency and consistency to your debugging. Keep your eyes open for good debugging tools. VBScript debug tools currently are far behind those for Visual Basic 4.0, but this language is still in its infancy, and you can expect support to increase. For now, scripts may take longer to debug than programs in other languages due to the lack of tools. But with patience, strategy, and some of the techniques discussed in this chapter, your debugging sessions still can be highly effective.

Review

This chapter provided important debugging techniques that can be applied to syntax and semantic errors. Syntax errors and semantic errors, both caused by incorrectly specifying your programs, were defined—and examples of both were illustrated. This chapter also demonstrated how VBScript provides the means to turn off the automatic generation of runtime error messages to the user and prevent the subsequent script termination. Tracing techniques can also be helpful in analyzing all types of errors. The various tracing techniques were summarized in this chapter.

If you're doing a lot of debugging, you'll probably want an even more powerful debug repertoire. You can obtain this by building your own debug routines. This chapter supplied several strategies you can incorporate in your own Web pages to analyze and prevent errors from occurring. While VBScript does not have a powerful set of debug tools like Visual Basic 4.0 does, there is enough in the language to craft your own effective debugging approach. The most important tools, however, are the same ones you supply for any language you must debug—your own persistence and patience.

In Chapter 13, "Dynamic Web Page Building," you will learn how to use Internet Explorer's Document object to create Web pages that dynamically alter the content of a Web page. You will also learn other techniques, such as writing the current date and time to a Web page, or dynamically changing the colors on a page. These techniques are very useful and helpful in VBScripting arsenal.

12

DEBUGGING

Dynamic Web Page Building

by Craig Eddy

IN THIS CHAPTER

CHAPTER 13

Perhaps the most exciting aspect of the World Wide Web is the amount of interactivity that can be provided. The advent of JavaScript and VBScript has furthered the cause of interactive Web sites. Using VBScript, it is possible to create a dynamic Web page without having to resort to server-side programming.

You create a dynamic Web page by taking a static HTML file and embedding VBScript code within it. The VBScript code provides the dynamic aspect by changing what is displayed on the page as well as how it is displayed. Your pages can be dynamic on a continuous basis (changing over time while the page is being viewed), or they can be dynamic at load time (the page that loads changes when it's loaded, but then is static). Once you have a grasp of what objects and functions are available to your scripts, you easily can design scripts that display dynamic information and change the page's presentation.

This chapter covers the basics of creating a dynamic Web page using VBScript. The first section covers the Internet Explorer's Document object, which contains properties and methods relative to the currently loaded Web page. Then the ActiveX Timer control is discussed. You can use this control to display messages, change the status bar text, or change the look of the page on a continuous basis. The chapter concludes with several sections describing specific ways to use VBScript to make your Web pages dynamic.

Using the Internet Explorer Document Object

The Internet Explorer exposes an entire hierarchy of objects to the scripts it is hosting. This hierarchy, or *object model*, provides your scripts with access to information about everything from the browser window itself (via the Window object) all the way down to an individual HTML form element (via the Forms collection of the Document object).

Because the topic of this chapter is dynamic Web pages, the Document object is the only object discussed here. This is not meant to imply that the other objects in the model aren't accessible or useful to VBScript, but they aren't necessary to create dynamic pages.

The Document object provides access to the HTML source code that exists on the page. Using the Document object, you can both read and write the HTML for the page. You also can control the document's color elements as well as access and modify the value of any HTML form elements contained within the document.

This section discusses the Document object's properties, collections, and methods in enough detail to use them in the examples presented throughout the rest of the chapter. You can find documentation on the Internet Explorer object model at http://www.microsoft.com/intdev/sdk/docs/scriptom/.

Properties and Collections

The Document object's properties and collections provide access to various HTML attributes for the Internet Explorer's currently loaded page. These attributes include the various color elements, the available HTML forms, a collection of links, a collection of anchors, and access to the client-side cookie file for the current page. *Cookies* are a means of storing information on the client's machine that can be retrieved later by the Web server when the client requests the page again.

The Color Properties

The current version of the HTML specification enables the Web page designer to specify the colors to be used to render certain elements on the page. You can control the text color used for links, the default foreground color (for text that is not a link), and the document's background color. Table 13.1 lists these properties.

Table 13.1. The Document object's color properties.

Property	Specifies
alinkColor	Color for an active link
bgColor	Color for the page background
fgColor	Color for text and other foreground items
linkColor	Color for a link
vlinkColor	Color for a visited link

> **NOTE**
>
> When the user holds down the mouse button over a link, that link is considered *active*. The link's color then changes to the color specified by the alinkColor property. Internet Explorer does not have this feature, however, so the link's color always remains the color specified by linkColor (or the default link color if linkColor is not specified).

The link color properties can be set only while the page is loading. The bgColor and fgColor properties can be set when the page loads as well as after the page has loaded. This capability enables you to create an on-the-fly color scheme for users. If they don't like the default colors you've chosen for the page, they can click a button, for example, to set a new color scheme. Or you can provide a drop-down list of available color schemes from which the user can choose. These are discussed in the section "Changing the Document's Colors," later in this chapter.

The Location Property

This property returns a string representation of the document's URL.

WARNING

The Microsoft Web site's Internet Explorer scripting object model documentation defines this property as a reference to a Location object. Internet Explorer, however, does not recognize this property as such, but simply as a string representing the URL for the document.

The LastModified Property

This property returns the date and time the document was last modified.

The Title Property

The document's title is returned by this property. This is the string specified between the HTML document's `<TITLE>...</TITLE>` tags.

The Referrer Property

This property provides the URL for the page the user was on when he clicked a link that brought him to the current page. If the user is on a page with URL `http://www.myserver.com/page1.htm`, for example, and he clicks a link that takes him to `http://www.myserver.com/page2.htm`, the Referrer property on the second page evaluates to `http://www.myserver.com/page1.htm`.

If the user opened the page by clicking a link in another page, the Referrer property returns NULL.

The Cookie Property

The term *cookie* refers to a piece of data stored on the user's machine. The data is relative to a certain Web page and is sent to Web servers that house the page the cookie belongs to when the page is requested by the browser. Cookies enable Web site designers to store user preferences and other information on the client's machine instead of on the Web server somewhere. You can store a cookie for the date and time the user last viewed a particular page, for example. When the user returns to the page, your VBScript code can access this cookie information and provide a message like Welcome back, it's been 10 days since your last visit.

Cookies are defined as a name and value associated with that name. Reading the Cookie property returns a string of all the names and values for the current page. This string separates each cookie name/value pair with a semicolon. To set a new cookie pair or modify an existing cookie's value, simply assign the pair to the `Cookie` property, as shown in this example:

```
Document.Cookie = strCookieName & "=" & strCookieValue
```

Here, `strCookieName` is a variable containing the name for the cookie and `strCookieValue` contains the value for the cookie. These variables can be replaced with hard-coded strings, of course.

Cookies also have an `expires` attribute that specifies the date after which the cookie no longer is valid. If an `expires` attribute is not specified, the cookie should expire at the end of the current browser session (that is, when the user exits the browser application). The `expires` attribute should be appended to the string assigned to the `Cookie` property. To set a cookie that expires on December 31, 1999 at midnight Greenwich mean time, for example, use this code:

```
Document.Cookie = strCookieName & "=" & strCookieValue & ";expires=31-Dec-99 GMT"
```

To remove a cookie from the client's machine, set its value to `NULL` and give it an `expires` attribute that matches some date in the past. For example:

```
Document.Cookie = strCookieName & "=NULL;expires=01-Aug-96"
```

removes the cookie specified in `strCookieName`.

The section "Using Cookies to Maintain User Information," later in this chapter, demonstrates in more detail how to access cookies using VBScript code. For a technical discussion of cookies in general, see the Netscape page describing them at `http://home.netscape.com/newsref/std/cookie_spec.html`.

NOTE

To use cookies, the page must be stored on and served by a Web server. This is due to the fact that cookies are actually a part of the HTTP specification and therefore require an HTTP client/server conversation in order to work. Therefore, cookies will not work when you are saving a page to a local hard drive and loading it using Internet Explorer's file browser.

The anchors Collection

The `anchors` collection is an array of the anchors contained in the document. An *anchor* is a named reference to a section of the document. Anchors are defined using the HTML tag `<a NAME=anchor-name>...</a>` and can be referenced in a link by `<a HTEF=page-url#anchor-name>`. This URL loads the page specified and transfers the user to the place where the anchor is specified.

The anchors collection has a length property. To determine how many anchors are contained in the document, use document.anchors.length. To reference the string for the first anchor in the document, use document.anchors[0].

The links Collection

The links collection is almost identical to the anchors collection. It also has a length property, and you reference items in the array using document.links[x]. The links array contains all the hyperlinks that take you to another page or to an anchor in the current document.

The forms Collection

The forms collection returns an array of all the HTML forms contained in the document. It also has a length property, and individual form objects are referenced using document.forms[x]. You then can reference an individual element of a form using document.forms[x].input1, for example.

Methods

The document object provides several useful methods that can be used to manipulate the contents of the document and open a new document.

The Write and Writeln Methods

These methods are used to print HTML text to the document. The text is printed at the point where the script is placed. The text is placed directly into the document and therefore must be formatted as HTML text. The difference between the two methods is that the Writeln method also appends a newline character to the end of the text written to the document.

The section "Writing the Current Date and Time to the Page," later in this chapter, gives you several examples of using the Write and Writeln methods. As a quick example, the HTML code in Listing 13.1 produces the Web page shown in Figure 13.1.

Listing 13.1. Writeln sample code.

```
<HTML><HEAD>
<TITLE>New Page</TITLE>
</HEAD><BODY>
<SCRIPT LANGUAGE="VBScript">
<!--
window.Document.Writeln "appCodeName: " & window.navigator.appCodeName & "<br>"
window.Document.Writeln "appName: " & window.navigator.appName & "<br>"
window.Document.Writeln "appVersion: " & window.navigator.appVersion & "<br>"
window.Document.Writeln "userAgent: " & window.navigator.UserAgent & "<br>"
window.Document.Writeln "LastModified: " & window.Document.LastModified & "<br>"
window.Document.Writeln "Referrer: " & window.Document.Referrer & "<br>"
window.Document.Writeln "Title: " & window.Document.Title & "<br>"
window.Document.Writeln "Location: " & window.Document.Location & "<br>"
```

```
-->
</SCRIPT>

<H1>Document.Writeln Example</H1>

<SCRIPT LANGUAGE="VBScript">
<!--
Document.Writeln "appCodeName: " & window.navigator.appCodeName & "<br>"
-->
</SCRIPT>
</BODY>
</HTML>
```

FIGURE 13.1.

The Writeln *example's resulting page.*

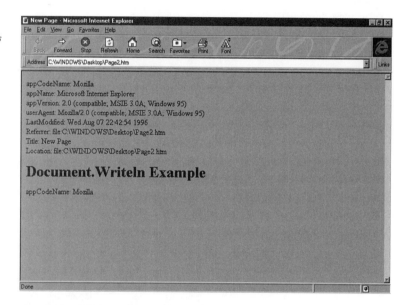

The Open, Close, and Clear Methods

The Open, Close, and Clear methods are used to create and write to a completely new document object. The Open method is used to start a new document. It clears the current document and prepares it for writing. The Close method is used after HTML text is written to the document to display all the text written to the document since the Open method was invoked. The text is not displayed until the Close method is used. The Clear method is used to clear the document of any existing data.

As a quick example, the code in Listing 13.2 produces the Web page shown in Figure 13.2. Note that only the text from the window_onLoad event code is shown—not the HTML contained in the <BODY>...</BODY> section of the listing. When the page loads, the <H1> section's text shows up briefly and then is replaced by the text from the onLoad event.

Listing 13.2. Using the Open and Close methods.

```
<HTML><HEAD>
<SCRIPT LANGUAGE="VBScript">
<!--
Sub window_onLoad()
window.document.open "text/html"
window.document.writeln "<H2>"
window.document.writeln "This text is from the window_onLoad event!"
window.document.writeln "</H2>"
window.document.close
end sub
-->
</SCRIPT>
<TITLE>New Page</TITLE>
</HEAD>
<BODY>
<H1>This Doesn't Show Up!!!</H1>
</BODY>
</HTML>
```

FIGURE 13.2.

The Open/Close *example's resulting page.*

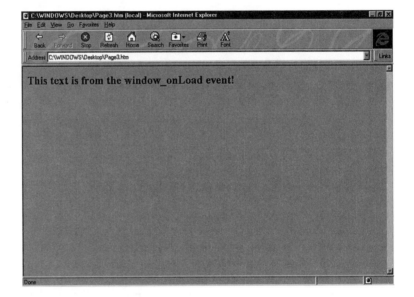

Using the ActiveX Timer Control

Now that you've learned how to manipulate the Document object, it's time to put that knowledge to use. This section describes the ActiveX Timer object and how to use it to create dynamic documents.

You can download the ActiveX Timer control from the Microsoft Web site at `http://www.microsoft.com/workshop/activex/gallery/ms/timer/sample.htm`. Before you go to the trouble, however, check to see whether you already have a copy on your system. The best way to do so is to run the ActiveX Control Pad and choose the Edit | Insert ActiveX Control menu. The Timer control appears as `Timer Object` in the Control Type list box.

The Timer control has three properties that are useful within VBScript code: `Interval`, `Enabled`, and `ID`. There is only one event: `Timer`. The `Interval` property determines the amount of time, in milliseconds, between calls of the `Timer` event. The `Enabled` property enables and disables the control. The `ID` property serves as the control's name. The `Timer` event is the event that fires with each passing of the time specified by the `Interval` property.

You can use the Timer control to create any type of dynamic effect you want. You can use it to randomly change the status bar text, open new documents, navigate to another Web page, and so on. The code in Listing 13.3 shows an example of opening a new document two seconds after the page loads and writing some text to it. Figure 13.3 shows the resulting page.

Listing 13.3. Using the ActiveX Timer control.

```
<HTML><HEAD>
<TITLE>New Page</TITLE>
</HEAD>
<BODY>
<H1>This Will Disappear Soon!!!</H1>
    <SCRIPT LANGUAGE="VBScript">
<!--
Sub IeTimer1_Timer()
window.document.open "text/html"
window.document.writeln "<H2>"
window.document.writeln "This text is from the "
window.document.writeln "Timer event!"
window.document.writeln "</H2>"
window.document.close
end sub
-->
</SCRIPT>
<OBJECT ID="IeTimer1" WIDTH=39 HEIGHT=39
 CLASSID="CLSID:59CCB4A0-727D-11CF-AC36-00AA00A47DD2">
    <PARAM NAME="_ExtentX" VALUE="1032">
    <PARAM NAME="_ExtentY" VALUE="1032">
    <PARAM NAME="Interval" VALUE="2000">
</OBJECT>
</BODY>
</HTML>
```

13

DYNAMIC WEB
PAGE BUILDING

FIGURE 13.3.

The resulting page from the ActiveX Timer control example.

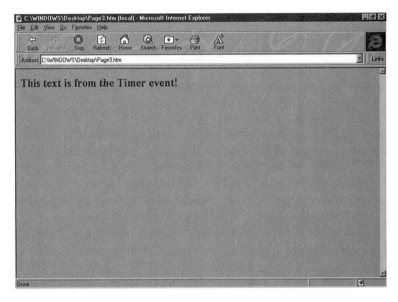

The page initially loads and displays the message This Will Disappear Soon!!!. After two seconds, the value of the Interval property, the IeTimer1_Timer event, fires. This event uses the Document object's Open, Writeln, and Close methods to create a new document and print the text This text is from the Timer event! Note that on the new document there is no Timer control, so the code executes only once. Because you're writing HTML to the document, however, you could have placed the Timer object and its associated code into the new document. This could be used to create a slide show but, due to the cascading nature of the code you'd have to enter into the script, it would be hard to maintain.

Writing the Current Date and Time to the Page

Perhaps one of the most useful features for creating dynamic Web pages is the capability to write the current date and time to the page. This is accomplished using the Document object's Writeln property and VBScript's various date and time functions.

The concept is simple: As the page loads, an embedded script uses the Document.writeln method to print a string containing the current date and time at the point in the HTML file where the script appears. Using the various date/time functions, you can format the string in any manner you want. The example presented in this section formats the date as Friday, August 9, 1996 and leaves the time in the format returned by the VBScript Time function.

Although the example presented here is not all that useful by itself, when combined with a "real" Web page, it provides a nice touch for your site. Figure 13.4 shows the output from the script. The code is presented in Listing 13.4.

FIGURE 13.4.

The current date/time written to the page.

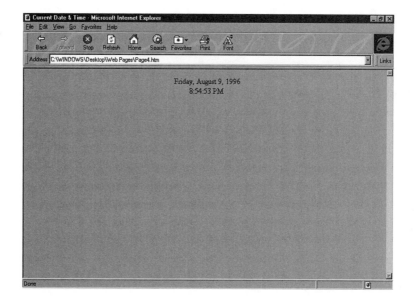

Listing 13.4. The code for the date/time example.

```
<HTML><HEAD>
<TITLE>Current Date & Time</TITLE>
</HEAD><BODY>
<center>
<SCRIPT LANGUAGE="VBScript">
<!--
Dim DayOfWeek
Dim MonthText
Dim strTemp

select case Weekday(Date)
  case 1
      DayOfWeek = "Sunday"
case 2
      DayOfWeek = "Monday"
case 3
      DayOfWeek = "Tuesday"
Case 4
      DayOfWeek = "Wednesday"
case 5
      DayOfWeek = "Thursday"
case 6
      DayOfWeek = "Friday"
case 7
      DayOfWeek = "Saturday"
end select
 Select Case Month(Date
 case
      MonthText = "January
```

continues

Listing 13.4. continued

```
case 2
      MonthText = "February"
case 3
      MonthText = "March"
case 4
      MonthText = "April"
case 5
      MonthText = "May"
case 6
      MonthText = "June"
case 7
      MonthText = "July"
case 8
      MonthText = "August"
case 9
      MonthText = "September"
case 10
      MonthText = "October"
case 11
      MonthText = "November"
case 12
      MonthText = "December"
end select
strTemp = DayOfWeek & ", " & MonthText & " "
strTemp = strTemp & Day(Date) & ", " & Year(Date) & "<br>"
document.writeln strTemp
document.writeln Time
-->
</SCRIPT>
</center>
</BODY></HTML>
```

The script code shown in Listing 13.4 is embedded within the HTML file's <BODY> section. This section contains the HTML that will be visible in the document window of the Web browser. The <CENTER> tag is used to center the date and time strings within the document window. The code begins by declaring three local variables: DayOfWeek, MonthText, and strTemp. These are used to construct the date string that will be displayed. The script then uses a Select Case construct to place the name of the current day of the week in DayOfWeek. The Weekday() function returns an integer corresponding to the day of the week for the date passed to it as its only parameter. In this case, the Date function is used; it returns the current date.

After the DayOfWeek value is assigned, another Select Case is used to assign a value to MonthText. This time, the Month() function is called in order to retrieve the number of the current month. Finally, the value for strTemp is assigned by combining the previous variables with the Day() and Year() functions. The value of strTemp is written to the document window using the writeln method. Then, the current time (returned by the Time function) also is written to the document.

Notice that this produces a static display. After the page is loaded, the date and time are not updated. If you want to create an updating date/time display, simply add ActiveX Label and Timer controls. Set the timer's Interval property to be the time between updates of the display and use 1000 for one second between updates. Then, in the Timer event, simply assign the strings created in the preceding example to the label's Caption property. Listing 13.5 provides an example of how this can be accomplished.

Listing 13.5. The code for the date/time using a label example.

```
<HTML>
<HEAD> <SCRIPT LANGUAGE="VBScript">
<!--
Sub window_onLoad()
Call IeTimer1_Timer
end sub
-->
</SCRIPT>
<TITLE>Updating Clock</TITLE>
</HEAD>
<BODY>
<CENTER>
<OBJECT ID="lblDate" WIDTH=259 HEIGHT=27
 CLASSID="CLSID:99B42120-6EC7-11CF-A6C7-00AA00A47DD2">
    <PARAM NAME="_ExtentX" VALUE="6853">
    <PARAM NAME="_ExtentY" VALUE="714">
    <PARAM NAME="Caption" VALUE="">
    <PARAM NAME="Angle" VALUE="0">
    <PARAM NAME="Alignment" VALUE="1">
    <PARAM NAME="Mode" VALUE="1">
    <PARAM NAME="FillStyle" VALUE="0">
    <PARAM NAME="FillStyle" VALUE="0">
    <PARAM NAME="ForeColor" VALUE="#000000">
    <PARAM NAME="BackColor" VALUE="#C0C0C0">
    <PARAM NAME="FontName" VALUE="Arial">
    <PARAM NAME="FontSize" VALUE="12">
    <PARAM NAME="FontItalic" VALUE="0">
    <PARAM NAME="FontBold" VALUE="0">
    <PARAM NAME="FontUnderline" VALUE="0">
    <PARAM NAME="FontStrikeout" VALUE="0">
    <PARAM NAME="TopPoints" VALUE="0">
    <PARAM NAME="BotPoints" VALUE="0">
</OBJECT>
<br>
<OBJECT ID="lblTime" WIDTH=259 HEIGHT=39
 CLASSID="CLSID:99B42120-6EC7-11CF-A6C7-00AA00A47DD2">
    <PARAM NAME="_ExtentX" VALUE="6853">
    <PARAM NAME="_ExtentY" VALUE="1032">
    <PARAM NAME="Caption" VALUE="">
    <PARAM NAME="Angle" VALUE="1">
    <PARAM NAME="Alignment" VALUE="1">
    <PARAM NAME="Mode" VALUE="1">
    <PARAM NAME="FillStyle" VALUE="0">
    <PARAM NAME="FillStyle" VALUE="0">
```

13

DYNAMIC WEB PAGE BUILDING

continues

Listing 13.5. continued

```
    <PARAM NAME="ForeColor" VALUE="#000000">
    <PARAM NAME="BackColor" VALUE="#C0C0C0">
    <PARAM NAME="FontName" VALUE="Arial">
    <PARAM NAME="FontSize" VALUE="12">
    <PARAM NAME="FontItalic" VALUE="0">
    <PARAM NAME="FontBold" VALUE="0">
    <PARAM NAME="FontUnderline" VALUE="0">
    <PARAM NAME="FontStrikeout" VALUE="0">
    <PARAM NAME="TopPoints" VALUE="0">
    <PARAM NAME="BotPoints" VALUE="0">
</OBJECT></CENTER>
<SCRIPT LANGUAGE="VBScript">
<!--
Sub IeTimer1_Timer()
Dim DayOfWeek
Dim MonthText
Dim strTemp

select case Weekday(Date)
  case 1
      DayOfWeek = "Sunday"
case 2
      DayOfWeek = "Monday"
case 3
      DayOfWeek = "Tuesday"
case 4
      DayOfWeek = "Wednesday"
case 5
      DayOfWeek = "Thursday"
case 6
      DayOfWeek = "Friday"
case 7
      DayOfWeek = "Saturday"
end select

Select Case Month(Date)
case 1
      MonthText = "January"
case 2
      MonthText = "February"
case 3
      MonthText = "March"
case 4
      MonthText = "April"
case 5
      MonthText = "May"
case 6
      MonthText = "June"
case 7
      MonthText = "July"
case 8
      MonthText = "August"
case 9
      MonthText = "September"
case 10
      MonthText = "October"
```

```
case 11
     MonthText = "November"
case 12
     MonthText = "December"
end select
strTemp = DayOfWeek & ", " & MonthText & " "
strTemp = strTemp & Day(Date) & ", " & Year(Date)
lblDate.Caption = strTemp
lblTime.Caption = Time
end sub
-->
</SCRIPT>
    <OBJECT ID="IeTimer1" WIDTH=39 HEIGHT=39
     CLASSID="CLSID:59CCB4A0-727D-11CF-AC36-00AA00A47DD2">
        <PARAM NAME="_ExtentX" VALUE="1005">
        <PARAM NAME="_ExtentY" VALUE="1005">
        <PARAM NAME="Interval" VALUE="1000">
    </OBJECT>
</BODY>
</HTML>
```

Creating a Random Frame Using Client-Side Refresh

Another method of creating dynamic Web pages is to use client-side refresh to periodically reload a Web page. By combining this HTML feature with VBScript code, you can produce a wonderfully dynamic page. This section describes how to use a Web page with two frames to produce a random famous quotation display. Figure 13.5 shows the resulting Web page.

FIGURE 13.5.

The Random Famous Quotes display page.

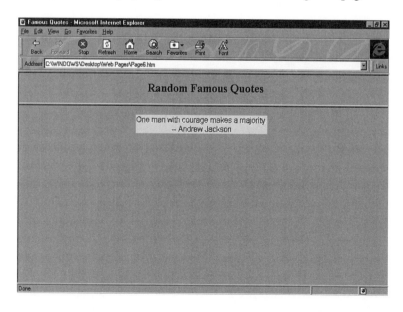

The main HTML file defines a frameset with two frames. Listing 13.6 contains the code for the file. The frameset refers to two frames: PAGE8.HTM and PAGE7.HTM.

Listing 13.6. HTML for the main page.

```
<HTML><HEAD><TITLE>Random Famous Quotes</TITLE></HEAD>
<BODY>
<Center><FRAMESET ROWS="15%, *" SCROLLING=NO>
<FRAME SRC="PAGE8.HTM" SCROLLING=NO>
<FRAME SRC="PAGE7.HTM"></FRAMESET></CENTER>
</BODY></HTML>
```

The top frame is static. It simply displays a heading. Listing 13.7 contains the code for this page. This file should be saved as PAGE8.HTM in the same directory as the main page.

Listing 13.7. HTML for the top frame.

```
<HTML>
<BODY><P>
<CENTER><H2>Random Famous Quotes</H2></CENTER>
</BODY></HTML>
```

The bottom frame is the dynamic one. Listing 13.8 contains the code for this page. This file should be saved as PAGE7.HTM in the same directory as the main page.

Listing 13.8. HTML for the dynamic frame.

```
<HTML><HEAD><META HTTP-EQUIV="Refresh" CONTENT="10">
</HEAD>
<BODY>
<script language="vbscript">
<!--
On Error Resume Next
DIM phrase(5)
lowerbound=0

phrase(0) = "When you have a choice and don't make it,"
phrase(0) = phrase(0) & "<br>that is, in itself, a choice.<br>"
phrase(0) = phrase(0) & "-- William James"
 phrase(1) = "If you tell the truth, you don't have to remember

phrase(1) = phrase(1) & "what you said.<br>"
phrase(1) = phrase(1) & "-- Mark Twain"
 phrase(2) = "None of my inventions came by accident.<br>
```

```
phrase(2) = phrase(2) & "They came by work.<br>-- Thomas Edison"
phrase(3) = "It is wonderful how much can be done<br>"
phrase(3) = phrase(3) & "if we are always doing.<br>-- Thomas Jefferson"
phrase(4) = "One man with courage makes a majority.<br>"
phrase(4) = phrase(4) & "-- Andrew Jackson"

upperbound=4
Randomize()
pick = Int((upperbound - lowerbound + 1) * Rnd + lowerbound)
 document.write "<CENTER><TD BGCOLOR=#EEEEEE ALIGN=CENTER><font size=3>"
 document.write phrase(pick
 document.write "</font></TD></CENTER>

-->
</script>
</BODY></HTML>
```

The HTML tag `<META HTTP-EQUIV="Refresh" CONTENT="10">` instructs the browser to reload the current document every 10 seconds. This is a browser feature and is supported by Internet Explorer.

Because the script is embedded into the `<BODY>` section, it executes when the page loads. The script first sets up an array of available quotations. Then the `Randomize()` and `Rnd` functions are used to generate a random number that serves as the index into the array of quotations. Finally, the `document.write` method is used to output the quotation and add some formatting.

Changing the Document's Colors

In addition to writing text to the HTML document, you can use VBScript to change the foreground and background colors on-the-fly. You also can change the color used to display links, but only when the page first loads. This section describes how to set the document colors within VBScript.

The example created in this section enables you to choose foreground and background colors from a drop-down listbox. You can choose from several color names in the listbox. After you make a selection, the appropriate color property (foreground or background) is set. The page created appears in Figure 13.6.

This page uses the Microsoft Forms 2.0 `ComboBox` ActiveX control as the drop-down listbox. Using the Microsoft ActiveX Control Pad currently is the easiest way to properly embed ActiveX controls into an HTML file. (The Control Pad is discussed in Chapter 8, "The ActiveX Control Pad.")

FIGURE 13.6.
The Color Picker Web page.

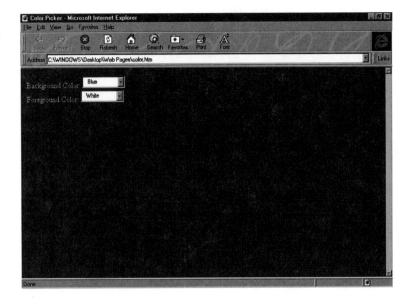

Listing 13.9 shows the code for the HTML file.

Listing 13.9. HTML for the Color Picker Web page.

```
<HTML><HEAD>
<SCRIPT LANGUAGE="VBScript">
<!--
Sub window_onLoad()
cboBGColor.AddItem "Black"
cboBGColor.AddItem "Red"
cboBGColor.AddItem "Green"
cboBGColor.AddItem "Blue"
cboBGColor.AddItem "White"
cboBGColor.ListIndex = 0

cboFGColor.AddItem "Black"
cboFGColor.AddItem "Red"
cboFGColor.AddItem "Green"
cboFGColor.AddItem "Blue"
cboFGColor.AddItem "White"
cboFGColor.ListIndex = 3

end sub
--
</SCRIPT>
<SCRIPT LANGUAGE="VBScript">
<!--
function GetColor(pstrColor)
select case pstrColor
case "Red"
   GetColor = "#FF0000"
```

```
Case "Green"
   GetColor = "#00FF00"
case "Black"
   GetColor = "#000000"
case "Blue"
   GetColor = "#0000FF"
case "White"
   GetColor = "#FFFFFF"
end select

end function
-->
</SCRIPT>
<TITLE>Color Picker</TITLE></HEAD>
<BODY>
<SCRIPT LANGUAGE="VBScript">
<!--
Sub cboBGColor_Click()
   window.document.bgColor = GetColor(cboBGColor.Text)
 end sub

-->
</SCRIPT>
Background Color
<OBJECT ID="cboBGColor" WIDTH=93 HEIGHT=2
      CLASSID="CLSID:8BD21D30-EC42-11CE-9E0D-00AA006002F3"

      <PARAM NAME="VariousPropertyBits" VALUE="75499547">
      <PARAM NAME="DisplayStyle" VALUE="7">
      <PARAM NAME="Size" VALUE="2455;635">
      <PARAM NAME="MatchEntry" VALUE="1">
      <PARAM NAME="ShowDropButtonWhen" VALUE="2">
      <PARAM NAME="FontCharSet" VALUE="0">
      <PARAM NAME="FontPitchAndFamily" VALUE="2">
      <PARAM NAME="FontWeight" VALUE="0">
</OBJECT>
<br>Foreground Color:
<SCRIPT LANGUAGE="VBScript">
<!--
Sub cboFGColor_Click()
  window.document.fgColor = GetColor(cboFGColor.Text)
end sub
-->
</SCRIPT>

<OBJECT ID="cboFGColor" WIDTH=93 HEIGHT=24
     CLASSID="CLSID:8BD21D30-EC42-11CE-9E0D-00AA006002F3">
      <PARAM NAME="VariousPropertyBits" VALUE="75499547">
      <PARAM NAME="DisplayStyle" VALUE="7">
      <PARAM NAME="Size" VALUE="2455;635">
      <PARAM NAME="MatchEntry" VALUE="1">
      <PARAM NAME="ShowDropButtonWhen" VALUE="2">
      <PARAM NAME="FontCharSet" VALUE="0">
      <PARAM NAME="FontPitchAndFamily" VALUE="2">
      <PARAM NAME="FontWeight" VALUE="0">
</OBJECT>
</BODY></HTML>
```

The script code begins execution with the window_onLoad event. This event is fired whenever the page is loaded. The code in this event adds the color names to the drop-down listboxes and sets their ListIndex properties. Doing so fires the respective Click events for the drop-down listboxes, setting the default colors to a black background with a blue foreground.

Next, a function named GetColor() is defined. This function takes a string parameter, pstrColor, and uses a Select Case to return the value for the chosen color. This function is called from the drop-down listboxes' Click event to determine the proper value to assign to the appropriate color property.

After this function, the <TITLE> tag defines the page's title and then the <BODY> portion of the HTML file starts. The first element after the <BODY> tag is another section of script code. This code is for the cboBGcolor_Click event. The code in this event sets the document object's bgColor property to the value returned by GetColor(cboBGColor.Text).

Next, some text is placed on the document to serve as a label for the background color drop-down listbox. Then the <OBJECT> element for the drop-down listbox is inserted. Note that most of the property information for this control is stored in the <PARAM NAME="VariousPropertyBits" VALUE="75499547"> element. This is obviously an encoded number. I used the ActiveX Control Pad to insert and edit this control. The assignment of this property was made by the Control Pad's Control Property feature, hiding the complexity from the Web page designer. In the Control Pad's Property window, I changed the Style property to 2 - DropDownList. This was the only property I modified from the default setting.

Next, the code for the foreground color drop-down listbox is defined. This is essentially identical to the cboBGColor_Click event except that the document object's fgColor property is used. There is then a label for the foreground color drop-down listbox and, finally, the <OBJECT> element for the drop-down listbox. This, except for the ID property (which is set to cboFGColor), is identical to the definition of the background color drop-down listbox.

After the HTML code is entered and saved, load the page into Internet Explorer. The page should load with a black background and a blue foreground. If it doesn't, first check the window_onLoad event to make sure that the proper strings are being used in the AddItem methods and the ListIndex property is being set correctly. Then check the Click event code for the drop-down listboxes and, finally, the GetColor() function. After the page loads properly, try changing the settings in the drop-down listbox. The appropriate color properties should change accordingly.

Using Cookies to Maintain User Information

Another extremely useful method for creating dynamic Web pages using VBScript is the use of cookies. A *cookie* is a set of information stored on the user's machine that is associated with a particular Web site. The HTTP protocol, which is the transport protocol for the World Wide

Web, provides for the setting and retrieving of these cookie files. You can access this information in your VBScript code using the document.cookie property first discussed in the section "The Internet Explorer Document Object," earlier in this chapter.

> **NOTE**
>
> Pages that use cookies must be stored on and retrieved using a Web server. This is because cookies are tied closely to the HTTP protocol. The example presented in this chapter will not function if the file is not saved on a Web server. If you attempt to save a cookie when not on a Web server page, you receive the runtime error number 438, object doesn't support this property or method.

The cookie property is set and retrieved as a string. It can be accessed at any time using your script code. A good use for cookies is the storage of user information relative to your Web page. If you have an order-entry page, for example, you might want to store the user's name and address so that when he returns to the page he won't have to enter it again. The script code reads the cookie property, parses out the name and address variables from it, and places the resulting information in the order-entry form's input boxes. You'll see a full-blown example of doing this in Chapter 25, "Order Entry."

Because the cookie stores multiple pieces of information within a single string, it is necessary to parse the string to retrieve the variable in which you are interested. The string is returned in the cookie property as a semicolon delimited string. Each portion of the string contains the variable name, an equal sign, and the variable's value. For example, First=Craig;Last=Eddy defines a cookie with two variables, First and Last, with values Craig and Eddy, respectively.

To parse the cookie string, I borrowed a function named ReadVariable() from Microsoft's Cookie Demo page (which you can find at http://www.microsoft.com/vbscript/us/vbssamp/cookies/extcookie.htm). This function takes as its only parameter the name of the variable to be retrieved from the cookie string. It returns the value of the variable or the string NOT_FOUND if the variable isn't found within the cookie string.

The simple example in this section stores the user's name and e-mail address in the cookie. It does so by providing Microsoft Forms 2.0 text boxes for the user input. After the user clicks the Save button, the information entered is stored in the cookie. Later, when the page is loaded again, the cookie information is read and if the name and e-mail variables are found, the text boxes are set to the values in the cookies.

Figure 13.7 shows the empty Web page as viewed with Internet Explorer. Listing 13.10 shows the HTML and VBScript code.

FIGURE 13.7.

The cookie example Web page.

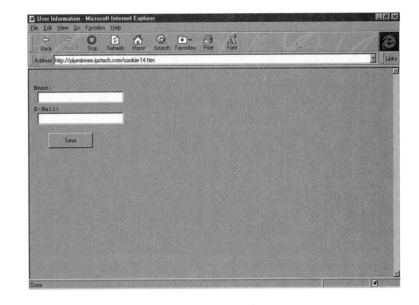

Listing 13.10. The HTML for cookie example.

```
<HTML><HEAD>
<SCRIPT LANGUAGE="VBScript">
<!--

dim  NOT_FOUND
NOT_FOUND = "NOT_FOUND"

Sub window_onLoad()
Dim lstrTemp, lstrVarName
lstrVarName = "Name"
lstrTemp = ReadVariable(lstrVarName)
if lstrTemp <> NOT_FOUND then txtName.Text = "" & lstrTemp
lstrTemp = ReadVariable("EMail")
if lstrTemp <> NOT_FOUND then txtEMail = cstr(lstrTemp)
end sub
Function ReadVariable(strVariableName)
'these five variables are used in the string manipulation
'code that finds the variable in the cookie.
Dim intLocation
Dim intNameLength

Dim intValueLength
Dim intNextSemicolon
Dim strTemp

'calculate length and location of variable name
intNameLength = Len(strVariableName)
intLocation = Instr(Document.Cookie, strVariableName)
```

```
'check for existence of variable name
If intLocation = 0 Then
    'variable not found, so it can't be read
    ReadVariable = NOT_FOUND
Else
    'get a smaller substring to work with
    strTemp = Right(Document.Cookie, Len(Document.Cookie) - intLocation + 1)

    'check to make sure we found the full string, not just a substring
    If Mid(strTemp, intNameLength + 1, 1) <> "=" Then
        'oops, only found substring, not good enough
        ReadVariable = NOT_FOUND
        'note that this will incorrectly give a not found result if and only if
        'a search for a variable whose name is a substring of a preceding
        'variable is undertaken.  For example, this will fail:
        '
        'search for: MyVar
        'cookie contains: MyVariable=2;MyVar=1
    Else
        'found full string
        intNextSemicolon = Instr(strTemp, ";")

        'if not found, then we need the last element of the cookie
        If intNextSemicolon = 0 Then intNextSemicolon = Len(strTemp) + 1

        'check for empty variable (Var1=;)
        If intNextSemicolon = (intNameLength + 2) Then
            'variable is empty
            ReadVariable = ""
        Else
            'calculate value normally
            intValueLength = intNextSemicolon - intNameLength - 2
            ReadVariable = Mid(strTemp, intNameLength + 2, intValueLength)
        End If
    End If
End If
end function

-->
</SCRIPT>
<TITLE>User Information</TITLE>
</HEAD><BODY><pre>
Name:   <br> <OBJECT ID="txtName" WIDTH=187 HEIGHT=24
 CLASSID="CLSID:8BD21D10-EC42-11CE-9E0D-00AA006002F3">
    <PARAM NAME="VariousPropertyBits" VALUE="746604571">
    <PARAM NAME="Size" VALUE="4948;635">
    <PARAM NAME="FontCharSet" VALUE="0">
    <PARAM NAME="FontPitchAndFamily" VALUE="2">
    <PARAM NAME="FontWeight" VALUE="0">
</OBJECT>
E-Mail: <br> <OBJECT ID="txtEMail" WIDTH=187 HEIGHT=24
 CLASSID="CLSID:8BD21D10-EC42-11CE-9E0D-00AA006002F3">
    <PARAM NAME="VariousPropertyBits" VALUE="746604571">
    <PARAM NAME="Size" VALUE="4948;635">
```

continues

Listing 13.10. continued

```
    <PARAM NAME="FontCharSet" VALUE="0">
    <PARAM NAME="FontPitchAndFamily" VALUE="2">
    <PARAM NAME="FontWeight" VALUE="0">
</OBJECT>
<SCRIPT LANGUAGE="VBScript">
<!--
Sub cmdSave_Click()
on error resume next
document.Cookie = "Name" & "=" & txtName
if err.number = 438 then
    msgbox "Error saving cookie: page is not located on a Web server!"
    err.clear
    exit sub
elseif err > 0 then
    msgbox "Error saving cookie: " & err.description
    err.clear
    exit sub
end if
document.Cookie = "EMail" & "=" & txtEMail
if err > 0 then
    msgbox "Error saving cookie: " & err.description
    err.clear
    exit sub
end if
MsgBox "Information saved!"
end sub
-->
</SCRIPT>
    <OBJECT ID="cmdSave" WIDTH=96 HEIGHT=32
     CLASSID="CLSID:D7053240-CE69-11CD-A777-00DD01143C57">
        <PARAM NAME="Caption" VALUE="Save">
        <PARAM NAME="Size" VALUE="2540;846">
        <PARAM NAME="FontCharSet" VALUE="0">
        <PARAM NAME="FontPitchAndFamily" VALUE="2">
        <PARAM NAME="ParagraphAlign" VALUE="3">
        <PARAM NAME="FontWeight" VALUE="0">
    </OBJECT>
</PRE></BODY></HTML>
```

In the window_onLoad event, the cookie information is read from the document.cookie property using the ReadVariable() function. If the cookie information (name and e-mail) is found, the data is placed in the appropriate text boxes.

The ReadVariable() parses the cookie property, searching for the variable name specified as the strVariableName parameter. It does this by using the Instr() function to locate the starting position of the string specified in strVariableName. If the string is not found, the constant value NOT_FOUND is returned. If the string is found, the ReadVariable() function then checks to make sure the variable name is not a substring of another variable name. If it passes this test, the value is parsed from the string by taking all the characters between the = and the next semicolon. This string is returned as the function's value.

Finally, the `cmdSave_Click` event code is responsible for saving the cookie information into the `cookie` property. It does so by assigning the string *variable_name=value* to the `cookie` property. Some error handling is in place to provide the user with any feedback that results from this operation. There are limits to how many cookies can be defined for a site and overstepping these limits would produce an error condition.

Review

This chapter provided you with loads of information useful in creating dynamic Web pages by using VBScript. The examples, although not full-blown applications by themselves, provide the framework for further enhancements. The remainder of this book covers special subjects such as animation and controlling Microsoft Office documents with VBScript code. The final part of the book builds on this part by presenting several real-world examples built using VBScript.

Customize Your Web Page with Cookies

by Evangelos Petroutsos

IN THIS CHAPTER

In Chapter 6, where we described the various properties of the `document` object, we mentioned briefly the `cookie` property, which lets you store information about your Web site on the client computer and recall it in a later session, or from within another page. The topic of cookies in Internet Explorer 3.0 deserves special attention, and we devote a separate chapter to it. This is another technique traditionally implemented on the server and so far required special software on the server, but now you can implement cookies on the client computer with the help of the `cookie` property of the `document` Object. Like image maps, it's another technique that moves from the server to client, simplifying the development of custom Webs.

The term *cookie*, another UNIX term if you're wondering, is a string, or token, which is contained in the document itself and which the browser can save on the local disk when a page is loaded. This token can be later retrieved by another page of the same Web. The cookie belongs to the Web, and each Web can leave its own cookies on the client computer. Every page belonging to the same Web will be able to access the cookie on the client computer. The next time the client connects to the same Web site, the home and other pages of the Web can read the cookie stored on the local computer during the previous session. This string may contain customization information, which may be as simple as setting the appearance of the page (background/text colors, favorite fonts, and so on), or a description of the action the viewer has taken in a previous section. For example, you can keep track of the software each user has downloaded from your site, or the ads they have already seen, so that the page can display a different ad every time it's opened by the particular client. You can store information about the user's interests in the cookie, and then use it to display relevant ads.

If you don't know how cookies work, or you want to see them in action, you should probably start by visiting a site that supports cookies and familiarize yourself with the possibilities. One such site is Microsoft's MSN page, at www.msn.com. Visit that site and click the Customize Start Page button area to go through the steps of customizing your start page. Figures 14.1 and 14.2 show the generic start page on www.msn.com and a customized start page on the same site. The customized page contains graphics that act as hyperlinks to the various topics (news, sports, and so on). Our examples aren't going to be that elaborate, but we'll demonstrate the basic principles of customizing Webs with cookies.

To understand how cookies are used and when to use them, let's look at the more traditional customization techniques. The simplest method of providing custom pages, so far, has been to force users to register the first time they hit your site and to log in with a user name and, possibly, a password. The registration information was stored in a database on the server, and each time a viewer came to the Web site, he or she would have to type a user ID and a password. After a CGI application checked the user input against the registration information, it would supply a custom page for the specific viewer. In other words, the server sends out a generic page, prompting the viewer to enter the site as a registered user. This approach is an inconvenience for the user and a significant burden for the server, because all the customization information about the client is stored on the server. The natural place to store customization information is the client computer, because the customization settings apply to the individual computer only. Even if the customization didn't have to take place on the client computer, the settings can be easily transferred to the server, where the custom page can be selected, or even created on-the-fly.

Figure 14.1.

This is what you'll see the first time you visit the MSN site.

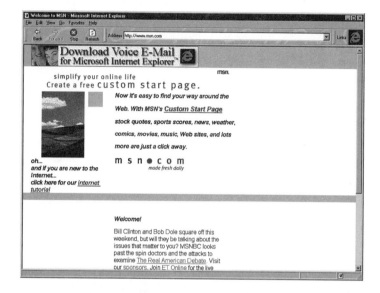

Figure 14.2.

The same site shown in Figure 14.1 after it was customized.

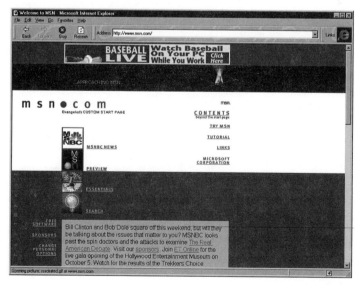

Safety Considerations

Cookies enable a Web to store information on the client computer. It doesn't have to be customization information, it could be anything (you can't store binary files, of course, but any string can be easily left on the client's disk). But is this safe? Will cookies impair the viewer's computer safety? Some people don't like the idea of browsers leaving information on their local disks. If, as a user, you are concerned about browsers leaving information on your disk without your permission, you can adjust your browser so that it warns you every time a document is about to store a cookie locally. Select the Options command in the View menu and, when the Options dialog box is displayed, click the Advanced tab, which is shown in Figure 14.3. If you check the box "Warn before accepting cookies," the browser won't store any cookies on your hard disk without warning you first. Check this button and then click the OK button to close the Options dialog box.

FIGURE 14.3.

The Advanced tab of the Options dialog box in Internet Explorer lets you specify how cookies will be handled.

If you set your system to warn you every time a cookie is about to be written to the local disk, Internet Explorer will issue a warning like the one shown in Figure 14.4. If you don't care about cookies, or if you don't plan to visit the site that's about to leave a cookie on your computer, click the No button to prevent the browser from storing the cookie on your hard disk.

FIGURE 14.4.

If you've set up your Internet Explorer to warn you before storing any cookies on your local disk, you'll see this dialog box every time a document attempts to store a cookie.

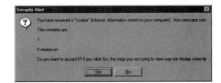

Actually, cookies are no threat for your computer because they are not executable files. Each site's cookies are stored in a separate text file in the Cookies folder under the Windows folder.

With the current implementation of client-side cookies, you can trust any site that leaves cookies to your computer. The basic principles of customizing a Web site with cookies are no different than customizing a service with the caller ID technique, which is used quite frequently by mail-order companies. Many companies that provide services to registered users (be it a computer sales company or a chain of pizza delivery places) use caller ID to offer "personalized service" (and cut down on their costs, too). When you call an 800 number to order diskettes, a new computer, or even a pizza, the operator (or the computerized system that handles the phones initially) knows who's calling before the phone is even picked up. He sees your caller ID (which is your telephone number) knows immediately who's calling, your address, even your most recent order. If you can put up with caller ID for the convenience of not having to repeat your name, telephone number, and address every time you order a computer component, or a pizza, you can certainly live with the idea of others leaving a few bytes of information on your computer so that you can view a site you visit frequently through custom pages.

What Are Cookies?

The document object and its properties and methods were discussed in Chapter 6, but we didn't say much about the cookie property there. Using cookies is a bit more complicated than using the other properties of the document object, not to mention that cookies require a server. A document that makes use of cookies can't be tested locally. In other words, you can't double-click its icon and expect to find a cookie on your own hard disk. The cookie will be created only if the document is furnished to the browser by a Web server. We'll discuss shortly the options for testing the examples of this section.

Let's start our discussion with an introduction to the concept of cookies. A cookie is like a tag you receive every time you check in baggage at the airport. When you check in your baggage, it's tagged with a special number, and you get a copy of the tag. When you arrive at your destination, you use the tag to get your baggage back. This tag uniquely identifies your own baggage. For instance, if your itinerary includes stopovers, your baggage will be handled by the airport crews and it will arrive at the same airport as you, where you can pick it up. Even if, by mistake, your baggage is loaded on the wrong plane, it will eventually arrive at the same destination, although not at the same time as you will. When you visit a Web site that needs to identify your site uniquely, it leaves a tag on a unique location on the hard disk. The next time you visit the same site, the pages of the site can check out this tag by looking at the same location. Each Web site has its own tag on the disk and its contents can be read or updated at any time, but by the pages of this site only. Each site has its own tag, stored in a separate file in the same folder as the tags of all other sites. The cookie is nothing more than a tag (with a fancy name). It's created once, and after that it's used every time you connect to the site that placed the cookie there.

If a Web site uses cookies to customize its pages for specific users, its pages look for the tag (cookie) left there during a previous session. If such a cookie is found, the pages customize themselves accordingly. For example, if a cookie with the user's name is found, all pages may display the user's name in a special box. Or, if a cookie with the user's favorite background color is found, all pages assume this background color (by setting the bgColor property of the document object, as discussed in Chapter 6). A cookie is a tag that uniquely identifies the client. Unlike airline tags, a cookie contains more than just a unique ID. It contains the ID, but it also contains other information that all the pages of a Web site are going to share in one session, or between sessions. Another, less obtrusive, use of cookies is to allow pages to exchange information. The current implementation of VBScript (and HTML) doesn't allow two pages to share information. With cookies, it is possible for all the pages of any given Web site to share information. You can think of cookies as global variables with a Web-wide scope.

Finally, there are two types of cookies: temporary cookies, which last for the duration of a single session and which the client computer doesn't remember the next time the user connects to the same server; and persistent cookies, which are actually stored on the local computer and can be retrieved in a future session. Temporary cookies are ideal for sharing information among the pages of a Web, because they are remembered by the browser, and they are not stored on the disk.

Creating Cookies

The cookie property of the document object accepts a string that consists of a variable and a value pair, similar to HTML attributes. A cookie that sets the color of the page's background to red would be

```
BackgroundColor = red
```

BackgoundColor is not a reserved keyword used in conjunction with cookies. You can use any variable name to describe a cookie. When a string like the previous one is assigned to the cookie property of the document object, the browser appends it to the file with the cookies for the current Web. You can append as many strings to the file with the cookies as you need.

The following VBScript lines will create a cookie file with three cookies:

```
cookie1="USERFNAME=Peter"
Document.cookie=cookie1
cookie2="USERLNAME=Evans"
Document.cookie=cookie2
cookie3="ZODIAC=Aquarius"
Document.cookie=cookie3
```

Once these lines are executed, a new cookie file will be created on the client computer. (If a cookie for this site exists already, the new values will either replace the existing ones, or append new variables to the existing cookie file.) This is a text file, and you can open it with any text editor to examine its contents. If you open your Windows | Cookies folder, you'll probably find cookies from other Web sites.

Your scripts can read the cookies placed earlier on a client computer by reading the `cookie` property of the `document` object. The following VBScript statements read the value of the document's `cookie` property, assign it to a variable, and then display the value of the variable with the `MsgBox()` function:

```
cookie=Document.cookie
MsgBox cookie
```

If these two lines are executed after the lines that set the three cookies of the previous example, the `MsgBox()` function will report the following string:

```
BGCOLOR=lightgray; FRCOLOR=blue; LINKS=red
```

Consecutive pairs of variables/values are separated by a semicolon. Every time a new cookie (variable/value pairs) is created, a new string of the form `Variable=Value` is appended to the cookie file. When you read the `cookie` property, though, VBScript returns a long string with all the cookies.

How to Test Pages with Cookies

You can test previous lines by placing them in the SCRIPT section of an HTML document. But the cookie mechanism will work only if the document is supplied by a server. If you just double-click an HTML document that contains VBScript lines that set the `cookies` property of the `document` object, VBScript will generate an error message to the effect that the object doesn't support the `cookies` property. The browser on its own can't create the cookies. The Web server's involvement is required.

> **NOTE**
>
> This chapter's projects can't be tested by simply opening them with Internet Explorer. To test the documents that contain cookies, you would need to be supplied by a Web Server, as explained in this section. If you double-click a project's icon to open it with Internet Explorer, the cookies will be blank strings.

To test the examples of this section on your computer, you must post the document that contains cookies on a Web. There are many ways to post a Web site and we'll present the simpler ones here. The simplest method is to set up your own Web server. You can install the FrontPage Personal Web Server and then place the document you want to test in the Content folder under the FrontPage Web folder and rename it to `Index.htm`. The FrontPage Personal Web Server is part of the Microsoft FrontPage package, which you can download from Microsoft's Web site. It's a time-bombed version (it will stop working after the last day of 1996, but you can visit this site for updates or a newer beta). To turn your Windows 95 machine into a Web server, all you have to do is run the Personal Web Server program. If you are connected to your Internet service provider when you start the program, other users will be able to access your site. If not, you'll still be able to test your pages locally.

If you are connected to an Internet service provider, you must find the IP address you were assigned when you connected to the Internet service provider's server. Run the WINIPCFG program, which will report your IP address. Open the Start menu, select Run, and in the dialog box that will be displayed type WINIPCFG. The IP address is a group of four numbers separated by periods. Notice that your IP address is different each time you connect to your ISP's server. The IP address reported by the WINPICFG application is valid for the current session, and the next time you connect you must find out your new IP address.

You must copy the document you want to test to the ISP's server. Most ISPs will give their subscribers a folder on their server where users can place their personal home pages. You must contact your ISP to find out where you should store the home page and accompanying documents and your address on the Internet. When you place a Web site on someone else's server, you get a URL such as www.someServer.com/users/~PEvans, where PEvans is your user name. The tilde character is always there and gives away the fact that you are renting space on someone else's server. You can also contact a Web service provider or Web hosting service that will give you all the space you need on a Web server, along with a registered name, such as www.pevans.com. Place the document with the cookie in your folder on the ISP's server and then connect to your own URL.

Finally, you can start Internet Explorer and enter the IP address of your computer in the Address box. If you are not connected to an ISP, you can type the IP address of the local host, which is always 127.0.0.1. When you connect to the address 127.0.0.1, the browser will be served by the Web server running on the local machine. If you are using the FrontPage Personal Web Server on Windows 95, or Internet Information Server on Windows NT, Internet Explorer will connect to the local host without accessing the Internet.

Because Microsoft FrontPage Personal Web Server is available for evaluation purposes for free, we'll use this server in our examples. Again, the other approaches are just as easy. You can use any Web server you may be using right now to test the examples of this chapter locally.

Let's build our first example, which will save a few cookies and their values and then read them. This example, shown in Figure 14.5, is called Cookies1.htm, and you will find it on the CD. It sets three cookies and reads their values, with the following code:

```
<HTML>
<HEAD>
<TITLE>Cookies Demo 1</TITLE>
<SCRIPT LANGUAGE="VBS">
Document.write "<CENTER><H1>Testing Cookies</H1></CENTER>"
cookie1="USERFNAME=Peter"
Document.cookie=cookie1
cookie2="USERLNAME=Evans"
Document.cookie=cookie2
cookie3="ZODIAC=Aquarius"
```

```
Document.cookie=cookie3
MsgBox "Cookies set. Click OK to read their values"
cookie=Document.cookie
msgbox cookie
</SCRIPT>
</HEAD>
<BODY>
</BODY>
</HTML>
```

FIGURE 14.5.

The Cookie1 project demonstrates how to save and recall cookies on the client computer.

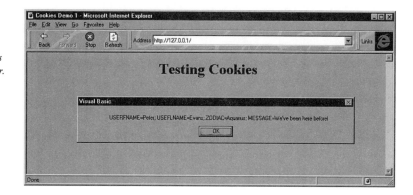

The VBScript code segment of this document sets the values of three cookies and then displays a message to inform the viewer that the cookies are set. Then, it reads their values and displays them in a dialog box. To test this application, copy the Cookies1.htm file in the Web's Root folder and rename it to Index.htm. (If your server is the Internet Information Server, rename it to Default.htm.) Then start Internet Explorer and connect to the Web server. If you are testing the cookies locally, connect to the IP address 127.0.0.1.

The first conclusion you can draw from this simple project is that, before you can use the cookies in your code, you must first extract them from the cookie property. Whereas individual cookies can be stored one at a time, you can't read a specific cookie, just the string that contains all of them. This takes a bit of code. We'll see shortly how this is done, but first let's explore the cookie property of the document object a little further.

Open the Cookie1.htm file (or Index.htm file if you've renamed it on the server) and change the value of one of the cookies. For example, change the value of the ZODIAC variable from Aquarius to Sagittarius:

```
cookie3="ZODIAC=Sagittarius"
```

Then, add a new cookie with the statements:

```
cookie4="MESSAGE=We've been here before"
Document.cookie=cookie4
```

14

CUSTOMIZE YOUR
WEB PAGE WITH
COOKIES

If you refresh the current document in Internet Explorer, the new value of the document's `cookie` property will be

```
USERFNAME=Peter;USEFLNAME=Evans;ZODIAC=Sagittarius;MESSAGE=We've been here before
```

There are two items worth noticing here. VBScript didn't create a new ZODIAC cookie. Instead, it replaced the value of the existing cookie. That was very nice, because we won't have to manipulate the strings ourselves every time we want to modify the value of a cookie. The other item is that the new cookie was appended at the end of the existing string.

The Cookie Folder

Storing and recalling cookies on the client computer is as easy as setting, or reading, the value of the `cookie` property of the `document` object. Even if you are using the same computer as server and client, nothing changes. The browser doesn't even know that it's being served by the same computer. The next question should be "where are the cookies, and what do they look like?"

The cookies you've created so far aren't stored on the local disk. To make a cookie persistent, you must append the string

```
;expires=<date>
```

to the cookie. `<date>` is an expression like `Wed, 01 Jan 1997 12:00:00 GMT`, which specifies when the cookie expires. If you don't specify the expiration date, the cookie expires at the session's end. The `expires` option makes the cookie persistent, which means it's saved on the local disk, in the Cookies folder under the Windows folder.

As we mentioned already, cookies are saved in text files in the Windows | Cookies folder. Each Web's cookies are stored in a single file, and the name of the file is your domain name. For an account name like `pevans@sams.com`, the cookie file's name would be `pevans@sams`. If you are connecting to the local host IP address, the cookie file will be named `anyuser@127_0_0_1` (it may be truncated, too). `anyuser` is a literal string, and it doesn't stand for a user name. Each Web site has a unique name which is used to create a unique cookie file on the client, so that all the pages belonging to the specific Web will access the same cookie file. The `anyuser@msn`, for instance, contains the cookies left on your system by the MSN site.

If you open the cookie file you just created with WordPad, you'll see something like the window of Figure 14.6. It contains the cookie names and their values on separate lines and a bunch of numbers inserted there by the browser, which you can safely ignore. The expiration date is stored there somewhere, but not in a way that is easy to see or tamper with. As you can see from the title of the document, it was tested locally with the FrontPage Personal Web Server.

FIGURE 14.6.

*The contents of the
cookie file generated by
the Cookie1 project.*

Now delete the cookie file. Right-click its icon and, from the Shortcut menu, select Delete. Then modify the document by deleting the lines that set the cookies (all the lines that begin with Document.cookie=) and the line with the first call to the MsgBox() function. Even better, comment out these lines and then save the Index.htm file again. Then return to your browser and refresh the current document (or open it again). The script will report the same cookies! You can visit other sites and then return to yours. The cookies will still be there. If the file is deleted, how does the browser know the values of the cookies? These values were cached when the page was first opened, and they will persist for the duration of the session. If you close Internet Explorer and then start it again and connect to the same host (most likely the local host), the values of the cookies will be lost. This time, the MsgBox function will report a blank string.

Extracting the Cookie Values

In order to use the cookies you have left on the client site during a previous session, you must read the cookie property of the document from within your code and extract the individual cookie values. The code for extracting each individual cookie is straightforward. Any way you implement it, this code makes extensive use of the string manipulation functions to isolate cookies and their values. The ReadCookies page (which can be found on this chapter's folder on the CD) contains a function that does exactly that. You can use this function as a starting point, or implement a different one, but the basic idea is to scan the entire cookie, locate pairs of variables and values, and extract them.

Figure 14.7 shows the Cookie2 document, which sets a few cookie values and then reads them from another page. Because both pages belong to the same Web, they can both access the same cookies. The first page creates the cookie; the second page reads them.

For a clean start, delete the cookies file from the folder Windows | Cookies and shut down Internet Explorer if it's running. Then copy the document CookiePage (in the Cookies folder on the CD) to the Web's root directory, rename it to Index.htm, and start Internet Explorer to connect to your host. The first time you connect to your server and the home page is displayed, you'll see a generic page, like the one in Figure 14.7. The second page of the cookie document is shown in Figure 14.8. This page can read the value of an individual cookie, or display all the cookies on a separate page, as shown in Figure 14.9.

FIGURE 14.7.

The first page of the Cookie2 Web creates a few persistent cookies.

FIGURE 14.8.

The page Cookie2a is the second page of the Cookie2 document.

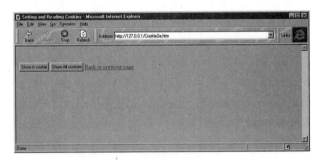

FIGURE 14.9.

This page extracts and displays all the cookies of the site.

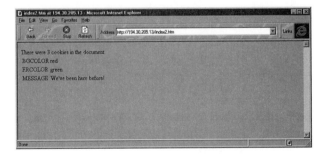

Now click the various buttons to create a few cookies. The program will prompt you to enter the values of certain settings with an InputBox, like the one shown in Figure 14.10. We used the InputBox function to simplify the code on the page. In a real-world application, you should design a good-looking page to obtain user input with the ActiveX controls discussed in the previous chapters.

FIGURE 14.10.

The Cookie2 page prompts the user to enter the value of each cookie, which is stored in a cookie file on the local computer.

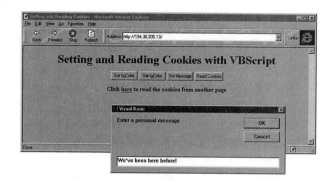

After all the cookie values have been set, the script will save the cookies on the local computer. Now click on the hyperlink on this page to switch to another page (shown in Figure 14.8) of the same Web. This page can access the cookies stored by the Web's home page. You can click the first Command button to find out the value of an existing cookie, or click the second Command button to see all the cookie values stored on the client computer by the home page.

When the first Command button is clicked, the code will prompt the user to enter the name of the variable he or she is interested in. Then it will retrieve the cookie, locate the value, and display it in a Message box. The second Command button reads the cookie, extracts all the variables and their values and displays them on a separate page, with the `write` method of the `document` object. The two useful procedures in this application are a function that finds the value of a variable in the cookie and a subroutine that scans the cookie and reports all the variables stored in it and their values.

Listing 14.1 shows the code of the `Cookie2` page.

Listing 14.1. The Cookie2 page.

```
 1: <HTML>
 2: <HEAD>
 3: <TITLE>Setting and Reading Cookies</TITLE>
 4: <SCRIPT LANGUAGE="VBS">
 5: Sub Button1_onClick()
 6:     bg=InputBox("Enter your favorite background color")
 7:     cookie1="BGCOLOR=" & bg
 8:     Document.cookie=cookie1
 9: End Sub
10: Sub Button2_onClick()
11:     fg=InputBox("Enter your favorite foreground color")
12:     cookie2="FRCOLOR=" & fg
13:     Document.cookie=cookie2
14: End Sub
15: Sub Button3_onClick()
16:     msg=InputBox("Enter a personal message")
17:     cookie3="MESSAGE=" & msg & ";expires=Wed, 01 Jan 1997 12:00:00 GMT"
18:     Document.cookie=cookie3
19: End Sub
```

14

CUSTOMIZE YOUR
WEB PAGE WITH
COOKIES

continues

Listing 14.1. continued

```
20: Sub Button4_onClick()
21:     cookie=Document.cookie
22:     msgbox cookie
23: End Sub
24: </SCRIPT>
25: </HEAD>
26: <BODY>
27: <CENTER>
28: <H1>Setting and Reading Cookies with VBScript</H1>
29: <INPUT TYPE="BUTTON" NAME="Button1" VALUE="Set bgColor">
30: <INPUT TYPE="BUTTON" NAME="Button2" VALUE="Set fgColor">
31: <INPUT TYPE="BUTTON" NAME="Button3" VALUE="Set Message">
32: <INPUT TYPE="BUTTON" NAME="Button4" VALUE="Read Cookies">
33: <BR><BR>
34: <H4>Click <A HREF=index2.htm>here</A> to read the cookies from another page
    </H4>
35: </CENTER>
36: </BODY>
37: </HTML>
```

The first three Command buttons on this page create three variables and store them in the cookie. The names of the variables are FGCOLOR, BGCOLOR, and MESSAGE. Their values are specified by the user with the help of an InputBox() function. You can set the value of each cookie as many times as you want, and the cookie property isn't going to create additional variables. Each time a new value is assigned to an existing variable, it replaces the existing value and does not create a new variable.

The destination of the hyperlink is the Index2.htm file, whose contents are shown in Listing 14.2.

Listing 14.2. The Index2.htm file.

```
 1: <HTML>
 2: <HEAD>
 3: <TITLE>Setting and Reading Cookies</TITLE>
 4: <HEAD>
 5: <SCRIPT LANGUAGE=VBS>
 6: Dim cookies(2,50)
 7:
 8: Function GetCookie(whichVariable)
 9:     cookie=Document.Cookie
10:     VarPosition=Instr(cookie, whichVariable)
11:     If VarPosition=0 then
12:         GetCookie=0
13:         Exit Function
14:     Else
15:         StartVarPosition=VarPosition+Len(whichVariable)
16:         EndVarPosition=Instr(StartVarPosition, cookie, ";")
17:         If EndVarPosition=0 then EndVarPosition=Len(cookie)+1
18:         GetCookie=Mid(cookie, StartVarPosition, EndVarPosition-
            StartVarPosition)
19:     End If
```

```
20: End Function
21:
22: Sub CButton1_onClick()
23:     ckVar=InputBox("Enter the name of the cookie")
24:     If ckVar<>"" Then
25:         ckVal=GetCookie(ckVar)
26:     End If
27:     If ckVal<>"" Then
28:         msgbox "The value of the " & ckVar & cookie & " is " & ckVal
29:     Else
30:         msgbox "No " & ckVar & "cookie found"
31:     End If
32: End Sub
33:
34: Sub CButton2_onClick()
35:     cookie=Document.cookie
36:     i=1
37:     While len(cookie)>0
38:         pos=Instr(cookie, "=")
39:         If pos>0 then
40:             ckVar=left(cookie, pos-1)
41:             cookie=mid(cookie,pos+1)
42:             pos=Instr(cookie,";")
43:             If pos=0 then
44:                 ckVal=cookie
45:                 cookie=""
46:             Else
47:                 ckVal=left(cookie,pos-1)
48:                 cookie=mid(cookie, pos+1)
49:             End If
50:             cookies(1,i)=ckVar
51:             cookies(2,i)=ckVal
52:         End If
53:         i=i+1
54:     Wend
55:     ncookies=i-1
56:
57:     Document.open
58:     Document.write "There were " & ncookies & " cookies in the document"
59:     Document.write "<TABLE>"
60:     For ck=1 to ncookies
61:         ckvar=cookies(1,ck)
62:         ckval=cookies(2,ck)
63:         Document.write "<TR>"
64:         Document.write "<TD>" & ckvar & "<TD>" & ckval
65:         Document.write "</TR>"
66:     Next
67:     Document.write "</TABLE>"
68:     Document.close
69: End Sub
70: </SCRIPT>
71: <BR><BR>
72: <INPUT TYPE=BUTTON NAME=CButton1 VALUE="Show A cookie">
73: <INPUT TYPE=BUTTON NAME=CButton2 VALUE="Show All cookies">
74: <A HREF=index.htm>Back to previous page</A>
75: </BODY>
76: </HTML>
```

14

CUSTOMIZE YOUR
WEB PAGE WITH
COOKIES

The GetCookie() function accepts the name of the cookie to extract as argument and extracts it from the Document.cookie property. First, it locates the variable's name in the cookie, and then it looks for the following semicolon. When GetCookie() finds the variable, it has in effect located the value following the variable name and returns it to the calling function. *VarPosition* is the position of the variable name in the cookie. After the variable name is found, the function looks in the rest of the cookie to find the following semicolon, which signals the end of the cookie's value (or the end of the string, if it happens to be the last cookie in the string). The *StartVarPosition* and *EndVarPosition* variables delimit the cookie's value in the string, and they are used to extract it.

The CButton2_onClick() subroutine works in a very similar manner. It starts at the left end of the string and treats everything to the first equal sign as the variable name. Then it locates the following semicolon, and everything between the equal sign and the semicolon is the value of the variable. With the first variable/value pair out of the way, it truncates the cookie by removing everything from the left up to (and including) the semicolon, and it repeats the same process over and over until the entire cookie has been searched.

Review

The customization techniques you learned in this chapter rely on the document itself and the browser. To create a highly customizable Web, like the MSN Web site for example, you must do some programming on the server. Let's say you have a number of home pages, each one for a specific category of users—a page for sports fans, another one for music lovers, another one for computer game addicts, and so on. To display the appropriate page to every client who has customized his or her home page, prepare a starting page with no content, or a simple design that informs the user that his or her custom page is being downloaded. This generic page should contain the VBScript code for grabbing the values of the cookies, place them in a hidden TextBox control, and then submit them to the server with the Form's Submit method. Or decide which of the many start pages suits the user's interest the best and request that page. If the cookie contains the string sports, the CustomSports page should be loaded. One way to do this is via the href property of the document's location object.

A customized site such as the MSN site uses a CGI application that creates the custom home page on-the-fly. Again, you can start with a generic home page, which reads the value of the cookie with all the settings, stores them in a hidden TextBox, and submits its contents to the server. The server will then generate a new home page on-the-fly, based on the viewer's preferences. There's quite a bit of overhead with this approach, because generating good-looking pages programmatically requires good programming skills and creativity. To simplify the task of setting up a custom page, you can use frames, some of which will be the same on all pages and the remaining ones will contain customized content. Frames will help you organize the information you want to place on the pages, without having to worry about sizing the pages and the positioning of the elements on them. The users will decide how big each frame will be.

The last approach of combining cookies and CGI applications to customize your Web is the most flexible approach, but the most demanding one in terms of authoring. If your goal, however, is to attract users to your site, this is the extra step that will place your site ahead of the others. You can also use this technique quite efficiently in an intranet environment to provide custom pages to certain groups of users. The users in the marketing department, for instance, will see the `Marketing.htm` page every time they start Internet Explorer, and users in the accounting department will see the `Accounting.htm` page.

IV
PART

Special Subjects

Creating Active Documents for Corporate Intranets

by Bill Schongar

IN THIS CHAPTER

Are intranets just a bunch of hype? Corporate networks for sharing resources between departments and across locations aren't anything new; local area networks (LANs) and wide area networks (WANs) have been in mainstream use for well over 10 years. The infrastructure and the technology used to turn a LAN into this amorphous thing called an "intranet" isn't anything new and spiffy either, because the basic communications protocol used to power an intranet, in the form of TCP/IP, has been around for quite a while as well. So what's so brand spankin' new that it needs all the publicity? The feeling of "new" comes from the way the network is being used.

If you think about a basic file-sharing network, you have a server (or any multiple of one that suits your needs) and a bunch of files resident on a drive. That's all you get. If you need the latest copy of the company financials, you have to make sure you get access to accounting's drive, figure out where the file is, figure out what its filename is, and then make sure that you have something to read that file format. What, you don't have XYZ accounting software? Back to square one. E-mail the folks in accounting and ask for a hard copy. What a welcome to the age of technology. To the end user there is no interrelation of data, no reasonably clear method of general organization (unless you count being able to decipher DOS-style 8.3 format filenames as an efficient method of organization), and no leeway for incompatible data formats. What you need is an intranet.

The relationship between, and organization of, pieces of information is just as important as being able to view the information in the first place. Intranets are built on organization and interrelation, because they're designed as a way to share information, not just files. When you look for the corporate financials, you might expect to find a link to performance by month or by quarter, maybe by department or product. These in turn may have other factors involved in their creation, and you should be able to track them all down with just a quick click of the mouse. When you want to submit a request, you shouldn't have to track down a paper copy of a form and then get it checked, processed, and tossed into the mysterious depths of getting approval. You should be able to go to an easy-to-find location, find the form you need, fill it out online, have error-checking done for you, receive confirmation that you submitted it, and be done with it. That's not too unreasonable, is it?

In short, an intranet is all about getting the most bang for your information buck. This is where ActiveX and VBScript make the difference. You can add powerful functionality and flexibility to your intranet without breaking a sweat. Users can update data in its native format, not worrying about conversion to some static chunk of HTML or a graphic. Want a spreadsheet? No problem. Want a multimedia slide show? You got it.

Want client-side processing, self-updating distributed applications, complete design flexibility, and some free time? You can have it all, and we'll show you how. In this chapter we'll focus on elements of ActiveX and VBScript that power your intranet to new levels, including

    Client-Side Processing

    Distributed Applications

Native Data Formats

Return on Investment

Whether you already have an intranet, or are trying to justify the expenses associated with creating or improving one, this chapter will show you how ActiveX will kick your site into high gear, at a price point you can live with and with functionality you won't be able to live without.

Client-Side Processing

1Mbps, 10Mbps, 100Mbps.... Let's face it, the network is never fast enough. No matter how fast you improve your network, something will come out that sucks up all the speed you have available, and then some. The more users you add to that lightning-fast server, the more all that speed seems like just another flash in the pan. The only way you can ever get a server to reach its true potential is to offload the menial tasks onto some other machine. Well, how about the users who are accessing the network? They have connected computers that could take on responsibility for their tasks, don't they?

Client-side processing is an increasingly important aspect of client/server computing. At first, it was enough that the two computers could talk to one another, and the server could be the processing powerhouse. That's akin to calling Julia Child and asking her to cook you dinner—if you have access to all the instructions and materials, why can't you do it yourself? Sure, an expert can probably do something faster and better, but if dozens of people call up with the same request over and over again, it's not going to be faster to wait for the expert than it would be to do the work yourself. Client-side processing gives the server a break, because it means you can download everything you need to do a job, and the server only has to process a fraction of what you really need, for tasks that require shared resources that your machine can't handle by itself.

ActiveX and VBScript are true client-side enabling technologies. You don't run embedded VBScript the way that you run a CGI program, where you call to the server, it thinks about it, it responds, and you repeat the cycle until you get what you want. VBScript is downloaded and run in your memory space, on your processor, with no network bandwidth taken up for paltry data operations like validating forms output. Do you really want to take up even a fraction of available server resources telling someone he forgot to enter an extension on his phone number, or a departmental billing number?

It's exactly these kinds of basic but necessary operations that VBScript and ActiveX can provide instant benefit in. Let's take the example of client-side forms validation in a little more detail, starting with the traditional method. First, the server has to download the form, which in and of itself is pretty static. Next, the user has to enter data. Any validation of that data has to initiate a connection to the server, the server has to start a process to evaluate the data, establish a connection to respond, and the end user has to receive it. Now, if this is a form that's accessed by one or two people twice a day, that's not very significant. If, on the other hand, this is one of a thousand such forms that on average get hit hundreds of times an hour, the processing savings for the server are significant, and the total performance benefit for users is extremely high. After all, what's faster—negotiating a conversation with a network server or communicating with a program resident in memory on your local machine?

Distributed Applications

Proceeding to the next level of client-side processing, you encounter distributed applications. More than just a script here and there, fully distributed applications provide the end user with all the files he needs to run a full-fledged application. Typical network installation of applications designed to be distributed is either localization of the programs' executables and support files on a drive that everyone runs them from, or asking users to go to that drive and download all those files locally. "Activated" applications can be fully functioning combinations of ActiveX and VBScript components working together, where it's downloaded once, automatically, and automatically updated to the latest version when it needs to be, by just a visit to a specific page.

What kinds of distributed applications are possible, and logical, for the corporate intranet environment? Here are just a few:

> Order Processing
>
> Training Materials
>
> Inventory Controls
>
> Data Warehousing Clients
>
> Scheduling Applications

The point of distributed applications is one you're already familiar with—keeping efficiency maximized. Fully distributed applications put the majority of the processing load on the client, rather than the server. This shouldn't be equated to isolation from the server. Far from it! Distributed applications don't need to be completely stand-alone applications, in that they would need to download a database file or similar shared resources, but the majority of the action taken on those resources should be done without the server's intervention. Record locking, error-checking—all these things should be done before the connection to the server kicks in.

Databases

Database functions are traditionally processor-intensive. Everyone needs them, for anything from orders and inventory control to holding employee information. The benefit of placing database operations in a distributed environment is that while the data exchange operations may take up a significant portion of the server's time, formatting the results is taken care of "offline," without tying up the server resources. As an example, let's consider a CGI program performing database operations.

First, there's the client side. A simple form or alternate interface provides data entry. No error-checking, no real interaction, just type and click. When the user submits the form, data is sent to the server where the server needs to start a process to handle the CGI program, barring the use of in-process server extensions for handling the request. The CGI program then decodes the URL-encoded information and generates something that functions as the calling convention for the database. Next, something needs to initiate a connection to the database, execute the data query, store the results, process the results, process output to match those results to the displayable needs of the client, encode the output, and send it back to the client. The client then loads the new HTML page and displays the static results. It works, and it's definitely a useful function, but there are a couple extra steps there.

With a VBScript and ActiveX solution, the client side takes care of all formatting and error-checking. Pass back a stream of database information, and let the client deal with it. Forgot an entry? Don't ever let the connection to the database open until everything is ready to go. Need more efficiency? Communicate directly with the database or its own special server, and bypass the need for an HTTP server as a middleman. It's not a matter of any less work being done, but rather the location and the efficiency of the work that makes the difference.

Even better, think of what you can do with the results. CGI returns come back as a standard text stream, with the possibility of some images and other content. ActiveX and VBScript could handle a streamed pile of data and fill dynamic listboxes or other UI features so that you can modify what you get, and send it back. Tried modifying a typical HTML page as the end user lately? Good luck. Taking tables of data, listboxes, and even images, you could modify them and then stream them back to the database. One-stop shopping for your database needs.

TIP

Open database connectivity (ODBC) over the Internet is a growing field. Companies have announced drivers and utilities that allow direct database connections through built-in drivers so that the database server is also the TCP/IP server for database requests. Large database vendors including Oracle, Sybase, and Informix are heavily involved in making all of this a reality, and you can expect to see ActiveX playing a big part in their strategy and in the strategies of people riding their coattails. If you're interested in a direct Internet-capable driver for your database, check with your database vendor to see what they have available. The results may surprise you.

Functionality and Flexibility

There's more possibility for functionality in ActiveX and VBScript combinations than you can easily shake a big stick at. The list of ActiveX controls grows by dozens a day, and that's a bare minimum. OLE and extension controls (like VBXs) have been made by thousands of individual software companies for C and Visual Basic, and the opening of a whole new marketplace has inspired them to new levels of productivity. Chances are quite good that no matter what type of ActiveX control you need, you can either find it already, find something close, or find the instructions to build it yourself. There are certain areas of functionality, however, that transcend specific controls, and fall into general categories of use to the intranet frame of mind. Let's look at a few.

Native Document Hosting

Have a lot of people creating material, but not a great way to convert it into HTML or some other arbitrary format? ActiveX is about to become your best friend. The whole concept behind OCX (and thus ActiveX) controls is to provide a generic container to which additional functionality can be added. The most obvious use of a generic container is to toss in different forms of content.

As an example, someone in your department has created a PowerPoint presentation. Now you'd like to share that with the rest of the company. You can either start taking screen captures and converting to HTML and JPEGs or GIFs, or you can take the easy and more functional way out. Not a tough decision. Microsoft came out with an ActiveX-enabled PowerPoint player, which allows you to embed the ActiveX player object in the HTML code, and reference a filename for the presentation itself. Suddenly, everyone who uses PowerPoint can place his or her presentations up for general use, with no conversion, no mess, no fuss!

The same holds true with other information types. Previously, the network involved hunting down the file you wanted, then hunting down the utility you need to open the document with. Now information is menued and organized, with logical text and links allowing information managers and employees in general to devise navigation that will lead people to relevant information without the hunt-and-peck of a flat file system.

Component Architecture

New functions are just an .OCX file away. Because ActiveX is an open software component environment, any new capabilities that you need can be built in quickly, efficiently, and painlessly. Each new function is capable of cooperation with existing components as well, so that a database program doesn't have to be a reporting software, and a slide show presenter doesn't have to understand HTML. Everything plugs together to form a seamless whole.

Third-Party Innovation

You don't have to think of everything. How are people supposed to sell you ideas and products if you've thought of, and implemented, everything you could possibly ever need? The number of developers out there who are creating ActiveX components is staggering. Pick up a copy of any magazine dedicated to Visual Basic, flip to the advertisements in the back, and you'll get some idea of what kind of industry already exists for add-on components. Because VBXs (the add-ons for Visual Basic) aren't too far away from ActiveX controls, the vast majority of these developers will be moving in that direction just as soon as they smell the money. And the smell is getting stronger by the day.

NOTE

Using ActiveX functions on your intranet may be initially limited by the platforms that comprise your network. ActiveX on UNIX, for example, wouldn't have been the best option in the first few months after ActiveX's release. At the time of this writing, in fact, going to UNIX was not even a possibility, though it was being hyped heavily as a future development. Macintosh was the first scheduled platform besides the native Windows implementations, and even that hadn't come to fruition by October. Rest assured, though, that Microsoft realizes that they'll lose a significant chunk of potential revenue if they only cater to Windows, and they'll do everything in their capabilities to make sure platforms aren't a problem.

Return on Investment (ROI)

"But what do we get back, financially?" It's a question heard all the time in companies big and small. Look at what you get so far—less wear and tear on the server, less maintenance, better performance, more functionality, and more expandability. Do these add up to big savings? You'd better believe it. And all of these contribute to two other significant improvements—employee efficiency and company image. Let's look at all of the fiscally friendly components.

Maintenance

We're not talking about cleaning the hard drive, or replacing monitors. Maintaining a corporate information system is all about keeping information up-to-date and accessible under any conditions. Fault-tolerant, mission-critical access is the kind of talk that people in high places like to hear. Maybe it's because they've been reading "Dilbert" and picked up some buzzwords, or maybe it's because they actually need those things; the jury's still out on that. Regardless of the real or perceived need, maintaining an information system comprised of data in a non-native format is time-consuming. Finding out about, getting hold of, converting, error-checking, and approving data before it goes anywhere is taking two steps forward and one step back every time you move. By allowing departments to leave documents in their native format, and using in-place document embedding through ActiveX controls or plain old OLE, responsibility for content can be narrowed down to two things: the accuracy of the original data, and the relocation of the data to the shared area. So, if there's a typo on line 3005 of this year's budget, let accounting fix it. If the new product schematic is missing a power cord, let R&D figure out where to put it and then have them modify the schematic. Isn't delegated responsibility great?

Reduced maintenance equals reduced costs, plain and simple. Less time lost from other revenue-generating projects, less time spent moaning and whining about not being able to get things converted properly, and fewer mistakes due to the conversion or modification by someone outside the originating department.

Expansibility and Integration

MIS Nightmare #23. You research, plan, design, recommend, specify, and purchase a state-of-the-art system that meets all your needs, only to have those needs completely change a week after you put everything together, and none of the vendor's partners ever come through on their original promises to develop what you need for the system you bought. While good planning can reduce the real instances of this nightmare, the underlying problem of technological obsolescence is anything but easily solvable through traditional methods. Scalability is what's needed, but it's often hard to scale a software solution because vendors change, new technology emerges, and everyone always wants what he or she read about that's currently not even in beta form yet. And, oh yes, it all has to work together with his or her existing stuff seamlessly.

ActiveX components give you the ability to say "No problem." What you're really building around when relying on ActiveX is a scalable software component architecture, like a modular server. Every time a new need arises, you've got plug-and-play expansibility by adding new components, and you know that each ActiveX component can communicate with the others easily and efficiently. You can even write custom code to integrate disparate elements in your own unique way, if you need to. This means that one department's need to have terminal emulation in a Web browser (shudder) and another department's need to integrate a proprietary legacy database format can both be accommodated, and even that some outside development company may already have done it for you with a component you can purchase.

Standards

When Microsoft decides to make a standard, and puts as much marketing power behind it as they have with ActiveX, you can be sure that it's not going to disappear in the near future. Before you bring up the inevitable subject of Microsoft's original failed foray into UNIX (called Xenix, for those of you who have forgotten that unfortunate incident), remember that ActiveX comes at a time and in a form that lots of people, especially Windows-centric developers, want very badly. They want to be able to make their applications Internet-ready with the addition of a file or two. They want to add other people's functions to their software without pain and frustration. And they want it right now. ActiveX delivers on all of those things and promises to deliver compatibility with Java as well.

That's what it comes down to, though, isn't it? Whose standard is going to become the one to follow, and which technologies are going to become tagalongs? Java made a splash the size of a tsunami when it first came out, and the rush continues. Why? Its goal in life is cross-platform compatibility and portability. This makes it a good choice for network computers and companies with diverse system types and the desire to program in a language slightly less cumbersome than C++, while still maintaining an object-oriented approach. Microsoft, however, is intent on making sure that if they can't conquer Java, they'll embrace it with ActiveX.

The first sign of this was the ActiveX scripting extensions that Microsoft built into Internet Explorer. Not just support for VBScript, their own scripting language, but support for JavaScript as well. In the same manner, scripting languages can communicate with ActiveX objects, and ActiveX objects should be able to communicate with Java classes and functions like Java Database Connectivity (JDBC). Countless companies are either already working on Java and ActiveX integrated solutions, have preliminary versions out, or have announced that they're going to pay very close attention to the marketplace.

Even in the worst case, where ActiveX competes with Java and causes a standards rift akin to the old Mac versus Windows debate, thousands of development houses whose bread and butter is made on Windows programming will be cranking out ActiveX components all the time. That adds up to a significant number of development resources that will continue to use ActiveX no matter what happens, which is better than what can be said for a variety of other new technologies that have fallen by the wayside in recent years.

Investment Protection

How many Windows programmers are there? How many Visual Basic developers are there? If you're a large corporation, chances are pretty good that you have one, the other, or both classes of those developers in-house. If you're a small company with a smaller budget, the chances of having a VB or Windows C++ programmer in-house are even higher, percentage-wise. If you, as a company or an individual, have invested significant time and effort into learning a certain programming language, the cost to switch you over to a new environment can be pretty high. ActiveX and VBScript aim to change that.

Because VBScript is a subset of Visual Basic, it's no trouble at all for a VB programmer to switch "down" to VBScript and learn what functions are no longer available to him, as well as learn ActiveX object syntax. Rather than a reduction in the toolset, it's an extension of what the programmer can already do, with no toolkits to buy, no distribution licensing to worry about, and plenty of possibilities.

While creating ActiveX controls isn't exactly a walk in the park, experienced C++ programmers (especially those with OLE and COM object experience) are just extending their knowledge base, not retraining themselves on a new language or a new set of tools. The same environments that they have on their systems, be they from Borland, Microsoft, or anyone else, will undoubtedly gain ActiveX built-in functions to make the development process easier, so future upgrades will roll in the ActiveX cost already.

In all cases, training and software resource costs for employees are kept to a minimum. This is bottom-line good news for any company, regardless of size. No need for extensive training, combined with the ability to maintain familiar development environments, means that ramp-up time for development is also kept to a minimum, yielding more profits sooner.

Employee Efficiency

Two choices: a huge pile of unorganized papers, or a filing cabinet that you know is organized and updated on a regular basis. While the former may aptly describe my desk, most of us would choose the latter as the best place to hunt down a specific piece of information that should already be stored there.

Distributed applications and client-side processing using ActiveX mean less time wasted when network traffic is high or a server is being obstinate, less time spent trying to figure out how the data presented on a page corresponds to the original information, and more time available for interpreting that original data in the way it was intended. Most important, employees will have increased the rate at which they can locate the information they need, when and how they need it.

Company Image

You're on the phone with someone at Company X, and you ask what you're sure is a question that he or she is not going to be able to handle. Expecting "Umm, let me transfer you…" or dreading the possible use of canned hold music while they hunt down someone from another department, you're shocked when he or she says it'll be no problem to look that up for you, continues discussing other tidbits with you, and then relays the answer you were looking for, and even offers to e-mail further documentation to you right now. Inspired, you ask a couple of other questions that some other companies you called last week still haven't gotten back to you on. Issue after issue, it's the same—the person you're talking to has all the information you need and then some.

What kind of image would you have of that company if you called them? Probably the same kind you'd want your customers to have of you—prompt, efficient, knowledgeable, and very well organized. The benefits of a corporate intranet don't stop at the company doors. If employees know they can track down the information they need, at times when they're the most desperate, they'll be more confident. Customers may not know you have an intranet, but they'll know you've got your stuff together, and it'll inspire confidence in them as well. All of these bolster your company's image to both employees and customers, which is in and of itself one of the most valuable returns you can get. A 10-person company can do business like it has a thousand employees, and a large company can provide a single point-of-contact to give customers a personal touch.

Review

This idealized version of the intranet is far from being just a daydream. New developments and a constant flood of interested consumers keep the desire for companies to develop intranet solutions very high. HTML itself was a good stepping stone for information, but intranets are becoming more than just static pages. They're now hosts for distributed applications and client-side data processing, with the need to represent the latest and greatest information on a minute-by-minute basis. ActiveX and VBScript can be combined to meet the needs of your corporate intranet easily, effectively, and cost-efficiently.

Controlling MS Office Documents in Web Pages

by Ramesh Chandak

IN THIS CHAPTER

The browser has revolutionized the way the Internet and Web are accessed. The key to this tremendous success is very simple—an easy-to-use interface coupled with the worldwide network of computers. A product with an easy-to-use interface has been instrumental to the success of several companies. Apple Computer made it big time with the introduction of Macintosh; the Macintosh interface was revolutionary to the people who had been so accustomed to the character-based DOS world. Next followed the Windows 3.1 interface. The most recent wave is the introduction of the browser, which has made it very easy to surf the Internet and the Web. In fact, the hyperlink hot spot concept implemented in the browser was first introduced as part of Hypercard on the Macintosh. But it did not hit the main street until the Web and the browser came together.

What Macintosh and Windows did for the desktop, the browser does for the Net. To begin with, the browser offers point-and-click graphical access to the Net. You can point to a site, link to another site, link to yet another site, and so on. It is the hyperlink capability that makes it so easy. Obviously, users expect more functionality from the browser than just the ability to point and surf! It has become the central point of navigation. It is only natural that a lot of features will be added to the browser in time.

The word processor is probably the most commonly used application in the world today. Again, it is only natural to expect direct links to your word processing documents from your browser. The alternative to this would be to switch to your word processing application, open it, select the document you wish to view, and click OK. This is a tedious and cumbersome task that hampers productivity. It is a lot easier and quicker to click the hot spot on your Web page that represents a word processing document and have it open automatically, without worrying about the format, type, and location of the document.

Along with its other Internet products, Microsoft has announced the release of its ActiveX technology. ActiveX is the level next to OLE. The data transfer technology has come a long way from the days of using Clipboard, to dynamic data exchange (DDE) protocol, to OLE, to now: ActiveX! ActiveX is based on Microsoft's Component Object Model (COM). The COM architecture specifies development of reusable software objects. Such objects can be written in completely different languages. They can reside on completely different platforms across completely different networks. Yet they can communicate and integrate with each other easily. This is the basic premise of the COM theory: creating reusable components that can interact with each other easily, irrespective of their language or location of origin. ActiveX is the result of Microsoft's five-year investment in research and development of the COM specification. Microsoft renamed OLE controls as ActiveX controls in an effort to push their Internet technology and standards aggressively.

ActiveX technology has multiple paradigms. You can create ActiveX controls and integrate them with your Windows applications. You can make your Web pages active by embedding ActiveX controls in them. An ActiveX control can also be downloaded by the user. As a corporate developer, you can create active documents using ActiveX. An active document is an ActiveX control representing Office documents such as Word, Excel, and PowerPoint.

Controlling MS Office Documents in Web Pages

CHAPTER 16

355

16

MS OFFICE
DOCUMENTS IN
WEB PAGES

Using active documents is the focus of this chapter. It discusses how you can make your browser a one-stop access point to your word processing, spreadsheet, and presentation documents.

Listing 16.1 shows HTML code for a sample Web page of this book, *VBScript Unleashed*, also shown in Figure 16.1. All the documents represented by the hot spots are stored in Microsoft Word 6.0 format.

Listing 16.1. HTML for a sample Web page of this book, *VBScript Unleashed*.

```
<!DOCTYPE HTML PUBLIC "-//IETF//DTD HTML//EN"><HTML><HEAD><TITLE>
VBScript Unleashed
</TITLE></HEAD><!--DocHeaderStart--><BODY leftmargin=8 bgcolor="#FFFFFF"
VLINK="#666666" LINK="#FF0000"><FONT FACE="ARIAL,HELVETICA" SIZE="2"><!--
DocHeaderEnd-->
<P><h2>VBScript Unleashed
</h2><P><!--DATE-->September 1, 1996<P><!--/DATE-->
<P><A HREF="vbs18or.doc">Controlling MS Office Documents in web pages<P>
<P><A HREF="vbs20or.doc">VBScript and Java<P>
<!--DocFooterStart--></FONT><FONT FACE="MS SANS SERIF" SIZE="1"
COLOR="BLACK"><A HREF="/Misc/cpyright.htm" target="_top">&#169;
1996 Sams.net</A></FONT><!--DocFooterEnd--></BODY></HTML>
```

FIGURE 16.1.

Sample Web page of this book, VBScript Unleashed.

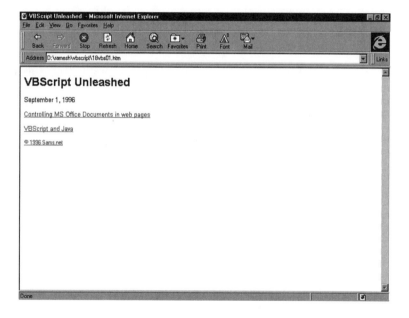

If you click the hot spot VBScript and Java, it opens the document in Microsoft Word 6.0 format within the Internet Explorer window. See Figure 16.2.

FIGURE 16.2.

A Microsoft Word document within the Internet Explorer window.

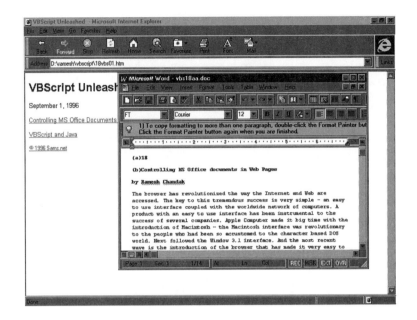

If you want to provide read-only access to your Word or Excel documents (such as human resource policies and employee handbooks), you can use the free application viewers (such as Microsoft PowerPoint Viewer, Microsoft Word Viewer, and Microsoft Excel Viewer).

This chapter provides a brief background on ActiveX technology. It focuses on how you can use ActiveX controls and VBScript to integrate Office documents into your Web pages. Although it specifically discusses Microsoft Office Suite products, the concept and steps involved in configuring them apply to other products such as Lotus Suite as well.

ActiveX

It all started with the need for applications to communicate with each other. In the good old days, data would be transferred between documents of the same application or between applications, using our beloved Clipboard. This changed in due course with the advent of dynamic data exchange (DDE) technology. The Clipboard and DDE eventually became the foundation for OLE. Microsoft actively and aggressively promoted this technology. It eventually became the de facto standard on the Windows platform. OLE made it very easy to embed a variety of documents into the host application. For example, a word processing document can contain a chart, graph, and spreadsheet. The word processing document is the container that holds other objects. Using OLE, applications can import information without the need to understand the format and origin of the data being imported. OLE helps improve the user's overall productivity. Users can focus on their tasks at hand and not worry about the format, origin, and location of the data. The popularity and widespread acceptance of OLE technology created a new industry, developing OCX controls. Hundreds of thousands of shareware and commercial OCX controls are available in the market today.

Having received a wake up call from Netscape and the wired community worldwide, Microsoft announced its own Internet strategy. In addition to introducing a variety of products and services aimed at Internet and intranet development, Microsoft seized this opportunity to promote its ActiveX technology. ActiveX is OLE and much more! ActiveX is OLE redefined for the Internet, and it goes beyond that. Traditional OCXs are large files, not suitable for deployment, and download over the Net. ActiveX is OLE optimized for the Net. It is all-encompassing. You can create ActiveX controls. Such controls can be integrated with your Web and other client/server applications. They can also be downloaded over the Net. Just as you have had hundreds of thousands of VBXs and OCXs integrate with your applications, built using programming tools such as PowerBuilder and Visual Basic, you now have ActiveX controls ready to be integrated with your Web, desktop, and network applications. With ActiveX you can also create active documents. Active documents are ActiveX controls representing Office documents such as Word, Excel, and PowerPoint. You can do ActiveX scripting. ActiveX scripting is writing scripts, using VBScript and ActiveX controls.

At the time of this writing, Microsoft is giving away a suite of ActiveX controls for the Internet. It is called the Internet Control Pack (ICP) and is available for download at `http://www.microsoft.com/icp/us/icpdown/icpdown.htm`. You can use these controls to develop your Internet and intranet applications quickly and easily.

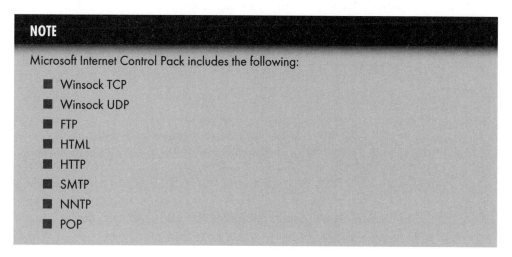

NOTE

Microsoft Internet Control Pack includes the following:

- Winsock TCP
- Winsock UDP
- FTP
- HTML
- HTTP
- SMTP
- NNTP
- POP

ActiveX is presently supported on the Windows platform. ActiveX on the Macintosh and UNIX platforms is expected by the end of 1996. Microsoft and Metrowerks are working together to include ActiveX support on the Macintosh. Microsoft, Mainsoft, and Bristol are working together to include ActiveX support on the UNIX platform. Microsoft Internet Explorer 3.0 is the only browser on the market today that includes full support for ActiveX and VBScript technology. You can use ActiveX controls with Netscape Navigator 3.0 if you use the ActiveX plug-in from NCompassLabs (`http://www.ncompasslabs.com`), a third-party software vendor.

> **NOTE**
>
> To stay current with ActiveX technology, visit Microsoft's ActiveX Web site at `http://www.microsoft.com/activex`.

ActiveX Scripting

ActiveX scripting is writing scripts, using a scripting language such as VBScript, JavaScript, and AppleScript, as well as ActiveX controls. You can integrate any type of object, including ActiveX objects, into your Web pages using the HTML <OBJECT> extension. The ability to integrate ActiveX objects lets you create active Web pages. Such Web pages can be dynamic and interactive in nature. Gone are the days of static Web pages where the surfer could only point, click, and read. You can now add animation and 3-D virtual reality experience to your Web pages and liven them up! If you are a corporate developer, you can integrate ActiveX controls that represent your Office documents on the intranet server. This lets users open Word, Excel, and PowerPoint documents directly, using their browser.

You can write ActiveX controls using programming tools such as Visual C++ and Borland C++ (the same tools that are used to write DLLs and OCX controls). Microsoft has released the ActiveX SDK, a Windows toolkit for Internet and intranet software development. In fact, the Microsoft Internet Explorer 3.0 is written completely using ActiveX SDK. Alternatively, you can buy third-party ActiveX controls developed by Microsoft and other independent software vendors.

You can download Microsoft's freebies—a suite of ActiveX controls—from its ActiveX home page (`http://www.microsoft.com/activex`). Table 16.1 lists descriptions of several of these controls.

Table 16.1. ActiveX freebies from Microsoft.

Name of control	Description
StockTicker	Continuously displays changing data. The control downloads the URL specified at regular intervals and displays that data. The data can be in text or XRT format.
Label	Displays given text at any specified angle. It can also render the text along user-defined curves.

Controlling MS Office Documents in Web Pages

CHAPTER 16

359

16

MS OFFICE
DOCUMENTS IN
WEB PAGES

Name of control	Description
Marquee	Scrolls, slides, and/or bounces URLs, within a user-defined window.
Chart	Enables you to draw various types of charts with different styles.
Timer	Invokes an event periodically and is invisible at runtime.

Listing 16.2 shows the object declaration for the chart control.

Listing 16.2. Object declaration for Microsoft's ActiveX chart control.

```
<OBJECT
     classid="clsid:FC25B780-75BE-11CF-8B01-444553540000"
     id=chart1
     width=400
     height=200
     align=center
     hspace=0
     vspace=0
>
<param name="hgridStyle" value="3">
<param name="vgridStyle" value="0">
<param name="colorscheme" value="0">
<param name="DisplayLegend" value="0">
<param name="BackStyle" value="1">
<param name="BackColor" value="#ffffff">
<param name="ForeColor" value="#0000ff">
<param name="Scale" value="100">
<param name="url" value="http://www.mycompany.com/chart.txt">
</OBJECT>
```

ActiveX Control Pad

ActiveX Control Pad is yet another Microsoft application. You can use it to design and develop your Web pages visually. Figure 16.3 shows the ActiveX Control Pad.

The Control Pad provides a visual way of accomplishing ActiveX scripting. Using the Pad, you can visually insert an ActiveX control into a Web page. Use the Edit | Insert ActiveX Control option to insert an ActiveX control. Figure 16.4 shows the Insert ActiveX Control dialog box.

Choose the appropriate control and click OK. The Properties dialog box is displayed. See Figure 16.5.

FIGURE 16.3.

The ActiveX Control Pad.

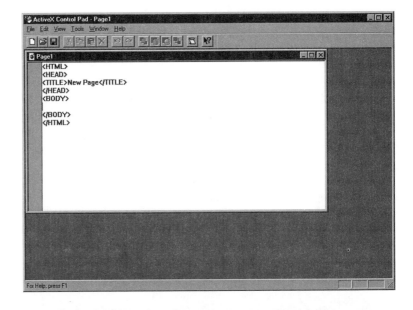

FIGURE 16.4.

Inserting an ActiveX control in your Web page using ActiveX Control Pad.

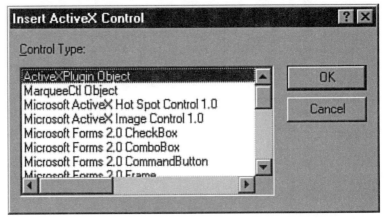

Use this dialog box to set the properties of the control per your application requirements. After you finish specifying the properties, close the Properties dialog box. The corresponding `<OBJECT>` code is added within your HTML code.

The following list outlines the steps required to include the ability to open Office documents such as Word, Excel, and PowerPoint within your browser window:

- Place all the required Office documents on the server in the appropriate directories.

- The host applications (Microsoft Word, Excel, and PowerPoint) should reside on the server or each client machine. Clearly, having them on the server is cost- and space-effective.

- If the users should have read-only access to the documents, set the access level of the directories to read-only. Alternatively, you can use the Office viewers instead of the complete applications.

- Use a tool such as ActiveX Control Pad to visually integrate ActiveX Office link controls into your HTML code.

- Use the control's Properties dialog box to set the name and location of the host application and the Office documents.

Figure 16.2, earlier in this chapter, shows an example of a Microsoft Word document within the Internet Explorer window.

FIGURE 16.5.

The ActiveX control properties dialog box.

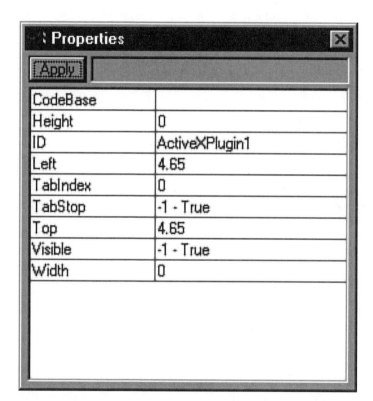

Properties	
Apply	
CodeBase	
Height	0
ID	ActiveXPlugin1
Left	4.65
TabIndex	0
TabStop	-1 - True
Top	4.65
Visible	-1 - True
Width	0

NOTE

If you do not have Microsoft Word installed on your system or on the Web server, you cannot view the word processing documents from your browser. The presence of the host application on the desktop or the network is required.

NOTE

Office viewers are available for download from Microsoft's Web site: http://
www.microsoft.com.

NOTE

Viewers are also helpful if you have not upgraded from version 2.0 to version 6.0 or 7.0. If you are still using Microsoft Word 2.0 for Windows and plan to upgrade later, you can use the Word Viewer for Windows in the meantime. The Word Viewer takes less resources than the full application and lets you view and print Word 6.0 documents. If you receive Word 6.0 documents from different sources, you can view and print them. Your Word 2.0 documents are upward-compatible with Word 6.0 for Windows.

Leveraging Your Investment

Microsoft Office Suite is *the* most popular software application package today. A number of corporations have invested in the Office Suite and used it to create a variety of documents, including reports, presentations, spreadsheets, and so on. These documents are the result of several man hours of work and effort that has been put in over the past several years. If you are building a company-wide intranet for your organization, it is highly beneficial if you provide easy access to such documents to your users. The popularity of the browser and the ability to use it as a one-stop point to access information from both the Internet and intranet makes it a natural candidate for linking it with your company documents.

Let us take a step back and review the OLE technology. Using OLE, you can embed a Microsoft Excel spreadsheet, for example, within your Microsoft Word document. This lets you open an Excel spreadsheet by double-clicking it within your Word document without having to explicitly open Microsoft Excel. In addition to spreadsheets, you can embed Word, PowerPoint, and other OLE-enabled documents. This improves productivity, because you don't need to worry about the format and location of the documents or the application needed to open such documents. Listing 16.3 shows the HTML code for a Web page displaying three types of documents: Microsoft Word, Microsoft Excel, and Microsoft PowerPoint. Figure 16.6 shows the resulting Web page. Notice the hot spots on the Web page. They do not really indicate the format of the document. If you click any hot spot, the appropriate application opens the document referenced.

Controlling MS Office Documents in Web Pages

CHAPTER 16

363

16

MS OFFICE
DOCUMENTS IN
WEB PAGES

Listing 16.3. HTML for a Web page displaying three types of documents.

```
<!DOCTYPE HTML PUBLIC "-//IETF//DTD HTML//EN"><HTML><HEAD><TITLE>
VBScript Unleashed
</TITLE></HEAD><!--DocHeaderStart--><BODY leftmargin=8 bgcolor="#FFFFFF"
VLINK="#666666" LINK="#FF0000"><FONT FACE="ARIAL,HELVETICA" SIZE="2"><!--
DocHeaderEnd-->
<P><h2>VBScript Unleashed
</h2><P><!--DATE-->September 1, 1996<P><!--/DATE-->
<P><A HREF="order.doc">This is a Microsoft Word document<P>
<P><A HREF="revenuesxls">This is a Microsoft Excel document<P>
<P><A HREF="vbscript.ppt">This is a Microsoft PowerPoint document<P>
<!--DocFooterStart--></FONT><FONT FACE="MS SANS SERIF" SIZE="1"
COLOR="BLACK"><A HREF="/Misc/cpyright.htm" target="_top">&#169;
1996 Sams.net</A></FONT><!--DocFooterEnd--></BODY></HTML>
```

FIGURE 16.6.

*A simple Web page
with hot spots to Word,
Excel, and PowerPoint
documents.*

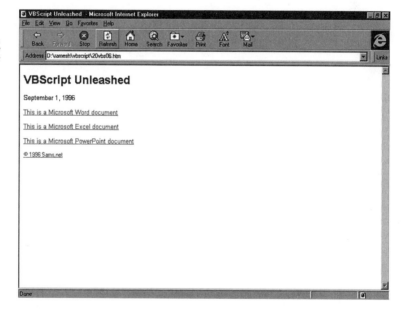

Using the browser as the one-stop point to access the Office documents helps improve productivity and provide an easy-to-use interface. Again, you don't need to worry about the format of the documents and the applications needed to open such documents. If your browser were not able to open your Office documents, you would have to switch from your browser window to your Windows desktop, open Microsoft Word or Microsoft Excel, open the application, and use the File | Open menu command to open the document of interest. Imagine if you had to do this for each and every Office document! It is a multistep process that affects productivity adversely.

The ability to provide access to your Office documents from the Web browser lets you leverage your investment in the Office Suite and documents created using it. You get an easy and simple to use access point and at the same time retain your investment in the office documents.

Integrating your browser with Office documents also lets you initiate some creative applications for your corporation. If your corporation has been distributing employee handbooks for several years, you can port the employee handbook onto your company-wide intranet. You can use Office Suite to create the electronic form of the employee handbook. Your company employees can view it using the browser. Similarly, the human resource department of your company can place its policies handbook on the intranet. These solutions offer significant cost savings. The cost of maintenance reduces substantially. Every year you can update your intranet-based employee and human resource policy handbooks easily and quickly. It virtually eliminates the cost of printing and distribution of such handbooks.

> **NOTE**
>
> Using an intranet for document sharing with a browser is more cost-effective than a specialized solution such as using Lotus Notes. Using a browser provides an easy-to-use, universal interface. It reduces the learning curve for the users. Using Lotus Notes requires investment of time and money in learning how to use and deploy it effectively.

Microsoft Office Suite

The Microsoft Office Suite is presently the most popular application in the marketplace. It offers a complete solution for your day-to-day business needs. New features such as the binder help you integrate your Word, Excel, and PowerPoint documents seamlessly into one document. On the other hand, the browser is presently the most popular user inteface in the marketplace. Its hyperlink capabilities, combined with the ease of use and presentation, makes it a great interface for navigating the Internet and intranet. It also make a great interface for browsing your desktop. In fact, there are indications that Microsoft is planning to integrate the browser interface into the next release of its Windows operating system and do away with the Windows Explorer and File Manager style interface. It remains to be seen if and when such technology becomes available. If your company has standardized on Microsoft Office Suite applications but has some Lotus or WordPerfect documents, you can still view them using your Office Suite applications. This is discussed in detail later in this chapter.

> **NOTE**
>
> Following are a few guidelines to follow when setting up your intranet for viewing Microsoft Office Suite documents using your favorite browser.

Controlling MS Office Documents in Web Pages

CHAPTER 16

365

16

MS OFFICE
DOCUMENTS IN
WEB PAGES

- Collect all the old and new documents and accumulate them in a single location. This includes Microsoft Office and non-Microsoft Office documents and documents created using older versions of Word, Excel, and PowerPoint. This would be a good point to discard all documents you think you do not need any more.

- If your company has standardized on the Microsoft Office Suite, consider upgrading the documents that were created using older versions of Word, Excel, and PowerPoint. This provides a common framework for all the documents.

- Consider converting any documents that were created using non-Microsoft Office Suite applications. For example you can convert Lotus AmiPro documents into Microsoft Word format. Although this type of conversion is not necessary, a standard format improves maintenance and ease of use.

- If your company has not standardized on a single package but uses several different suites in different departments, consider including all format specifications.

- Organize your documents by functionality or department, depending on how your organization works.

When you open a Word or Excel document from your browser, a local copy is opened. The master copy resides on the server. Therefore, any changes made are reflected only in the local copy and not in the master copy. Using your browser to read Office documents promotes collaborative work. Documents can be shared between group members freely and easily. For example, if you are working on a sales spreadsheet and the sales data should be made available to everyone else in your group, you can upload its copy onto the server. The uploaded document becomes available to everyone else in the group who can access it directly from their Web browser.

NOTE

Because the document opened by the browser is a local copy, this setup does not support collaborative work in the true sense. It is still a very cost-effective solution, compared to the price points of some specialized groupware applications such as Lotus Notes.

NOTE

If the browser displays an error message indicating it cannot load the Microsoft Word document, try this:

- Check available system resources
- Close any other Windows applications that may be open

Applications such as Word for Windows are very resource-hungry.

NOTE

Make sure you have set the right access for the network directories that contain the Office documents. If you want to provide read-only access to these documents, make the directory read-only.

NOTE

Microsoft's Internet Assistants for Word, Excel, and PowerPoint help you convert word processing, spreadsheet, and presentation documents into HTML and vice versa. These Internet assistants can be downloaded from Microsoft's Web site.

Relevant Web Sites

Table 16.2 lists a few relevant Web sites. There are plenty of resources and examples available on the Net.

Table 16.2. Relevant Web sites.

Site Name	Site URL
Microsoft	`http://www.microsoft.com/activex`
ZD Net	`http://www.zdnet.com/activexfiles/`
ActiveX Developer Support	`http://activex.adsp.or.jp/`
CMP Media Inc.	`http://www.activextra.com/`

Review

Microsoft Office is the most popular Office Suite product in the market today. Office products including Word, Excel, and PowerPoint have been in use since before the introduction of the browser. By extending your browser to access Word, Excel, and PowerPoint documents, you can leverage your investment in Office products and provide an easy-to-use, one-stop interface to your users. This boosts productivity tremendously.

Keep in mind the following guidelines when configuring your intranet for viewing Microsoft Office Suite documents using your favorite browser:

■ Collect all old and new documents and accumulate them in a single location. Discard any documents you think you do not need any more.

■ If your company has standardized on the Microsoft Office Suite, upgrade the documents that were created using older versions of Word, Excel, and PowerPoint.

■ Convert any documents that were created using non-Microsoft Office Suite applications.

If you want to provide read-only access to your documents, consider using the free application viewers from Microsoft. They can be downloaded from Microsoft's Web site: `http://www.microsoft.com`.

This chapter discussed how you can use ActiveX Control Pad to integrate ActiveX controls into your Web pages. Microsoft Internet Explorer 3.0 includes full support for VBScript and ActiveX controls.

From here, refer to the following chapters for further reading:

■ Chapter 15, "Creating Active Documents for Corporate Intranets," to learn how to create active documents on your corporate intranets.

■ Chapter 21, "Safety and Security," to learn how to maintain security and safety when deploying VBScript-based Web applications.

■ Chapters 23–27 include examples of VBScript-based applications. Review the code to understand how VBScript meshes with HTML.

Animation

by Paul Lagasse

IN THIS CHAPTER

Now that you understand how to allocate variables and explicitly call functions in VBScript, you might be wondering how to use this new tool to effectively enhance the Web site you have or master the Web site you have in mind. The answer to that question is simple: animation. Nothing captures the attention of the transient Net surfer faster than a Web site with a lot of visual and audio data that doesn't slow down the connection.

One of the biggest drawbacks of the Internet, in its current incarnation, is the lack of effective multimedia data that can be transferred from a Web site to a local host. Without 30 frames per second animation and audio that doesn't stutter over a 28.8 modem connection, the information superhighway will never supersede the television as the world's favorite pastime and source of information. However, Internet development is happening rapidly and will soon overcome these obvious deficiencies. Tools like VBScript will be used to control the flow of this information to and from your Web site.

VBScript does not have internal structures or data types that allow it to handle digital video and audio playback, but coupled with Microsoft's ActiveX controls, many impressive types of animation can be achieved. Not only can you display an array of visual and audio data, from MPEGs to Stock Quotes, but many applications can have a level of interactivity far beyond simple frame-by-frame playback, by using Visual Basic logic. The following examples will give you some guidelines for setting up this interactivity.

ActiveX Controls Capable of Animation

We will look at a list of the current controls that Microsoft freely distributes from their Web site (http://www.microsoft.com/activex/gallery) at the time of this writing. Using these controls together and "gluing" them with VBScript, we can accomplish some very promising animation. As well, many updated controls are being created daily by Microsoft and third-party developers, which will make this list seem small and limited in the near future. The current animation-capable controls include

- Image. This control allows the display of a variety of bitmapped image formats. In conjunction with a timer, the control can be used to create a frame-based animation or collage of images that can be manipulated by a user at runtime.

- Gradient. This control displays a rectangle with a smooth gradient fill from a start color to an end color. With a timer, this control too can be used to generate a color-cycling animation.

- Marquee. The Internet Explorer Marquee control can auto-scroll (vertically or horizontally) an HTML page in a region defined by the user. The speed of the scrolling and direction are user definable and adjustable at runtime using VBScript.

- Timer. The Timer is invisible at runtime and generates a specific timer event at a predefined interval. The timer event can be used to trigger activity in other controls and allows for a wide range of animation possibilities.

17

- Stock Ticker. This control is used to display data from a URL at a given interval. This data can change frequently and will provide the user with updated information on a regular basis. The data can be in a text or XRT format on a Web site.

- Label. This control displays text on an HTML page as well as responding to several types of mouse interactivity. It can be used to display the text at an angle that can be modified at runtime.

- Active Movie. The Active Movie format has recently hit the scene with Internet Explorer 3.0 and allows any tools that support ActiveX to display a wide variety of digital audio and visual data. Not only does it support AVI and MPEG playback but WAV and AU audio playback as well, with little to no programming overhead.

Each one of these controls can display information statically, but in conjunction with other controls it is possible to create some fairly sophisticated animation quickly and easily. The example we will first discuss uses the Timer and Image controls to display frames of a 3-D animation rendered as Windows bitmaps. The frames of this animation can be in any bitmap format the Image control supports, which gives you the ability to display images from several sources.

Frame Animation with Image and Timer Controls

The examples in this chapter assume you are familiar with Microsoft's ActiveX Control Pad, which is an invaluable tool for laying out an HTML page that supports ActiveX controls and VBScript.

The Image control allows you to display bitmapped images in an HTML page; however, when you combine the control with a timer, it allows you to display your bitmaps as frames in an animation. The playback of these frames is completely customizable, including the order of the frames, the rate of play, and the types of images displayed.

First, the example displays an HTML layout (shown in Listing 17.1) called TimerAni that contains an Image control called Image1 and a Timer object named Timer1. These control names are the defaults generated by the ActiveX Control Pad and have not been modified to avoid any confusion.

Listing 17.1. HTML code segment to launch image control animation.

```
 :  <HTML>
 :  <HEAD>
 :  <TITLE>Image Control / Timer Sample</TITLE>
 :  </HEAD>
 :  <BODY>
 :  <OBJECT CLASSID="CLSID:812AE312-8B8E-11CF-93C8-00AA00C08FDF"
 :  ID="TimerAni_alx" STYLE="LEFT:0;TOP:0">
 :  <PARAM NAME="ALXPATH" REF VALUE="TimerAni.alx">
 :   </OBJECT>
10:  </BODY>
11:  </HTML>
```

When the layout is displayed, the Visual Basic Script will allocate two global variables to handle the processing. (See Listing 17.2.) The first, called Count, records the current frame index referenced in the second variable array, called Images(). Images() stores the names of the bitmapped graphics that contain the bulk of the animation. They are stored in consecutive order so that the frames of the animation appear to happen smoothly, but the order of the images could just as easily have been switched around, in order to make a collage of images instead of a smooth animation. When you become familiar with this example, you can try rearranging the order.

Listing 17.2. ActiveX Layout control code for the Image/Timer animation.

```
 1: <SCRIPT LANGUAGE="VBScript">
 2: <!--
 3: 'Global Variables
 4: dim Count      'Keep track of current image index
 5: dim Images(16)      'Store the names of the bitmaps for the animation
 6: Images(1) = "VBSA0000.BMP"
 7: Images(2) = "VBSA0001.BMP"
 8: Images(3) = "VBSA0002.BMP"
 9: Images(4) = "VBSA0003.BMP"
10: Images(5) = "VBSA0004.BMP"
11: Images(6) = "VBSA0005.BMP"
12: Images(7) = "VBSA0006.BMP"
13: Images(8) = "VBSA0007.BMP"
14: Images(9) = "VBSA0008.BMP"
15: Images(10) = "VBSA0009.BMP"
16: Images(11) = "VBSA0010.BMP"
17: Images(12) = "VBSA0011.BMP"
18: Images(13) = "VBSA0012.BMP"
19: Images(14) = "VBSA0013.BMP"
20: Images(15) = "VBSA0014.BMP"
21: Images(16) = "VBSA0015.BMP"
22: -->
23: </SCRIPT>
24: <SCRIPT LANGUAGE="VBScript">
25: <!--
26: Sub Timer1_Timer()
27: 'When Timer1 generates the timer event, we want to change the graphic that is
    currently being'displayed. To do this we set the picture path variable of
    Image1 by referencing the array Images()
28: 'at the current index stored in Count
29: If Count = 16 Then Count = 0      'Make sure the Animation loops when it hits the
    last frame
30: Count = Count + 1                              'Increment the current frame count
31: Image1.PicturePath="C:\VBSCRIPT\IMAGES\" & Images(Count) 'concatenate the
current Array
32:      'index the full path to the
33:      'images.
34: end sub
35: -->
36: </SCRIPT>
37: <DIV ID="Layout1" STYLE="LAYOUT:FIXED;WIDTH:597pt;HEIGHT:362pt;">
38:      <OBJECT ID="Image1"
39:        CLASSID="CLSID:D4A97620-8E8F-11CF-93CD-00AA00C08FDF"
          STYLE="TOP:17pt;LEFT:33pt;WIDTH:120pt;HEIGHT:75pt;ZINDEX:0;">
```

```
40:            <PARAM NAME="PicturePath" VALUE="C:\VBSCRIPT\IMAGES\VBSA0000.BMP">
41:            <PARAM NAME="BorderStyle" VALUE="0">
42:            <PARAM NAME="SizeMode" VALUE="1">
43:            <PARAM NAME="SpecialEffect" VALUE="2">
44:            <PARAM NAME="Size" VALUE="4233;2646">
45:        </OBJECT>
46:        <OBJECT ID="Timer1"
47:         CLASSID="CLSID:59CCB4A0-727D-11CF-AC36-00AA00A47DD2"
           STYLE="TOP:17pt;LEFT:165pt;WIDTH:29pt;HEIGHT:29pt;ZINDEX:1;">
48:            <PARAM NAME="_ExtentX" VALUE="1005">
49:            <PARAM NAME="_ExtentY" VALUE="1005">
50:            <PARAM NAME="Interval" VALUE="30">
51:        </OBJECT>
52:        <OBJECT ID="Label1"
53:         CLASSID="CLSID:978C9E23-D4B0-11CE-BF2D-00AA003F40D0"
           STYLE="TOP:99pt;LEFT:25pt;WIDTH:363pt;HEIGHT:18pt;ZINDEX:2;">
54:            <PARAM NAME="Caption" VALUE="Simple Animation Sample using Image
               Control and Timer">
55:            <PARAM NAME="Size" VALUE="12806;635">
56:            <PARAM NAME="FontEffects" VALUE="1073741825">
57:            <PARAM NAME="FontHeight" VALUE="240">
58:            <PARAM NAME="FontCharSet" VALUE="0">
59:            <PARAM NAME="FontPitchAndFamily" VALUE="2">
60:            <PARAM NAME="FontWeight" VALUE="700">
61:        </OBJECT>
62: </DIV>
```

FIGURE 17.1.

Embossed images displayed as animation frames.

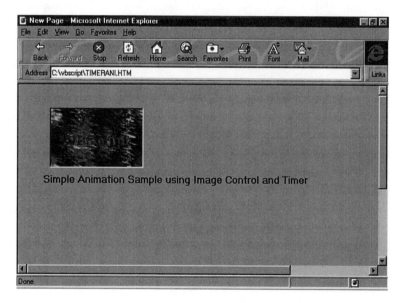

You will notice that the main bulk of the processing is handled in the `Timer1_Timer()` subroutine. This `_Timer` event occurs every time the interval defined in the timer object is reached. The process is very straightforward; every time the timer generates an event, we increment our current frame index by 1. As long as the index does not go beyond the maximum number of frames the array contains, the `Picture` path is updated to point to a new image. This new image is named by joining the full path to the image (which could just as easily be a URL like `http://www.samples.com/images` instead of a local hard disk) and the current array element using the & operator. In this animation, the limit is set at 16 so the `IF` structure will reset the frame index to 0 whenever the animation hits the sixteenth frame.

Can you see how the animation can be very easily controlled using VBScript? By changing the order of the elements of the array, you can adjust the order of play. By changing the interval defined in the `Timer1` object, you can increase or decrease the speed of playback and each frame of the animation can be a different image format—even a different size image. Best of all, the animation will continue to play properly, even when the HTML page has finished loading, and will remain active and customizable at runtime. It is possible to display an animated GIF in the same fashion, but there is no way to have the GIF change its order at the touch of a button. To show you this kind of interactivity coupled with animation, the next example displays rotating text, using Microsoft's Internet Explorer Label control and a timer. This time, however, the user will be able to change the course of the rotation by clicking Button controls available on the page.

> **NOTE**
>
> It is always good to keep in mind the size of the files you are downloading and the performance you can expect to achieve using them. Coming off a hard disk or CD-ROM, this example will work fine—but over a slow Internet connection, waiting for the images to download could take quite some time. To see the difference locally, rename the images to `VBSAC000*.BMP` and try the example again. The first set of images used are rendered at 16 million colors and are rather large. The second set are rendered at 256 colors and can save a large amount of load time. If you wanted to get even better performance from an Internet connection, you could try converting the images to a compressed format, like JPG. Having a much smaller file size than an uncompressed BMP can save time and increase performance.

Rotating Text with the Label Control

This example relies on some of the basic functionality described in the first example but expands upon the interactivity that VBScript provides. The example manipulates the Internet Explorer Label control to create a rotating text animation that cycles clockwise and counterclockwise. Input is retrieved from the user in the form of two Button controls. When the user clicks either button, the direction of the animation will be adjusted accordingly. This example was set up using the ActiveX Control Pad. Listing 17.3 details the HTML header that loads the HTML Layout, and Listing 17.4 shows the contents of the layout (ALX) file.

Listing 17.3. Label control animation.

```
 1: <HTML>
 2: <HEAD>
 3: <TITLE>Label / Timer Sample</TITLE>
 4: </HEAD>
 5: <BODY>
 6: <OBJECT CLASSID="CLSID:812AE312-8B8E-11CF-93C8-00AA00C08FDF"
 7: ID="TimrLabl_alx" STYLE="LEFT:0;TOP:0">
 8: <PARAM NAME="ALXPATH" REF VALUE="file:C:\VBSCRIPT\TimrLabl.alx">
 9:   </OBJECT>
10: </BODY>
11: </HTML>
```

Once the page is loaded, the text will begin cycling clockwise. (See Figure 17.2.) The spinning effect is caused by incrementing the value stored in the Degree variable by 2 each time the _timer event is triggered. The Angle property of the ieLabel causes the caption of the label to be displayed at an elevated or declinated position, based on the value of the angle stored in the Degree variable. A value of 180 will cause the text to be displayed upside down. By running through this loop, we are able to achieve the effect of the text spinning at its center.

Listing 17.4. ActiveX Layout code for Label and Timer animation.

```
 1: <SCRIPT LANGUAGE="VBScript">
 2: <!--
 3: dim Direction
 4: dim Degree
 5: Direction = "ClockWise"
 6: -->
 7: </SCRIPT>
 8: <SCRIPT LANGUAGE="VBScript">
 9: <!--
10: Sub IeTimer1_Timer()
11: Select Case Direction
12:
13:     Case "ClockWise" 'Decrement the degree counter by two
14:         Degree = Degree - 2
15:         If Degree = 361 Then Degree = 0
16:     Case "Counter-ClockWise" 'Increment the degree counter by two
17:         Degree = Degree + 2
18:         If Degree = 0 then Degree = 360
19: End Select
20: ieLabel1.Angle = Degree
21: end sub
22: -->
23: </SCRIPT>
24: <SCRIPT LANGUAGE="VBScript">
25: <!--
26: Sub CommandButton2_Click()
27: Direction = "Counter-ClockWise"
28: end sub
29: -->
```

continues

Listing 17.4. continued

```
30: </SCRIPT>
31: <SCRIPT LANGUAGE="VBScript">
32: <!--
33: Sub CommandButton1_Click()
34: Direction = "ClockWise"
35: end sub
36: -->
37:
38: </SCRIPT>
39: <DIV ID="Layout1" STYLE="LAYOUT:FIXED;WIDTH:477pt;HEIGHT:272pt;">
40:     <OBJECT ID="IeTimer1"
41:      CLASSID="CLSID:59CCB4A0-727D-11CF-AC36-00AA00A47DD2"
         STYLE="TOP:33pt;LEFT:165pt;WIDTH:25pt;HEIGHT:29pt;ZINDEX:0;">
42:         <PARAM NAME="_ExtentX" VALUE="873">
43:         <PARAM NAME="_ExtentY" VALUE="1032">
44:         <PARAM NAME="Interval" VALUE="2">
45:     </OBJECT>
46:     <OBJECT ID="IeLabel1"
47:      CLASSID="CLSID:99B42120-6EC7-11CF-A6C7-00AA00A47DD2"
         STYLE="TOP:8pt;LEFT:17pt;WIDTH:140pt;HEIGHT:99pt;ZINDEX:1;">
48:         <PARAM NAME="_ExtentX" VALUE="4948">
49:         <PARAM NAME="_ExtentY" VALUE="3493">
50:         <PARAM NAME="Caption" VALUE="Rotating Text Example">
51:         <PARAM NAME="Angle" VALUE="0">
52:         <PARAM NAME="Alignment" VALUE="4">
53:         <PARAM NAME="Mode" VALUE="1">
54:         <PARAM NAME="FillStyle" VALUE="0">
55:         <PARAM NAME="FillStyle" VALUE="0">
56:         <PARAM NAME="ForeColor" VALUE="#000000">
57:         <PARAM NAME="BackColor" VALUE="#000000">
58:         <PARAM NAME="FontName" VALUE="Arial">
59:         <PARAM NAME="FontSize" VALUE="12">
60:         <PARAM NAME="FontItalic" VALUE="0">
61:         <PARAM NAME="FontBold" VALUE="1">
62:         <PARAM NAME="FontUnderline" VALUE="0">
63:         <PARAM NAME="FontStrikeout" VALUE="0">
64:         <PARAM NAME="TopPoints" VALUE="0">
65:         <PARAM NAME="BotPoints" VALUE="0">
66:     </OBJECT>
67:     <OBJECT ID="CommandButton1"
68:      CLASSID="CLSID:D7053240-CE69-11CD-A777-00DD01143C57"
         STYLE="TOP:116pt;LEFT:8pt;WIDTH:83pt;HEIGHT:25pt;TABINDEX:0;ZINDEX:2;">
69:         <PARAM NAME="Caption" VALUE="ClockWise">
70:         <PARAM NAME="Size" VALUE="2911;873">
71:         <PARAM NAME="FontCharSet" VALUE="0">
72:         <PARAM NAME="FontPitchAndFamily" VALUE="2">
73:         <PARAM NAME="ParagraphAlign" VALUE="3">
74:         <PARAM NAME="FontWeight" VALUE="0">
75:     </OBJECT>.
76:     <OBJECT ID="CommandButton2"
77:      CLASSID="CLSID:D7053240-CE69-11CD-A777-00DD01143C57"
         STYLE="TOP:116pt;LEFT:99pt;WIDTH:83pt;HEIGHT:25pt;TABINDEX:1;ZINDEX:3;">
78:         <PARAM NAME="Caption" VALUE="Counter-ClockWise">
79:         <PARAM NAME="Size" VALUE="2910;873">
80:         <PARAM NAME="FontCharSet" VALUE="0">
```

```
81:            <PARAM NAME="FontPitchAndFamily" VALUE="2">
82:            <PARAM NAME="ParagraphAlign" VALUE="3">
83:            <PARAM NAME="FontWeight" VALUE="0">
84:      </OBJECT>
85: </DIV>.
```

FIGURE 17.2.

*Rotating label modified
with user input through
Button controls.*

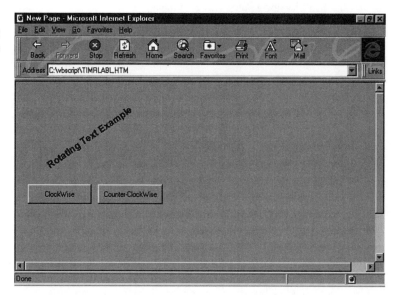

Looking at the sample carefully, you will notice that it is not very complicated. Each time the
_timer event is triggered, the angle of the ieLabel is updated. Whether the value of the angle
is incremented or decremented is determined by the state of the Direction variable. The
Direction variable changes only when the user clicks either of the button controls. When the
_click event occurs, the global variable Direction is changed and the _timer event updates the
value of Degree using the Select… Case method to handle the program flow.

Using Active Movie for Digital Audio and Video

Okay, you are fairly impressed that you can control ActiveX controls so effortlessly using
VBScript, but now you want to know how you can add real multimedia content to a Web site.
You have seen many Web sites displaying impressive video files and kicking off a comical sound
file whenever a button is pressed. How can you do this with VBScript? The answer is Microsoft's
Active Movie control. It is a fully featured multimedia control that handles a multitude of video
and audio file formats, including .mov, .mpg, .avi, .wav, .au, and .aiff. These file types are
some of the most commonly seen on the Internet, which makes Active Movie a superb addition to Internet Explorer and VBScript. The following example will display a Video for

Windows file in the Internet Explorer Window. This example (see Listings 17.5 and 17.6, as well as Figure 17.3) uses the default popup controls of the Active Movie driver to display the video that will allow the user a high level of interactivity with little programming.

Listing 17.5. HTML for Active Movie control example.

```
 1: <HTML>
 2: <HEAD>
 3: <TITLE>Active Movie Demonstration</TITLE>
 4: </HEAD>
 5: <BODY>
 6: <OBJECT CLASSID="CLSID:812AE312-8B8E-11CF-93C8-00AA00C08FDF"
 7: ID="AMovie_alx" STYLE="LEFT:0;TOP:0">
 8: <PARAM NAME="ALXPATH" REF VALUE="file:C:\VBScript\AMovie.alx">
 9:  </OBJECT>
10: </BODY>
11: </HTML>
```

It's important to remember that all of the content files used to run the animation are loaded into the cache directory of your browser. That is why some sites take an exceptionally long time to load the first time you connect to them. All of the video and audio files are downloaded to the local machine and run from there when they are addressed. Caching information in this way removes much overhead that would be generated by extended communication with a server. This is good and bad for multimedia apps. It is great for your application once the files have downloaded, but the download times can be extraordinarily long when a lot of information is involved. The second time you connect to a cached site, your browser will look locally for content files and will display these files as quickly as the hardware on your machine will allow.

"Streaming" technology will allow an application to retrieve information from a server in small parts and play them back as they are loaded, but this requires a reliable connection to the Internet and can generate a lot of traffic. Relying on the local PC to run the content is called *client-side networking*. Once the data is downloaded, the local machine is responsible for handling the playback of data. Active Movie is a good example of a client-side control that relies on the local hardware and operating system to process multimedia data. An AVI downloaded into the Internet Explorer and run on one machine might perform differently on another.

Listing 17.6. ActiveX layout code for ActiveMovie playback.

```
 1: <DIV ID="Layout1" STYLE="LAYOUT:FIXED;WIDTH:597pt;HEIGHT:362pt;">
 2:     <OBJECT ID="ActiveMovie1"
 3:       CLASSID="CLSID:05589FA1-C356-11CE-BF01-00AA0055595A"
          STYLE="TOP:8pt;LEFT:8pt;WIDTH:200pt;HEIGHT:151pt;TABINDEX:0;ZINDEX:0;">
 4:         <PARAM NAME="_ExtentX" VALUE="7038">
 5:         <PARAM NAME="_ExtentY" VALUE="5318">
 6:         <PARAM NAME="MovieWindowWidth" VALUE="160">
 7:         <PARAM NAME="MovieWindowHeight" VALUE="124">
```

```
 8:            <PARAM NAME="Appearance" VALUE="0">
 9:            <PARAM NAME="BorderStyle" VALUE="0">
10:            <PARAM NAME="FileName" VALUE="C:\VBSCRIPT\IMAGES\VBSAMP.AVI">
11:        </OBJECT>
12:        <OBJECT ID="Label1"
13:         CLASSID="CLSID:978C9E23-D4B0-11CE-BF2D-00AA003F40D0"
            STYLE="TOP:165pt;LEFT:8pt;WIDTH:470pt;HEIGHT:25pt;ZINDEX:1;">
14:            <PARAM NAME="Caption" VALUE="Active Movie allows playback of a
                multitude of file formats">
15:            <PARAM NAME="Size" VALUE="16589;873">
16:            <PARAM NAME="FontHeight" VALUE="360">
17:            <PARAM NAME="FontCharSet" VALUE="0">
18:            <PARAM NAME="FontPitchAndFamily" VALUE="2">
19:            <PARAM NAME="FontWeight" VALUE="0">
20:        </OBJECT>
21: </DIV>
```

FIGURE 17.3.

Default Active Movie control displaying AVI.

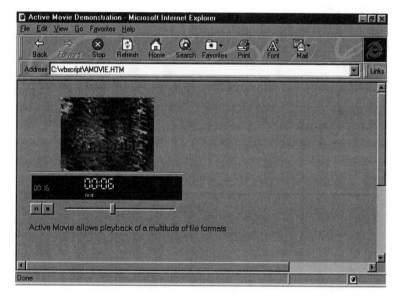

You might notice that the Active Movie control provides quite a bit of extra functionality that doesn't need to be programmed in at all. Not only does the driver support many multimedia file formats, but it has built-in controls that can report information about the currently displayed files and control functionality, such as Pause and Resume. Using buttons or similar controls on a page makes it simple to create an interactive Audio or Video player (by addressing the properties of the Active Movie object). Changing the filename of the Active Movie object will allow you to download and display another video or audio file at the touch of a button, and MovieWindowSize will allow you to control how much of the screen the video takes up. It is simple to embed this type of functionality into your HTML layout using VBScript.

The Marquee Control for Scrolling Pages

The final example included in the animated ActiveX control discussion is the Internet Explorer Marquee control. It is a very simple tool with a lot of potential and allows a VBScript developer to display scrolling HTML text within an HTML page without frames. This is a very nice feature. Developers who are familiar with HTML layout can take advantage of this control to effortlessly display scrolling HTML data on one side of a page while having static HTML text remain visible and scrollable on the same page. That alone is helpful if you want to display an updated list of information for your users to see; but the example adds another level of interactivity by allowing the user to determine which way the marquee scrolls by clicking on one of four directional buttons. Listing 17.7 and Figure 17.4 show an example of how you can put the marquee to work in your page.

> **NOTE**
>
> This example was written without the ActiveX Control Pad, so you will notice some subtle differences. The object names are not simply control1, control2, or control3. Each button corresponds to its functionality, and the events in the script match the controls of the same name. This makes it easier to follow the flow of the example. On a more complex script, however, it a good idea to invest in some standards. A better idea for a more complex project would be to name each button control with the BTN_ prefix. For example, the Up button would be called BTN_UP or something similar that makes sense to you. If you looked through the code of a larger application, you would see why this makes sense, because a specific object type is usually the most readily available form of information. When debugging a script, you might know what type of object you are looking for but not necessarily which one.

Listing 17.7. HTML code for a directional Marquee control.

```
 1: <HTML>
 2:  <OBJECT
 3:          align=CENTER
 4:          classid="clsid:1a4da620-6217-11cf-be62-0080c72edd2d"
 5:          width=640 height=200 BORDER=1 HSPACE=5
 6:          id="Marquee"
 7:  >
 8:  <PARAM NAME="ScrollStyleX" VALUE="Circular">
 9:  <PARAM NAME="ScrollStyleY" VALUE="Circular">
10:  <PARAM NAME="szURL" VALUE="c:\vbscript\marqdoc.htm">
11:  <PARAM NAME="ScrollDelay" VALUE=1000>
12:  <PARAM NAME="LoopsX" VALUE=-1>
13:  <PARAM NAME="LoopsY" VALUE=-1>
14:  <PARAM NAME="ScrollPixelsX" VALUE=0>
15:  <PARAM NAME="ScrollPixelsY" VALUE=0>
16:  <PARAM NAME="DrawImmediately" VALUE=1>
```

```
17:     <PARAM NAME="Whitespace" VALUE=0>
18:     <PARAM NAME="PageFlippingOn" VALUE=1>
19:     <PARAM NAME="Zoom" VALUE=100>
20:     <PARAM NAME="WidthOfPage" VALUE=640>
21:   </OBJECT>
22: <HR>
23:     <OBJECT ID="UP"
24:       CLASSID="CLSID:D7053240-CE69-11CD-A777-00DD01143C57"
           STYLE="TOP:149pt;LEFT:83pt;WIDTH:41pt;HEIGHT:25pt;TABINDEX:0;ZINDEX:0;">
25:         <PARAM NAME="Caption" VALUE="Up">
26:         <PARAM NAME="Size" VALUE="1455;873">
27:         <PARAM NAME="FontCharSet" VALUE="0">
28:         <PARAM NAME="FontPitchAndFamily" VALUE="2">
29:         <PARAM NAME="ParagraphAlign" VALUE="3">
30:         <PARAM NAME="FontWeight" VALUE="0">
31:     </OBJECT>
32:     <OBJECT ID="DOWN"
33:       CLASSID="CLSID:D7053240-CE69-11CD-A777-00DD01143C57"
           STYLE="TOP:182pt;LEFT:50pt;WIDTH:41pt;HEIGHT:25pt;TABINDEX:1;ZINDEX:1;">
34:         <PARAM NAME="Caption" VALUE="Down">
35:         <PARAM NAME="Size" VALUE="1455;873">
36:         <PARAM NAME="FontCharSet" VALUE="0">
37:         <PARAM NAME="FontPitchAndFamily" VALUE="2">
38:         <PARAM NAME="ParagraphAlign" VALUE="3">
39:         <PARAM NAME="FontWeight" VALUE="0">
40:     </OBJECT>
41:     <OBJECT ID="LEFT"
42:       CLASSID="CLSID:D7053240-CE69-11CD-A777-00DD01143C57"
           STYLE="TOP:182pt;LEFT:116pt;WIDTH:41pt;HEIGHT:25pt;TABINDEX:2;ZINDEX:2;">
43:         <PARAM NAME="Caption" VALUE="Left">
44:         <PARAM NAME="Size" VALUE="1455;873">
45:         <PARAM NAME="FontCharSet" VALUE="0">
46:         <PARAM NAME="FontPitchAndFamily" VALUE="2">
47:         <PARAM NAME="ParagraphAlign" VALUE="3">
48:         <PARAM NAME="FontWeight" VALUE="0">
49:     </OBJECT>
50:     <OBJECT ID="RIGHT"
51:       CLASSID="CLSID:D7053240-CE69-11CD-A777-00DD01143C57"
           STYLE="TOP:215pt;LEFT:83pt;WIDTH:41pt;HEIGHT:25pt;TABINDEX:3;ZINDEX:3;">
52:         <PARAM NAME="Caption" VALUE="Right">
53:         <PARAM NAME="Size" VALUE="1455;873">
54:         <PARAM NAME="FontCharSet" VALUE="0">
55:         <PARAM NAME="FontPitchAndFamily" VALUE="2">
56:         <PARAM NAME="ParagraphAlign" VALUE="3">
57:         <PARAM NAME="FontWeight" VALUE="0">
58:     </OBJECT>
59: <SCRIPT LANGUAGE="VBScript">
60: <!--
61: -->
62: </SCRIPT>
63: <SCRIPT LANGUAGE="VBScript">
64: <!--
65: Sub UP_Click()
66: Marquee.ScrollPixelsX = "0"
67: Marquee.ScrollPixelsY = "-50"
68: end sub
69: -->
```

17

ANIMATION

continues

Listing 17.7. continued

```
70: </SCRIPT>
71: <SCRIPT LANGUAGE="VBScript">
72: <!--
73: Sub DOWN_Click()
74: Marquee.ScrollPixelsX = "0"
75: Marquee.ScrollPixelsY = "50"
76: end sub
77: -->
78: </SCRIPT>
79: <SCRIPT LANGUAGE="VBScript">
80: <!--
81: Sub LEFT_Click()
82: Marquee.ScrollPixelsX = "-50"
83: Marquee.ScrollPixelsY = "0"
84: end sub
85: -->
86: </SCRIPT>
87: <SCRIPT LANGUAGE="VBScript">
88: <!--
89: Sub RIGHT_Click()
90: Marquee.ScrollPixelsX = "50"
91: Marquee.ScrollPixelsY = "0"
92: end sub
93: -->
94: </SCRIPT>
95: </HTML>
```

FIGURE 17.4.

*Marquee example
shows a scrolling
HTML document.*

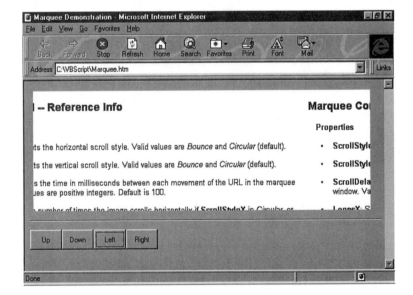

Once again, by simply changing the properties of the ActiveX control, I can change the functionality that is seen in the animation. The important things to note are the fact that `ScrollPixelsX` and `ScrollPixelsY` properties control the number of pixels the marquee will display at each interval. The interval is set at 1000 milliseconds when the object is defined, and the name of the URL that holds the HTML file to display is also set. Both of these properties could be changed at runtime with buttons or scrollbars to affect the rate at which the animation runs and which file is displaying.

Do you see a pattern in the examples? Almost all of the functionality built into the ActiveX controls is handled for you. VBScript can affect the properties and produce the types of animations that make a Web site interesting. Creating animations with VBScript is not really a matter of calling a particular series of functions but of creatively using the objects that are at hand. As mentioned before, more and more objects will become available, and some will handle more traditional style path and frame-based animations—but with simple property manipulation you can achieve some interesting and powerful results. Look at the `StockTicker` and `Gradient` controls. The `Stockticker` can display information much the same way the marquee can, but it uses a completely different type of file format, which is good for business applications. Can you see a way to make color-cycling animated page breaks using the gradient object? By using a `Timer` object and adjusting the `StartColor` and `EndColor` properties, it is a sure bet that you can create an HTML page that has content separators that no one has ever seen before.

Other HTML Tags that Provide Multimedia Playback

Most of this chapter has dealt with providing animation control through ActiveX, which is the most logical way to perform the operation with VBScript because you can use VBScript to address the properties of the objects and make changes at runtime. There are several tags not supported by all browsers that allow playback of multimedia files. You cannot use VBScript to change the properties of these tags, but if you are using VBScript to generate HTML pages on the fly it is a good idea to know about them. Once again, the standards are changing even in the world of HTML tags, and those of you with extensive HTML building knowledge will already know these; but the most current tags are as follows:

- ■ `<img>`   Using the `src` property, you can display a GIF or JPG image. This is nearly the same as using the Image control, but your best bet for animating the image is to use an animated GIF and a browser that supports GIFs.

- ■ Using the `dynsrc` property, you can display video files. The string `<img dynsrc="myvideo.avi" start="mouseover">` will put the first frame of `myvideo.avi` on your page and begin displaying it when you move the mouse over it.

- ■ <body> Supports a background property that allows you to display a graphic as a tiled wallpaper.

- ■ <bgsound> Used much like the <img> tag, this tag lets you specify a source (src) file that is a Wave audio (.WAV) or MIDI (.MID) file so you can play audio on your HTML page. The loop property sets the number of times a MIDI file will play. -1 indicates infinite playback as long as the page is loaded, and a positive integer will set the number of times the file plays.

Using these tags in conjunction with the VBScript Document.Write method, you can generate HTML pages on the fly that actually contain multimedia content. Too bad all the Web pages out there that use CGI scripts don't do that.

VBScript and Java

by Ramesh Chandak

IN THIS CHAPTER

Among all the Internet buzzwords you hear today, I am sure one of them has been Java. What is Java? Why is it so *hot*? What is all the hype about? Why is everyone saying Java has revolutionized the computer and information industry? Where did it come from? If Microsoft didn't make it, who did? All this and much more. Never before has the computing industry undergone such a transformation in so little time. First the Internet, then Netscape Navigator, and now Java! The Internet has completely changed the development and distribution paradigm.

Java is a product from JavaSoft, the software division of Sun Microsystems. With the advent of browser technology and Web authoring tools, creating and navigating the Web pages has become very easy. But these pages have been mostly static, with very little or no interactivity, as if they had no life of their own. They were straight rendering of text and graphics. Static pages generate very little interest for the surfer. There was a need for something that would liven up the experience of surfing the Internet. Then comes along Java!

What is Java? Java is an object-oriented programming language. Java is multithreaded, secure, and portable. It is based on C++, the object-oriented programming language that has been in use for several years now. You can create portable, interactive Web pages using Java. The Java Virtual Machine (JVM) is the core of the Java runtime system. It is a software-based microprocessor and translates Java executables into platform-specific instructions. Java code itself is machine-independent, but JVM is not. JVM is machine-specific. The Java compiler compiles your Java program into compiled bytecodes. A bytecode is a runtime form that executes on the JVM. The extra layer of JVM makes Java programs sluggish compared to native programs written in C or C++. Java applications are portable because of the JVM implementation but are comparatively slower. Just-In-Time (JIT) compilers have addressed this issue. A JIT compiler compiles the bytecodes into native code on-the-fly. It acts as the intermediate layer between the JVM and the target machine. A Java-enabled browser means the JVM is built into it. When the browser comes across the <APPLET> tag, it downloads and executes it using its built-in JVM.

Java and JavaScript are different. Java is an object-oriented programming language. JavaScript is an object-based scripting language. Using Java, you can build standalone applications and applets. Using JavaScript, you cannot build Java applications and applets. JavaScript, originally called LiveScript, is a technology from Netscape. Java is a technology from Sun Microsystems. JavaScript can be considered an extension to HTML. HTML is good for straight rendering of text and graphics, but lacks the capability to make the surfing experience interactive. There are certain things you cannot do using pure HTML—for example, validating user response. Using just HTML, you would have to use CGI scripts or programs at the server end to process and validate user responses and return the results to the browser. Using JavaScript, you can do this directly within HTML without having to send the data back and forth. This reduces network traffic and improves overall response. Only validated data is sent to the server. You can do much more with JavaScript. You can add animation to your Web pages. You can display alert windows and message boxes if the user does not enter the correct data or correct format of the data. Simply put, you can build interactive Web pages using HTML and JavaScript.

According to a recent *ComputerWorld* survey, there are approximately 3 million programmers around the world (and still growing!) who use Visual Basic as their primary programming language. On the other hand, there are approximately 1.1 million programmers who use C/C++ as their primary programming language. Those 3 million programmers would benefit from VBScript, Microsoft's scripting language for the Web. Because VBScript is a subset of Visual Basic, these programmers would find it easy to use. Most of all, VBScript would benefit the non-programmers, whose background is not strictly programming. Non-programmers who are interested in creating their own interactive Web pages would find it easy to program using VBScript since the programming structure is based on the BASIC language. The VBScript learning curve would be a lot shorter compared to JavaScript for a non-programmer.

It is important to understand that both JavaScript and VBScript have their advantages and disadvantages. Java is portable and object-oriented. VBScript is not truly object-oriented. Unless you are an expert in object-oriented and C++ programming, Java involves a steeper learning curve.

Scripting using VBScript and JavaScript is easier than programming in C and C++. Take a look at the HyperCard community for the Macintosh. The introduction of HyperCard and its scripting language, HyperScript, revolutionized the Macintosh world of programming. A whole new generation of applications has been developed by a variety of people—both programmers and non-programmers.

As of this writing, only Microsoft Internet Explorer 3.0 supports VBScript. In contrast, JavaScript is supported by Netscape Navigator 3.0, Microsoft Internet Explorer 3.0, and HotJava 1.0, Sun Microsystem's browser.

This chapter introduces Java and its features, as well as JavaScript and its programming syntax and structure. It also discusses Java applets and Java classes. It further discusses VBScript and its syntax and structure. After reading this chapter, you will have gained a good understanding of Java, JavaScript, and VBScript, and how they compare with each other. This chapter is not a programming reference guide on JavaScript and VBScript. It does not include all the programming structures and conventions available in these scripting languages. Instead, it discusses the main features of each language, including functions, subroutines, arithmetic, and logical and comparison operators, and compares and contrasts them. This chapter also discusses a Web page example written using both JavaScript and VBScript. By comparing both the scripts, you will gain a better insight into these languages.

What Is Java?

Java is an object-oriented programming language. Java includes a runtime interpreter, an Application Programming Interface (API), and a set of development tools. Java is distributed as JDK—the Java Developer's Kit. As of this writing, the latest version of JDK is 1.1. You can download JDK from JavaSoft's Web site: http://java.sun.com. Figure 18.1 shows the JavaSoft home page.

FIGURE 18.1.

Java home page hosted by JavaSoft, the software division of Sun Microsystems. It is one of the most popular Web sites, visited by millions of programmers, developers, and others.

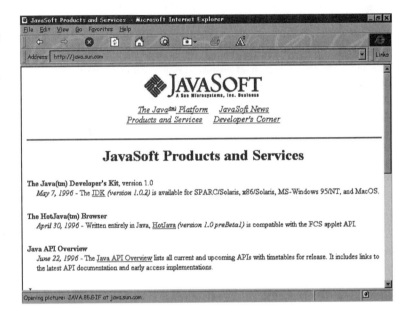

Java is secure. Java is multithreaded. Java is derived from C/C++. If you are an experienced C/C++ programmer, you will find it easy to get started with Java. It includes the Java Application Programming Interface—a library of methods for developing platform-independent, distributed applications that include full networking and windowing support.

> **NOTE**
>
> If you are an experienced C++ programmer, you will appreciate Java and its features, including built-in networking, platform-independent API class library, and robust exception handling. When programming in Java, you no longer have to deal with pointers. Java understands object-oriented structure only. Everything you define and use in Java *must* be an *object.*

Figure 18.2 shows the Java development framework. The Java source code utilizes the Java API and user-defined classes. The source code is compiled into Java runtime bytecode by the Java compiler. The runtime bytecode runs on the Java Virtual Machine (JVM), a software-based microprocessor. The JVM is an interpreter and can reside on any platform, including Windows 3.1, Windows 95, UNIX, Macintosh, and so on, thus making Java applications platform-independent.

FIGURE 18.2.

The Java Developer's Kit (JDK). Java is distributed as the JDK. The JDK includes the runtime interpreter, the Java Virtual Machine (JVM), and the Java API.

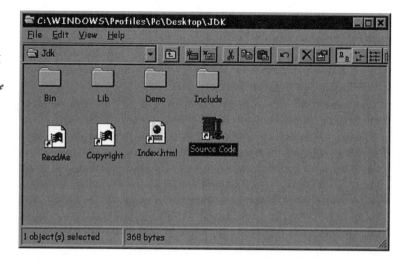

The Java Developer's Kit contains a variety of tools and Java development information. Following is a list of the main components of the JDK:

- The Runtime Interpreter
- The Compiler
- The Applet Viewer
- The Debugger
- The Class File Disassembler
- The Header and Stub File Generator
- The Documentation Generator
- Applet Demos
- API Source Code

The Java API includes class definitions and methods that provide links into the native windowing and networking capabilities of the host operating system. It is the common thread between Java programs and any host operating system. The Java runtime system and API make Java portable. The Java runtime system is not tied to any particular operating system. It has been developed from scratch. The Java API is a universal API for writing applications targeted at all operating systems.

Java is supported by both industry standard browsers—Netscape Navigator and Microsoft Internet Explorer. There are several applications that have been written using Java. HotJava, Sun Microsystem's Web browser, is written completely using Java. You can develop a variety of applications using Java. Using Java you can write multithreaded applications and secure, distributed, multiplatform applications. You can also write object-oriented Web applications.

You can write applets using Java. An applet is not a standalone application; it cannot run on its own. A browser or an applet viewer needs to be used to run an applet. When the browser encounters the <APPLET> tag, it downloads the applet and the JVM embedded within the browser executes it.

Figure 18.3 describes the Java API structure. The Java API consists of two types of packages: packages that are built-in and packages that a Java programmer can define and use.

FIGURE 18.3.

Java API consists of packages. It comes with a predefined set of packages. You can also define your own packages.

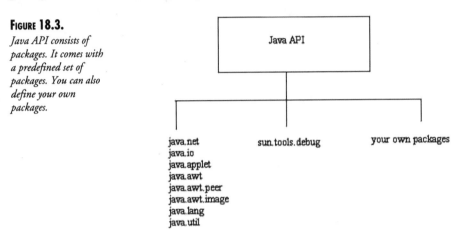

A Java package is a group of related interfaces, classes, and exceptions. The grouping is done simply for ease of understanding and convenience. See Figure 18.4.

FIGURE 18.4.

A Java package includes interfaces, classes, and exceptions.

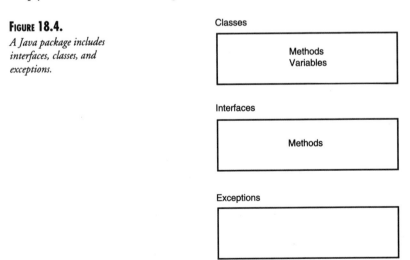

Java is object-oriented. Anything you define and use must be an object. A class is the basic object-oriented component in Java. An interface is a collection of related methods. An exception is an event that alters the normal course of program execution.

Class: A class is the basic object-oriented component in Java. It includes methods and variables. Variables store data. Methods are functions that operate on the classes and variables. For example, the `checkbox` class in the `java.awt` package is used to implement checkbox and radio button GUI controls in Java applications. The `file` class in the `java.io` package is used to provide system-independent access to a file or a directory on the host operating system. The `applet` class in the `java.applet` package is used to implement Java applets.

Interface: An interface is a collection of related methods. For example, the `imageproducer` is a set of functions for classes that produce images. The `imageproducer` methods are used to reconstruct or modify an image being produced.

Exception: An exception is an event that alters the normal course of program execution.

The Java Developer's Kit comes with a number of examples. Figure 18.5 shows a tic-tac-toe example, written as a Java applet and executed using Microsoft Internet Explorer.

FIGURE 18.5.

The tic-tac-toe Java applet. It comes with the JDK. The JDK can be downloaded from Sun's home page: `java.sun.com.`

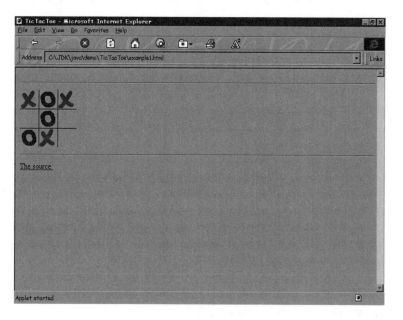

The file `tictactoe.java` on the enclosed CD-ROM includes the source code for the tic-tac-toe Java applet.

Java, Java Applets, and JavaScript

A Java-enabled browser means the Java runtime interpreter and Java Virtual Machine are integrated within the browser. Applets are Java programs that are linked to the Web browser. An applet may be used to enhance a Web document by displaying animation or playing sound. It cannot modify the state of the HTML document being displayed. It is executed by the Java runtime interpreter that is integrated with the browser.

An applet is specified by the `<applet>... </applet>` tags within the HTML code. When the browser encounters the `<applet>` tag, it downloads the applet, runs a number of security tests on it and passes it to the runtime interpreter and Java Virtual Machine that execute it locally. Applets are executed within a well-defined area of the browser. It is similar to running a command-line program. The browser does not execute the applet. The runtime interpreter executes the applet. You can think of the runtime interpreter as a plug-in or helper application to the browser.

Java and JavaScript are not the same. Nor are they competitors to each other. Java is an object-oriented *programming* language. JavaScript is a *scripting* language. You can use Java to write object-oriented, network, distributed, secure, multithreaded Java applications. The source code files have `.java` extensions. Java source code is compiled and stored in `.class` files. See Figure 18.6.

FIGURE 18.6.

The Java source code is stored in `.java` files. The compiled code is stored in `.class` files.

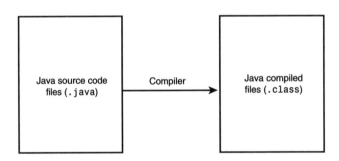

JavaScript is embedded within your HTML code. It is an extension to your HTML code. You can change the appearance and behavior of your Web pages dynamically using JavaScript. You can process mouse events such as mouse click or the mouse moving over a certain part of the Web page and initiate certain actions on such events. For example, you can display different background bitmaps, depending on the day of the week. You can process form data when the user clicks the submit button and alert the user of any invalid data. Java supports static binding. When writing code using Java, you must declare the types of variables before you can use them. JavaScript supports dynamic binding. With JavaScript it is not necessary to declare the type. If you do not declare the type of the variable, JavaScript interprets it at runtime, based on the context in which it is used. For example, if a variable is used to perform addition of numbers, it is interpreted as a number. If a variable is used to perform string concatenation, it is interpreted as a string. Such loose binding makes JavaScript lightweight and portable. Similarly, if you declare functions in JavaScript, it is not necessary to specify the type of the return value of the function. On the other hand, you must declare the type of the return value of the function in Java. Java applets can also be executed using any of the three browsers. Java is available as JDK from JavaSoft's Web site. If you download and install Netscape Navigator, Microsoft Internet Explorer, or HotJava, you have basically everything you need to use JavaScript.

> **NOTE**
>
> You can use Java to develop non-Web-based applications. Since JavaScript and VBScript are extensions to HTML, they are used primarily to create Web applications. However, VBScript can be used as a component in other Windows applications.

Listing 18.1 shows a HelloWorld program written in Java.

Listing 18.1. A HelloWorld program written in Java.

```java
import java.lang.System;
class HelloWorld {
   public static void main (String args[]) {
      System.out.println("Hello World!");
   }
}
```

Compare the preceding Java code to JavaScript and VBScript code for writing the same HelloWorld program. Listing 18.3 shows an example of a HelloWorld program written in JavaScript.

Java Classes

The Java API includes the following packages. A Java package includes interface, classes, and exceptions.

`java.net:`	A library of classes and methods for implementing socket-based client/server networking
`java.io:`	A library of classes and methods for stream-based I/O
`java.applet:`	A library of classes and interfaces for applet development

`java.awt:`	A library of windowing classes and methods called Abstract Windowing Toolkit (AWT)
`java.awt.image:`	A library of classes for managing image data, including color models, cropping, and color filtering
`java.awt.peer:`	A library of interface definitions that map platform-independent AWT classes to their native platform-dependent implementations; it does not include any classes
`java.lang:`	A library of methods and classes for applet, console, and window programming
`java.util:`	A library of Java utilities
`sun.tools.debug:`	A library of debugging tools and utilities

> **NOTE**
>
> To keep abreast of the latest on Java, visit Javasoft's home page regularly.

JavaScript Objects

JavaScript is an object-based scripting language. Even though it is object-based, JavaScript does not support inheritance. You can define your own objects in JavaScript and use them together with JavaScript's built-in objects to write Web pages. As of this writing, there are a total of 17 JavaScript objects. Table 18.1 lists them.

Table 18.1. JavaScript objects.

Object	*Meaning*
`navigator`	Base class for all HTML objects
`window`	Base class for the `document` object
`document`	Contains information about all HTML properties inside the current page
`history`	Contains browser's URL history list
`form`	Contains information about the defined form
`date`	Contains date information, including system date function
`math`	Includes `math` constants and functions
`string`	Contains information about `string` functions
`radio`	Contains information about a form's radio button
`checkbox`	Contains information about a form's checkbox button

Object	Meaning
select	Represents a form's list as an array
button	Contains information about a form's button; it could represent a form's reset, submit, or custom button
text, textarea	Contains information about a form's text box
location	Contains information about the current URL location

JavaScript Language Structure

Listing 18.2 shows an example of HTML code that includes a JavaScript function. The JavaScript code is identified by the <SCRIPT> tag. The code is embedded between the beginning and ending <SCRIPT> tags.

Listing 18.2. Basic structure of a JavaScript function.

```
<SCRIPT LANGUAGE="JavaScript">
<!--

    function <function_name> {
    ...
      }

// -->
</SCRIPT>
```

Listing 18.3 shows a JavaScript-based HelloWorld function.

Listing 18.3. JavaScript HelloWorld function.

```
<SCRIPT LANGUAGE="JavaScript">
<!--

    function HelloWorld() {
      alert("Hello World!");

    }
// -->
</SCRIPT>
```

The LANGUAGE attribute indicates the scripting language that is used. The browser interprets the code accordingly. Microsoft Internet Explorer 3.0 can interpret both JavaScript and VBScript. Netscape Navigator and HotJava can interpret only JavaScript.

> **NOTE**
>
> Although currently only Microsoft Internet Explorer supports VBScript, other browsers are expected to include support for interpreting VBScript code.

JavaScript functions can be placed anywhere inside the HTML code, including the HEAD and BODY sections. It is recommended you place all your functions and procedures in one location, usually toward the end of the BODY section, before the </BODY> tag.

JavaScript Operators

JavaScript operators include arithmetic, comparison, logical, and bit operators. Table 18.2 shows the JavaScript arithmetic operators.

Table 18.2. JavaScript arithmetic operators.

Operator	Meaning
+	Addition
-	Subtraction/negation
*	Multiplication
/	Division
++	Increment
--	Decrement
%	Modulus

Table 18.3 shows the JavaScript comparison operators.

Table 18.3. JavaScript comparison operators.

Operator	Meaning
!=	Non-equality
>	Greater than
>=	Greater than or equal to
<	Less than
<=	Less than or equal to

Table 18.4 shows the JavaScript logical operators.

Table 18.4. JavaScript logical operators.

Operator	Meaning
&&	Logical AND
¦¦	Logical OR
!	Logical NOT

Table 18.5 shows the JavaScript bit operators.

Table 18.5. JavaScript bit operators.

Operator	Meaning
&	Bitwise AND
¦	Bitwise OR
^	Bitwise XOR

A single = is the assignment operator. It is used to store a value into a variable.

JavaScript Flow of Control Statements

Table 18.6 shows the JavaScript flow of control statements.

Table 18.6. JavaScript flow of control statements.

Statement	Meaning
```For ([initial_expression;][condition;][increment_expression]) { statement 1 ... statement N }```	Execute the code within the loop for N times where N is specified in the For loop
```For Each...Next```	Execute the code within the loop for each item in the specified collection

continues

18

VBSCRIPT AND JAVA

Table 18.6. continued

Statement	Meaning
| ```
If (condition) {
   statement 1...
   statement N}
   [else {
   statement 2}]
``` | If...Else statement |
| ```
while (condition) {
  statement 1
   ...
  statement N
  }
``` | Execute the code within the loop as long as the specified condition is true |

VBScript Language Structure

VBScript is a lightweight portable subset of Visual Basic, the language, and Visual Basic for Applications, the scripting language used in Microsoft Excel and Word. It is a scripting language that can be used as part of your HTML code for designing and modifying Web pages. Similar to JavaScript, you can change the appearance and behavior of your Web pages dynamically using VBScript. You can process mouse events such as a mouse click or the mouse moving over a certain part of the Web page and initiate certain actions on such events. For instance, you can display different background bitmaps, depending on the day of the week. You can process form data when the user clicks the Submit button and alert the user of any invalid data. VBScript can also be used as part of other applications that use ActiveX controls, OLE Automation servers, and Java applets. As of this writing, VBScript is available only as part of Microsoft Internet Explorer 3.0.

If you are already familiar with Visual Basic, the programming language, you will be able to quickly and easily grasp VBScript. There are a few important differences, though. VBScript does not support strict data types. It supports only variants. It does not support file I/O. Nor does it include direct access to the underlying operating system.

How does VBScript compare with JavaScript? Well, it is directly comparable to JavaScript. In fact, VBScript is a competitor to JavaScript. Both languages have their advantages and disadvantages. Visual Basic has been around for quite some time. Java is relatively new. According to a recent *ComputerWorld* survey, there are approximately 3 million programmers who use Visual Basic as their primary programming language. The introduction of VBScript is clearly a welcome sign for these programmers. A lot of them would find it easier to use VBScript with their HTML code than to learn a new language, JavaScript. Neither JavaScript nor VBScript can produce standalone applets. However, they can be used to add intelligence and interactivity to HTML documents.

> **NOTE**
>
> If you are an experienced Visual Basic programmer you will find it easy to learn and understand the lightweight subset of Visual Basic, VBScript.

Presently, VBScript is available for Windows 95, Windows NT, Windows 3.1, and Power Macintosh platforms. UNIX versions of VBScript for Sun, HP, Digital, and IBM platforms are under development. VBScript can be used with HTML code with or without ActiveX controls.

Using JavaScript and VBScript with your HTML code reduces Internet traffic. You can perform data validation on the client side instead of sending the data over to the server to be processed by CGI scripts. Only valid data is transmitted over the Net. This is similar to a client/server environment using PowerBuilder or Visual Basic and Sybase where the data validation is performed by the GUI front end and Sybase receives only validated data to work with.

> **NOTE**
>
> CGI allows Web browsers to interact with the server programs. You can use CGI and other similar technologies, including ISAPI, NSAPI, OLE, and IDC, to perform tasks such as querying the database. For more on CGI, see Chapter 20, "CGI and VBScript."

18

VBSCRIPT AND JAVA

VBScript Examples

Listing 18.4 shows HTML code that includes a VBScript function. The VBScript code is identified by the <SCRIPT> tag. It is embedded between the beginning and ending <SCRIPT> tags.

Listing 18.4. VBScript function.

```
<SCRIPT LANGUAGE="VBScript">
<!--

    Function

    End Function

-->
</SCRIPT>
```

Listing 18.5 shows HTML code that includes a VBScript subroutine. If you know Visual Basic, you realize that VBScript coding is very similar because it is a subset of Visual Basic.

Listing 18.5. VBScript HelloWorld function.

```
<SCRIPT LANGUAGE="VBScript">
<!--

    Sub HelloWorld
        Msgbox "Hello World!"
    End Sub

-->
</SCRIPT>
```

VBScript supports procedures or subroutines just as Visual Basic does. Subroutines are defined in VBScript using the sub keyword. Use the Call statement to initiate a call to the VBScript subroutine. Listing 18.6 shows a Call statement to the HelloWorld subroutine declared in Listing 18.5.

Listing 18.6. Calling a VBScript subroutine.

```
<SCRIPT LANGUAGE="VBScript">
<!--
    Call HelloWorld

    Sub HelloWorld
        Msgbox "Hello World!"
    End Sub

-->
</SCRIPT>
```

Listing 18.7 demonstrates the use of comments inside your VBScript code.

Listing 18.7. Use of comments in VBScript.

```
<SCRIPT LANGUAGE="VBScript">
<!--

    'Call the HelloWorld subroutine          'this is the commented line
    Call HelloWorld

    Sub HelloWorld
        Msgbox "Hello World!"
    End Sub

-->
</SCRIPT>
```

Not all browsers support VBScript. Therefore, the VBScript functions and procedures are embedded within the comment tags (`<!--` and `-->`). Any browser that does not interpret VBScript can bypass the VBScript functions and procedures without displaying the code.

VBScript functions and procedures can be placed anywhere inside the HTML code, including the HEAD and BODY sections. It is recommended you place all your functions and procedures in one location, usually toward the end of the BODY section before the `</BODY>` tag, similar to JavaScript coding.

> **NOTE**
>
> VBScript can be used to control and integrate both HTML intrinsic controls and ActiveX controls.

VBScript Variables

VBScript supports arrays and collections of variables, similar to Visual Basic.

VBScript Operators

VBScript operators include arithmetic, comparison, and logical operators. Table 18.7 shows the VBScript arithmetic operators.

Table 18.7. VBScript arithmetic operators.

Operator	Meaning
+	Addition
-	Subtraction/negation
*	Multiplication
/	Division
\	Integer division
&	String concatenation
^	Exponentiation
mod	Remainder on division

Table 18.8 shows the VBScript comparison operators.

Table 18.8. VBScript comparison operators.

Operator	Meaning
=	Equality
<>	Non-equality
>	Greater than
>=	Greater than or equal to
<	Less than
<=	Less than or equal to
Is	Object equivalence

Table 18.9 shows the VBScript logical operators.

Table 18.9. VBScript logical operators.

Operator	Meaning
And	Logical AND
Or	Logical OR
Not	Logical NOT
Xor	Logical exclusion
Eqv	Logical equivalence
Imp	Logical implication

VBScript Err Object

The VBScript error object Err is built into it. It can be used to track runtime errors. It has several properties that can be used to track and handle runtime errors.

VBScript Variant Data Type

The only data type VBScript supports is a variant. It is a *one for all* data type. A single data type makes the language lightweight and portable. It also makes it easier and faster to download.

A variant is a special kind of data type that can contain different kinds of information, depending on the context in which it is used. If it is used in numeric context, a variant data type contains numeric data. If it is used in string context, a variant data type contains string data.

Table 18.10 shows the VBScript variant data types.

Table 18.10. VBScript variant data types.

Data Type	Meaning
integer	Integer value between -32,768 and 32,767.
long integer	Integer in the range -2,147,483,648 to 2,147,483,648.
double	Double-precision, floating-point number. The range for negative values is -1.7976931348232E308 to -4.940656458412E-324. The range for positive values is 4.940656458412347E-324 to .79769313486232E308.
single	Single precision floating-point number. The range for negative values is -3.402823E38 to -.1401298E-45. The range for positive values is 1.401298E-45 to 3.402823E38.
date	Date.
empty	If it represents a number, its value is 0. If it represents a string, its value is "".
string	Variable length string; it can hold up to 2 billion characters in length.
null	Contains no valid data.
boolean	True or false.
byte	Integer range: 0–255.
object	Object.
error	Error number.

You can use the function vartype to return information about the type of data stored in a variant.

VBScript Constants

You can define constants in your VBScript code using the DIM statement. Listing 18.8 shows an example of declaring a constant MyString. The assignment statement determines the data type of the constant. In this case the variant MyString is of type string.

Listing 18.8. Assign a string to a variant.

```
Dim MyString
MyString = "This is my string".
```

If you assign a number, MyString represents a numeric data type. Listing 18.9 shows an example of assigning a number to a variant.

Listing 18.9. Assign a number to a variant.

```
Dim MyString
MyString = 786
```

If you assign a number as a quoted string, MyString represents a string data type. Listing 18.10 shows an example of assigning a number as a quoted string to a variant.

Listing 18.10. Assign a number as a quoted string to a variant.

```
Dim MyString
MyString = "786"
```

Date and Time literals are represented by enclosing them within # signs. Listing 18.11 shows an example of assigning a date to a variant.

Listing 18.11. Assign a date to a variant.

```
Dim DepartureDate
DepartureDate = #08-23-96#
```

VBScript Flow of Control Statements

Table 18.11 shows the VBScript flow of control statements.

Table 18.11. VBScript flow of control statements.

Statement	Meaning
For.Next	Execute the code within the loop for N times, where N is specified in the For loop.

Statement	Meaning
`For Each.Next`	Execute the code within the loop once for each item in the specified collection.
`If.Then`	Simple `If.Then` statement.
`If.Then.Else.End If`	The standard `If.Then.Else.End If` statement.
`Select`	Select `Case` test expression. `Case` `Case` `End Select`
`Do.Loop`	Execute the code within the loop as long as the loop expression is true.
`While.Wend`	Execute the code within the loop as long as the specified condition is true.

VBScript Functions

VBScript supports functions just like Visual Basic does. Functions are defined in VBScript using the `Function` keyword. Similar to variables, VBScript functions are also loosely typed. You need not explicitly define the type of return value of a function. The type of return value is automatically set, based on the context in which it is used.

VBScript Procedures

VBScript supports procedures just as Visual Basic does. Procedures are defined in VBScript using the `sub` keyword. JavaScript does not support procedures.

ActiveX

VBScript can integrate both HTML intrinsic and ActiveX controls easily. As of this writing, JavaScript does not support integration of ActiveX controls.

18
VBSCRIPT AND JAVA

> **NOTE**
>
> Microsoft's ActiveX Control Pad offers a visual editing environment that lets you develop Web pages interactively. You can also integrate ActiveX and other HTML intrinsic controls easily using ActiveX Control Pad.

Standards and Conventions

This section discusses the importance of having a set of standards and conventions when programming using JavaScript and VBScript. It outlines the advantages of using coding guidelines. It recommends the approach that best suits your company. This section is not intended to be a reference guide on the coding standards for JavaScript and VBScript. However, it recommends a list of steps that you should consider when establishing the standards and conventions for your company.

If your company does not have a coding convention, you should seriously consider establishing one. Establishing and using corporate-wide scripting standards and conventions is critical to the long-term success of any mission-critical project involving JavaScript and VBScript. Coding guidelines encourage reusability and improve project maintenance. They improve team communication and the debugging process. In this fast-changing world, developers move from one project to another. A set of standards and conventions helps make such moves easy. If a developer starts working on a project that has already been in the works for quite some time, being familiar with the coding standards and conventions from the previous project reduces the learning curve involved with the new project.

Typically the norm is to continue with your established coding conventions and adapt them to JavaScript and VBScript. For example, if you have been using 4GL tools such as Visual Basic and PowerBuilder for client/server application development and have been following certain guidelines when writing applications using such tools, it makes sense to adopt such guidelines and modify them as necessary for JavaScript and VBScript scripting. This approach maintains as much uniformity as possible across coding guidelines using different tools and languages.

An interesting twist to using JavaScript and VBScript is the ability to share your code worldwide. Any Web page designed and placed on the Internet is accessible to developers and programmers worldwide, along with its source code. Although there is no official worldwide set of standards and conventions, those set forth by JavaSoft and Microsoft can be considered as the worldwide set of standards and conventions.

> **NOTE**
>
> Microsoft's suggested standards and conventions for VBScript are available for download at http://www.microsoft.com/vbscript. JavaSoft's suggested standards and conventions for JavaScript are available for download at http://home.netscape.com/comprod/ products/navigator/version_2.0/script/index.html.

Establishing a set of standards and conventions includes, but is not limited to, the following steps:

- ■ Use descriptive variable names. For example, instead of using `nm` for the name of a sponsor, consider using `sponsor_name`. Some companies use mixed-case variable names, for example `Sponsor_Name`. If you have been using mixed-case variable names in your previous projects, continue with it for your JavaScript and VBScript projects as well.

- ■ Use all caps to represent constants. You can prefix them with the appropriate letter to indicate whether it is an integer, a string, and so on. For example `iNUMBERCONNECTIONS` is an integer constant representing the number of connections.

- ■ Comment your code well, including revision history. It helps to know the kinds of changes a program has undergone and how it has evolved over time. A new developer on the project can quickly understand the nature of change requests.

- ■ Similar to the approach of naming variables, use descriptive names for objects, procedures, and functions you declare. For example, a text box control can be named `txtAddress1`, where `txt` indicates it is a text box control and `Address1` indicates it is used to store the first line of the address. Similarly, use descriptive names for procedures and functions.

- ■ Structure your script appropriately. After the script tag `<SCRIPT>`, an HTML comment should appear on the next line. This comment is for the old browsers that do not support any scripting language (although it would be hard to find anyone using an old browser!). If you use an HTML comment on the next line, the browser does not display the script code. When possible, use one script rather than multiple script sections throughout the page. Generally your code should appear inside the `<HEAD>...</HEAD>` tags. It can also appear at the bottom of your page, just before the `</BODY>` end-of-body tag. Having all your script in one place helps you locate it quickly and easily.

Comparing Java, JavaScript, and VBScript: A Summary

Table 18.12 summarizes the different features of Java, JavaScript, and VBScript.

Table 18.12. Java, JavaScript, and VBScript: A summary.

Java	*JavaScript*	*VBScript*
Programming language	Scripting language	Scripting language
Object-oriented	Object-based	Not object-based

continues

Table 18.12. continued

Java	JavaScript	VBScript
Strongly typed	Loosely typed	Loosely typed
No support for functions	Supports functions	Supports functions
Interacts with browser as applet	Supports functions	Extension to HTML
Secure	Secure	Secure
Derived from C/C++	C/C++ based	Subset of Visual Basic
Supported by all three browsers	Supported by all three browsers	Presently supported by only Internet Explorer
Steeper learning curve if not familiar with C/C++	Easy to learn	Based on BASIC

Examples

In this section, we'll review and analyze a VBScript example downloaded from the Web site http://www.microsoft.com/vbscript. We will also review and analyze the JavaScript code for the same example. Figure 18.7 shows a simple Web page created by the HTML code included in the file msftd.html on the companion CD-ROM. This HTML displays an order form that lets you place orders for flowers. You specify the occasion and enter the name and address where the flowers should be sent.

Let us look at the code part by part. Listing 18.12 is all HTML code that is used to set up the form. Three radio buttons are displayed to let the user select from Birthday (default), Anniversary, and Get Well Soon occasions. These buttons are displayed using the <Input Type> tag.

Next, the data entry fields for entering the name and address of the destination are added. The <Input> tag is used to add these fields. Three buttons, Submit, Clear, and Init, are added at the bottom. The Submit button sends the order. The Clear button clears the name and address fields. The Init button initializes the data entry fields.

Listing 18.12. HTML code for setting up the form for ordering flowers.

```
<HEAD><TITLE>VBScript sample:  Ordering Flowers</TITLE></HEAD>
<BODY>

<TABLE  WIDTH="80%">
<TR VALIGN=bottom>
<TD WIDTH="40%"><IMG SRC="/vbscript/us/vbssamp/msftd/msftd.gif" ALIGN=center></TD>
<TD WIDTH="60%"><FONT SIZE=12><I>Order Flowers</I></FONT></TD>
</TR>
</TABLE>
```

```
<FONT FACE="Times New Roman" SIZE=4>What is the occasion?</FONT><BR>
<PRE>
<INPUT TYPE=RADIO NAME=OptOccasion CHECKED> Birthday

<INPUT TYPE=RADIO NAME=OptOccasion> Anniversary

<INPUT TYPE=RADIO NAME=OptOccasion> Get well soon
</PRE>

<FONT FACE="Times New Roman" SIZE=4>When and where should the flowers be sent?</
➥FONT><BR>
<PRE>
Date      <INPUT NAME=TxtDate   SIZE=60>

Name      <INPUT NAME=TxtName   SIZE=60>

Address   <INPUT NAME=TxtAddress SIZE=60>

City      <INPUT NAME=TxtCity SIZE=60>

State     <INPUT NAME=TxtState SIZE=60>

Zip code <INPUT NAME=TxtZip SIZE=60>

          <INPUT TYPE=BUTTON VALUE="Submit" NAME="BtnSubmit">  <INPUT TYPE=BUTTON
          ➥VALUE="Clear" NAME="BtnClear">  <INPUT TYPE=BUTTON VALUE="Init" NAME=
          ➥"BtnInit"><BR></PRE>
```

18

Figure 18.7.

An ordering flowers Web page created using HTML and VBScript.

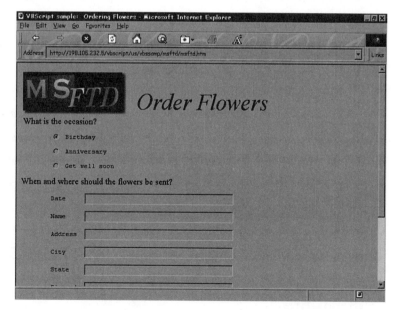

Listing 18.13 shows the VBScript code that is used to process the data entered by the user. It is also used to process the mouse click events when the user clicks the Submit, Clear, or Init button. Before the days of JavaScript and VBScript, such processing would be done on the server, using CGI programs and scripts. VBScript extends the HTML code and validates user input before it is sent to the server. This reduces network traffic and improves the overall performance of your Web page.

There are two variants declared: strMsgBoxTitle and bValidOrder. Note that the types of these variables have not been defined. One can guess from the names of the variables that strMsgBoxTitle is likely to store string data and bValidOrder is expected to store a Boolean value that is true or false.

There are six procedures defined in this VBScript code: Window_OnLoad, BtnInit_OnClick, BtnSubmit_OnClick, ValidateDeliveryDate, CheckSpecified, and BtnClear_OnClick.

The subroutine Window_OnLoad is executed when the Web page window is first loaded by the browser. It assigns the value MSFID to the variant strMsgBoxTitle. The variant StrMsgBoxTitle is assigned a string value and therefore it is now a string variable. The strMsgBoxTitle is used to display the title for the message box. Next, the subroutine Window_OnLoad calls the BtnInit_OnClick procedure. This procedure initializes the data entry fields.

The procedure BtnInit_OnClick initializes the data entry fields. It is executed when the Web page window is first loaded. It is also executed when the user clicks the Init button.

The procedure BtnSubmit_OnClick is executed when the user clicks the Submit button. It checks whether the data entered is valid. If it is valid, the variable bValidOrder that is initialized to true at the beginning of this procedure retains its initialized value. If bValidOrder is true, the order is sent. If the data entered is not valid, bValidOrder is set to false and the control is returned to the user on the Web page.

The procedure ValidDeliveryDate checks whether the value specified in the date field is valid.

The procedure CheckSpecified is actually called by the BtnSubmit_OnClick procedure. It checks whether the data entered in name and address fields is valid.

The procedure BtnClear_OnClick is executed when the user clicks the Clear button. It clears the data entry fields.

Listing 18.13. VBScript code.

```
<SCRIPT LANGUAGE="VBScript">
<!--
Option Explicit

Dim strMsgBoxTitle
Dim bValidOrder

Sub Window_OnLoad
    strMsgBoxTitle = "MSFTD"
    Call BtnInit_OnClick
End Sub
```

```
Sub BtnInit_OnClick
    TxtName.Value = "Joe Smith"
    TxtAddress.Value = "1 Main Street"
    TxtCity.Value = "Springfield"
    TxtState.Value = "Washington"
    TxtZip.Value = "12345"
    TxtDate.Value = Date + 3
End Sub

Sub BtnSubmit_OnClick
    bValidOrder = True
    Call CheckSpecified(txtName.Value, "Please specify a name.")
    Call CheckSpecified(txtAddress.Value, "Please specify an address.")
    Call CheckSpecified(txtCity.Value, "Please specify a city.")
    Call CheckSpecified(txtState.Value, "Please specify a state.")
    Call CheckSpecified(txtZip.Value, "Please specify a zip code.")
    Call CheckSpecified(txtDate.Value, "Please specify a date.")
    Call ValidateDeliveryDate
    If bValidOrder Then
        MsgBox "Thank you for your order!", 0, strMsgBoxTitle

        ' TODO:  Actually send the order.
    End If
End Sub

Sub ValidateDeliveryDate
    Dim SoonestWeCanDeliver
    Dim RequestedDate

    If Not bValidOrder Then Exit Sub

    SoonestWeCanDeliver = Date + 2
    RequestedDate = CDate(TxtDate.Value)
    If RequestedDate < SoonestWeCanDeliver Then
        bValidOrder = False
        MsgBox "Not even we can deliver that fast!", 0, strMsgBoxTitle
    End If
End Sub

Sub CheckSpecified(ByVal strFieldValue, ByVal strMsg)
    If strFieldValue = "" And bValidOrder Then
        MsgBox strMsg, 0, strMsgBoxTitle
        bValidOrder = False
    End If
End Sub

Sub BtnClear_OnClick
    TxtName.Value = ""
    TxtAddress.Value = ""
    TxtCity.Value = ""
    TxtState.Value = ""
    TxtZip.Value = ""
    TxtDate.Value = ""
End Sub

-->
</SCRIPT>
```

18

VBSCRIPT AND
JAVA

The remaining part of the code is again all HTML. In this example all the VBScript code is encapsulated between the `<SCRIPT>` and `</SCRIPT>` tags. The entire code resides in a single location within the body of the HTML code. This makes the code modular and easy to locate. The VBScript code is listed in the `<BODY>` section of the HTML code.

Now let us look at the JavaScript code for the same example. The JavaScript code is included in the file `jsftd.html` on the companion CD-ROM. The top part of the file is again all HTML code. The only difference is in the way the buttons are declared. You'll notice an additional criteria in the `<Input>` tag line—`OnClick`. `OnClick` is an event associated with the buttons. It is activated when the user clicks the button.

The second half of the file is the JavaScript code. One important difference you'll notice immediately is that everything is declared as a function, whereas we had procedures (that is, subroutines) declared in the VBScript code. JavaScript does not support procedures. It supports functions only. Every function returns a value. In this example, a return value of `0` indicates success. Overall, the form and structure of the JavaScript code are similar to the VBScript code.

Relevant Web Sites

Refer to the following Web sites for more information on Java, JavaScript, and VBScript. There are plenty of JavaScript and VBScript resources and examples available on the Net for download. Both JavaScript and VBScript are relatively new languages. You can certainly expect enhancements and bug fixes as these languages mature and gain developer support. Table 18.13 lists a few Web sites that would be excellent bookmarks for keeping up-to-date with the Java, JavaScript, and VBScript world.

Table 18.13. Web sites for Java, JavaScript, and VBScript.

Site name	*Site URL*
Netscape JavaScript	`http://home.netscape.com/comprod/ products/navigator/version_2.0/script/ index.html`
JavaScript Developer Tools	`http://home.netscape.com/comprod/ products/navigator/version_2.0/script/ javascript_tools.html`
JavaScript Authoring Guide	`http://home.netscape.com/eng/ mozilla/2.0/handbook/javascript/ index.html`
JavaScript Resources and Examples	`http://home.netscape.com/comprod/ products/navigator/version_2.0/script/ script_info/index.html`

Site name	*Site URL*
JavaScript	`http://home.netscape.com/eng/mozilla/` `2.0/handbook/javascript/index.html`
VBScript	`http://www.microsoft.com/vbscript`
VBScript links	`http://www.microsoft.com/vbscript/` `us/vbsmain/vbslinks.htm`

Review

In this chapter you learned about Java and JavaScript. Although Java's portability and object-oriented capabilities are beneficial, there are approximately 3 million programmers who use Visual Basic as their primary programming language and who would benefit from using VBScript with their HTML code. Since VBScript is a subset of Visual Basic, these programmers would be able to port their Visual Basic code. Programming in Basic is a lot easier than in C/C++ for a number of the non-programmers. Clearly there is a need for VBScript—an easy-to-use scripting language that even non-programmers can use to build highly interactive Web pages.

In this chapter, you also learned about VBScript's programming syntax and structure. Presently VBScript is available only as part of Internet Explorer 3.0. It is available for the Windows 95, Windows NT, Windows 3.1, and Power Macintosh platforms. UNIX versions of VBScript for Sun, HP, Digital, and IBM platforms are under development. VBScript can be used with HTML code with or without ActiveX controls. It supports only one data type—a variant. You can use the function `vartype` to return information about the type of data stored in a variant. You can define constants in VBScript using the `DIM` statement. VBScript operators include arithmetic, logical, and comparison operators. The VBScript error object `Err` is built into it. It can be used to track runtime errors. The `Err` object has several properties that can be used to track and handle runtime errors. VBScript supports functions and procedures just like Visual Basic does. Functions are defined using the `Function` keyword. Procedures or subroutines are defined using the `sub` keyword. JavaScript does not support procedures.

Whether you should use Java, JavaScript, or VBScript, depends on the nature of your application and your prior programming knowledge. If you are a proficient C++ programmer, you would find Java and JavaScript interesting and easy to catch on. On the other hand, if you are a Visual Basic guru, you would appreciate its lightweight portable subset: VBScript.

18

VBSCRIPT AND JAVA

VBScript and DLLs

by Ramesh Chandak

IN THIS CHAPTER

The concept of DLL, which stands for dynamic link library, first appeared with the release of the Windows operating system. Simply put, a DLL is a collection of functions. It is dynamically linked at runtime with your application's executable and helps you extend the functionality of the base function call library of any Windows application. (See Figure 19.1.) This chapter introduces DLLs and discusses their advantages and disadvantages. It compares and contrasts DLLs with static libraries. You will learn more about the structure of a DLL. You will also learn about where and how you can define your own functions within a DLL. This chapter discusses VBScript's lack of support for DLLs and how it affects your code.

FIGURE 19.1.

A dynamic link library is loaded into memory at runtime.

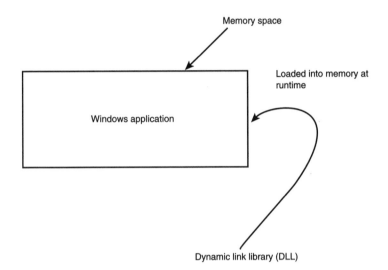

DLLs are likely to create distribution nightmares. Just like any other software, a DLL will probably get upgraded over time. Consequently, you end up having several different versions of DLLs. When writing your installation utility, you need to consider the possibility of older versions of DLLs residing on your user's system and be careful when you install new versions of the same DLLs. With the introduction of 32-bit–based Windows 95, programmers and developers have to be aware of the 16- and 32-bit versions of the same DLLs. DLL management becomes important in such cases.

DLLs might have any file extension (`.res`, `.fon`, `.exe`, or `.dll`, for example). A DLL program does not include the `main()` or `winmain()` functions. Instead, it contains the functions `Entry`, `LibMain`, and `Exit`.

A large pool of third-party developers for Visual Basic and other Microsoft programming tools have created a tremendous number of enhanced controls and libraries for use with your Windows applications. Most of these controls and libraries are nothing but DLLs. Developers have created DLLs that handle not only complex mathematical calculations, but also provide enhanced user interface controls. A DLL is usually written using C or C++, which is a big advantage because it provides speed and efficiency. Using DLLs to handle numeric-intensive tasks, while using your favorite GUI tool for the user interface of your application, is highly recommended as it offers code modularity, speed, and efficiency.

Windows 95 has three main DLLs : `gdi32.exe`, `user32.exe`, and `kernel32.exe`. Windows 3.1 comprises of the same three DLLs, but uses their 16-bit versions: `gdi.exe`, `user.exe`, and `kernel.exe`.

> **NOTE**
>
> Usually DLL files have the `.dll` extension. Windows DLLs have the `.exe` extension; however, they are still DLLs.

Each DLL consists of function calls that constitute the entire Windows function call library. By default, these DLLs reside in the `system` subdirectory of your Windows directory (`c:\windows\system`, for example).

Windows 3.1 is a single-threaded, cooperative multitasking system. Unlike OS/2 or Windows NT, only one thread of execution can be active at any given time in a given application. The primary difference between a Windows application and a Windows DLL is that Windows tasks get entered into TDB—the task database. The task database is an internal Windows object. Therefore, a Windows application gets the resources, such as stack segment, message queue, file handle table, DOS path, and environment block, but a DLL does not get these items directly. The DLL borrows them from the Windows application that calls it.

Static Versus Dynamic Library

A static library is linked into your executable code. It is part of the executable, thus creating a larger executable file. A larger executable file requires more RAM and disk space. On the other hand, a static library is faster than a DLL because it has already linked into the executable and loaded into memory when the executable is first run. Before it can be used, a programmer-defined DLL must be loaded into memory, if that has not already occurred.

> **NOTE**
>
> A Windows DLL is already loaded when Windows starts up, so it does not have to be specifically loaded into memory at runtime.

19

VBSCRIPT AND DLLs

A large executable takes more time to load into memory. Also, the static library has to have a link into every executable that needs it. Consequently, if you have three different executables that need a static library, this static library must be linked into all three executables. And if all three executables run at the same time, you have three copies of the static library loaded into the memory space, which makes for inefficient use of memory space. No code sharing exists across applications, which is where dynamic link libraries come into picture. A dynamic link library is loaded only at runtime. And only one copy of the library needs to get loaded into the memory space. The library can be shared across applications if more than one application needs it. An application can even unload the DLL if it is not needed at any given point in time, and thus free up some memory.

The executable file contains *references* to the functions in the DLL. If you create ten different programs that use the same library, you need to create only one DLL, which saves memory and disk space. Primarily, a DLL works to reduce the load image of an EXE, as well as share resources across multiple executables or instances of an executable. You can update these DLLs without re-linking because the executable contains references and not the actual code.

> **NOTE**
>
> Static libraries offer better performance. DLLs offer better memory management.

DLLs have been known to create distribution nightmares. Just like any other application is upgraded over time, a DLL is also likely to be upgraded. You may add new functions to a DLL or enhance existing ones. You may port a 16-bit DLL to a 32-bit or upgrade simply because the host application has been upgraded. To accommodate such scenarios, you need to consider in your installation utility that older versions of DLLs might reside on your user's system—so be careful when you install new versions of the same DLLs. Consider this real-world example. A Visual Basic 3.0 application was designed using Microsoft Access 1.1 as the back-end database. Another Visual Basic 3.0 application was designed that uses Microsoft Access 2.0 as the back-end database and the Jet Engine compatibility layer to make Visual Basic 3.0 talk to Microsoft Access 2.0. After installing the second application on the same machine as the first one, the first application stopped working. It gave an error message, Reserved Error (which is not documented in any of the Visual Basic or Microsoft Access documentation). It became very difficult to debug. Later it was realized that the first application did not work anymore because it was using the Jet Engine compatibility layer, although the database was still version 1.1—not upgraded to version 2.0. It was using the Access version 2.0 DLLs when in fact it should have been using the version 1.1 DLLs. The version 2.0 DLLs were resident in the same directory as the version 1.1 DLLs—the \windows\system directory.

Both static and dynamic libraries have advantages and disadvantages. The trend in Windows development utilizes DLLs. DLL technology is developed and promoted by Microsoft. Microsoft anticipates, expects, and hopes every user will use its products, from Microsoft Word to Visual FoxPro to Microsoft Access. Many of these applications utilize the same DLLs, which supports why DLL technology makes sense. If you are using Microsoft Word and Microsoft Excel, for example, and they utilize the same three DLLs, only one copy of each DLL gets loaded into memory.

In order for you to run a program that uses a dynamic library, the library must be present on the disk, either in the current directory, a directory accessible through the PATH string in MS-DOS, the Windows directory, or the SYSTEM subdirectory of the Windows directory. If the library does not appear in any of these locations, you get a runtime application error. The best place to install your application DLLs is in your application directory, and you should include it in the PATH string. Any Windows DLLs must be installed in the \windows\system directory.

With the introduction of 32-bit–based Windows 95, programmers and developers have to think about the 16- and 32-bit versions of the same DLLs. DLL management becomes important in such cases.

> **NOTE**
>
> DLL distribution and management becomes critical for the success of any DLL-based application. When you release upgrades and fixes, make sure the installation utility does not cause any unnecessary overwrites and deletes of existing DLLs.

Structure of a DLL

Any standard Windows application includes the main() or winmain() function. You can run an application by double-clicking its executable (.exe). The main() or winmain() function is the starting point for the application. Within the main() function, you include all the code necessary to perform the required tasks, including calling other functions or functions within a DLL. On the other hand, you cannot run a DLL simply by double-clicking on it.

The Entry Function

Once the Windows loader has loaded a DLL into memory, it transfers execution to the DLL's entry-point function, which performs whatever initialization the DLL needs to function properly. The name of LibEntry.Obj is different for different platforms. LibEntry's most important task is to initialize the DLL's local heap, if it has one. Without a local heap the DLL cannot use any of Windows' local memory management APIs. Once it has initialized the DLL's local heap, LibEntry usually calls a programmer-specified function to perform any additional initialization required by the DLL.

You may wonder why all initialization does not occur in LibEntry instead of calling a programmer-specified function. LibEntry is written in Assembly language for performance reasons. Any changes or additions to the LibEntry.Obj have to occur in Assembly language. Programming is easier in a high-level language, such as C or C++, than in Assembly language.

Writing the minimum code necessary in LibEntry using Assembly language is easier; then you call a function and write that function in a high-level language. LibEntry.Obj, a runtime object file, is linked by the built-in C++ compiler at build time. If this function fails, Windows unloads the DLL from memory; otherwise it calls LibMain. If LibMain returns false, Windows unloads the DLL from memory. Note that you cannot have multiple instances of the same DLL in memory; moreover, LibEntry and LibMain get called only once, no matter how many applications share the same DLL. If you want to perform additional initialization for each instance of your application, you should provide an exported function and call that function instead.

The LibMain Function

LibMain is a programmer-defined initialization function called by LibEntry. Because LibEntry performs initializations that are common to all DLLs, you can write your DLL-specific initialization in LibMain. Because this represents a separate function from LibEntry, you can write it in a high-level language instead of writing in Assembly language. Listing 19.1 shows the LibMain function.

Listing 19.1. The LibMain function.

```
/* You may modify it in any way you wish but do not remove Libmain and WEP.
Without them you will be  unable to link your DLL. */
#include <windows.h>
int _export LibMain( HANDLE hmod, WORD dataseg, WORD heap, LPSTR cmdline)
{
    hmod = hmod;                    // these assignments generate no code
    dataseg = dataseg;             // but prevent compiler warnings about
    heap = heap;                   // unreferenced variables
    cmdline = cmdline;
    return( 1 );
}
```

Remember that this function is called only once. It can only perform an initialization that is independent of the application instances. You may want to use it to load resources, such as bitmaps or icons, or to create data structures that the DLL manages. Remember, however, not to write code in LibMain that depends on other previously loaded DLLs, because when several DLLs are to be loaded at one time, Windows does not load them in any guaranteed order.

The Exit Function

Windows Exit Procedure (WEP) is the last function of a DLL to be called before Windows unloads the DLL from memory. WEP performs any cleanup a DLL needs to do before it is unloaded and is called only once. When a DLL's usage count drops to zero, the Windows loader calls the DLL's WEP and then unloads the DLL. The usage count for an implicitly loaded DLL becomes zero after all instances of all applications that are currently using it exit. Listing 19.2 shows the WEP function.

Listing 19.2. The Windows Exit Procedure (WEP).

```
int _export WEP( int res )
{
    res = res;
    return( 1 );
}
```

Windows 3.0 requires this function for all DLLs. In Windows 3.1 and later versions, WEP is optional.

Programmer-Defined Functions

These functions enable you to actually implement the functionality you want—they represent the real workhorses of the DLL. Programmer-defined functions implement the functionality of DLLs in two varieties: exported and non-exported.

When declaring functions within a DLL, certain conventions should be followed, as specified in the Windows SDK. You need to use the ANSI keywords far, pascal, and export.

The FAR declaration helps Windows change the code segment of any program as required by the memory manager. The references to specific keywords such as FAR or NEAR do not apply in a 32-bit environment.

PASCAL function calls are more efficient than C function calls. With PASCAL function calls, the responsibility of managing parameters and cleaning up the stack remains with the called procedure. Under C function calls, the calling procedure takes this responsibility. Thus, the PASCAL function calls eliminate any duplication of code because multiple instances could exist of one procedure calling a single instance of another procedure.

The EXPORT keyword tells the compiler what functions in the DLL should be made visible and accessible to the world outside the DLL.

Exported Functions

Exported functions define the programming interface of a DLL and are meant to be called by applications and other DLLs. They usually represent the highest abstraction level a DLL provides to its callers. To implement these high-level services, exported functions often call non-exported functions that perform the necessary operations to support their functionality.

Exported functions must be declared as far because they do not reside in the segments from which they are called. They may, however, use any naming and parameter-passing conventions that pass parameters on the stack. Two popular conventions are pascal and cdecl. Conventions that pass parameters in the CPU's registers may not be used because prolog code uses the CPU's registers when the function is called. Also note that exported functions that return floating-point values or structures and objects larger than 4 bytes must use the pascal calling convention.

Non-Exported (Internal) Functions

Internal functions can only be called by other functions within the same DLL; applications and other DLLs cannot call them and do not need to be aware that they even exist. Because they are internal to a DLL, you can use only non-exported functions to implement the functionality of the DLL's initialization, termination, and exported functions. Non-exported functions should be used in DLLs just as they are in applications—to build a modular structure and to break down the complexity. Internal functions in DLLs can use any naming and parameter-passing conventions supported by your compiler.

Why Use DLLs?

DLLs represent important technology that has gained widespread use and acceptance since its inception. Many advantages to using DLLs exist. DLLs provide better memory management. A dynamic link library gets loaded only at runtime, and only one copy of the library needs to be loaded into the memory space. If more than one application needs it, the library is shared across applications. An application can even unload the DLL if it is not needed at any given time, which frees up memory. Consequently, you make efficient use of your system memory.

A wave of third-party libraries has hit the marketplace. Utilizing these existing DLLs directly with your application saves you a great deal of time and effort. It enables you to focus on the core of your application because the DLLs take care of some of the intricacies of your application.

A DLL is usually written using C or C++. Programs written in C or C++ operate quickly and efficiently, which improves the speed and response time of your application tremendously.

Consider this example. Your application involves complex mathematical calculations, and you are using a front-end GUI tool, such as Visual Basic or PowerBuilder, to build the user interface for your application. You can implement the mathematical calculations in two ways. You can write them as functions directly in Visual Basic or PowerBuilder, not the most efficient way to do it. On the other hand, you can write them as C or C++ functions embedded within a DLL, which is fast and efficient. Moreover, a DLL comprised of such functions can be used across different applications. You write it once and you use it multiple times, which encourages code sharing and reusability. Implementing the mathematical calculations this way makes the structure of your application modular. Furthermore, you can modify the functions within the DLL (without changing the name references) and do not have to worry about re-creating the executable. All you have to do is update your user's system with the latest version of the DLL.

A large pool of third-party developers exists for Visual Basic, the development environment for Windows. These developers have created a large number of third-party controls and libraries for Visual Basic. Most of these controls and libraries are nothing but DLLs. The developers have created DLLs that not only handle complex mathematical and geometrical calculations, but also provide enhanced user interface controls. Visual Basic 3.0's release included a basic set of user interface controls that left a big void to be later filled by the third-party developers. Examples of such controls include dropdown calendar, spin control, progress bar, etc. These controls can be programmed and created as part of a DLL, thus making them reusable across different applications. If you are using a third-party DLL, make sure you have all the necessary documentation on the DLL. Without proper documentation, you would have a hard time figuring out what functions are included within the DLL and what types of arguments those functions take.

> **NOTE**
>
> Even with the advent of OCX and ActiveX technologies, DLLs will exist for quite some time. The large established base of DLL-based applications cannot disappear so easily and quickly.

Disadvantages of Using DLLs

Although DLLs offer significant advantages, you need to know about certain drawbacks. Because DLLs are usually written in C or C++, a good programming knowledge of C or C++ becomes essential. Programming using C or C++ is not the easiest task. It has a steep learning curve, and understanding pointers and pointer management is important.

19

VBSCRIPT AND DLLs

As indicated earlier, DLLs are likely to create distribution nightmares. For more on this topic, refer to the section titled "Static Versus Dynamic Library," earlier in this chapter.

Integrating DLLs with a front-end application written in a 4GL language calls for an effective implementation of error-checking protocol. An added component to debugging exists—in addition to debugging your front-end application, you also have to debug your DLL code if necessary.

A Sample DLL

Listing 19.3 shows the three main files for creating a DLL using any C++ compiler. These three files have the following extensions: cpp, def, and .rc. Listing 19.3 also shows the block of code that goes into these three files. Use the export keyword to denote what functions can be called by the calling application. Any function not declared with the export keyword is an internal function and cannot be called by the calling application.

Listing 19.3. The three main files for creating a Windows DLL.

```
BEGIN FILE : <dll.cpp>
#include <windows.h>

/*** Windows DLL Entrance & Exit Functions ***/
int FAR PASCAL LibMain  (HANDLE hInst, WORD wDataSeg, WORD wHeapSize, LPSTR
lpszCmdLine)
{
if (wHeapSize > 0 )
    UnLockData(0);
return 1;
}

int FAR PASCAL _export WEP(bSystemExit)
int      bSystemExit;
{
    return 1;
}

/* enter the code for your function here */
int FAR PASCAL _export your_function(<param1, param2, param3,… ,paramN>)
{
    <the code for this function goes here>
}
END FILE dll.cpp

BEGIN FILE : dll.def            /* module definition file */
Library        dll_function     /* For WINDOWS EXE, use NAME */
                                /* For WINDOWS DLL, use LIBRARY */
Exetype        WINDOWS
Description    'WINDOWS Sample DLL'
Stub           'WINSTUB.EXE'
```

```
Code            Shared Moveable Discardable Preload
Data            Single Moveable Preload
HeapSize        1024
StackSize       8192
Exports         WEP               /* identify the functions */
                dll_function      /* that are being exported */
END FILE dll.def

BEGIN FILE : dll.rc
Q7inf    RCData
Begin
    0x4337, 0x444D, 0x03E8, 0,0,0,0
End
StringTable
Begin
    1000:"dll_function,1000"
End
END FILE dll.rc
```

> **NOTE**
>
> Creating a Windows DLL involves the use of three main files: `.cpp`, the C++ source code file; `.def`, the module definition file; and `.rc`, the resource file.

Next, you will undertake the task of writing an investment formula DLL. Depositing funds in an interest-bearing account represents a traditional method for accumulating savings. To quickly determine how much time is required to double a sum of money, you can apply an estimate commonly known as the *Rule of 72*. This estimate provides an approximation. The exact time depends on the compounding method being used.

The *Rule of 72* says you divide 72 by the stated interest rate. The result shows the approximate number of years required to double a deposit. Listing 19.4 shows the Rule of 72 formula.

Listing 19.4. The Rule of 72 formula.

```
Formula : rule of 72
72 / Interest Rate = Years to double
```

For example, you deposit $5,000 in an account that pays 8 percent interest. It will take 9 years (= 72/8) to double to $10,000. Listing 19.5 shows the source code files for this DLL.

Listing 19.5. Source code for `rule72.dll`.

```
BEGIN FILE : rule72.cpp
#include <windows.h>

/*** Windows DLL Entrance & Exit Functions ***/
 int FAR PASCAL LibMain  (HANDLE hInst, WORD wDataSeg, WORD wHeapSize, LPSTR
 ➥lpszCmdLine)
{
if (wHeapSize > 0 )
    UnLockData(0);
return 1;
}

int FAR PASCAL _export WEP(bSystemExit)
int     bSystemExit;
{
   return 1;
}

/* To simplify calculations integer values are used */
int FAR PASCAL _export rule72(int intrate)
{
   return(72/intrate);
}
END FILE rule72.cpp

BEGIN FILE : rule72.def           /* module definition file */
Library         rule72            /* For WINDOWS EXE, use NAME */
                                  /* For WINDOWS DLL, use LIBRARY */
Exetype         WINDOWS
Description      'WINDOWS Sample DLL'
Stub            'WINSTUB.EXE'
Code            Shared Moveable Discardable Preload
Data            Single Moveable Preload
HeapSize        1024
StackSize       8192
Exports         WEP               /* identify the functions */
                RULE72            /* that are being exported */
END FILE rule72.def

BEGIN FILE : rule72.rc
Q7inf    RCData
Begin
    0x4337, 0x444D, 0x03E8, 0,0,0,0
End
StringTable
Begin
    1000:"RULE72(),1000"
End
END FILE rule72.rc
```

Use the small or medium memory model for compiling and creating Windows DLLs.

VBScript and DLLs

VBScript is a subset of Visual Basic, the programming language. Visual Basic uses the following convention for declaring and calling DLL functions. Because DLL procedures reside in a file external to your application, you have to give your application some information so that it can find and execute the DLL procedures you want to use. You provide this information with the `Declare` statement. Once you have declared a DLL procedure, you can use it in your code like any other procedure. Listing 19.6 shows the syntax for the `Declare` statement.

Listing 19.6. Syntax for `Declare` statement in Visual Basic.

```
Declare Sub publicname Lib "libname" [Alias "alias"] [([[ByVal] variable_ [As type]
[,[ByVal] variable
➡[As type]]…])]
or
Declare Function publicname Lib "libname" [Alias "alias"] [([[ByVal] variable_ [As
type] [,[ByVal]
➡variable [As type]]…])] As Type
```

If the procedure does not return a value, declare it as a `Sub` procedure. For example, Listing 19.7 shows the declaration of a subroutine, `InvertRect`, from the Windows DLL, `user.exe`.

Listing 19.7. Declaring the procedure—`InvertRect`.

```
Declare Sub InvertRect Lib "User" (ByVal hDC as integer, aRect as Rect)
```

If the procedure returns a value, declare it as a `Function`. For example, Listing 19.8 shows the declaration of a function, `GetSystemMetrics`, from the Windows DLL, `user.exe`.

Listing 19.8. Declaring the function—`GetSystemMetrics`.

```
Declare Function GetSystemMetrics Lib "User" (ByVal n as Integer) as Integer
```

Because VBScript is a subset of Visual Basic, you would expect that it supports the calling of DLLs. Unfortunately, as of this writing VBScript does not support it. This might change in the future. VBScript is the new kid on the block and continues to evolve as it gains wider acceptance. Future releases of VBScript might support DLL integration.

As previously stated, lack of support for DLL integration limits VBScript. Thousands of DLLs exist that can be utilized and integrated very easily. With no support for DLL integration, you may wonder what options you have. You would have to use the built-in structures for

19

VBSCRIPT AND DLLs

declaring VBScript functions and procedures instead. For example, you would have to define your own function, `rule72()`, in VBScript to replace the `rule72.dll`'s functionality. Listing 19.9 shows the VBScript `rule72()` function.

Listing 19.9. VBScript function `rule72()`.

```
<SCRIPT LANGUAGE="VBScript">
<!--Option Explicit

    Dim strMsgBoxTitle
    Dim bValidOrder
    Dim nyears

    Function rule72(int_rate)
        nyears = 72 / int_rate
        return nyears
    End Function

    Sub Window_OnLoad
        strMsgBoxTitle = "MSFTD"
        Call BtnInit_OnClick
    End Sub

....
....
....

-->
</SCRIPT>
```

> **NOTE**
>
> If Microsoft decides to include support for DLLs, you would probably use syntax and format similar to the preceding example for declaring them and calling the DLL procedures.

Another option is to use ActiveX controls. VBScript supports integration of ActiveX controls with HTML. In fact, Microsoft Internet Explorer 3.0 is the only browser in today's market that includes full support for ActiveX controls and VBScript. You can use Visual C++ or Borland C++ to write ActiveX controls—the same tools that you use to write DLLs.

> **NOTE**
>
> Microsoft might not include support for DLLs in VBScript because it is actively promoting its ActiveX technology. In such a case, you would need to convert existing DLLs into ActiveX controls for use with your VBScript code.

Relevant Web Sites

Table 19.1 lists Web sites for more information on DLLs and VBScript. Many resources and examples exist on the Internet.

Table 19.1. Relevant Web sites.

Purpose	*Site URL*
Overview of dynamic link libraries	`http://ipserve.com/jzhuk/` `dll.html`
Using Windows to create DLLs	`http://www.awu.id.` `ethz.ch/~didi/wxwin/` `wx/wx53.html`
Windows Developer FAQ on DLLs	`http://www.r2m.com/win-` `developer-FAQ/dlls`
VBScript	`http://www.microsoft.com/` `vbscript`
VBScript links	`http://www.microsoft.com/` `vbscript/us/vbsmain/` `vbslinks.htm`

Review

DLLs represent important technology that has gained wide acceptance over the years. Although DLL technology is a precursor to OLE and ActiveX, it is still very much in wide use. Understanding how to write DLLs helps you extend the capabilities of your application and maintain code modularity.

You can link a library with the executable in two ways: statically and dynamically. Static linking provides better performance. In the case of a DLL, it has to be first loaded before it can be used. In static linking, you do not have to worry about maintaining different versions of the library because it is completely embedded and linked into the executable. In dynamic linking, DLL maintenance becomes critical, because you would end up having different versions of the same DLL over time.

DLLs may have any file extension (`res`, `fon`, `exe`, or `dll`). A DLL program does not include the `main()` or `winmain()` function. Instead it contains the functions `Entry`, `LibMain`, and `Exit`.

A pool of third-party developers for Visual Basic and other Microsoft programming tools has created a large volume of enhanced controls and libraries that you can use with your Windows applications. Most of these controls and libraries are nothing but DLLs. A DLL is usually written using C or C++, which provides speed and efficiency. You should perform mathematically intensive tasks using DLLs, and use your favorite GUI tool for building the user interface. Your application gains improved speed and response time. And code modularity is maintained.

As of this writing, the current release of VBScript does not support DLL integration, which indicates a very serious limitation in VBScript. If and when Microsoft includes support for DLLs, the syntax and format for declaring them and calling the DLL procedures would probably be similar to that discussed in the "VBScript and DLLs" section. Another option is to convert existing DLLs into ActiveX controls and integrate them with your VBScript code.

CGI and VBScript

by Ramesh Chandak

IN THIS CHAPTER

CHAPTER 20

The very first Web pages lacked interactivity. Users could only browse through them and use hyperlinks to jump from one page to another. Common Gateway Interface (CGI) is one of several ways you can use to add interactivity to your Web pages. Other methods include using Java, JavaScript, VBScript, ActiveX, and plug-ins.

CGI represents a simple protocol of communication between the Web forms and the programs that reside on the Web server. A CGI script or program gets its input from the Web forms, processes it, and sends the results back to your browser. CGI is *not* a programming language; it is a script or a program that resides on the server. You can create a CGI script or program using almost any programming language, such as C/C++, Visual Basic, Perl, FORTRAN, or AppleScript, that supports standard input and output processing. This chapter introduces you to the concept of CGI, discusses why CGI was invented, and explains the different CGI environment variables. It also discusses the basic architecture of a CGI-based Web application and how data is communicated in such an architecture. This chapter further discusses the process of building a CGI application and how you can use VBScript to perform certain processing on the client side thus eliminating the need for CGI scripts or programs for some common tasks.

The CGI programs should process data and respond quickly. Remember, CGI programs get their input from the Web forms. The user is awaiting response while the data is being processed. Therefore, the CGI programs must respond quickly. Because the CGI programs reside on the server, you benefit from the server's processing power.

Early on during the design of your project consider the following two points:

- Does your application demand the use of CGI?

  A static, information-only Web page might not need a CGI program. An interactive Web page would probably use CGI programs.

- How would you protect your CGI programs?

  Because the CGI program is invoked as a result of user actions through the browser, consider necessary security precautions. The CGI programs should be under direct control of the Webmaster *only;* all others, including users, should have only *execute* rights. The users should not have delete, modify, rename, or move rights for the CGI programs.

Understanding CGI

The best way to understand CGI and what it does comes from examples. The following example demonstrates the results obtained using CGI and without CGI. In this example, an order form is created and placed online to enable customers to order products from anywhere in the world.

Listing 20.1 shows the HTML code that uses the `mailto:` command to send the order information from the browser to the Web server when the customer clicks the Send button.

The company, product, and price information included in Listing 20.1 is fictitious and exists for demonstration purposes. Notice the following line in Listing 20.1:

```
<FORM method=POST  ACTION="mailto:xyz@rksoftware.com">
```

The preceding line indicates to the browser the information being sent to the specified e-mail address when the user clicks the Send button using the `mailto:` command.

Figure 20.1 shows part of the HTML page resulting from Listing 20.1.

Listing 20.1. HTML sample using the `mailto:` command for ordering software.

```
<html>
<head>
<title>Order Desk

</title>
</head>
<BODY background="wrbgrnd6.gif"
bgproperties="fixed">
<center>
<h1>    Order Desk <a href="ita.html">
<img border=0 align="middle" src="itlogo2f.gif" alt="RK Software logo"></a>
<img src="amex.gif"> <img src="mastercd.gif">  <img src="visacard.gif">
</h1>
<br><a href="order.html"><img src="ordpgbu7.gif" align="middle"
alt="Go to DOWNLOADABLES Order Form" border=0></a> .
<a href="customer_service.html"><img src="custsbut.gif"
border=0 align="middle" alt="Customer Servie / FAQ">
</a>
</center>
<hr>
<br><b>USE OF THIS FORM</B>
<br>
<br>
This page is for ordering software on <b>diskettes and CD-ROM</b>.

<br>
<br>Click <a href="order.html">HERE</a> to go to a page where
you can order software and <b>forms</b> which you can <b>download</b>,
including a truncated version of <a href="abc_soft.html">ABC Software</a> for
Windows ("Personal Edition").
<br>
<br>Order on-line using this form
or email your responses to this form to XYZ Company at
<a href="mailto:xyz@rksoftware.com">xyz@rksoftware.com</a> or
call (800)555-5555 or +1(123)876-9876 or fax to (123)876-9876.<r>

<br><b>*** A 10% restocking charge will be applied to all returns
***</b>
<br>
```

20

CGI AND
VBSCRIPT

continues

Listing 20.1. continued

```
<br>Please add shipping charges where indicated. We look forward to serving you.
<hr>
You can also order by mail with a check or money order. Make sure to include
shipping/handling charges, as shown below, in US dollars to:<br><br>RK Software,
Inc.

<br>555 Anywhere St.
<br>Beautyville FL 32256 USA
<hr>

<FORM method=POST  ACTION="mailto:74172.1154@compuserve.com">

<INPUT TYPE="hidden" NAME="recipient" VALUE="xyz@rksoftware.com">

<INPUT TYPE="hidden" NAME="Subject" VALUE="Software Order">


<pre><b>Select one</b> (required): <INPUT TYPE="radio" NAME="card_type"
VALUE="VISA" CHECKED>VISA <INPUT TYPE="radio" NAME="card_type"
VALUE="MC" >MasterCard <INPUT TYPE="radio" NAME="card_type"
VALUE="AMEX" >American Express</pre>

</menu>

<PRE><b>Credit Card Number</b> (required):
<INPUT TYPE="text" NAME="Credit_Card_Number" SIZE=25>
<b>Expiration date</b> (required):
<INPUT TYPE="text" NAME="Expiration" SIZE=5>

<b>Shipping address</b>:

    <b>Ship To Name</b>
(required):          <INPUT TYPE="text" NAME="Ship_To_Name" SIZE=40>

<b>Company Name</b>: <INPUT TYPE="text" NAME="Company_Name" SIZE=40>
    <b>Street Address </b> (required):
<INPUT TYPE="text" NAME="Ship_To_Addr_(line_1)" SIZE=40>

FedEx will not deliver to U.S. Post Office Box
    <b>Ship To Address (line 2)</b>:                <INPUT TYPE="text"
NAME="Ship_To_Addr_(line_2)" SIZE=40>
    <b>Ship To City</b> (required):                <INPUT TYPE="text"
NAME="Ship_To_City" SIZE=40>
    <b>Ship To State/Province</b> (required):       <INPUT TYPE="text"
NAME="Ship_To_State/Province" SIZE=12>
    <b>Ship To Zip/Postal Code</b> (required):      <INPUT TYPE="text"
NAME="Ship_To_Zip/Postal_Code" SIZE=10>
    <b>Ship To Country</b> (required):             <INPUT TYPE="text"
NAME="Ship_To_Country" SIZE=15>
    <b>Telephone number</b> (required):            <INPUT TYPE="text"
NAME="Telephone" SIZE=13>
    <b>Fax number</b>:                              <INPUT TYPE="text" NAME="fax"
SIZE=13>
    <b>E-mail address</b>:                          <INPUT TYPE="text" NAME=
                                                ➡"e-mail" SIZE=25>
```

```
<br><b>Please enter the billing address of your credit card, if different from the
➥shipping address.</b>
<b>(Please enter your name AS IT APPEARs ON YOUR CREDIT CARD)</b>
     <b>Name:</b>
<INPUT TYPE="text" NAME="Name" SIZE=40>
     <b>Address (line 1):</b>
<INPUT TYPE="text" NAME="Address_(line_1)" SIZE=40>
     <b>Address (line 2):
</b>              <INPUT TYPE="text" NAME="Address_(line_2)" SIZE=40>

<b>City:</b>
<INPUT TYPE="text" NAME="City_or_town" SIZE=40>
     <b>State or Province:</b>
<INPUT TYPE="text" NAME="State_or_Province" SIZE=12>
     <b>Zip/Postal Code:</b>
<INPUT TYPE="text" NAME="Zip/Postal_Code:" SIZE=10>
     <b>Country:</b>
<INPUT TYPE="text" NAME="Country" SIZE=15>
</PRE>
     <p>
     </menu>

<p>Please indicate the program(s) you wish to order by checking them off:<br>
     <p>

<b> <INPUT TYPE="checkbox" NAME="programs_ordered" VALUE="My Software Lite
CD-ROM- $99"><a href="my_soft.html">My Software Lite</a> v.2.0 for Windows CD-ROM -
- $99 <br>
</b>--> For additional licences at the same location or on a network please call,
write or fax our office.
<br>     --><i> My Software Lite </i> comes with a 60-day return guarantee. A 10%
➥restocking fee applies <br>
--> to all returns.
Shipping & handling charges are not refundable.
<br><br>
<b>
<INPUT TYPE="checkbox" NAME="programs_ordered" VALUE="My Software Pro -
- $149"><a href="my_softpro.html"> My Software Pro </a>
v. 2.0 for Windows -diskettes - - - - - $149</b>

<br>     --><i>
My Software Pro </i> comes with a 30-day return guarantee.
A 10% restocking fee applies
<br>     --> to all returns.
Shipping & handling charges are not refundable.
<br>     -->
You can also order a <b> downloadable</b>, truncated version of
My Software Pro, called <br>     --> <i> My Software Pro
<b>Personal Edition</b></i> for <b> only $69 (non-refundable)
<a href="order.html"> ¦HERE¦</a></b>
<br><br>

<br><br>
<hr>
<b><i><u>Shipping and Handling Charges:
</u></i></b>
```

continues

20

CGI AND
VBSCRIPT

Listing 20.1. continued

```
<br><i>My Software Lite</i> and <i>My Software Pro</i> are shipped by <b>Federal
➥Express courier</b>. Other products "best way".<br><br>

Add <b>$12</b> for delivery of <i>My Software Lite</i> or <i>My Software Pro</i>
within the U.S. or <b>$25</b> to Mexico and Canada, <b>$45 - $75</b> outside N.
America, depending on location, except Demo and where otherwise indicated.

<br><br>
Overseas demo shipment costs $5 (total $10). <br>

<p><hr>How did you come upon our home page, or who referred you here? Any comments
or questions?<br>

<TEXTAREA name="Referred_by" rows=3 cols=60></TEXTAREA>

<p>
<hr>Thank you for your order!
     <p><INPUT
TYPE="hidden" NAME="WebFormID" VALUE="2">
     <p>Click
here to <INPUT TYPE="submit" VALUE="Send Your Order Now"> .................... or
<INPUT TYPE="reset" VALUE="Clear"> the form and start over.</FORM>
<p>

<hr>

Return to <a href="index.html"><img src="central3.gif" alt="RK
Software logo">RK Software Home Page</a>

<hr><FONT SIZE=-2>(C)1996
RK Software.</FONT>
</body>
You are visitor <img src="/cgi-bin/Count.cgi?ft=3&dd=C&frgb=0;0;0¦df=rksoft-
index.dat" align=absmiddl> since 1-Dec-1995
</html>
```

Listing 20.2 shows the results obtained by using the `mailto:` command.

Listing 20.2 Results obtained by using the `mailto:` command.

```
Subject: Form posted from AIR Mosaic
Content-type: application/x-www-form-urlencoded
Content-length: 567
X-Mailer: AIR Mosaic (16-bit) version 1.00.198.07
WebFormID=2&Referred_by=&programs_ordered=My%20Software%20Lite%20%0D%0ACD-ROM-
  %20%2499&Country=&Zip/Postal_Code:=&State_or_Province=&City_or_town=&Address_
  (line_2)=&Address_(line_1)=&Name=&email=&fax=&Telephone=&Ship_To_Country=USA&Ship_To_Zip/
  Postal_Code=45632&Ship_To_State/Province=FL&Ship_To_City=Bonnesville&Ship_To_
  Addr_(line_2)=&Ship_To_Addr_(line_1)=456%20Whatever%20Street&Company_
  Name=XYZ%20Corporation&Ship_To_Name=XYZ%20Corporation&Expiration=9%2F99&Credit_
  Card_Number=1234567890123456&card_type=VISA&Subject=Software%20Order&recipient=
  xyz@rksoftware.com
```

FIGURE 20.1.

HTML page created using Listing 20.2's code.

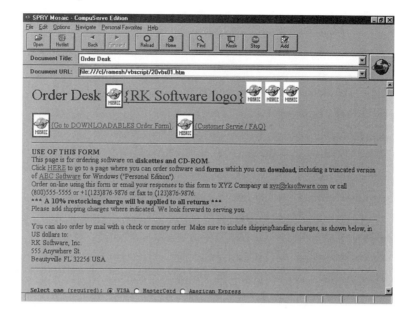

As you can see, the e-mail received using the `mailto:` command is not easily readable. It needs to be parsed before you can decipher what it contains. A CGI script or program comes in handy here because a CGI script would parse the message into a readable format before it is sent.

Listing 20.3 shows the HTML code that uses a CGI script to send the same order information from the browser to the Web server. Notice the following line in Listing 20.3:

```
<FORM method=POST  ACTION="http://www.rksoft.net/cgi-bin/formmail.pl">
```

The preceding line invokes the CGI script, `formmail.pl`, written in Perl and residing on the Web server in the cgi-bin directory.

Listing 20.3. HTML sample using CGI for ordering software.

```
<html>
<head>
<title>Order Desk

</title>
</head>
<BODY background="wrbgrnd6.gif"
bgproperties="fixed">
<center>
<h1>   Order Desk <a href="ita.html">
<img border=0 align="middle" src="itlogo2f.gif" alt="RK Software logo"></a>
<img src="amex.gif"> <img src="mastercd.gif">  <img src="visacard.gif">
</h1>
```

20

CGI AND
VBSCRIPT

continues

Listing 20.3. continued

```
<br><a href="order.html"><img src="ordpgbu7.gif" align="middle"
alt="Go to DOWNLOADABLES Order Form" border=0></a> .
<a href="customer_service.html"><img src="custsbut.gif"
border=0 align="middle" alt="Customer Service / FAQ">
</a>
</center>
<hr>
<br><b>USE OF THIS FORM</B>
<br>
<br>
This page is for ordering software on <b>diskettes and CD-ROM</b>.

<br>
<br>Click <a href="order.html">HERE</a> to go to a page where
you can order software and <b>forms</b> which you can <b>download</b>,
including a truncated version of <a href="abc_soft.html">ABC Software</a> for
Windows ("Personal Edition").
<br>
<br>Order on-line using this form or email your responses to this form to XYZ
Company at <a href="mailto:xyz@rksoftware.com">xyz@rksoftware.com</a> or
call (800)555-5555 or +1(123)876-9876 or fax to (123)876-9876.<r>

<br><b>*** A 10% restocking charge will be applied to all returns
***</b>
<br>
<br>Please add shipping charges where indicated. We look forward to serving you.
<hr>
You can also order by mail with a check or money order. Make sure to include
shipping/handling charges, as shown below, in US dollars to:<br><br>RK Software,
Inc.

<br>555 Anywhere St.
<br>Beautyville FL 32256 USA
<hr>

<FORM method=POST  ACTION="http://www.rksoft.net/cgi-bin/formmail.pl">

<INPUT TYPE="hidden" NAME="recipient" VALUE="xyz@rksoftware.com">

<INPUT TYPE="hidden" NAME="Subject" VALUE="Software Order">

<pre><b>Select one</b> (required): <INPUT TYPE="radio" NAME="card_type"
VALUE="VISA" CHECKED>VISA <INPUT TYPE="radio" NAME="card_type"
VALUE="MC" >MasterCard <INPUT TYPE="radio" NAME="card_type"
VALUE="AMEX" >American Express</pre>

</menu>

<PRE><b>Credit Card Number</b> (required):
<INPUT TYPE="text" NAME="Credit_Card_Number" SIZE=25>
<b>Expiration date</b> (required):
<INPUT TYPE="text" NAME="Expiration" SIZE=5>

<b>Shipping address</b>:

    <b>Ship To Name</b>
(required):                     <INPUT TYPE="text" NAME="Ship_To_Name" SIZE=40>
```

```
        <b>Company Name</b>:                                <INPUT TYPE="text"
NAME="Company_Name" SIZE=40>
        <b>Street Address </b> (required):
<INPUT TYPE="text" NAME="Ship_To_Addr_(line_1)" SIZE=40>

FedEx will not deliver to U.S. Post Office Box
        <b>Ship To Address (line 2)</b>:                    <INPUT TYPE="text"
NAME="Ship_To_Addr_(line_2)" SIZE=40>
        <b>Ship To City</b> (required):                     <INPUT TYPE="text"
NAME="Ship_To_City" SIZE=40>
        <b>Ship To State/Province</b> (required):           <INPUT TYPE="text"
NAME="Ship_To_State/Province" SIZE=12>
        <b>Ship To Zip/Postal Code</b> (required):          <INPUT TYPE="text"
NAME="Ship_To_Zip/Postal_Code" SIZE=10>
        <b>Ship To Country</b> (required):                  <INPUT TYPE="text"
NAME="Ship_To_Country" SIZE=15>
        <b>Telephone number</b> (required):                 <INPUT TYPE="text"
NAME="Telephone" SIZE=13>
        <b>Fax number</b>:                                  <INPUT TYPE="text" NAME="fax"
SIZE=13>
        <b>E-mail address</b>:                              <INPUT TYPE="text" NAME=
                                                         ➥"e-mail" SIZE=25>
<br><b>Please enter the billing address of your credit card, if different from the
shipping address.</b>
<b>(Please enter your name AS IT APPEARs ON YOUR CREDIT CARD)</b>
        <b>Name:</b>
<INPUT TYPE="text" NAME="Name" SIZE=40>
        <b>Address (line 1):</b>
<INPUT TYPE="text" NAME="Address_(line_1)" SIZE=40>
        <b>Address (line 2):
</b>            <INPUT TYPE="text" NAME="Address_(line_2)" SIZE=40>

<b>City:</b>
<INPUT TYPE="text" NAME="City_or_town" SIZE=40>
        <b>State or Province:</b>
<INPUT TYPE="text" NAME="State_or_Province" SIZE=12>
        <b>Zip/Postal Code:</b>
<INPUT TYPE="text" NAME="Zip/Postal_Code:" SIZE=10>
        <b>Country:</b>
<INPUT TYPE="text" NAME="Country" SIZE=15>
</PRE>
        <p>
        </menu>

<p>Please indicate the program(s) you wish to order by checking them off:<br>
        <p>

<b> <INPUT TYPE="checkbox" NAME="programs_ordered" VALUE="My Software Lite
CD-ROM- $99"><a href="my_soft.html">My Software Lite</a> v.2.0 for Windows CD-ROM -
- $99 <br>
</b>--> For additional licences at the same location or on a network please call,
write or fax our office. <br>    --><i> My Software Lite </i> comes with a 60-day
return guarantee. A 10% restocking fee applies <br>    --> to all returns.
Shipping & handling charges are not refundable. <br><br>
<b>
```

continues

Listing 20.3. continued

```
<INPUT TYPE="checkbox" NAME="programs_ordered" VALUE="My Software Pro -
- $149"><a href="my_softpro.html"> My Software Pro </a>
v. 2.0 for Windows -diskettes - - - - - $149</b>

<br>    --><i>
My Software Pro </i> comes with a 30-day return guarantee. A 10% restocking fee
applies <br>    --> to all returns. Shipping & handling charges are not refundable.
<br>    -->
You can also order a <b> downloadable</b>, truncated version of My Software Pro,
called <br>    --> <i> My Software Pro <b>Personal Edition</b></i> for <b> only $69
(non-refundable) <a href="order.html">
¦HERE¦</a></b><br><br>

<br><br>
<hr>
<b><i><u>Shipping and Handling Charges:
</u></i></b>
<br><i>My Software Lite</i> and <i>My Software Pro</i> are shipped by <b>Federal
Express courier</b>. Other products "best way".<br><br>

Add <b>$12</b> for delivery of <i>My Software Lite</i> or <i>My Software Pro</i>
within the U.S. or <b>$25</b> to Mexico and Canada, <b>$45 - $75</b> outside N.
America, depending on location, except Demo and where otherwise indicated.

<br><br>
Overseas demo shipment costs $5 (total $10). <br>

<p><hr>How did you come upon our home page, or who referred you here? Any comments
or questions?<br>

<TEXTAREA name="Referred_by" rows=3 cols=60></TEXTAREA>

<p>
<hr>Thank you for your order!
    <p><INPUT
TYPE="hidden" NAME="WebFormID" VALUE="2">
    <p>Click here to <INPUT TYPE="submit" VALUE="Send Your Order Now">
.................... or <INPUT TYPE="reset" VALUE="Clear"> the form and start over.
</FORM>
<p>

<hr>

Return to <a href="index.html"><img src="central3.gif" alt="RK Software logo">RK
Software Home Page</a>

<hr><FONT SIZE=-2>(C)1996
RK Software.</FONT>
</body>
You are visitor <img src="/cgi-bin/Count.cgi?ft=3&dd=C&frgb=0;0;0¦df=rksoft-
index.dat" align=absmiddl> since 1-Dec-1995
</html>
```

Listing 20.4 shows the results obtained by using a CGI script.

Listing 20.4. Results obtained by using a CGI script.

```
Subject: Form posted from AIR Mosaic
Content-type: application/x-www-form-urlencoded
Content-length: 567
X-Mailer: AIR Mosaic (16-bit) version 1.00.198.07
WebFormID=2
Referred_by=
programs_ordered=My Software Lite CD-ROM
Country=
Zip/Postal_Code:=
State_or_Province=
City_or_town=
Address_(line_2)=
Address_(line_1)=
Name=
email=
fax=
Telephone=
Ship_To_Country=USA
Ship_To_Zip/Postal_Code=45632
Ship_To_State/Province=FL
Ship_To_City=Bonnesville
Ship_To_Addr_(line_2)=
Ship_To_Addr_(line_1)=456 Whatever Street
Company_Name=XYZ Corporation
Ship_To_Name=XYZ Corporation
Expiration=9/99
Credit_Card_Number=1234567890123456
card_type=VISA
Subject=Software Order
recipient=xyz@rksoftware.com
```

This result appears much more readable! The CGI script included in Listing 20.4 processes the data received from the Web form and e-mails it to you in a meaningful form. You receive the customer order as simple ASCII text that is easily readable.

CGI scripting performs this kind of task and much more. CGI scripts help connect your Web site to a relational database, which enables visitors and customers to easily browse and search your product catalog. Airlines can set up sites that let their customers inquire about flight schedules and make reservations online. Banks can set up Web sites that enable their customers to check balances and make transfers. Libraries can set up sites that enable readers to search for books and magazines. A CGI program can send data back to the browser, making the communication a two-way traffic.

CGI is not a programming language. It represents a simple communication protocol that establishes the communication layer between the server and the server-side applications. Figure 20.2 shows the architecture of a CGI-based Web application.

20

**CGI AND
VBSCRIPT**

A CGI program is nothing but a simple application that accepts input, processes it, and sends the resulting output to its appropriate destination. Therefore, you can use any standard programming or scripting language that supports input/output processing to write your CGI programs. Potential candidates include C/C++, Visual Basic, Perl, or FORTRAN. If you use C/C++ or Visual Basic, you create a *CGI program*. A CGI program is an executable, similar to the executables you create for your desktop client/server applications. If you use a scripting language such as Perl or AppleScript, you create a *CGI script*. You will find it easier to create and maintain a script. Any changes made to a program must undergo the compile, link, and build process before the program can be executed. Whether you choose to create a program or script depends on the tool you plan to use. The choice of tool depends on your familiarity with the tool and its programming syntax and structure. If you programmed with C/C++ all your life, you may feel better using C/C++ to write your CGI programs. In fact, you may be able to reuse your library of C/C++ routines for some of your CGI programs. On the other hand, if you are an avid Visual Basic developer, you probably want to continue using it to write your CGI programs.

CGI programs reside on the server. They benefit from faster and better processing power of the server. The more powerful the server, the better execution and response time you get from your CGI programs. At the same time, you should pay special attention when writing your CGI program code. The code should be efficient and fast. In the preceding example, if the CGI program takes a long time to convert the order form data into simple ASCII, you would get all your e-mail notifications late. Your ability to process the orders on a timely basis would suffer. The standard programming rules to write clean, modular, and efficient code also apply to CGI programming.

CGI Specification

The CGI specification came from Rob McCool of Netscape Communications. At the moment, the specification is under the supervision of the World Wide Web Consortium (W3C—http://www.w3.org).

The CGI specification enables you to expand the capabilities of your server. It serves as a gateway between the Web server and other server processes including databases.

NOTE

Other server APIs exist in the marketplace in addition to the CGI API. These include Netscape's NSAPI (Netscape Server Application Programming Interface) and Microsoft's ISAPI (Internet Server Application Programming Interface).

The Web server captures the HTML form data into environment variables. A CGI script reads the environment variables, processes the data, and sends the response back to the browser. The form data is received as a set of name-value pairs. These pairs are separated by the & sign. The name and value tags are separated by the = sign. Because each `name=value` pair is URL encoded, the following conversion must occur:

1. Convert all + characters to spaces.
2. Convert all `%xx` sequences to the single character whose ASCII value is xx in hexadecimal form.

The form data gets stored in the environment variable `QUERY_STRING` if the `GET` method is used in the `FORM` tag for submission. If the `POST` method is used in the `FORM` tag for submission, the form data is not stored in any environment variables. You get it from `STDIN`. Because the server does not send an `EOF` at the end of the data, use the environment variable `CONTENT_LENGTH` to determine the number of bytes to be read. The next section, "CGI Environment Variables," outlines the different variables available for storing and processing data.

A number of scripts exist on the World Wide Web that do the preceding conversion. These scripts come in a number of different languages, including the Bourne Shell, C, Perl, Perl5, TCL, and many more.

You can send different types of data back to the browser including HTML, GIF, and other MIME Content-Types. For example, to send HTML data, use the Content-Type of `text/html`. To send a GIF image, use the Content-Type of `image/gif`.

The Win-CGI standard is a CGI standard supported by some Windows-based Web servers.

> **NOTE**
>
> In the Win-CGI standard, the data gets stored in INI files instead of environment variables. The use of INI files is widespread and very common on the Windows platform.

If you write CGI programs (executables, for example), the executables usually appear in the `\cgi-bin\` directory on the server and the source code is stored in the `\cgi-src\` directory. Security measures must exist to control access to both these directories.

If you write CGI scripts, they usually get stored in the `\cgi-bin\` directory. Because the script is its own source, you don't need to store anything in the `\cgi-src\` directory. Again, security measures must exist to control access to the `\cgi-bin\` directory—especially in this case, because the script is the source code itself.

CGI Environment Variables

The following CGI environment variables are set for all requests:

- GATEWAY_INTERFACE: The revision of the CGI specification to which this server complies.
- SERVER_NAME: The server's host name, DNS alias, or IP address as it appears in self-referencing URLs.
- SERVER_SOFTWARE: The name and version of the information server software answering the request and running the gateway. Format: *name/version.*

The following environment variables are specific to the request being fulfilled by the gateway program:

- AUTH_TYPE: If the server supports user authentication and the script is protected, this is the protocol-specific authentication method used to validate the user.
- CONTENT_TYPE: For queries which have attached information, such as HTTP POST and PUT, this is the content type of the data.
- CONTENT_LENGTH: The length of the said content as given by the client. In addition to this, the header lines received from the client, if any, are placed into the environment with the prefix HTTP_ followed by the header name. Any - characters in the header name get changed to characters. The server may exclude any headers which it has already processed, such as Authorization, Content-Type, and Content-length. If necessary, the server may choose to exclude any or all of these headers if including them would exceed any system environment limits.

  An example of this is the HTTP_ACCEPT variable, which was defined in CGI/1.0. Another example is the header User-agent.
- HTTP_ACCEPT: The MIME types that the client will accept, as given by HTTP headers. Other protocols might need to get this information from elsewhere. Each item in this list should be separated by commas as per the HTTP spec. Format: *type/subtype, type/subtype.*
- HTTP_USER_AGENT: The browser the client uses to send the request. General format: *software/version library/version.*
- PATH_INFO: The extra path information as specified by the client. Scripts can be accessed by their virtual pathname, followed by extra information at the end of this path. The extra information is sent as PATH_INFO. The server should decode this information if it comes from a URL before it is passed to the CGI script.
- PATH_TRANSLATED: The server provides a translated version of PATH_INFO, which takes the path and does any virtual-to-physical mapping to it.

- QUERY_STRING: The information following the ? that referenced this script. The query information should not be decoded in any fashion. This variable should always be set when query information exists, regardless of command-line decoding.

- REMOTE_ADDR: The IP address of the remote host making the request.

- REMOTE_HOST: The host name making the request. If the server does not have this information, it should set REMOTE_ADDR and not set this variable.

- REMOTE_IDENT: If the HTTP server supports RFC 931 identification, this variable is set to the remote user name retrieved from the server. Usage of this variable should be limited to logging only.

- REQUEST_METHOD: The method with which the request was made. For HTTP, the request methods are GET, HEAD, POST, and so on.

- REMOTE_USER: If the server supports user authentication and the script is protected, this is the user name that has been authenticated.

- SCRIPT_NAME: A virtual path to the script being executed; used for self-referencing URLs.

- SERVER_PROTOCOL: The name and revision of the information protocol this request came in with.

- SERVER_PORT: The port number to which the request was sent.

Architecture of a CGI Application

In order to pass data about the information request from the server to the script, the server uses command-line arguments, as well as environment variables. These environment variables get set when the server executes the gateway program.

Figure 20.2 describes the World Wide Web architecture of which CGI is one part. The Web browser is the client and it can interact with other applications such as Microsoft Word, Microsoft Excel, and Microsoft PowerPoint, depending on the nature of the application. The client connects to the Web server via the network. Several applications can reside on the server. The CGI interface acts as the gateway between the Web server and the server-side processes. One of the server-side processes could be a relational database. Although CGI acts as a gateway between any type of Web server and server-side applications, it has been more commonly implemented with the HTTPd server.

The client browser invokes the CGI script and waits until the CGI script completes its process. Thus, the CGI script must execute fast enough to have no perceived delay in the response time.

The drawback of using CGI is that every time a CGI script is invoked, the Web server spawns a new process. This setup becomes a problem when a given Web site gets frequently accessed by several users. It results in the Web server spawning a plethora of processes.

FIGURE 20.2.

Architecture of a CGI application.

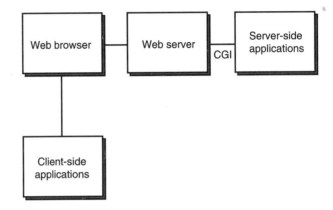

In the previous example, the CGI script processes the form order and notifies the company about receiving a customer order. You can extend the script further to dial into a credit card bureau and check the validity of the credit card number provided by the customer. The script can notify the customer about the acceptance or denial of the order. If the order gets accepted, the customer receives an order reference number. If the order is not accepted, the denial reasons are indicated.

CGI Versus VBScript

Certain tasks exist that could be easily performed on the client side with VBScript, thus avoiding the use of CGI programs. For example, processing mouse clicks and validating user input, come to mind. Consider the example of validating user input on the client side itself before the data goes to the server. Validating user input before it goes to the server represents good programming practice because the server's processing power can be better utilized for other important tasks.

Not everything can be implemented using VBScript. In some cases, you still need to consider CGI as a possible option for your application. For example, if your application needs to communicate with a back-end database, CGI provides one way to implement it, whereas VBScript doesn't work for such tasks. Whether you use VBScript or CGI, or both, depends on the nature of your application, as well as your familiarity with VBScript and CGI.

NOTE

VBScript programming is much simpler than CGI programming. If this represents your first foray into Web programming using CGI, expect a significant learning curve using and experimenting with CGI. On the other hand, VBScript coding is simpler because of the BASIC language syntax it follows.

Examples

This section reviews and analyzes a VBScript example downloaded from the Web site `http://www.microsoft.com/vbscript`. Figure 20.3 shows a simple Web page created by the HTML code included in the file `msftd.html` on the companion CD-ROM. This HTML displays an order form that enables you to place orders for flowers. You specify the occasion and enter the name and address where the flowers should be sent.

FIGURE 20.3.

Ordering flowers Web page created using HTML and VBScript.

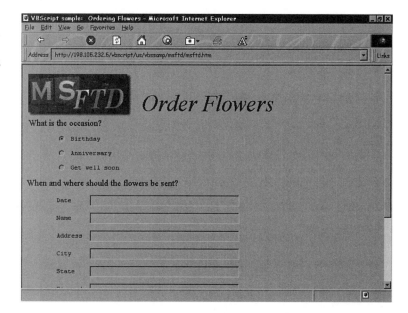

Look at the code part by part. Listing 20.5 represents all the HTML code used to set up the form. Three radio buttons are displayed so the user can select Birthday (default), Anniversary, or Get well soon. These buttons are displayed using the `<Input Type>` tag. This part of the code remains the same no matter whether you use CGI or VBScript.

Next, you add the data-entry fields for entering name and address of the destination. The `<Input>` tag is used to add these fields. Three buttons—Submit, Clear, and Init—are added at the bottom. The Submit button sends the order. The Clear button clears the name and address fields. The Init button initializes the data-entry fields.

If you use CGI scripts to process user input and mouse clicks, you would include reference to those scripts in your HTML code. For example, the Submit button would include a reference to a CGI script residing on the server. This script is invoked when the user clicks the Submit button. The mouse click gets processed on the server and the results are transmitted back to the browser. This process becomes expensive because every such event would be processed on the server. It also increases network traffic and loads the server with trivial tasks that could easily be processed on the client side. Consequently, you have a very inefficient use of the server and its processing power.

Listing 20.5. HTML code for setting up the form for ordering flowers.

```
<HEAD><TITLE>VBScript sample:  Ordering Flowers</TITLE></HEAD>
<BODY>

<TABLE  WIDTH="80%">
<TR VALIGN=bottom>
<TD WIDTH="40%"><IMG SRC="/vbscript/us/vbssamp/msftd/msftd.gif" ALIGN=center></TD>
<TD WIDTH="60%"><FONT SIZE=12><I>Order Flowers</I></FONT></TD>
</TR>
</TABLE>

<FONT FACE="Times New Roman" SIZE=4>What is the occasion?</FONT><BR>
<PRE>
<INPUT TYPE=RADIO NAME=OptOccasion CHECKED> Birthday

<INPUT TYPE=RADIO NAME=OptOccasion> Anniversary

<INPUT TYPE=RADIO NAME=OptOccasion> Get well soon
</PRE>

<FONT FACE="Times New Roman" SIZE=4>When and where should the flowers be sent?
</FONT><BR>
<PRE>
Date       <INPUT NAME=TxtDate   SIZE=60>

Name       <INPUT NAME=TxtName   SIZE=60>

Address   <INPUT NAME=TxtAddress SIZE=60>

City       <INPUT NAME=TxtCity SIZE=60>

State      <INPUT NAME=TxtState SIZE=60>

Zip code <INPUT NAME=TxtZip SIZE=60>

<INPUT TYPE=BUTTON VALUE="Submit" NAME="BtnSubmit">  <INPUT TYPE=BUTTON
VALUE="Clear" NAME="BtnClear">  <INPUT TYPE=BUTTON VALUE="Init" NAME="BtnInit"><BR>
</PRE>
```

Listing 20.6 shows the VBScript code used to process the data entered by the user. This code also processes the mouse click events when the user clicks the Submit, Clear, or Init buttons. Prior to JavaScript and VBScript, such processing would occur on the server using CGI programs and scripts. VBScript extends the HTML code and validates user input before it is sent to the server. This setup reduces network traffic, decreases server load, and improves the overall performance of your Web page.

Two variants and six procedures get defined: strMsgBoxTitle and bValidOrder and Window_OnLoad, BtnInit_OnClick, BtnSubmit_OnClick, ValidateDeliveryDate, CheckSpecified, and BtnClear_OnClick.

The subroutine Window_OnLoad gets executed when the Web page window is first loaded by the browser. It assigns the value MSFID to the variant strMsgBoxTitle. The variant StrMsgBoxTitle is assigned a string value; therefore, it is now a string variable. The strMsgBoxTitle is used to display the title for the message box. Next the subroutine Window_OnLoad calls the BtnInit_OnClick procedure. This procedure initializes the data-entry fields.

The procedure BtnInit_OnClick initializes the data-entry fields. It is executed when the Web page window is first loaded. It also gets executed when the user clicks the Init button.

The procedure BtnSubmit_OnClick gets executed when the user clicks the Submit button. It checks to make sure if the data entered is valid. If it is valid, the variable bValidOrder is initialized to true at the beginning of this procedure and retains its initialized value. If bValidOrder is true, the order gets sent. If the data entered is invalid, bValidOrder is set to false and the control is returned to the user on the Web page.

The procedure ValidDeliveryDate determines whether the value specified in the date field is valid.

The procedure CheckSpecified is actually called by the BtnSubmit_OnClick procedure. It determines whether the data entered in name and address fields is valid.

The procedure BtnClear_OnClick is executed when the user clicks the Clear button. It clears the data-entry fields.

Listing 20.6. VBScript code for processing mouse clicks and user input.

```
<SCRIPT LANGUAGE="VBScript">
<!--
Option Explicit

Dim strMsgBoxTitle
Dim bValidOrder

Sub Window_OnLoad
    strMsgBoxTitle = "MSFTD"
    Call BtnInit_OnClick
End Sub

Sub BtnInit_OnClick
    TxtName.Value = "Joe Smith"
    TxtAddress.Value = "1 Main Street"
    TxtCity.Value = "Springfield"
    TxtState.Value = "Washington"
    TxtZip.Value = "12345"
    TxtDate.Value = Date + 3
End Sub
```

20

CGI AND
VBSCRIPT

continues

Listing 20.6. continued

```
Sub BtnSubmit_OnClick
    bValidOrder = True
    Call CheckSpecified(txtName.Value, "Please specify a name.")
    Call CheckSpecified(txtAddress.Value, "Please specify an address.")
    Call CheckSpecified(txtCity.Value, "Please specify a city.")
    Call CheckSpecified(txtState.Value, "Please specify a state.")
    Call CheckSpecified(txtZip.Value, "Please specify a zip code.")
    Call CheckSpecified(txtDate.Value, "Please specify a date.")
    Call ValidateDeliveryDate
    If bValidOrder Then
        MsgBox "Thank you for your order!", 0, strMsgBoxTitle

        ' TODO:  Actually send the order.
    End If
End Sub

Sub ValidateDeliveryDate
    Dim SoonestWeCanDeliver
    Dim RequestedDate

    If Not bValidOrder Then Exit Sub

    SoonestWeCanDeliver = Date + 2
    RequestedDate = CDate(TxtDate.Value)
    If RequestedDate < SoonestWeCanDeliver Then
        bValidOrder = False
        MsgBox "Not even we can deliver that fast!", 0, strMsgBoxTitle
    End If
End Sub

Sub CheckSpecified(ByVal strFieldValue, ByVal strMsg)
    If strFieldValue = "" And bValidOrder Then
        MsgBox strMsg, 0, strMsgBoxTitle
        bValidOrder = False
    End If
End Sub

Sub BtnClear_OnClick
    TxtName.Value = ""
    TxtAddress.Value = ""
    TxtCity.Value = ""
    TxtState.Value = ""
    TxtZip.Value = ""
    TxtDate.Value = ""
End Sub

-->
</SCRIPT>
```

The remaining part of the code is again all HTML. It remains the same no matter whether you use CGI or VBScript. In this example, all the VBScript code is encapsulated between the `<SCRIPT>` and `</SCRIPT>` tags. The entire code resides in a single location within the body of the HTML code, making the code modular and easy to locate. The VBScript code is listed in the `<BODY>` section of the HTML code.

Relevant Web Sites

Table 20.1 lists few Web sites for more information on CGI and VBScript. Plenty of resources and examples exist on the Internet.

Table 20.1. Relevant Web sites.

Site Name	Site URL
World Wide Web Consortium	`http://www.w3.org`
Perl CGI scripts for Internet Retailers	`http://phoenixrise.com/CCC/cindex.html`
VBScript	`http://www.microsoft.com/vbscript`
VBScript links	`http://www.microsoft.com/vbscript/us/vbsmain/vbslinks.htm`

Review

CGI represents a simple protocol of communication between the Web forms and your programs that reside on the Web server. A CGI script or program gets its input from the Web forms, processes it, and sends the results back to your browser. CGI is *not* a programming language; it is a script or a program that resides on the server. You can create a CGI script or program using almost any programming language that supports standard input and output processing. For example, you can use C/C++, Visual Basic, Perl, or FORTRAN to write your CGI programs. The best language to use is the one that you feel familiar with and comfortable using. Whatever you choose, make sure your CGI programs process data efficiently and respond quickly. Remember, CGI programs get their input from the Web forms, and the user waits for the response while the data is being processed. Therefore, the CGI programs need to respond quickly.

You have two important decisions to make about CGI early on for your project. First, decide whether your project demands the use of CGI. Then, you have to decide how to protect the CGI programs. Because a CGI program is invoked as a result of user action through the browser, you need to undertake necessary security precautions. The CGI programs should be under direct control of the Webmaster only and all others should have only *execute* rights.

VBScript programming is simpler than CGI programming. This chapter introduced CGI and explained the different CGI environment variables. It compared CGI with VBScript and identified how VBScript can be used to handle some of the processing on the client side, thus eliminating or reducing the need for CGI scripts and reducing the load on the network and server. Data communication in a CGI-based web architecture was also discussed. This chapter also included examples of VBScript code for processing mouse clicks and user input. There is plenty of resources and examples available on the Net. A list of few relevant and useful web sites is included in this chapter. Be sure to visit the Microsoft VBScript site regularly to keep abreast of the latest on Microsoft Internet Explorer and VBScript. VBScript is the new kid on the block and it is expected to grow and evolve over time.

If you use CGI scripts to process user input and mouse clicks, you load the server with many trivial tasks that could very easily be handled on the client side. You also increase network traffic. This setup creates an inefficient use of the server and its processing power. Using VBScript to handle such tasks reduces network traffic and server load.

Safety and Security

by Bill Schongar and Paul Lagasse

It's hard to protect yourself against every possible thing that could happen. To give ourselves a feeling of security, we surround ourselves with walls. Of course we have to get in and out, so we put doors in those walls. Because the doors become the weak link, we put locks on them. Now our wall is not as strong as the original wall, but it's more convenient, and we feel okay about it. But, we also feel a little claustrophobic, so we need some windows to get light inside. That puts more holes in the walls, albeit with a little glass standing between us and the outside world, but it's definitely no deterrent to someone who wants to get in. And we still feel secure? It's a sacrifice of security for convenience.

Dealing with computers, and most definitely dealing with the Internet, is a little like a house. You can be pretty certain that when you first get your computer set up it doesn't have anything nasty lurking in it. As you start opening up more connections to the outside world and bringing back things you've found, you're taking a chance. Is that chance worth it for the convenience you gain? Is there too much danger? Well, take a look.

VBScript and ActiveX are two recent entries into the exuberant chaos of the Internet, and as new visitors there's a lot that you might or might not know about their potential for causing trouble. We're now going to examine all the possible hazards you could be facing, and show you that although the potential for danger is there, a great deal of effort has been put into making VBScript and ActiveX as safe and secure as possible. You'll look at the following:

- Trust and the Internet
- VBScript's built-in safeguards
- Internet Component Download
- Authenticode
- Paranoia, self-defense, and reasonable risk

One thing to keep in mind while going through this chapter is that there's inherent danger in everything you do. There's always a chance something can be misused, that something can go wrong. But risks are normally weighed against benefits, and the same needs to hold true when dealing with VBScript and ActiveX. Much has been done to make both elements of Microsoft's Internet plans as safe as possible, but it's better for you to know all the possibilities so you can be prepared.

A Matter of Trust...

Who do you trust? Whether you're considering buying a used car, investing in some financial venture, or buying software, the decision ends up being a combination of a number of factors. What's the reputation of the person or group you're dealing with? What do you know about the product, service, or information you're getting? What's your gut instinct? There's a lot to consider.

The wide and often weird world of the Internet makes trust a more difficult commodity to come by. There's now a lot of distance between you and whomever you're dealing with. You might or might not have the benefit of knowing the reputations of the folks on the other end of the arrangement, or even if you're dealing with whom you think you are. Anonymous remailers, purloined passwords, and the inherently insecure nature of an unsecured public network are all just parts of the chances you're taking.

Don't think that you're alone, though. If you're on one end of the conversation, think about what's going on if there's another person like you on the other side. They feel they're trustworthy, but what do they know about you? How can they be sure that you're who you say you are? If you're writing any kind of software code for them, how can they be absolutely sure there's nothing nasty hidden in it? What about things such as unforeseen circumstances, like bugs in the code that weren't tested or encountered?

Can VBScript Security Hold Up?

Sounds ominous, but don't get your knickers in a twist just yet. At the time of this writing, there were no publicly known security holes, but the same was true of JavaScript and Java for a while, too. It stands to reason that somewhere, sometime, someone will discover a trick or a bug that manifests itself as a nasty possibility for security breach. They might or might not make it public, depending on if they're well-known security researchers at a university or someone with something slightly less ethical driving their hunt for such a "feature."

The software is continuously changing, as well. Not necessarily VBScript, but what's used to run it. The basic premise of VBScript is that with a few DLLs or some source code, some other application could run VBScript code. Depending on how someone else implements VBScript functionality, the security features of VBScript could end up being compromised, either due to errors, incompatibility, or just the need of the other application for more functionality. NCompass Labs was the first company to dare tread those waters by developing ScriptActive, a plug-in that allows VBScript to function in Netscape Navigator. While it's unlikely that any adverse interactions could happen in ScriptActive's use of VBScript, it's just an example that VBScript language and functions will find their way into a variety of operating systems and general environments. That leaves a lot of room for an open door.

If you've followed the plans of Microsoft and the other big industry players, you've also seen that one of the big pushes is to integrate the Internet and everyone's machines. Microsoft plans an integrated desktop, where you're browsing the Net and your hard drive at the same time. You can bet that will mean more built-in functions that could possibly be accessed by scripting languages. And that means more possibilities for dangerous situations. The hope is that new security technologies and the basic built-in safeguards of VBScript will make Net surfing safe for a long time yet to come. So far, it doesn't look too scary.

VBScript's Built-In Safeguards

Safety and security in VBScript would seem to be a dead-end topic. After all, didn't Microsoft say in all their original VBScript documentation that "all potentially unsafe operations have been removed from the language"? The following list shows some commonly used Visual Basic function categories that you won't find in VBScript.

File I/O (all of it)

DDE

Object Instantiation

Direct Database Access (DAO)

DLL execution

While certainly not an exhaustive summary, you can see that a lot was removed in the name of security. You can't create an object, you can't do real file input and output—what could possibly be potentially harmful or unsafe? Well, because you ask, take a look.

Safety in VBScript is a relative term. The good news is, you really can't purposefully do anything that will have a significant harmful effect on any user's system. That's because of the language limitations we just looked at in the previous list. If File I/O had been left in, or even some of the other inter-application communications processes, there would be a lot that you might need to worry about. However, it's still easily possible to annoy people. For example, we'll show you an obnoxious implementation of a Message Box. It would certainly be a way to discourage people with VBScript-enabled browsers from visiting your page, but other than that its actual practical use is pretty much nil. So don't try this at home, unless you really want to inconvenience yourself.

Listing 21.1. VBScript Inconvenience Script—What not to do in VBScript.

```
 1: <script language="vbscript">
 2: <!--
 3: ' Don't run this in your browser!
 4: ' The purpose of this script is just to show how even
 5: ' basic "safe" functions in VBScript can cause
 6: ' problems...
 7: while (1=1)
 8: {
 9:     value = MsgBox("Yuck.", 1 + 16 + 4096)
10: }
11: -- >
12: </script>
```

If you had run the script in Listing 21.1, you would get a screen that looks similar to that shown in Figure 21.1, where a message box pops up on the screen with the message and style that had been selected with the MsgBox function. The problem here is that this function is in an endless loop; every time you click OK in the message box, another message box comes up. No problem; just switch pages and kill the task. Nice try, but one of the reasons this is so inconvenient is that you can't do that.

The parameters on the end of the MsgBox function do more than just control the appearance, they include a parameter (the 4096 part of the MsgBox statement, to be specific) that makes the Message Box System-Modal. For those of you who haven't done much in the realm of Windows programming, this means that everything else on the system stops until this message box is cleared. Under Windows 95, you're not completely stuck—you can go into your other applications and save files, open files, and go about your business as normal, but that annoying message box will still remain on top of your other tasks. Because it's in an infinite loop, it doesn't stop with just one message box, which means your system is somewhat stuck until you very explicitly tell it to stop.

This is just an annoyance example, one that doesn't do anything to your system that's permanent or really disruptive (other than tying up your computer and possibly causing you to reboot, of course), but demonstrates unsafe code. It does something that isn't harmful, but doesn't function as intended, and was probably never tested if it's part of a larger script. Remember, "safety" is a relative term— being "safe" to run a piece of code might mean complete security to one person, and bug-free code to another.

As a general rule, though, VBScript by itself can't do any significant damage. Microsoft was very careful to remove potentially unsafe elements, and without those elements in place the VBScript code is trapped within the confines of the browser. It's certainly possible that new additions to the browser could change that, or that a bug or security hole could open up, but that possibility is about as small as it can reasonably be expected to be.

Flirting with Danger—ActiveX Components

Microsoft is pushing ActiveX components like a bulldozer moves dirt and small rocks: relentless and unstoppable. This created an immediate response from vendors of OLE-capable controls that had previously been developed for C++ and Visual Basic use. The number of ActiveX controls on the market and in development just exploded over a short period of time. You already know the reason—the capability to integrate ActiveX components with VBScript adds a lot of possibilities to the list of what can be done with an otherwise limited scripting environment. They open almost every door that was closed by limiting VBScript operations in the first place. Don't have File I/O? Make use of an ActiveX component. Can't tell the system to do things? You got it…ActiveX to the rescue.

With this proliferation of controls on Web pages, more and more sites will be adding functional controls to their internal and external sites. From a functionality standpoint, having this cornucopia of controls is great, but from a security standpoint, the same proliferation is fright-ening. You're talking about legions of controls that are automatically downloaded onto your system, installed, configured, and there for anyone to use in their VBScript code. All any VBScript author needs to do is look for the unique CLASSID number that corresponds to the object, and hey, presto! They now have instant access to that control within their VBScript code, or through another ActiveX control. With so many controls popping up at once, it's hard to believe that no one will find bugs or even as-designed features, which let someone get away with something that you might not want them to.

Imagine for a moment that you want to prevent someone from doing something. Isolating them will normally make some progress on that front because they can only affect their immediate surroundings. That is, unless you provide them with a method of communicating to someone or something outside their isolation. Give someone a phone and a capable outside accomplice that they call, and all you've done is prevented the isolated person from doing the dirty work themselves. The same holds true for the seemingly incarcerated VBScript and its ActiveX cohorts. If someone can find a way to get a control of theirs on your system, or knows of a legitimate control that can be coerced into doing something that suits their purposes, you could be in trouble.

Looking at the basic array of ActiveX controls, you might scoff at first. What can someone do, toss an extra button on your browser screen? Shove unwanted streaming video at you? Spawn unwanted URLs in new windows? Hmm, doesn't sound too terribly frightening, does it? Be-fore you doze off into peaceful dreams of the safe world VBScript lives in, you might want to try looking under the bed.

Authentic Controls—Friend or Foe?

In the race to inspire confidence in online consumers, the software industry constantly looks for the best way to assure people that what they're getting hold of is authentic and safe. People like going into a store and knowing they're not buying some cheap copy of something when they're paying the price for the original, and they like feeling that they can trust the vendor of the software. But how do you assure people over the Internet?

You start by giving them something reasonably tangible. The Internet is an anonymous place, where people can pretend they're anyone they want, because you can't see them. If you need to convince consumers that your software is safe, you first need to convince them that you're who you say you are. The tangible proof that someone can get when an ActiveX control comes into play arrives in the form of an authentication certificate. While it's just one item to the user, there's a lot more behind this certificate than just one step.

Internet Component Download

The first step that precedes the certificate is Internet Component Download. Unlike the traditional plug-ins, but like Java applications, ActiveX components can be automatically downloaded, installed, configured, and run on an end-user's machine, all automatically. The HTML `<OBJECT>` tag that outlines what the ActiveX control is, as well as what parameters the object has, includes support for specifying a location through a `CODEBASE` parameter. If the unique class ID (CLSID)of the object isn't found on the user's system, the browser goes out to the site specified in the `CODEBASE` parameter and downloads the required file or files.

When the component is downloaded, a few basic checks are made on the integrity of the file to ensure that it isn't immediately doing something it shouldn't, but it can't possibly test the component exhaustively. What Microsoft and other vendors would like to accomplish is giving end users the same sense of security and assurance that they have when buying a shrink-wrapped piece of software in a store. You know who it's from, you know what it's supposed to be, and you know who to yell at if it doesn't perform as expected. To make us all feel safe, components are secured using what's called Authenticode technology.

Authenticode

Knowing that you're getting what you asked for is where Authenticode kicks in. Part of the mechanism for downloading the ActiveX component seamlessly involves a basic security check on the thing that's being obtained. One of the best ways to promote security in these transactions is to have a piece of code digitally "signed" by the manufacturer, so you know it's reasonably authentic, and not just someone claiming to be IBM or Microsoft, or some modification of their code. Besides that, it can check the integrity of the download, making sure that the transfer didn't get corrupted along the way.

The hows and whys behind the general use of Authenticode are pretty simple. You create a piece of code, and then you tag it with a digital signature that contains information about the file, including a cryptographic checksum. A what? A Cryptographic checksum is basically a summary of the file itself, such as how big it is and some interior inherent data, which is then encoded and stored. When the file integrity is checked, the same information is gathered and encrypted again. If the two encrypted portions match, it's a pretty sure bet that the code hasn't been tampered with or corrupted during download.

But what if someone else tries to sign a name that's not theirs to a piece of code? Well, that's where a signing authority steps in.

Signing Authority

To prevent digital forgery, a signing authority is used in conjunction with the Authenticode process to ensure that the person or company signing the code is legitimate. The first signing authority entrusted with this task of keeping signatures intact is VeriSign, Inc. For a fee, they'll check your company out and provide a way for you to uniquely identify your products electronically, preventing tampering. What this buys you, as an established vendor, is the capability to provide a reasonable level of assurance to customers and visitors that you are who you say you are, the code is what you say it is, and someone else will vouch for you.

So, if you, as a software author, develop a component or a series of components, you'd prove to a Signing Authority that you are who you say you are. They might ask for a Dun and Bradstreet number, some tax information, or other documents, just to be certain. When they're convinced, they give you a unique digital stamp that you can use to encrypt your software. When you stamp your software this way, someone on the other end will see a certificate that contains the public information contained in that stamp—who your company is, what the software is, and who vouches for you. While all possibilities of forgery can't be avoided, the combination is pretty effective, and enough to inspire a reasonable level of confidence in erstwhile consumers. After all, that's the goal—you're downloading only "friendly" components that have been checked and that someone takes responsibility for.

They Do What They Were Meant To

Don't be fooled into thinking that ActiveX controls are harmless, even the ones that do what you think they do and come from people you can trust. Someone you trust could give you a knife set as a present, but if someone breaks into your house they could still use it against you. The danger isn't necessarily in the original source of the object in question, but any subsequent use of that object could potentially be by someone you don't trust.

As an example, imagine an ActiveX-based FTP control. Great for automated download pages, especially in intranets. You could branch your VBScript application to different files based on questionnaires, or any number of other choices, and process it in the background so users could continue to do other things on the page. While the control itself is extremely useful, imagine the possibilities for abuse. Someone could download any file they want to your system, possibly even bypassing prompts to check and see what you want to do with the file. Far worse, FTP is a two-way street—they could bundle and upload a variety of system files from your machine, or other random files that could be of use to them. If they were really devious, they could just replace a typical system file with a copy of their own, to capture passwords and other data.

Rogue Controls

Pretend, for a moment, that you're a computer whiz with a desire to experiment, and have temporarily misplaced any ethical qualms about doing weird things to other people's systems. Oh go on, we won't tell anybody about your dark side. From this new (hopefully) vantage point, ActiveX could be a big temptation to play with. You've got millions of people downloading software that they've never even heard of, often times without even realizing it. Sure, it's harder than making a virus or following a how-to guide for packet-based denial-of-service attacks, but, oh, the possibilities. And you were looking for a real challenge for your free time, anyway...so you decide to hack some ActiveX controls.

Threats from the Outside

There are a lot of highly skilled individuals out there who aren't pretending. They know code inside and out, backwards and forwards, and they could easily see mucking about with ActiveX and its associated security as a great thing to add to their resume. There are also distinct groups of them. Some are in it just for the challenge, not for the damage—to them it's not a question of malice or ethics, but something new and cool to figure out and understand. They might make a few controls that do things they shouldn't, but they'll probably give them to friends, or show them off. Another group might follow that path slightly further, being interested in just what they can do, and where that knowledge gets them. They'd probably build something to collect tidbits about you from your hard drive, send it back to them, and bounce you an anonymous e-mail saying they've done it.

Other groups end up with far more malicious intents—they might want to trash your hard drive, get financial data, or break into your corporate network to get things that will ruin your whole day. Some of it might be subtle, planted for later, and other things could be blatant, but for them the challenge isn't just to know how to do it, it's to do it, use it, and get away with it.

The popularity of ActiveX makes it too tempting a target to be ignored. No matter who does it first, or how they do it, someone will create controls that are designed to breach the security of your system. These "rogue" controls could take any form, but the most obvious ones have already been mentioned—system corruption, private information gathering, and stepping stones for further security breaches.

Can you defend against these kinds of people? Sure, don't download anything, ever. This is paranoid, fatalistic, but unfortunately, true. Insidious hostile controls, like those that serve a real purpose but have hostile code embedded deep within, will be the worst. While it inspires a sense of paranoia to think you have to question everyone, it's just part of the cost you pay for the convenience of the Internet.

Threats from Within

The worst possible case of rogue controls would be that of intentional tampering of a company's controls by a member of that company. This would be someone who could change the code, or switch it for something else entirely, and authenticate the new code. Because the trust in authenticode technology is geared more towards trusting a company, rather than an individual, dissent within the ranks hits the consumers through what they thought was a safe back door. As mentioned in the "Authentic Controls" section of this chapter, users might have already established that future; authenticated source code from a particular company or agency should not inform them of future component downloads. So, if someone tampers with what is already registered as a "friendly" product.

Another possibility would be the cracking of the authenticode scheme on either the signing end or the user end. Imagine what someone could do if they got hold of Microsoft's signing key—suddenly you're prompted to download the latest version of an Internet Explorer control, and the certificate looks perfectly valid, if you see it at all. This breach of the underlying security would cause a real break of faith in the trust that Authenticode and other digital signing technologies want to inspire in end users.

Defending Against Friendly Fire and Nasties

Preventing your system from these kinds of attacks is pretty tough to do all by yourself. Sure, you can disable the use of ActiveX controls, but that's the "stick your head in the sand" approach to safety, and won't move you into the next generation of functionality very quickly. Your real best defense is to put only those controls on your system that you need, and keep up with the latest versions of browsers and controls. This gives you the best chance to have the properly functioning versions of controls and the latest security measures available in your browser.

Be sure to take advantage of the security measures wherever possible. Don't disable them because they're annoying or inconvenient—they're built in for a reason. A common trap is to disable the certificate checking for other software packages from the same company or signing authority. Give yourself a fighting chance—let yourself know what people are shoving on your system.

Remember, though, that at the heart of the legitimate controls are people with safety and functionality as their primary goals. They're not out to mess your system up or give people a way to cause you problems. They want to give you functions that you want and need. It's in their best interest to give you a sense of confidence in what they produce and not let you be scared off by possible threats. This means you've got a lot of people behind the scenes working for your security and safety, both by improving the reliability of their own controls and security and by fending off attacks on the ActiveX security mechanisms by outside sources. It's like having your own personal Internet Police Force—and it's a good thing to have.

Paranoia, Self-Defense, and Reasonable Risk

Combining functionality and safety is a tough job. In Biotechnology and other fields, you often encounter the term Best Available Technology (BAT) when dealing with potential risks and their solutions. It means that a better solution may come along in the future, but if you're dealing with the issue right now, a better solution doesn't come to mind. VBScript and ActiveX take advantage of the Best Available Technology for protecting themselves and for protecting you. Like any security measures, there is always a way around them, but just like putting doors and windows in your house, you sacrifice complete security for convenience, aesthetics, and functionality.

Don't box yourself in without an opening into the functionality that VBScript and ActiveX provide. As a developer, you can't afford not to think about security, but you can't hope to have a 100% secure solution. If problems and security breaches occur, your duty to the end users is to protect them from potential problems that are within your control, and try to keep your use of controls reasonable, so as not to crowd their systems and possibly breach their defenses. As an end user, you need to act as a careful consumer. Don't let things onto your system that you question, but don't be afraid of every new thing that comes out. You can always disable Java, ActiveX, and VBScript in your browser if you're nervous, but for the benefits that you'll get by leaving them all enabled, it sure seems like a reasonable risk.

VBScript as a Component in Other Applications

by Bill Schonger and Paul Lagasse

CHAPTER 22

Browsers are great, but what if you want to take VBScript along with you to another application to add some scripting support? No problem, if you're a programmer at heart. ActiveX Scripting, which VBScript is a part of, is designed to allow a lot of mobility in the use of the code. Whether it's upgrading the code to Visual Basic for Applications or Visual Basic itself, or building your own program which interprets VBScript, you have a lot of options. In this chapter, we'll cover a variety of those options and how you can use them to your benefit, including some further details on ActiveX Scripting methods themselves. Topics covered include

- Porting VBScript to VBA and Visual Basic
- ActiveX Scripting Engine Requirements
- ActiveX Scripting Host Requirements
- VBScript Binary and Source Code Licensing
- Spruuids— Microsoft's Example of VBScript Hosting

Understanding what VBScript really is behind the scenes isn't tough, but going out and creating your own container to integrate VBScript is another matter entirely. It requires a pretty good familiarity with COM and OLE programming, which in and of themselves imply a lengthy history of Windows programming expertise. Rather than assuming you have all that background, we'll look at the general concepts behind ActiveX scripting engines and hosts, but we'll also be sure to provide enough specifics and references, in case you're on the advanced track and need the implementation specifics.

Porting VBScript to VBA and Visual Basic

Application development in VBScript can be a two-way street. Conversion utilities exist to take the extended functionality of VBA and Visual Basic applications and chop them down into ActiveX/VBScript hybrids, but it's just as easy to port your application up the evolutionary ladder. This isn't to say that you'll want to prototype your applications in VBScript and then move them up, but it makes a very attractive upgrade path available for developers or people who are introduced to Visual Basic by way of VBScript. After all, isn't attracting developers to Visual Basic syntax a big reason why Microsoft will put a lot of effort into making VBScript a standard? It just means that there will be more developers who won't want to move out of the syntax they learned and are comfortable with. Talk about an easy sell…

There are significant differences between VBScript, its older sibling VBA, and the parent Visual Basic language set. The most obvious is the increase in available features. For each step you move up the VB evolutionary chain, you gain a number of functions that were previously too insecure for use in one or the other of the language subsets. File Input and Output jumps out immediately as a powerful addition, but inter-process communications and general systems functions are also important.

A consideration to keep in mind when "moving up" your code is that you have more flexibility in performance, and a lot more to worry about with error checking. Variants are the primary data type in VBScript, but once you get into the bigger siblings, you have to worry about matching up data types and converting back and forth, to make sure you don't get any problems.

All About ActiveX Scripting

To give people the most flexibility in being able to run different scripts in different programs on different operating systems, Microsoft developed the ActiveX Scripting specification, of which VBScript is just one implementation of the idea. Consisting of two components, the scripting engine and the scripting host, ActiveX Scripting allows a lot of interchangability, both in what kind of script or programming language can be used and what applications can use it.

Script Engines

The component that actually interprets the scripting language is the script engine. Whether the language in question is VBScript, Perl, TCL/TK, or Joe Bob's Discount Script, an engine is specifically geared toward that one language and carries out whatever interpretive tasks are required in order for the script to be understood. In addition, it also has to be friendly enough to get along with applications that are instructing it to run.

Assuming for the moment that you're not too worried about languages other than VBScript, let's take a moment to look at just how the whole Scripting Engine thing works. At its root, a scripting engine is an OLE (object linking and embedding) control that supports the right combination of entry points, or "hooks," for other properly OLE-enabled ActiveX containers to talk to it and trade information about what's going on in the script. If either one is missing specific hooks, or doesn't adhere closely to the necessary standards, things are going to get messy real quick.

When you embed a script into an HTML page with the <SCRIPT> tag, what you're really doing is setting a flag for the browser to say "Oh geez, what do I do with this?". When the browser reaches that tag, it takes a quick look at the LANGUAGE parameter inside the <SCRIPT> tag, and determines whether it knows how to handle that particular language, either based on an OBJECT tag pointing the browser to a new interpreter, or if the browser's built-in table of languages says "Hey, we know that language, we can handle it." In the case of Internet Explorer 3.0, the languages that the browser can handle without questions are JavaScript (or JScript, as Microsoft likes to call it) and, of course, VBScript.

> **NOTE**
>
> If you were to build an engine for your own special scripting language, you could use an
> <OBJECT> tag to make sure that your special scripting engine was downloaded onto the
> user's system if it wasn't already there. This would require giving it a unique class ID
> (CLSID), just like any other ActiveX object, and hoping that the user trusts you enough to
> download the component just to run your script. You did say your scripting language was
> secure, didn't you?

Just like the plug-and-play architecture of Windows 95 and Macintosh systems, ActiveX scripting engines provide plug-and-play support for any language you'd care to dream up an interpreter for.

Scripting Engine OLE Interfaces

The innards of the scripting engines don't need to be too terribly complex—just enough to safely handle the language that will be interpreted, and to provide the basic hooks that are expected by the browser. If you've written an OLE COM object before, you're more than halfway there! To make sure you have the information you need to finish the other half, we'll take a look at what hooks, in this case OLE interfaces, are needed in the scripting engine itself. If you haven't written an OLE COM object before, or don't intend to soon, there's a significant amount of distance you'll need to go before tackling your first scripting engine, and you might want to skip over the next few paragraphs and jump right to Scripting Hosts.

The primary interface for a scripting engine is IActiveScript. This in turn provides the subsequent hooks for all information to be passed between a host and the internals of the engine in an orderly fashion. The header information for IActiveScript would be defined as shown in Listing 22.1, with each component serving a particular need.

Listing 22.1. Header information for IActiveScript.

```
 1: Interface IActiveScript : IUnknown
 2:  {
 3:   HRESULT SetScriptSite([in] IActiveScriptSite *pScriptSite);
 4:   HRESULT GetScriptSite([in] REFIID iid, [out] void **ppvScriptSite);
 5:   HRESULT SetScriptState([in] SCRIPTSTATE   ss);
 6:   HRESULT GetScriptState([out] SCRIPTSTATE *pss);
 7:   HRESULT Close();
 8:   HRESULT AddNamedItem([in] LPCOLESTR pstrName, [in] DWORD dwFlags);
 9:   HRESULT AddTypeLib([in] REFGUID guidTypeLib, [in] WORD wMaj, [in] WORD wMin,
        [in] DWORD dwFlags);
10:   HRESULT GetScriptDispatch([in] LPCOLESTR pstrItemName, [out] IDispatch
        **ppdisp);
11:   HRESULT GetCurrentScriptThreadID([out] SCRIPTTHREADID *pstid);
12:   HRESULT GetScriptThreadID([in] DWORD dwWin32ThreadID, [out] SCRIPTTHREADID
        *pstid);
```

```
13:    HRESULT GetScriptThreadState([in] SCRIPTTHREADID stid, [out]
       SCRIPTTHREADSTATE *psts);
14:    HRESULT InterruptScriptThread([in] SCRIPTTHREADID stid, [in] EXCEPINFO *pei,
       [in] DWORD dFlags);
15:    HRESULT Clone([out] IActiveScript **ppscript);
16:    };
```

NOTE

If you're familiar with header information and declarations, you'll notice that the interface that all functions are bound to, for both scripting engines and later on in scripting hosts, is the IUnknown interface. This is the heart of what defines an ActiveX control—the capability to accept and support the IUnknown interface so that future controls and functions have a generic entry point to assess information through.

THREADING AND SCRIPTING ENGINES

ActiveX Scripting engines are normally designed to be free-threading OLE COM objects, where methods contained in IActiveScript and all underlying interfaces can be called without marshalling. What in the world is marshalling? It's a special process for packaging and unpackaging parameters to allow a remote procedure call to happen. In essence, you have to manage synchronization and other processes by yourself, because you want the Scripting Engine to be as flexible as possible, without forcing more work on the Scripting Host. To do this with a little less pain and agony, two primary restrictions are placed on IActiveScriptSite's use within the engine: 1) The script site will never call itself through a thread it created, and 2) The script site will never be called from within a simple state control method for threads (like Clone()). What does all this buy you? A little more safety in dealing with threads, and more flexibility in the use of Scripting hosts.

The next big interface is IActiveScriptParse. It's not normally required, but if the scripting language is going to allow expression text to be evaluated, or dynamic pieces of scripting code to be added during runtime, it becomes mandatory. Listing 22.2 shows how the interface would be defined in your code.

Listing 22.2. Header information for IActiveScriptParse.

```
1: Interface IActiveScriptParse : IUnknown
2:    {
3:    HRESULT InitNew();
4:    HRESULT AddScriptlet(
```

continues

Listing 22.2. continued

```
 5:        LPCOLESTR  pstrDefaultName,
 6:        LPCOLESTR  pstrCode,
 7:        LPCOLESTR  pstrItemName,
 8:        LPCOLESTR  pstrSubItemName,
 9:        LPCOLESTR  pstrEventName,
10:        LPCOLESTR  pstrEndDelimiter,
11:        DWORD      dwFlags,
12:        BSTR       *pbstrName,
13:        EXCEPINFO  *pexcepinfo);
14:     HRESULT ParseScriptText(
15:        LPCOLESTR  pstrCode,
16:        LPCOLESTR  pstrItemName,
17:        IUnknown   *punkContext,
18:        LPCOLESTR  pstrEndDelimiter,
19:        DWORD      dwFlags,
20:        VARIANT    *pvarResult,
21:        EXCEPINFO  *pexcepinfo);
22:     };
```

> **NOTE**
>
> With the exception of BSTR, EXCEPINFO, and VARIANT, all parameters for
> IActiveScriptParse are passed into the function.

Last, but not least, is the scripting engine's persistence information, IPersist. This retains parameters, object ClassID data, and other incoming data so that it can be held and used by the engine and the script for whatever purpose that information was intended for. IPersist can actually come in three flavors: IPersistStorage, IPersistStream, and IPersistFile. The use of one type of IPersist interface over the other varies by situation. For example, if you were using a custom scripting engine, you could include a data= parameter to open a connection and bind the data to storage, making use of the IPersistStorage interface. It's all a matter of use, so you should be prepared for any of them.

Scripting Engine Programming Considerations

In "Communications Between Scripting Engines and Hosts," later in this chapter, we'll look at just how communications flow between scripting hosts and scripting engines. For the moment, though, there are some other important considerations to keep in mind if you're planning on taking the big leap and programming your own scripting engine.

First and foremost, think about threading. Your scripting engine will have a lot of work to do, and you can't consider it secure and robust if your execution threads are tripping over one another. That's terribly inconvenient. Since each scripting engine is a free-threaded OLE COM object, and the host doesn't help untangle the threads, you'll have to be careful to perform synchronization methods on your own, and properly.

Next, consider the language you're thinking of writing the engine for. If it's a company project and you have to build a proprietary language interpreter for your intranet, that's one situation. If, on the other hand, you really like some language and wish you could use it in your Web pages, that's another thing entirely. Remember, you're going to have to take into account all the possible security holes, what functions just can't be done (not that there will be too many of them, if you don't care about security), and who your target audience is. No one's really going to want to download a 1MB scripting engine just to look at your page and the whiz-bang things you can do with your own scripting language. Sure, it'd make a cool project for a computer science major or someone with a real desire to experiment, but it's not horrendously practical.

Languages that are in popular use but don't have scripting engines available yet are good targets for people trying to gain widespread financial or ego-boosting return on their investment of time. Perl and TCL/TK, at the time of writing, were the two most likely candidates for engines that would be widely used. If you haven't seen any engines out there for them by the time you read this, maybe you can give Larry Wall or Sun Microsystems a call and have a long talk with them about lending a hand.

Last, but not least, is security. It's been mentioned before, and it will keep being mentioned. People want to know that what they're using won't compromise their system's integrity. They also want the utility or language they're using to do everything except make toast, so there's a little conflict there. You have to logically balance security issues with functionality, and then test the heck out of the engine to avoid glaring security holes. It'd be pretty embarrassing to get your system trashed by someone else using a security hole in your scripting engine.

Script Hosts

If script engines are what provide the locomotive power, script hosts are the chassis, the wheels, the steering, and the brakes of the whole traveling entourage. They provide the space for engines to come alive, and provide open links so that data can pass back and forth between the engine and the host itself. Even Microsoft's Internet Explorer is nothing more than a glorified scripting host—it has the links in and out, and it takes advantage of them just like any other application can if it wants to. You just have to know what's involved.

Scripting Host OLE Interfaces

In OLE terms, a scripting host is a container that is aware of specific OLE interfaces—IActiveScriptSite and IActiveScriptSiteWindow, to be specific. IActiveScriptSite is the big kahuna of hooks, since it creates a place for the scripting engine to run in the server's namespace, store any extra data, and open the channel for events to be processed inside the script engine itself, not just the host interface. IActiveScriptSiteWindow is actually optional, and is only used by those scripting hosts that want to support User_Interface (UI) interactions on the same object as IActiveScriptSite.

Since IActiveScriptSite is the primary interface and mandatory for the whole thing to function, we'll look at it in more detail. This interface has to make a number of different functions available for passing control over the script back and forth, while being open enough to allow synchronization between the scripting engine and the host. The operations available in IActiveScriptSite can be defined in a header, as shown in Listing 22.3.

Listing 22.3. Header information for IActiveScriptSite.

```
 1: interface IActiveScriptSite : IUnknown
 2:   {
 3:   HRESULT GetLCID([out] LCID *plcid);
 4:   HRESULT GetItemInfo(
 5:       [in]  LPCOLESTR    pstrName,
 6:       [in]  DWORD        dwReturnMask,
 7:       [out] IUnknown   **ppunkItem,
 8:       [out] ITypeInfo **ppTypeInfo);
 9:   HRESULT GetDocVersionString([out] BSTR *pstrVersionString);
10:   HRESULT OnScriptTerminate([in] VARIANT *pvarResult, [in] EXCEPINFO
       *pexcepinfo);
11:   HRESULT OnStateChange([in] SCRIPTSTATE ssScriptState);
12:   HRESULT OnScriptError([in] IActiveScriptError *pase);
13:   HRESUT    OnEnterScript();
14:   HRESULT   OnLeaveScript();
15:   };
```

Knowing what each of those components is there for will make understanding the host creation process a lot easier, so let's take a moment to get introduced to each one. GetLCID is pretty straightforward, as it returns the localization string associated with the scripting host's user interface, so that any error messages or other data that get sent back appear in the correct language on the end user's machine.

GetItemInfo allows the script to go outside its boundaries and collect additional information about an object and related interface information, which it then stores in its three return parameters. GetDocVersionString is basic version checking, which returns a unique identifier (from the script host's point of view) to identify the version of the currently running script. The purpose of OnScriptTerminate is pretty self-explanatory; it informs the host when the script has finished executing. OnStateChange is used to monitor the current state of the script, whether it's running, waiting, stopped, or done. OnScriptError notifies the host that something bad has happened, and passes it an object reference from which the host can extract further information, as well as instructions to either continue, terminate, or re-initialize the script itself. OnEnterScript is called when the script is first executed and must be called every time event handling passes to an object. Just as OnEnterScript must be called every time an entry or re-entry occurs into the script, `OnLeaveScript` must be called to prepare the script for such an occasion. Think of them as opening and closing brackets— you have to make sure you have matching sets, or you'll get nasty errors.

`IActiveScriptSiteWindow` is much less involved than `IActiveScriptSite`, as can be witnessed by looking at Listing 22.4, showing the header information used by the interface. All it does is perform two actions: obtain the window that can function as the owner for all pop-ups (performed by `GetWindow`), and enable or disable the modality of the main window and any dialog boxes (through `EnableModeless`).

Listing 22.4. Header information for `IActiveScriptSiteWindow`.

```
1: interface IActiveScriptSiteWindow : IUnknown
2:    {
3:    HRESULT GetWindow(HWND *phwnd);
4:    HRESULT EnableModeless(BOOL fEnable);
5:    };
```

Communications Between Scripting Engines and Hosts

With all the interfaces in place, communications can take place between the scripting engine and the scripting host. There are a number of behind-the-scenes steps involved, so let's look at the order in which they take place.

First, an instance of the scripting engine needs to be created in memory. To do this, the scripting host calls the `CoCreateInstance()` function. This function uses the class ID (CLSID) of the scripting language to identify the engine to be used. If one can't be found, the host will need to create a URL moniker (file address) for the engine, then download and bind it with the `BindToObject()` function.

Next, the script is loaded in preparation for interpretation. This is where the persistence of the scripting engine and host come into play. If the script has previously been lodged in memory, an `IPersist` method is called to bring the script directly into the scripting host. Otherwise, a new instance of the script itself is created, either through an `IPersist` method or by using `IActiveScriptParse` if information is being dynamically appended.

Once the script is locked and loaded, any pages, forms, or other entities that are top-level named entities are then directly imported into the script engine's namespace through the `AddNamedItem()` function of `IActiveScript`. This means that while forms and OLE objects from an HTML page would be loaded, HTML controls and other inherent elements wouldn't be. They would be referenced individually later, through the `ITypeInfo` and `Idispatch` methods.

Now it's time to initialize the script and let it loose. By calling `SetScriptState` through `IActiveScript`, the scripting host essentially executes the `Main()` equivalent in the scripting engine. This would include any prerequisite event polling, data binding, and other such supporting function work. This dirty work initiated by the SetScriptState call, which has to occur before the actual script begins its execution, involves using a function such as GetItemInfo from IActiveScriptSite, and methods such as IConnectionPoint and Idispatch's Invoke() function, to make sure that data, function entry points, and events are all properly handled to avoid exception errors.

And now the script is running! While it seems like a lot of work, once the functions are added into the code, everything is reasonably automatic, barring some catastrophe of programming typos.

Licensing

There are three basic ways to implement VBScript support in your application, depending on your level of coding expertise. The simplest is to wait for someone else to develop a function that takes care of it for you. Far from being a facetious statement, this is the absolute truth: If you can license or out and out purchase a well-built method of supporting VBScript in the manner you need, you're far better off going this route. An excellent example would be NCompass Labs' creation of ScriptActive, a Netscape Navigator browser plug-in that enables VBScript support where none previously existed. To you, as a developer, this provides seamless support—you write your code, and it functions as you expect. It's all just plug and play, like an additional ActiveX component.

In fact, this may be the route that a number of companies follow—waiting for the creation of a generic ActiveX control that serves as just a runtime VBScript interpreter and provides simple but effective hooks into it for non-programmers. After all, not everyone will want to go out and code in C just to get the functionality of VBScript into something that doesn't support it. But for those of you who do want to do some intricate coding, there are the other two options to consider.

The Binary Route

One step down the ease-of-use ladder from the "wait for someone else" approach is the use of the precompiled VBScript binary. In the form of VBScript.DLL, Microsoft provides you with the pieces you need to pass data back and forth while interpreting VBScript code. The advantage to this route is pretty clear—you're being provided with a be-all and end-all interpreter for the VBScript functions you want to use, and all you have to do is tie it in through function calls. By providing you with the DLL and some header files (and eventually, maybe some documentation), Microsoft expects that you'll be able to do the tough stuff without too much pain and agony. This is both the recommended and the most logical method for building VBScript into any application, be it a word processor, database application, or something of your own devising.

A benefit of using the VBScript binary is that users can download the latest copy of the binary itself from Microsoft, instantly adding features and fixing bugs whenever an update is available. By sharing a common DLL between potential scripting hosts, this also leads to shared use of that DLL resource. So when Internet Explorer and your newly created VBScript-enabled application reach for that same space of memory, everyone can get along peacefully. You also get the benefit of building your application to the general ActiveX scripting host specifications, which means you could plug in any other ActiveX scripting engine that was developed later on. Instant upgradability, no hassles.

By filling out the VBScript binary licensing agreement, you essentially agree to distribute VBScript binaries only in their original form, that you won't pick them apart to see how they work, and that you can send the distributable files out royalty-free. Pretty nice arrangement, huh? Don't take our word for it, though, make sure you check out the legal agreement word for word at `http://www.microsoft.com/VBScript/us/vbsdown/vbseula.htm` before you decide to do something with it. Don't expect to find much hidden in the agreement, though. Microsoft's statement on the whole thing is summed up in two sentences: "Licensing the VBScript binary for use in your application is very easy—simply acknowledge Microsoft in the "About Box" of your application. There is no charge for this license."

An important consideration is that getting hold of the VBScript binary is really just obtaining a pre-packaged item. Microsoft can sell the same package to countless developers, without incurring really significant costs or efforts to track down what's done with it, or answer too many questions. If you're looking for the cheap way out, this is definitely it. As we mentioned, barring any redistribution which isn't explicitly mentioned in the VBScript binary licensing agreement, it's free! Otherwise, you take the next step, the one that requires the involvement of the Microsoft legal department.

Source Code

Porting VBScript to another platform, or doing other things that require you to get at the very innards of VBScript itself, will require the VBScript runtime source code, which can be modified, tweaked, or mucked about with however you see fit. As you could probably guess, there are a large number of restrictions that get placed on you when you decide to go this route. If you develop a new technology, get a patent, or benefit in any number of ways from your hard work, Microsoft does too. In fact, if you look at the licensing, they become your partner. Not a "let's split it 50-50" partner, but rather a partner with as much ownership as you over what you've created and the rights to redistribute, sell, relicense, or otherwise make a tidy sum off your work. And did we mention that any profit they make is solely theirs?

Ownership considerations aside, VBScript Source Code licensing is not a common option. It's much more likely that your needs can be served by either porting your own scripting language or by using the VBScript binary licensing arrangement to take advantage of the binary convenience and price difference.

Putting It All Together—Microsoft's "Spruuids" Example

While different reasons exist for putting together a scripting host, the folks at Microsoft thought a game would be a neat way to demonstrate it all. "Spruuids" is one of the examples included in the ActiveX Developer's Kit, but it's in kit form, and some assembly is required to make it work. If you have the ActiveX SDK, or if you obtain it from Microsoft, you'll have all the files and sample code you need to get a jump start on creating your own host. Although it's not possible to cover everything that's done in the Spruuids sample, we'll look at a few pieces of it so that you can get an idea of what the creators of this whole hosting thing had in mind.

First, depending on the version of your ActiveX Developer's Kit, you may or may not be easily able to find the sample. In earlier editions, references were included in the online Infoviewer text, but later editions hid the reference a little deeper. If you have sample code installed, you'll find everything you really need in the `Samples/AXScript/Spruuids/Src` directory. If you don't have the sample code, try getting hold of the latest ActiveX Developer's Kit from `http://www.microsoft.com/activex`, or through a subscription to the Microsoft Developer's Network (any level).

The first stop on the tour is the `README` file found in the `Src` directory. This provides the outline of what performs what task so that you can skip over the pieces that you don't want to know about yet and jump to the heart of the matter. The three files to pay close attention to for their relation to ActiveX script hosting are:

- `Game.h`, the ActiveX scripting header file
- `VBSGuids.h`, which contains the registered `CLASSID` of VBScript
- `Game.cpp`, the heart of the ActiveX scripting code

> **NOTE**
>
> If you did check the `Readme.txt` file, and then looked at that list, you might be a bit confused. According to the `Readme` file, there's supposed to be an `ActivScp.h` file that serves as the ActiveX scripting header file. That may have been true in a previous release, but in recent releases, `Game.h` has taken its place and contains the header information for `IActiveScriptSite`. In the rush to get the ActiveX Developer's Kit out the door in answer to the demands for it, that's a small change that was overlooked and might be corrected by the time you get your development kit.

Inside `Game.h`, it's pretty easy to spot the section that deals with ActiveX scripting support—Microsoft puts a big comment line before and after the section, as shown in Listing 22.5.

Listing 22.5. Contents of Game.h header file.

```
 1: // ##### BEGIN ACTIVEX SCRIPTING SUPPORT #####
 2:   // *** IActiveScriptSite methods ***
 3:   STDMETHOD(GetLCID)(LCID *plcid);
 4:   STDMETHOD(GetItemInfo)(LPCOLESTR pstrName, DWORD dwReturnMask, IUnknown
       **ppiunkItem, ITypeInfo **ppti);
 5:   STDMETHOD(GetDocVersionString)(BSTR *pszVersion);
 6:   STDMETHOD(RequestItems)(void);
 7:   STDMETHOD(RequestTypeLibs)(void);
 8:   STDMETHOD(OnScriptTerminate)(const VARIANT *pvarResult, const EXCEPINFO
       *pexcepinfo);
 9:   STDMETHOD(OnStateChange)(SCRIPTSTATE ssScriptState);
10:   STDMETHOD(OnScriptError)(IActiveScriptError *pscripterror);
11:   STDMETHOD(OnEnterScript)(void);
12:   STDMETHOD(OnLeaveScript)(void);
13:   // *** IActiveScriptSiteWindow methods ***
14:   STDMETHOD(GetWindow)(HWND *phwnd);
15:   STDMETHOD(EnableModeless)(BOOL fEnable);
16: // #####  END  ACTIVEX SCRIPTING SUPPORT #####
```

This provides the hooks that Game.cpp is going to need, and that we've explored before. Since the idea of the program is to have a user interface (it is a game, after all), IActiveScriptingWindow is included, to allow interaction with the UI windows.

The contents of VBSGuids.h is really one item—the Globally Unique Identifier (GUID or Class ID) of the VBScript engine itself—{B54F3741-5B07-11cf-A4B0-00AA004A55E8}. Try saying that two times fast.

Inside Game.cpp is the heart and soul of the interactions, but if you tear it apart you'll see it's not really that mysterious. Neat, yes. Fun, yes. But not overwhelming. Again, it's going to require a real knowledge of C++ programming to get an idea of what's going on, but picking out the pieces that enable the ActiveX scripting support is about as easy as it gets—they're delineated, as shown in Listing 22.6.

Listing 22.6. What ActiveX scripting sections of Game.cpp look like.

```
 1: // ##### BEGIN ACTIVEX SCRIPTING SUPPORT #####
 2: // Add the Game as a Named Item & load its code
 3:   g_clineOffset = 0;
 4:   hr = pgame->ParseFile(g_pszCodeFile, L"Game");
 5:   if (hr)
 6:     {
 7:     MessageBox(g_papp->m_hwndDlg, s_pszError ? s_pszError : "Unspecified
       Error", "Spruuids", MB_OK ¦ MB_ICONEXCLAMATION);
 8:     return hr;
 9:     }
10: // #####  END  ACTIVEX SCRIPTING SUPPORT #####
```

Future Hosts

Developers are already starting to build ActiveX scripting hosts for a variety of purposes. When Netscape didn't jump at providing ActiveX scripting support, NCompass Labs created the ScriptActive plug-in, which serves as a scripting host that builds seamless VBScript support right into Netscape Navigator. It's a perfect example of how extensibility on all fronts can provide quite an opportunity for developers. What will the next scripting hosts be? Anything from ActiveX plug-n-play components all the way to complete tools built around ActiveX scripting as their internal scripting language for access to functions. The possibilities are endless.

The big question is how many other languages will follow suit, and whether the extensibility of ActiveX scripting hosts will overpower or just complement existing JavaScript development. All that remains to be seen is who builds what people want, and how soon they do it.

V

PART

VBScript Sample Projects

Conversions and Calculations

by Evangelos Petroutsos

IN THIS CHAPTER

CHAPTER 23

The last part of the book contains a collection of examples you will find useful both in learning VBScript and applying it to your projects. These examples demonstrate key features of the language, some of them rather trivial and others more advanced. All the examples in this section were designed to show how to handle common situations in application development with a language like VBScript, as well as how to use some of the more advanced ActiveX controls. Converting metric units, for instance, is a trivial operation that can be carried out with a single multiplication. The Conversions utility of the next section, however, deploys an elaborate user interface based on the TabStrip control. In the discussion of the examples, you will see how this control is used in building a user interface. Even if you're not interested in learning how to write calculators, in the following chapters you will certainly find useful and practical information and VBScript programming techniques.

The first example of this chapter discusses a unit conversion utility. As simple as the actual conversions may be, the program was designed so that you can easily expand it to perform additional conversions. The second example is a financial calculator. Again, the main topic isn't the actual code for calculating monthly payments, but how to manipulate dates programmatically, a common task in financial calculations. The last example in this chapter is a math calculator. You will see the basics for developing a calculator that performs the basic arithmetic operations, and you learn how to simulate a hand-held calculator. Again, this application was designed so that it can be easily expanded, and you will see how to enhance the basic calculator by making it capable of manipulating hexadecimal numbers.

Metric Conversions

The first example presents a utility that converts metric units. The actual calculations are trivial, but the example provides a few programming issues to explore. The first issue is the user interface. As you can see in Figure 23.1, the Conversions utility deploys a sophisticated user interface based on the TabStrip control. You could have designed this application in many different ways, but the one suggested here has distinctive advantages.

The User Interface

First, the application's window stays quite small. Placing all the units on a single layout would result in a waste of valuable screen estate, not to mention that you can fit only so much in a window.

By grouping the various units as Figure 23.1 shows, the application becomes easier to use. People usually want to convert specific units from one system to another; they don't convert units at large, just for the sake of it. The user of the Conversions application will activate the appropriate tab and see on it the units he or she wants to convert.

Finally, once you have implemented the application, you can easily add tabs to accommodate other types of units. You just repeat the existing code and replace the prompts on the layout.

FIGURE 23.1.

The Conversions utility lets the user convert different types of units, grouped by category.

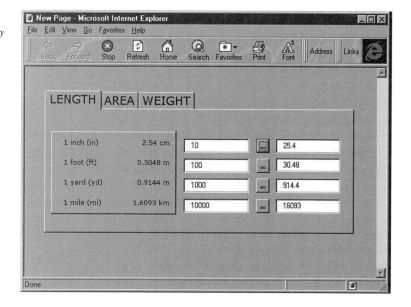

The Conversions application relies on the TabStrip control, which comes with Internet Explorer 3.0 and is one of topics discussed in this chapter. The TabStrip control is a collection of tabbed pages that contain related information. Each page in a TabStrip control contains identically structured information corresponding to a different group. If you wanted to display statistical data about various cities on a TabStrip control, you would use a different page per city. The structure of the data for each city is the same, just the data is different. In other words, all pages will contain the same controls, but different data. Of course, you can have variations on the basic structure of the data displayed on a TabStrip control. For instance, some cities may have unique features that must be displayed on separate controls, which will be visible on certain tabs and invisible on others.

The TabStrip Control

Now start by designing the application's user interface with the ActiveX Control Pad. Start with Control Pad, select New HTML Layout from the File menu, and when the new Layout appears on-screen, select the TabStrip tool and draw a relatively large TabStrip control on the Form. When you place a new TabStrip on an HTML Layout, it has two tabs, named Tab1 and Tab2. To change their names or add new tabs, right-click one of the tabs, and the shortcut menu seen in Figure 23.2 appears. The four commands on this shortcut menu enable you to

- Insert a new tab at the location of the current tab.
- Delete the current tab.

- Rename the current tab.

- Move the current tab to another location. If you choose Move, you'll be presented with a list of the tabs on the control. Select the tab you want to relocate and move it up and down the list.

Figure 23.2.

To add, remove, or rearrange the tabs on a TabStrip control, right-click one of the tabs, and you see this shortcut menu.

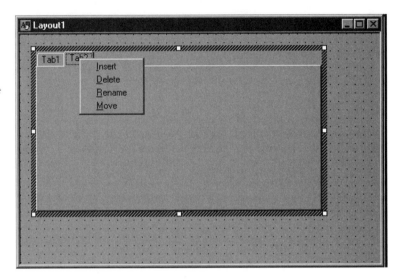

Create an additional tab and name the three tabs Length, Weight, and Area. (Refer back to Figure 23.1.)

TabStrip Control's Properties

You can also adjust the appearance of the tabs on the TabStrip control using the Properties window. The Style property determines the look of the tabs and can have one of the following values (see Figure 23.3):

    0 (default): Each page is identified with a tab.
    1: Each page is identified with a button.
    3: Pages have no marks on them.

Figure 23.3 illustrates the three possible values of the Style property. If the Style property is 0, you must select the page to appear on top of the others programmatically. If the control contains too many pages and their tabs, or buttons, can't be displayed in a single row, two buttons with arrows to the left and right are automatically attached next to the tabs; these arrows enable users to scroll and locate the one they need. If you prefer, you can set the MultiRow property to True, to make all tabs visible, even if they have to occupy multiple lines. This arrangement works in address book types of applications, as shown in Figure 23.4. The tabs on the TabStrip control of Figure 23.4 appear to the right side of the control by setting the TabOrientation to 3 (Right). The other values of the TabOrientation property are 0 (top), 1 (bottom), and 2 (left).

FIGURE 23.3.

There are three styles you can choose for your TabStrip *control.*

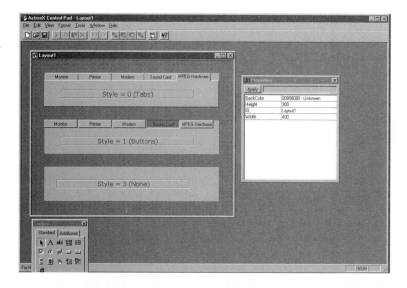

FIGURE 23.4.

The TabStrip *control is ideal for address book types of applications.*

Finally, you can set the width and height of each tab with the `TabFixedWidth` and `TabFixedHeight` properties respectively (both properties are expressed in pixels). By default, each tab can have its own dimensions, depending on the caption displayed. To set all tabs to the same width, set these two properties to a value large enough to accommodate all the tabs.

TabStrip Control's Methods

So far you have seen the properties for adjusting the appearance of the control at design time. To control the `TabStrip` programmatically, you must first understand the nature of this control, which is a bit unusual. The `TabStrip` control represents a collection of `Tab` objects, and each `Tab` object in the collection has its own index in the `Tabs` collection. `Tabs` is an array, whose elements are the individual tabs. To access the first tab and read or set its properties with VBScript commands, use the expression

```
TabStrip1.Tabs(0)
```

where *TabStrip1* is the name of the control. The second tab has index 1, and so on.

The `Tabs` collection has a single property, `Count`, which returns the total number of tabs. To manipulate the control's tags at runtime, the `Tabs` collection provides four methods, which correspond to the commands of its shortcut menu. (See Figure 23.2.) The `Tabs` collection's methods are

> **Add** adds a new tab to the `Tabs` collection.
> **Clear** removes all objects from the `Tabs` collection.
> **Item** returns a member of the `Tabs` collection.
> **Remove** removes a `Tab` object from the collection.

To add a new tab at runtime, use a statement like

```
Set TabObject = TabStrip1.Tabs.Add([ Name [, Caption [, index]]])
```

where *TabStrip1* is the name of the control and the bracket indicates that the arguments enclosed are optional. The simplest form of the `Add` method is

```
TabStrip1.Tabs.Add
```

which appends a new tab to the control and names it *Tabx*, where x is a number. If the control already has 2 tabs, `Tab1` and `Tab2`, the previous call to the `Add` method will add a third one and name it `Tab3`. You can specify the name, caption, and order of the tabs added to the collection.

The `Clear` method removes all the tabs from the control, similar to the `Clear` method of the `ListBox` control, which removes all items in a `List` control. The `Remove` method removes a `Tab` object from the collection, and its syntax is

```
TabStrip1.Tabs.Remove(index)
```

where *index* is the order of the tab to be removed in the collection. The statement

```
TabStrip1.Tabs.Remove(0)
```

removes the first tab of the `TabStrip1` control.

Finally, the `Item` method returns a member of the `Tabs` collection, and its syntax is

```
Set ThisTab = TabStrip1.Tabs.Item(index)
```

The `Caption` property controls the string that identifies each member of the Tabs collection. To set the caption of the first tab in the `TabStrip1` control, you can use the statement

```
TabStrip1.Tabs(0).Caption = "Printers"
```

or extract the appropriate member of the collection and then set the property:

```
ThisTab=TabStrip1.Tabs(0).Item
ThisTab.Caption = "Printers"
```

Implementing the Conversions Utility

Place a `TabStrip` control on the layout and add a third tab with the `Add` command of the shortcut menu. Then change the captions of all three tabs to match the ones shown in Figure 23.1. To change the font of the captions, right-click the control and select properties from the shortcut menu that will appear. In the Properties window, set the `Font` property to the appropriate value.

Now you're ready to place the various controls on the `TabStrip` control. The controls aren't really placed on the `TabStrip` control. Instead, they are placed on the layout and the `TabStrip` control enables them to appear. You can draw each one of the controls on the Layout outside the `TabStrip` control and then move them with the mouse to their places. You can also move the `TabStrip` control out of view while creating the rest of the user interface, and then place it on top of the controls and resize it. If the `TabStrip` hides the remaining controls, place it behind the other controls with the Send to Back command of the Format menu.

The box on which the conversion factors are placed is an `ImageBox`. The `ImageBox` control contains eight labels in two columns: the Label controls of the first column are named `Units11`, `Units12`, `Units13`, and `Units14`, and the labels of the second column are named `Units21`, `Units22`, `Units23`, and `Units24`. They hold the conversion factors for various pairs of units. The captions of these labels must change every time the user clicks a different tab, so they must be set from within the code. Don't bother to change them at this point. Just notice that the captions of the labels in the first column are left-aligned, and those of the second column are right-aligned.

Then, place the `TextBox` controls where the user will enter the amounts to be converted. Place the Command buttons and the `TextBox` controls where the results will be displayed. The `TextBox` controls on the first column are named `From1`, `From2`, `From3`, and `From4`, and the controls on the second column are named `To1`, `To2`, `To3`, and `To4`. These text boxes hold the units to be converted and the equivalent amount in the new system. Place all the controls on the form, align them with the commands of the Format menu, and assign a common font name and size for them all.

Programming the Application

Now you can look at the code of the application. First, you must supply the subroutine that changes the captions of the Label controls. This subroutine must be invoked every time the user clicks a tab, an action signaled by the TabStrip control's Click event. The subroutine for this event provides an argument, which is the index of the tab that was clicked. Depending on the value of the Index argument, the captions are set to different values:

```
Sub TabStrip1_Click(Index)
    If Index=0 Then
        Unit11.Caption="1 inch (in)"
        Unit12.Caption="1 foot (ft)"
        Unit13.Caption="1 yard (yd)"
        Unit14.Caption="1 mile (mi)"
        Unit21.Caption="2.54 cm"
        Unit22.Caption="0.3048 m"
        Unit23.Caption="0.9144 m"
        Unit24.Caption="1.6093 km"
        ClearBoxes
    End If

    If Index=1 Then
        Unit11.Caption="1 sq. inch"
        Unit12.Caption="1 sq. foot"
        Unit13.Caption="1 sq. yard"
        Unit14.Caption="1 acre"
        Unit21.Caption="6.4526 sq. cm"
        Unit22.Caption="0.093 sq. m"
        Unit23.Caption="0.8361 sq. m"
        Unit24.Caption="4046.86 sq. m"
        ClearBoxes
    End If

    If Index=2 Then
        Unit11.Caption="1 ounce (oz)"
        Unit12.Caption="1 pound (lb)"
        Unit13.Caption="1 short ton"
        Unit14.Caption="1 long ton"
        Unit21.Caption="28.35 gr"
        Unit22.Caption="0.4536 kg"
        Unit23.Caption="0.9072 t"
        Unit24.Caption="1.0161 t"
        ClearBoxes
    End If
End Sub
```

The ClearBoxes() subroutine clears the contents of the TextBox controls every time a new tab is displayed, because the amounts converted earlier wouldn't agree with the new units on the page. This subroutine takes care of all the elements that change as the user switches to a different page. When the layout is loaded for the first time, this subroutine must also be called, or else the labels will be blank until the user actually clicks on one of them. In the window_OnLoad event, enter the following lines:

```
Sub Window_onLoad()
    TabStrip1_Click(0)
End Sub
```

Finally, the actual unit conversions take place every time the user clicks on the corresponding Command button. The subroutines behind each Command button could be long Select Case statements (or series of If statements), but a simpler and more elegant way of converting the units exists. The conversion factor for each unit is always stored in the caption of the corresponding label in the second column. You can extract this number from the label's Caption property and use it in the calculations. The result is a short subroutine that is totally independent of the converted units. The program reads the conversion factor from the corresponding label and then the number of units (the number entered by the user in the appropriate TextBox control). Then it multiplies the two values (units times conversion factor) and stores the result to the other TextBox control (in the column with the results). You can add more tabs to the control or change the units on each page, and you won't have to touch the code. It will always work, as long as the conversion can be carried out with a simple multiplication. Here's the code behind the first Command button:

```
Sub CommandButton1_Click()
    If NOT IsNumeric(From1.Text) Then Exit Sub
    SpacePos=Instr(Unit21, " ")
    factor=left(Unit21, SpacePos-1)
    To1.Text=CDbl(From1.Text) * factor
End Sub
```

The code behind the remaining Command buttons is nearly identical, except for the names of the From and To TextBox controls. The first line makes sure the TextBox contains a valid number; if not, the execution of the subroutine is aborted. Then, it isolates the first element in the string, which is the conversion factor, and assigns it to the factor variable. This variable gets multiplied by the contents of the first TextBox, and the result is assigned to the second TextBox.

To run and test your application, save the layout as Conversions.alx, open a new HTML file, and insert the layout with the Insert HTML Layout command on the Edit menu. After the insertion of the HTML layout, the new document will display as follows:

```
<HTML>
<HEAD>
<TITLE>New Page</TITLE>
</HEAD>
<BODY>

<OBJECT CLASSID="CLSID:812AE312-8B8E-11CF-93C8-00AA00C08FDF"
ID="conversions_alx" STYLE="LEFT:0;TOP:0">
<PARAM NAME="ALXPATH" REF
VALUE="file:C:\WINDOWS\Desktop\Projects\Calc\conversions.alx">
</OBJECT>

</BODY>
</HTML>
```

Notice that the ActiveX Control Pad inserted the complete path name in the definition of the HTML Layout object. If your HTML files and the layouts they contain are stored in the same folder, you should edit the HTML file and remove the path name, or replace it with a relative path, such as ..\Layouts\Conversions.alx.

A Financial Calculator

In this and the following section, you build two calculators: a financial one and a simple math calculator. Calculators, among the most common utilities in every environment, certainly have their place on the Web. The financial calculator is a simple application that enables you to enter the various parameters of a loan (starting and ending dates, amount, interest rate, and monthly payment) and calculates the one you haven't specified. For example, you can enter the amount, the duration, and the interest rate; then ask the program to calculate your monthly payment. Or, instead of the loan's duration, you can enter the monthly payment you can afford to pay, and the program will calculate how long it will take you to pay off the loan. This example can begin as a starting point for a more advanced financial calculator. As usual, the calculations are simple (provided you know about loans, mortgages, and so on), but you will see a few interesting points about VBScript's date manipulation functions demonstrated in this example. Financial calculations rely on date manipulation operations, and VBScript's date functions can simplify your code a good deal.

The User Interface

The user interface of the Financial Calculator application appears in Figure 23.5. It's much simpler than the one from the previous example and should be fairly easy to implement. It consists of five Label controls and five TextBox controls next to them. The user may enter values in some of the TextBox controls and then click the Command button next to the quantity to be calculated. Even if the corresponding box contains a value from previous calculations, the program will ignore it and calculate based on the values of the other controls.

FIGURE 23.5.

The Financial Calculator utility calculates the duration of a loan, or the monthly payment, according to the date you provide.

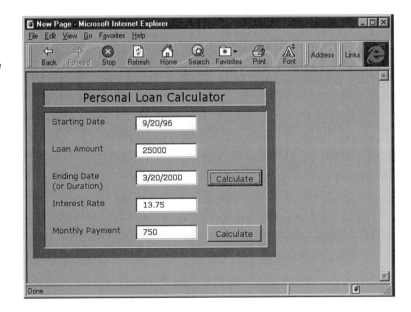

The application has straightforward code, except perhaps for the actual calculations. The functions that calculate the loan's parameters are a bit involved, but the goal here is not to teach you the secrets of banking. If you develop financial applications, you will find the calculations trivial. Even if you've never written any financial applications in the past, you can still follow this example. Just treat the `CalculatePayment()` and `CalculateMonths()` functions as black boxes, which calculate the loan's monthly payment and duration in months, respectively. The goal of this project is to show you a few interesting VBScript programming techniques, and not teach you how to calculate loans. The duration of a loan's amortization is calculated with the formula:

```
MPay=LoanAmount * RRate / (1-(1+RRate)^-N))
```

where `MPay` is the monthly payment, `LoanAmount` is the principal (the loan's initial amount), `N` is the loan's duration in months and `RRate` is given by

```
RRate=Interest/1200
```

where `Interest` is the interest rate. To calculate the duration of the loan in months, the previous equation is solved for `N`.

With the calculations out of the way, we can concentrate on the application's user interface, by adding some flexibility to it. The user will have the option to enter either the duration of the loan (in months) or the ending date. If the user supplies the duration of the loan, the starting date field will be ignored. If, however, the user wants to calculate the duration of the loan and has entered a starting date, the program will display the ending date.

VBScript Date Functions

Before understanding the actual code of the application, you should review the VBScript date manipulation functions. The `Date` and `Time` functions return the current date and time, respectively, and the `Now` function returns both date and time. The `Date` function will get used from within the window's `OnLoad` event to display the current date in the `Starting Date` field:

```
Sub window_OnLoad()
    Date1.Text=Date
End Sub
```

Date calculations have been a sore point in programming for many years and with nearly every language. The built-in support for manipulating dates was minimal, and programmers had to supply lengthy procedures for operations, such as the difference between two days, or to calculate the date 60 days from today. VBScript simplifies date manipulation with the `DateValue()` and `SerialDate()` functions. The `DateValue()` function accepts a date value as an argument and returns a numeric value, which represents the date. Using the `DateValue()` function, you can perform arithmetic operations with dates. For example, to calculate the number of days between two dates, you can use the following statements:

```
date1="3/8/95"
date2="9/21/97"
Difference=DateValue(date2)-DateValue(date1)
```

(The value of the `Difference` variable after the execution of the previous lines becomes `928`.) If you attempt to subtract two dates directly, you get an error message instead.

The `DateSerial()` function accepts three numeric arguments that correspond to a year, a month, and a day value and returns the corresponding date. The statement

```
MsgBox DateSerial(1995, 10, 3)
```

will display the string `10/3/95` in a message box.

Like the `DateValue()` function, the `DateSerial()` function can handle arithmetic operations with dates. For example, you can find out what date it will be on the 90th day of the year by calling `DateSerial` with the following arguments:

```
DateSerial(1996, 1, 90)
```

(`30/3/96`, if you are curious). To find out the date 1,000 days from now, call the `DateSerial()` function as

```
DateSerial(Year(Date), Month(Date), Day(Date)+1000)
```

You can also add (or subtract) a number of months to the month argument and a number of years to the year argument. Say that the duration of a loan made on August 23, 1996 goes 75 months. You can calculate the exact day of the loan's final payment with the statement

```
FinalDate=DateSerial(1996, 8+75, 23)
```

The variable `FinalDate` is a date variable (`11/23/2002`, to be exact). Because hardcoding data does not represent a good programming technique, a more complicated statement that enables you to calculate the date *M* months from today appears next:

```
NewDate=DateSerial(Year(Date), Month(Date)+M, Day(Date))
```

where *M* is the number of months between the two dates; it can be negative, too, if you want to calculate a date in the past.

> **TIP**
>
> VBScript provides two similar functions for manipulating time: the `TimeValue()` and `TimeSerial()` functions. These functions won't be used in this example, but they function identically to the date functions, except that they use hours, minutes, and seconds, instead of years, months, and days.

With this background on the VBScript date functions, you can examine the Financial Calculator application. The user interface is quite simple. You must place five `Label` and five `Textbox` controls next to each other, and two Command buttons next to the Ending Date and Monthly Payment fields. The labels indicate the type of input that each TextBox accepts. The user must supply a date to all fields that don't have a Command button next to them and to one of the other two. Then, the user may click one of two Command buttons to calculate the ending date or the monthly payment for the specified amount.

Notice that users can enter not only the duration of the loan in months, but they can enter an ending date, too. The program will use the duration of the loan in the first case, and it calculates the duration by subtracting the starting date from the ending date in the second case. The result also gets displayed in two formats. If the Starting Date field has no information, the program prints the duration of the loan in months. If the Starting Date field contains a valid date, the program displays the ending date.

Programming the Application

Now you can look at the code of the application. The code behind the Click event of the two Command buttons remains quite simple:

```
Sub CalcMonths_Click()
    PayMonths=Int(CalculateMonths()+0.5)
    if IsDate(Date1.Text) Then
        Date2.Text=DateSerial(Year(Date1.Text), Month(Date1.Text)+PayMonths,
        Day(Date1.Text))
    Else
        Date2.Text=PayMonths
    End If
End Sub

Sub CalcPayment_Click()
    MPayment.Text=Int((CalculatePayment()+0.5)*100)/100
End Sub
```

The CalcMonths Command button calls the CalculateMonths() function, which reads the data from the controls and calculates the duration of the loan. Then it displays the duration in the third TextBox in two different formats, depending on the contents of the first TextBox. If the first TextBox control contains a valid date, the result appears as a date. The CalculateMonths() function returns the duration of the loan in months, and the program figures out the date so many months from the starting date by adding the duration of the loan to the starting date; then the program displays it. If the first TextBox doesn't contain a valid date, the duration is displayed in months.

The CalcPayment Command button calls the CalculatePayment() function, which also reads the data from the controls and calculates the monthly payment. The amount of the monthly payment is rounded to two decimal digits and displays on the last TextBox.

Both the CalculateMonths() and CalculatePayment() functions assume that the interest is compounded daily. The actual calculations don't matter for the example. If you make your living by approving loans, you should double check the program, or supply your own functions for calculating the loan parameters. The CalculateMonths() function appears next:

```
Function CalculateMonths()
    MPay=MPayment.Text
    LoanAmount=Amount.Text
    IRate=Rate.Text
    RRate=IRate/1200
    If LoanAmount*RRate/MPay >= 1 Then
        MsgBox "Too small monthly payment for the amount requested"
        CalculateMonths=0
        Exit Function
    End If
    T1=log(1-LoanAmount*RRate/MPay)
    T2=log(1+RRate)
    CalculateMonths=-T1/T2
End Function
```

Notice the If statement that compares the quantity LoanAmount*RRate/Mpay to 1. If this quantity is larger than 1, the argument of the logarithm in the formula for calculating T1 is negative, and the logarithm of a negative number can't be calculated. To prevent an error message, make sure that the logarithm can be computed before going to this line. If the arguments are such that the logarithm of the quantity 1-LoanAmount*RRate/Mpay can't be calculated, the function ends prematurely and returns the value zero. In practice, this result will happen if you attempt to pay off a loan with a monthly payment that doesn't even cover the monthly interest. The monthly payment should be such that the total amount you owe to the bank (principal and interest) decreases every month. Otherwise, you have made a loan that will never be paid off, and then why bother making payments?

The CalculatePayment() function starts by computing the duration of the loan and then proceeds with the calculations. The DateDifference() function reads the values of the controls and returns the duration of the loan in months (you see shortly the implementation of the DateDifference() function). This number then gets used in the calculations of the monthly payment.

```
Function CalculatePayment()
    Duration=DateDifference()
    If Duration<0 Then Exit Function
    LoanAmount=Amount.Text
    IRate=Rate.Text
    RRate=IRate/1200
    MPay=LoanAmount*RRate/(1-(1+RRate)^(-Duration))
    CalculatePayment=MPay
End Function
```

The DateDifference() function is the most interesting one in this application. It uses the DateValue() function to compute the difference between the starting and ending dates in months and returns this value to the calling program. First, it checks the contents of the Date2 TextBox control to see if it contains a valid date. If the user has specified the ending date of the loan instead of its duration, the program subtracts the two dates and divides the result by 30 to come up with the duration of the loan in months. If the `Date2` field contains a number, the program uses this value as the duration of the loan. Finally, if the `Date2` field contains neither a date nor a numeric value, the program lets the user know he has made an invalid entry, and then doesn't proceed with the calculations. The following text shows the code for the `DateDifference()` function.

```
Function DateDifference()
    Difference=-1
    If IsDate(date2) then
        Difference=int((DateValue(Date2)-DateValue(Date1))/30+0.5)
    Else
        if IsNumeric(date2) then
            Difference=date2
        else
            MsgBox "Please enter a valid ending date or a duration for the loan"
        End If
    End If
    DateDifference=Difference
End Function
```

A Math Calculator

The last example in this chapter is a math calculator. As you probably expect, the code for carrying out the operations represents the simplest part of the application. This calculator only performs basic arithmetic operations, such as addition and subtraction; however, it's not a trivial application. As you will see, the application has a design you can easily expand and customize. After looking at the code of the application, you build a hexadecimal calculator based on this example by adding a few lines of code.

The User Interface

The application is called Calculator, and its user interface appears in Figure 23.6. The calculator has a Label control display, which means that users can't enter data by typing it. They must click the calculator's buttons with the mouse. In addition to the 10 digits, the period, and the usual arithmetic operators, a few additional buttons exist for keeping running totals. The M+ button adds the current number (the number currently displayed) to a running total in memory, the MR button recalls the total from the memory, and the MC button resets the memory.

The user interface of the Calculator application might seem trivial, but it will take you a while. To speed things up, design one Command button for a digit, set its size, font, and any other common properties; then copy and paste it on the layout over and over. Just change the Caption property of each new Command button pasted. Once all the buttons appear on the layout, use the Align commands of the Format menu to align the Command button controls (refer to Figure 23.6). If you don't like this arrangement, place the buttons in a way that suits you.

FIGURE 23.6.

The Calculator utility mimics a hand-held calculator from within any Web page.

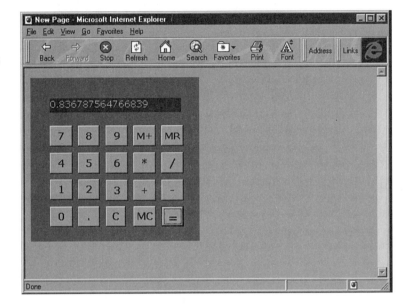

There are situations in which you may have to align a large number of controls on a layout, like the command buttons of the Calculator application. To align a large number of controls in a tabular arrangement on a layout, you must first make all the controls the same size, then make the horizontal and vertical spacing between adjacent controls the same and finally, adjust the lefts of the controls on the same column, and the tops of the controls on the same row.

Select all the controls you want to align with the mouse while holding down the Shift key. You can also select multiple controls by drawing a rectangle that encloses all the controls you want to adjust with the mouse. Then select the Make Same Size command of the Format menu.

Next, select all the buttons of the first row and align their tops with the Align/Tops command of the Format menu. Then make the spacing between pairs of adjacent buttons the same, using the Horizontal Spacing/Make Equal command from the Format menu. Do the same with the buttons in the first column. This time, align their left sides and make the vertical spacing the same. Once the buttons of the first row and column are in place, you can easily align the rest of them. Select all the button in each row and align their tops, and select all buttons in each column and align their left sides. Just make sure that the first button you select has the alignment you want applied to the other ones.

Programming the Application

The code of the Calculator application mimics the operation of a hand-held calculator. It expects the user to type a number (the first operand), then the symbol of an operation (the operator), and then another number (the second operand). These three entities then get combined to produce the result as follows:

```
result=operand1 operator operand2
```

As the user clicks on digit buttons, the corresponding digit displays. This result occurs by appending the new digit to the label's Caption property. When the user clicks an operator's button, the current number is stored in a global variable, and the display clears in anticipation for the second operand. The subroutine for the Command button's Click event is

```
Sub Digit1_Click()
    DisplayDigit("1")
End Sub
```

The subroutines for the Click events of the other digit buttons are similar.

The DidplayDigit() subroutine does more than just append a digit to the display. It checks the global variable *MustClear* to see if the display must be cleared first:

```
Sub DisplayDigit(digit)
    If MustClear Then
        Display.Caption=""
        MustClear=False
    End If
    Display.Caption=Display.Caption+digit
End Sub
```

The variable MustClear is set to True every time an operator's button is clicked. Say the user enters the number 381 and then clicks the Addition button to signal the intention to add two numbers. The display doesn't clear immediately after the Plus button gets clicked. Instead, the MustClear variable is set to True and the display actually clears only when the user clicks the next digit button (the first digit of the second operand). The code for the Plus button's Click event appears next:

```
Sub Plus_Click()
    op1=Display.Caption
    MustClear=True
    op="PLUS"
End Sub
```

op1 and op are global variables, whose values are set by the various subroutines of the application; they get used during the calculation of the result. When the user clicks the Plus button, the contents of the display become the first operand, the operator is set according to the button that was pressed, and the MustClear variable is set to True. This variable must be set to True so that the next time the user clicks a digit button, the display clears and a new number is entered.

All the action takes place from within the Equals button's Click event. That subroutine appears in the following code:

```
Sub Equals_Click()
    Op2=Display.Caption
    Select Case Op
    Case "PLUS":
        result = CDbl(op1) + CDbl(op2)
    Case "MINUS":
        result = CDbl(op1) - CDbl(op2)
    Case "TIMES":
        result = CDbl(op1) * CDbl(op2)
    Case "DIV":
        If CDbl(op2) = 0 Then
            Display.Caption="ERROR!"
        Else
            result = CDbl(op1) / CDbl(op2)
        End If
    End Select
    If Display.Caption<>"ERROR!" then Display.Caption=result
    MustClear=True
End Sub
```

As soon as the Equals button is clicked, the number currently displayed becomes the second operand and the program checks the value of the op variable. If op is PLUS, it adds the two operands. If it is MINUS, the program subtracts the second from the first operand. If op is TIMES, it multiplies the two operands. In all cases, the result is stored in the result variable and gets displayed later.

If the value of the op variable is DIV, however, the program tests the value of the second operand against zero to prevent a runtime error (the Division by zero error). If the second operand is non-zero, it performs the division and displays the result. If it is zero, the program displays the string ERROR! instead of the result.

Finally, the memory buttons manipulate the contents of another global variable, the memory variable. The M+ button adds the current number to the memory variable, the MR button displays the current value of the memory variable, and the MC button resets the value to zero. The three subroutines appear next:

```
Sub MemAdd_Click()
    memory=memory + Display.Caption
    MustClear=True
End Sub

Sub MemRecall_Click()
    Display.Caption=memory
    MustClear=True
End Sub

Sub MemClear_Click()
    memory=0
    MustClear=True
End Sub
```

The code of the Calculator application is fairly straightforward. The actual calculations only require a few lines of code, and most of the code handles the display. You can easily expand the bare bones application presented here to include more operations. For example, you can add a +/- button that inverts the sign of the current number. This button can be implemented with a single line of code:

```
Display.Caption="-" & Display.Caption
```

Improving the Calculator

You can easily turn this utility into a scientific calculator. You will spend the most time adjusting the user interface to include more buttons, because the operations are straightforward. For instance, if you add a COS button (for calculating the cosine of a number) on the layout, you must enter the following line in the button's `Click` event:

```
Display.Caption=cos(CDbl(Display.Caption))
```

When the user clicks the COS button, the cosine of the displayed value is calculated and appears on the calculator's display. You can add trigonometric functions, square roots, and powers, because these operations don't require two operands. They just read the current value, calculate a function of the number and display the result. You must, however, add a good deal of error checking code so that the program won't attempt to calculate the square root or logarithm of a negative number.

Another useful variation of the basic Calculator application is a hexadecimal calculator, like the one shown in Figure 23.7. If you add a few more buttons for the hexadecimal digits A through F, you can perform the same operations, only in the hexadecimal number system. In the hexadecimal system, however, you can work with integers only. To perform operations in the hexadecimal system, you must prefix the numbers with the symbols `&H` and then take their value with the `CInt` function, which converts its argument to an integer. The arithmetic operations will be carried out in the decimal system and the result gets converted to the hexadecimal system with the function `Hex`.

The HexCalculator application, shown in Figure 23.7, is a variation on the Calculator that performs hexadecimal calculations. The `Equals_Click()` subroutine looks slightly different than before:

```
Sub Equals_Click()
    Op2="&H" & Display.Caption
    Select Case Op
    Case "PLUS":
        result = CInt(op1) + CInt(op2)
    Case "MINUS":
        result = CInt(op1) - CInt(op2)
    Case "TIMES":
        result = CInt(op1) * CInt(op2)
    Case "DIV":
        if CInt(op2) = 0 Then
```

23

CONVERSIONS
AND
CALCULATIONS

```
            Display.Caption="ERROR!"
        else
            result = CInt(op1) / CInt(op2)
        End If
    End Select
    If Display.Caption<>"ERROR!" then Display.Caption=Hex(result)
    MustClear=True

End Sub
```

When you prefix the operands with the `"&H"` string, they get converted to hexadecimal numbers. The `CInt()` function converts these hex numbers to decimals, performs the operation, and then converts the result back to a hex number before displaying it.

Further Improvements

As you can see, it didn't take much to convert the simple decimal calculator into a hexadecimal one. To summarize, all you had to do was add the extra hex digits, convert the arguments to decimal numbers to carry out the calculations, and then convert the result back to a hexadecimal number to display the result. You can now try to combine both calculators in one by adding a toggle button that switches the mode of the calculator between the two systems. When the calculator is in decimal mode, you should disable the hex digits on the layout and restore them when the calculator is switched back to hexadecimal mode. As far as the calculations are concerned, you can copy both subroutines for the Equals button we presented earlier in your code and call one of them, depending on the calculator's current mode.

Review

In this chapter's examples you were shown how to design applications that perform simple calculations, like converting units between systems, or more complicated calculations like math operations. As you have realized by now, the functions that do the actual calculations are usually the shortest and simplest part of the application. The real challenge in programming in a visually rich environment like Windows 95 is to provide the simplest, most functional user interface. This requires visual design skills, as well as programming skills.

The code behind the various buttons of the Calculator application wasn't simple, considering what it accomplishes. Arranging the buttons on the layout and coming up with an attractive user interface will probably take you longer than writing the code. After the code of the Calculator application was written, it was surprisingly simple to add support for hexadecimal digits to the application, as well as extend it to handle trigonometric and other advanced math functions.

The Conversions utility is another typical example. Writing the code for converting units between systems is trivial, but with a well-designed user interface we were able to create a usable application (one that doesn't overwhelm the user with options). At the same time, by displaying the conversion factors on the program's form, we were able to design an application that can be expanded without actually touching the code that performs the calculations. You can add more options to the program by simply adding new labels with conversion factors. The logic of converting the units has been built into the application, and you needn't worry about it unless the conversion isn't as simple as a multiplication. The display of the conversion factors on the form not only simplifies the code but provides useful information to the user.

The types of applications we explored in this chapter were rather simple ones, but they are quite common and it's likely that you'll incorporate a similar functionality to some of your applications. No doubt, you've seen numerous applications that perform financial or arithmetic calculations. What will make the difference between yours and the other applications is simplicity and ease of use. Our examples weren't the ultimate examples of simplicity or flexibility, but they demonstrated some of the key features you should incorporate in even the simplest applications.

CHAPTER 24

WWW Personal Information Manager

by Owen Graupman

IN THIS CHAPTER

Overview

Personal information managers have always been one of the most popular applications for a computer. This chapter will show you how to make a World Wide Web–based personal information manager that allows the user to store to-do's, appointments, and e-mail addresses with a few simple clicks of the mouse.

Two very important techniques are used to create this interactive page:

■ Dynamic page creation
■ Persistent storage through cookies

Dynamic page creation is one of the hottest topics in page creation. A dynamic page changes in response to the environment, user input, or a variety of other information. The WWW PIM uses VBScript to generate the entire page based on the current date and information stored by the user.

Persistent storage through cookies allows visitors to this page to store their appointments in small text files called *cookies*, which reside on their local computer and can be recalled at any time. Many sites today use cookies to store information about the user. Some of the most common uses are to store color preferences or information provided by the user like their name and address. Because a cookie is just a text file managed by the browser, client-side security is very good. Even if a miscreant person was able to place a virus in a cookie, the file contains headers and footers that would prevent the code from running and infecting your system.

Before you go running off to explore cookies, keep in mind that cookies will only work when the page is loaded from an HTTPD server. Loading this page locally will produce a blank page that will not store any data.

How It Works

When a user loads this page from the Internet, VBScript goes to work parsing through the cookie to pull out information for each of the categories of data. It then formats this information into HTML and writes it directly into the document context as HTML.

When a user clicks on any item, whether it's a to-do, address, or appointment, message boxes prompt the user through creating a new item. The information is then placed into the cookie and the page reloaded.

You can see how the finished example looks in Figure 24.1, and the entire HTML and VBScript code in Listing 24.1.

FIGURE 24.1.

The finished WWW Personal Information Manager.

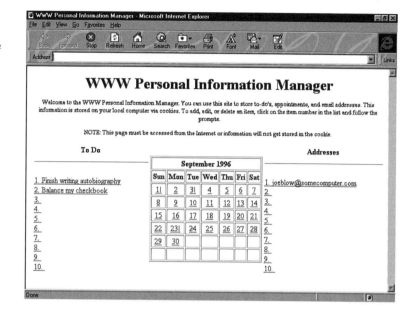

Listing 24.1. The WWW Personal Information Manager code listing.

```
1: <!DOCTYPE HTML PUBLIC "-//IETF//DTD HTML//EN">
2:
3: <HTML>
4:
5: <HEAD>
6: <TITLE>WWW Personal Information Manager</title>
7: </HEAD>
8:
9: <BODY BGCOLOR="#FFFFFF" LANGUAGE="VBSCRIPT">
10: <H1 ALIGN=CENTER>WWW Personal Information Manager</H1>
11: <P ALIGN=CENTER><FONT SIZE=2>Welcome to the WWW Personal Information Manager.
    You can use this site to store to-do's, appointments,
12: and email addresses. This information is stored on your local computer via
    cookies. To add, edit, or delete an item, click on the item
13: number in the list and follow the prompts.</FONT></P>
14: <P ALIGN=CENTER><FONT SIZE=2>NOTE: This page must be accessed from the Internet
    or information will not get stored in the cookie. </FONT></P>
15: <CENTER>
16: <TABLE CELLPADDING=0 CELLSPACING=5 WIDTH=100%>
17: <SCRIPT LANGUAGE="VBSCRIPT"><!--
18: Call docCreate
19:
20: Sub setVariable(sVariableName, varVariableValue)
21: Document.Cookie = sVariableName & "=" & varVariableValue & ";expires=Monday,
    28-Sep-98 12:00:00 GMT"
22: end sub
23:
24: Function readVariable(sVariableName)
25: Dim iLocation
```

continues

24

PERSONAL
INFORMATION
MANAGER

Listing 24.1. continued

```
26: Dim iNameLength
27: Dim iValueLength
28: Dim iNextSemicolon
29: Dim sTemp
30:
31: iNameLength = Len(sVariableName)
32: iLocation = InStr(Document.Cookie, sVariableName)
33: If iLocation = 0 Then
34:     readVariable = ""
35: Else
36:     sTemp = Right(Document.Cookie, Len(Document.Cookie) - iLocation + 1)
37:     If Mid(sTemp, iNameLength + 1, 1) <> "=" Then
38:         readVariable = ""
39:     Else
40:         iNextSemicolon = InStr(sTemp, ";")
41:         If iNextSemicolon = 0 Then iNextSemicolon = Len(sTemp) + 1
42:         If iNextSemicolon = (iNameLength + 2) Then
43:             readVariable = ""
44:         Else
45:             iValueLength = iNextSemicolon - iNameLength - 2
46:             readVariable = Mid(sTemp, iNameLength + 2, iValueLength)
47:         End If
48:     End If
49: End if
50: end function
51:
52: Sub killVariable(sVariableName)
53: setVariable sVariableName, "NULL;expires=Monday, 01-Jan-95 12:00:00 GMT"
54: end sub
55:
56: Sub addTodo(iRecord)
57: Dim sTodo
58: Dim iChoice
59:
60: iChoice = MsgBox("Do you want to add or delete this item? Click yes to add or
    no to delete.", 3, "Add/Delete Item")
61: Select Case iChoice
62:     Case 6
63:         sTodo = InputBox("What do you want to do?", "Add To-Do")
64:         Call setVariable("%%TD" & Trim(iRecord), sTodo)
65:     Case 7
66:         killVariable "%%TD" & Trim(iRecord)
67:     Case 2
68:         Exit Sub
69: End Select
70: window.navigate "wwwpim.htm"
71: End Sub
72:
73: Sub addAppt(m,d,y)
74: Dim sAppt
75: Dim TempAppt
76:
77: TempAppt = readVariable("%%AP" & Trim(m) & "/" & Trim(d) & "/" & Trim(y))
78:
79: If Len(Trim(TempAppt)) > 0 Then
```

```
80:     sAppt = InputBox("Please enter or edit your appointment list for today",
        "Add/Edit Appointment", readVariable("%%AP" & Trim(m) & "/" & Trim(d) & "/"
        & Trim(y)))
81: Else
82:     sAppt = InputBox("Please enter or edit your appointment list for today",
        "Add/Edit Appointment")
83: End If
84: If Len(Trim(sAppt)) > 0 Then
85:     Call setVariable("%%AP" & Trim(m) & "/" & Trim(d) & "/" & Trim(y), sAppt)
86: Else
87:     killVariable("%%AP" & Trim(m) & "/" & Trim(d) & "/" & Trim(y))
88: End If
89: window.navigate "wwwpim.htm"
90: End Sub
91:
92: Sub addAddr(iRecord)
93: Dim Addr
94: Dim iChoice
95: iChoice = MsgBox("Do you want to add or delete this item? Click yes to add or
    no to delete.", 3,"Add/Delete Item")
96:
97: Select Case iChoice
98:     Case 6
99:         Addr=InputBox("What address do you want to add?", "Add Email Address")
100:        Call setVariable("%%AD" & Trim(iRecord), Addr)
101:    Case 7
102:        killVariable "%%AD" & Trim(iRecord)
103:    Case 2
104:        Exit Sub
105: End Select
106: window.navigate "wwwpim.htm"
107: End Sub
108:
109: Sub ApptStat(m,d,y)
110: Dim sTemp
111:
112: sTemp   = CStr(d & " " & readVariable("%%AP" & m & "/" & d & "/" & y))
113: If Len(Trim(sTemp)) > 0 AND readVariable("%%AP" & m & "/" & d & "/" & y) <>
     "NULL" Then
114:     window.status = sTemp
115: Else
116:     window.status = CStr(d)
117: End If
118: End Sub
119:
120: Function makTD_URL(iRecord)
121: If Trim(readVariable("%%TD" & Trim(iRecord))) <> "NULL" Then
122:     makTD_URL = "<A LANGUAGE=VBScript HREF=#null onClick=addTodo(" &
         Trim(iRecord) & ")>" & iRecord & ". " & readVariable("%%TD" &
         Trim(iRecord)) & "</A>"
123: Else
124:     makTD_URL = "<A LANGUAGE=VBScript HREF=#null onClick=addTodo(" &
         Trim(iRecord) & ")>" & iRecord & ". </A>"
125: End If
126: End Function
127:
```

24

PERSONAL
INFORMATION
MANAGER

continues

Listing 24.1. continued

```
128: Function makAD_URL(iRecord)
129: If Trim(readVariable("%%AD" & Trim(iRecord))) <> "NULL" Then
130:     makAD_URL = "<A LANGUAGE=VBScript HREF=#null onClick=addAddr(" &
         Trim(iRecord) & ")>" & iRecord & ". " & "</a>" & "<A HREF=mailto:" &
         readVariable("%%AD" & Trim(iRecord)) & ">" & readVariable("%%AD" &
         Trim(iRecord)) & "</A>"
131: Else
132:     makAD_URL = "<A LANGUAGE=VBScript HREF=#null onClick=addAddr(" &
         Trim(iRecord) & ")>" & iRecord & ". " & "</A>"
133: End If
134: End Function
135:
136: Function makAP_URL(m,d,y)
137: Dim stAppt
138:
139: stAppt = readVariable("%%AP" & m & "/" & d & "/" & y)
140: If Len(Trim(stAppt)) > 0 AND Trim(stAppt) <> "NULL" Then
141:     sTemp = "<A LANGUAGE=VBScript HREF=#null onClick="
142:     sTemp = sTemp & Chr(34)
143:     sTemp = sTemp & "Call addAppt(" & m & ", " & d & ", " & y & ")"
144:     sTemp = sTemp & Chr(34)
145:     sTemp = sTemp & " onMouseOver="
146:     sTemp = sTemp & Chr(34)
147:     sTemp = sTemp & "Call ApptStat(" & m & ", " & d & ", " & y & ")" & Chr(34)
         & ">"
148:     sTemp = sTemp & d & "!</a>"
149: Else
150:     sTemp = "<A LANGUAGE=VBScript HREF=#null onClick="
151:     sTemp = sTemp & Chr(34)
152:     sTemp = sTemp & "Call addAppt(" & m & ", " & d & ", " & y & ")"
153:     sTemp = sTemp & Chr(34)
154:     sTemp = sTemp & " onMouseOver="
155:     sTemp = sTemp & Chr(34)
156:     sTemp = sTemp & "Call ApptStat(" & m & ", " & d & ", " & y & ")" & Chr(34)
         & ">"
157:     sTemp = sTemp & d & "</A>"
158: End If
159: makAP_URL = sTemp
160: End Function
161:
162: Sub docCreate
163: Dim sDocument
164: sDocument = "<TD ALIGN=LEFT VALIGN=TOP WIDTH=35%><CENTER><B>To Do</B></
     CENTER>"
165: sDocument = sDocument & Chr(13) & Chr(10) & "<HR>"
166: For i = 1 to 10
167:     sDocument = sDocument & "<BR>" & makTD_URL(i)
168: Next
169: sDocument = sDocument & "</TD><TD ALIGN=CENTER VALIGN=MIDDLE WIDTH=30%>"
170: sDocument = sDocument & makCalendar()
171: sDocument = sDocument & "</TD><TD ALIGN=LEFT VALIGN=TOP WIDTH=35%>"
172: sDocument = sDocument & "<CENTER><B>ADDRESSES</B></CENTER>"
173: sDocument = sDocument & Chr(13) & Chr(10) & "<HR>"
174: For j = 1 to 10
175:     sDocument = sDocument & "<BR>" & makAD_URL(j)
```

```
176: Next
177:
178: sDocument = sDocument & "</TD></TR>"
179: sDocument = sDocument & Chr(13) & Chr(10) & "</TABLE>"
180:
181: Document.Write sDocument
182:
183: End Sub
184:
185: Function makCalendar()
186: m=Month(Now())
187: y=Year(Now())
188:
189: FirstDay = WeekDay(Dateserial(y,m,1))
190: DaysInMonth= Day(Dateserial(y,m+1,1)-1)
191: ThisMonth=GMonth(Month(Dateserial(y,m,1)), true) & " " &
     Year(Dateserial(y,m,1))
192:
193: sCalendar=""
194: sCalendar=sCalendar & "<CENTER><TABLE BORDER=1 CELLPADDING=2>"
195: sCalendar=sCalendar & "<TR><TH COLSPAN=7>" & ThisMonth & "</TH>"
196: sCalendar=sCalendar & "<TR><TH WIDTH=50 ALIGN=CENTER>Sun</TH><TH WIDTH=50
     ALIGN=CENTER>Mon</TH><TH WIDTH=50 ALIGN=CENTER>Tue</TH><TH WIDTH=50
     ALIGN=CENTER>Wed</TH><TH WIDTH=50 ALIGN=CENTER>Thu</TH><TH WIDTH=50
     ALIGN=CENTER>Fri</TH><TH WIDTH=50 ALIGN=CENTER>Sat</TH></TR>"
197:
198: ictrDay=0
199: For Row=1 to 6
200:     sCalendar=sCalendar & "<TR>"
201:     For Col=1 to 7
202:         sCalendar=sCalendar & "<TD WIDTH=50 ALIGN=CENTER>"
203:         If Row=1 AND Col=FirstDay then
204:             ictrDay=1
205:         End If
206:         If ictrDay = 0 Then
207:             sCalendar=sCalendar &  " "
208:         End If
209:         If ictrDay <> 0 Then
210:             If ictrDay <= DaysInMonth Then
211:                 sCalendar=sCalendar & makAP_URL(m,ictrDay,y)
212:             End If
213:             If ictrDay > DaysInMonth Then
214:                 sCalendar=sCalendar &  " "
215:             End If
216:         ictrDay=ictrDay+1
217:         End if
218:         sCalendar=sCalendar &  "</TD>"
219:     Next
220:     sCalendar=sCalendar &  "</TR>"
221: Next
222: sCalendar=sCalendar &  "</TABLE>"
223: makCalendar = sCalendar
224: End Function
225:
226: Function GMonth(iMonth, fLongShort)
227: Select Case iMonth
```

24

PERSONAL
INFORMATION
MANAGER

continues

Listing 24.1. continued

```
228: Case 1
229:     If fLongShort = true then GMonth="January" else GMonth="Jan"
230: Case 2
231:     If fLongShort = true then GMonth="February" else GMonth="Feb"
232: Case 3
233:     If fLongShort = true then GMonth="March" else GMonth="Mar"
234: Case 4
235:     If fLongShort = true then GMonth="April" else GMonth="Apr"
236: Case 5
237:     If fLongShort = true then GMonth="May" else GMonth="May"
238: Case 6
239:     If fLongShort = true then GMonth="June" else GMonth="Jun"
240: Case 7
241:     If fLongShort = true then GMonth="July" else GMonth="Jul"
242: Case 8
243:     If fLongShort = true then GMonth="August" else GMonth="Aug"
244: Case 9
245:     If fLongShort = true then GMonth="September" else GMonth="Sep"
246: Case 10
247:     If fLongShort = true then GMonth="October" else GMonth="Oct"
248: Case 11
249:     If fLongShort = true then GMonth="November" else GMonth="Nov"
250: Case 12
251:     If fLongShort = true then GMonth="December"   else GMonth="Dec"
252: End Select
253: End Function
254:
255: --></SCRIPT>
256: </TABLE>
257: </CENTER>
258: </BODY>
259:
260: </HTML>
261:
```

Creating the Page

Looking at the source reveals quite a bit of VBScript code and very little HTML. Almost the entire page is generated by VBScript as it is loaded. We accomplish this feat through several routines, which are broken up into the following areas:

- Working with cookies
- Creating dynamic HTML
- Presenting information
- Tying it all together

Working with Cookies

Cookies (or more properly, magic cookies) provide a means for browsers to store persistent information without the need for access to CGI scripts, custom executables, or other means of data storage and retrieval. I use a 'variable' metaphor for working with cookies as described in the following sections:

- The Variable Metaphor
- Reading Variables
- Writing and Deleting Variables

The Variable Metaphor

An easy way to access random pieces of information from a cookie is through variable assignment. By assigning a recognizable name to persistent information, you can easily pull out relevant pieces from the cookie using a simple subroutine.

The WWW PIM uses three different types of variables to store information. It uses %%TD*x* where *x* is the record number to store to-do's, %%AD*x* where *x* is the record number for addresses, and, finally, %%AP*mm*/*dd*/*yyyy* for appointment dates.

Reading Variables

The code in Listing 24.2 is used to read a variable from within the cookie.

Listing 24.2. The `readVariable()` function.

```
 1: Function readVariable(sVariableName)
 2: Dim iLocation
 3: Dim iNameLength
 4: Dim iValueLength
 5: Dim iNextSemicolon
 6: Dim sTemp
 7:
 8: iNameLength = Len(sVariableName)
 9: iLocation = InStr(Document.Cookie, sVariableName)
10: If iLocation = 0 Then
11:     readVariable = ""
12: Else
13:     sTemp = Right(Document.Cookie, Len(Document.Cookie) - iLocation + 1)
14:     If Mid(sTemp, iNameLength + 1, 1) <> "=" Then
15:         readVariable = ""
16:     Else
17:         iNextSemicolon = InStr(sTemp, ";")
18:         If iNextSemicolon = 0 Then iNextSemicolon = Len(sTemp) + 1
19:         If iNextSemicolon = (iNameLength + 2) Then
20:             readVariable = ""
```

continues

Listing 24.2. continued

```
21:          Else
22:                iValueLength = iNextSemicolon - iNameLength - 2
23:                readVariable = Mid(sTemp, iNameLength + 2, iValueLength)
24:          End If
25:      End If
26: End if
27: end function
28:
```

The readVariable() function takes a single parameter—the variable name to read—and returns the value of that variable. The readVariable() function accomplishes this through several iterations of InStr and Mid. This works fine for storing numerical information, but you run into a problem when storing random character information. Let's say you create a variable called Appt, which stores appointment information. Now if a user enters Dentist Appt in their appointment information, InStr can return the wrong chunk of information, or worse, complete garbage. The readVariable() function attempts to reduce this possibility by searching for an equal sign (=) immediately after the string being sought. To further reduce the chances of this problem occurring, routines append %% to the beginning of each variable name.

Writing and Deleting Variables

The page uses the same subroutine to both write and delete variables from the cookie. Just like those found on the store shelves, all magic cookies have expiration dates. By default, an entry in a cookie will expire when the browser is closed, which isn't very persistent. Imagine what would happen if your daily planner erased itself every time you closed the cover.

The setVariable routine in Listing 24.3 takes a pair of parameters: The former is the variable name, and the latter its corresponding value. It then appends an expiration date of September 28, 1998, to the end of the cookie.

Listing 24.3. The setVariable routine.

```
1:
2: Sub setVariable(sVariableName, varVariableValue)
3: Document.Cookie = sVariableName & "=" & varVariableValue & ";expires=Monday, 28-
   Sep-98 12:00:00 GMT"
4: end sub
5:
```

Correspondingly, the killVariable routine in Listing 24.4 sets the variable to NULL, appends an expiration date of January 1, 1995, and then calls the setVariable routine. Watchful readers will note that using killVariable will create an entry with two expiration dates. Fortunately for us, the second date is ignored and then deleted.

Listing 24.4. The `killVariable` routine.

```
1:
2: Sub killVariable(sVariableName)
3: setVariable sVariableName, "NULL;expires=Monday, 01-Jan-95 12:00:00 GMT"
4: end sub
```

Creating Dynamic HTML

The code uses five functions to create the statements needed to display the information in HTML format. These functions are divided into two related areas:

- Creating HREF functions
- Creating the calendar functions

The first set of functions is used to create a single `<A HREF>` statement that displays the stored data, if any, and provides the necessary code to edit the item.

The second set of functions is similar to the first, but also generates a table in addition to one of the HREF functions.

Creating HREFs from Scratch

The following three functions in Listings 24.5, 24.6, and 24.7 are used to create a single `<A HREF>` statement. The first two take only the record number as a parameter and pass back a formatted string that can be written directly into the document. Listing 24.7, `makAP_URL()`, takes the month, day, and year for the current record.

The code in Listing 24.6, which is used to create the address code, takes the address provided and converts it to a `mailto:` directive so that a user can easily mail someone on the address list by clicking on the address, or edit the record by clicking on the number.

In addition to the code to edit an appointment, the `makAP_URL()` function also contains an `onMouseOver` event to place the current appointment in the status bar.

Listing 24.5. The `makTD_URL()` function.

```
1:
2: Function makTD_URL(iRecord)
3: If Trim(readVariable("%%TD" & Trim(iRecord))) <> "NULL" Then
4:     makTD_URL = "<A LANGUAGE=VBScript HREF=#null onClick=addTodo(" &
        Trim(iRecord) & ")>" & iRecord & ". " & readVariable("%%TD" &
        Trim(iRecord)) & "</A>"
5: Else
6:     makTD_URL = "<A LANGUAGE=VBScript HREF=#null onClick=addTodo(" &
        Trim(iRecord) & ")>" & iRecord & ". </A>"
7: End If
8: End Function
9:
```

24

Listing 24.6. The makAD_URL() function.

```
1:
2: Function makAD_URL(iRecord)
3: If Trim(readVariable("%%AD" & Trim(iRecord))) <> "NULL" Then
4:      makAD_URL = "<A LANGUAGE=VBScript HREF=#null onClick=addAddr(" &
         Trim(iRecord) & ")>" & iRecord & ". " & "</a>" & "<A HREF=mailto:" &
         readVariable("%%AD" & Trim(iRecord)) & ">" & readVariable("%%AD" &
         Trim(iRecord)) & "</A>"
5: Else
6:      makAD_URL = "<A LANGUAGE=VBScript HREF=#null onClick=addAddr(" &
   Trim(iRecord) & ")>" & iRecord & ". " & "</A>"
7: End If
8: End Function
9:
```

Listing 24.7. The makAP_URL() function.

```
 1:
 2: Function makAP_URL(m,d,y)
 3: Dim stAppt
 4:
 5: stAppt = readVariable("%%AP" & m & "/" & d & "/" & y)
 6: If Len(Trim(stAppt)) > 0 AND Trim(stAppt) <> "NULL" Then
 7:      sTemp = "<A LANGUAGE=VBScript HREF=#null onClick="
 8:      sTemp = sTemp & Chr(34)
 9:      sTemp = sTemp & "Call addAppt(" & m & ", " & d & ", " & y & ")"
10:      sTemp = sTemp & Chr(34)
11:      sTemp = sTemp & " onMouseOver="
12:      sTemp = sTemp & Chr(34)
13:      sTemp = sTemp & "Call ApptStat(" & m & ", " & d & ", " & y & ")" & Chr(34)
         & ">"
14:      sTemp = sTemp & d & "!</a>"
15: Else
16:      sTemp = "<A LANGUAGE=VBScript HREF=#null onClick="
17:      sTemp = sTemp & Chr(34)
18:      sTemp = sTemp & "Call addAppt(" & m & ", " & d & ", " & y & ")"
19:      sTemp = sTemp & Chr(34)
20:      sTemp = sTemp & " onMouseOver="
21:      sTemp = sTemp & Chr(34)
22:      sTemp = sTemp & "Call ApptStat(" & m & ", " & d & ", " & y & ")" & Chr(34)
         & ">"
23:      sTemp = sTemp & d & "</A>"
24: End If
25: makAP_URL = sTemp
26: End Function
```

Creating the Calendar

The final set of HREF functions is the makCalendar() function (see Listing 24.8), which iterates through several loops to create a calendar out of an embedded table based on the current month and year, and the GMonth() function (see Listing 24.9), which provides the month names for makCalendar().

Listing 24.8. The makCalendar() function.

```
 1:
 2: Function makCalendar()
 3: m=Month(Now())
 4: y=Year(Now())
 5:
 6: FirstDay = WeekDay(Dateserial(y,m,1))
 7: DaysInMonth= Day(Dateserial(y,m+1,1)-1)
 8: ThisMonth=GMonth(Month(Dateserial(y,m,1)), true) & " " & Year(Dateserial(y,m,1))
 9:
10: sCalendar=""
11: sCalendar=sCalendar & "<CENTER><TABLE BORDER=1 CELLPADDING=2>"
12: sCalendar=sCalendar & "<TR><TH COLSPAN=7>" & ThisMonth & "</TH>"
13: sCalendar=sCalendar & "<TR><TH WIDTH=50 ALIGN=CENTER>Sun</TH><TH WIDTH=50
➡    ALIGN=CENTER>Mon</TH><TH WIDTH=50 ALIGN=CENTER>Tue</TH><TH WIDTH=50
➡    ALIGN=CENTER>Wed</TH><TH WIDTH=50 ALIGN=CENTER>Thu</TH><TH WIDTH=50
➡    ALIGN=CENTER>Fri</TH><TH WIDTH=50 ALIGN=CENTER>Sat</TH></TR>"
14:
15: ictrDay=0
16: For Row=1 to 6
17:     sCalendar=sCalendar & "<TR>"
18:     For Col=1 to 7
19:         sCalendar=sCalendar & "<TD WIDTH=50 ALIGN=CENTER>"
20:         If Row=1 AND Col=FirstDay then
21:             ictrDay=1
22:         End If
23:         If ictrDay = 0 Then
24:             sCalendar=sCalendar & " "
25:         End If
26:         If ictrDay <> 0 Then
27:             If ictrDay <= DaysInMonth Then
28:                 sCalendar=sCalendar & makAP_URL(m,ictrDay,y)
29:             End If
30:             If ictrDay > DaysInMonth Then
31:                 sCalendar=sCalendar & " "
32:             End If
33:             ictrDay=ictrDay+1
34:         End if
35:         sCalendar=sCalendar & "</TD>"
36:     Next
37:     sCalendar=sCalendar & "</TR>"
38: Next
39: sCalendar=sCalendar & "</TABLE>"
40: makCalendar = sCalendar
41: End Function
42:
```

The makCalendar()function creates a table definition, creates the month banner and the seven weekday columns, and then loops through the remaining rows and columns, calling the makAP_URL() function from Listing 24.7 to place the date. The makAP_URL() function appends an exclamation mark to the end of a date that contains an appointment.

The GMonth() function takes a pair of arguments, the month number, and a boolean value to determine whether it should return a long month like January or a short month like Jan. Although the short month is not used, it produces a value that can be used in the expiration field of a cookie so that you can expand this example to create time-sensitive to-do's.

Listing 24.9. The GMonth() function.

```
 1: Function GMonth(iMonth, fLongShort)
 2: Select Case iMonth
 3: Case 1
 4:    If fLongShort = true then GMonth="January" else GMonth="Jan"
 5: Case 2
 6:    If fLongShort = true then GMonth="February" else GMonth="Feb"
 7: Case 3
 8:    If fLongShort = true then GMonth="March" else GMonth="Mar"
 9: Case 4
10:    If fLongShort = true then GMonth="April" else GMonth="Apr"
11: Case 5
12:    If fLongShort = true then GMonth="May" else GMonth="May"
13: Case 6
14:    If fLongShort = true then GMonth="June" else GMonth="Jun"
15: Case 7
16:    If fLongShort = true then GMonth="July" else GMonth="Jul"
17: Case 8
18:    If fLongShort = true then GMonth="August" else GMonth="Aug"
19: Case 9
20:    If fLongShort = true then GMonth="September" else GMonth="Sep"
21: Case 10
22:    If fLongShort = true then GMonth="October" else GMonth="Oct"
23: Case 11
24:    If fLongShort = true then GMonth="November" else GMonth="Nov"
25: Case 12
26:    If fLongShort = true then GMonth="December"  else GMonth="Dec"
27: End Select
28: End Function
29:
```

Presenting Information

An application is completely useless if it doesn't provide the user any feedback. In order to keep the WWW PIM from being completely useless, we need to add some code that creates an interface for the user to edit and view information from the page. This code is broken down into two separate groups:

- The add routines
- The ApptStat routine

The add Routines

The add routines in Listings 24.10, 24.11, and 24.12 provide an interface for the user to input, edit, or delete information. Each routine displays one or more message boxes and prompts the user for the necessary information. Depending on whether the user is adding, editing, or deleting information, each routine then calls either setVariable or killVariable.

The addTodo and addAddr routines both display a generic message box like the one in Figure 24.2.

FIGURE 24.2.

The Add/Delete Item message box.

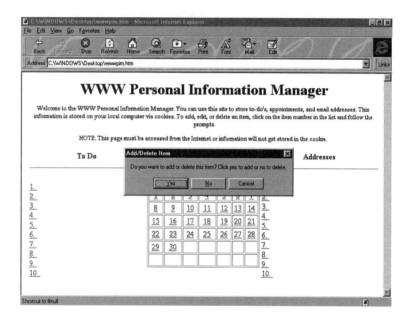

Listing 24.10. The addTodo routine.

```
1:
2: Sub addTodo(iRecord)
3: Dim sTodo
4: Dim iChoice
5:
6: iChoice = MsgBox("Do you want to add or delete this item? Click yes to add or no
➥ to delete.", 3, "Add/Delete Item")
7: Select Case iChoice
8:     Case 6
9:         sTodo = InputBox("What do you want to do?", "Add To-Do")
10:         Call setVariable("%%TD" & Trim(iRecord), sTodo)
11:     Case 7
12:         killVariable "%%TD" & Trim(iRecord)
13:     Case 2
14:         Exit Sub
15: End Select
16: window.navigate "wwwpim.htm"
17: End Sub
18:
```

Listing 24.10 displays an input box that looks like Figure 24.3.

FIGURE 24.3.

The Add To-Do dialog.

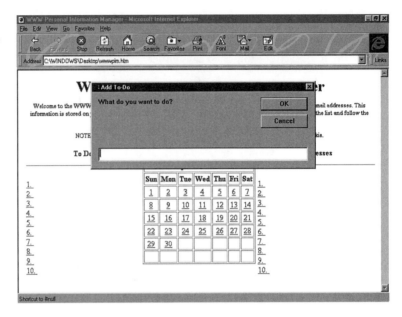

Listing 24.11. The addAppt routine.

```
1:
2: Sub addAppt(m,d,y)
3: Dim sAppt
4: Dim TempAppt
5:
6: TempAppt = readVariable("%%AP" & Trim(m) & "/" & Trim(d) & "/" & Trim(y))
7:
8: If Len(Trim(TempAppt)) > 0 Then
9:     sAppt = InputBox("Please enter or edit your appointment list for today", ➥
➥      "Add/Edit Appointment", readVariable("%%AP" & Trim(m) & "/" & Trim(d) & "/"
➥      & Trim(y)))
10: Else
11:     sAppt = InputBox("Please enter or edit your appointment list for today",
➥      "Add/Edit Appointment")
12: End If
13: If Len(Trim(sAppt)) > 0 Then
14:     Call setVariable("%%AP" & Trim(m) & "/" & Trim(d) & "/" & Trim(y), sAppt)
15: Else
16:     killVariable("%%AP" & Trim(m) & "/" & Trim(d) & "/" & Trim(y))
17: End If
18: window.navigate "wwwpim.htm"
19: End Sub
20:
```

Listing 24.11 displays an input box like the one in Figure 24.4.

FIGURE 24.4.
The Add/Edit Appointment dialog.

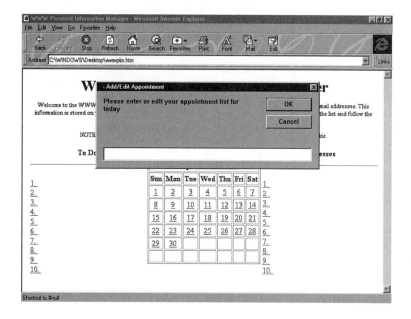

Listing 24.12 displays an input box like the one in Figure 24.5.

Listing 24.12. The addAddr routine.

```
1:
2: Sub addAddr(iRecord)
3: Dim Addr
4: Dim iChoice
5: iChoice = MsgBox("Do you want to add or delete this item? Click yes to add or no
➥to delete.", 3,"Add/Delete Item")
6:
7: Select Case iChoice
8:     Case 6
9:         Addr=InputBox("What address do you want to add?", "Add Email Address")
10:        Call setVariable("%%AD" & Trim(iRecord), Addr)
11:    Case 7
12:        killVariable "%%AD" & Trim(iRecord)
13:    Case 2
14:        Exit Sub
15: End Select
16: window.navigate "wwwpim.htm"
17: End Sub
18:
```

24

PERSONAL
INFORMATION
MANAGER

Figure 24.5.

The Add/Delete address routine.

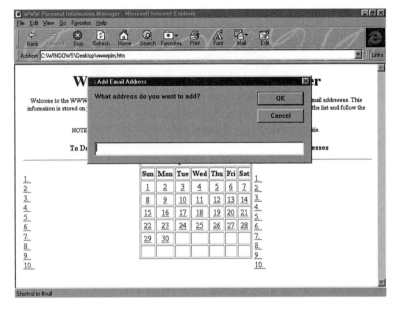

The ApptStat Routine

The `ApptStat` routine (see Listing 24.13) is called by the `onMouseOver` event associated with each day. When the mouse passes over a date, this routine is called and the current appointment is placed in the status bar.

Listing 24.13. The ApptStat routine.

```
1:
2: Sub ApptStat(m,d,y)
3: Dim sTemp
4:
5: sTemp     = CStr(d & " " & readVariable("%%AP" & m & "/" & d & "/" & y))
6: If Len(Trim(sTemp)) > 0 AND readVariable("%%AP" & m & "/" & d & "/" & y) <>
➥"NULL" Then
7:      window.status = sTemp
8: Else
9:      window.status = CStr(d)
10: End If
11: End Sub
```

Tying It All Together

Now that we've covered all the routines that support generation of the page, we have one last procedure to cover, the `docCreate` routine.

The docCreate Procedure

The docCreate procedure in Listing 24.14 encapsulates all the previous functions to generate all of the HTML for the page. It creates each column one at a time, filling in each cell with an <HREF> from one of the mak() functions, and then it calls document.write to append the new content to the document.

Listing 24.14. The docCreate procedure.

```
1:
2: Sub docCreate
3: Dim sDocument
4: sDocument = "<TD ALIGN=LEFT VALIGN=TOP WIDTH=35%><CENTER><B>To Do</B></CENTER>"
5: sDocument = sDocument & Chr(13) & Chr(10) & "<HR>"
6: For i = 1 to 10
7:     sDocument = sDocument & "<BR>" & makTD_URL(i)
8: Next
9: sDocument = sDocument & "</TD><TD ALIGN=CENTER VALIGN=MIDDLE WIDTH=30%>"
10: sDocument = sDocument & makCalendar()
11: sDocument = sDocument & "</TD><TD ALIGN=LEFT VALIGN=TOP WIDTH=35%>"
12: sDocument = sDocument & "<CENTER><B>ADDRESSES</B></CENTER>"
13: sDocument = sDocument & Chr(13) & Chr(10) & "<HR>"
14: For j = 1 to 10
15:     sDocument = sDocument & "<BR>" & makAD_URL(j)
16: Next
17:
18: sDocument = sDocument & "</TD></TR>"
19: sDocument = sDocument & Chr(13) & Chr(10) & "</TABLE>"
20:
21: Document.Write sDocument
22:
23: End Sub
24:
```

Review

After trying this sample, you can see how to create Web applications that can easily store and retrieve complex sets of information and display them to the user.

Here's a few challenges for you to extend your WWW Personal Information Manager:

- Extend functionality by allowing you to create as many to-do's and addresses as you want, place appointments for future dates, or add more information like phone and street addresses.
- Add a notification capability that tells you when appointments are due or forthcoming.
- Convert the page to use ActiveX controls to give it a sleek and modern look.

24

PERSONAL
INFORMATION
MANAGER

Order Entry

by Craig Eddy

IN THIS CHAPTER

CHAPTER 25

Perhaps the biggest boon to the growth of the Internet, despite the complaints of many of the Internet's early pioneers, has been the advent of electronic commerce. The World Wide Web has been used for marketing purposes for a few years now. The availability of safe and accurate Web-based ordering is just now becoming a reality, however.

This chapter presents an example of a Web-based order entry application. It is written using a combination of HTML forms and VBScript code. The products available on this order form are *static*—that is, there is no connection to a database of available products. This makes the Web page easier to design and implement. To add such a connection requires using a server-side application to generate the HTML form and the appropriate VBScript code. This example won't delve into such detail.

The VBScript code in this order entry application performs the following functions:

- Accesses the document's `cookie` property to save and retrieve information about the user of the order entry form
- Calculates subtotals, shipping charges, and sales tax
- Validates the information entered, such as ZIP code
- Submits the validated information to the server-side process, which accepts the order data

This chapter begins with an overview of security as it relates to Web-based commerce such as online ordering. Then, a brief review of HTTP cookies is presented, which were discussed in Chapter 14, "Customize Your Web Page with Cookies." Finally, you'll see the example application itself.

Ensuring Secure Transactions on the Web

When you discuss the Internet, the first and most hotly debated topic to enter the conversation is the subject of security. The concerns about security on the Web are well-founded given the ease with which a hacker can use well-documented methods to steal information from machines located on or communication occurring on a computer network such as the Internet. Although security isn't required to build and run the VBScript application presented in this chapter, a brief overview of various security concerns seems appropriate.

The typical concerns when dealing with electronic commerce follow:

- Verifying that the merchant is authentic
- Authenticating the user
- Preventing unauthorized access to information

These three concerns and possible solutions are touched on in the following sections. Another very good source of information is the Microsoft Internet Security Framework site located at `http://www.microsoft.com/intdev/security/default.htm`.

Authenticating the Merchant

It is necessary to authenticate the merchant (or simply the Web site being accessed) because just about anyone these days can post a Web site and use a variety of methods to request credit card numbers or electronic cash payments. As a potential purchaser of products and services on the Web, you'd like to know that companies you're about to purchase from are who they say they are.

The current trend in merchant authentication is to use *site certificates.* These are issued by an agency that takes the responsibility to verify that organizations requesting the site certificates are who they say they are. Internet Explorer 3.0 supports the use of site certificates for authentication. Figure 25.1 shows a sample site certificate. Notice the small padlock at the right-hand side of the status bar. This indicates that Internet Explorer currently is viewing a secure and verified site.

FIGURE 25.1.

A sample site certificate for a secure Web site.

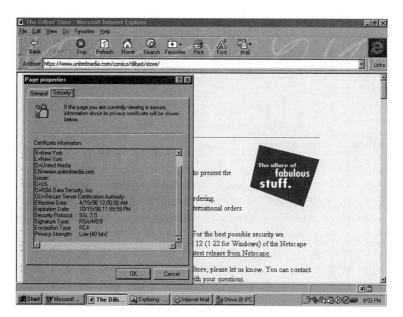

Authenticating the Purchaser

Just as you as a purchaser are concerned with the authenticity of the Web site, the merchant also wants to ensure that you are who you say you are. This is less of a concern than authenticating the merchant because the merchant almost always verifies your ability to pay before providing the product or service. Still, with the possibility of credit card fraud and possible means of counterfeiting electronic cash, merchants still want to be able to verify your identity as a purchaser at their Web sites.

Internet Explorer 3.0 supports personal certificates. These are similar to site certificates and also are issued by an agency that verifies you are, indeed, who you claim to be. Currently, personal certificates are provided by an agency named VeriSign. Its Web site provides a very good overview of personal certificates and how they are obtained and used. The URL for the page is `http://digitalid.verisign.com/brw_intr.htm`.

Encrypting Web Communications

Obviously, if you are willing to send credit card information across a public network like the Internet, you want to know that no one else can view that information. The same holds true for personal information such as household income. Several encryption standards currently are being debated, and some are in place within Web browsers today. Eventually, one or two standards will win out; until at least one gains general acceptance, everyday purchasing on the Web will remain a fantasy. Site certificates also play a vital role in securing the channels of communication.

Reviewing Cookies

The term *cookie*, when used in reference to a Web page, refers to a string of characters that is stored for the particular Web page or site. The cookie can store any type of information you want. Typically, cookies store information that identifies the user of the Web browser (name, address, and phone number) or retain some state information (when the user last accessed the page, what his personal preferences related to the page are, and so on).

Using VBScript, you can access the cookie for a page using the `document.cookie` property. The format of the string is *variable_name=value*. Multiple variable/value pairs are stored by separating the pairs with a semicolon. For example, the `cookie` property may evaluate to this:

`LastName=Eddy;FirstName=Craig;FavoriteColor=Green`

This cookie has three variables stored: `LastName`, `FirstName`, and `FavoriteColor`.

You set the cookie for a page by assigning a string formatted as *variable_name=value* to the `document.cookie` property. For example,

`document.cookie = "FavoriteColor=Yellow"`

assigns or changes the setting for the variable `FavoriteColor`.

Cookie variables also can be set to expire at a certain time. This is accomplished by appending the string `;expires=`*date/time*. The cookie variable then is invalid after the date/time specified.

To remove a cookie variable, set its value to the string `NULL` and append an `expires` with a value set to some date in the past.

> **NOTE**
>
> Cookies are valid only if the page being accessed is stored on a Web server. This is due to the fact that cookies are actually part of the transport protocol used to communicate on the Web. If you attempt to assign a value to the cookie property for a page not located on a Web server, your script code produces a trappable runtime error.

Designing the Order Entry Form

The order entry form created in this chapter is an order form that is static. For the sake of simplicity, no attempt is made to retrieve data from a product database and assemble an order form from that data.

The products sold using this form are framed portraits of United States presidents (hey, why not?). The user will be able to order any quantity of the available portraits. Shipping and handling, as well as sales tax, are calculated by the VBScript code so that users always know exactly how much the purchase will cost them. The script code also verifies the entered phone number and ZIP code for proper formatting before submitting the form data.

Figure 25.2 shows the order entry form. The top of the form contains header information: customer name, address, and phone number. This is followed by the order form that gives the user the details about each portrait: description, cost, and shipping charge. The user enters the quantity of each portrait to be ordered, and the script code updates the various subtotals and the grand total. The shipping cost, product total cost, and grand total are displayed in a separate frame that always appears at the bottom of the browser, regardless of where the user has scrolled to on the order form.

Listing 25.1 shows the HTML used to create the frames. You can type it in or copy it from the CD-ROM. Save it to a Web server directory if possible. The name is irrelevant, but you'll need to remember what it is because this is the file that you'll open with Internet Explorer when it's time to test the application.

Listing 25.1. The frame container for the order entry page.

```
<HTML>
<HEAD>
<TITLE>Portrait Order Form</TITLE>
</HEAD>
<BODY>
<FRAMESET FRAMEBORDER=NO ROWS="90,10">
<FRAME SCROLLING=YES SRC=25-3.htm>
<FRAME SCROLLING=NO MARGINHEIGHT=5 MARGINWIDTH=5 SRC=25-2.HTM>
</FRAMESET>
</BODY>
</HTML>
```

25

ORDER ENTRY

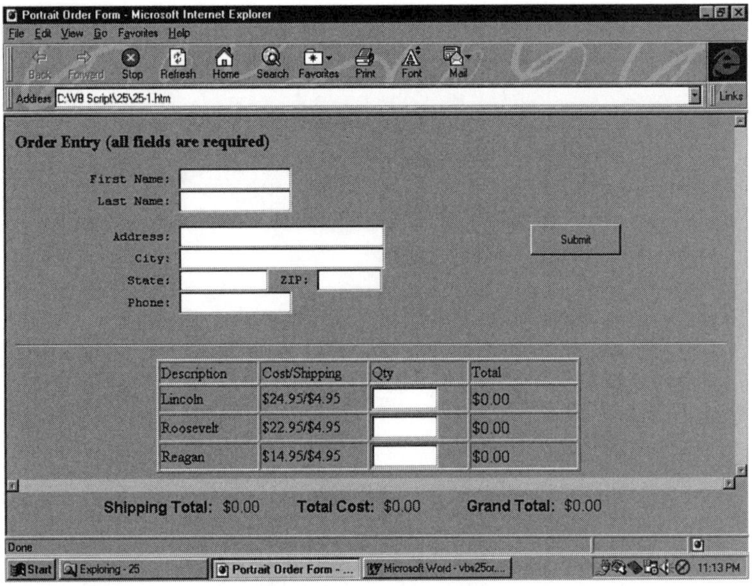

FIGURE 25.2.

The order entry form displayed with Internet Explorer.

This Web page makes pretty basic use of frames. The <FRAMESET> tag specifies the start of a frame definition. The FRAMEBORDER=NO specifies that there should be no borders around the frames. ROWS="90,10" specifies that the frames will be stacked vertically. The top frame will take up 90 percent of the browser's viewing area, and the bottom frame uses 10 percent.

The <FRAME SCROLLING=YES SRC=25-3.htm> tag for the first frame in the frameset specifies that the frame is to be scrollable and that a file named 25-3.htm should be used as the content for the frame.

The <FRAME SCROLLING=NO MARGINHEIGHT=5 MARGINWIDTH=5 SRC=25-2.htm> tag for the second frame in the frameset specifies that the frame is not scrollable and that a file named 25-2.htm should be used as the content for the frame. This is the bottom frame shown in Figure 25.2.

Next, Listing 25.2 shows the HTML code for the bottom frame (25-2.htm). You can type the code, use the ActiveX Control Pad to assist in inserting the Label controls, or copy the code from the accompanying CD-ROM. Save the file as 25-1.htm in the same directory as the code from Listing 25.1.

Listing 25.2. The bottom frame of the order entry page.

```
<HTML><HEAD><TITLE>New Page</TITLE></HEAD>
<BODY><CENTER>
   <OBJECT ID="IeLabel1" WIDTH=127 HEIGHT=27
 CLASSID="CLSID:99B42120-6EC7-11CF-A6C7-00AA00A47DD2">
   <PARAM NAME="_ExtentX" VALUE="3334">
   <PARAM NAME="_ExtentY" VALUE="714">
```

```
        <PARAM NAME="Caption" VALUE="Shipping Total:">
        <PARAM NAME="Angle" VALUE="0">
        <PARAM NAME="Alignment" VALUE="0">
        <PARAM NAME="Mode" VALUE="1">
        <PARAM NAME="FillStyle" VALUE="0">
        <PARAM NAME="FillStyle" VALUE="0">
        <PARAM NAME="ForeColor" VALUE="#000000">
        <PARAM NAME="BackColor" VALUE="#C0C0C0">
        <PARAM NAME="FontName" VALUE="Arial">
        <PARAM NAME="FontSize" VALUE="12">
        <PARAM NAME="FontItalic" VALUE="0">
        <PARAM NAME="FontBold" VALUE="1">
        <PARAM NAME="FontUnderline" VALUE="0">
        <PARAM NAME="FontStrikeout" VALUE="0">
        <PARAM NAME="TopPoints" VALUE="0">
        <PARAM NAME="BotPoints" VALUE="0">
</OBJECT>    <OBJECT ID="lblShipTot" WIDTH=80 HEIGHT=27
 CLASSID="CLSID:99B42120-6EC7-11CF-A6C7-00AA00A47DD2">
        <PARAM NAME="_ExtentX" VALUE="1879">
        <PARAM NAME="_ExtentY" VALUE="714">
        <PARAM NAME="Caption" VALUE="$0.00">
        <PARAM NAME="Angle" VALUE="0">
        <PARAM NAME="Alignment" VALUE="0">
        <PARAM NAME="Mode" VALUE="1">
        <PARAM NAME="FillStyle" VALUE="0">
        <PARAM NAME="FillStyle" VALUE="0">
        <PARAM NAME="ForeColor" VALUE="#000000">
        <PARAM NAME="BackColor" VALUE="#C0C0C0">
        <PARAM NAME="FontName" VALUE="Arial">
        <PARAM NAME="FontSize" VALUE="12">
        <PARAM NAME="FontItalic" VALUE="0">
        <PARAM NAME="FontBold" VALUE="0">
        <PARAM NAME="FontUnderline" VALUE="0">
        <PARAM NAME="FontStrikeout" VALUE="0">
        <PARAM NAME="TopPoints" VALUE="0">
        <PARAM NAME="BotPoints" VALUE="0">
</OBJECT>      <OBJECT ID="IeLabel2" WIDTH=93 HEIGHT=27
 CLASSID="CLSID:99B42120-6EC7-11CF-A6C7-00AA00A47DD2">
        <PARAM NAME="_ExtentX" VALUE="2461">
        <PARAM NAME="_ExtentY" VALUE="714">
        <PARAM NAME="Caption" VALUE="Total Cost:">
        <PARAM NAME="Angle" VALUE="0">
        <PARAM NAME="Alignment" VALUE="0">
        <PARAM NAME="Mode" VALUE="1">
        <PARAM NAME="FillStyle" VALUE="0">
        <PARAM NAME="FillStyle" VALUE="0">
        <PARAM NAME="ForeColor" VALUE="#000000">
        <PARAM NAME="BackColor" VALUE="#C0C0C0">
        <PARAM NAME="FontName" VALUE="Arial">
        <PARAM NAME="FontSize" VALUE="12">
        <PARAM NAME="FontItalic" VALUE="0">
        <PARAM NAME="FontBold" VALUE="1">
        <PARAM NAME="FontUnderline" VALUE="0">
        <PARAM NAME="FontStrikeout" VALUE="0">
        <PARAM NAME="TopPoints" VALUE="0">
        <PARAM NAME="BotPoints" VALUE="0">
```

25

ORDER ENTRY

continues

Listing 25.2. continued

```
</OBJECT>    <OBJECT ID="lblCostTot" WIDTH=90 HEIGHT=27
     CLASSID="CLSID:99B42120-6EC7-11CF-A6C7-00AA00A47DD2">
          <PARAM NAME="_ExtentX" VALUE="3360">
          <PARAM NAME="_ExtentY" VALUE="423">
          <PARAM NAME="Caption" VALUE="$0.00">
          <PARAM NAME="Angle" VALUE="0">
          <PARAM NAME="Alignment" VALUE="0">
          <PARAM NAME="Mode" VALUE="1">
          <PARAM NAME="FillStyle" VALUE="0">
          <PARAM NAME="FillStyle" VALUE="0">
          <PARAM NAME="ForeColor" VALUE="#000000">
          <PARAM NAME="BackColor" VALUE="#C0C0C0">
          <PARAM NAME="FontName" VALUE="Arial">
          <PARAM NAME="FontSize" VALUE="12">
          <PARAM NAME="FontItalic" VALUE="0">
          <PARAM NAME="FontBold" VALUE="0">
          <PARAM NAME="FontUnderline" VALUE="0">
          <PARAM NAME="FontStrikeout" VALUE="0">
          <PARAM NAME="TopPoints" VALUE="0">
          <PARAM NAME="BotPoints" VALUE="0">
   </OBJECT> <OBJECT ID="IeLabel3" WIDTH=104 HEIGHT=27
 CLASSID="CLSID:99B42120-6EC7-11CF-A6C7-00AA00A47DD2">
     <PARAM NAME="_ExtentX" VALUE="2752">
     <PARAM NAME="_ExtentY" VALUE="714">
     <PARAM NAME="Caption" VALUE="Grand Total:">
     <PARAM NAME="Angle" VALUE="0">
     <PARAM NAME="Alignment" VALUE="0">
     <PARAM NAME="Mode" VALUE="1">
     <PARAM NAME="FillStyle" VALUE="0">
     <PARAM NAME="FillStyle" VALUE="0">
     <PARAM NAME="ForeColor" VALUE="#000000">
     <PARAM NAME="BackColor" VALUE="#C0C0C0">
     <PARAM NAME="FontName" VALUE="Arial">
     <PARAM NAME="FontSize" VALUE="12">
     <PARAM NAME="FontItalic" VALUE="0">
     <PARAM NAME="FontBold" VALUE="1">
     <PARAM NAME="FontUnderline" VALUE="0">
     <PARAM NAME="FontStrikeout" VALUE="0">
     <PARAM NAME="TopPoints" VALUE="0">
     <PARAM NAME="BotPoints" VALUE="0">
</OBJECT>    <OBJECT ID="lblGrandTot" WIDTH=90 HEIGHT=27
     CLASSID="CLSID:99B42120-6EC7-11CF-A6C7-00AA00A47DD2">
          <PARAM NAME="_ExtentX" VALUE="3360">
          <PARAM NAME="_ExtentY" VALUE="423">
          <PARAM NAME="Caption" VALUE="$0.00">
          <PARAM NAME="Angle" VALUE="0">
          <PARAM NAME="Alignment" VALUE="0">
          <PARAM NAME="Mode" VALUE="1">
          <PARAM NAME="FillStyle" VALUE="0">
          <PARAM NAME="FillStyle" VALUE="0">
          <PARAM NAME="ForeColor" VALUE="#000000">
          <PARAM NAME="BackColor" VALUE="#C0C0C0">
          <PARAM NAME="FontName" VALUE="Arial">
          <PARAM NAME="FontSize" VALUE="12">
          <PARAM NAME="FontItalic" VALUE="0">
```

```
        <PARAM NAME="FontBold" VALUE="0">
        <PARAM NAME="FontUnderline" VALUE="0">
        <PARAM NAME="FontStrikeout" VALUE="0">
        <PARAM NAME="TopPoints" VALUE="0">
        <PARAM NAME="BotPoints" VALUE="0">
    </OBJECT></CENTER></BODY></HTML>
```

This HTML file is simply a set of six ActiveX Label controls. You can readily obtain these controls from the Microsoft ActiveX Control Gallery at `http://www.microsoft.com` if they don't already exist on your machine. Note that if you cannot guarantee that users have these controls installed on their machines, you should specify the CODEBASE property. The value of the property provides the location of where the control can be downloaded and installed.

Note that the ID properties specified as `lblShipTot`, `lblCostTot`, and `lblGrandTot` should not be modified without a corresponding change in `25-3.htm` that sets the Caption properties for these labels. Also, you should not modify the Width or Height properties. Giving the labels different Height properties from one another makes them appear in different places on the page as opposed to in a line, as shown in Figure 25.2.

Because the HTML for the main order form is mostly VBScript code, `25-3.htm` is discussed in the next section.

Creating the Order Entry Form

This section discusses the creation of the main order form. Most of the HTML file is comprised of the script code. Most of the document is contained within the HTML <FORM> container. The ACTION element specified for the form should be the URL to the back-end program that is servicing the order entry process. In my example, I've used a simple ISAPI application that simply returns the data found on the HTML form.

The document is formatted with two tables. The top of the document has a table with one row (<TR> ... </TR>) and two columns (<TD> ... </TD>). The left-hand column contains the customer information input boxes. The right-hand column only contains the Submit button. Note that this is not an HTML form input of type Submit. This is actually an ActiveX command button control. This is necessary because, after this button is clicked, the VBScript code does some data-validation work before submitting the form's data to the back-end program. If the validation checks fail, the form's Submit method is not invoked and the user is given the opportunity to correct any errors.

The top and bottom portions of the form are separated with a horizontal rule (<HR>), which is simply a line that runs horizontally across the browser window. The bottom part of the document contains another table. Each row in this table has text describing the portraits and their costs. There is also a Microsoft Forms 2.0 ActiveX text box control, a hidden HTML input box, and an ActiveX Label control for each item in the table.

The ActiveX text box enables the user to enter an integer quantity specifying how many of each portrait to purchase. VBScript code verifies that the value entered is indeed an integer. After a quantity is entered, the total for the line is calculated. This total is displayed in the ActiveX label. Then the overall totals displayed in the bottom frame are updated. You'll see this when you delve into the VBScript code in the next section.

Examining the VBScript Code

This section describes the actual script code for the order entry application. Listing 25.3 shows the HTML for 25-3.htm. This section discusses the VBScript code but not the HTML contained in Listing 25.3. Most of the HTML is fairly standard.

Listing 25.3. The main frame for the order entry page.

```
<!DOCTYPE HTML PUBLIC "-//IETF//DTD HTML//EN">
<HTML><HEAD>
    <SCRIPT LANGUAGE="VBScript">
<!--
Sub window_onLoad()
Dim lstrTemp

lstrTemp = ReadVariable("FirstName")
if lstrTemp <> NOT_FOUND then Document.ORDER.FirstName.Value = lstrTemp
lstrTemp = ReadVariable("LastName")
if lstrTemp <> NOT_FOUND then Document.ORDER.LastName.Value = lstrTemp
lstrTemp = ReadVariable("Address")
if lstrTemp <> NOT_FOUND then Document.ORDER.Address.Value = lstrTemp
lstrTemp = ReadVariable("City")
if lstrTemp <> NOT_FOUND then Document.ORDER.City.Value = lstrTemp
lstrTemp = ReadVariable("State")
if lstrTemp <> NOT_FOUND then Document.ORDER.State.Value = lstrTemp
lstrTemp = ReadVariable("ZIP")
if lstrTemp <> NOT_FOUND then Document.ORDER.ZIP.Value = lstrTemp
lstrTemp = ReadVariable("Phone")
if lstrTemp <> NOT_FOUND then Document.ORDER.Phone.Value = lstrTemp

Document.ORDER.FirstName.focus()

end sub

Function ReadVariable(strVariableName)
'these five variables are used in the string manipulation
'code that finds the variable in the cookie.
Dim intLocation
Dim intNameLength
Dim intValueLength
Dim intNextSemicolon
Dim strTemp

'calculate length and location of variable name
intNameLength = Len(strVariableName)
intLocation = Instr(Document.Cookie, strVariableName)
```

```
         'check for existence of variable name

If intLocation = 0 Then
     'variable not found, so it can't be read
     ReadVariable = NOT_FOUND
Else
     'get a smaller substring to work with
     strTemp = Right(Document.Cookie, Len(Document.Cookie) - intLocation + 1)

     'check to make sure we found the full string, not just a substring
     If Mid(strTemp, intNameLength + 1, 1) <> "=" Then
         'oops, only found substring, not good enough
         ReadVariable = NOT_FOUND

         'note that this will incorrectly give a not found result if and only if
         'a search for a variable whose name is a substring of a preceding
         'variable is undertaken.  For example, this will fail:
         '
         'search for: MyVar
         'cookie contains: MyVariable=2;MyVar=1
     Else
         'found full string
         intNextSemicolon = Instr(strTemp, ";")

         'if not found, then we need the last element of the cookie
         If intNextSemicolon = 0 Then intNextSemicolon = Len(strTemp) + 1

         'check for empty variable (Var1=;)
         If intNextSemicolon = (intNameLength + 2) Then
             'variable is empty
             ReadVariable = ""
         Else
             'calculate value normally
             intValueLength = intNextSemicolon - intNameLength - 2
             ReadVariable = Mid(strTemp, intNameLength + 2, intValueLength)
         End If
     End If
End If
End If
end function

dim  NOT_FOUND
NOT_FOUND = "NOT_FOUND"

-->
    </SCRIPT>
<TITLE>Main Frame in Order Entry</TITLE ></HEAD>
<BODY>
<H3>Order Entry (all fields are required)</H3><p>
 <div align=center><center><table width=80% align=center><tr><td width=75%>
     <FORM ACTION="http://pipestream.ipctech.com/cgi-win/spitback.dll"
     METHOD="POST" NAME="ORDER">
<pre><p>First Name: <input type=text size=20 maxlength=256 name="FirstName">
 Last Name: <INPUT TYPE=text SIZE=20 NAME="LastName" maxlength=256>
<br>   Address: <INPUT TYPE=text SIZE=40 NAME="Address" maxlength=256>
      City: <INPUT TYPE=text SIZE=40 NAME="City" maxlength=256>
     State: <INPUT TYPE=text SIZE=15 NAME="State" maxlength=256> ZIP: <INPUT
```

25

continues

Listing 25.3. continued

```
TYPE=text SIZE=10 NAME="ZIP" maxlength=10>
      Phone: <INPUT TYPE=text SIZE=20 NAME="Phone" maxlength=256></pre></td>
<td width=25%><CENTER><OBJECT ID="cmdSubmit" WIDTH=96 HEIGHT=32
      CLASSID="CLSID:D7053240-CE69-11CD-A777-00DD01143C57">
        <PARAM NAME="Caption" VALUE="Submit">
        <PARAM NAME="Size" VALUE="2540;846">
        <PARAM NAME="FontCharSet" VALUE="0">
        <PARAM NAME="FontPitchAndFamily" VALUE="2">
        <PARAM NAME="ParagraphAlign" VALUE="3">
        <PARAM NAME="FontWeight" VALUE="0">
    </OBJECT></CENTER></td>
</tr></table></center></div>
 <hr>
<div align=center><center>
<table width=60% BORDER=1>
<tr><td width=25%>Description</td><td width=25%>Cost/Shipping</td>
<td width=25%>Qty</td><td width=25%>Total</td></tr>
<tr><td width=25%>Lincoln</td><td width=25%>$24.95/$4.95</td><td width=25%>
<!-- MORE SCRIPT CODE -->
<SCRIPT LANGUAGE="VBScript">
<!--
Function GetPrice(pzQtyText, pzQtyHidden, pdPrice)
Dim lExtPrice
GetPrice = -1
If instr(pzQtyText.Text, ".") then
    pzQtyText.Text = pzQtyHidden.value
    MsgBox "Please enter a vaid integer quantity!"
    Exit Function
end if
if not(isNumeric(pzQtyText.Text)) then
    pzQtyText.Text = pzQtyHidden.value
    MsgBox "Please enter a vaid integer quantity!"
    exit function
end if
lExtPrice = pdPrice * pzQtyText.Text
pzQtyHidden.value = pzQtyText.Text
GetPrice = FormatCurrency(lExtPrice)
end function

Function FormatCurrency(ptInputValue)
Dim ltValue
ltValue = ptInputValue
if instr(ltValue,".") = 0 then
    ltValue = ltValue & ".00"
elseif instr(ltValue,".") = Len(ltValue) - 1 then
    ltValue = ltValue & "0"
end if
ltValue = "$" & ltValue
FormatCurrency = ltValue
end function

Sub UpdateTotals()
dim lTmp
lTmp = CInt(document.order.LincolnQty.Value )
lTmp = lTmp + CInt(document.order.RooseveltQty.Value)
lTmp = lTmp + CInt(document.order.ReaganQty.Value)
```

```
lTmp = lTmp * 4.95
window.parent.frames(1).lblShipTot.Caption = cstr(FormatCurrency(lTmp))

Dim lTmp2
lTmp2 = CDbl(document.order.lblLincolnExt.Caption)
lTmp2 = lTmp2 + CDbl(document.order.lblRooseveltExt.Caption)
lTmp2 = lTmp2 + CDbl(document.order.lblReaganExt.Caption)
window.parent.frames(1).lblCostTot.Caption = cstr(FormatCurrency(lTmp2))

window.parent.frames(1).lblGrandTot.Caption = cstr(FormatCurrency(lTmp + ltmp2))
end sub

Sub txtLincolnQty_Change()
Dim lExtPrice
lExtPrice = GetPrice(document.order.txtLincolnQty, document.order.LincolnQty,
24.95)
if lExtPrice = -1 then exit sub
Document.ORDER.lblLincolnExt.caption = cstr(lExtPrice)
Call UpdateTotals()
end sub

Sub txtRooseveltQty_Change()
Dim lExtPrice
lExtPrice = GetPrice(document.order.txtRooseveltQty, document.order.RooseveltQty,
22.95)
if lExtPrice = -1 then exit sub
Document.ORDER.lblRooseveltExt.caption = cstr(lExtPrice)
Call UpdateTotals()
end sub

Sub txtReaganQty_Change()
Dim lExtPrice
lExtPrice = GetPrice(document.order.txtReaganQty, document.order.ReaganQty, 14.95)
if lExtPrice = -1 then exit sub
Document.ORDER.lblReaganExt.caption = cstr(lExtPrice)
Call UpdateTotals()
end sub
-->
        </SCRIPT>
        <OBJECT ID="txtLincolnQty" WIDTH=71 HEIGHT=24
         CLASSID="CLSID:8BD21D10-EC42-11CE-9E0D-00AA006002F3">
            <PARAM NAME="VariousPropertyBits" VALUE="746604571">
            <PARAM NAME="Size" VALUE="1873;635">
            <PARAM NAME="FontCharSet" VALUE="0">
            <PARAM NAME="FontPitchAndFamily" VALUE="2">
            <PARAM NAME="FontWeight" VALUE="0">
        </OBJECT>
        <INPUT TYPE=hidden VALUE="0" SIZE=5 NAME="LincolnQty" maxlength=256>
</td><td width=25%>
        <OBJECT ID="lblLincolnExt" WIDTH=83 HEIGHT=16
         CLASSID="CLSID:99B42120-6EC7-11CF-A6C7-00AA00A47DD2">
            <PARAM NAME="_ExtentX" VALUE="2196">
            <PARAM NAME="_ExtentY" VALUE="423">
            <PARAM NAME="Caption" VALUE="$0.00">
            <PARAM NAME="Angle" VALUE="0">
            <PARAM NAME="Alignment" VALUE="0">
```

25

ORDER ENTRY

continues

Listing 25.3. continued

```
                <PARAM NAME="Mode" VALUE="1">
                <PARAM NAME="FillStyle" VALUE="0">
                <PARAM NAME="FillStyle" VALUE="0">
                <PARAM NAME="ForeColor" VALUE="#000000">
                <PARAM NAME="BackColor" VALUE="#C0C0C0">
                <PARAM NAME="FontName" VALUE="Arial">
                <PARAM NAME="FontSize" VALUE="12">
                <PARAM NAME="FontItalic" VALUE="0">
                <PARAM NAME="FontBold" VALUE="0">
                <PARAM NAME="FontUnderline" VALUE="0">
                <PARAM NAME="FontStrikeout" VALUE="0">
                <PARAM NAME="TopPoints" VALUE="0">
                <PARAM NAME="BotPoints" VALUE="0">
            </OBJECT>
</td></tr>
<tr><td width=25%>Roosevelt</td><td width=25%>$22.95/$4.95</td><td width=25%>
            <OBJECT ID="txtRooseveltQty" WIDTH=71 HEIGHT=24
             CLASSID="CLSID:8BD21D10-EC42-11CE-9E0D-00AA006002F3">
                <PARAM NAME="VariousPropertyBits" VALUE="746604571">
                <PARAM NAME="Size" VALUE="1873;635">
                <PARAM NAME="FontCharSet" VALUE="0">
                <PARAM NAME="FontPitchAndFamily" VALUE="2">
                <PARAM NAME="FontWeight" VALUE="0">
            </OBJECT>
            <INPUT TYPE=hidden VALUE="0" SIZE=5 NAME="RooseveltQty" maxlength=256>
</td><td width=25%>
            <OBJECT ID="lblRooseveltExt" WIDTH=83 HEIGHT=16
             CLASSID="CLSID:99B42120-6EC7-11CF-A6C7-00AA00A47DD2">
                <PARAM NAME="_ExtentX" VALUE="2196">
                <PARAM NAME="_ExtentY" VALUE="423">
                <PARAM NAME="Caption" VALUE="$0.00">
                <PARAM NAME="Angle" VALUE="0">
                <PARAM NAME="Alignment" VALUE="0">
                <PARAM NAME="Mode" VALUE="1">
                <PARAM NAME="FillStyle" VALUE="0">
                <PARAM NAME="FillStyle" VALUE="0">
                <PARAM NAME="ForeColor" VALUE="#000000">
                <PARAM NAME="BackColor" VALUE="#C0C0C0">
                <PARAM NAME="FontName" VALUE="Arial">
                <PARAM NAME="FontSize" VALUE="12">
                <PARAM NAME="FontItalic" VALUE="0">
                <PARAM NAME="FontBold" VALUE="0">
                <PARAM NAME="FontUnderline" VALUE="0">
                <PARAM NAME="FontStrikeout" VALUE="0">
                <PARAM NAME="TopPoints" VALUE="0">
                <PARAM NAME="BotPoints" VALUE="0">
            </OBJECT>
</td></tr>
<tr><td width=25%>Reagan</td><td width=25%>$14.95/$4.95</td><td width=25%>
            <OBJECT ID="txtReaganQty" WIDTH=71 HEIGHT=24
             CLASSID="CLSID:8BD21D10-EC42-11CE-9E0D-00AA006002F3">
                <PARAM NAME="VariousPropertyBits" VALUE="746604571">
                <PARAM NAME="Size" VALUE="1873;635">
                <PARAM NAME="FontCharSet" VALUE="0">
                <PARAM NAME="FontPitchAndFamily" VALUE="2">
                <PARAM NAME="FontWeight" VALUE="0">
            </OBJECT>
```

```
            <INPUT TYPE=hidden VALUE="0" SIZE=5 NAME="ReaganQty" maxlength=256>
</td><td width=25%>
        <OBJECT ID="lblReaganExt" WIDTH=83 HEIGHT=16
         CLASSID="CLSID:99B42120-6EC7-11CF-A6C7-00AA00A47DD2">
            <PARAM NAME="_ExtentX" VALUE="2196">
            <PARAM NAME="_ExtentY" VALUE="423">
            <PARAM NAME="Caption" VALUE="$0.00">
            <PARAM NAME="Angle" VALUE="0">
            <PARAM NAME="Alignment" VALUE="0">
            <PARAM NAME="Mode" VALUE="1">
            <PARAM NAME="FillStyle" VALUE="0">
            <PARAM NAME="FillStyle" VALUE="0">
            <PARAM NAME="ForeColor" VALUE="#000000">
            <PARAM NAME="BackColor" VALUE="#C0C0C0">
            <PARAM NAME="FontName" VALUE="Arial">
            <PARAM NAME="FontSize" VALUE="12">
            <PARAM NAME="FontItalic" VALUE="0">
            <PARAM NAME="FontBold" VALUE="0">
            <PARAM NAME="FontUnderline" VALUE="0">
            <PARAM NAME="FontStrikeout" VALUE="0">
            <PARAM NAME="TopPoints" VALUE="0">
            <PARAM NAME="BotPoints" VALUE="0">
        </OBJECT>
</td></tr>
</table>
</center></div>
    </FORM>
<!-- FINAL SCRIPT SECTION -->
<SCRIPT LANGUAGE="VBScript">
<!--
Sub cmdSubmit_Click()
dim lTmp
if ValidateLen(Document.Order.FirstName, "First Name") = 0 then exit sub
if ValidateLen(Document.Order.LastName, "Last Name") = 0 then exit sub
if ValidateLen(Document.Order.Address, "Address") = 0 then exit sub
if ValidateLen(Document.Order.City, "City") = 0 then exit sub
if ValidateLen(Document.Order.State, "State") = 0 then exit sub
if ValidateLen(Document.Order.ZIP, "ZIP Code") = 0 then exit sub

lTmp = (Document.ORDER.ZIP.value)
select case Len(lTmp)
case 5
    if not isnumeric(lTmp)  then
        Call ErrorOnZIP()
        exit sub
    end if

case 10
    if mid(lTmp,6,1) <> "-" then
        call ErrorOnZIP()
        exit sub
    end if
    if not IsNumeric(left(lTmp,5)) then
        Call ErrorOnZIP()
        exit sub
    end if
    if not isnumeric(right(lTmp,4)) then
```

25

ORDER ENTRY

continues

Listing 25.3. continued

```
            Call ErrorOnZIP()
            exit sub
        end if
case else
    Call ErrorOnZIP()
    exit sub
end select

Document.Cookie = "FirstName=" & document.order.FirstName.Value
Document.Cookie = "LastName=" & Document.Order.LastName.Value
Document.Cookie = "Address=" & Document.Order.Address.Value
Document.Cookie = "City=" & Document.Order.City.Value
Document.Cookie = "State=" & Document.Order.State.Value
Document.Cookie = "ZIP=" & Document.Order.ZIP.Value
Document.Cookie = "Phone=" & Document.Order.Phone.Value
Document.Cookie = "LastOrderDate=" & CStr(Now)

call Document.ORDER.submit()
end sub

Function ValidateLen(pzField, ptMessage)
if Len(pzField.value) = 0 then
    MsgBox ptMessage & " is required!"
    call pzField.Focus()
    ValidateLen = 0
    exit function
end if
ValidateLen = 1
end function

Sub ErrorOnZIP()
    MsgBox "ZIP Code invalid!"
    call Document.ORDER.ZIP.Select
    call Document.ORDER.ZIP.focus()
end sub
-->
    </SCRIPT>
</BODY></html>
```

The script code begins with the window_onLoad event. The first step of the script is to load any cookie data that exists for the order entry page. The cookie data is saved when the user clicks the Submit button. The onLoad event calls the ReadVariable() function discussed in Chapter 14. This function reads a cookie variable from the cookie property and returns the cookie's value. The cookie data then is placed into the appropriate text boxes on the form.

After the cookie data is loaded, the focus is set to the first name text box by invoking the focus() method. This is necessary because you cannot guarantee that the first name box will receive focus when the page loads. Usually, one of the ActiveX text boxes receives focus before the HTML form does.

Scrolling further down the listing, find the comment `<!-- MORE SCRIPT CODE -->`. This section of code is where calculations are made based on the quantities entered by the user. The first function, `GetPrice()`, ensures that the user entered an integer and then calculates the total price for the line on which the quantity was entered. Note the use of the `IsNumeric()` function. Because the Visual Basic `val()` function does not appear to work within VBScript, you should use `IsNumeric()` instead of `if val(variable_name) = 0` to determine whether *variable_name* stores a numeric value.

Next comes the `FormatCurrency()` function. Because VBScript lacks the Visual Basic `format$()` function, you must manually format strings. The `FormatCurrency()` function takes a string and formats it as `$#.00` would in the `format$()` function.

Next comes the `UpdateTotals` procedure. This procedure updates the ActiveX labels found in the bottom frame. The first section of code in Listing 25.3 updates the label that displays the total shipping cost. The second section updates the total cost of the portraits, not including shipping. The final line of code updates the label displaying the grand total.

Finally, the `change` event code is used for the three ActiveX text boxes. All three event procedures perform the same tasks. First, the `GetPrice()` function is called to obtain the total product cost for the current portrait. If the quantity entered was valid, the ActiveX label displaying the extended cost for the portrait (quantity multiplied by price) is updated. Finally, the `UpdateTotals` procedure is called to update the bottom frame.

The final section of code appears after the `<!-- FINAL SCRIPT SECTION -->` comment. This code is responsible for validating the data entered into the form. The validation rules follow:

- All user information fields must have values.
- The ZIP code entered must be in ##### format or #####-#### format.

> **WARNING**
>
> Early versions of Internet Explorer 3.0 appear to submit an HTML form whenever the user presses the Enter key, bypassing the validation code placed in the command button's `Click` event. If you come up with a clever way to avoid this, e-mail me at craige@pipestream.ipctech.com.

The Submit button is not an HTML form's Submit button but rather an ActiveX command button control. Clicking this button fires the `cmdSubmit_click` event. This event first uses a function named `ValidateLen()` to check the existence of data in the specified text box. If the text box is empty, a message box is displayed and the function returns a 0. The HTML form data is not submitted in this case. After all the user information boxes are validated as having data, the ZIP code field is checked to make sure that the data is in the proper format.

After all the validation checks have passed, the script updates the cookie data. The current values entered in the text boxes are stored into the cookie. The current date/time also is stored in a cookie to store the date/time of the user's last order submission.

Finally, the form's submit() method is invoked to send the form's data to the back-end process that is servicing the order entry application.

Testing the Application

After you save or copy the code for the three listings from the CD-ROM, you can test the script. If you want to use the cookie feature, you must save the files to a Web server's content directory because cookies depend on a Web server for their operation.

Load the file 25-1.htm. It should appear as in Figure 25.2. Enter information into all the user information boxes at the top of the page. Try entering some invalid ZIP codes and clicking the Submit button. If you don't receive a message box informing you that the ZIP code is invalid, check the code in the cmdSubmit_click event. Also, if you can leave a user information field blank without receiving a message box, check to make sure that the field is included in the calls to ValidateLen().

Next, try entering some quantities into the table at the bottom of the form. You should see the appropriate label captions change. Try entering a number other than an integer. A message box should appear asking you to enter an integer. If not, check the code in the GetPrice() function.

After testing the other portions and successfully submitting the form, reload the page. The user information text boxes should contain the data previously entered. If not, first check the cmdSubmit_click event to make sure that the cookie property is being set for any missing information. If everything looks fine there, check the window_onLoad event to make sure that the data is being read for the missing field. If all fields are missing, check the code in ReadVariable() and make sure that you're using the Web server to provide the page, instead of using Internet Explorer's File | Open menu to load the operating system.

Review

The example in this chapter provides the basis for a fully operational order entry Web application. The only piece you must add is the back-end application that processes the submitted data. This is another subject for another book. *Web Programming with Visual Basic*, published by Sams.net, is an excellent source for learning how to program back-end Web server applications using Visual Basic.

RTFEditor

by Evangelos Petroutsos

IN THIS CHAPTER

Using OCX Controls with VBScript

You've seen examples of ActiveX controls, which were designed specifically for VBScript and Web applications. Controls are not new to the Windows environment, though. They are the basic building blocks of the Windows user interface and as such existed long before VBScript, and were called OCX controls. If you have programmed in the Windows environment, you are familiar with OCX controls. ActiveX is a new specification for building controls that can be used both on the desktop and within a browser. Eventually, all the existing OCX controls will be converted to ActiveX format and you'll be able to use them on your Web pages or desktop applications written in most languages, like Visual Basic or Visual C++. As of this writing, however, there aren't many ActiveX controls. Over the next year, numerous ActiveX controls will become available from Microsoft and other companies. They will be more flexible than the existing ones, and you'll find in them all the functionality you want to incorporate into your VBScript applications.

This chapter covers some of the old OCX controls in Web page design. OCX controls aren't meant to be used with VBScript, but they work and you'll get a good idea of the kind of functionality they can add to your applications. To follow the examples of this and the following chapter, you must have certain OCX controls installed on your system. Windows programming languages, such as Visual Basic and Visual C++, will automatically install these OCX controls on your system. If you don't have one of these programming tools installed on your system, you should wait for the ActiveX versions of these controls or consider purchasing Visual Basic. The upcoming version of Visual Basic (version 5.0) will be an ideal complement to VBScript. You should also check Microsoft's Workshop site (`www.microsoft.com/workshop`) for new ActiveX controls and updates.

The RTFEditor Application

The first OCX control discussed is the Rich Textbox control. The Rich Textbox control is in a small but very flexible word processor that combines the functionality of a Textbox control with formatting capabilities. If you want the Textbox control to display multiple fonts and styles, the Rich Textbox control is what you need. The application we are going to build in this chapter is called RTFEditor, and you can find it in this chapter's folder on the CD-ROM. Apart from showing you how to use the Rich Textbox control to build a word processor, the RTFEditor application demonstrates how to use command buttons and the Popup Menu control to build a user interface with menus. As long as HTML layouts can't have a menu structure of their own similar to the one you see on practically every Windows application, you'll have to use the Popup Menu control to creatively provide your users with the means to interact with your applications.

The RTFEditor application, shown in Figure 26.1, is a functional word processor that runs from within Internet Explorer's environment. Users can type text and edit it using the common editing operations (such as cut and paste) and the editing keys common to any text editing application in the Windows environment (like Home and Ctrl-C). In addition, they can use the menus behind the command buttons to format the text.

FIGURE 26.1.

RTFEditor is a functional word processing application that can be placed on a Web page and operated from within Internet Explorer 3.0.

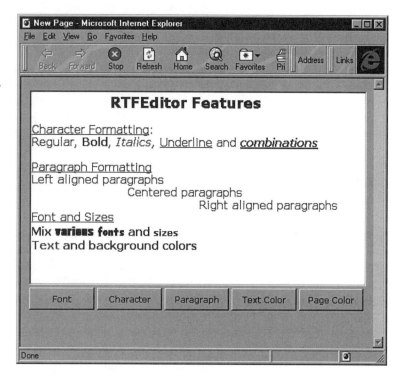

The command buttons at the bottom of the page act as triggers for popup menus, with the various formatting options. The popup menus that correspond to each command button are shown in Figure 26.2. We have included a few very basic formatting commands to demonstrate the capabilities of the Rich Textbox control, and you can add more formatting options on your own. Even with the basic functionality we've built into it, RTFEditor is a functional application that provides most of the functionality of a word processor needed by the average user on a daily basis.

You can open the RTFEditor application and familiarize yourself with it. Every time the RTFEditor page is loaded, Internet Explorer 3.0 will issue a warning to the effect that the application contains controls that might not be safe for your system, shown in Figure 26.3. This warning means that the page contains controls that Internet Explorer can handle, but they are

not ActiveX controls and have not been verified for safety on the Web. The controls we are
going to use are common Windows controls, and you can safely put them on your pages; so
click the Yes to All button to continue. You just have to live with the inconvenience of seeing
this message every time the page is loaded.

FIGURE 26.2.

*The options of the
RTFEditor
application's popup
menus.*

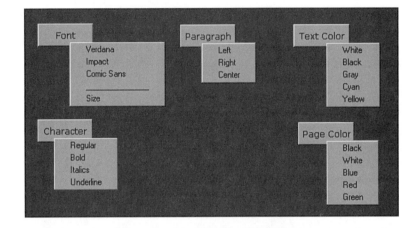

FIGURE 26.3.

*By default, Internet
Explorer will warn you
with this message box
each time it's about to
load a Web page with
an OCX control.*

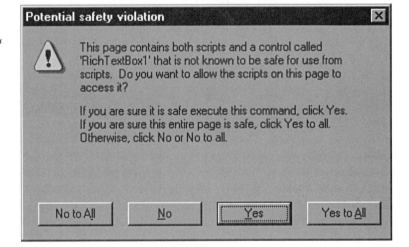

NOTE

You can bypass this warning through the safety settings of Internet Explorer, but we don't
recommend changing the browser's settings while you surf the Web. If you follow the
procedure outlined here, make sure you restore the original settings before you load other
people's pages.

To change the safety level of Internet Explorer, open the Options dialog box by selecting Options from the View menu. Then click the Security tab and on the new page click Safety Level to bring up the Safety Level window of Figure 26.4.

FIGURE 26.4.
The Safety Level settings let you specify how Internet Explorer will handle potential security and safety problems.

Click the None radio button and then click the OK button twice to close the Options dialog box. Now you can load the pages of this and the next chapter without the inconvenience of the warning of Figure 26.2.

You're now ready to look at the application. First, however, let's review the Rich Textbox control, its properties, and its methods that we are going to use in the example.

The Rich Textbox Control

Let's start by looking at the various properties of the control that we'll use in building the RTFEditor application. The basic property of the Rich Textbox control is its RTFText property. RTF stands for rich text format and is a language for describing formatted documents, not unlike HTML. Like HTML, RTF was designed to create portable formatted documents that can be displayed on different systems. The RTF language uses tags to describe the document's format. For example, the tag for italics is \i, and its scope is delimited with the next character formatting tag (which in most cases is the \plain tag, which restores the text style to plain). The following RTF line will produce a sentence with a few words in italics:

```
RTF is a language for creating \i portable formatted\plain documents
```

The equivalent HTML code would be

```
RTF is a language for creating <I>portable formatted</I> documents
```

RTF, however, is much more complicated than HTML because RTF was meant to be used internally by applications. Just as you need a browser to view HTML documents, you need an RTF-capable application to view RTF documents. WordPad, for instance, supports RTF and can save a document in RTF format and read RTF files. But you're not expected to supply your own RTF code to produce a document.

To demonstrate the principles of RTF and how to create portable documents in RTF, let's create a simple formatted document with WordPad and then look at the source code. Start WordPad, enter some text, and format it any way you can with the program's tools. Figure 26.5 shows the same document contained in the Rich Textbox control of Figure 26.1, after it was copied from the RTFEditor application (with the Ctrl-C keystroke) and pasted into a Word document (with the Ctrl-V keystroke). The text was actually transferred in RTF format, which shows you that RTF is indeed a universal language, at least in the Windows environment. If you can exchange RTF files with other types of operating systems, you'll realize that RTF is indeed a universal file format for exchanging formatted files. You can also try to modify the text in Word, copy it, and paste it into the RTFEditor's window.

Now you can save the text in RTF format too. Select the Save As command from the File menu, and in the dialog box that will be displayed on the screen select Rich Text Format. Then save the file as Document.rtf. (You don't have to supply the extension.) You can find the RTF code for the document of Figure 26.5 in the folder with this chapter's examples on the CD-ROM. If you open this file with a text editor (any application that can't interpret RTF code), you'll see the actual code that produced the document:

```
{\rtf1\ansi\deff0\deftab720{\fonttbl{\f0\fnil MS Sans Serif;}{\f1\fnil\fcharset2
Symbol;}
{\f2\fswiss\fprq2 System;}{\f3\fnil Times New Roman;}{\f4\fnil\fprq2
Verdana;}{\f5\fnil\fprq2 Impact;}
{\f6\fnil\fprq2 Comic Sans MS;}}
{\colortbl\red0\green0\blue0;\red16\green16\blue255;\red255\green16\blue16;}
\deflang1033\pard\qc\plain\f4\fs32\cf1\b RTFEditor Features\plain\f4\fs32\b
\par \pard\plain\f4\fs24
\par \plain\f4\fs24\ul Character Formatting\plain\f4\fs24 :
\par Regular, \plain\f4\fs24\b Bold\plain\f4\fs24 , \plain\f4\fs24\i
Italics,\plain\f4\fs24
\plain\f4\fs24\ul Underline\plain\f4\fs24  and \plain\f4\fs24\b\i\ul combinations
\par \plain\f4\fs24
```

```
\par \plain\f4\fs24\ul Paragraph Formatting\plain\f4\fs24
\par Left aligned paragraphs
\par \pard\qc\plain\f4\fs24 Centered paragraphs
\par \pard\qr\plain\f4\fs24 Right aligned paragraphs
\par \pard\plain\f4\fs24\ul Font and Sizes\plain\f4\fs24
\par Mix \plain\f5\fs24 various\plain\f4\fs24  \plain\f6\fs24 fonts\plain\f4\fs24
and \plain\f4\fs20 sizes\plain\f4\fs24
\par \plain\f4\fs24\cf2 Text\plain\f4\fs24  \plain\f4\fs24\cf1 and background
colors\plain\f4\fs24
\par \pard\plain\f3\fs20
\par }
```

Figure 26.5.

The Rich Textbox control lets you exchange formatted documents with other Windows applications, like Word.

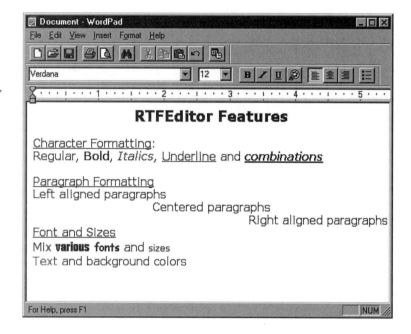

If you look carefully at the RTF code, you'll be able to see where the text and the formatting tags are. The \par tag inserts a paragraph similar to the <P> tag in HTML. The \bold tag delimits text to be displayed in bold. The file's header holds information about the fonts used in the document. The designation f4 corresponds to the Verdana font and appears quite frequently in the text.

The RTF format makes it possible to format text on a Rich Textbox control. But producing cryptic text as in the RTF code segment shown previously to display a few lines of formatted text isn't VBScript's way of doing things. Indeed, the Rich Textbox control simplifies this process by providing a number of properties for formatting the text.

Text Manipulation Properties

The Rich Textbox control has many properties, the most important of them being the ones that manipulate the selected text. All these properties start with the prefix `Sel`. `SelText` is the selected text. To assign the selected text to a variable, use the statement

```
SText=RichTextbox1.SelText
```

where `RichTextbox1` is the name of the control. You can also modify the selected text by assigning a new value to the `SelText` property. The statement

```
RichTextbox1.SelText=UCase(RichTextbox1.SelText)
```

converts the selected text to uppercase. If you assign a string to the `SelText` property, the selected text in the control will be replaced. The statement

```
RichTextbox1.SelText="replacement string"
```

will replace the current selection on the `RichTextbox1` control with the string `"replacement string"`. If no text was selected, the same statement will insert the string at the location of the pointer. It is possible, therefore, to automatically insert text by assigning a string to the `SelText` property. This technique is quite useful in displaying some initial text on the control.

To simplify the manipulation and formatting of the text on the control, there are two additional properties, the `SelStart` and `SelLength` properties, which report the position of the first selected character in the text and the length of the selection respectively. You can also set the values of these properties to select a piece of text from within your code. One obvious use of these properties is to select (and highlight) the entire text:

```
RichTextBox1.SelStart=0
RichTextBox1.SelLength=Len(RichTextBox1.Text)
```

The `Text` property returns the text on the control, just like the `Text` property of the TextBox control.

Text Formatting Properties

The properties for formatting the selected text are `SelBold`, `SelItalic`, and `SelUnderline`. You can read the value of these properties to check the formatting of the selected text from within your code or set them to change the formatting accordingly. The statements

```
RichTextbox1.SelBold=True
RichTextbox1.SelItalic=True
```

turn on the bold and italic attributes of the selected text. Again, if no text is selected, the attributes are set for the character at the current location of the pointer. By setting the character formatting properties accordingly, the user is in effect changing the style of the text he or she is about to type.

The character formatting properties are used as toggles. Every time the user clicks the Bold button (or selects Bold from the application's menu), the following code is executed:

```
RichTextbox1.SelBold=NOT RichTextbox1.SelBold
```

If the selected text is in bold, it's turned back to normal; if it's normal, it's turned to bold. As you have noticed, there is no property to reset the text style back to normal. To do so, you must manually set all three properties to `False`:

```
RichTextbox1.SelBold=False
RichTextbox1.SelItalic=False
RichTextbox1.SelUnderline=False
```

The `SelAlignment` property lets you read or change the alignment of one or more paragraphs, and it can have one of the following values:

0   (Default) Left aligns selected paragraph(s)
1   Right aligns selected paragraph(s)
2   Centers selected paragraph(s)

Notice that the user doesn't have to actually select the entire paragraph to be aligned. Placing the pointer anywhere on the paragraph to be reformatted or selecting a few characters in the paragraph will do, because there is no way to align part of the paragraph only.

To change the font and style of the selected text, use the properties `SelFontName` and `SelFontSize`. The following statements will render the selected text in Verdana font, 24 points:

```
RICHTEXT.SelFontName = "Verdana"
RICHTEXT.SelFontSize = 24
```

You must supply a font name that exists on the client computer, or a similar font will be substituted. As of now, it's not possible for VBScript to read the names of the fonts installed on the client computer and present them to the viewer to select one.

Finally, there are two properties for creating bulleted items: the `SelBullet` property—and controlling the text's baseline, the `SelOffset` property. If the `SelBullet` property is set to `True`, the selected paragraphs are formatted with a bullet style, similar to the UL tag in HTML. To create a list of bullet items, select them with the pointer and assign the value `True` to the `SelBullet` property. To restore a list of bullet items to normal text, select the items and assign the value `False` to the `SelBullet` property.

The `SelOffset` property determines whether the selected characters appear on, above, or below the normal text baseline. Normally, text appears on the baseline. You can raise its baseline to create superscripts (you must also reduce its size a point or two) or lower it to create subscripts. To lower the baseline of the selected text, assign a negative number to the `SelOffset` property. This value must be expressed in twips. (A twip corresponds to one-twentieth of a point, and there are 72 points in an inch.)

As you have realized, creating a functional, even fancy, word processor based on the Rich Textbox control is quite simple. You must provide a convenient user interface that lets the user select text and apply attributes and styles to it, and then set the control's properties accordingly. This is exactly what this chapter's application does.

Designing the User Interface

The RTFEditor's user interface is rather simple because VBScript doesn't provide the elaborate menu structures you need to build an application of this type. The commands for manipulating the text are placed in Popup Menu controls, which are activated by clicking the various command buttons below the Rich Textbox control. As usual, we'll start with the design of the layout and then look at the code.

To create the layout of Figure 26.1, create a new HTML document and place a Rich Textbox control on it with the Insert ActiveX control command of the Edit menu. When the Insert ActiveX Control window (shown in Figure 26.6) appears on the screen, locate the item Microsoft Rich Textbox Control and click the OK button.

FIGURE 26.6.

The Insert ActiveX Control window can be used to insert OCX controls on an HTML document.

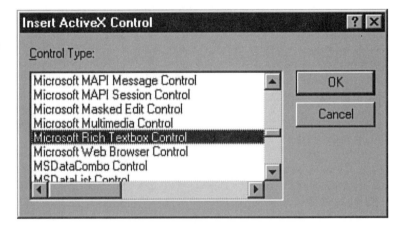

Although it's possible to add this control to the Control Pad's toolbox and then draw a new control directly on the HTML layout, Internet Explorer will refuse to load the control at runtime. Instead, it will display the error message shown in Figure 26.7. This is a stubborn message you can't avoid no matter what your settings for safety and security are. The only way to avoid this message is to place the OCX control directly on the HTML document, with the Insert ActiveX Control command. When the application is loaded, you'll be warned that the document contains a control that may not be safe for your system, but it will at least give you the option to load the unsafe control.

FIGURE 26.7.

If you place a Rich Textbox control directly on a layout, Internet Explorer will refuse to load it.

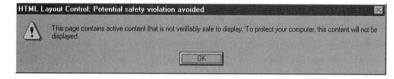

When the Edit ActiveX Control window appears, adjust the size of the control and set the default font. You must also set its Scrollbars property to 2 (Vertical) or 3 (Both) so that the users will be able to quickly move to any location in a long document. After you have adjusted the size and the properties of the control, VBScript will insert an object definition like the following one in the HTML file:

```
<OBJECT ID="RichTextBox1" WIDTH=100 HEIGHT=51
 CLASSID="CLSID:3B7C8860-D78F-101B-B9B5-04021C009402">
    <PARAM NAME="_Version" VALUE="65536">
    <PARAM NAME="_ExtentX" VALUE="2646">
    <PARAM NAME="_ExtentY" VALUE="1323">
    <PARAM NAME="_StockProps" VALUE="69">
    <PARAM NAME="BackColor" VALUE="-2147483643">
    <PARAM NAME="ScrollBars" VALUE="2">
    <PARAM NAME="TextRTF" VALUE="{\rtf1\ansi\deff0\deftab720{\fonttbl{\f0\fnil MS
Sans Serif;}{\f1\fnil\fcharset2 Symbol;}{\f2\fswiss\fprq2 System;}{\f3\fnil\fprq2
MS Sans Serif;}}
{\colortbl\red0\green0\blue0;}
\deflang1033\pard\plain\f3\fs17
\par }
">
</OBJECT>
```

The TextRTF property contains some initial settings for the control's RTF text. The last parameter must be deleted or you will not be able to read the RTF code of the document on the control. (The TextRTF property will always return its initial value.) As you will see later in the chapter, we are going to add a command that displays the RTF description of the document on the control.

There's another property you must add manually to this definition, and this is the RightMargin property. This property determines the right margin of the text on the control and should be slightly less than the _ExtentX property. The right margin isn't specified as the distance of the text from the right edge of the control. Instead, it's the distance of the text's right margin from the left edge of the control. You should make it smaller than the _ExtentX property to accommodate the vertical scrollbar that will be attached to the control when the text's length exceeds the length of the Rich Textbox control.

You can also specify a right margin larger than the control's width. In this case, the users will be able to type lines longer than the control's width. Just make sure that a horizontal scrollbar will be attached to the control so that the user will be able to scroll the text right and left. The exact values of these two properties for the RTFEditor example are

```
<PARAM NAME="_ExtentX" VALUE="14000">
<PARAM NAME="RightMargin" VALUE="12500">
```

Next place the command buttons below the Rich Textbox control. Because you are not working on an HTML layout control, where you can visually place the various controls and align them, you must edit the HTML file manually and create a table structure for aligning the command buttons. Because HTML lacks the tags for precise placement of the elements on a Web page, using a table to align them is a very common practice. The table in which the Rich Textbox and command button controls will be placed has two rows and five columns. The Rich Textbox control takes up the entire first row (all five columns), and the command buttons take up the second row of the table. Each one is placed in its own cell. The command buttons are aligned perfectly with the Rich Textbox control, even when the user resizes the browser's window. Here's the modified HTML document with all the controls:

```
<HTML>
<HEAD>
<TITLE>New Page</TITLE>
</HEAD>
<BODY>
<TABLE>
<TR>
<TD COLSPAN=5>
    <OBJECT ID="RichTextBox1" WIDTH=500 HEIGHT=280
     CLASSID="CLSID:3B7C8860-D78F-101B-B9B5-04021C009402">
        <PARAM NAME="_Version" VALUE="65536">
        <PARAM NAME="_ExtentX" VALUE="14000">
        <PARAM NAME="_ExtentY" VALUE="7408">
        <PARAM NAME="_StockProps" VALUE="69">
        <PARAM NAME="BackColor" VALUE="-2147483643">
        <PARAM NAME="ScrollBars" VALUE="3">
        <PARAM NAME="RightMargin" VALUE="12500">
    </OBJECT>
</TR>

<TR>

<TD>
    <OBJECT ID="FontMenu" WIDTH=96 HEIGHT=32
     CLASSID="CLSID:D7053240-CE69-11CD-A777-00DD01143C57">
        <PARAM NAME="Caption" VALUE="Font">
        <PARAM NAME="Size" VALUE="2540;846">
        <PARAM NAME="FontName" VALUE="Verdana">
        <PARAM NAME="FontHeight" VALUE="180">
        <PARAM NAME="FontCharSet" VALUE="0">
        <PARAM NAME="FontPitchAndFamily" VALUE="2">
        <PARAM NAME="ParagraphAlign" VALUE="3">
        <PARAM NAME="FontWeight" VALUE="0">
    </OBJECT>
```

```
<TD>
    <OBJECT ID="CharacterMenu" WIDTH=96 HEIGHT=32
     CLASSID="CLSID:D7053240-CE69-11CD-A777-00DD01143C57">
        <PARAM NAME="Caption" VALUE="Character">
        <PARAM NAME="Size" VALUE="2540;846">
        <PARAM NAME="FontName" VALUE="Verdana">
        <PARAM NAME="FontHeight" VALUE="180">
        <PARAM NAME="FontCharSet" VALUE="0">
        <PARAM NAME="FontPitchAndFamily" VALUE="2">
        <PARAM NAME="ParagraphAlign" VALUE="3">
        <PARAM NAME="FontWeight" VALUE="0">
    </OBJECT>
<TD>
    <OBJECT ID="ParagraphMenu" WIDTH=96 HEIGHT=32
     CLASSID="CLSID:D7053240-CE69-11CD-A777-00DD01143C57">
        <PARAM NAME="Caption" VALUE="Paragraph">
        <PARAM NAME="Size" VALUE="2540;846">
        <PARAM NAME="FontName" VALUE="Verdana">
        <PARAM NAME="FontHeight" VALUE="180">
        <PARAM NAME="FontCharSet" VALUE="0">
        <PARAM NAME="FontPitchAndFamily" VALUE="2">
        <PARAM NAME="ParagraphAlign" VALUE="3">
        <PARAM NAME="FontWeight" VALUE="0">
    </OBJECT>
<TD>
    <OBJECT ID="TextMenu" WIDTH=96 HEIGHT=32
     CLASSID="CLSID:D7053240-CE69-11CD-A777-00DD01143C57">
        <PARAM NAME="Caption" VALUE="Text Color">
        <PARAM NAME="Size" VALUE="2540;846">
        <PARAM NAME="FontName" VALUE="Verdana">
        <PARAM NAME="FontHeight" VALUE="180">
        <PARAM NAME="FontCharSet" VALUE="0">
        <PARAM NAME="FontPitchAndFamily" VALUE="2">
        <PARAM NAME="ParagraphAlign" VALUE="3">
        <PARAM NAME="FontWeight" VALUE="0">
    </OBJECT>
<TD>
    <OBJECT ID="PageMenu" WIDTH=96 HEIGHT=32
     CLASSID="CLSID:D7053240-CE69-11CD-A777-00DD01143C57">
        <PARAM NAME="Caption" VALUE="Page Color">
        <PARAM NAME="Size" VALUE="2540;846">
        <PARAM NAME="FontName" VALUE="Verdana">
        <PARAM NAME="FontHeight" VALUE="180">
        <PARAM NAME="FontCharSet" VALUE="0">
        <PARAM NAME="FontPitchAndFamily" VALUE="2">
        <PARAM NAME="ParagraphAlign" VALUE="3">
        <PARAM NAME="FontWeight" VALUE="0">
    </OBJECT>
</TABLE>

</OBJECT>
<OBJECT ID="IEPOP1" WIDTH=0 HEIGHT=0
    CLASSID="CLSID:7823A620-9DD9-11CF-A662-00AA00C066D2">
        <PARAM NAME="_ExtentX" VALUE="0">
        <PARAM NAME="_ExtentY" VALUE="0">
    </OBJECT>
```

```
<OBJECT ID="IEPOP2" WIDTH=0 HEIGHT=0
  CLASSID="CLSID:7823A620-9DD9-11CF-A662-00AA00C066D2">
      <PARAM NAME="_ExtentX" VALUE="0">
      <PARAM NAME="_ExtentY" VALUE="0">
  </OBJECT>
</BODY>
</HTML>
```

This is the RTFEdit.htm file in this chapter's folder on the CD. Notice that it contains two Popup Menu controls too, the IEPOP1 and IEPOP2 controls. Each command button causes a menu to pop up on the screen, and this is the IEPOP1 control. One of the options in the Font menu is Size, which leads to a second popup menu, the IEPOP2.

The Code Behind the Scenes

Now we are ready to look at the code. Each one of the command buttons at the bottom of the page triggers a Popup Menu control, which contains the corresponding options. Because we are using a single Popup Menu control, we must adjust its contents dynamically and keep track of which menu is displayed with a global variable. Here is the Click event of the Paragraph menu:

```
Sub ParagraphMenu_Click()
    WhichMenu="PARAGRAPH"
    IEPOP1.Clear
    IEPOP1.AddItem "Left"
    IEPOP1.AddItem "Right"
    IEPOP1.AddItem "Center"
    IEPOP1.Popup
End Sub
```

First this code sets the WhichMenu global variable, so that we'll know later which menu was opened and which option on this menu was selected. The Click events of the Character, Paragraph, Text Color, and Page Color menus are quite similar. They just use a different value for the WhichMenu variable and assign different content to the menu. After the menu's options are added, the menu is displayed with the Popup method.

Once a user has made a selection, the Click event of the IEPOP1 control is triggered, and this is where all the action takes place. The IEPOP1 Menu control is also used to implement a shortcut menu on the Rich Textbox control. Every time the user right-clicks the editor's window, the shortcut menu of Figure 26.8 is displayed.

The shortcut menu is displayed every time the user right-clicks the editor's window, an action that is signaled to the program by the control's MouseDown event. Here's the handler for this event:

```
Sub RichTextBox1_MouseDown(Button, Shift, x, y)
    If Button<>2 then Exit Sub
    IEPOP1.Clear
    WhichMenu="EDITOR"
    IEPOP1.AddItem "Copy"
    IEPOP1.AddItem "Cut"
```

```
        IEPOP1.AddItem "Paste"
        IEPOP1.AddItem "Delete"
        IEPOP1.AddItem "Select All"
        IEPOP1.AddItem "Show RTF Code"
        IEPOP1.Popup
End Sub
```

Figure 26.8.

This shortcut menu contains the most commonly used commands for text manipulation.

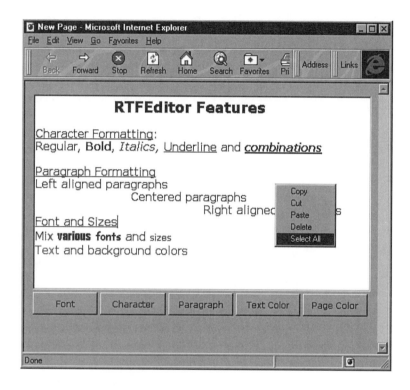

Any selection the user makes on the IEPOP1 control is reported to the application by means of the control's `Click` event. The IPEOP1 control's `Click` event is the lengthier subroutine, where all the action takes place:

```
Sub IEPOP1_Click(item)
    Select Case WhichMenu
    Case "FONT":
        If item=1 then RichTextBox1.SelFontName="Verdana"
        If item=2 then RichTextBox1.SelFontName="Impact"
        If item=3 then RichTextBox1.SelFontName="Comic Sans MS"
        If item=5 then
            IEPOP2.Clear
            IEPOP2.AddItem "10 points"
            IEPOP2.AddItem "12 points"
            IEPOP2.AddItem "14 points"
            IEPOP2.AddItem "16 points"
            IEPOP2.AddItem "18 points"
            IEPOP2.Popup
        End If
```

```
    Case "CHAR":
        If item=1 Then
            RichTextBox1.SelBold=0
            RichTextBox1.SelItalic=0
            RichTextBox1.SelUnderline=0
        End If
        If item=2 then RichTextBox1.SelBold=NOT RichTextBox1.SelBold
        If item=3 then RichTextBox1.SelItalic=NOT RichTextBox1.SelItalic
        If item=4 then RichtextBox1.SelUnderline=NOT RichtextBox1.SelUnderline
    Case "PARAGRAPH":
        RichTextBox1.SelAlignment=item-1
    Case "TEXT":
        If item=1 then RichTextBox1.SelColor=&H000000
        If item=2 then RichTextBox1.SelColor=&HFFFFFF
        If item=3 then RichTextBox1.SelColor=&HFF1010
        If item=4 then RichTextBox1.SelColor=&H1010FF
        If item=5 then RichTextBox1.SelColor=&H10FF10
    Case "PAGE":
        If item=1 then RichTextBox1.BackColor=&HFFFFFF
        If item=2 then RichTextBox1.BackColor=&H000000
        If item=3 then RichTextBox1.BackColor=&HA0A0A0
        If item=4 then RichTextBox1.BackColor=&HFFFF01
        If item=5 then RichTextBox1.BackColor=&H40F0F0
    Case "EDITOR":
        If item=1 then TempText=RichTextBox1.SelText
        If item=2 then
            TempText=RichTextBox1.SelText
            RichTextBox1.SelText=""
        End If
        If item=3 then RichTextBox1.SelText=TempText
        If item=4 then RichTextBox1.SelText=""
        If item=5 then
            RichTextBox1.SelStart=0
            RichTextBox1.SelLength=Len(RichTextBox1.Text)
        End If
        If Item=6 Then
            MsgBox RichTextBox1.TextRTF
        End If
    End Select
End Sub
```

This subroutine is a big Select Case statement, which examines the value of the WhichMenu variable and carries out the action depending on the selected option. If the user selected an option from the Character menu (WhichMenu="PARAGRAPH"), the code sets the SelBold, SelItalic, and SelUnderline properties accordingly. If the user selected an option to change the color of the text or the page on which the text is displayed, the code sets the TextColor and BackColor properties.

Most of the code is straightforward, with the exception of the Size selection of the Font menu. This option leads to another submenu, with various font sizes. The program adds a number of options (font sizes) to the IEPOP2 control and then displays it. When the user makes a selection from this menu, the following subroutine is executed:

```
Sub IEPOP2_Click(item)
    RichTextBox1.SelFontSize=10+(item-1)*2
End Sub
```

Here, we use the index of the selected item in the IEPOP2 control to set the font size of the selected text.

The last segment of the IEPOP1_Click() subroutine we'd like to discuss is the implementation of the editor's shortcut menu. The Copy, Cut, and Paste commands don't use the Clipboard to temporarily store some text. Instead, the copied text is stored in a global variable, TempText, which is then pasted onto the control with the Paste command. This approach isolates the RTFEditor application from the rest of the system and all the editing is done locally. It is possible to exchange data with other applications, however, with the Ctrl-X (cut), Ctrl-C (copy), and Ctrl-V (paste) keystrokes. This functionality is built into the controls and Windows itself, and you don't have to do anything about it.

The last option in the shortcut menu displays the RTF code of the document in a message box, as shown in Figure 26.9. This option is included for your experimentation with RTF code, and you should use it with very small documents. If the editor's window contains many lines of code, the message box will overflow and not display anything.

FIGURE 26.9.

The last command in the shortcut menu displays the document's RTF code in a message box.

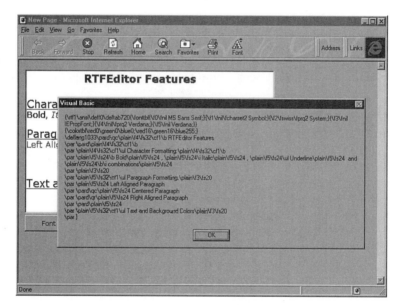

Saving and Recalling RTF Documents

RTFEditor is a practical tool, but what good is an editor if it can't store the documents into disk files and recall them later? Indeed, this application lacks two very important functions, which we are going to add momentarily. Even without the benefit of storing files on disk, you have learned how to present nicely formatted information to the user. You can use a word processor to produce the RTF code and then place it on a RichTextbox control. With some programming effort, you can allow the users to annotate the document, right on their screens.

You can also place a RichTextbox control on a Web page and collect information from your viewers. To do so, you can copy the TextRTF property to a hidden textbox and submit it to the server. Or you can use it in conjunction with Exchange, to let users create formatted e-mail messages. The Rich Textbox control comes in very handy for developing intranet applications. Once the commands for saving and opening files are implemented, RTFEditor will become a handy utility for your Web pages.

The Rich Textbox control provides two methods for saving and loading documents to and from files. These methods are called SaveFile and LoadFile, and they can save documents in RTF or text format. The syntax of the SaveFile method is

```
RichTextBox1.SaveFile filename, filetype
```

where *filename* is the full name of the file in which the document will be stored and *filetype* indicates whether the document will be stored in RTF format (*filetype=0*) or plain text (*filetype=1*). The syntax of the LoadFile method is similar:

```
RichTextBox1.LoadFile filename, filetype
```

The Open and Save As commands can be implemented with a single statement. But hardcoding the name of the file won't take you far. A well-behaved Windows application must prompt the user for the name of the file to be opened or saved on disk. This is done with another OCX control, the Common Dialogs control, which we'll explore in the next section.

The Common Dialogs Control

The Common Dialogs control is a peculiar one because it's not displayed on the layout at runtime. It's a control that provides its services to the applications, but it need not be displayed, just like the Timer control. The services provided by the Common Dialogs control are the common Windows 95 dialog boxes, like the Open and Save As dialog boxes, which let the user select a filename; the Color dialog box, which lets the user select a color; the Font dialog box, which lets the user select a font; and so on. After you learn how to display the Save As and Open dialog boxes, you can try substituting the Font popup menu of the RTFEditor application with the standard Font dialog box and the two color menus with the Choose Color dialog box. Figures 26.10 and 26.11 show the two Common Dialog boxes we use in our example: the Save As and Open dialog boxes.

To call on the services of the Common Dialogs control, you must first place an instance of the control on the layout. Use the Insert ActiveX control command of the Edit menu, and in the Insert ActiveX control box that will appear (refer to Figure 26.6) locate the Common Dialogs control. Then click the OK button to place it on the layout. Notice that you can't adjust its size, because the Common Dialogs control remains hidden at runtime. However, you can set several properties to adjust its function on the layout, like the font to be used, a default filename to appear when the Open or Save As dialog boxes are displayed, and so on.

FIGURE 26.10.
The Save As dialog box.

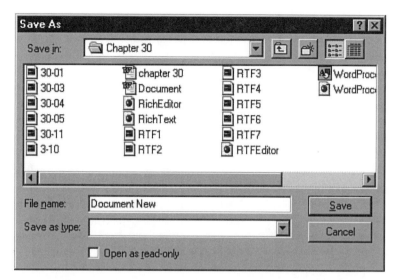

FIGURE 26.11.
The Open dialog box.

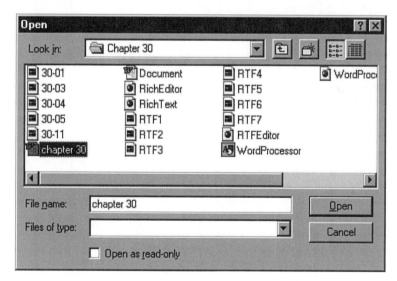

Control Pad will insert the following object definition in the HTML file for the Common Dialogs control:

```
<OBJECT ID="CommonDialog1" WIDTH=32 HEIGHT=32
 CLASSID="CLSID:F9043C85-F6F2-101A-A3C9-08002B2F49FB">
    <PARAM NAME="_Version" VALUE="65536">
    <PARAM NAME="_ExtentX" VALUE="847">
    <PARAM NAME="_ExtentY" VALUE="847">
    <PARAM NAME="_StockProps" VALUE="0">
</OBJECT>
```

Once the Common Dialogs control has been placed on the layout, you can use its Action property to display any of the Windows dialog boxes. The Action property may have one of the following values:

1 Displays the Open dialog box
2 Displays the Save As dialog box
3 Displays the Color dialog box
4 Displays the Font dialog box
5 Displays the Printer dialog box

Once you assign a value to the Action property, the corresponding dialog box will appear on the screen and the execution of the program will be suspended until the dialog box is closed. The user can traverse the entire structure of his or her hard disk and locate the desired filename. Once the Open or Save button has been clicked, the control is returned to your application, which can read the name of the file selected by the user (property FileName) and use it to open the file or store the current document.

The Open and Save As Commands

Let's see how the File Open and File Save options were added to the application. The new project is called RTFEditor1. (We didn't want to add to the RTFEditor application and make it more complicated than necessary.) Open the RTFEditor.htm file with the ActiveX Control Pad and save it as RTFEditor1. First, you must edit the HTML file to add a sixth command button, as shown in Figure 26.12. This entails some adjustments to the table because there will be six rows now. You can open RTFEditor1.htm and look at the source code. It's quite similar to the RTFEditor application, and we need not repeat the HTML code here.

The new command button functions just like the others. Each time the command button is clicked, a Popup Menu control with the following options is displayed: New File, Load File, and Save File. Here's how the three options are added to the menu from within the IEPOP1_Click() subroutine:

```
Sub FileMenu_Click()
    WhichMenu="FILE"
    IEPOP1.Clear
    IEPOP1.AddItem "New File"
    IEPOP1.AddItem "Open File"
    IEPOP1.AddItem "Save File"
    IEPOP1.Popup
End Sub
```

The New File command simply clears the contents of the textbox and is implemented with a single statement:

```
RichTextbox1.Text=""
```

The code of the File Open option in the popup menu causes the Open File Common Control dialog box to be displayed with the following lines:

```
CommonDialog1.Action=1
RichTextBox1.LoadFile CommonDialog1.FileName, 0
```

And the code of the File Save option is just as simple:

```
CommonDialog1.Action=2
RichTextBox1.SaveFile CommonDialog1.FileName, 0
```

FIGURE 26.12.

The improved RTFEditor application can save and load documents to and from the local disk with the File menu's options.

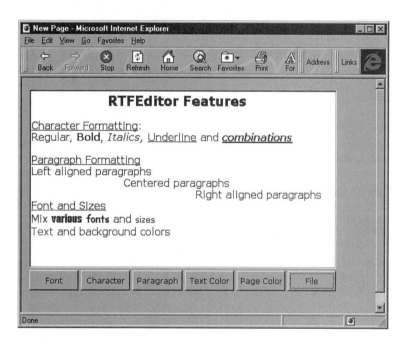

To add file-handling capabilities to your application, insert the following Case statement in the existing Select Case structure:

```
Case "FILE":
    If item=1 Then RichTextbox1.Text=""
    If item=2 Then
        CommonDialog1.Action=1
        RichTextBox1.LoadFile CommonDialog1.FileName, 0
    End If
    If item=3 Then
        CommonDialog1.Action=2
        RichTextBox1.SaveFile CommonDialog1.FileName, 0
    End If
```

The implementation of the file-related commands is quite simple, but it should be a bit lengthier. For example, what will happen if the user clicked the Cancel button? The Common Dialogs control returns an empty string. Here's a better way to implement the File Open command:

```
If item=2 Then
    CommonDialog1.Action=1
    Filename=CommonDialog1.FileName
    If FileName="" Then Exit Sub
    RichTextBox1.LoadFile CommonDialog1.FileName, 0
End If
```

Similar changes must be made to the File Save command's code so that the program will not attempt to save the current document under an invalid filename. In the case of the File Save command you can also prompt the users with an Input Box as to whether they want to save the current document in RTF (`filetype=0`) or text (`filetype=1`) format.

Safety Considerations

As we mentioned earlier, Internet Explorer will issue a warning every time it's about to load a page with an OCX control. OCX controls aren't unsafe for the client system, but they are not ActiveX controls, and they haven't been verified for security. The RTFEditor application could be considered doubly unsafe because it saves data on the local disk. People are very reluctant to allow an application that they ran into on the Internet to leave anything on their disk. Applications that make use of OCX controls are quite safe for an intranet environment, but you should think twice before placing them on public Web pages. When the ActiveX versions of these controls become available the situation will change. It's not known how these controls will handle security, but some mechanisms will be built into the controls to protect the viewers. Even a simple warning will help because the user will be able to control which application saves data to the local disk, and when.

Review

Until all the existing controls are converted to ActiveX format, you can use the OCX controls to develop quite powerful utilities for the Web pages you plan to post on your intranet. The RichTextbox control, for example, provides all the functionality you need to build a simple word processor for everyone in the company. If you plan to use OCX controls on your pages, you should consider purchasing Visual Basic and consult the documentation for additional features of the various OCX controls. The Rich Textbox control, for example, provides methods for searching the text on the control, various ways of selecting text (from the location of the pointer to the end of the line, for example), a method for printing the text, and so on. One final suggestion is to customize each user's editor with cookies. For instance, you can provide a first-level menu that lets the users select the type of document they want to create, and you can bring up the RTFEditor application with a predefined template document, the user's settings (colors, font), the user's name, the current date, and so on. There are Microsoft Office applications that will do all that, but right now none of them can be invoked and customized from within a Web page as easily as the RTFEditor application—not to mention that the average user will find a custom editor like this one easier to learn and use.

Of course, the users of your applications that make use of regular OCX controls must be aware of the warning that Internet Explorer will issue and ignore it. This is more likely to happen in an intranet environment rather than the World Wide Web. We expect to see ActiveX versions of the OCX controls discussed in this and the following chapter shortly after this book hits the market.

The next chapter continues the exploration of OCX controls and how they can be used in Internet Explorer's environment by showing you how to build a spreadsheet application. The GraphData application uses the Grid OCX control to let the user enter data on a spreadsheet and then plots the data on the Graph control (which is actually an ActiveX control).

The Chart and Grid Controls

by Evangelos Petroutsos

IN THIS CHAPTER

CHAPTER 27

The examples in this chapter demonstrate the Chart and Grid controls. We explored the Chart control in Chapter 9, "More ActiveX Controls," but in this chapter we are going to develop a much more elaborate document that not only graphs data but accepts user-supplied data and then graphs it. The examples of this chapter are complete, functional applications that can run from within Internet Explorer (and soon from within other browsers, too). They demonstrate the kind of functionality you can add to your Web pages with VBScript and ActiveX controls.

The first application relies on ActiveX controls and can be safely posted on the Web. The Chart application, shown in Figure 27.1, is a data-graphing application that lets the user enter data in the TextBox controls at the layout's lower-right corner. Each time the user changes a value in one of the values, the graph is updated automatically. The group of TextBox controls used for data entry was arranged as a spreadsheet, but since each cell requires its own TextBox control and the corresponding code, we couldn't place too many cells on the layout with this approach. We are going to eliminate this limitation later with the Grid control.

FIGURE 27.1.

The Chart application graph's user-supplied data at runtime.

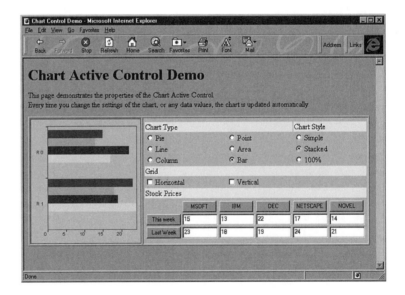

For a real data-entry and graphing application, you need a Grid control. A Grid control is an old OLE control, which will already be installed on your system if you have Visual Basic or Visual C++. It's a miniature spreadsheet, with most of the functionality you need to implement a data-entry and graphing application, like the one shown in Figure 27.2. This example is called GridChart, and you'll see how it was implemented in the second half of this chapter. The code is more compact than the code of the Grid application, because we don't have to repeat identical subroutines for each cell and we can provide as many cells as necessary for the user to enter data.

FIGURE 27.2.

The GridChart application provides a Grid control, where the user can enter the data to be graphed.

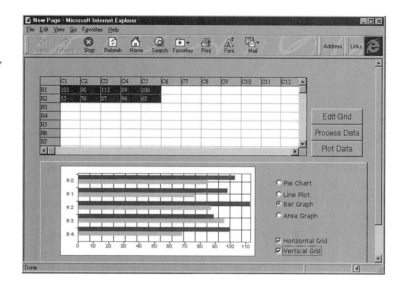

The drawback of the GridChart application is that it can only be used locally or in an intranet environment, because it makes use of an old OLE control that does not come with Internet Explorer, and many users might not have it. We are assuming that you have Visual Basic installed on your system and you have access to this control. Besides, it won't be long before an ActiveX version of the Grid control becomes available. (Keep an eye on Microsoft's Workshop site, at www.microsoft.com/workshop.)

There's one more reason why the two controls are combined in the GridChart example. The data graphed by the Graph control is stored into the control in a two-dimensional array. The rows of the array correspond to different datasets and its columns to the individual points in each dataset. The structure of the Grid control is quite similar. The Grid control is a tabular arrangement of cells. The GridChart application maps the rows of the grid to datasets of the Chart control. The similarities between the two controls are not limited to the surface. The methods for accessing data points in the Chart control and cells in the Grid control are quite similar. In essence, you must first set the row and column index of the element you want to access. These two values uniquely identify an element (a cell in the Grid control and a data point in the Chart control). Then, you can access the element (read or set its value) with the Text property of the Grid control, or the DataItem of the Chart control. The remaining properties of both controls determine the appearance of the control (the appearance of the graph or the placement and look of the data in the grid's cells). They have intuitive names, and you can easily figure out their purpose. Even if you don't, you can look up the help files and experiment with their settings to get what you want. The important thing is to understand the basic mechanism for accessing the elements of these two controls, and you'll be able to use them very efficiently.

The Chart Example

The Chart application is a demonstration of the various properties of the Chart control. It also shows how to change the control's data at runtime, by plugging new values into the control's data array. The user interface of the application consists of a Chart control, a number of OptionButton and CheckBox controls that control the graph's appearance, and a number of TextBox controls where the user may change the data values.

The OptionButton controls that control the appearance of the graph are by far less than the actual graph types, but when combined, they can specify all graph types. The settings of the GraphType property let you specify only eight different charts (Pie, Point, Line, Area, Column, Bar, HLC, OHLC chart), but each one comes in three flavors: simple, stacked, and full (100%). The Chart application lets you select separately the type of the graph and its variation, thus eliminating the need for 20 different Option buttons.

The Chart application was implemented as an HTML document. There are no layouts on the page of Figure 27.1. The various controls were aligned with an elaborate table structure, which you may ignore if you are not familiar with HTML. Placing the controls on a layout is actually simpler. The code of the application is shown in Listing 27.1.

Listing 27.1. The Chart project's complete code.

```
 1:
 2: <HTML>
 3: <HEAD>
 4: <TITLE>Chart Control Demo</TITLE>
 5: <SCRIPT LANGUAGE="VBS">
 6:     Sub DoChartType(CType)
 7:     Chart.ChartType=CType
 8:     End Sub
 9:     Sub DoChartStyle(CStyle)
10:         if Chart.ChartType < 2 then Exit Sub
11:     currentStyle=Chart.ChartType
12:     if CStyle = 0 then
13:         if (currentStyle-2) mod 2 = 0 then Exit Sub
14:         if (currentStyle-3) mod 2 = 0 then Chart.ChartType=currentStyle - 1
15:         if (currentStyle-4) mod 2 = 0 then Chart.ChartType=currentStyle - 2
16:         Exit Sub
17:     end if
18:     if CStyle = 1 then
19:         if (currentStyle-2) mod 2 = 0 then Chart.ChartType=currentStyle + 1
20:         if (currentStyle-3) mod 2 = 0 then Exit Sub
21:         if (currentStyle-4) mod 2 = 0 then Chart.ChartType=currentStyle + 1
22:         Exit Sub
23:     end if
24:     if CStyle = 2 then
25:         if (currentStyle-2) mod 2 = 0 then Chart.ChartType=currentStyle + 2
26:         if (currentStyle-3) mod 2 = 0 then Chart.ChartType=currentStyle + 1
27:         if (currentStyle-4) mod 2 = 0 then Exit Sub
28:         Exit Sub
29:     End if
30:     End Sub
```

```
31:    Sub HorizontalGrid(HGrid)
32:        if HGrid.Checked = 1 then
33:            Chart.HGridStyle = 1
34:        else
35:            Chart.HGridStyle = 0
36:        end if
37:    End Sub
38:    Sub VerticalGrid(VGrid)
39:        if VGrid.Checked = 1 then
40:            Chart.VGridStyle = 1
41:        else
42:            Chart.VGridStyle = 0
43:        end if
44:    End Sub
45:
46:    Sub NewData(row, col, Data)
47:            Chart.RowIndex = row
48:            Chart.ColumnIndex = col
49:            Chart.DataItem =Data.Value
50:    End Sub
51: </SCRIPT>
52: </HEAD>
53: <BODY>
54: <H1>Chart Active Control Demo</H1>
55: This page demonstrates the properties of the Chart Active Control.<BR>
56: Every time you change the settings of the chart, or any data values, the chart
    ➥is updated automatically.
57: <P>
58: <TABLE BORDER>
59: <TR><TD>
60: <OBJECT
61:     classid="clsid:FC25B780-75BE-11CF-8B01-444553540000"
62:     id=Chart
63:     width=240
64:     height=260
65:         align=center
66:     hspace=0
67:     vspace=0>
68:     <param name="BackColor" value="14737632">
69:     <param name="ChartStyle" value="0">
70:     <param name="ChartType" value="4">
71:     <param name="HGridStyle" value="0">
72:     <param name="VGridStyle" value="0">
73:     <param name="ColorScheme" value="0">
74:     <param name="Rows" value="2">
75:     <param name="Columns" value="5">
76:     <param name="data[0][0]" value="15">
77:     <param name="data[0][1]" value="13">
78:     <param name="data[0][2]" value="22">
79:     <param name="data[0][3]" value="17">
80:     <param name="data[0][4]" value="14">
81:     <param name="data[1][0]" value="23">
82:     <param name="data[1][1]" value="18">
83:     <param name="data[1][2]" value="19">
84:     <param name="data[1][3]" value="24">
85:     <param name="data[1][4]" value="21">
86:
```

27

THE CHART AND
GRID CONTROLS

continues

Listing 27.1. continued

```
 87: </OBJECT>
 88: <TD BGCOLOR=#E0E0E0>
 89: <FORM>
 90: <TABLE>
 91: <TR>
 92: <TD COLSPAN=2 BGCOLOR=#FFFFCC>Chart Type</TD>
 93: <TD BGCOLOR=#FFFFCC>Chart Style</TD>
 94: </TR>
 95: <TR>
 96: <TD><INPUT TYPE="RADIO" NAME="TypeGroup" onClick="DoChartType(0)">Pie</TD>
 97: <TD><INPUT TYPE="RADIO" NAME="TypeGroup" onClick="DoChartType(2)">Point</TD>
 98: <TD><INPUT TYPE="RADIO" checked NAME="StyleGroup"
     ➥onClick="DoChartStyle(0)">Simple
 99: </TR>
100: <TR>
101: <TD><INPUT TYPE="RADIO" NAME="TypeGroup" onClick="DoChartType(5)">Line</TD>
102: <TD><INPUT TYPE="RADIO" NAME="TypeGroup" onClick="DoChartType(8)">Area</TD>
103: <TD><INPUT TYPE="RADIO" NAME="StyleGroup" onClick="DoChartStyle(1)">Stacked
104: </TR>
105: <TR>
106: <TD><INPUT TYPE="RADIO" NAME="TypeGroup" CHECKED
     ➥onClick="DoChartType(11)">Column</TD>
107: <TD><INPUT TYPE="RADIO" NAME="TypeGroup" onClick="DoChartType(14)">Bar</TD>
108: <TD><INPUT TYPE="RADIO" NAME="StyleGroup"
     ➥onClick="DoChartStyle(2)">100%</TD></TD>
109: </TR>
110: <TR>
111: <TD COLSPAN=3 BGCOLOR=#FFFFCC>Grid</TD>
112: </TR>
113: <TR>
114: <TD><INPUT TYPE="CHECKBOX" NAME="HGrid"
     ➥onClick="HorizontalGrid(HGrid)">Horizontal</TD>
115: <TD><INPUT TYPE="CHECKBOX" NAME="VGrid"
     ➥onClick="VerticalGrid(VGrid)">Vertical</TD>
116: <TD></TD>
117: <TR>
118: <TD COLSPAN=3 BGCOLOR=#FFFFCC>Stock Prices</TD>
119: <TR>
120: <TD COLSPAN=3>
121: <TABLE>
122: <TD></TD>
123: <TD><INPUT TYPE="BUTTON" VALUE="MSOFT"></TD>
124: <TD><INPUT TYPE="BUTTON" VALUE="IBM"></TD>
125: <TD><INPUT TYPE="BUTTON" VALUE="DEC"></TD>
126: <TD><INPUT TYPE="BUTtON" VALUE="NETSCAPE"></TD>
127: <TD><INPUT TYPE="BUTTON" VALUE="NOVEL"></TD>
128: <TR>
129: <TD><INPUT TYPE="Button" VALUE="This week"></TD>
130: <TD><INPUT TYPE="Text" NAME="d00" SIZE=11 VALUE="15"
     ➥onChange="NewData 0, 0, d00"></TD>
131: <TD><INPUT TYPE="Text" NAME="d01" SIZE=11 VALUE="13"
     ➥onChange="NewData 0, 1, d01"></TD>
132: <TD><INPUT TYPE="Text" NAME="d02" SIZE=11 VALUE="22"
     ➥onChange="NewData 0, 2, d02"></TD>
133: <TD><INPUT TYPE="Text" NAME="d03" SIZE=11 VALUE="17"
     ➥onChange="NewData 0, 3, d03"></TD>
```

```
134: <TD><INPUT TYPE="Text" NAME="d04" SIZE=11 VALUE="14"
     ➥onChange="NewData 0, 4, d04"></TD>
135: <TR>
136: <TD><INPUT TYPE="Button" VALUE="Last Week"></TD>
137: <TD><INPUT TYPE="Text" NAME="d10" SIZE=11 VALUE="23"
     ➥onChange="NewData 1, 0, d10"></TD>
138: <TD><INPUT TYPE="Text" NAME="d11" SIZE=11 VALUE="18"
     ➥onChange="NewData 1, 1, d11"></TD>
139: <TD><INPUT TYPE="Text" NAME="d12" SIZE=11 VALUE="19"
     ➥onChange="NewData 1, 2, d12"></TD>
140: <TD><INPUT TYPE="Text" NAME="d13" SIZE=11 VALUE="24"
     ➥onChange="NewData 1, 3, d13"></TD>
141: <TD><INPUT TYPE="Text" NAME="d14" SIZE=11 VALUE="21"
     ➥onChange="NewData 1, 4, d14"></TD>
142: </TR>
143: </TABLE>
144: </TD>
145: </TR>
146: </TABLE>
147: </FORM>
148: </TD>
149: </TR>
150: </TABLE>
151: </BODY>
152: </HTML>
```

Notice that the OptionButton controls contain the onChange attribute in their definitions, which specifies the name of the procedure to be executed every time the user checks, or clears, them. The subroutines DoChartType() and DoChartStyle() do all the work in this program. The DoChartType() subroutine sets the basic type of the graph and the DoStyleChart() subroutine sets the flavor of the basic type. They both accept an argument, which is a number representing the chart's type and style. Both subroutines examine the value of their argument and set the value of the GraphType property accordingly. The DoChartType() subroutine accepts an integer argument, which is the value of the GraphType property for the simple version of the desired type (0 for pie charts, 2 for line plots, 5 for point plots, and so on). The DoChartStyle() subroutine accepts an integer which is 0 for simple charts, 1 for stacked charts, and 2 for full charts.

The same method of invoking the proper subroutine is used when a TextBox's value changes, too. This time we used the onChange attribute, which calls the specified subroutine each time the control's value changes. When the value changes, all TextBox controls call the NewData() subroutine, with three arguments: the dataset and datapoint number and the new value. The dataset number is 0 or 1, depending on the row of the TextBox, and the datapoint number is a value between 0 and 4. (There are five datapoints in each dataset.)

The rest of the code is rather trivial, in the sense that it sets the various properties of the Chart control to adjust the graph's appearance. You might want to examine the DoChartStyle() subroutine, which sets the graph's type based on the arguments it receives when called.

The GridChart Example

The GridChart document we are going to implement in this chapter is shown in Figure 27.1, and you will find it on the CD. It's one of the lengthiest applications presented in this book, and it demonstrates not only a few controls but the type of functionality you add to your VBScript applications with the help of ActiveX controls. As you will soon realize, the code is rather straightforward, once you understand the concepts of manipulating the Grid and Chart controls. Fortunately, there are many similarities between the two controls, and this will simplify the code too.

The GridChart project is similar in principle to the Grid project, except the data-entry aspect of the application has been vastly improved with the functionality of the Grid control. The drawback of this application is that you can't use it unless you have the Grid control installed on your system. (It's an OLE control that comes with Microsoft's languages and can be freely distributed with the application.) Moreover, the user will see a warning every time Internet Explorer loads the control, as discussed in the previous chapters. When the warning appears, click Yes to load the control. As long as you have the source code and can verify that you are loading a Microsoft control, there's no security risk for your computer.

The user interface of the GridChart project is straightforward. The grid is where the user enters data and the various command buttons perform a few basic operations. The Edit Grid button displays a pop-up menu, with the following commands:

Delete current row	Deletes all the cells in the current row.
Delete current column	Deletes all the cells in the current column.
Fill current row	Fills all the cells in the current row with a user-supplied value.
Fill current column	Fills all the cells in the current column with a user-supplied value.
Clear Grid	Clears the contents of the grid.

These commands are quite easy to implement, and they demonstrate the types of operations you can perform on the Grid control.

The Process Data button leads to another pop-up menu, with the following commands:

MEAN of selected cells
MIN of selected cells
MAX of selected cells

These commands have not been implemented, but you will see how you can detect the selected cells in the grid and access their values shortly. Then you'll be able to implement these, as well as other, more complicated calculations with the selected cells.

The last button, Plot Data, copies the values of the selected cells to the Chart control, which plots them immediately.

The OptionButton and CheckButton controls next to the Chart control control the appearance of the graph. They simply set the `GraphType`, `HGridStyle`, and `VGridStyle` properties of the Grid accordingly—and you'll probably want to add more options to better control your graphs.

The Grid Control

The Grid control is a simple spreadsheet you can place on your layouts to either display or accept data from the user. It looks a lot like a spreadsheet, with cells arranged in a table, and each cell can be addressed via a row and a column number. The Grid control was designed for presenting data to the user and doesn't provide any means for accepting user input. This problem, however, is easily fixed by taking control of the `KeyPress` events on the control. You can supply some VBScript code in the Grid's `KeyPress` event to convert the user's keystrokes to digits and display them in the current cell.

Figure 27.3 shows a Grid control as it appears on a layout, in the ActiveX Control Pad. To place a Grid control on a layout, you must first add its icon to the toolbox, with the help of the Additional controls commands of its shortcut menu. In the Insert ActiveX control dialog box, select Grid Object and a little grid icon will be placed on the toolbox. (You can see it in the toolbox of Figure 27.3.) Use this icon to place Grid controls on your layouts just like all other controls.

FIGURE 27.3.

A Grid control placed on a layout with the ActiveX Control Pad.

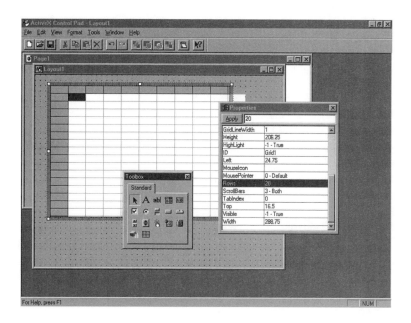

The cells of the first row and column have a gray background because they were meant to be used as titles for the corresponding columns and rows. The unique feature of these cells is that they don't scroll along with the rest of the cells, so the titles always remain visible. You can change the number of title rows and columns with the FixedCols and FixedRows properties. Another characteristic of the title row and column is that when one of their cells is clicked, the entire row or column is selected.

Let's start by looking at the Grid control's properties, which we are going to use in the code. The number of visible columns and rows on the control is set by the Rows and Cols properties. Depending on the size of the control and the number and size of the cells, it's possible that not all cells will fit within the control's dimensions. In this case, you can attach a vertical and/or a horizontal scrollbar, to let the user quickly locate the section of the grid he or she wants to view. The scrollbars will not be visible during the design of the project and will appear when the document is opened with Internet Explorer only if they are needed.

Each column in the grid may have its own width, which is controlled by the ColWidth property. To set the width of the first column (the title column), use the statement

```
Grid1.ColWidth(0)=500
```

The width's value is expressed in twips, and there are 20 twips in a point. The previous statement sets the width of the first column to approximately 25 points. Likewise, each row may have a different height, which is controlled by the RowHeight property, whose syntax is quite similar. Notice that the user can change the width of columns and height of rows at runtime, by dragging the column and row separators with the mouse. If you place the mouse over a dividing line between two columns (or rows) and in the title section of the grid, it will assume the shape of a double arrow, indicating that it can be dragged to resize a row or column of cells.

To access a specific cell, assign its coordinates to the Row and Col properties of the control and then access its Text property. The Text property can be read or set. As you might recall, the same approach is used with the Chart control to assign values to its Data array, which holds the datapoints to be plotted. As with the Chart control, the indexing of the Grid control's rows and columns starts at 0. To read the value of the fifth cell on the second column, use the statements

```
Grid1.Row=4
Grid1.Col=1
thisnumber=Grid1.Text
```

or replace the third statement with one like the following to assign a new value to the cell:

```
Grid1.Text=100.01
```

To read all the values in the fourth row and store them in an array, you must use a loop like this one:

```
Grid1.Row=3
For icol=1 to MaxRows
```

```
    Grid1.Col=icol
    a(icol)=Grid1.Text
Next
```

If you want to read multiple rows and store them in a two-dimensional array, use two nested loops, the outer one scanning the selected rows and the inner one scanning the selected columns in each row. As you might have guessed already, we'll use a similar loop to copy the values of the selected cells on the grid to the chart's data array.

The SelStartRow and SelStartCol properties return the number of the first and last selected rows respectively. Likewise, the SelStartCol and SelEndCol properties return the first and last selected columns in the grid. Because the user will rarely fill in all the cells in a grid, use these four properties to limit the area of the grid you work with. When the user is ready to plot the grid's data, he or she must first select a range of cells with the mouse and then click on the Plot Data button. The program assumes that each dataset corresponds to a row of the grid and the columns are the datapoints. The code that copies the values from the grid to the Chart control's data array is shown here:

```
StartRow=Grid1.SelStartRow
StartCol=Grid1.SelStartCol
EndRow=Grid1.SelEndRow
EndCol=Grid1.SelEndCol

IEChart1.Columns=EndRow-StartRow+1
IEChart1.Rows=EndCol-StartCol+1

ccol=0
For irow=StartRow to EndRow
    crow=0
    For icol=StartCol to EndCol
        Grid1.Row=irow
        Grid1.Col=icol
        IEChart1.RowIndex=crow
        IEChart1.ColumnIndex=ccol
        IEChart1.DataItem=Grid1.Text
        crow=crow+1
    Next
    ccol=ccol+1
Next
```

First it sets the StartRow, EndRow, StartCol, and EndCol properties that delimit the area of the grid we are interested in. Then, it sets the Columns and Rows properties of the Chart control so that the correct number of datasets and data points in each dataset will be plotted. The two loops do the actual copying of the values from the Grid to the Chart control. Notice the similarities in the commands that select the current cell in the grid and the current data point in the current dataset in the Chart control. For both controls, we set a column and a row value, which identify a single element (a cell in the case of the Grid control and a data value in the case of the Graph control). Then we use the Text property to read the value of the current cell in the Grid control and the `DataItem` property of the Chart control to set the value of the current data point in the Graph control. As soon as all the values have been copied, the Chart control's graph will be updated. This code must be placed in the Plot Data Command button's `Click` event and is probably the most challenging (and most interesting) part of the application. Most of the remaining code simply sets the various properties of the controls.

Implementing the Application

The first problem to deal with is how to make the Grid control accept user data. By default, the Grid control does not let the user enter data. But it recognizes the various `Keyboard` events, so it shouldn't be difficult to simulate data-entry operations. Indeed, you can place a few lines of VBScript code in the control `KeyPress` event to capture the keystrokes and translate them to digits to be displayed on the current cell. The code is fairly simple; it has to check the key pressed and make sure that it was a valid alphanumeric symbol and then append it to the current cell's contents. Providing the functionality of the various editing keys, especially mouse operations, is quite complicated, so we decided to let the user edit the cells' contents with the Backspace key only. Here's the code of the Grid's `KeyPress` event handler:

```
Sub Grid1_KeyPress(ByVal KeyAscii)
If KeyAscii=8 and Len(Grid1.Text)>0 Then
    Grid1.Text=Left(Grid1.Text, Len(Grid1.Text)-1)
    Exit Sub
End If
If KeyAscii<32 Then
    Exit Sub
End If
Grid1.Text=Grid1.Text+chr(KeyAscii)
End Sub
```

The first `If` structure checks for the Backspace key. If the Backspace key was pressed and the cell contains text, it deletes the rightmost character. If the key pressed does not correspond to a printable character, the keystroke is ignored. If you open the GridChart application and test-drive it for a few minutes, you'll realize that this short code works quite well.

The various commands of the Edit pop-up menu are straightforward, too. They make use of the `Cols` and `Rows` properties of the Grid control to assign values to a range of cells with a `For...Next` loop. The subroutine that fills a row with a user-supplied value is

```
Sub FillRow()
    Entry=InputBox("Please enter value to copy into current row")
    irow=Grid1.Row
    For icol=1 to Grid1.Cols-1
        Grid1.Col=icol
        Grid1.Text=Entry
    Next
End Sub
```

The code for deleting the contents of the cells in a given row is

```
Sub DelRow()
    irow=Grid1.Row
```

```
   For icol=1 to Grid1.Cols-1
      Grid1.Col=icol
      Grid1.Text=""
   Next
End Sub
```

We have already examined the code behind the Plot Data button, which copies the values of the selected cells from the Grid to the Chart control. The complete code of the GridChart project is shown in Listing 27.2.

Listing 27.2. The GridChart project's complete code.

```
 1: <SCRIPT LANGUAGE="VBScript">
 2: <!--
 3: Sub Form_onLoad()
 4:     Grid1.Row=0
 5:     For icol=1 to Grid1.Cols-1
 6:         Grid1.Col=icol
 7:         title="C" & icol
 8:         Grid1.Text=title
 9:     Next
10:     Grid1.Col=0
11:     For icol=1 to Grid1.Rows-1
12:         Grid1.Row=icol
13:         Grid1.Text="R" & icol
14:     Next
15: End Sub
16:
17: Sub CommandButton1_Click()
18:     call EditMenu.Popup()
19: End Sub
20:
21: Sub Grid1_KeyPress(ByVal KeyAscii)
22: If KeyAscii=8 and Len(Grid1.Text)>0 Then
23:     Grid1.Text=Left(Grid1.Text, Len(Grid1.Text)-1)
24:     Exit Sub
25: End If
26: If KeyAscii<32 Then
27:     Exit Sub
28: End If
29: Grid1.Text=Grid1.Text+chr(KeyAscii)
30: End Sub
31:
32: Sub DelRow()
33:     irow=Grid1.Row
34:     For icol=1 to Grid1.Cols-1
35:         Grid1.Col=icol
36:         Grid1.Text=""
37:     Next
38: End Sub
39:
40: Sub DelColumn()
41:     icol=Grid1.Column
42:     For irow=1 to Grid1.Rows-1
```

continues

Listing 27.2. continued

```
43:        Grid1.Row=irow
44:        Grid1.Text=""
45:    Next
46: End Sub
47:
48: Sub FillRow()
49:    Entry=InputBox("Please enter value to copy into current row")
50:    irow=Grid1.Row
51:    For icol=1 to Grid1.Cols-1
52:        Grid1.Col=icol
53:        Grid1.Text=Entry
54:    Next
55: End Sub
56:
57: sub FillColumn()
58:    Value=InputBox("Please enter value to copy into current column")
59:    icol=Grid1.Col
60:    for irow=1 to Grid1.Rows-1
61:        Grid1.Row=irow
62:        Grid1.Text=Value
63:    next
64: End sub
65:
66: sub ClearGrid()
67:    for icol=1 to Grid1.Cols
68:        for irow=1 to Grid1.Rows-1
69:            Grid1.Row=irow
70:            Grid1.Col=icol
71:            Grid1.Text=""
72:        next
73:    next
74: End sub
75:
76: Sub EditMenu_Click(ByVal item)
77:    if item=1 then DelRow()
78:    if item=2 then DelColumn()
79:    if item=3 then FillRow()
80:    if item=4 then FillColumn()
81:    if item=5 then ClearGrid()
82: End Sub
83:
84: Sub Mean()
85: msgbox "ENTER MEAN CALCULATIONS HERE"
86: End Sub
87:
88: Sub Max()
89: msgbox "ENTER MAX CALCULATIONS HERE"
90: End Sub
91:
92: Sub Min()
93: msgbox "ENTER MIN CALCULATIONS HERE"
94: End Sub
95:
96: Sub ProcessMenu_Click(ByVal item)
97:    if item=1 then Mean()
```

```
 98:     if item=2 then Max()
 99:     if item=3 then Min()
100: End Sub
101:
102: Sub CommandButton2_Click()
103: StartRow=Grid1.SelStartRow
104: StartCol=Grid1.SelStartCol
105: EndRow=Grid1.SelEndRow
106: EndCol=Grid1.SelEndCol
107:
108: IEChart1.Columns=EndRow-StartRow+1
109: IEChart1.Rows=EndCol-StartCol+1
110:
111: ccol=0
112: For irow=StartRow to EndRow
113:     crow=0
114:     For icol=StartCol to EndCol
115:         Grid1.Row=irow
116:         Grid1.Col=icol
117:         IEChart1.RowIndex=crow
118:         IEChart1.ColumnIndex=ccol
119:         IEChart1.DataItem=Grid1.Text
120:         crow=crow+1
121:     Next
122:     ccol=ccol+1
123: Next
124: End Sub
125:
126: Sub CommandButton3_Click()
127: ProcessMenu.PopUp()
128: end Sub
129:
130: Sub OptionButton1_Change()
131:     IEChart1.ChartType=1
132: End Sub
133:
134: Sub OptionButton2_Change()
135:     IEChart1.ChartType=5
136: End Sub
137:
138: Sub OptionButton3_Change()
139:     IEChart1.ChartType=14
140: End Sub
141:
142: Sub OptionButton4_Change()
143:     IEChart1.ChartType=8
144: End Sub
145:
146: Sub CheckBox1_Change()
147:     If CheckBox1.Value Then
148:         IEChart1.HGridStyle=1
149:     Else
150:         IEChart1.HGridStyle=0
151:     End If
152: End Sub
153:
```

27

THE CHART AND GRID CONTROLS

continues

Listing 27.2. continued

```
154: Sub CheckBox2_Change()
155:     If CheckBox2.Value Then
156:         IEChart1.VGridStyle=1
157:     Else
158:         IEChart1.VGridStyle=0
159:     End If
160: End Sub
161:
162: -->
163: </SCRIPT>
164: <DIV STYLE="LAYOUT:FIXED;WIDTH:556pt;HEIGHT:314pt;">
165:     <OBJECT ID="Image1"
166:     CLASSID="CLSID:D4A97620-8E8F-11CF-93CD-00AA00C08FDF"
            ➥STYLE="TOP:149pt;LEFT:17pt;WIDTH:528pt;HEIGHT:165pt;ZINDEX:0;">
167:         <PARAM NAME="BorderStyle" VALUE="0">
168:         <PARAM NAME="SizeMode" VALUE="3">
169:         <PARAM NAME="SpecialEffect" VALUE="1">
170:         <PARAM NAME="Size" VALUE="18627;5821">
171:         <PARAM NAME="PictureAlignment" VALUE="0">
172:         <PARAM NAME="VariousPropertyBits" VALUE="19">
173:     </OBJECT>
174:     <OBJECT ID="Grid1"
175:     CLASSID="CLSID:A8C3B720-0B5A-101B-B22E-00AA0037B2FC"
            ➥STYLE="TOP:17pt;LEFT:17pt;WIDTH:429pt;HEIGHT:123pt;ZINDEX:1;">
176:         <PARAM NAME="_Version" VALUE="65536">
177:         <PARAM NAME="_ExtentX" VALUE="15134">
178:         <PARAM NAME="_ExtentY" VALUE="4339">
179:         <PARAM NAME="_StockProps" VALUE="77">
180:         <PARAM NAME="BackColor" VALUE="16777215">
181:         <PARAM NAME="Rows" VALUE="20">
182:         <PARAM NAME="Cols" VALUE="20">
183:     </OBJECT>
184:     <OBJECT ID="CommandButton1"
185:     CLASSID="CLSID:D7053240-CE69-11CD-A777-00DD01143C57"
            ➥STYLE="TOP:66pt;LEFT:454pt;WIDTH:83pt;HEIGHT:25pt;TABINDEX:1;
            ➥ZINDEX:2;">
186:         <PARAM NAME="Caption" VALUE="Edit Grid">
187:         <PARAM NAME="Size" VALUE="2911;882">
188:         <PARAM NAME="FontHeight" VALUE="240">
189:         <PARAM NAME="FontCharSet" VALUE="0">
190:         <PARAM NAME="FontPitchAndFamily" VALUE="2">
191:         <PARAM NAME="ParagraphAlign" VALUE="3">
192:         <PARAM NAME="FontWeight" VALUE="0">
193:     </OBJECT>
194:     <OBJECT ID="CommandButton2"
195:     CLASSID="CLSID:D7053240-CE69-11CD-A777-00DD01143C57"
            ➥STYLE="TOP:116pt;LEFT:454pt;WIDTH:83pt;HEIGHT:25pt;TABINDEX:2;ZINDEX:3;">
196:         <PARAM NAME="Caption" VALUE="Plot Data">
197:         <PARAM NAME="Size" VALUE="2911;882">
198:         <PARAM NAME="FontHeight" VALUE="240">
199:         <PARAM NAME="FontCharSet" VALUE="0">
200:         <PARAM NAME="FontPitchAndFamily" VALUE="2">
201:         <PARAM NAME="ParagraphAlign" VALUE="3">
202:         <PARAM NAME="FontWeight" VALUE="0">
203:     </OBJECT>
204:     <OBJECT ID="CommandButton3"
```

```
205:        CLASSID="CLSID:D7053240-CE69-11CD-A777-00DD01143C57"
            ➡STYLE="TOP:91pt;LEFT:454pt;WIDTH:83pt;HEIGHT:25pt;TABINDEX:3;
            ➡ZINDEX:4;">
206:          <PARAM NAME="Caption" VALUE="Process Data">
207:          <PARAM NAME="Size" VALUE="2911;882">
208:          <PARAM NAME="FontHeight" VALUE="240">
209:          <PARAM NAME="FontCharSet" VALUE="0">
210:          <PARAM NAME="FontPitchAndFamily" VALUE="2">
211:          <PARAM NAME="ParagraphAlign" VALUE="3">
212:          <PARAM NAME="FontWeight" VALUE="0">
213:        </OBJECT>
214:        <OBJECT ID="iechart1"
215:         CLASSID="CLSID:FC25B780-75BE-11CF-8B01-444553540000"
            ➡STYLE="TOP:157pt;LEFT:50pt;WIDTH:313pt;HEIGHT:140pt;ZINDEX:5;">
216:          <PARAM NAME="_ExtentX" VALUE="11033">
217:          <PARAM NAME="_ExtentY" VALUE="4948">
218:          <PARAM NAME="Rows" VALUE="4">
219:          <PARAM NAME="Columns" VALUE="3">
220:          <PARAM NAME="ChartType" VALUE="8">
221:          <PARAM NAME="Data[0][0]" VALUE="0">
222:          <PARAM NAME="Data[0][1]" VALUE="10">
223:          <PARAM NAME="Data[0][2]" VALUE="11">
224:          <PARAM NAME="Data[1][0]" VALUE="7">
225:          <PARAM NAME="Data[1][1]" VALUE="11">
226:          <PARAM NAME="Data[1][2]" VALUE="12">
227:          <PARAM NAME="Data[2][0]" VALUE="6">
228:          <PARAM NAME="Data[2][1]" VALUE="12">
229:          <PARAM NAME="Data[2][2]" VALUE="13">
230:          <PARAM NAME="Data[3][0]" VALUE="11">
231:          <PARAM NAME="Data[3][1]" VALUE="13">
232:          <PARAM NAME="Data[3][2]" VALUE="14">
233:          <PARAM NAME="HorizontalAxis" VALUE="0">
234:          <PARAM NAME="VerticalAxis" VALUE="0">
235:          <PARAM NAME="hgridStyle" VALUE="0">
236:          <PARAM NAME="vgridStyle" VALUE="0">
237:          <PARAM NAME="ColorScheme" VALUE="0">
238:          <PARAM NAME="BackStyle" VALUE="1">
239:          <PARAM NAME="Scale" VALUE="100">
240:          <PARAM NAME="DisplayLegend" VALUE="1">
241:          <PARAM NAME="BackColor" VALUE="16777215">
242:          <PARAM NAME="ForeColor" VALUE="32768">
243:        </OBJECT>
244:        <OBJECT ID="OptionButton1"
245:         CLASSID="CLSID:8BD21D50-EC42-11CE-9E0D-00AA006002F3"
            ➡STYLE="TOP:173pt;LEFT:396pt;WIDTH:108pt;HEIGHT:18pt;TABINDEX:4;
            ➡ZINDEX:6;">
246:          <PARAM NAME="BackColor" VALUE="2147483663">
247:          <PARAM NAME="ForeColor" VALUE="2147483666">
248:          <PARAM NAME="DisplayStyle" VALUE="5">
249:          <PARAM NAME="Size" VALUE="3810;635">
250:          <PARAM NAME="Caption" VALUE="Pie Chart">
251:          <PARAM NAME="FontName" VALUE="Verdana">
252:          <PARAM NAME="FontHeight" VALUE="200">
253:          <PARAM NAME="FontCharSet" VALUE="0">
254:          <PARAM NAME="FontPitchAndFamily" VALUE="2">
255:          <PARAM NAME="FontWeight" VALUE="0">
256:        </OBJECT>
257:        <OBJECT ID="OptionButton2"
```

27

THE CHART AND
GRID CONTROLS

continues

Listing 27.2. continued

```
258:        CLASSID="CLSID:8BD21D50-EC42-11CE-9E0D-00AA006002F3"
            ➥STYLE="TOP:191pt;LEFT:396pt;WIDTH:108pt;HEIGHT:18pt;TABINDEX:5;
            ➥ZINDEX:7;">
259:          <PARAM NAME="BackColor" VALUE="2147483663">
260:          <PARAM NAME="ForeColor" VALUE="2147483666">
261:          <PARAM NAME="DisplayStyle" VALUE="5">
262:          <PARAM NAME="Size" VALUE="3810;635">
263:          <PARAM NAME="Caption" VALUE="Line Plot">
264:          <PARAM NAME="FontName" VALUE="Verdana">
265:          <PARAM NAME="FontHeight" VALUE="200">
266:          <PARAM NAME="FontCharSet" VALUE="0">
267:          <PARAM NAME="FontPitchAndFamily" VALUE="2">
268:          <PARAM NAME="FontWeight" VALUE="0">
269:        </OBJECT>
270:        <OBJECT ID="OptionButton3"
271:         CLASSID="CLSID:8BD21D50-EC42-11CE-9E0D-00AA006002F3"
            ➥STYLE="TOP:206pt;LEFT:396pt;WIDTH:108pt;HEIGHT:18pt;TABINDEX:6;
            ➥ZINDEX:8;">
272:          <PARAM NAME="BackColor" VALUE="2147483663">
273:          <PARAM NAME="ForeColor" VALUE="2147483666">
274:          <PARAM NAME="DisplayStyle" VALUE="5">
275:          <PARAM NAME="Size" VALUE="3810;635">
276:          <PARAM NAME="Caption" VALUE="Bar Graph">
277:          <PARAM NAME="FontName" VALUE="Verdana">
278:          <PARAM NAME="FontHeight" VALUE="200">
279:          <PARAM NAME="FontCharSet" VALUE="0">
280:          <PARAM NAME="FontPitchAndFamily" VALUE="2">
281:          <PARAM NAME="FontWeight" VALUE="0">
282:        </OBJECT>
283:        <OBJECT ID="OptionButton4"
284:         CLASSID="CLSID:8BD21D50-EC42-11CE-9E0D-00AA006002F3"
            ➥STYLE="TOP:224pt;LEFT:396pt;WIDTH:108pt;HEIGHT:18pt;TABINDEX:7;
            ➥ZINDEX:9;">
285:          <PARAM NAME="BackColor" VALUE="2147483663">
286:          <PARAM NAME="ForeColor" VALUE="2147483666">
287:          <PARAM NAME="DisplayStyle" VALUE="5">
288:          <PARAM NAME="Size" VALUE="3810;635">
289:          <PARAM NAME="Caption" VALUE="Area Graph">
290:          <PARAM NAME="FontName" VALUE="Verdana">
291:          <PARAM NAME="FontHeight" VALUE="200">
292:          <PARAM NAME="FontCharSet" VALUE="0">
293:          <PARAM NAME="FontPitchAndFamily" VALUE="2">
294:          <PARAM NAME="FontWeight" VALUE="0">
295:        </OBJECT>
296:        <OBJECT ID="CheckBox1"
297:         CLASSID="CLSID:8BD21D40-EC42-11CE-9E0D-00AA006002F3"
            ➥STYLE="TOP:264pt;LEFT:396pt;WIDTH:99pt;HEIGHT:17pt;TABINDEX:8;
            ➥ZINDEX:10;">
298:          <PARAM NAME="BackColor" VALUE="2147483663">
299:          <PARAM NAME="ForeColor" VALUE="2147483666">
300:          <PARAM NAME="DisplayStyle" VALUE="4">
301:          <PARAM NAME="Size" VALUE="3493;600">
302:          <PARAM NAME="Caption" VALUE="Horizontal Grid">
303:          <PARAM NAME="FontName" VALUE="Verdana">
304:          <PARAM NAME="FontHeight" VALUE="200">
305:          <PARAM NAME="FontCharSet" VALUE="0">
306:          <PARAM NAME="FontPitchAndFamily" VALUE="2">
307:          <PARAM NAME="FontWeight" VALUE="0">
```

```
308:      </OBJECT>
309:      <OBJECT ID="CheckBox2"
310:        CLASSID="CLSID:8BD21D40-EC42-11CE-9E0D-00AA006002F3"
          ➥STYLE="TOP:280pt;LEFT:396pt;WIDTH:99pt;HEIGHT:17pt;TABINDEX:9;
          ➥ZINDEX:11;">
311:        <PARAM NAME="BackColor" VALUE="2147483663">
312:        <PARAM NAME="ForeColor" VALUE="2147483666">
313:        <PARAM NAME="DisplayStyle" VALUE="4">
314:        <PARAM NAME="Size" VALUE="3493;600">
315:        <PARAM NAME="Caption" VALUE="Vertical Grid">
316:        <PARAM NAME="FontName" VALUE="Verdana">
317:        <PARAM NAME="FontHeight" VALUE="200">
318:        <PARAM NAME="FontCharSet" VALUE="0">
319:        <PARAM NAME="FontPitchAndFamily" VALUE="2">
320:        <PARAM NAME="FontWeight" VALUE="0">
321:      </OBJECT>
322: </DIV>
```

Notice that the definition of the Chart object contains random data. You can remove the PARAM tags that assign values to the Data array, or assign the same values to this array and the first few cells of the grid so that when the document is loaded, the graph will match the data on the grid.

Another item worth noticing is the assignment of titles to the grid's fixed cells. This action takes place when the layout is loaded. Because the cells of the first column and row are fixed, the user cannot edit them at runtime.

The GridChart application doesn't contain any error handlers. For example, it assumes that the user has already selected a range of cells before he or she attempts to plot them, and that they contain numeric data. If this isn't true, an error message will be displayed and the program will stop. There's a lot you can do to improve not only the application's interface and appearance, but its operation too. GridChart is a good starting point for a data-plotting applications, but there is quite a bit of error checking you can add to the program.

Review

The last example of this section demonstrates two very flexible controls that are commonly used together: the Grid control and the Chart control. Although the Grid control was designed to facilitate the display of data in a spreadsheet arrangement, with a few lines of code in its KeyDown and KeyPress events, you can turn it into a data-entry tool. The Chart control displays numeric data, like the ones stored on a Grid control, as graphs.

The two controls have more functional similarities, too. They both manipulate data stored in a two-dimensional array. The two-dimensional structure of the Grid's data is rather obvious. The Chart control uses a similar arrangement for storing multiple datasets, with as many data points per dataset. To access a cell in a grid, you must specify its address, which is the row and column number of the cell. To access a data point in a Chart control, you must specify the dataset it belongs to, and its order in the dataset. The address of a cell in a Grid control is specified with the help of the Row and Col properties, and a data point in a Chart control is specified with the RowIndex and ColIndex properties. Once the address of an element has been specified with the properties mentioned here, you can use the Text property of the Grid control or the DataItem property of the Chart control to read or set its value. The two controls provide a number of properties for specifying the appearance of the data or the chart, but you can easily figure out most of them, or experiment with the various settings to get what you want.

Appendix

VI
PART

VBScript Language Reference

IN THIS APPENDIX

Variables, Constants, and Expressions

Variables and constants are similar in that they both refer to a location in memory that contains a value. A constant has a value that remains the same throughout the execution of the program. A variable, on the other hand, is modified during the execution. Every constant and variable is assigned a name that uniquely identifies it and must follow the conventions listed here:

- Must begin with an alphabetic character
- Cannot contain an embedded period or type-declaration character
- Must be unique in the same scope
- Must not exceed 255 characters

A constant may be a string or numeric literal, another constant, or any combination that includes arithmetic or logical operators. For example:

```
Const Ident = "This is Freds script"
```

Possible variable subtypes as well as their data ranges are shown in Table A.1. Other reserved terms when describing data types are shown in Table A.2.

Table A.1. Variant subtypes.

Subtype	*Range*
Byte	0 to 255.
Boolean	True or False.
Integer	-32,768 to 32,767.
Long	-2,147,483,648 to 2,147,483,647.
Single	-3.402823E38 to -1.401298E-45 for negative values; 1.401298E-45 to 3.402823E38 for positive values.
Double	-1.79769313486232E308 to -4.94065645841247E-324 for negative values; 4.94065645841247E-324 to 1.79769313486232E308 for positive values.
Currency	-922,337,203,685,477.5808 to 922,337,203,685,477.5807.
Date	January 1, 100 to December 31, 9999, inclusive.
Object	Any Object reference.
String	Variable-length strings may range in length from 0 to approximately 2 billion characters (approximately 65,535 for Microsoft Windows version 3.1 and earlier).

Table A.2. Data type reserved terms.

Term	Description
Nothing	A value that indicates that an object variable is no longer associated with any actual object.
Null	A value indicating that a variable contains no valid data.
Empty	A value that indicates that no beginning value has been assigned to a variable (0 for a numeric subtype or a zero-length string).

Operators

When several operations occur in an expression, each part is evaluated and resolved in a predetermined order known as *operator precedence.* (See Table A.3.) Parentheses can be used to override this order. When the precedence is equal (that is, addition and subtraction, multiplication and division, all comparison operators), the expressions are evaluated from left to right.

Table A.3. Operator precedence.

Symbol	Description	Type
^	Exponentiation	Arithmetic
-	Negation	Arithmetic
*	Multiplication	Arithmetic
/	Division	Arithmetic
\	Integer division	Arithmetic
Mod	Modulo arithmetic	Arithmetic
+	Addition	Arithmetic
-	Subtraction	Arithmetic
&	String concatenation	Arithmetic
=	Equality	Comparison
<>	Inequality	Comparison
<	Less than	Comparison
>	Greater than	Comparison
<=	Less than or equal to	Comparison
>=	Greater than or equal to	Comparison

continues

A

VBSCRIPT LANGUAGE REFERENCE

Table A.3. continued

Symbol	Description	Type
IS	Same object	Comparison
NOT	Negation	Logical
AND	Bitwise conjunction	Logical
OR	Bitwise disjunction	Logical
XOR	Bitwise exclusion	Logical
EQV	Bitwise equivalence	Logical
IMP	Bitwise implication	Logical

Arithmetic Operators

Arithmetic operators are used in expressions to perform mathematical calculations. The following general rules are involved in the operations:

■ If one or both operands are Null expressions, the result is Null.

■ If an operand is Empty, it is treated as a 0.

+ (Addition) Operator

This operator determines the sum of two numbers. Its usage is

```
sum = expr1 + expr2
```

where sum is a numeric variable, and expr1 and expr2 are any expressions.

> **NOTE**
>
> Though the + operator can be used to concatenate two character strings, its usage as a concatenation operator is discouraged. The & operator should be used for that purpose.

If both expressions in the operation are strings, a concatenation of these strings will occur. Otherwise, an addition will be performed.

The general rules apply. If both expressions are Empty, the result is an Integer subtype equal to 0.

- (Subtraction) Operator

The subtraction operator will yield the difference between two numbers when used as

```
result = number1 - number2
```

where `result` is a numeric variable, and `number1` and `number2` are numeric expressions.

This operator can also be used as the unary negation operator to change to the negative value of a numeric expression. In this case its usage is

```
-number
```

where `number` is a numeric expression.

The general rules apply.

* (Multiplication) Operator

The multiplication operator will yield the product of two numbers. Its usage is

```
result = multiplier1 * multiplier2
```

where `result` is a numeric variable, and `multiplier1` and `multiplier2` are numeric expressions.

The general rules apply.

/ (Division) Operator

The division operator will yield the quotient of two numbers. Its usage is

```
quotient = dividend / divisor
```

where `quotient` is a numeric floating-point variable, and `dividend` and `divisor` are numeric expressions.

The general rules apply.

\ (Integer Division) Operator

The integer division operator divides two numbers and return an integer result. Its usage is

```
quotient = dividend \ divisor
```

where `quotient` is a numeric variable, and `dividend` and `divisor` are numeric expressions.

Numeric expressions are rounded to `Byte`, `Integer`, or `Long` subtype expressions. Then the general rules apply.

^ (Exponentiation) Operator

The exponentiation operator will yield the power of a number raised to an exponent. Its usage is

```
result = number ^ exponent
```

where `result` is a numeric variable, and `number` and `exponent` are numeric expressions.

As well as the general rules, exponent must be an integer if `number` is a negative value.

Mod (Modulus) Operator

The modulus operator determines the remainder from the division of two numbers. Its usage is

```
result = dividend Mod divisor
```

where `result` is any numeric variable, and `dividend` and `divisor` are numeric expressions. If the dividend or divisor is a floating-point number, it is rounded to an integer before the operation. The general rules apply.

Concatenation Operators

Concatenation operators combine strings. The general rules are

- Any non-string operands are converted to a `String` subtype before the operation.
- Any operand that is `Null` or `Empty` is treated as a zero-length string.
- If both operands are `Null`, the result is `Null`.

& (Concatenation) Operator

The & concatenation operator will combine two expressions into a string result. Its usage is

```
result = expr1 & expr2
```

where `result` is any variable, and `expr1` and `expr2` are any expressions.

+ (Concatenation) Operator

The + concatenation operator functions in the same manner as the & concatenation operator when either operand is a `String` subtype. Its usage is

```
result = expr1 + expr2
```

where `result` is any variable, and either `expr1` or `expr2` is a `String` variable.

> **NOTE**
>
> Use of the + concatenation operator is not recommended. Use the & operator to eliminate ambiguity.

Logical Operators

Logical operators perform logical comparison and algebraic bitwise operations. Some general rules are

- A Null expression is treated as a numeric zero in these operations.
- A nonzero value (or bit) is True.
- A zero value (or bit) is False.

AND Operator

The AND operator can perform a logical conjunctive comparison on two expressions as well as perform a bitwise algebraic conjunctive operation. Its usage is

```
result = expr1 AND expr2
```

where result is any numeric variable, and expr1 and expr2 are any expressions. When the AND operator performs a bitwise comparison of two numeric expressions, it sets the corresponding bit in result according to the truth table in Figure A.1. When used as a logical comparison operator, result is set according to the truth table in Figure A.1 also.

FIGURE A.1.

AND *operator truth tables.*

Bitwise	0	1
0	0	0
1	0	1

Logical	True	False
True	True	False
False	False	False

OR Operator

The OR operator can perform a logical disjunctive comparison on two expressions as well as perform a bitwise algebraic disjunctive operation. Its usage is

```
result = expr1 OR expr2
```

where result is any numeric variable, and expr1 and expr2 are any expressions. When the OR operator performs a bitwise comparison of two numeric expressions, it sets the corresponding bit in result according to the truth table in Figure A.2. When used as a logical comparison operator, result is set according to the truth table in Figure A.2 also.

A

VBSCRIPT LANGUAGE REFERENCE

FIGURE A.2.

OR *operator truth tables.*

Bitwise	0	1
0	0	1
1	1	1

Logical	True	False
True	True	True
False	True	False

XOR Operator

The XOR operator can perform a logical exclusive comparison of two expressions as well as perform a bitwise exclusive algebraic operation. Its usage is

```
result = expr1 XOR expr2
```

where result is any numeric variable, and expr1 and expr2 are any expressions. When the XOR operator performs a bitwise comparison of two numeric expressions, it sets the corresponding bit in result according to the truth table in Figure A.3. When used as a logical comparison operator, result is set according to the truth table in Figure A.3 also.

FIGURE A.3.

XOR *operator truth tables.*

Bitwise	0	1
0	0	1
1	1	0

Logical	True	False
True	False	True
False	True	False

EQV Operator

The EQV operator can perform a logical equivalence comparison of two expressions as well as perform a bitwise equivalence algebraic operation. Its usage is

```
result = expr1 EQV expr2
```

where result is any numeric variable, and expr1 and expr2 are any expressions. When the EQV operator performs a bitwise comparison of two numeric expressions, it sets the corresponding bit in result according to the truth table in Figure A.4. When used as a logical comparison operator, result is set according to the truth table in Figure A.4 also.

FIGURE A.4.

EQV *operator truth tables.*

Bitwise	0	1
0	1	0
1	0	1

Logical	True	False
True	True	False
False	False	True

IMP Operator

The IMP operator can perform a logical implication comparison of two expressions as well as perform a bitwise implication algebraic operation. Its usage is

```
result = expr1 IMP expr2
```

where result is any numeric variable, and expr1 and expr2 are any expressions. When the IMP operator performs a bitwise comparison of two numeric expressions, it sets the corresponding bit in result according to the truth table in Figure A.5. When used as a logical comparison operator, result is set according to the truth table in Figure A.5 also.

FIGURE A.5.

EQV *operator truth tables.*

Bitwise		
	0	1
0	1	1
1	0	1

Logical		
	True	False
True	True	False
False	True	True

- (Negation) Operator

The negation operator can indicate the negative value of a numeric expression. Its usage is

```
-number
```

where number is any numeric expression.

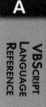

> **NOTE**
>
> The syntax of the usage distinguishes between the negation operator and the subtraction operator.

NOT Operator

The NOT operator can perform a logical negation of an expression as well as an algebraic bitwise reversal of an expression. Its usage is

```
result = NOT expr
```

where result is a numeric variable and expr is any expression. When used as a negation operator, if expr is True, result will be False. If expr is False, result will be True. If expr is Null, result will be Null.

When used as an algebraic operator, each bit in result will be cleared if set in expr or set if clear in expr.

Comparison Operators

Comparison operators match two expressions and provide alternative program execution flow. Their usage is

```
result = expr1 op expr2
result = obj1 IS obj2
result = string LIKE pattern
```

where op is the comparison operator, `result` is a numeric variable, `expr1` and `expr2` are expressions, `obj1` and `obj2` are objects, `string` is a string variable, and `pattern` is a string expression.

> **NOTE**
>
> The logical operators can also be used as comparison operators.

The general rules for comparisons are

- If both expressions are numeric, a numeric comparison is performed.
- If both expressions are strings, a string comparison is performed.
- When comparing a string to a numeric, the numeric expression is always the lesser of the two.
- If one expression is `Empty` and the other is a numeric expression, the `Empty` expression is treated as a numeric 0. If both are `Empty`, then they are both treated as numeric 0 and are equal.
- If one expression is `Empty` and the other is a string expression, the `Empty` expression is treated as a `Null` string.
- If either expression is `Null`, the result is `Null`.
- If both expressions are `Empty`, the expressions are equal.

< (Less than) Operator

The less than operator's usage is

```
expr1 < expr2
```

and a `True` result is yielded when `expr1` is arithmetically less than `expr2`.

<= (Less than or equal to) Operator

The less than or equal to operator's usage is

```
expr1 <= expr2
```

and a `True` result is yielded when `expr1` is arithmetically less than or equal to `expr2`.

> (Greater than) Operator

The greater than operator's usage is

`expr1 > expr2`

and a `True` result is yielded when `expr1` is arithmetically greater than `expr2`.

>= (Greater than or Equal to) Operator

The greater than or equal to operator's usage is

`expr1 >= expr2`

and a `True` result is yielded when `expr1` is arithmetically greater than or equal to `expr2`.

= (Equal to) Operator

The equal to operator's usage is

`expr1 = expr2`

and a `True` result is yielded when `expr1` is arithmetically equal to `expr2`.

<> (Not Equal to) Operator

The not equal to operator's usage is

`expr1 <> expr2`

and a `True` result is yielded when `expr1` is arithmetically not equal to `expr2`.

Is Operator

The `Is` operator compares two object reference variables. Its usage is

`obj1 Is obj2`

where `obj1` and `obj2` are object names. If `obj1` and `obj2` both refer to the same object, the condition is `True`. Two variables can be made to refer to the same object by using the `Set` statement.

Statements

This section describes the statement syntax for the VBScript language. In the descriptions the use of brackets ([]) indicates an optional entry or keyword.

Call Statement

The Call statement transfers control to a Sub procedure or Function procedure. Its usage is

```
Call name ([[ByVal] arg1, [ByVal] arg2, ... [ByVal] argn])
[result =] name [[ByVal] arg1, [ByVal] arg2, ... [ByVal] argn]
```

where name is the name of the procedure to call, arg1 through argn are a comma-delimited list of expressions to pass to the procedure, and result is any numeric variable. If the ByVal keyword precedes a variable in the argument list , the argument is being passed to the procedure by value and the procedure being called may change the value of the variable. In the first syntax, the argument list must be enclosed in parentheses and a result is not available.

Dim Statement

The Dim statement declares variables and allocates storage space. Its usage is

```
Dim var1[([subs])][, var2[([subs])]] . . .
```

where var1 and var2 are names of variables to be declared and subs are upper-bound dimensions for an array variable. An array can have up to 60 dimensions. The lower bound of an array is always 0. Scoping rules will apply to the variables declared. When variables are initialized, a numeric variable is initialized to 0 and a string is initialized to a zero-length string (" ").

If the subs fields are not specified (empty parentheses), a dynamic array is indicated. In this case the ReDim statement can be used later to define the number of dimensions and elements in the array.

Do...Loop Statement

The Do loop repeats a block of statements while a condition is True or until a condition becomes True. The two possible usages are

```
Do [{While ¦ Until} condition]
    [statements]
Loop
Do
    [statements]
Loop [{While ¦ Until} condition]
```

where condition is an expression that can be evaluated to True or False. Statements are various statements that are repeated while or until condition is True. To exit the loop immediately, use the Exit Do statement.

Erase Statement

The Erase statement will free the storage used by a dynamic array. If the array is fixed size, the elements in the array will be reset. Its usage is

```
Erase array
```

where array is the name of the array to be erased.

Exit Statement

The Exit statement is used to escape from a block of code. The statement varies depending on the type of block involved. Its usages are

```
Exit Do
Exit For
Exit Function
Exit Sub
```

For...Next Statement

The For...Next loop repeats a group of statements a specified number of times and optionally varies a variable within the loop. Its usage is

```
For count = start To end [Step step]
    [statements]
Next
```

where count is a numeric variable used as a loop counter, start is the beginning value for count, end is the ending value, and step is the amount count is to change (defaulting to 1) for each iteration of the loop. Statements is the block of code to be executed on each iteration. The sequence of loop iterations can be either positive or negative, depending upon the step value.

The Exit For statement can be used to escape from the loop.

For Each...Next Statement

The For Each...Next statement is a variation of the For loop that can repeat a block of code for each element in an array. Its usage is

```
For Each entry In array
    [statements]
Next [entry]
```

where entry is a variable used to iterate through the elements of the array, array is the name of a collection or array, and statements is a block of code to be executed on each iteration. An Exit For can be used to escape from the loop.

Function Statement

The Function statement defines the block of code that makes up a function procedure. It encompasses the name and arguments of that procedure. Its usage is

```
Function name [[ByVal] arg1, [ByVal] arg2, ... [ByVal] argn]
    [statements]
    [name = expression]
End Function
```

where name is the name of the function, arg1 through argn is a list of variables passed to the procedure, and statements is a block of code to be executed. The name = expression optional

A

line returns a value to the caller of the function. The ByVal keyword indicates an argument whose value may be changed during the procedure.

An Exit Function statement can be used to escape from the function at any point.

If...Then Statement

The If...Then statement provides alternative statement execution depending upon varying conditions that may be present. Its usage is

```
If condition-1 Then
    [statements]
[ElseIf condition-2 Then
    [elifstatements]]
[Else
    [elstatements]]
End If
```

where condition-1 and condition-2 are conditional expressions (see comparison and logical operators above), statements is a block of code executed when condition-1 is True, elifstatements is a block of code executed when condition-1 is False and condition-2 is True, and elstatements is a block of code that is executed when neither condition-1 nor condition-2 is True.

> **NOTE**
>
> A single line form of the If statement is available; however, its use is discouraged for readability reasons.

On Error Statement

The On Error statement identifies an error-handling routine and specifies the location of the routine within a procedure. It can also be used to disable an error-handling routine. Its usage is

```
On Error Resume Next
```

Randomize Statement

The Randomize statement sets a new seed value into the random-number generator. Its usage is

```
Randomize [number]
```

where number is a numeric expression.

ReDim Statement

The ReDim statement declares dynamic-array variables and allocates or reallocates storage space. Its usage is

```
ReDim [Preserve] name(subs) [,name(subs)] . . .
```

where Preserve indicates that the existing values in an array are to be saved when changing the size of the last dimension, name is the name of a variable, and subs are the redimensions of an array variable.

Rem Statement

The Rem statement is a nonexecutable statement and provides documentary remarks in a program. Its usages are

```
Rem comment
```

or

```
' comment
```

where comment is the text of any remarks you want to include.

Select Case Statement

Select Case executes one of several groups of statements, depending on the value of an expression. Its usage is

```
Select Case testexpr
    [Case expr1
        [statements1]]
    [Case expr2
        [statements2]]
    .
    .
    .
    [Case exprn
        [statementsn]]
    [Case Else
        [elstatements]]
End Select
```

where testexpr is any expression; expr1, expr2, ..., and exprn are alternative values for testexpr; and statements1, statements2, ..., and statementsn are blocks of code that are executed when the value of testexpr matches the respective case expression. elstatements is a block of code that is executed when testexpr doesn't match any of the case expressions.

Set Statement

The Set statement assigns an object reference to a variable or property. Its usage is

```
Set objectvar = { objectexpr ¦ Nothing}
```

where objectvar is the name of a variable and objectexpr is the name of an object, a variable of an object type, or a function that returns an object of an object type. If Nothing is specified, the name of the object is disassociated from objectvar.

Sub Statement

The Sub statement defines the block of code that makes up a subroutine. It encompasses the name and arguments of that routine. Its usage is

```
Sub name [[ByVal] arg1, [ByVal] arg2, ... [ByVal] argn]
    [statements]
End Sub
```

where name is the name of the subroutine, arg1 through argn is a list of variables passed to the procedure, and statements is a block of code to be executed. Unlike a procedure, a subroutine cannot be used on the right side of a statement and does not return a value. The ByVal keyword indicates an argument whose value may be changed during the procedure.

An Exit Sub statement can be used to escape from the function at any point.

While...Wend Statement

The While statement is similar to the Do While statement and executes a block of code while a condition is True. Its usage is

```
While condition
    [statements]
Wend
```

where condition is a comparison or logical expression that can be evaluated to True or False and statements is the block of code to be executed.

Functions

The VBScript language offers a number of built-in procedures that are used to extend the functionality of the language. These are implemented as functions and as such will return a value that can be used in expressions. For convenience these functions can be grouped by purpose.

Variable and Conversion Functions

The variable and conversion functions deal directly with the types of variables and offer ways to convert these variables from one type to another. Refer to Table A.1 for more information.

CBool Function

The CBool function returns a Boolean value that depends on the value of the argument. Its usage is

```
result = CBool(expr)
```

where result is an expression that is a Variant of subtype Boolean and expr is a valid expression that can be evaluated to a numeric value. If expr is 0, the function returns False; otherwise, it returns True. If expr cannot be evaluated to a numeric value, the function causes a runtime error.

CByte Function

The CByte function converts an expression into a byte value. Its usage is

```
result = CByte(expr)
```

where result is a Variant of subtype Byte and expr is a valid expression with a value in the byte range. If expr is not in the byte range, an error occurs.

CDbl Function

The CDbl function returns an expression that has been converted to a Variant of subtype Double. Its usage is

```
result = CDbl(expr)
```

where result is a Variant of subtype Double and expr is a valid expression with a value in the double range.

Chr Function

The Chr function converts an ANSI character code into a character. Its usage is

```
result = Chr(charcode)
```

where result is a character and charcode is a number that identifies an ANSI character.

> **NOTE**
>
> Another function (ChrB) is provided for use with byte data contained in a string. Instead of returning a character, which may be one or two bytes, ChrB always returns a single byte. ChrW is provided for 32-bit platforms that use Unicode characters. Its argument is a Unicode (wide) character code, thereby avoiding the conversion from ANSI to Unicode.

ChrB Function

The ChrB function converts an ANSI character code into a single byte. Its usage is

```
result = ChrB(charcode)
```

where result is a byte subtype and charcode is a number that identifies an ANSI character.

ChrW Function

The ChrW function converts an ANSI character code into a Unicode character. Its usage is

```
result = ChrW(charcode)
```

where result is a Unicode character (2 byte) and charcode is a number that identifies an ANSI character.

> **NOTE**
>
> This function is valid only on platforms that support Unicode characters.

CInt Function

The CInt function converts an expression to a Variant of subtype Integer. Its usage is

```
result = CInt(expr)
```

where result is an Integer subtype and expr is a valid expression. If expr is not within an integer range, a runtime error occurs. During the operation, expr is rounded to the nearest whole number.

CLng Function

The CLng function converts an expression to a Variant of subtype Long. Its usage is

```
result = CLng(expr)
```

where result is a Long subtype and expr is a valid expression. If expr is outside the range for a Long, a runtime error occurs. During the operation, expr is rounded to the nearest whole number.

CSng Function

The CSng function converts an expression to a Variant of subtype Single. Its usage is

```
result = CSng(expr)
```

where result a Variant of subtype Single and expr is a valid expression. If expr is not in the range for a Single, a runtime error occurs.

CStr Function

The CStr function converts an expression into a string. Its usage is

```
result = CStr(expr)
```

where result is a Variant of subtype String and expr is a valid expression. The value of result will vary depending on the subtype of expr as shown in the following table:

Expr *Subtype*	*Result*
Boolean	True or False.
Date	A date in short-date format.
Error	The word *Error* and the error number.
Any numeric	The number in string format.

If expr is Null, a runtime error occurs. If it is Empty, result is a zero-length string (""").

Hex Function

The Hex function converts a number into a string representing the hexadecimal value of that number. Its usage is

```
str = Hex(number)
```

where str is a string variable containing a hexadecimal representation and number is any valid numeric expression. The limit of the number is 8 hexadecimal characters (4 bytes).

LBound Function

The LBound function identifies the smallest subscript for the particular dimension of an array. Its usage is

```
result = LBound(arrayname[, dimension])
```

where result is the smallest subscript, arrayname is the name of the array, and dimension indicates the desired dimension.

Oct Function

The Oct function converts a number into a string representing the octal value of that number. Its usage is

```
str = Oct(number)
```

where str is a string variable containing an octal representation and number is any valid numeric expression. The limit of the number is 11 octal characters (4 bytes).

UBound Function

The UBound function identifies the largest subscript for the particular dimension of an array. Its usage is

```
result = UBound(arrayname[, dimension])
```

where result is the largest subscript, arrayname is the name of the array, and dimension indicates the desired dimension.

VarType Function

The VarType function returns an integer indicating the subtype of a variable. Its usage is

```
result = VarType(varname)
```

where result is an integer and varname is the name of a variable. Possible values for result are as follows.

Result	varname *Type*
0	Empty (uninitialized).
1	Null (no valid data).
2	Integer.
3	Long integer.
4	Single-precision floating-point number.
5	Double-precision floating-point number.
6	Currency.
7	Date.
8	String.
9	Automation object.
10	Error.
11	Boolean.
12	Variant (used only with arrays of Variants).
13	Non-automation object.
17	Byte.
8192	Array (added to value above).

Date/Time Functions

The date and time functions deal with various procedures that support conversions of these values. Within these routines, the days of the week have the following coded values:

Value	Day of Week
1	Sunday
2	Monday
3	Tuesday
4	Wednesday
5	Thursday
6	Friday
7	Saturday

CDate Function

The CDate function converts an expression that has been converted to a Date subtype. Its usage is

```
result = CDate(expr)
```

where result is a Variant of subtype Date and expr is a valid date expression.

> **NOTE**
>
> The IsDate function can be used to determine if the expression to be converted is valid.

Date Function

The Date function retrieves the current system date. Its usage is

```
result = Date
```

where result is a Variant of subtype Date.

DateSerial Function

The DateSerial function sets a date value in a Date variable. Its usage is

```
result = DateSerial(year, month, day)
```

where result is a Variant of subtype Date, year is a number between 100 and 9999, month is a number between 1 and 12, and day is a number between 1 and 31. A numeric expression in the correct range may be used as an argument. If the expression is not valid, it is incremented to the next larger number.

DateValue Function

The `DateValue` function converts an expression into a `Date` subtype. Its usage is

```
result = DateValue(expr)
```

where result is a `Variant` of subtype `Date` and expr is a string expression representing a date, such as November 30, 1997 or 11/30/1997.

Day Function

The `Day` function extracts a day value from an expression representing a date. Its usage is

```
result = Day(expr)
```

where `result` is a whole number between 1 and 31, and expr is any expression that can represent a date. If expr is `Null`, `Null` is returned.

Hour Function

The `Hour` function extracts an hour value from an expression representing a time. Its usage is

```
result = Hour(expr)
```

where `result` is a whole number between 0 and 23, and expr is any expression that can represent a time. If expr is `Null`, `Null` is returned.

Minute Function

The `Minute` function extracts a minute value from an expression representing a time. Its usage is

```
result = Minute(expr)
```

where `result` is a whole number between 0 and 59, and expr is any expression that can represent a time. If expr is `Null`, `Null` is returned.

Month Function

The `Month` function extracts a month value from an expression representing a date. `Month` returns a whole number between 1 and 12, inclusive, representing the month of the year. Its usage is

```
result = Month(date)
```

where `result` is a whole number between 1 and 12, and expr is any expression that can represent a date. If expr contains `Null`, `Null` is returned.

Now Function

The Now function retrieves the current date and time according to the current setting of the computer's date and time. Its usage is

```
result = Now
```

where result is an expression containing the date and time.

Second Function

The Second function extracts the second value from an expression. Its usage is

```
result = Second(expr)
```

where result is a whole number between 0 and 59 and expr is any expression that can represent a time. If expr contains Null, Null is returned.

Time Function

The Time function retrieves the current system time. Its usage is

```
result = Time
```

where result is a Variant of subtype Date.

TimeSerial Function

The TimeSerial function sets a time value in a Date variable. TimeSerial returns a Variant of subtype Date containing the time for a specific hour, minute, and second. Its usage is

```
result = TimeSerial(hour, minute, second)
```

where result is a Variant of subtype Date, hour is a number between 0 and 23, minute is a number between 0 and 59, and second is a number between 0 and 59. A numeric expression in the correct range may be used as an argument. If the expression is not valid, it is incremented to the next larger number.

TimeValue Function

The TimeValue function retrieves a time from an expression indicating a time. Its usage is

```
result = TimeValue(expr)
```

where result is a Variant of subtype Date and expr is a string expression representing a time.

Weekday Function

The `Weekday` function determines the day of the week for a particular date. Its usage is

```
result = Weekday(expr, [firstdayofweek])
```

where `result` is a whole number representing the day of the week (see weekday values in the earlier table), `expr` is an expression representing a date. If `expr` contains `Null`, `Null` is returned. The optional `firstdayofweek` argument identifies the value assumed for the first day.

Year Function

The `Year` function extracts the year value from an expression. Its usage is

```
result = Year(expr)
```

where `result` is a whole number representing the year and `expr` is any expression that can represent a date. If `expr` is `Null`, `Null` is returned.

Conditional Functions

The conditional functions facilitate the testing of certain variable conditions. Each of these functions returns a Boolean value (`True` or `False`) depending upon the implicit test being performed.

IsArray Function

The `IsArray` function determines whether a particular variable is an array subtype. Its usage is

```
bool = IsArray(varname)
```

where `bool` is `True` if the specified `varname` is an array; otherwise, the function returns `False`.

IsDate Function

The `IsDate` function determines if an expression can be converted to a date. Its usage is

```
bool = IsDate(expr)
```

where `bool` is `True` if the specified `expr` is recognizable as a date or time.

IsEmpty Function

The `IsEmpty` function determines whether a variable has been initialized. Its usage is

```
bool = IsEmpty(varname)
```

where `bool` is `True` if the specified `varname` has been initialized or set to a value.

IsNull Function

The IsNull function determines whether a variable contains valid data (not Null). Its usage is

```
bool = IsNull(varname)
```

where bool is True if the specified varname is Null, that is, contains no valid data. Because a variable containing Null will yield Null when used in a conditional expression, the use of IsNull is encouraged when the possibility exists for a variable to be Null.

IsNumeric Function

The IsNumeric function determines whether a variable has a numeric subtype or an expression can be evaluated as a numeric. Its usage is

```
bool = IsNumeric(expr)
```

where bool is True if expr can be evaluated as a number.

IsObject Function

The IsObject function determines whether a variable is an object subtype. Its usage is

```
bool = IsObject(varname)
```

where bool is True if the specified varname is a valid OLE Automation object.

StrComp Function

Unlike the other comparison operators the StrComp function compares two strings for equality or alphabetic sequence. Its usage is

```
result = StrComp(str1, str2[, bin])
```

where result is a signed numeric variable and str1 and str2 are string expressions. The optional bin argument specifies whether a binary (indicated with a True value), rather than an alphabetic, comparison is to be performed. If either str1 or str2 is Null, result will be Null. Otherwise the value of result will be set according to the following list:

Condition	result *value*
str1 < str2	-1
str1 = str2	0
str1 > str2	+1

String Functions

String functions provides functionality when dealing with string variables.

Asc Function

The Asc function extracts the ANSI character code for the first letter in a string. Its usage is

```
result = Asc(string)
```

where result is the character code and string is any valid string expression. If string is Empty, a runtime error occurs.

AscB Function

The AscB function extracts the first byte in a string. Its usage is

```
result = AscB(string)
```

where result is a Byte subtype and string is any valid string expression. If string is Empty, a runtime error occurs.

AscW Function

The AscW function extracts the Unicode character code for the first letter in a string. Its usage is

```
result = AscW(string)
```

where result is the Unicode and string is any valid string expression. If string is Empty, a runtime error occurs.

InStr Function

The InStr function identifies the beginning character position of a token within a string. Its usage is

```
newstart = InStr([start, ]source, token[, compare])
```

where newstart is the character location where the token was found in the string (0 if not located), start is the starting position for the search, source is the string to be searched, token is the string to be located, and compare is the type of comparison (0 for a binary compare, 1 for a textual, case-insensitive compare).

InStrB Function

The InStrB function is the byte version of the InStr function and identifies the beginning byte position of a token within a string. Its usage is

```
newstart = InStr([start, ]source, token[, compare])
```

where newstart is the byte location where the token was found in the string (0 if not located), start is the starting position for the search, source is the string to be searched, token is the string to be located, and compare is the type of comparison (0 for a binary compare, 1 for a textual, case-insensitive compare).

LCase Function

The LCase function converts a string to lowercase. Its usage is

```
result = LCase(string)
```

where result is a lowercase string and string is any valid string expression.

Left Function

The Left function extracts a specified number of characters from the beginning of a string. Its usage is

```
result = Left(string, length)
```

where result is a string variable, string is a valid string expression, and length is a numeric expression indicating how many characters to return.

> **NOTE**
>
> Another function (LeftB) is provided for use with byte data contained in a string. Instead of specifying the number of characters to return, length specifies the number of bytes.

LeftB Function

The LeftB function, similar to the Left function, extracts a specified number of bytes from the beginning of a string. Its usage is

```
result = LeftB(string, length)
```

where result is a string variable, string is a valid string expression, and length is a numeric expression indicating the number of bytes to extract.

Len Function

The Len function determines the size of a string or determines how many characters are needed to store a variable. Its usage is

```
result = Len(string ¦ varname)
```

where result is the number of characters in a string or the number of bytes required to store a variable, string is any valid string expression, and varname is a variable name.

LenB Function

The LenB function determines the size of a string or determines how many bytes are needed to store a variable. Its usage is

```
result = LenB(string ¦ varname)
```

where result is the number of bytes in a string or the number of bytes required to store a variable, string is any valid string expression, and varname is a variable name.

LTrim Function

The LTrim function copies a string while stripping leading spaces. Its usage is

```
result = LTrim(string)
```

where result is the stripped string and string is a valid string expression from which the spaces are to be removed.

Mid Function

The Mid function copies a specified number of characters from a position within a string. Its usage is

```
result = Mid(string, start[, length])
```

where result is the resultant string, string is the expression from which characters are to be copied, start is the position in string where the part to be taken begins, and length is the number of characters to copy.

MidB Function

The MidB function is the byte version of the Mid function. It copies a specified number of bytes from a position within a string. Its usage is

```
result = MidB(string, start[, length])
```

where result is the resultant string, string is the expression from which bytes are to be copied, start is the position in string where the part to be taken begins, and length is the number of bytes to copy.

Right Function

The Right function copies a specified number of characters from the trailing portion of a string. Its usage is

```
result = Right(string, length)
```

where result is the resultant string, string is the expression from which the characters are to be copied, and length is a numeric expression indicating how many characters to copy.

RightB Function

The RightB function is the byte version of the Right function. It copies a specified number of bytes from the trailing portion of a string. Its usage is

```
result = RightB(string, length)
```

where result is the resultant string, string is the expression from which the bytes are to be copied, and length is a numeric expression indicating how many bytes to copy.

RTrim Function

The RTrim function copies a string while stripping trailing spaces. Its usage is

```
result = RTrim(string)
```

where result is the stripped string and string is a valid string expression from which the spaces are to be removed.

String Function

The String function builds a string containing multiple copies of the same character. Its usage is

```
result = String(number, character)
```

where result is a string variable, number is the length of the returned string, and character is the character code used to build the return string.

Trim Function

The Trim function copies a string while stripping leading and trailing spaces. Its usage is

```
result = Trim(string)
```

where result is the copied string and string is a valid string expression from which the spaces are to be removed.

UCase Function

The UCase function copies a string while converting all characters to uppercase. Its usage is

```
result = UCase(string)
```

where result is the resultant string and string is any valid string expression.

Input Functions

Input functions are procedures that automate and simplify the display and preparation of input for a script. They make it easy to provide dialog boxes and other Windows controls.

InputBox Function

The InputBox function prompts the user for input. It displays dialog box containing a prompt or other controls and then waits for the user to reply. Its usage is

```
result = InputBox(prompt[, title][, default][, x][, y][, help, context])
```

where result is the string entered by the user, prompt is the message to be displayed, title is a string to be displayed in the title bar, default is the preloaded response for the user, x and y are the coordinates—in twips (1/20th of a point)—for placement of the dialog box, help identifies the Help file to use to provide context-sensitive Help for the dialog box, and context is the Help context number for the appropriate Help topic. When a Help file is specified, a Help button is automatically added to the dialog box.

Upon return from the procedure, result will contain the contents of the text box (if the user chooses OK) or a zero-length string (if the user selects Cancel).

MsgBox Function

The MsgBox function displays a message in a dialog box with buttons and returns a value indicating which button the user has chosen. Its usage is

```
result = MsgBox(prompt[, buttons][, title][, help, context])
```

where result is the value of the button selected by the user (see Table A.4), prompt is the string to be displayed in the dialog box, buttons is a number indicating the buttons and types to be displayed as depicted in Table A.5, title is the string to be displayed in the title bar of the dialog box, help identifies the Help file to use to provide context-sensitive Help for the dialog box, and context is the Help context number for the appropriate Help topic. When a Help file is specified, a Help button is automatically added to the dialog box.

Table A.4. result values.

Value	Description
1	OK
2	Cancel
3	Abort
4	Retry
5	Ignore
6	Yes
7	No

Table A.5. `buttons` settings.

Setting	Description
Button settings	
0	OK button only
1	OK and Cancel buttons
2	Abort, Retry, and Ignore buttons
3	Yes, No, and Cancel buttons
4	Yes and No buttons
5	Retry and Cancel buttons
Icon settings	
16	Critical Message icon
32	Warning Query icon
48	Warning Message icon
64	Information Message icon
Default settings	
0	First button is default
256	Second button is default
512	Third button is default
768	Fourth button is default
Dialog type	
0	Application modal
4096	System modal

A

VBSCRIPT LANGUAGE REFERENCE

Mathematical Functions

The mathematical functions simplify the programming of tasks involving mathematical and geometric procedures. When using these functions, remember that some functions may be derived from other functions.

Some useful formulas are shown below:

```
radians = degrees * PI / 180
degrees = radians * 180 / PI
PI = 3.1415926535897932
natural log:  e = 2.718282
Sin(α) = a / c
Cos(α) = b / c
Tan(α) = a / b
```

```
Sec(α) = 1 / Cos(α)
Cosec(α) = 1 / Sin(α)
Cotan(α) = 1 / Tan(α)
Arcsin(X) = Atn(X / Sqr(-X * X + 1))
Arccos(X) = Atn(-X / Sqr(-X * X + 1)) + 2 * Atn(1)
Arcsec(X) = Atn(X / Sqr(X * X - 1)) + Sgn((X) -1) * (2 * Atn(1))
Arccosec(X) = Atn(X / Sqr(X * X - 1)) + (Sgn(X) - 1) * (2 * Atn(1))
Arccotan(X) = Atn(X) + 2 * Atn(1)
HSin(X) = (Exp(X) - Exp(-X)) / 2
HCos(X) = (Exp(X) + Exp(-X)) / 2
HTan(X) = (Exp(X) - Exp(-X)) / (Exp(X) + Exp(-X))
HSec(X) = 2 / (Exp(X) + Exp(-X))
HCosec(X) = 2 / (Exp(X) - Exp(-X))
HCotan(X) = (Exp(X) + Exp(-X)) / (Exp(X) - Exp(-X))
HArcsin(X) = Log(X + Sqr(X * X + 1))
HArccos(X) = Log(X + Sqr(X * X - 1))
HArctan(X) = Log((1 + X) / (1 - X)) / 2
HArcsec(X) = Log((Sqr(-X * X + 1) + 1) / X)
HArccosec(X) = Log((Sgn(X) * Sqr(X * X + 1) +1) / X)
HArccotan(X) = Log((X + 1) / (X - 1)) / 2
LogN(x) = Log(x) / Log(n)
```

Abs Function

The Abs function obtains the absolute value of a number. Its usage is

```
result = Abs(number)
```

where result is the absolute value of the number argument.

Atn Function

The Atn function obtains the arctangent of a number. Its usage is

```
result = Atn(number)
```

where result is the angle in radians that corresponds to the tangent number argument.

Cos Function

The Cos function obtains the cosine of an angle. Its usage is

```
result = Cos(number)
```

where result is the ratio of the length of the side adjacent to the angle divided by the length of the hypotenuse and number is an angle in radians.

Exp Function

The Exp function obtains the base of natural logarithms raised to a power. Its usage is

```
result = Exp(number)
```

where result is the antilog of the number argument.

Fix Function

The Fix function obtains the integer portion of a number. Its usage is

```
result = Fix(number)
```

where result is the integer portion of the number argument.

Int Function

The Int function obtains the integer portion of a number. Its usage is

```
result = Int(number)
```

where result is the integer portion of the number argument.

Log Function

The Log function obtains the natural logarithm of a number. Its usage is

```
result = Log(number)
```

where result is the logarithmic value of the number argument.

Rnd Function

The Rnd function obtains a random number. Its usage is

```
result = Rnd[(switch)]
```

where result is a random number and switch indicates how the random number is to be determined. A positive number for switch indicates that the next random number in the sequence should be returned.

Before calling this function, the random number generator should be initialized by using the Randomize statement.

Sgn Function

The Sgn function obtains the sign of a number. Its usage is

```
result = Sgn(number)
```

where result is 1 if the number argument is positive, 0 if number is 0, and -1 if number is negative.

Sin Function

The Sin function obtains the sine of an angle. Its usage is

```
result = Sin(number)
```

where `result` is the ratio of the length of the side opposite the angle divided by the length of the hypotenuse and `number` is an angle in radians.

Sqr Function

The `Sqr` function obtains the square root of a number. Its usage is

```
result = Sqr(number)
```

where `result` is the square root of the `number` argument.

Tan Function

The `Tan` function obtains the tangent of an angle. Its usage is

```
result = Tan(number)
```

where `result` is the ratio of the length of the side opposite the angle divided by the length of the side adjacent to the angle and `number` is an angle in radians.

I

INDEX